Scotland
BED & BREAKFAST

Published by the Scottish Tourist Board
P.O. Box 705, Edinburgh EH4 3EU

CHAIRMAN'S WELCOME

This guide is intended to help you take the first steps on what I know will be an unforgettable journey — a holiday in Scotland.

This guide to Bed and Breakfast accommodation will assist you in getting the most from this magnificent country. It is not my purpose here to tell you about the history, the heritage, the scenery, the people, the places and the activities. They are yours to discover.

I believe that whether you are a first time visitor or one of the many who return again and again, you will enjoy an experience that is incomparable anywhere in the world.

We have 172 Tourist Information Centres, where you can find people who will introduce you to the secrets and attractions of their area.

In the following pages I would like to highlight the range and quality of accommodation available to you during your visit to Scotland.

I would particularly commend to you the establishments in this guide which have been inspected and "graded" by the Scottish Tourist Board. They are colour coded in red to draw to your attention the quality and level of facilities on offer.

I hope that your visit leaves you and your companions with memories that will bring you back to Scotland. If you do, you can always be sure that a warm welcome awaits you.

Ian Grant
Chairman

ABOUT THIS BOOK

For more than thirty years **Where to Stay** has been the Scottish Tourist Board's official guide to holiday accommodation in Scotland. Bed & Breakfast in Scotland is one of the cheapest and most convenient forms of holiday accommodation and is excellent value for money.

Bed & Breakfast places and university accommodation in all parts of Scotland are listed here in alphabetical order by place-names, or, in the case of isolated countryside locations, under the nearest town or village.

If you are looking for accommodation in a particular area, the map section on pages xxvii to xxxii will enable you to identify locations.

Telephone numbers. The telephone number, exchange name and dialling code (in brackets) are given immediately below the address. The dialling code applies to calls made anywhere in the UK except for local calls. If in doubt, call the operator by dialling 100.

Telephone Dialling Codes. There are several changes to telephone dialling codes throughout Scotland this year. Where possible we have printed the most up-to-date codes, but some may have changed since going to print.

If you are having difficulty contacting an establishment, phone British Telecom directory enquiries on 192 and they will be happy to advise you of the correct number.

Map References. These are given against each place name listed in the guide. The first figure refers to the map number, the latter two figures give the grid reference.

DISABLED VISITORS

Many places listed in this book welcome disabled visitors. Those which have been inspected under the Scottish Tourist Board's Grading and Classification Scheme have their access facilities shown thus:

   Access for wheelchair users without assistance
 A Access for wheelchair users with assistance
 P Access for ambulant disabled
 R Access for residents only

It is always advisable to telephone the establishment in advance for further information.

Details of the criteria used for these symbols are shown on page 312. Further details from STB.

The undernoted organisations are also able to provide further information and advice:–
Disability Scotland
Information Dept
Princes House
5 Shandwick Place
EDINBURGH EH2 4RG
Tel: 031-229 8632

Holiday Care Service
2 Old Bank Chambers
Station Road
HORLEY
Surrey RH6 9HW
Tel: Horley (02934) 74535

BOOKING

It is always advisable to book accommodation in advance. This applies particularly during Easter and July and August.

Your travel agent will always be delighted to help you and to take care of your travel arrangements.

For those visitors who have not booked their accommodation in advance, Tourist Information Centres across Scotland provide a very useful accommodation booking service. For more details see page xv.

There are about 170 Tourist Information Centres in Scotland, a list of which is given on pages xv to xxv. All operate the Book a Bed Ahead scheme and local accommodation booking, while many operate an advance reservations service in addition. Tourist Information Centres are always glad to help with any accommodation problems.

RESERVATIONS

Accommodation should be booked directly through the hotel or guest house, through a travel agent or through a Tourist Information Centre. While the Scottish Tourist Board can give advice and information about any aspect of holidays in Scotland, it is *not* in a position to arrange accommodation or to make reservations.

ABOUT THIS BOOK

Accepting accommodation by telephone or in writing means you have entered into a legally binding contract with the proprietor of the establishment. A deposit is usually requested in order to secure your booking. This deposit does not necessarily represent compensation for the loss of a booking, and should you cancel or fail to take up the accommodation, for whatever reason, the proprietor may request further compensation. You should always check cancellation terms in advance and, if you must cancel a booking, advise the management immediately. We strongly advise taking out a holiday insurance policy to cover any such eventuality.

COMPLAINTS

Any complaints or criticisms about individual establishments should be taken up immediately with the management. In most cases the problems can be dealt with satisfactorily, thus avoiding any prolonged unhappiness during your stay.

If this procedure fails to remedy the grievance to your satisfaction, and particularly where serious complaints are concerned, please write giving full details to the local Area Tourist Board (see pages xv-xxv) or to the Customer Liaison Department at the Scottish Tourist Board where appropriate.

VALUE ADDED TAX (VAT)

Please note that VAT is calculated by establishments for this publication at a rate of $17^1/_2$%. Any subsequent changes in this rate will affect the price you will be charged.

PRICES

The prices of accommodation, services and facilities stated in this guide are based on information received from the relevant advertisers. To the best of the Board's knowledge the information received was correct at the time of going to press. The Board can accept no responsibility for any errors or omissions.

To make this guide available at the earliest possible and practical time for 1994, the information received has had to be submitted well in advance of the 1994 holiday season. The prices stated are therefore not guaranteed to be the prices that will be charged throughout the holiday season. The prices are estimates at the time of going to press of the prices that establishments expect to apply but are subject to change without further notice. As there may have been amendments to prices, you should check with the establishment before making a booking or otherwise relying on the information.

Subject to the proviso that they are estimates and subject to change as stated above, the prices quoted in this guide are per person and normally represent the minimum (low season) and/or the maximum (high season) charges expected to apply to the majority of rooms in the establishment and include service charges, if any, and Value Added Tax as applicable. In addition, prices often vary according to season and are usually lower outside the peak holiday weeks. In a few cases where breakfast is normally charged separately, the rates quoted include this charge; it is normally for full breakfast, but as some establishments only provide Continental breakfast, this should be checked at the time of booking. In many cases, double/twin bedded rooms can accommodate families; the availability of these and of family rooms is shown, along with other details.

There is a statutory requirement for establishments to display overnight accommodation charges. When you arrive at the place you are going to stay it is in your interests to check prices.

September 1993

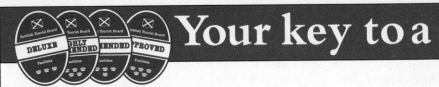

When you're choosing your holiday from home, quality and comfort are too important to leave to chance.

That's why, since 1985, STB has been annually inspecting self catering accommodation, defining the standards that our visitors expect and helping owners and operators meet those standards. Self catering accommodation all over the country, from the simplest to the most sophisticated is GRADED for quality and CLASSIFIED for its facilities.

Here's how it works.

Look out for the blue oval sign displayed by members of the GRADING and CLASSIFICATION Scheme.

The centre panel of the sign tells you if the property is APPROVED (an acceptable standard), COMMENDED (offering a good standard), HIGHLY COMMENDED (offering a very good standard) or DELUXE (offering an excellent standard).

The GRADES are awarded by the STB inspectors once they have checked all the important factors that contribute to quality in a property. Just as you would, they look for clean, comfortable surroundings, well furnished and heated. They check all practical aspects, including utensils and equipment. Like you, they appreciate atmosphere and location and a friendly smile of welcome.

great holiday!

The lower section of the sign displays the CROWN Classification, denoting the range of facilities and services on offer. From a basic 1 CROWN, up to 5 CROWNS can be added. The criteria are cumulative and must be provided in full up to the level of the CROWNS displayed.

The following table gives an indication of some of the facilities to be expected at each level. For a full list of all CROWN Classification criteria, contact: STB, 23 Ravelston Terrace, Edinburgh EH4 3EU. Tel: 031 332 2423.

	1	2	3	4	5
Clean, comfortable and sound accommodation	●	●	●	●	●
Adequate means of heating at all times	●	●	●	●	●
B/W TV available free or for hire	●	●	●	●	●
Typewritten brochure available		●	●	●	●
Bedroom with dressing table, mirror, light, wardrobe		●	●	●	●
Refrigerator		●	●	●	●
Linen and towels available			●	●	●
Bathrooms to have a heater			●	●	●
Colour TV in property			●	●	●
All properties self contained			●	●	●
At least 1 bathroom with bath				●	●
Automatic clothes washing machine and				●	●
Tumble dryer in unit or on site				●	●
Dishwasher, fridge/freezer, microwave					●
Thermostatically controlled heating throughout					●
Telephone for incoming and outgoing calls					●

Over 1,650 self catering establishments, 4,300 properties, are members of the Grading and Classification Scheme and they are to be found in all parts of Scotland.

BOOKING DIRECT? BOOKING THROUGH THE TOURIST INFORMATION CENTRE? REMEMBER ALWAYS CHECK THE GRADING AND CROWN CLASSIFICATION OF YOUR CHOSEN ESTABLISHMENT.

OÙ SE LOGER EN ECOSSE

Bienvenue en Ecosse!

Voici le guide touristique officiel, publié par l'Office écossais du tourisme Revu chaque année, ce guide est reconnu depuis trente ans comme le plus complet en son genre. Des hôtels, pensions de famille et résidences universitaires de toutes les régions de l'Ecosse y sont classés selon l'ordre alphabétique des localités. Sauf indication contraire, l'indicatif téléphonique est celui de la localité.

Au moment de mettre sous presse, il ne nous est pas possible de donner des prix définitifs; il est vivement conseillé aux visiteurs de demander confirmation des prix lorsqu'ils effectuent la réservation.

Nous avons signalé à l'attention des gourmets les hôtels qui offrent les spécialités de la cuisine écossaise (recettes écossaises traditionnelles à base de produits écossais de haute qualité).

NB. L'Office écossais du tourisme (Scottish Tourist Board) décline toute responsabilité en cas d'erruers ou d'omissions.

AVERTISSEMENT: CHIENS ETC.

Il est rappelé aux visiteurs étrangers que l'introduction d'animaux domestiques en Grande-Bretagne est soumise à une réglementation très stricte, qui prévoit une longue période de quarantaine. Etant donné le danger de propagation du virus rabique, des peines très sévères sont prévues pour toute infraction aux réglements.

SUR LES ROUTES D'ECOSSE

Veillez à attacher votre ceinture de sécurité, si votre voiture en est munie. Le port de la ceinture est obligatoire en Grande Bretagne.

La légende des symboles se trouve au volet de la couverture, qui fait aussi office de signet.

Logez a l'enseigne de l'hospitalité Ecossaise voir page 308.

DEUTSCH

WO ÜBERNACHTET MAN IN SCHOTTLAND

Willkommen in Schottland!

Dieses Buch ist der offizielle Führer des Schottischen Touristenbüros. Seit dreißig Jahren wird dieses Buch als das umfassendste seiner Art anerkannt. Es wird jedes Jahr auf den neuesten Stand gebracht. Hotels, Gasthäuser und Unterbringung in den Universitäten in allen Teilen Schottlands sind hier nach Ortsnamen in alphabetischer Reihenfolge aufgeführt. Die jeweilige Vorwahlnummer ist unter dem Ortsnamen zu finden, außer, wenn sie extra angegeben ist.

Zu Beginn der Drucklegung dieses Buches ist es noch nicht möglich, feste Preise anzugeben, und Besuchern wird daher geraten, sich nach den Tarifen zu erkundigen, wenn sie Buchungen vornehmen.

Das Schottische Touristenbüro (Scottish Tourist Board) kann keine Verantwortung für eventuelle Fehler oder Auslassung von Preisen und Einrichtungen übernehmen.

Als weitere Hilfe haben wir die echte Privatpensionen gekennzeichnet, die echte schottische Küche – Taste of Scotland – anbieten. Das bedeutet, daß hier traditionell schottische Rezepte verwandt werden unter Benutzung schottischer Produkte von hoher Qualität.

HUNDE

Das Mitbringen von Tieren jeder Art aus dem Ausland ist wegen Tollwutgefahr strengstens untersagt. Die Übertretung dieses Gesetzes wird mit hohen Strafen belegt.

AUTOFAHREN IN SCHOTTLAND

Schnallen Sie sich immer an! Es wird nun zur Pflicht. (Vorausgesetzt, Ihr Auto ist mit Sicherheitsgurt ausgestattet.)

Die Zeichenerklärungen befinden sich im eingeklebten Faltblatt am Ende des Buches.

Ubernachten sie dort, wo sie das Zeichen für echt Schottische Gastlichkeit Sehen Seihe Seite 310.

YOUR HOLIDAY IN SCOTLAND

USEFUL INFORMATION ABOUT SCOTLAND

TRAVEL

Bookings for rail, sea and air travel to Scotland and within Scotland should be made through your travel agent, or directly to British Rail, airlines and ferry companies. The Scottish Tourist Board will be glad to give you information but cannot make your bookings for you.

Seats may be booked in advance on the main long-distance coaches, aircraft and for berths and cabins in the steamers to the islands. Sleeping berths on trains should always be booked well in advance. It is necessary to book seats for 'extended' coach tours and also for day coach outings operated from most holiday and touring centres.

Car hire bookings should also be made in advance wherever possible, especially for July and August. Taxis are readily available in Edinburgh, Glasgow, and other major centres at controlled charges. Taxis are generally available in most communities, but in smaller, less populous areas charges may vary considerably.

DRIVING

The 'Rules of the Road' are the same in Scotland as in the rest of the U.K. While there is limited motorway mileage in Scotland, the roads are uniformly good.

DRIVING ON SINGLE-TRACK ROADS

A few stretches of road are still single track, mainly in the north-west and on some of the islands. They demand a careful technique. When two vehicles approach from opposite directions, the car which first reaches a passing place should pull in or stop opposite the passing place to allow safe passage. Passing places are also used to let another vehicle overtake. It is an offence to hold up a following vehicle and not give way. It could, for example, be the local doctor on his or her way to an accident. At all times consideration should be shown for other road users. Finally, please note that passing places should never be used as parking places.

When touring in the far north and west particularly, remember that petrol stations are comparatively few, and distances between them may be considerable. This is particularly true if your car uses unleaded petrol. Some petrol stations close on Sundays. Fill your tank in good time, and keep it as full as possible.

Remember, it is now law that the driver and front passenger must wear seat belts, and in the back where they are fitted.

PUBLIC HOLIDAYS

The Bank Holidays which are also general holidays in England do not apply in Scotland. Most Bank Holidays apply to banks and to some professional and commercial offices only, although Christmas Day and New Year's Day are usually taken as holidays by everyone. Scottish banks are closed in 1994 on 1 and 4 January, 1 April, 2 and 30 May, 1 August and 27 and 28 December. In place of the general holidays, Scottish cities and towns normally have a Spring Holiday and an Autumn Holiday. The dates of these holidays vary from place to place, but they are almost invariably on a Monday.

MONEY

Currency, coinage and postal rates in Scotland are the same as in the rest of the U.K. Scotland differs from England in that Scottish banks issue their own notes. These are acceptable in England, at face value, as are Bank of England notes in Scotland. Main banks are open during the following hours:
Monday-Friday 0915/0930 -1600/1645 (depending on bank). Most banks are open later on a Thursday evening (until 1730). In smaller towns and villages branches may close over the lunchtime period, usually from 1230 -1330.

Some city centre banks are open daily 0930 -1530 and on Saturdays. In rural areas, banks post their hours clearly outside and travelling banks call regularly.

USEFUL INFORMATION ABOUT SCOTLAND

SHOPPING

The normal shopping hours in Scotland are 0900-1730, although bakeries, dairies and newsagents open earlier. Many shops have an early closing day (1300) each week, but the actual day varies from place to place and in cities from district to district.

Many city centre shops also stay open late on one evening each week.

A TASTE OF SCOTLAND

Guides are indispensable tools in planning a holiday or even a meal or overnight stop. There are thousands of eating establishments and nobody on the move has time to try out a large selection until a suitable one is found. In Scotland, therefore, it is natural to turn to the Taste of Scotland Guide for help. Within it are listed a wide range of highly recommended hotels and restaurants, ranging from five star hotels to farmhouses. All have been inspected and selected because they meet the exacting requirements of the Taste of Scotland Scheme. And the choice is wide so that there will be something for everyone at whatever price level they seek. The prime concern of the Scheme is to concentrate on aspects of hospitality and welcome, but particularly to ensure that food is of the highest possible standard compatible with the prices charged. To this end there is strong emphasis on the use of the fresh local produce for which Scotland is famed. Food prepared from the pick of the crop and presented with panache.

For convenience, however, the Scottish Tourist Board's classification and grading assessments are also listed, where applicable. Many establishments feature regularly or occasionally some of the mouth-watering regional specialities which are of particular interest to the visitor. The 1994 edition of the **Taste of Scotland Guide** lists many new members, and has dropped several which have failed to maintain standards or have changed ownership. The Guide may be obtained direct from Taste of Scotland, 33 Melville Street, Edinburgh EH3 7JF. (£4.50 including post and packing). Also available from Scottish Tourist Board in London, and from many Tourist Information Centres and bookshops and through the British Travel Centre in London. Use it to help plan your travels – and maximise your enjoyment.

LICENSING LAWS

Currently in Scotland, the hours that public houses and hotel bars are open to serve drinks are the same all over the country. 'Pubs' are open from 1100 to 1430 and from 1700 to about 2300 hours, Monday to Saturday inclusive and most are now licensed to open on Sundays. In addition, some establishments may have obtained extended licences for afternoon or late night opening.

Hotel bars have the same hours as 'pubs', and are open on Sundays from 1230 to 1430 and 1830 to 2300. Residents in licensed hotels may have drinks served at any time. Some restaurants and hotels have extended licences allowing them to serve drinks with meals until 0100 in the morning. Persons under the age of 18 are not allowed to drink in licensed premises.

CHURCHES

The established Church of Scotland is Presbyterian, but the Roman Catholic and other denominations have very considerable numbers of adherents. The Episcopal Church of Scotland is in full communion with the Church of England, and uses a similar form of worship. In the far north and west of Scotland, particularly in the islands, many people belong to the Free Church of Scotland and appreciate it when their views on the Sabbath as a day when there should be no recreational or other unnecessary activity are respected by visitors.

Times of services of the various denominations are usually intimated on hotel notice boards, as well as outside the churches and, of course, visitors are always welcome.

USEFUL INFORMATION ABOUT SCOTLAND

COMING FROM OVERSEAS?

Visitors to Scotland from overseas require to observe the same regulations as for other parts of the U.K. As a general rule they must have a valid passport, and, in certain cases, visas issued by British Consular authorities overseas: check with a local Travel Agent, or where appropriate, the overseas offices of the British Tourist Authority.

Currency: Overseas visitors who require information about the import and export of currency, cars, or other goods, on personal purchases and belongings, shopping concessions, etc., should consult a Travel Agent or Bank or the overseas offices of the B.T.A.

Driving: Motorists coming from overseas who are members of a motoring organisation in their own country may obtain from them full details of the regulations for importing cars, motor cycles, etc. for holiday and touring purposes into the U.K. They can drive in Britain on a current Driving Licence from their own country, or with an international Driving Permit, for a maximum period of 12 months. Otherwise, a British Driving Licence must be obtained: until the Driving Test is passed it is essential to be accompanied by a driver with a British Licence.

Seat belts: Drivers and front seat passengers must wear safety belts while driving in Britain, by law. Rear seat passengers must also wear seat belts, where fitted.

VAT: Value Added Tax, currently charged at 17.5% on many goods, can sometimes be reclaimed by overseas visitors who buy items for export. Visitors should ask the shopkeeper about the retail export schemes before making a purchase, and will be required to fill in special forms.

SCOTTISH YOUTH HOSTELS

There are over 80 youth hostels in Scotland offering simple, low-cost self catering accommodation to all people, but especially the young, Youth Hostels may be in a castle or in a mansion, or a timber building way out in the wild. All have dormitories, washrooms, common room and kitchen. Some hostels also offer accommodation for families with children under five. Telephone: (0786) 451181.

There are also over 35 hostels in Scotland for backpackers and independent travellers, telephone: (04562) 807.

PETS

Where pets are permitted, owners are asked to take responsibility for pets' behaviour. In particular, please keep dogs under control in the presence of farm animals. To identify those establishments which may accept pets, look out for the 🐕 symbol within the establishment entry. Please confirm the acceptance of your pet when making your booking.

RABIES

Britain is very concerned to prevent the spread of rabies. Strict quarantine regulations apply to animals brought into Britain from abroad and severe penalties are enforced if they are broken or ignored. Dogs and cats are subject to 6 months quarantine in an approved quarantine centre. Full details from the Department of Agriculture and Fisheries for Scotland, Chesser House, 500 Gorgie Road, Edinburgh EH1 3AW. The restrictions do not apply to animals from Eire, Northern Ireland, the Isle of Man or the Channel Islands.

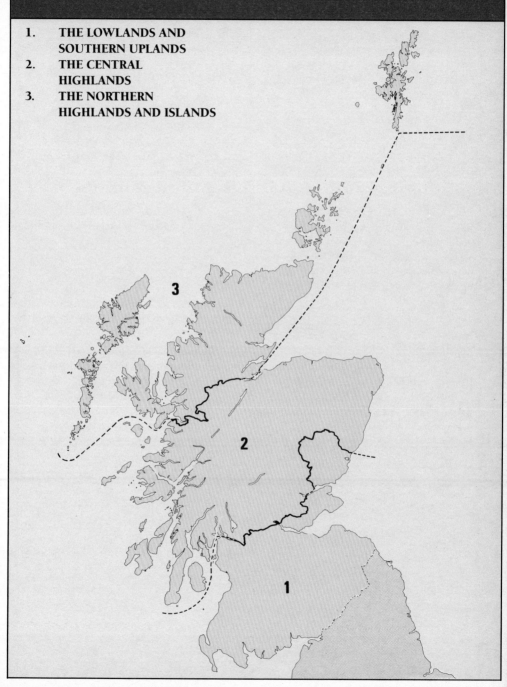

SCOTLAND'S TOURIST AREAS

1. **THE LOWLANDS AND SOUTHERN UPLANDS**
2. **THE CENTRAL HIGHLANDS**
3. **THE NORTHERN HIGHLANDS AND ISLANDS**

TOURIST INFORMATION CENTRES

Where you see the information 𝒾 you are guaranteed a welcome by people who really know their country. Information Centres form a linked network which can guide you all around Scotland.

Among the wide range of services now available are:

𝒾 Free information and advice on the local area, and on the whole of Scotland – events, routes, things to see and places to visit.

𝒾 Accommodation booking – whether locally, or in any other part of Scotland. A small fee will be charged for national reservations and may be charged for local bookings. Ask for Scottish Tourist Board Graded accommodation for a guarantee of high quality and a warm welcome.

𝒾 Maps and books – guide books, reference books, and often a wide range of Scottish literature for your holiday reading.

𝒾 Tickets for events and activities, both local and national – season tickets for a wide range of attractions, including Historic Scotland and National Trust for Scotland properties.

𝒾 Local excursions, tours and travel tickets.

𝒾 Many major Information Centres now offer a bureau de change service.

𝒾 Films, souvenirs and local craft items.

✉ This symbol indicates those information centes which will respond to written enquiries.

WHERE TO FIND OUT MORE ABOUT SCOTLAND

Scottish Tourist Board, Central Information. Tel: 031-332 2433

Also, from August 1993:
24-hr Scottish Tourist Board Information Line. Tel: 0891 666465.
(Calls are charged at 36p a minute cheap rate, 48p a minute at all other times)

In England, the following centres provide full information on Scotland:

Scottish Tourist Board London Office
19 Cockspur Street, Trafalgar Square
London SW1Y 5BL
Tel: (071) 930 8661

Southwaite Tourist Information Centre
M6 Service Area (North Bound)
Southwaite, by Carlisle CA4 0NS
Tel: (069) 747 3445

Tyne Commission Quay
Tourist Information Centre
Ferry Terminal, North Shields
by Newcastle upon Tyne NE29 6EN
Tel: (091) 257 9800

Gretna Gateway to Scotland
M74 Service Area
CA6 5HQ
Tel: (0461) 38500

1. THE LOWLANDS AND SOUTHERN UPLANDS

Angus Tourist Board

ARBROATH
Market Place
Arbroath
Angus DD11 1HR
Tel: (0241) 72609
Jan-Dec

CARNOUSTIE
The Library
High Street
Carnoustie
Tel: (0241) 52258
Apr-early Oct

KIRRIEMUIR
17 High Street
Kirriemuir
Forfar
Tel: (0575) 74097
Apr-early Oct

BRECHIN
St Ninians Place
Brechin
Angus
Tel: (0356) 623050
Apr-early Oct

FORFAR
The Library
West High Street
Forfar
Tel: (0307) 467876
Apr-early Oct

MONTROSE
The Library
High Street
Montrose
Tel: (0674) 72000
Apr-early Oct

Ayrshire Tourist Board

ARDROSSAN &
Ferry Terminal Building
The Harbour, Ardrossan
Ayrshire
Tel: (0294) 601063
Apr-Oct

LARGS ✉
Promenade, Largs
Ayrshire KA30 8BG
Tel: (0475) 673765
Jan-Dec

TROON
Municipal Buildings
South Beach
Troon
Ayrshire
Tel: (0292) 317696
Easter-Sept

AYR ✉
39 Sandgate
Ayr KA7 1BG
Tel: (0292) 284196
Jan-Dec

MAUCHLINE
National Burns Memorial Tower
Kilmarnock Road, Mauchline
Ayrshire
Tel: (0290) 51916
Jan-Dec

GIRVAN
Bridge Street, Girvan
Ayrshire
Tel: (0465) 4950
Apr-Oct

MILLPORT &
Stuart Street, Millport
Isle of Cumbrie
Tel: (0475) 530753
Easter-Sept

KILMARNOCK ✉
62 Bank Street
Kilmarnock
Ayrshire
Tel: (0563) 39090
Jan-Dec

PRESTWICK
Boydfield Gardens
Prestwick
Ayrshire
Tel: (0292) 79946
June-Sept

City of Dundee Tourist Board

DUNDEE ✉ &
4 City Square
Dundee DD1 3BA
Tel: (0382) 27723
Jan-Dec

 When you visit a Tourist Information Centre you are guaranteed a welcome by people who really know their country.

For information, maps, holiday reading, accommodation bookings and much more, look for the information 🛈

Clyde Valley Tourist Board

ABINGTON
Welcome Break Service Area
Junction 13, M74
Abington
Tel: (08642) 436
Easter-Oct

BIGGAR ♿
155 High Street
Biggar
Lanarkshire
Tel: (0899) 21066
Easter-Oct

HAMILTON ♿
Road Chef Services
M74 Northbound
Hamilton
Tel: (0698)285590
Jan-Dec

LANARK ✉ ♿
Horsemarket
Ladyacre Road
Lanark ML11 7LQ
Tel: (0555) 661661
Jan-Dec

COATBRIDGE
The Time Capsule
Buchanan Street
Coatbridge
Tel: (0236) 431133
Apr-Oct

MOTHERWELL ✉
Motherwell Library
Hamilton Road
Motherwell
Tel: (0698) 251311
Jan-Dec

STRATHAVEN ♿
Town Mill Arts Centre
Stonehouse Road
Strathaven
Tel: (0357) 29650
Apr-Oct

Dumfries and Galloway Tourist Board

CASTLE DOUGLAS ✉
Markethill
Castle Douglas
Tel: (0556) 2611
Easter-Oct

DALBEATTIE ✉
Town Hall
Dalbeattie
Tel: (0556) 610117
Easter-early Oct

DUMFRIES ✉
Whitesands
Dumfries
Tel: (0387) 53862
Jan-Dec

GATEHOUSE OF FLEET ✉
Car Park
Gatehouse of Fleet
Tel: (0557) 814212
Easter-Oct

GRETNA GREEN ✉ ♿
Old Blacksmith's Shop
Gretna Green
Tel: (0461) 37834
Easter-Oct

GRETNA – Gateway to Scotland
M74 Service Area
CA6 5HQ
Tel: (0461) 38500
Jan-Dec

KIRKCUDBRIGHT ✉ ♿
Harbour Square
Kirkcudbright
Tel: (0557) 30494
Easter-Oct

LANGHOLM ✉
High Street
Langholm
Tel: (03873) 80976
Easter-early Oct

MOFFAT ✉ ♿
Churchgate
Moffat
Tel: (0683) 20620
Easter-Oct

NEWTON STEWART ✉
Dashwood Square
Newton Stewart
Tel: (0671) 2431
Easter-Oct

SANQUHAR ✉ ♿
Tolbooth, High Street
Sanquhar
Tel: (0659) 50185
Easter-early Oct

STRANRAER ✉ ♿
Port Rodie Car Park
Stranraer
Tel: (0776) 2595
Easter-Oct

East Lothian Tourist Board

DUNBAR ✉ ♿
143 High Street
Dunbar
Tel: (0368) 63353
Jan-Dec

MUSSELBURGH ✉ ♿
Brunton Hall
Musselburgh
East Lothian
Tel: (031) 665 6597
June-end Sept

NORTH BERWICK ✉ ♿
Quality Street
North Berwick
Tel: (0620) 2197
Jan-Dec

OLDCRAIGHALL ✉ ♿
Granada Service Area
Oldcraighall
Musselburgh
Tel: (031) 653 6172
Jan-Dec

PENCRAIG ✉
A1
By East Linton
East Lothian
Tel: (0620) 860063
Apr-end Sept

Edinburgh Tourist Board

EDINBURGH AND SCOTLAND
INFORMATION CENTRE ♿
3 Princes Street
Edinburgh EH2 2QP
Tel: (031) 557 1700
Jan-Dec

EDINBURGH AIRPORT ♿
Tourist Information Desk
Edinburgh Airport
Edinburgh EH12 9DN
Tel: (031) 333 2167
Jan-Dec

Forth Valley Tourist Board

BO'NESS
Hamilton's Cottage, by Bo'ness
Station
Union Road
Bo'ness
Tel: (0506) 826626
May-Sept

FORTH ROAD BRIDGE ✉
Queensferry Lodge Hotel
St Margarets Head
North Queensferry
Tel: (0383) 417759
Jan-Dec

DUNFERMLINE ✉
Abbot House
Maygate
Dunfermline
Tel: (0383) 720999
Easter-Sept

KINCARDINE BRIDGE ✉
Pine 'N' Oak Lay-by
Airth
By Falkirk
Tel: (0324) 417759
Easter-Sept

FALKIRK ✉
The Steeple
High Street
Falkirk
Tel: (0324) 20244
Jan-Dec

LINLITHGOW ✉
Burgh Halls
The Cross
Linlithgow
Tel: (0506) 844600
Jan-Dec

Greater Glasgow Tourist Board

GLASGOW ✉
35 St Vincent Place
Glasgow G1 2ER
Tel: (041) 204 4400
Jan-Dec

GOUROCK
Pierhead
Gourock
Tel: (0475) 39467
Mar-Oct

GLASGOW AIRPORT
Tourist Information Desk
Glasgow Airport
Paisley PA3 2ST
Tel: (041) 848 4440
Jan-Dec

PAISLEY
Town Hall
Abbey Close
Paisley PA1 1JS
Tel: (041) 889 0711
Jan-Dec

Kirkcaldy District Council

BURNTISLAND ✉
. 4 Kirkgate
Burntisland
Tel: (0592) 872667
Jan-Dec

KIRKCALDY ✉
19 Whytescauseway
Tel: (0592) 267775
Jan-Dec

GLENROTHES
Lyon Square
Kingdom Centre
Glenrothes, Fife
Tel: (0592) 610784
Jan-Dec

LEVEN ✉
South Street
Leven
Tel: (0333) 429464
Jan-Dec

Midlothian Tourism Association

BONNYRIGG ♿
Polton Street
Bonnyrigg
Midlothian
Tel: (031) 660 6814
Jan-Dec

PENICUIK
The Library
3 Bellman's Road
Penicuik
Midlothian
Tel: (0968) 673286/672340
Jan-Dec

DALKEITH ♿
The Library
White Hart Street
Dalkeith
Midlothian
Tel: (031) 660 6818
Jan-Dec

St Andrews and North East Fife Tourist Board

ANSTRUTHER
Scottish Fisheries Museum
Anstruther KY10
Tel: (0333) 311073
Easter, May-Sept

CRAIL
Museum & Heritage Centre
Marketgate
Crail KY10
Tel: (0333) 50869
June-Sept

CUPAR &
Fluthers Car Park
Cupar
Fife KY15
Tel: (0334) 52874

ST ANDREWS ✉
78 South Street
St Andrews KY16 9JX
Tel: (0334) 72021
Jan-Dec

Scottish Borders Tourist Board

COLDSTREAM ✉ &
Henderson Park
Coldstream
Tel: (0890) 882607
Apr-Oct

EYEMOUTH ✉ &
Auld Kirk
Manse Road
Eyemouth TD14
Tel: (08907) 50678
Apr-Oct

GALASHIELS ✉ &
Bank Street
Galashiels TD1
Tel: (0896) 55551
Apr-Oct

HAWICK ✉
Common Haugh
Hawick TD9
Tel: (0450) 72547
Apr-Oct

JEDBURGH ✉ &
Murrays Green
Jedburgh TD8 6BE
Tel: (0835) 863435
Jan-Dec

KELSO ✉ &
Turret House
Abbey Court
Kelso TD5 7AX
Tel: (0573) 223464
Apr-Oct

MELROSE ✉ &
Priorwood Gardens
Melrose
Kelso TD6
Tel: (089682) 2555
Apr-Oct

PEEBLES ✉ &
High Street, Peebles
Kelso
Tel: (0721) 720138
Apr-Oct

SELKIRK ✉ &
Halliwells House
Selkirk TD7
Tel: (0750) 20054
Apr-Oct

2. THE CENTRAL HIGHLANDS

Aviemore and Spey Valley Tourist Board

AVIEMORE ✉ &
Grampian Road
Aviemore
Inverness-shire
Tel: (0479) 810363
Jan-Dec

CARRBRIDGE ✉
Main Street
Carrbridge
Inverness-shire
Tel: (0479) 84630
May-Sept

GRANTOWN-ON-SPEY ✉ &
High Street
Grantown-on-Spey
Morayshire
Tel: (0479) 2773
April-Oct

KINGUSSIE ✉
King Street
Kingussie
Tel: (0540) 661 297
May-Sept

RALIA ✉ &
A9, Nr Newtonmore
Inverness-shire
Tel: (0540) 673253
Apr-Oct

Banff and Buchan Tourist Board

ADEN
Aden Country Park
Mintlaw AB4 8LD
Tel: (0771) 23037
Apr-Oct

BANFF ✉
Collie Lodge
Banff AB45 1AU
Tel: (0261) 812419
Apr-Oct

FRASERBURGH
Saltoun Square
Fraserburgh AB4 5DA
Tel: (0346) 518315
Apr-Oct

PETERHEAD
54 Broad Street
Peterhead AB4 6BX
Tel: (0779) 71904
Apr-Oct

TURRIFF
Swimming Pool Car Park
Queens Road
Turriff
Tel: (0888) 63001
Apr-Oct

City of Aberdeen Tourist Board

ABERDEEN
St Nicholas House
Broad Street
Aberdeen AB9 1DE
Tel: (0224) 632727
Jan-Dec

Bute and Cowal Tourist Board

DUNOON
7 Alexandra Parade
Dunoon PA23 8AB
Tel: (0369) 3785
Jan-Dec

Fort William and Lochaber Tourist Board

BALLACHULISH
Ballachulish
Argyll
Tel: (08552) 296
Apr-Oct

FORT WILLIAM
Cameron Square
Fort William
Tel: (0397) 703781
Jan-Dec

KILCHOAN
Argyll
Tel: (09723) 222
Apr-Sept

MALLAIG
Mallaig
Inverness-shire
Tel: (0687) 2170
Apr-Sept

SPEAN BRIDGE
Spean Bridge
Inverness-shire
Tel: (0397) 81576
Apr-Oct

STRONTIAN
Strontian
Argyll
Tel: (0967) 2131
May-Sept

Gordon District Tourist Board

ALFORD
Railway Museum
Station Yard
Alford AB3 8AD
Tel: (09755) 62052
Mid Apr-Oct

ELLON
Maket Street Car Park
Ellon AB4 8JD
Tel: (0358) 20730
Late March-Oct

HUNTLY
7A The Square
Huntly AB5 5AE
Tel: (0466) 792255
Mid Apr-Oct

INVERURIE
Town Hall
Market Place
Inverurie AB5 9SN
Tel: (0467) 20600
Mid Apr-Oct

Inverness, Loch Ness and Nairn Tourist Board

DAVIOT WOOD
A9
By Inverness
Tel: (0463) 772203
Apr-Oct

INVERNESS
Castle Wynd
Inverness IV1 1EZ
Tel: (0463) 234353
Jan-Dec

FORT AUGUSTUS
The Car Park
Fort Augustus
Tel: (0320) 6367
Apr-Oct

NAIRN
62 King Street
Nairn
Tel: (0667) 52753
Apr-Oct

Isle of Arran Tourist Board

BRODICK
The Pier
Brodick
Isle of Arran
Tel: (0770) 2140/2401
Jan-Dec

LOCHRANZA
The Pier
Lochranza
Isle of Arran
Tel: (0770) 83320
May-Oct

Kincardine and Deeside Tourist Board

ABOYNE
Ballater Road Car Park
Aboyne
Tel: (03398) 86060
Easter-Sept

BANCHORY
Bellfield Car Park
Banchory
Tel: (0330) 822000
Easter-end Oct

CRATHIE
Car Park
Crathie
Tel: (03397) 42414
May-Sept

BALLATER
Station Square
Ballater
Tel: (03397) 55306
Easter-end Oct

BRAEMAR
The Mews
Mar Road
Braemar
Tel: (03397) 41600
March-Nov
weekends in ski season

STONEHAVEN
66 Allardice Street
Stonehaven
Tel: (0569) 62806
Easter-Oct

Loch Lomond, Stirling and Trossachs Tourist Board

ABERFOYLE ✉ ♿
Main Street
Aberfoyle
Perthshire FK8 3TH
Tel: (08772) 352
Apr-Oct

BALLOCH ✉ ♿
Balloch Road
Balloch
Dumbartonshire G83
Tel: (0389) 53533
March-Nov

CALLANDER ✉ ♿
Rob Roy & Trossachs Visitor Centre
Ancaster Square
Callander
Perthshire
Tel: (0877) 30342
March-Dec

DRYMEN
The Square
Tel: (0360) 60068
Jan-Dec

DUMBARTON ✉
A82 Northbound
Milton
Dumbarton
Tel: (0389) 42306
Apr-Oct

DUNBLANE ✉ ♿
Stirling Road
Dunblane
Stirlingshire FK15
Tel: (0786) 824428
May-Sept

HELENSBURGH ✉ ♿
The Clock Tower
Helensburgh
Dumbartonshire
Tel: (0436) 72642
Apr-Oct

KILLIN ✉ ♿
Main Street
Killin
Perthshire
Tel: (05672) 820254
Apr-Oct

STIRLING ✉ ♿
Dumbarton Road
Stirling FK8 2QQ
Tel: (0786) 75019
Jan-Dec

STIRLING – Pirnhall ✉ ♿
Pirnhall
By Stirling
Tel: (0786) 814111
March-Nov

TARBET – Loch Lomond ✉
Main Street
Tarbet
Dumbartonshire
Tel: (03012) 260
Apr-Oct

TILLICOULTRY ✉ ♿
Clock Mill
Upper Mill Street
Tillicoultry
FK13 6AX
Tel: (0259) 752176
Apr-Oct

TYNDRUM ✉ ♿
Main Street
Tyndrum
Perthshire FK20 8RY
Tel: (08384) 246
Apr-Oct

Moray Tourist Board

BUCKIE
Cluny Square
Buckie AB56 1AG
Tel: (0542) 34853
Mid May-Sept

CULLEN
20 Seafield Street
Cullen AB56 2SH
Tel: (0542) 40757
Mid May-Sept

DUFFTOWN
Clock Tower
The Square
Dufftown AB55 4AD
Tel: (0340) 20501
Easter-Oct

ELGIN ✉
17 High Street
Elgin IV30 1EG
Tel: (0343) 542666/543388
Jan-Dec

FORRES
Falconer Museum
Tolbooth Street
Forres IV36 0PH
Tel: (0309) 672938
Mid May-Oct

KEITH
Church Road
Keith AB55 3BR
Tel: (05422) 2634
Mid May-Sept

LOSSIEMOUTH
Station Park
Pitgaveny Street
Lossiemouth IV31 6NT
Tel: (034381) 814804
Mid May-mid Sept

TOMINTOUL
The Square
Tomintoul AB37 9ET
Tel: (08074) 580285
Easter-Oct

 When you visit a Tourist Information Centre you are guaranteed a welcome by people who really know their country.

For information, maps, holiday reading, accommodation bookings and much more, look for the information *i*

Perthshire Tourist Board

ABERFELDY
The Square
Aberfeldy PH15 2DA
Tel: (0887) 820276
Jan-Dec

AUCHTERARDER
90 High Street
Auchterarder PH3 1BJ
Tel: (0764) 663450
Jan-Dec

BLAIRGOWRIE
26 Wellmeadow
Blairgowrie
Perthshire PH10 6AS
Tel: (0250) 872960/873701
from Nov 91

CRIEFF
Town Hall
High Street
Crieff PH7 3HU
Tel: (0764) 652578
Jan-Dec

DUNKELD
The Cross
Dunkeld
Perthshire PH8 0AN
Tel: (0350) 727688
from mid 92
March-Oct

KINROSS
Service Area Junction 6
M90
Kinross
Tel: (0577) 863680
Jan-Dec

PERTH
45 High Street
Perth PH1 5TJ
Tel: (0738) 38353
Jan-Dec

PERTH – Inveralmond
Inveralmond
A9 Western City By-pass
Perth
Tel: (0738) 38481
Easter-Oct

PITLOCHRY
22 Atholl Road
Pitlochry
Perthshire PH16 5BX
Tel: (0796) 472215/472751
Jan-Dec

West Highlands, and Islands of Argyll Tourist Board

BOWMORE
The Square
Bowmore
Isle of Islay
Tel: (049681) 254
Jan-Dec

CAMPBELTOWN
Mackinnon House
The Pier
Campbeltown
Tel: (0586) 552056
Jan-Dec

CRAIGNURE
The Pierhead
Craignure
Isle of Mull
Tel: (06802) 377
April-Oct

INVERARAY
Front Street
Inveraray
Argyll
Tel: (0499) 2063
Jan-Dec

LOCHGILPHEAD
Lochnell Street
Lochgilphead
Argyll
Tel: (0546) 602344
April-Oct

TARBERT
Harbour Street
Tarbert
Argyll
Tel: (0880) 820429
April-Oct

OBAN
Boswell House
Argyll Square
Oban
Tel: (0631) 63122
Jan-Dec

TOBERMORY
Main Street
Tobermory
Isle of Mull
Tel: (0688) 2182
Jan-Dec

3. THE NORTHERN HIGHLANDS AND ISLANDS

Caithness Tourist Board

JOHN O'GROATS
County Road
John O'Groats
Tel: (0955) 81373
Apr-Oct

THURSO
Riverside
Thurso
Tel: (0847) 62371
Apr-Oct

WICK
Whitechapel Road
Wick
Tel: (0955) 2596
Jan-Dec

Isle of Skye and South West Ross

BROADFORD
Car Park
Broadford
Isle of Skye
Tel: (0471822) 361
Apr-Oct

GLENSHIEL
Glenshiel
Kyle of Lochalsh
Ross-shire
Tel: (059981) 264
Apr-Sept

KYLE OF LOCHALSH
Car Park
Kyle of Lochalsh
Ross-shire
Tel: (0599) 4276
Apr-Oct

PORTREE
Meall House
Portree
Isle of Skye IV51 9BZ
Tel: (0478) 2137
Jan-Dec

Orkney Tourist Board

KIRKWALL
6 Broad Street
Kirkwall
Orkney
Tel: (0856) 872856
Jan-Dec

STROMNESS
Ferry Terminal Building
Stromness
Orkney
Tel: (0856) 850716
Jan-Dec

Ross and Cromarty Tourist Board

GAIRLOCH
Auchtercairn
Gairloch
Ross-shire
Tel: (0445) 2130
Jan-Dec

LOCHCARRON
Main Street
Lochcarron
Ross-shire
Tel: (05202) 357
April-Oct

NORTH KESSOCK
North Kessock
Ross-shire
Tel: (0463) 73505
Jan-Dec

STRATHPEFFER
The Square
Strathpeffer
Ross-shire
Tel: (0997) 421415
Easter-Nov

ULLAPOOL
Shore Street
Ullapool
Tel: (0854) 612135
Easter-Nov

Shetland Islands Tourism

LERWICK
Market Cross
Lerwick
Shetland ZE1 0LU
Tel: (0595) 3434
Jan-Dec

Sutherland Tourist Board

BETTYHILL ♿
Clachan
Bettyhill
Sutherland
Tel: (06412) 342
Apr-Sept

DORNOCH ✉
The Square
Dornoch
Sutherland IV25 3SD
Tel: (0862) 810400
Jan-Dec

HELMSDALE ♿
Coupar Park
Helmsdale
Sutherland
Tel: (04312) 640
Late Mar-Sept

BONAR BRIDGE ✉ ♿
Bonar Bridge
Sutherland
Tel: (08632) 333
Apr-Sept

DURNESS ♿
Sango
Durness
Sutherland
Tel: (0971) 511259
Late Mar-Oct

LOCHINVER ♿
Main Street
Lochinver
Sutherland
Tel: (05714) 330
Late Mar-Oct

Western Isles Tourist Board

CASTLEBAY
Main Street
Castlebay
Isle of Barra
Tel: (08714) 336
Easter-Oct

TARBERT
Pier Road
Tarbert
Isle of Harris
Tel: (0859) 2011

LOCHMADDY
Pier Road
Lochmaddy
Isle of North Uist
Tel: (08763) 321
Easter-Oct

STORNOWAY ✉
4 South Beach Street
Stornoway
Isle of Lewis PA87 2XY
Tel: (0851) 703088
Jan-Dec

LOCHBOISDALE
Pier Road
Lochboisdale
Isle of South Uist
Tel: (08784) 286
Easter-Oct

ALPHABETICAL INDEX OF SCOTTISH ISLANDS

Many visitors to Scotland are keen to stay on islands. In this guide, the locations on small islands are listed under the names of the islands: Isle of Eigg etc. On the larger islands, locations are listed under the name of the nearest town or village. If you want to stay on Arran, for instance, this index will show you the locations to check in the guide: Blackwaterfoot, Kildonan and so on. The number beside each place-name refers to the Maps on pages xxvii-xxxii, eg. 5B10= Map 5, grid reference B10.

ALPHABETICAL INDEX OF SCOTTISH ISLANDS

MAPS

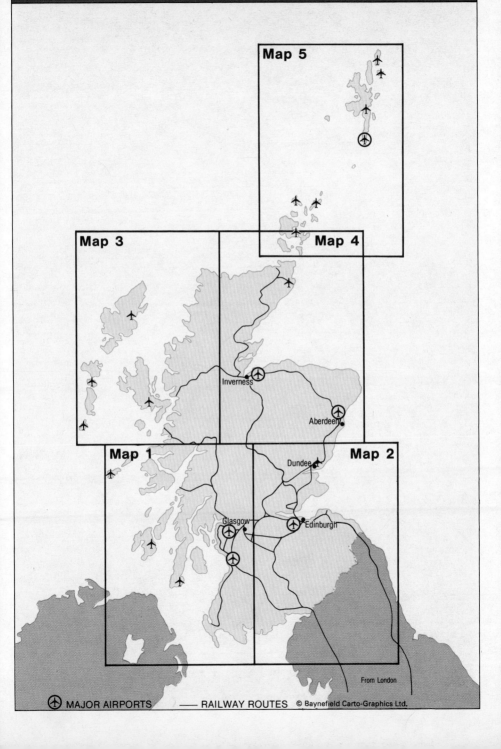

Map 5

Map 3

Map 4

Inverness

Aberdeen

Map 1

Dundee

Map 2

Glasgow

Edinburgh

From London

⊕ MAJOR AIRPORTS   —— RAILWAY ROUTES   © Bayenfield Carto-Graphics Ltd.

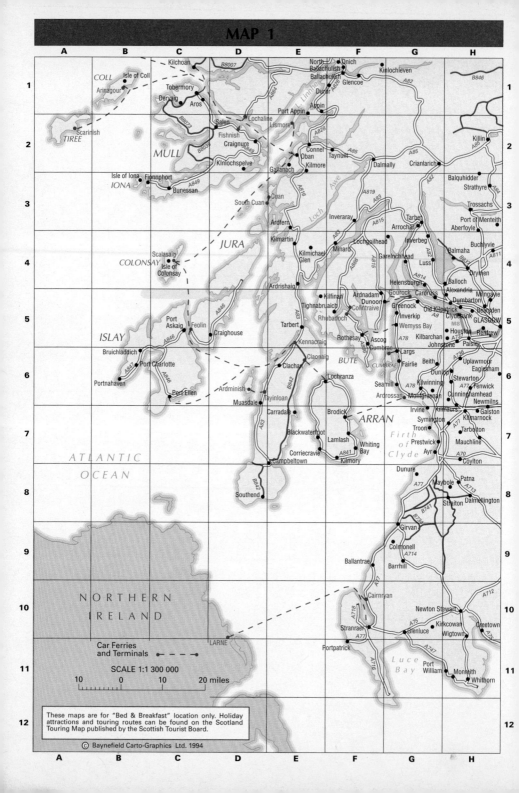

MAP 2

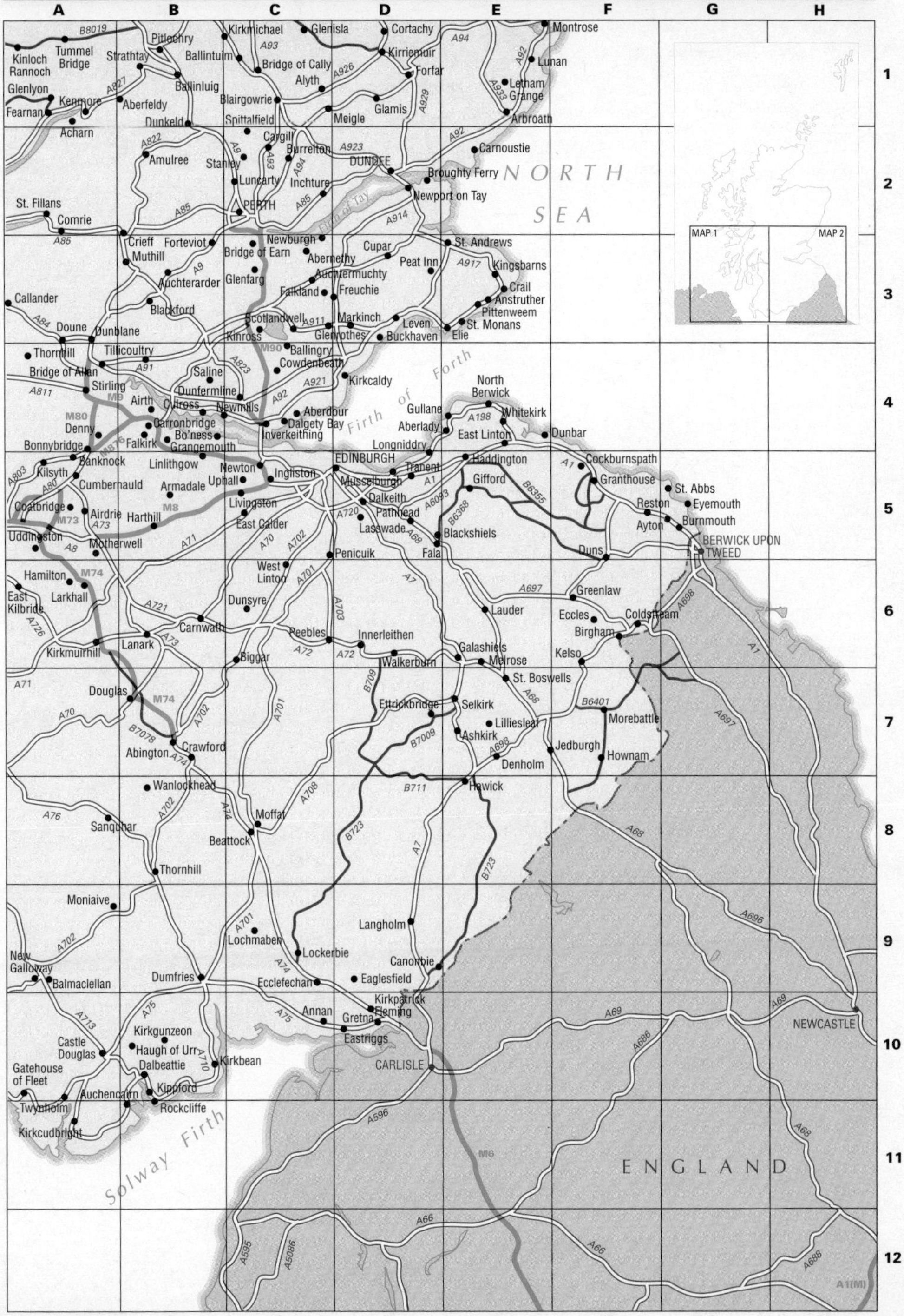

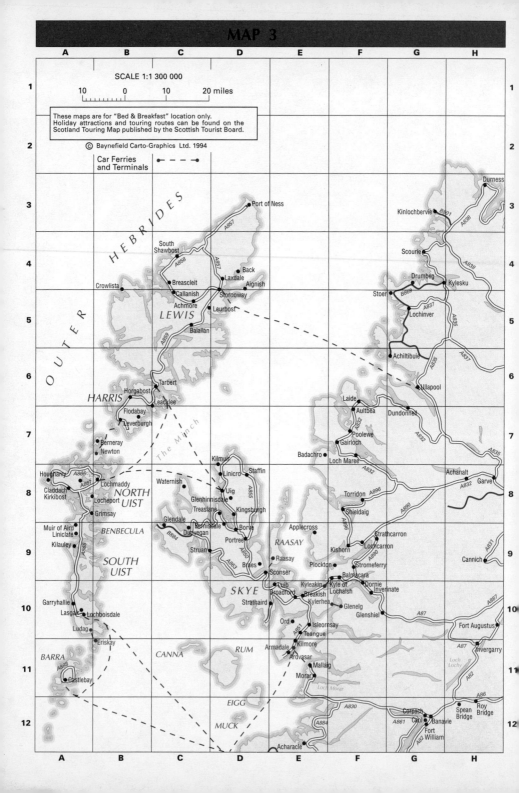

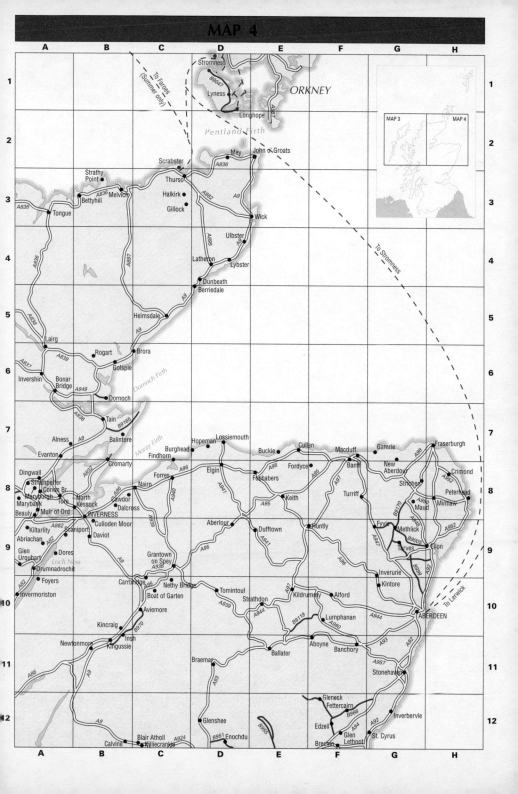

MAP 4

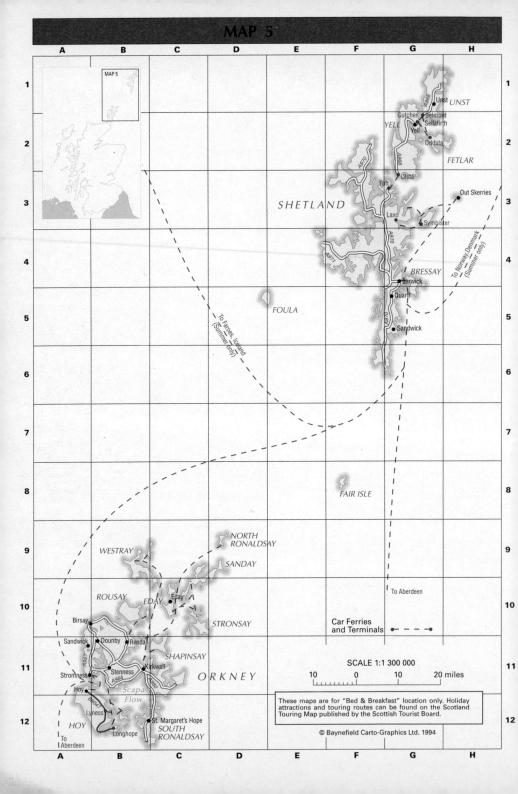

MAP 5

Scotland

BED & BREAKFAST

1994

ABERCHIRDER, by Huntly Banffshire	Map 4 F8						
Mrs E Gregor Skeibhill Farm Aberchirder Banffshire AB54 5TT Tel: (Aberchirder) 0466 780301		COMMENDED Listed	2 Family	1 Pub.Bath/Show	B&B per person from £12.00 Single from £11.00 Double	Open Jan-Dec Dinner 1800-2000 B&B + Eve. Meal from £17.00	

Home cooking and baking on friendly working family farm. Close to Castle and Whisky Trail. 8 miles (13kms) from Banff; 11 miles (17kms) from Huntly.

ABERDEEN	Map 4 G1						
The Angel Islington Guest House 191 Bon Accord Street Aberdeen AB1 2UA Tel: (Aberdeen) 0224 587043		COMMENDED Listed	2 Single 1 Twin 2 Double 1 Family	1 En Suite fac 3 Pub.Bath/Show	B&B per person £18.00-£25.00 Single £14.00-£18.00 Double	Open Jan-Dec	

Semi-detached granite built Victorian house in residential area on south side of city. Shops, railway station and Duthie Park within 1 mile (2kms).

| Ashgrove Guest House
34 Ashgrove Road
Aberdeen
AB2 5AD
Tel: (Aberdeen) 0224 484861 | | APPROVED
Listed | 3 Single
2 Family | 1 En Suite fac
1 Limited ensuite
1 Pub.Bath/Show | B&B per person
from £16.00 Single
from £15.00 Double | Open Jan-Dec | |

Conveniently located for airport and local hospitals, with easy access to city centre. Television in all bedrooms.

| Bimini
69 Constitution Street
Aberdeen
AB2 1ET
Tel: (Aberdeen) 0224 646912 | | COMMENDED
♛ | 1 Single
4 Twin
1 Double
1 Family | 2 Pub.Bath/Show | B&B per person
£16.00-£20.00 Single
£15.00-£17.00 Double | Open Jan-Dec | |

Personally run guest house. In residential area close to centre and all local amenities. Car park to rear.

| Denmore Guest House
166 Bon-Accord Street
Aberdeen
AB1 2TX
Tel: (Aberdeen) 0224 587751
Fax: 0224 587751 | | COMMENDED
♛ | 3 Single
2 Twin
2 Double
2 Family | 3 Pub.Bath/Show | B&B per person
£18.00-£25.00 Single
£15.00-£16.00 Double | Open Jan-Dec | |

Victorian semi-detached house in quiet tree-lined residential street. Close to city centre, railway station and ferry terminal.

FURAIN GUEST HOUSE

North Deeside Road, Peterculter, Aberdeen AB1 0QN
Telephone: 0224 732189

FURAIN GUEST HOUSE, on the A93, 8 miles west of Aberdeen centre, close to several historic castles and convenient for touring some of the most beautiful countryside in the UK.

We give a full Scottish Breakfast with choice and an optional three-course evening meal, home cooked, again with choice — table licence.

| Furain Guest House
92 North Deeside Road
Peterculter
Aberdeen
AB1 0QN
Tel: (Aberdeen) 0224 732189 | | COMMENDED
♛ ♛ | 1 Single
3 Twin
2 Double
2 Family | 8 En Suite fac
1 Pub.Bath/Show | B&B per person
£25.00-£27.00 Single
£18.00-£19.50 Double | Open Jan-Dec
Dinner 1900-2100
B&B + Eve. Meal
£26.00-£38.00 | |

Late Victorian house built of red granite. Family run, convenient for town, Royal Deeside and the Castle Trail. Private car parking.

Gushetneuk Guest House 3 Belvidere Street Aberdeen AB2 4QS Tel: (Aberdeen) 0224 636435	Map 4	COMMENDED Listed	2 Single 2 Twin 1 Double 1 Family	1 Pub.Bath/Show	B&B per person from £22.00 Single from £17.00 Double	Open Jan-Dec	

Terraced granite house in residential area close to local public parks.
Convenient for Aberdeen Royal Infirmary and bus routes to city centre.

| Klibreck Guest House
410 Great Western Road
Aberdeen
AB1 6NR
Tel: (Aberdeen) 0224 316115 | | COMMENDED | 1 Single
3 Twin
1 Double
1 Family | 2 Pub.Bath/Show | B&B per person
from £18.00 Single
from £14.50 Double | Open Jan-Dec | |

Granite building, corner site in residential area in city's West End.
On main bus route to city centre and Royal Deeside. Off road parking.

| Mount Pleasant
Guest House
28 Abbotswell Crescent
Aberdeen
AB1 5AR
Tel: (Aberdeen) 0224 871788 | | COMMENDED
Listed | 4 Single
3 Twin
4 Double
1 Family | 1 En Suite fac
4 Pub.Bath/Show | B&B per person
£17.50-£22.50 Single
£14.00-£17.50 Double | Open Jan-Dec
Dinner at 1830
B&B + Eve. Meal
£25.50-£30.50 | |

Recently modernised bungalow with garden. Close to industrial estate
and only 1.5 miles (2.5kms) from city centre.

| Salisbury Guest House
12 Salisbury Terrace
Aberdeen
AB1 6QH
Tel: (Aberdeen) 0224 590447 | | COMMENDED | 1 Single
1 Twin
1 Double
1 Family | 3 Pub.Bath/Show | B&B per person
from £16.00 Single
from £15.00 Double | Open Jan-Dec
Dinner from 1700
B&B + Eve. Meal
£21.00-£22.00 | |

Family run guest house in quiet street near to city centre
and to main bus routes. Home cooking.

| Strathboyne Guest House
26 Abergeldie Terrace
Aberdeen
AB1 6EE
Tel: (Aberdeen) 0224 593400 | | COMMENDED | 4 Single
1 Twin
1 Double
1 Family | 2 En Suite fac
2 Pub.Bath/Show | B&B per person
£17.00-£23.00 Single
£15.00-£16.00 Double | Open Jan-Dec
Dinner 1750-1800
B&B + Eve. Meal
from £24.00 | |

Semi-detached house in residential area, close to local park.
Breakfast menu and evening tea. Near bus route and 10 minutes walk to city centre.

| Strathisla Guest House
408 Great Western Road
Aberdeen
AB1 6NR
Tel: (Aberdeen) 0224 321026 | | COMMENDED
Listed | 2 Single
1 Twin
1 Double
1 Family | 5 En Suite fac | B&B per person
£25.00-£30.00 Single
£20.00-£22.00 Double | Open Jan-Dec | |

Personally run guest house in west end of Aberdeen. Totally smoke-free environment.

| Mrs Margaret Laing
20 Louisville Avenue
Aberdeen
AB1 6TX
Tel: (Aberdeen) 0224
319812 | | COMMENDED | 1 Single
1 Twin
1 Family | 1 Pub.Bath/Show | B&B per person
£16.00-£18.00 Single
£15.00-£17.00 Double | Open Jan-Dec | |

Terraced granite house in quiet residential area 2 miles (3 kms) from city centre.
Close to main Inverness, Braemar and Perth roads.

| Mr and Mrs J A G McHardy
33 Carden Place
Aberdeen
AB1 1UN
Tel: (Aberdeen) 0224 645191 | | COMMENDED
Listed | 1 Single
2 Double | 1 Pub.Bath/Show | B&B per person
£18.00-£20.00 Single
£16.00-£18.00 Double | Open Jan-Dec | |

Victorian terraced house in west end of city within easy walking
distance of city centre. Unrestricted parking. Non smoking house.

Mrs Mann Bellfield Farm, Kingswells Aberdeen AB1 8PX Tel: (Aberdeen) 0224 740239	COMMENDED 👑	1 Twin 1 Double 1 Family	2 Pub.Bath/Show	B&B per person £18.00-£20.00 Single £17.00-£18.00 Double	Open Jan-Nov
		200 year old farmhouse on working farm, situated on western outskirts of Aberdeen on A944. 4 miles (6kms) to city centre by bus.			
Mrs Marshall Elmdale 8 Elm Place Aberdeen AB2 3SU Tel: (Aberdeen) 0224 635549	APPROVED Listed	1 Single 1 Twin 1 Double 1 Family	4 Limited ensuite 1 Pub.Bath/Show	B&B per person £26.50-£29.50 Single £16.25-£18.75 Double	Open Jan-Dec Dinner 1730-1930 B&B + Eve. Meal £26.20-£29.20
		Quiet guest house near hospital and city centre. Lunches and dinner available on request.			
Norman & Mary Marshall Manorville 252 Great Western Road Aberdeen AB1 6PJ Tel: (Aberdeen) 0224 594190	COMMENDED 👑👑	1 Twin 1 Double 1 Family	3 En Suite fac	B&B per person £22.00-£25.00 Single £18.00-£20.00 Double	Open Jan-Dec
		Granite dwelling house in close proximity to town centre on main bus route to Deeside. All rooms ensuite.			
Mrs E Noble 39 Desswood Place Aberdeen AB2 4EE Tel: (Aberdeen) 0224 646571	APPROVED Listed	1 Single 1 Double 1 Family	1 Pub.Bath/Show	B&B per person £17.00-£18.00 Single £15.00-£16.00 Double	Open Jan-Dec
		Granite terraced house in residential West end of city on bus route to city centre.			
Mrs D Spalding 9 Morningside Terrace Mannofield Aberdeen AB1 7NZ Tel: (Aberdeen) 0224 315213	COMMENDED Listed	2 Single	1 Pub.Bath/Show	B&B per person £16.00-£18.00 Single	Open Jan-Dec
		Modern detached house in quiet residential area, easy parking. Non smoking establishment.			
Mrs A Watt St Elmo, 64 Hilton Drive Aberdeen AB2 2NP Tel: (Aberdeen) 0224 483065	APPROVED Listed	2 Twin	1 Pub.Bath/Show	B&B per person £17.00-£21.00 Single £13.00-£15.00 Double	Open Jan-Dec
		Detached bungalow in residental area with frequent bus service. City centre 2 miles (3 kms). No smoking.			

BY ABERDEEN — Map 4 G1

Mrs Goudriaan Blackdog Heights Bridge of Don, Aberdeen Aberdeenshire AB23 8BT Tel: (Aberdeen) 0224 704287	COMMENDED Listed	2 Single 1 Twin 1 Double	1 Pub.Bath/Show	B&B per person £14.00-£15.00 Single from £14.00 Double	Open Jan-Dec
		Large modern bungalow in own grounds 5 miles (8kms) from Aberdeen, 2 miles (3kms) from Exhibition Centre. Handy for main A92 and near the beach.			

HAWKCRAIG HOUSE

HAWKCRAIG POINT, ABERDOUR, FIFE KY3 0TZ
Telephone: (0383) 860 335

HAWKCRAIG is an old ferryman's house at water's edge overlooking
Aberdour Harbour and Inchcolm Island.
Only 30 minutes from Edinburgh by road or rail.
Accommodation, on the ground floor, comprises one twin with private
shower, toilet etc., one double with private bath, toilet etc., and
guests' sitting room.

Mrs E Barrie Hawkcraig House Hawkcraig Point Aberdour Fife KY3 0TZ Tel: (Aberdour) 0383 860335	**HIGHLY COMMENDED** 👑 👑	1 Twin 1 Double	2 En Suite fac	B&B per person £22.00-£24.00 Single £18.00-£20.00 Double	Open Mar-Oct Dinner from 1900 B&B + Eve. Meal £35.00-£37.00
		Old ferryman's house situated at waters edge overlooking Aberdour Harbour and Inchcolm Island. Steep access. Taste of Scotland member.			
Mrs S Knott Dunraggie, Murrell Road Aberdour Fife KY3 0XN Tel: (Aberdour) 0383 860136	**COMMENDED** 👑	1 Single 1 Double 1 Family	1 En Suite fac 1 Priv. NOT ensuite 1 Pub. Bath/Show	B&B per person £15.00-£16.00 Single £15.00-£17.00 Double	Open Apr-Sep
		Comfortable, warm and quiet; ideal for all ages. Lovely views over River Forth.			
Mrs Janet Lonie Flock House, Seaside Place Aberdour Fife KY3 0TX Tel: (Aberdour) 0383 860777		1 Twin 1 Family	2 Priv. NOT ensuite 1 Pub. Bath/Show	B&B per person £15.00-£17.00 Single £14.00-£15.00 Double	Open Jan-Dec
Mrs Pauleen Norman Forth View, Hawkcraig Point Aberdour Fife KY3 0TZ Tel: (Aberdour) 0383 860402		1 Single 2 Twin 1 Double 1 Family	3 En Suite fac 2 Pub. Bath/Show	B&B per person £16.00-£25.00 Single £18.50-£20.00 Double	Open Apr-Oct Dinner at 1900

TELEPHONE DIALLING CODES

Many telephone dialling codes
have changed this year. If you
experience difficulty in
connecting a call, please call
Directory Enquiries — **192** —
where someone will issue the
correct number.

Please note: a charge will be
placed for this service when
using a private telephone.

Map 2
B1

Dunolly House

Taybridge Drive, Aberfeldy, Perthshire PH15 2BP.
Telephone: (0887) 820298

A warm welcome awaits you at this delightful 'Heart of the Highlands' Tay riverside location. Ideal family holiday accommodation and touring base. Attractive twin, double or family rooms including en-suite facilities, TV in rooms, games room, laundry, drying room. Rural setting but close to shops, recreation centre, golf and fishing centres. Popular walking, pony trekking, watersports country. Activity programmes arranged (s.a.e. for details).

**B&B from £12 pp per night
(en-suite from £17.50)**

Dunolly House Taybridge Drive Aberfeldy Perthshire PH15 2BP Tel: (Aberfeldy) 0887 820298	Award Pending	1 Single 2 Twin 5 Double 8 Family	5 En Suite fac 1 Limited ensuite 6 Pub. Bath/Show	B&B per person £15.00 Single £14.00-£18.50 Double	Open Jan-Dec Dinner 1900-2030 B&B + Eve. Meal £22.50-£26.50
Fernbank House Kenmore Street Aberfeldy Perthshire PH15 2BL Tel: (Aberfeldy) 0887 820345	Award Pending	1 Single 1 Twin 3 Double 2 Family	7 En Suite fac	B&B per person from £19.50 Single £19.50-£22.50 Double	Open Jan-Dec
Tigh'n Eilean Guest House Taybridge Drive Aberfeldy Perthshire PH15 2BP Tel: (Aberfeldy) 0887 820109	HIGHLY COMMENDED	1 Twin 2 Double	2 En Suite fac 1 Priv. NOT ensuite	B&B per person £16.00-£19.00 Single £16.00-£19.00 Double	Open Jan-Dec Dinner 1800-1900 B&B + Eve. Meal £25.00-£29.00
		Elegant Victorian house overlooking the river. Warm and comfortable; homecooking. One room with jacuzzi.			
Mrs Bassett-Smith Handa, Taybridge Road Aberfeldy Perthshire PH15 2BH Tel: (Aberfeldy) 0887 820334	COMMENDED	1 Twin 1 Double	2 En Suite fac	B&B per person £15.00-£16.00 Double	Open Jan-Dec Dinner 1800-1930 B&B + Eve. Meal £21.00-£22.00
		Semi-detached house with fine views over Wade's Bridge to Weem Rock. Putting green next door, golf course and tennis court 100 yards.			
Mrs Bell-Campbell Carn Dris by Aberfeldy Perthshire PH15 2LB Tel: (Aberfeldy) 0887 820250	Award Pending	1 Single 1 Twin 2 Double	1 En Suite fac 1 Pub. Bath/Show	B&B per person from £15.00 Single £15.00-£20.00 Double	Open Apr-Oct
Mr and Mrs Malcolm Novar, 2 Home Street Aberfeldy Perthshire PH15 2AJ Tel: (Aberfeldy) 0887 820779		1 Twin 1 Family	1 En Suite fac 1 Priv.NOT ensuite	B&B per person £15.00-£17.00 Single £15.00-£17.00 Double	Open Apr-Oct

Mr & Mrs P Nunn Mavisbank, Taybridge Drive Aberfeldy Perthshire PH15 2BP Tel: (Aberfeldy) 0887 820223			1 Twin 1 Double	1 Pub. Bath/Show	B&B per person from £15.00 Single from £15.00 Double	Open Mar-Oct	
Mr D & Mrs J Parmley Nessbank, Crieff Road Aberfeldy Perthshire PH15 2BJ Tel: (Aberfeldy) 0887 829503		**HIGHLY COMMENDED** 👑 👑	2 Twin 1 Double	3 En Suite fac	B&B per person £20.00-£22.00 Single £18.00-£20.00 Double	Open Jan-Dec	
			Victorian house on the edge of the town yet 5 minutes walk from the shops. Close to Moness Burn and scenic bank walks.				
Mrs Ross 2 Rannoch Road Aberfeldy Perthshire PH15 2BU Tel: (Aberfeldy) 0887 820770			1 Twin 2 Double	1 Pub.Bath/Show	B&B per person £13.00-£14.50 Double	Open Mar-Oct Dinner from 1900 B&B + Eve. Meal £20.00-£22.00	
Mr Mark Williams Glengyle, Taybridge Terrace Aberfeldy Perthshire PH15 2BS Tel: (Aberfeldy) 0887 820350			1 Single 1 Twin 1 Double	2 Pub.Bath/Show	B&B per person £14.00-£16.00 Single £14.00-£16.00 Double	Open Jan-Dec	
ABERFOYLE **Perthshire** Mrs A Jennings The Bield, Trossachs Road Aberfoyle Perthshire FK8 3SX Tel: (Aberfoyle) 08772 351	Map 1 H3		1 Single 2 Double 1 Family	1 En Suite fac 1 Pub.Bath/Show	B&B per person to £12.50 Single £12.50-£15.00 Double	Open Apr-Oct	
Mrs M More Keith House, Trossachs Road Aberfoyle Perthshire FK8 3SX Tel: (Aberfoyle) 08772 470			1 Twin 1 Double	1 Pub.Bath/Show	B&B per person £15.00 Single £12.50 Double	Open May-Sep Dinner from 1830 B&B + Eve. Meal £18.50	
BY ABERFOYLE **Perthshire** Andrew and Pauline Carter Creag-Ard House B&B Milton, near Aberfoyle Perthshire FK8 3TQ Tel: (Aberfoyle) 0877 382297	Map 1 H3	**COMMENDED** Listed	1 Single 4 Twin 2 Double	4 En Suite fac 1 Pub.Bath/Show	B&B per person £15.00 Single £15.00-£20.00 Double	Open Jan-Dec	
			Detached Victorian house with superb views over Loch Ard and Ben Lomond beyond. Private fishing and boating. En suite bedrooms.				
ABERLADY **East Lothian** Mrs J Pyle Luffness Croft Aberlady East Lothian EH32 0QA Tel: (Aberlady) 08757 275	Map 2 E4		1 Twin 1 Double 1 Family	1 En Suite fac 1 Pub.Bath/Show	B&B per person £20.00-£25.00 Single £15.00-£20.00 Double	Open Jan-Dec Dinner 1700-2130 B&B + Eve. Meal £20.00-£28.00	

ABERLOUR **Banffshire** Mr Alexander Henderson The Haven, Mary Avenue Aberlour Banffshire AB38 9QN Tel: (Aberlour) 0340 871205	Map 4 D9		2 Twin 1 Double	1 En Suite fac 1 Pub.Bath/Show	B&B per person £15.00-£18.00 Single £13.00-£17.00 Double	Open Jan-Dec Dinner 1830-2000 B&B + Eve. Meal £24.00-£50.00	
BY ABERLOUR **Banffshire** Mrs Agnes Thom Kinermony Farm Aberlour Banffshire AB38 9LX Tel: (Aberlour) 0340 871818	Map 4 D9		2 Twin 1 Family	2 Pub.Bath/Show	B&B per person £12.00 Single £12.00 Double	Open Jan-Dec Dinner 1900-2000 B&B + Eve. Meal £20.00	
ABERNETHY **Perthshire** Mrs MacKenzie Gattaway Farm Abernethy Perthshire PH2 9LQ Tel: (Perth) 0738 85746	Map 2 C3		1 Twin 1 Double	2 En Suite fac 1 Pub.Bath/Show	B&B per person to £14.50 Double	Open Jan-Dec Dinner 1800-2100	
ABINGTON **Lanarkshire** Mrs C Craig Townfoot Roberton, by Abington Lanarkshire ML12 6RS Tel: (Lamington) 08995 655	Map 2 B7	**COMMENDED** Listed	2 Twin	1 Pub.Bath/Show	B&B per person £12.00-£14.00 Single £12.00-£14.00 Double	Open Jan-Dec Dinner 1800-2000 B&B + Eve. Meal £18.00-£20.00	
			In a delightfully quiet position, set back from the main road, small and friendly with comfortable rooms. Some annex accomm for self catering.				
Mrs A Hodge Gilkerscleugh Mains Farm Abington Lanarkshire Tel: (Crawford) 08642 388		**Award** **Pending**	1 Twin 1 Double	2 En Suite fac	B&B per person £15.00-£17.00 Single £15.00-£17.00 Double	Open May-Oct Dinner 1800-2000 B&B + Eve. Meal £26.50-£28.50	
Mrs Mary Hodge Craighead Farm Abington Lanarkshire ML12 6SQ Tel: (Crawford) 08642 356		**Award** **Pending**	1 Twin 1 Double	1 Pub.Bath/Show	B&B per person £14.00-£15.50 Single £14.00-£15.50 Double	Open May-Sep Dinner 1800-1900 B&B + Eve. Meal £20.00-£21.00	
Mrs J Hyslop Glentewing Farm Crawfordjohn, Biggar Lanarkshire Tel: (Crawfordjohn) 08644 221		**HIGHLY** **COMMENDED**	1 Twin 1 Double	2 En Suite fac 1 Pub.Bath/Show	B&B per person £16.00-£20.00 Double	Open Jan-Dec Dinner 1830-1930 B&B + Eve. Meal £23.00-£28.00	
			Early 20c stone farmhouse set in a glen with extensive view towards Tinto Hill. Far from the madding crowd yet only 5 miles (8 kms) from M74.				
Mrs Lillias Hyslop Netherton Farmhouse Abington, by Biggar Lanarkshire ML12 6RU Tel: (Crawford) 08642 321		**Award** **Pending**	1 Twin 1 Double 1 Family	1 En Suite fac 2 Pub.Bath/Show	B&B per person £13.00-£16.00 Single £13.00-£16.00 Double	Open Jan-Dec Dinner 1800-2000 B&B + Eve. Meal £19.00-£22.00	

Mrs W Wales Kersdale, 2 Edinburgh Road Abington, Biggar Lanarkshire ML12 6SY Tel: (Crawford) 08642 323			1 Single 1 Twin 1 Family	1 Limited ensuite 2 Pub.Bath/Show	B&B per person £14.00-£18.00 Single £12.00-£14.00 Double	Open Jan-Dec Dinner 1700-2100 B&B + Eve. Meal £18.00-£20.00	▣ symbols

| ABOYNE
Aberdeenshire | Map 4
F1 | | | | | | |

ARBOR LODGE
BALLATER ROAD · ABOYNE AB34 5HY
Telephone: 03398 86951

ARBOR LODGE is a large luxury home set in a woodland garden in the picturesque village of Aboyne. All bedrooms have en-suite bathrooms, teamaking facilities and television. Ideally located for touring Royal Deeside. Activities include golf, fishing, bowling, tennis, gliding, water skiing, swimming, squash and hill-walking.

Arbor Lodge Ballater Road Aboyne Aberdeenshire AB34 5HY Tel: (Aboyne) 03398 86951	DELUXE 👑 👑	3 Twin	3 En Suite fac	B&B per person £25.00 Single £20.00 Double	Open Mar-Oct Dinner 1830-1930 B&B + Eve. Meal £35.00	symbols
		A newly built spacious house of character with large garden and wooded area. **Near centre of village. All bedrooms ensuite.**				
Chesterton House Formaston Park Aboyne Aberdeenshire AB34 5HF Tel: (Aboyne) 03398 86740		3 Twin	1 En Suite fac 1 Pub.Bath/Show	B&B per person £18.00-£20.00 Single £16.00-£18.00 Double	Open Jan-Dec Dinner 1800-2000 B&B + Eve. Meal £26.00-£30.00	symbols
Hazlehurst Lodge Ballater Road Aboyne Aberdeenshire AB34 5HY Tel: (Aboyne) 03398 86921	DELUXE 👑 👑 👑	1 Twin 2 Double	3 En Suite fac	B&B per person £28.00-£56.00 Single £28.00-£30.00 Double	Open Jan-Dec Dinner 1930-2130 B&B + Eve. Meal from £38.00	symbols
		Former Coachman's Lodge to Aboyne Castle with small restaurant **and large garden. Ideal for touring Royal Deeside.**				

STRUAN HALL
BALLATER ROAD, ABOYNE AB34 5HY
Telephone: (03398) 87241

We provide quality accommodation in a lovely village in the heart of Royal Deeside. Struan Hall is ideally situated for touring the area bounded by Perth, Inverness and Aberdeen. Quiet roads provide access to wonderful scenery, distilleries, castles, gardens and a full range of sporting and outdoor activities.

Struan Hall Ballater Road Aboyne Aberdeenshire AB34 5HY Tel: (Aboyne) 03398 87241	DELUXE 👑 👑	2 Twin 1 Double	3 En Suite fac	B&B per person £22.00-£27.00 Single to £22.00 Double	Open Feb-Nov	symbols
		Stone built house c1870, situated near centre of village, **recently refurbished to a high standard, with a warm and friendly welcome.**				

Name & Address	Grading	Rooms	Facilities	B&B Details	Prices	Opening
Mrs Eileen Barton Alltdinnie, Birse Aboyne Aberdeenshire AB34 5ES Tel: (Aboyne) 03398 86323		1 Single 1 Twin 1 Double	2 Priv.NOT ensuite 1 Pub.Bath/Show	B&B per person £18.00–£20.00 Single £20.00–£22.00 Double	Open Apr-Oct Dinner 1900-2000 B&B + Eve. Meal £30.00–£35.00	
Mr & Mrs Lawson Springfield, Old Ballater Road Aboyne Aberdeenshire AB34 5HN Tel: (Aboyne) 03398 86158	COMMENDED	1 Twin 1 Double 1 Family	1 En Suite fac 2 Priv.NOT ensuite	B&B per person £16.00–£18.00 Double	Open Apr-Oct	

Victorian house in cul-de-sac with views across Dee Valley. Convenient for golf, hill-walking, touring. Non-smoking. Relaxed friendly atmosphere.

Name & Address	Grading	Rooms	Facilities	B&B Details	Prices	Opening
Mr Moffat Alford House Restaurant, Ballater Road Aboyne Aberdeenshire AB34 5HT Tel: (Aboyne) 03398 86249		1 Single 1 Twin 1 Double	1 Pub.Bath/Show	B&B per person £14.00–£15.00 Single £14.00–£15.00 Double	Open Jan-Dec Dinner at 1800 B&B + Eve. Meal £20.00–£22.00	
Mrs E L Thorburn Birkwood Lodge, Gordon Crescent Aboyne Aberdeenshire AB34 5HJ Tel: (Aboyne) 03398 86347	HIGHLY COMMENDED	2 Twin 1 Double	2 En Suite fac 1 Priv.NOT ensuite	B&B per person £22.50–£25.00 Single £18.00–£20.00 Double	Open Jan-Dec Dinner 1900-2000 B&B + Eve. Meal £33.00–£40.00	

Quiet situation overlooking village green. Friendly Scottish hospitality and log fire. Emphasis on home cooking using fresh local produce.

Name & Address	Map	Grading	Rooms	Facilities	B&B Details	Prices	Opening
ABRIACHAN Inverness-shire Miss Lorna Lumsden Wester Altourie, Blackfold Abriachan Inverness-shire IV3 6LB Tel: (Dochgarroch) 046386 203 Fax: 046386 247	Map 4 A9	Award Pending	2 Twin	1 Pub.Bath/Show	B&B per person £16.00 Double	Open Jan-Dec Dinner from 1800 B&B + Eve. Meal £24.00	
ACHANALT Ross-shire	Map 3 H8						

Name & Address	Grading	Rooms	Facilities	B&B Details	Prices	Opening
Mr Peter Davidson Achanalt House Achanalt, by Garve Ross-shire IV23 2QD Tel: (Garve) 0997 414283 Fax: 0997 414283	Award Pending	1 Single 1 Twin 1 Double 1 Family	2 Pub.Bath/Show	B&B per person £14.00–£15.00 Single £13.00–£15.00 Double	Open Jan-Dec Dinner at 1930 B&B + Eve. Meal £20.00–£22.00	

ACHARACLE, Ardnamurchan Argyll	Map 3 E1

BELMONT
ACHARACLE, ARDNAMURCHAN, ARGYLL PH36 4JT
Telephone: 096785 266

Good food and a warm welcome await you at Belmont, a converted manse overlooking Loch Shiel and the Moidart Hills. This family run establishment is the ideal centre for exploring the unspoilt Ardnamurchan Peninsula, with its abundant wildlife, excellent beaches and numerous walks. En-suite facilities. Children welcome.

Mrs C L Learmouth Belmont Acharacle, Ardnamurchan Argyll PH36 4JT Tel: (Salen) 096785 266		Award Pending	1 Single 1 Twin 1 Double	1 Pub.Bath/Show	B&B per person £16.50-£17.00 Single £14.00-£14.50 Double	Open Jan-Dec Dinner 1800-2100 B&B + Eve. Meal £23.50-£24.50

ACHARN, by Kenmore Perthshire Mrs Brodie Old School House Acharn, Aberfeldy Perthshire PH15 2HS Tel: (Kenmore) 0887 830307	Map 2 A1	COMMENDED	1 Twin 2 Double	2 En Suite fac 1 Limited ensuite 1 Pub.Bath/Show	B&B per person £14.00-£16.00 Double	Open Apr-Oct

Converted and fully modernised old schoolhouse by Loch Tay. Convenient for many water sports; excellent local walks; golf and fishing.

ACHILTIBUIE Ross-shire Mrs M W MacLeod Dornie House Achiltibuie Ross-shire IV26 2YP Tel: (Achiltibuie) 085482 271	Map 3 G6		2 Double	2 Pub.Bath/Show	B&B per person from £12.00 Double	Open Apr-Sep

ACHMORE Lewis, Western Isles Mrs W Golder Lochview, 35b Achmore Achmore Lewis, Western Isles PA86 9DU Tel: (Crossbost) 085186 205	Map 3 C5	COMMENDED	1 Twin 2 Double	2 Pub.Bath/Show	B&B per person to £15.00 Single to £15.00 Double	Open Jan-Dec Dinner 1800-1900 B&B + Eve. Meal to £22.50

Detached bungalow in a rural location overlooking Loch Achmore. Callanish Standing Stones about 5 miles (8kms). Good touring centre for west coast.

AIGNISH, Point Lewis, Western Isles Mrs L G MacDonald Ceol-Na-Mara, 1A Aignish Point Lewis, Western Isles PA86 0PB Tel: (Garrabost) 0851 870339	Map 3 D4	COMMENDED	1 Twin 1 Double 1 Family	2 Pub.Bath/Show	B&B per person £15.00 Single £14.00 Double	Open Jan-Dec Dinner 1830-2000 B&B + Eve. Meal £20.00-£21.00

Comfortable modern home in pleasant rural Stornoway across the causeway on the Eye Peninsula. Home cooking and baking.

Mrs C I McLeod 3 Aignish, Point Stornoway Lewis, Western Isles PA86 0PB Tel: (Garrabost) 0851 870900			1 Double 2 Family	2 Pub.Bath/Show	B&B per person to £14.00 Single to £14.00 Double	Open Jan-Dec Dinner 1800-2000 B&B + Eve. Meal to £20.00

AIRDRIE	Map 2						
Lanarkshire	A5						
Rosslee Guest House		COMMENDED	1 Single	3 En Suite fac	B&B per person	Open Jan-Dec	
107 Forest Street		✿ ✿	3 Twin	2 Pub.Bath/Show	£17.00-£21.00 Single	Dinner 1730-1830	
Airdrie			1 Double		£17.00-£21.00 Double	B&B + Eve. Meal	
Lanarkshire			1 Family			£24.00-£28.00	
ML6 7AR							
Tel: (Airdrie) 0236 765865							

Former church manse, now family run guest house with comfortable rooms.
Central situation for Edinburgh or Glasgow.

Mrs M Dunbar			1 Single	2 Pub.Bath/Show	B&B per person	Open Jan-Dec	
Braidenhill Farm			1 Double		£14.00-£14.50 Single		
Glenmavis, Airdrie			1 Family		£14.00-£14.50 Double		
Lanarkshire							
ML6 0PJ							
Tel: (Glenboig) 0236 872319							

Easter Glentore Farm
GREENGAIRS, AIRDRIE, LANARKSHIRE ML6 7TJ
Telephone: 0236 830243

Farm dates back to 1705, located in scenic setting. All rooms on ground floor, 1 en-suite, 2 with washbasins, all with tea/coffee facilities. Guests own bathroom, lounge with colour TV; evening meal optional. Warm, friendly, homely atmosphere with good home cooking and baking. Best B&B award-winner. Excellent touring base.

✿ ✿ **Highly Commended**   Alastair and Elsie Hunter

Mrs E Hunter		HIGHLY	3 Double	1 En Suite fac	B&B per person	Open Jan-Dec	
Easter Glentore Farm		COMMENDED		1 Pub.Bath/Show	from £19.50 Single	Dinner 1700-2000	
Greengairs, by Airdrie		✿ ✿			from £17.00 Double	B&B + Eve. Meal	
Lanarkshire						from £26.50	
ML6 7TJ							
Tel: (Greengairs)							
0236 830243							

Working stock rearing farm only 15 miles (24kms) from the centre of Glasgow.
Warm welcome, home cooking and homely atmosphere.

AIRTH	Map 2						
Stirlingshire	B4						
Mr N A Dixon		Award	2 Twin	1 En Suite fac	B&B per person	Open Jan-Dec	
Viewforth House, Main Street		Pending	1 Double	2 Priv.NOT ensuite	£22.00-£24.00 Single	Dinner 1700-1900	
Airth				1 Pub.Bath/Show	£18.00-£20.00 Double	B&B + Eve. Meal	
Stirlingshire						£29.50-£31.50	
FK2 8JJ							
Tel: (Airth) 0324 831711							

ALEXANDRIA	Map 1						
Dunbartonshire	H5						
Mrs Barbara O'Donnell			1 Single	2 Pub.Bath/Show	B&B per person	Open Jan-Dec	
Ashbank, 258 Main Street			1 Twin		£13.50-£14.00 Single	Dinner 1800-2000	
Alexandria			1 Family		£13.00-£13.50 Double	B&B + Eve. Meal	
Dunbartonshire						£18.00-£18.50	
G83 0NU							
Tel: (Alexandria) 0389 52356							

BY ALFORD	Map 4						
Aberdeenshire	F1						
Mrs C E Braiden		COMMENDED	1 Twin	1 Pub.Bath/Show	B&B per person	Open Jan-Dec	
Macbrae Lodge		Listed	1 Double		£14.00 Single		
Mongarrie, Alford			1 Family		£14.00 Double		
Aberdeenshire							
AB33 8AX							
Tel: (Alford) 09755 63421							

In quiet position, with lovely views of open countryside. Comfortable accommodation and home-baking. Ideal for Castle and Whisky trails.

Mrs Rosemarie MacKie Whiteside, Tullnessle Alford Aberdeenshire AB33 8DE Tel: (Alford) 09755 62024		APPROVED Listed	1 Twin 1 Double	1 Pub.Bath/Show	B&B per person £12.00-£13.00 Single from £12.00 Double	Open Apr-Sep Dinner 1900-2000 B&B + Eve. Meal £18.00-£19.00

Friendly farmhouse B&B on working dairy farm. Home-cooking. Pleasant country walks.

ALNESS **Ross-shire** Mrs Dorothy MacDougall Averon Bank Cottage, Ardross Road Alness Ross-shire IV17 0QA Tel: (Alness) 0349 882392	Map 4 B7	COMMENDED Listed	2 Single 1 Twin	2 Pub.Bath/Show	B&B per person £13.00-£14.00 Single £13.00-£14.00 Double	Open Jan-Dec

Detached cottage in small cul-de-sac on the outskirts of the village with private garden area.

ALYTH **Perthshire** Mrs Ann Ferguson Bruceton Farm Alyth, Blairgowrie Perthshire PH11 8JT Tel: (Craigton) 05753 201	Map 2 C1		1 Single 1 Twin 1 Double	1 Priv.NOT ensuite 1 Pub.Bath/Show	B&B per person from £14.00 Single from £17.00 Double	Open Mar-Nov

Mrs McBain Old Stables, 2 Losset Road Alyth Perthshire PH11 8BT Tel: (Alyth) 08283 2547		HIGHLY COMMENDED	2 Twin 1 Double	3 En Suite fac	B&B per person £16.00-£20.00 Single £16.00-£20.00 Double	Open Jan-Dec

Warm and friendly welcome assured in this striking conversion of 19C stable.
Log fireplace and sauna. Private car park close to town centre.

Mrs Jean Rimmer Lintrathen, St Ninians Road Alyth Perthshire PH11 8AR Tel: (Alyth) 08283 2785		COMMENDED Listed	1 Single 1 Double	1 Pub.Bath/Show	B&B per person £11.00-£12.00 Single £11.00-£12.00 Double	Open Jan-Dec

Modern bungalow at the edge of the town. Good touring area. Ample car parking.

AMULREE, by Aberfeldy **Perthshire** Mrs Simpkins Tirchardie Farm, Glenquaich Amulree, by Dunkeld Perthshire PH8 0DE Tel: (Amulree) 0350 725266	Map 2 B2		1 Single 1 Double 1 Family	2 Pub.Bath/Show	B&B per person £12.50 Single £12.50 Double	Open Jan-Dec Dinner 1900-2200 B&B + Eve. Meal £16.50

ANCRUM, by Jedburgh **Roxburghshire** Mrs Hensens Ancrum Craig Ancrum, Jedburgh Roxburghshire TD8 6UN Tel: (Ancrum) 08353 830280	Map 2 E7	COMMENDED	1 Twin 1 Double	1 En Suite fac 1 Priv.NOT ensuite	B&B per person £15.00-£20.00 Double	Open Mar-Oct

19C house in rural location with large garden and magnificent views of
surrounding countryside. Private bathrooms. Open fire.

ANNAN **Dumfriesshire** Mrs S Anderson The Craig, 18 St Johns Road Annan Dumfriesshire DG12 6AW Tel: (Annan) 0461 204665	Map 2 C1		1 Twin 1 Double 1 Family	2 Pub. Bath/Show	B&B per person £13.00-£14.00 Single £15.00-£16.00 Double	Open Jan-Dec Dinner 1800-1900 B&B + Eve. Meal £19.00-£20.00
BY ANNAN **Dumfriesshire** Mrs Forrest Hurkledale Farm, Cummertrees Annan Dumfriesshire DG12 5QA Tel: (Cummertrees) 04617 228	Map 2 C1	COMMENDED 👑 👑	1 Twin 2 Double	1 En Suite fac 1 Pub. Bath/Show	B&B per person from £17.00 Single £15.00-£20.00 Double	Open Jan-Dec Dinner 1830-1930 B&B + Eve. Meal £22.00-£27.00
			Old farmhouse on extensive mixed farm at village outskirts, with panoramic views across the Solway Firth to England.			
ANSTRUTHER **Fife** The Hermitage Ladywalk Anstruther Fife KY10 3EX Tel: (Anstruther) 0333 310909	Map 2 E3	Award Pending	1 Twin 3 Double	2 Pub. Bath/Show	B&B per person £22.00-£26.00 Double	Open Mar-Dec Dinner from 1900 B&B + Eve. Meal £32.00-£38.00

The Spindrift

PITTENWEEM ROAD, ANSTRUTHER, FIFE KY10 3DT
Telephone: 0333 310573

An imposing Victorian house with 8 luxury en-suite bedrooms, elegant public rooms and freshly prepared cuisine. Situated in the picturesque East Neuk — a golfer's paradise. We are a no-smoking house. **PRICES FROM £25 B&B**

For brochure contact Eric and Moyra McFarlane.

The Spindrift Pittenweem Road Anstruther Fife KY10 3DT Tel: (Anstruther) 0333 310573		HIGHLY COMMENDED 👑 👑 👑	2 Twin 3 Double 3 Family	8 En Suite fac	B&B per person £25.00-£30.00 Double	Open Jan-Dec Dinner 1800-1930 B&B + Eve. Meal £35.00-£40.00
			Stone built Victorian house with wealth of original features, set in fishing village. Short walk from town centre. Ideal touring base. Non smoking.			
Mrs C Dickson The Tea Clipper, 15 East Green Anstruther Fife KY10 3AA Tel: (Anstruther) 0333 310377			1 Single 1 Twin 1 Double	2 Pub. Bath/Show	B&B per person £13.00-£14.00 Single £13.00-£14.00 Double	Open Jan-Dec
Mrs E MacGeachy The Dykes, 69 Pittenweem Road Anstruther Fife KY10 3DT Tel: (Anstruther) 0333 310537		COMMENDED 👑	1 Double 1 Family	1 Pub. Bath/Show	B&B per person £15.00 Double	Open Mar-Sep
			Detached bungalow on edge of village. Views over golf course to the sea. Attractive well maintained garden. Non-smoking house.			
Mrs B Ritchie The Sheiling, 32 Glenogil Gardens Anstruther Fife KY10 3ET Tel: (Anstruther) 0333 310697		COMMENDED Listed	2 Double	1 Pub. Bath/Show	B&B per person £13.00-£15.00 Double	Open Apr-Sep
			Pretty, white semi-detached bungalow in quiet area near harbour. Attractive gardens. Homemade shortbread, jams and marmalade.			

BY APPIN Argyll	Map 1 E1

LOCHSIDE COTTAGE

FASNACLOICH, APPIN, ARGYLL PA38 4BJ   063173 216

Enjoy the West Highlands and Islands. The tranquil setting of Lochside Cottage (wonderful walks from cottage garden), combined with the friendly atmosphere of the Broadbent's home, ensures a pleasant relaxing holiday away from the hurly burly of modern life. Comfortable, attractive bedrooms, sittingroom and delicious home cooking. Local information readily available.

Mrs Stella M Broadbent Lochside Cottage Fasnacloich, by Appin Argyll PA38 4BJ Tel: (Appin) 063173 216	Award Pending	1 Twin 1 Double	2 Priv. NOT ensuite	B&B per person £16.00-£19.00 Double	Open Mar-Oct Dinner 1900-2000 B&B + Eve. Meal £26.00-£30.00

APPLECROSS Ross-shire Mrs J A Gillies Camustiel Applecross Ross-shire IV40 8LT Tel: (Applecross) 05204 229	Map 3 E9	2 Double	1 Pub. Bath/Show	B&B per person £14.00 Single £14.00 Double	Open Apr-Oct

Mrs Griffin The Kennels Applecross Ross-shire IV54 8ND Tel: (Applecross) 05204 247	APPROVED Listed	1 Single 1 Family	1 Pub. Bath/Show	B&B per person £12.00-£13.00 Single £12.00-£13.00 Double	Open Mar-Sep Dinner 1800-1900 B&B + Eve. Meal £18.00-£19.00

Stone built stalkers house on private estate, situated near peaceful west coast village: wild deer, home cooking.

Mrs J Thomson Raon-Mor, Camustiel Applecross Ross-shire IV54 8LT Tel: (Applecross) 05204 260		1 Twin 2 Double	1 Pub. Bath/Show	B&B per person from £13.00 Double	Open Apr-Oct

ARBROATH Angus Kingsley Guest House 29-31 Marketgate Arbroath Angus DD11 1AU Tel: (Arbroath) 0241 73933	Map 2 E1 APPROVED	3 Single 3 Twin 4 Double 4 Family	5 Pub. Bath/Show	B&B per person £14.00-£15.00 Single £12.00-£12.50 Double	Open Jan-Dec Dinner 1730-1900 B&B + Eve. Meal £17.00-£20.00

Family run guest house, in town centre, close to fishing harbour and beach. Games room. Minibus trips available to surrounding districts free of charge.

Sandhutton Guest House 16 Addison Place Arbroath Angus DD11 2AX Tel: (Arbroath) 0241 72007	HIGHLY COMMENDED	2 Twin 1 Double	1 Priv. NOT ensuite 2 Pub. Bath/Show	B&B per person from £16.00 Single from £14.00 Double	Open Apr-Oct

Victorian villa offering a warm welcome and comfortable non-smoking accommodation with modern facilities. Centrally located for amenities.

Susan Burness Beechcroft, 18c Viewfield Road Arbroath Angus DD11 2BU Tel: (Arbroath) 0241 71399		1 Twin 2 Double	1 En Suite fac 1 Pub. Bath/Show	B&B per person £12.00-£14.00 Double	Open Apr-Oct

---

Details of Grading and Classification are on page vi.   Key to symbols is on back flap.

Mrs J Caldwell Grange of Conon Arbroath Angus DD11 3SD Tel: (Carmyllie) 02416 202 Fax: 02416 202		**HIGHLY COMMENDED** 👑 👑	2 Twin 1 Family	1 Priv.NOT ensuite 2 Pub.Bath/Show	B&B per person to £27.50 Single to £22.50 Double	Open Jan-Dec	
			Family house on working arable farm in quiet location on outskirts of Arbroath. Close to golf courses and ideal for touring coast and Angus glens.				
Mrs H M Henderson Ashlea, 27 Bellevue Gardens Arbroath Angus DD11 5BE Tel: (Arbroath) 0241 74816			1 Twin 1 Double	1 Pub. Bath/Show	B&B per person £12.00-£12.50 Double	Open Apr-Oct	
BY ARBROATH Angus Mrs L E Storey The Old Inn Leysmill, by Arbroath Angus DD11 4RR Tel: (Friockheim) 0241 828436	Map 2 E1		1 Double 1 Family	1 Pub. Bath/Show	B&B per person £14.00 Single £14.00 Double	Open Jan-Dec Dinner 1800-1900 B&B + Eve. Meal £22.00	
ARDFERN Argyll C Lindsay-MacDougall of Lunga Lunga Ardfern, by Lochgilphead Argyll PA31 8QR Tel: (Barbreck) 08525 237 Fax: 08525 639	Map 1 E3		1 Single 1 Twin 1 Double	1 Pub. Bath/Show	B&B per person £14.00-£21.00 Single £14.00-£21.00 Double	Open Jan-Dec Dinner from 2000 B&B + Eve. Meal £24.00-£33.00	
ARDNADAM, by Dunoon Argyll Anchorage Guest House Shore Road, Ardnadam by Dunoon Argyll PA23 8QD Tel: (Dunoon) 0369 5108	Map 1 F5		2 Double 1 Family	3 En Suite fac	B&B per person £24.00-£32.00 Single £14.00-£22.00 Double	Open Jan-Dec Dinner 1900-2100 B&B + Eve. Meal £26.00-£44.00	
ARDRISHAIG, by Lochgilphead Argyll Mrs Hamilton Seaview, St Claire Road Ardrishaig, by Lochgilphead Argyll Tel: (Lochgilphead) 0546 603300	Map 1 E4	Award Pending	1 Twin 2 Double 1 Family	2 Pub. Bath/Show	B&B per person £12.00 Single to £12.00 Double	Open Jan-Dec	
ARDVASAR, Sleat Isle of Skye, Inverness-shire Mrs Barton Hazelwood Ardvasar, Sleat Isle of Skye, Inverness-shire IV45 8RS Tel: (Ardvasar) 04714 200	Map 3 E1		1 Twin 1 Double	1 Pub. Bath/Show	B&B per person from £15.00 Double	Open Jan-Dec	
Mrs R Houlton Home Leigh, 3 Calgary Ardvasar, Sleat Isle of Skye, Inverness-shire Tel: (Ardvasar) 04714 361			3 Twin	3 En Suite fac	B&B per person £15.00-£18.00 Single £15.00-£18.00 Double	Open Mar-Nov Dinner 1800-1900 B&B + Eve. Meal £23.00-£26.00	

ARMADALE, by Bathgate **West Lothian** Mrs Frances Gibb Tarrareoch Farm Armadale, nr Bathgate West Lothian EH48 3BJ Tel: (Armadale) 0501 730404	Map 2 B5		1 Single 2 Twin	1 Pub. Bath/Show	B&B per person £15.00-£17.00 Single £12.50-£15.00 Double	B&B + Eve. Meal £19.00-£20.00	Open Jan-Dec

AROS **Isle of Mull, Argyll** Mrs C Stephens Kentallen Farm Aros Isle of Mull, Argyll Tel: (Aros) 0680 300427	Map 1 C1	HIGHLY COMMENDED	3 Double	2 En Suite fac 1 Pub. Bath/Show	B&B per person £16.00-£21.50 Double	Open May-Sep	
		Traditional stone built house on working farm, 7 miles (11kms) south of Tobermory. Stunning views over Sound of Mull to Ardnamurchan.					

ARROCHAR **Dunbartonshire** Greenbank Guest House Greenbank Arrochar Dunbartonshire G83 7AA Tel: (Arrochar) 03012 305/513	Map 1 G3		1 Single 1 Twin 1 Double 1 Family	3 En Suite fac 1 Limited ensuite 1 Pub. Bath/Show	B&B per person £15.00-£17.50 Single £15.00-£17.50 Double	Open Jan-Dec Dinner 1700-2200	

Lochside Guest House Arrochar Dunbartonshire G83 7AA Tel: (Arrochar) 03012 467		APPROVED	1 Single 1 Twin 3 Double 2 Family	3 En Suite fac 1 Priv.NOT ensuite 3 Pub. Bath/Show	B&B per person £15.00-£16.00 Single £15.00-£18.00 Double	Open Jan-Dec Dinner 1800-1930 B&B + Eve. Meal £24.00-£28.00	
		Friendly atmosphere in this guest house on the shore of Loch Long with view across the Loch to the Cobbler.					

Rossmay Guest House Arrochar Dunbartonshire G83 7AH Tel: (Arrochar) 03012 250		COMMENDED	1 Single 1 Twin 2 Double 1 Family	4 En Suite fac 1 Priv. NOT ensuite	B&B per person £18.00-£22.00 Single £16.00-£18.00 Double	Open Feb-Nov Dinner from 1900 B&B + Eve. Meal £24.00-£26.00	
		Small, friendly guest house tranquilly situated on shores of Loch Long with panoramic views across the Loch. Home cooking and a warm welcome.					

Mrs Armstrong Succoth Farm House, Succoth Arrochar Dunbartonshire G83 7AL Tel: (Arrochar) 03012 591		HIGHLY COMMENDED	1 Twin 2 Double	1 En Suite fac 2 Pub. Bath/Show	B&B per person £13.50-£15.00 Double	Open Easter-Oct	
		19C stone farmhouse with spectacular mountain scenery and views across Loch Long.					

| ARROCHAR | Map 1 |
| Dunbartonshire | G3 |

FERRY COTTAGE
ARROCHAR, DUNBARTONSHIRE G83 7AH
Telephone: (03012) 428   Fax: (03012) 699

This 200-year-old house, fully refurbished by a local craftsman, is central for touring and all outdoor activities. Our scenic views across Loch Long and the Arrochar Alps are second to none.

Bedroom facilities include tea/coffee, hairdryers, en-suites and firm beds to ensure a restful night. One features a "FOUR POSTER WATER BED". Central heating throughout. Cosy lounge and PAY PHONE. For your peace of mind there is private parking and a Fire Certificate.

★ OPEN ALL YEAR ★. Colour TV in all bedrooms. 5 minutes drive from Loch Lomond.

NON-SMOKING ESTABLISHMENT!
Situated 1 mile south of Arrochar on the A814.

| Mrs C Bennetton
Ferry Cottage
Ardmay, Arrochar
Dunbartonshire
G83 7AH
Tel: (Arrochar) 03012 428
Fax: 03012 699 | COMMENDED
👑 👑 | 1 Twin
1 Double
1 Family | 3 En Suite fac | B&B per person
£15.00-£21.50 Double | Open Jan-Dec
Dinner at 1930
B&B + Eve. Meal
£23.50-£30.00 |
| | | Refurbished 200 year old house with attractive bedrooms and en-suite showerooms. Scenic views across Loch Long. | | | |

MORELAGGAN HOUSE
ARROCHAR, DUNBARTONSHIRE G83 7AH
Telephone: 03012 317

Situated beside Loch Long with spectacular views over the Arrochar Mountains and Argyle Forest. Easy access to Loch Lomond, Glasgow, Stirling, Oban and the Highlands, with their wide range of leisure facilities. Morelaggan is a family home in secluded countryside offering comfortable accommodation, evening meals and a special Scottish welcome.

Mrs J V Carter Morelaggan House Arrochar Dunbartonshire G83 7AH Tel: (Arrochar) 03012 317		1 Twin 1 Family	1 Pub. Bath/Show	B&B per person £15.00-£17.50 Single £12.50-£15.00 Double	Open Mar-Oct Dinner from 1800
Mrs Gallacher Rowantree Cottage, Main Road Arrochar Dunbartonshire G83 7AA Tel: (Arrochar) 03012 540	Award Pending	3 Double	3 En Suite fac	B&B per person £20.00-£25.00 Single £17.00-£19.50 Double	Open Jan-Dec Dinner 1800-1930 B&B + Eve. Meal £28.50-£32.50
ASCOG **Isle of Bute** Mrs Watson Ascog Farm Ascog, Rothesay Isle of Bute PA20 9LL Tel: (Rothesay) 0700 503372	Map 1 F5	1 Single 2 Double	1 Pub. Bath/Show	B&B per person £13.00 Single £13.00 Double	Open Jan-Dec

	Map 3						
AULTBEA **Ross-shire** Mellondale Guest House 47 Mellon Charles Aultbea Ross-shire IV22 2JL Tel: (Aultbea) 0445 731326	F7	**HIGHLY COMMENDED** 👑 👑 👑	2 Twin 3 Double	4 En Suite fac 1 Limited ensuite 2 Pub. Bath/Show	B&B per person from £15.00 Single from £15.00 Double	Open Feb-Nov Dinner from 1830 B&B + Eve. Meal from £23.00	

Modern family guest house set in 4 acres with views of Loch Ewe.
9 miles (14kms) from Inverewe Gardens. Ideal walking centre.

Mrs Anne Jones Cnoc Donn, Badfearn Aultbea Ross-shire IV22 2JB Tel: (Aultbea) 0445 731485			1 Twin 2 Double	2 En Suite fac 1 Pub. Bath/Show	B&B per person £12.50-£15.00 Single £12.50-£15.00 Double	Open Apr-Oct Dinner 1830-2030 B&B + Eve. Meal £19.00-£21.50	

Tom & Helen Lister Oran na Mara Drumchork, Aultbea Ross-shire IV22 2HU Tel: (Aultbea) 0445 731394		**COMMENDED** 👑 👑	3 Family	1 En Suite fac 1 Pub. Bath/Show	B&B per person from £16.00 Single £13.00-£19.00 Double	Open Jan-Dec Dinner at 1900	

Bungalow in elevated position, bedrooms with impressive views over Loch Ewe.
Traditional and vegetarian breakfasts. Vegetarian evening meals only.

Mrs MacDonald Roselea, 6 Pier Road Aultbea Ross-shire IV22 2JQ Tel: (Aultbea) 0445 731251			1 Double 1 Family	2 Pub. Bath/Show	B&B per person from £12.00 Single from £12.00 Double	Open May-Sep	

Mrs A MacLennan Sandale, 5 Pier Road Aultbea Ross-shire IV22 2JQ Tel: (Aultbea) 0445 731336		**COMMENDED** 👑	1 Single 1 Twin 1 Family	2 Pub. Bath/Show	B&B per person £13.00-£15.00 Single	Open Mar-Nov Dinner 1800-2000 B&B + Eve. Meal £22.00-£24.00	

House with sun lounge and views over Loch Ewe, set in a colourful garden.
Traditional Scottish hospitality. Good home cooking.

Mrs H McLeod The Croft Aultbea Ross-shire IV22 2JA Tel: (Aultbea) 0445 731352		**COMMENDED** Listed	1 Twin 2 Double	1 Pub. Bath/Show	B&B per person £13.50 Single £13.50 Double	Open Jan-Dec Dinner 1900-2000 B&B + Eve. Meal from £22.50	

Detached house situated in elevated position overlooking Aultbea and Loch Ewe,
with views of Torridon Hills. Trad. Scottish cooking & hospitality.

Mrs MacNeill Buena Vista Aultbea Ross-shire IV22 2HU Tel: (Aultbea) 0445 731374		**COMMENDED** 👑	1 Twin 1 Double	1 Pub. Bath/Show	B&B per person from £14.00 Single from £14.00 Double	Open Apr-Oct Dinner 1830-1900 B&B + Eve. Meal from £22.00	

Stone built 19c Highland house in peaceful rural setting, on edge of village,
with views westwards over Loch Ewe.

Mrs P MacRae Cove View, Mellon Charles Aultbea Ross-shire Tel: (Aultbea) 0445 731351			4 Double	2 Priv. NOT ensuite 2 Pub. Bath/Show	B&B per person from £13.00 Double	Open Jan-Dec Dinner 1800-1900	

AVIEMORE

	Map 4					
AVIEMORE **Inverness-shire** Ardlogie Guest House Dalfaber Road Aviemore Inverness-shire PH22 1PU Tel: (Aviemore) 0479 810747	C1	COMMENDED Listed	1 Twin 4 Double	3 En Suite fac 2 Pub. Bath/Show	B&B per person £14.00-£17.00 Double	Open Jan-Dec
			Semi-detached house in quiet road, 5 minutes walk from centre with its many facilities. Ideal for skiing, walking and touring.			
Craiglea Guest House Grampian Road, Aviemore Inverness-shire PH22 1RH Tel: (Aviemore) 0479 810210			1 Single 3 Twin 3 Double 4 Family	1 En Suite fac 3 Pub. Bath/Show	B&B per person £14.00-£16.00 Single £14.00-£16.00 Double	Open Jan-Dec

KINAPOL GUEST HOUSE

Dalfaber Road, Aviemore, Inverness-shire PH22 1PY
Tel: 0479 810513 👑 *Commended*

Small modern guest house in quiet situation, only 5 minutes' walk to station, buses and Aviemore Centre. All bedrooms have H&C, electric blankets, tea/coffee trays etc., and most have views of Cairngorm Mountains. Large bright guests' lounge with TV and hot drinks trolley. Large garden with access to river. Drying cupboard and ski store. Some bicycles for guests' use. Reduced rates for week bookings.

Kinapol Guest House Dalfaber Road Aviemore Inverness-shire PH22 1PY Tel: (Aviemore) 0479 810513	COMMENDED 👑	1 Twin 3 Double 1 Family	2 Pub. Bath/Show	B&B per person £13.00-£20.00 Single £13.00-£14.00 Double	Open Jan-Dec
		Friendly welcome at modern house in large garden with views of Cairngorms. Quiet location but only 5 minutes walk to the town centre.			
Lynwilg House Aviemore Inverness-shire PH22 1PZ Tel: (Aviemore) 0479 811685	Award Pending	1 Single 1 Twin 1 Double 1 Family	3 En Suite fac 1 Priv. NOT ensuite 1 Pub. Bath/Show	B&B per person £16.00-£20.00 Single £18.00-£22.00 Double	Open Jan-Nov Dinner 1900-2000 B&B + Eve. Meal £28.00-£32.00
Ravenscraig Guest House Aviemore Inverness-shire PH22 1RP Tel: (Aviemore) 0479 810278	COMMENDED 👑 👑	1 Single 4 Twin 5 Double 2 Family	12 En Suite fac	B&B per person £16.00-£19.00 Single £16.00-£19.00 Double	Open Jan-Dec
		Situated on edge of village, within a few minutes walk of Aviemore centre. All rooms en suite. Some ground floor annexe accommodation.			
Mr and Mrs S Carruthers 18 Morlich Place Aviemore Inverness-shire PH22 1TH Tel: (Aviemore) 0479 810941		2 Twin 1 Double	2 Pub. Bath/Show	B&B per person to £18.00 Single £14.00-£15.00 Double	Open Jan-Dec, exc Xmas
Mrs E Clark Sonas, 19 Muirton Aviemore Inverness-shire PH22 1SF Tel: (Aviemore) 0479 810409	HIGHLY COMMENDED Listed	1 Twin 2 Double	2 Pub. Bath/Show	B&B per person from £15.00 Single from £14.00 Double	Open Jan-Dec
		Modern detached bungalow in quiet residential area of village. All bedrooms have washbasins, colour TV's and tea/coffee making facilities.			

Mrs A M Ferguson Cairn Eilrig, Glenmore Aviemore Inverness-shire PH22 1QU Tel: (Cairngorm) 0479 861223		COMMENDED Listed	1 Twin 1 Family	1 Pub. Bath/Show	B&B per person from £13.00 Double	Open Jan-Dec

Bungalow situated in Glenmore Forest Park with superb open views of the Cairngorms. Warm Highland hospitality guaranteed. Ski lifts 2 miles (3 kms)

Mrs M Harper 32 Seafield Place Aviemore Inverness-shire PH22 1RZ Tel: (Aviemore) 0479 810433			1 Double 1 Family	1 Pub. Bath/Show	B&B per person £12.00-£13.00 Double	Open Jan-Dec

Mrs J McCombie Avalon, Coylumbridge Aviemore Inverness-shire PH22 1RD Tel: (Aviemore) 0479 810158			1 Twin 1 Double	2 En Suite fac	B&B per person £14.00-£15.00 Double	Open Jan-Dec

Mrs Dorothy Whelan 17 Craig-na-Gower Avenue Aviemore Inverness-shire PH22 1RW Tel: (Aviemore) 0479 810031		COMMENDED	1 Twin 1 Double	2 En Suite fac	B&B per person from £15.00 Single from £13.00 Double	Open Jan-Dec

Modern semi-detached bungalow, with garden, in quiet residential area with off-road parking. En suite rooms. A non-smoking house.

AYR Armadale Guest House 33 Bellevue Crescent Ayr KA7 2DP Tel: (Ayr) 0292 264320/282404	Map 1 G7	COMMENDED Listed	1 Twin 1 Double 1 Family	2 Limited ensuite 1 Pub. Bath/Show	B&B per person from £15.00 Double	Open Jan-Dec

Personally run Edwardian terraced house in quiet residential are yet convenient for beach, town centre and railway station.

Langley Bank Guest House 39 Carrick Road Ayr KA7 2RD Tel: (Ayr) 0292 264246		HIGHLY COMMENDED Listed	1 Single 2 Twin 2 Double 1 Family	4 En Suite fac 2 Pub. Bath/Show	B&B per person £15.00-£30.00 Single £15.00-£25.00 Double	Open Jan-Dec

Elegantly refurbished Victorian house close to all amenities. Most roomshave private facilities and telephones. Good base for touring Ayrshire.

Mr & Mrs H W Anton Clyde Cottage, 1 Arran Terrace Ayr KA7 1JF Tel: (Ayr) 0292 267368		COMMENDED	1 Twin 1 Double 1 Family	1 Pub. Bath/Show	B&B per person £14.00-£16.00 Single £14.00-£16.00 Double	Open Jan-Dec Dinner from 1800 B&B + Eve. Meal £18.00-£20.00

Homely welcome at Listed stone-built house with large garden in Conservation Area. 200 yards from seafront, easy walk to town. Private parking.

Mrs W Campbell Ferguslea, 98 New Road Ayr Ayrshire KA8 8JG Tel: (Ayr) 0292 268551		COMMENDED	1 Single 2 Twin	1 Priv. NOT ensuite 1 Pub. Bath/Show	B&B per person £13.00-£15.00 Single £13.00-£15.00 Double	Open Jan-Dec

Traditional Scottish hospitality in comfortable family home, within 10 minutes walk of town centre and all amenities.

Mrs T Filippi Coilbank Villa 32 Castlehill Road Ayr KA7 2HZ Tel: (Ayr) 0292 262936		COMMENDED Listed	1 Single 2 Twin	2 Pub. Bath/Show	B&B per person £15.00-£16.00 Single £14.00-£15.00 Double	Open Apr-Sep

Stone built Victorian town house with large garden, convenient for town centre and beach. Near railway station.

Details of Grading and Classification are on page vi. | Key to symbols is on back flap. |

Mrs Agnes Gemmell Dunduff Farm, Dunure Ayr Ayrshire KA7 4LH Tel: (Dunure) 029250 225/450225		**HIGHLY COMMENDED** 👑 👑	1 Twin 2 Double	2 En Suite fac 1 Pub. Bath/Show	B&B per person £20.00-£25.00 Single £16.00-£25.00 Double	Open Apr-Oct	

17C farmhouse on working farm in elevated position 5 miles (8kms) south of
Ayr with fine views over Firth of Clyde to Arran. Private trout loch.

Mr & Mrs L Hainey Leslie-Anne, 13 Castlehill Road Ayr KA7 2HX Tel: (Ayr) 0292 265646			1 Twin 1 Double 1 Family	3 En Suite fac 1 Pub. Bath/Show	B&B per person from £19.00 Double	Open Jan-Dec	

Mr & Mrs I McDonald 26 The Crescent 26 Bellevue Crescent Ayr KA7 2DR Tel: (Ayr) 0292 287329		**HIGHLY COMMENDED** 👑 👑	1 Twin 2 Double	3 En Suite fac	B&B per person £25.00-£30.00 Single £20.00-£24.00 Double	Open Jan-Nov Dinner 1900-1930 B&B + Eve. Meal £35.00-£45.00	

Refurbished Victorian terrace house in quiet location with easy access
for town centre and beach. Evening meals by arrangement.

Mrs J B Mair Laggan, 42 Craigie Road Ayr KA8 0EZ Tel: (Ayr) 0292 264947		**COMMENDED** 👑	1 Double 1 Family	1 Pub. Bath/Show	B&B per person from £14.50 Single from £15.50 Double	Open Apr-Sep	

Semi-detached villa in residential area, close to racecourse and public parks.
15 minutes walk from town centre and its amenities.

Mrs Wilson Deanbank 44 Ashgrove Street Ayr KA7 3BG Tel: (Ayr) 0292 263745		**HIGHLY COMMENDED** 👑	1 Double 1 Family	1 Pub. Bath/Show	B&B per person £16.00-£18.00 Single £15.00-£17.00 Double	Open Jan-Dec	

Friendly, semi-detached home with many additional comforts.
In a quiet residential situation, yet convenient for town centre.

Mrs Margaret D Wilson Knoxville, 105 Prestwick Road Ayr KA8 8LJ Tel: (Ayr) 0292 284594			2 Twin 1 Double	2 Pub. Bath/Show	B&B per person from £14.00 Single from £14.00 Double	Open Jan-Dec	

BY AYR Mrs Reid Lagg Farm Dunure Ayrshire KA7 4LE Tel: (Dunure) 029250 647	**Map 1 G7**	**HIGHLY COMMENDED** 👑	1 Twin 1 Double	1 Pub. Bath/Show	B&B per person from £14.00 Double	Open Apr-Sep	

Attractive white farmhouse with panoramic views of Heads of Ayr bay.
5 miles (8kms) from Ayr town centre. Good base for touring and walking.

AYTON, by Eyemouth Berwickshire Mrs N Ferguson Towerwoods, The Crofts Ayton Berwickshire TD14 5QT Tel: (Coldingham) 08907 81529	**Map 2 G5**		1 Single 2 Twin	1 En Suite fac 2 Pub. Bath/Show	B&B per person £13.50 Single £13.50-£14.50 Double	Open Jan-Dec	

Mrs Riach Ayton Mains Farm House Ayton Berwickshire TD14 5RE Tel: (Ayton) 08907 81336		COMMENDED Listed	2 Single 1 Twin 1 Double	1 Priv. NOT ensuite 1 Pub. Bath/Show	B&B per person £14.00-£15.00 Single £13.00-£14.00 Double	Open Apr-Oct

On the main Eyemouth to Ayton road, this traditional farmhouse built in 1840 has delightful gardens. A non-smoking house.

Mrs A Steel Ayton Cocklaw Ayton, Eyemouth Berwickshire TD14 5RJ Tel: (Ayton) 08907 81236		COMMENDED Listed	1 Double 1 Family	1 Pub. Bath/Show	B&B per person £14.00-£16.00 Single	Open Apr-Oct

Stone built farmhouse on mixed working farm, with large garden and original duck pond. Friendly atmosphere, home cooking and farm walks.

Mrs Stevens Springbank Cottage Beanburn Ayton Berwickshire TD14 5QZ Tel: (Ayton) 08907 81263		COMMENDED Listed	1 Twin 1 Family	1 Pub. Bath/Show	B&B per person £14.00-£20.00 Single £14.00-£16.00 Double	Open Jan-Dec

Victorian cottage in peaceful village convenient for A1. Ideal centre for touring Borders and Edinburgh. Close to Coastal Nature Reserve.

BACK **Lewis, Western Isles** Mrs M Fraser Seaside Villa Back Lewis, Western Isles PA86 Tel: (Back) 085182 208	Map 3 D4	COMMENDED 👑👑	1 Twin 1 Double 1 Family	1 En Suite fac 1 Limited ensuite 1 Pub. Bath/Show	B&B per person from £14.00 Single from £14.00 Double	Open Jan-Dec Dinner from 1800 B&B + Eve. Meal £21.00

Modern house on working croft, friendly atmosphere with home baking and cooking, 7 miles (11kms) from Stornoway. Lovely sea views.

BADACHRO **Ross-shire** Badachro Inn Badachro Gairloch Ross-shire IV21 2AA Tel: (Badachro) 044583 255	Map 3 E7		1 Single 1 Twin	1 Priv. NOT ensuite 1 Pub. Bath/Show	B&B per person £15.00-£18.00 Single £15.00-£18.00 Double	Open Jan-Dec Dinner 1700-2200

Mrs D Moore Hazel Cottage, Leacnasaide Badachro, Gairloch Ross-shire Tel: (Badachro) 044583 300		COMMENDED 👑👑	1 Twin 2 Double	2 En Suite fac 1 Priv. NOT ensuite 1 Pub. Bath/Show	B&B per person £15.00 Double	Open May-Sep

Modern detached house with garden. On quiet wooded road. 1 mile (2kms) Badachro. 4 miles (6kms) Gairloch.

Mr & Mrs G Willey Harbour View Badachro Ross-shire IV21 2AA Tel: (Badachro) 044583 316		COMMENDED 👑👑👑	1 Twin 3 Double	4 En Suite fac 1 Pub. Bath/Show	B&B per person £17.00-£18.50 Double	Open Feb-Nov Dinner at 1900 B&B + Eve. Meal £26.00-£27.50

With superb views over Badachro Bay, this extended fisherman's cottage, having small rooms and combe ceilings, retains its original period charm.

BALALLAN **Lewis, Western Isles** Mrs Mary MacAulay 40 Balallan Balallan Isle of Lewis, Western Isles Tel: (Balallan) 085183 326	Map 3 C5		1 Single 1 Twin 1 Family	2 Pub. Bath/Show	B&B per person from £12.00 Single from £12.00 Double	Open Jan-Dec Dinner 1800-2100 B&B + Eve. Meal £15.00-£17.00

Details of Grading and Classification are on page vi.

Key to symbols is on back flap.

BALINTORE, Tain **Ross-shire** Mr & Mrs Arthur The Sycamores Balintore, Tain Ross-shire IV20 1XW Tel: (Fearn) 0862 832322	Map 4 B7	COMMENDED 👑👑👑	1 Twin 1 Family	1 En Suite fac 1 Priv. NOT ensuite	B&B per person £15.00 Single £15.00 Double	Open Jan-Dec Dinner 1900-2030 B&B + Eve. Meal £15.00-£25.00	
			With superb views over Badachro Bay, this extended fisherman's cottage, having fine sandy beaches. Access to friendly farm animals. Children welcome.				

Mrs C Paterson Croma, Hilton Fearn Ross-shire IV20 1UZ Tel: (Fearn) 0862 832282		COMMENDED Listed	1 Single 1 Twin 1 Double	2 Pub. Bath/Show	B&B per person £13.50-£14.50 Single £13.50-£14.50 Double	Open Jan-Dec Dinner 1730-2030 B&B + Eve. Meal £16.50-£18.50	
			Mr and Mrs Paterson with their love of antiques have created a warm and stylish home for holiday makers and travellers.				

BALLACHULISH **Argyll**	Map 1 F1	

Craiglinnhe Guest House

BALLACHULISH, ARGYLL PA39 4JX
Tel: (08552) 270

Craiglinnhe, situated close to the water's edge amidst magnificent scenery, provides an excellent touring base for the Western Highlands. Set in beautiful gardens, this small, personally managed guest house offers traditional Scottish hospitality in extremely well-appointed accommodation. An ideal setting in which to relax and unwind.
Brochure on request.   **Commended 👑👑👑**

Craiglinnhe Guest House Ballachulish Argyll PA39 4JX Tel: (Ballachulish) 08552 270		COMMENDED 👑👑👑	4 Twin 2 Double	6 En Suite fac	B&B per person from £18.00 Double	Open Dec-Oct Dinner from 1900 B&B + Eve. Meal from £27.00	
			Family run guest house overlooking Loch Linnhe and the mountains beyond. Hill walking and mountaineering in the area. Good centre for touring.				

Fern Villa Guest House Ballachulish Argyll PA39 4JE Tel: (Ballachulish) 08552 393		COMMENDED 👑👑👑	2 Twin 3 Double	5 En Suite fac	B&B per person from £15.50 Double	Open Jan-Dec Dinner from 1900 B&B + Eve. Meal from £25.00	
			Non-smoking. Traditional granite built house in this typical West Highland village on Loch Leven by Glencoe. Fort William 15 miles (24 kms).				

Lyn-Leven Guest House Ballachulish Argyll PA39 4JP Tel: (Ballachulish) 08552 392		COMMENDED 👑👑👑	4 Twin 3 Double 1 Family	8 En Suite fac 1 Pub. Bath/Show	B&B per person £16.00-£22.00 Single £16.00-£18.50 Double	Open Jan-Dec Dinner from 1830 B&B + Eve. Meal £24.00-£27.50	
			Small, modern, family run guest house located in Ballachulish village and overlooking Loch Leven. All home cooking.				

Mrs Dow Tigh-ard, Brecklet Ballachulish Argyll PA39 4JG Tel: (Ballachulish) 08552 328			1 Twin 1 Double	2 Pub. Bath/Show	B&B per person from £13.00 Double	Open Apr-Oct	

VAT is shown at 17.5%: changes in this rate may affect prices. Prices shown are for guidance only. Please send SAE with each enquiry.

Name / Address	Grading	Rooms	Facilities	B&B	Opening
Mrs Sheana Hall Cnap an Tairbh, by Lochside Cottages Ballachulish Argyll Tel: (Ballachulish) 08552 575		1 Twin 1 Double	2 En Suite fac	B&B per person from £13.50 Double	Open Jan-Dec
Mr & Mrs M MacAskill Park View, 18 Park Road Ballachulish Argyll PA39 4JS Tel: (Ballachulish) 08552 560	Award Pending	1 Twin 2 Double	2 Pub. Bath/Show	B&B per person from £11.00 Double	Open Jan-Dec

Ballachulish Home Farm
BALLACHULISH, ARGYLL PA39 4JX

This is a brand new, traditional style farmhouse, situated on an elevated site amid naturally wooded parkland, giving a sense of peace and quietness. Accommodation includes three double rooms, all en-suite, bright spacious lounge, separate dining room and drying facilities. Very central for touring West Highlands.

For details contact Mrs J. McLauchlan. Tel: (08552) 792.

Name / Address	Grading	Rooms	Facilities	B&B	Opening
Mrs McLauchlan Ballachulish Home Farm Ballachulish Argyll PA39 4JX Tel: (Ballachulish) 08552 792	Award Pending	1 Twin 2 Double	3 En Suite fac	B&B per person from £20.00 Double	Open Apr-Oct
Mrs J Watt Riverside House Ballachulish Argyll PA39 4JE Tel: (Ballachulish) 08552 473	Award Pending	1 Twin 2 Double	1 En Suite fac 1 Priv. NOT ensuite 1 Pub. Bath/Show	B&B per person from £13.50 Single from £13.50 Double	Open Feb-Oct
BALLANTRAE **Ayrshire** Balkissock Lodge Ballantrae Ayrshire KA26 0LP Tel: (Ballantrae) 046583 537 Fax: 0465 83537	Map 1 F9 Award Pending	1 Twin 1 Double 1 Family	3 En Suite fac	B&B per person £25.00-£30.00 Double Dinner 1900-2100 B&B + Eve. Meal £35.00-£55.00	Open Jan-Dec
Mrs J Campbell Craigalbert Farm Ballantrae Ayrshire KA26 0PD Tel: (Ballantrae) 046583 289	COMMENDED Listed	1 Twin 2 Double	1 En Suite fac 2 Pub. Bath/Show	B&B per person from £13.00 Single from £13.00 Double	Open May-Oct

Bungalow style farmhouse on 180 acre beef and sheep farm 2 miles (3kms) from village. Rural and sea views. Good base for touring and walking.

Name / Address	Grading	Rooms	Facilities	B&B	Opening
Mrs Drummond Ardstinchar Cottage Main Street Ballantrae Ayrshire KA26 0NJ Tel: (Ballantrae) 046583 343	COMMENDED	1 Twin 2 Double	1 Pub. Bath/Show	B&B per person £15.00-£20.00 Single £13.00-£16.00 Double	Open Jan-Dec

Comfortable accommodation in family home, within 20 minutes drive from Irish ferries.

Mrs H McClung Elsanjac, 46 Main Street Ballantrae Ayrshire KA26 0NB Tel: (Ballantrae) 046583 376	COMMENDED 👑 👑	1 Double 1 Family	1 Priv. NOT ensuite 1 Pub. Bath/Show	B&B per person £12.50-£15.00 Double	Open Apr-Oct
		Pretty cottage convenient for ferry ports. One room has private facilities. Sea angling; golf; near to Culzean Castle and Burns country.			
Mrs E McIntyre Downan Farm Ballantrae Ayrshire KA26 0PB Tel: (Ballantrae) 046583 226	COMMENDED Listed	1 Double 1 Family	1 Pub. Bath/Show	B&B per person from £15.00 Single from £13.00 Double	Open May-Oct
		100 acre stock farm situated on coast just South of Ballantrae with fine views over Firth of Clyde towards Kintyre and Arran.			
Mrs Georgina McKinley Laggan Farm Ballantrae, Girvan Ayrshire KA26 0JZ Tel: (Ballantrae) 046583 402	COMMENDED 👑 👑	1 Double 1 Family	1 En Suite fac 1 Pub. Bath/Show	B&B per person £14.00-£17.00 Single £14.00-£17.00 Double	Open May-Oct Dinner 1700-1900 B&B + Eve. Meal £22.00-£25.00
		Family run dairy farm 0.5 miles (1km) south of Ballantrae on the Ayrshire coast. Woodland walks, fishing by arrangement.			
BALLATER **Aberdeenshire** Craig Gowan 53 Golf Road Ballater Aberdeenshire AB35 5RU Tel: (Ballater) 03397 55008	Map 4 E1 COMMENDED 👑 👑 👑	1 Single 3 Twin 2 Double	3 En Suite fac 2 Pub. Bath/Show	B&B per person £17.00-£20.00 Single £17.00-£20.00 Double	Open Jan-Dec Dinner from 1900 B&B + Eve. Meal £26.00-£29.00
		Victorian villa in quiet residential area, two minutes walk from golf course, bowling green, tennis courts and shops. Personally run.			
Gairnshiel Lodge Glengairn Ballater Aberdeenshire AB35 5UQ Tel: (Ballater) 03397 55582	COMMENDED 👑 👑 👑	1 Single 4 Twin 2 Double 4 Family	6 En Suite fac 2 Pub. Bath/Show	B&B per person £15.50-£19.50 Single £15.50-£19.50 Double	Open Jan-Dec Dinner 1900-2000 B&B + Eve. Meal £26.00-£30.00
		Traditional, stone built, former hunting lodge 4.5 acres of ground, 6 miles (10kms) from Ballater and Balmoral. Home cooking.			
Glenbardie Guest House Braemar Road Ballater Aberdeenshire AB35 5RQ Tel: (Ballater) 03397 55537		2 Twin 1 Double 2 Family	2 En Suite fac 2 Pub. Bath/Show	B&B per person £18.00-£22.00 Single £15.00-£18.00 Double	Open May-Oct
Moorside Guest House Braemar Road Ballater Aberdeenshire AB35 5RL Tel: (Ballater) 03397 55492 Fax: 03397 55492	COMMENDED 👑 👑	4 Twin 2 Double 3 Family	9 En Suite fac	B&B per person £27.00-£30.00 Single £18.00-£20.00 Double	Open Mar-Nov
		Friendly family run guest house offering all rooms with ensuite facilities, TVs and courtesy trays. Large garden and car park.			

BALLATER continued	Map 4 E1

Netherley Guest House

NETHERLEY PLACE, BALLATER, ABERDEENSHIRE AB35 5QE
Telephone: 03397 55792

A pretty town near Balmoral, Ballater is an ideal base for exploring the beautiful Grampian Mountains, walking, angling, gliding or skiing. Centrally located, the Netherley is a family-run guest house providing a friendly, comfortable stay. *Contact Maria Franklin Netherley Guest House, Netherley Place, Ballater AB35 5QE.*

Netherley Guest House 2 Netherley Place Ballater Aberdeenshire AB35 5QE Tel: (Ballater) 03397 55792	COMMENDED	2 Single 2 Twin 2 Double 3 Family	4 En Suite fac 2 Pub. Bath/Show	B&B per person £17.00-£19.00 Single £15.00-£20.00 Double	Open Feb-Oct
		Family run guest house in a quiet location in the centre of a renowned village. Close to shops and amenities.			
Evelyn M Gray "Dee Valley" 26 Viewfield Road Ballater Aberdeenshire AB35 5RD Tel: (Ballater) 03397 55408	COMMENDED	1 Twin 2 Double	1 En Suite fac 2 Pub. Bath/Show	B&B per person £15.00-£17.00 Double	Open Apr-Oct
		Detached house in quiet residential area, close to village centre, bus station and golf course. Home cooking.			
Mrs A P Henchie Morven Lodge 29 Braemar Road Ballater Aberdeenshire AB35 5RQ Tel: (Ballater) 03397 55373	COMMENDED	1 Twin 1 Double 1 Family	1 Priv. NOT ensuite 2 Pub. Bath/Show	B&B per person £15.00-£16.00 Double	Open May-Oct
		Former rectory situated close to the town centre. Convenient base for touring Deeside.			
Mrs C J Strachan Osborne House 4 Dunarroch Road Ballater Aberdeenshire AB35 5RP Tel: (Ballater) 03397 56031	HIGHLY COMMENDED	2 Twin 1 Double	3 En Suite fac	B&B per person £30.00-£50.00 Single £18.00-£28.00 Double	Open Apr-Oct Dinner at 1845 B&B + Eve. Meal £29.00-£39.00
		Late Victorian granite house with feature portico; private grounds and parking. Quiet residential area close to centre and golf course. No smoking.			
Mrs E Wilkie Darrochlee 5A Monaltrie Road Ballater Aberdeenshire AB35 5QE Tel: (Ballater) 03397 55287		1 Twin 2 Family	2 Pub. Bath/Show	B&B per person from £20.00 Single £14.00-£15.00 Double	Open Jan-Dec
BY BALLATER **Aberdeenshire** Roger & Fiona Barnes The Willows Cambus O'May, by Ballater Aberdeenshire AB35 5SD Tel: (Ballater) 03397 55892	Map 4 E1 COMMENDED	1 Double 1 Family	2 En Suite fac	B&B per person £17.00-£21.00 Single £16.00-£20.00 Double	Open Jan-Dec Dinner 1630-1900 B&B + Eve. Meal £24.00-£28.00
		Stone built, Edwardian house with large garden situated in heart of Royal Deeside; 10 miles (16kms) from Balmoral. Coffee shop.			

BALLINGRY, by Loch Leven Fife	Map 2 C4

NAVITIE HOUSE
BALLINGRY · Nr LOCH LEVEN · FIFE KY5 8LR
Telephone: 0592 860295

This period mansion, set in 4 acres of ground, offers large rooms with en-suite facilities, home cooking, sauna and excellent views over the Forth Valley. Situated 4 miles off the M90 and only 25 minutes drive from Edinburgh. Many golf courses within a short drive.

B&B £18 per night. Discounts for children.

Navitie House Ballingry, by Loch Leven Fife KY5 8LR Tel: (Ballingry) 0592 860295	APPROVED ♛♛♛	1 Single 2 Twin 3 Double 3 Family	7 En Suite fac 1 Pub. Bath/Show	B&B per person £20.00 Single £18.00 Double	Open Jan-Dec Dinner 1900-2100 B&B + Eve. Meal £25.00

Detached house in its own grounds overlooking Ballingry village.
Only 4miles (6kms) from the Edinburgh to Perth motorway.

BALLINLUIG, by Pitlochry Perthshire Mrs Forbes Craggandarroch Ballinluig Perthshire PH9 0NG Tel: (Ballinluig) 0796 482633	Map 2 B1	1 Twin 1 Double	1 Pub. Bath/Show	B&B per person £12.00 Double	Open Jan-Dec

BALLINTUIM, by Blairgowrie Perthshire Mrs Alison J Constable Tomlea Farm Ballintuim,by Blairgowrie Perthshire PH10 7NL Tel: (Strathardle) 0250 881383	Map 2 C1	1 Twin 1 Double	2 Pub. Bath/Show	B&B per person £13.00-£15.00 Single £12.00-£13.00 Double	Open Jan-Dec Dinner 1830-2000 B&B + Eve. Meal £20.00-£22.00

BALLOCH Dunbartonshire Anchorage Guest House Balloch Road Balloch Dunbartonshire G83 8SS Tel: (Alexandria) 0389 53336	Map 1 H4	2 Twin 4 Double 1 Family	4 En Suite fac 2 Pub. Bath/Show	B&B per person £15.00-£17.00 Double	Open Jan-Dec

Gowanlea Guest House Drymen Road Balloch Dunbartonshire G83 8HS Tel: (Alexandria) 0389 52456	HIGHLY COMMENDED ♛♛	1 Twin 2 Double	3 En Suite fac	B&B per person £18.00-£25.00 Single £18.00-£22.00 Double	Open Jan-Dec

Situated in residential area of Balloch, close to world famous Loch Lomond.
Friendly welcome, all rooms en suite.

Mrs M Brown 6 McLean Crescent Lomond Road Estate Balloch Dunbartonshire G83 8HW Tel: (Alexandria) 0389 52855		COMMENDED Listed	1 Twin 1 Double	1 Pub. Bath/Show	B&B per person £15.00-£16.00 Single £13.00-£13.50 Double	Open Jan-Dec Dinner from 1800 B&B + Eve. Meal £20.00-£20.50

Modern family villa on quiet residential estate offering a warm and friendly welcome. 30 minute drive from Glasgow airport.

M Burgess Megave, 13 Tullichewan Road Balloch Dunbartonshire G83 8GH Tel: (Alexandria) 0389 50341			1 Twin 2 Double	2 Pub. Bath/Show	B&B per person from £14.00 Double	Open Jan-Dec
Mr Alistair Elder Kinnoul, Drymen Road Balloch Dunbartonshire G83 8HS Tel: (Alexandria) 0389 21116		Award Pending	1 Family	1 En Suite fac	B&B per person £20.00 Single £17.00 Double	Open Jan-Dec

Mrs Margot Foulger Beulah, Fisherwood Road Balloch Dunbartonshire G83 8SW Tel: (Alexandria) 0389 53022		COMMENDED	1 Twin 1 Double	2 En Suite fac	B&B per person £16.00-£17.00 Double	Open Jan-Dec

Family home set in secluded mature garden. Private parking and convenient for shops and railway station to Glasgow.

Mr M Harris Cameron Cottage Old Luss Road Balloch Dunbartonshire Tel: (Balloch) 0389 59779			2 Single 2 Double	3 En Suite fac 1 Pub. Bath/Show	B&B per person £14.00-£18.00 Single £15.00-£20.00 Double	Open Jan-Dec Dinner 1800-2100 B&B + Eve. Meal £20.00-£30.00
Mrs Hyland Arbor Travel Lodge Old Luss Road Balloch Dunbartonshire G83 8QW Tel: (Balloch) 0389 56233 Fax: 0389 58988			2 Twin 2 Double	4 En Suite fac	B&B per person £20.00-£22.00 Double	Open Jan-Dec
Mrs Sandra McBride Argyll Lodge 16 Luss Road Balloch Dunbartonshire Tel: (Alexandria) 0389 59020			1 Single 1 Twin 1 Family	2 Pub. Bath/Show	B&B per person £15.00 Single £15.00 Double	Open Jan-Dec Dinner 1800-2000 B&B + Eve. Meal £21.00
Mrs H McIntyre 56 Hardie Street, Levenvale Balloch Dunbartonshire G83 0RX Tel: (Alexandria) 0389 56816			1 Twin 1 Double	1 Pub. Bath/Show	B&B per person £12.00-£14.00 Double	Open Jan-Dec

Mrs Margo J Ross Glyndale, 6 McKenzie Dr Lomond Rd Est. Balloch Dunbartonshire G83 8HL Tel: (Alexandria) 0389 58238		COMMENDED Listed	1 Twin 1 Double	1 Pub. Bath/Show	B&B per person £13.00-£13.50 Double	Open Mar-Nov

Semi-detached house in residential area, 5 minutes walk from Balloch Park. 30 minute drive from Glasgow airport.

| Mr L Verrecchia
La Sosta, Balloch Road
Balloch
Dunbartonshire
Tel: (Alexandria) 0389 58247 | | Award
Pending | 3 Twin
2 Double | 5 En Suite fac | B&B per person
from £19.00 Double | Open Jan-Dec
Dinner 1700-2300 | |

| BALLYGRANT
Isle of Islay, Argyll | Map 1
C5 | | | | | | |

KILMENY FARMHOUSE
BALLYGRANT, ISLE OF ISLAY,
ARGYLL PA45 7QW   Tel: 049 684 668

Traditional family-run business, established 1976, offering you comfort, friendliness and peace. All rooms furnished to STB Highly Commended standard. Choice of menu; ALL home cooking, ALL home baking, marmalades etc. Sittingroom available all day. Commanding views of the surrounding countryside.

Ideal base for walks and island exploration.   **Brochure available.**

| Mrs M Rozga
Kilmeny Farmhouse
Ballygrant
Isle of Islay, Argyll
PA45 7QW
Tel: (Port Askaig) 049684 668 | | HIGHLY
COMMENDED
🏅🏅 | 1 Twin
1 Double | 1 En Suite fac
1 Pub. Bath/Show | B&B per person
£17.00-£21.00 Double | Open Jan-Dec
Dinner 1730-2000
B&B + Eve. Meal
£27.00-£31.00 | |

On working farm, with excellent views over surrounding farmland. Friendly atmosphere and home cooking, with a choice of menu.

| BALMACARA
Ross-shire
Mrs A Gordon
Ashgrove
Balmacara Square
Balmacara
by Kyle of Lochalsh
Ross-shire
IV40 8DJ
Tel: (Balmacara) 059986 259 | Map 3
F9 | | 1 Twin
1 Double
1 Family | 1 Pub. Bath/Show | B&B per person
£13.00-£14.00 Double | Open Jan-Dec | |

SGURR MOR LODGE
BALMACARA, by KYLE OF LOCHALSH IV40 8DH
Margaret McGlennon   Telephone: 059 986 242

Beautifully situated overlooking Lochalsh and Skye, Sgurr Mor is a comfortable, centrally heated house 200 yards off main road to Skye. Surrounded by large garden, it is quiet and peaceful.

All rooms en-suite, residents' lounge with tea and coffee-making facilities and separate dining room. Ample safe parking.

| Mrs M McGlennon
Sgurr-Mor Lodge, Reraig
Balmacara
by Kyle of Lochalsh
Ross-shire
IV40 8DH
Tel: (Balmacara) 059986 242 | | COMMENDED
🏅🏅 | 1 Single
3 Twin
1 Double | 5 En Suite fac | B&B per person
£18.00-£19.50 Single
£18.00-£19.50 Double | Open Mar-Oct | |

Modern Highland lodge, with large south facing garden, overlooking Loch Alsh, towards Skye. All rooms with private facilities. Parking.

VAT is shown at 17.5%: changes in this rate may affect prices.   Prices shown are for guidance only.   Please send SAE with each enquiry.

BALMACLELLAN Kirkcudbrightshire	Map 2 A9

HIGH PARK FARM
Balmaclellan, Castle Douglas DG7 3PT
Telephone: New Galloway (06442) 298

HIGH PARK is a comfortable stone-built farmhouse built in 1838. The 171-acre dairy, sheep and stock rearing farm is situated by Loch Ken on the A713 amidst Galloway's beautiful scenery within easy reach of hills and coast. Good food guaranteed. All bedrooms have washbasins, shaver points, tea/coffee facilities. Pets welcome.

STB Commended ☜   **Brochure: Mrs Jessie E. Shaw at above address**

Mrs J Shaw High Park Balmaclellan Kirkcudbrightshire DG7 3PT Tel: (New Galloway) 06442 298	COMMENDED ☜	1 Twin 2 Double	1 Pub. Bath/Show	B&B per person £13.00-£14.00 Single £13.00-£14.00 Double	Open Apr-Oct Dinner from 1900 B&B + Eve. Meal £20.00-£21.00	
		Early 19C farmhouse on working dairy and sheep farm, situated by Loch Kenoff A713 amidst beautiful Galloway scenery.				

BALMAHA, by Drymen Stirlingshire	Map 1 H4					
Mrs Bates Bay Cottage Balmaha, by Drymen Stirlingshire G63 Tel: (Balmaha) 036087 346		1 Single 1 Twin 1 Family	1 En Suite fac 1 Limited ensuite 2 Pub. Bath/Show	B&B per person £17.50-£18.50 Single £17.50-£18.50 Double	Open Apr-Oct Dinner 1800-2000 B&B + Eve. Meal £27.50-£28.50	
Mrs E Craik Lomond Bank Balmaha Stirlingshire G63 0JQ Tel: (Balmaha) 036087 213	HIGHLY COMMENDED ☜ ☜	1 Twin 2 Double	1 En Suite fac 2 Pub. Bath/Show	B&B per person £20.00 Single £16.50-£19.50 Double	Open Apr-Oct	
		Comfortable, Victorian country house, on the shores of Loch Lomond. Magnificent views and extensive grounds. One bedroom en-suite.				
Mrs B Crooks Arrochoile Balmaha, by Drymen Stirlingshire G63 0JG Tel: (Balmaha) 0360 87231		2 Twin 1 Double	3 En Suite fac	B&B per person from £20.00 Double	Open Apr-Oct Dinner 1800-1930 B&B + Eve. Meal from £30.00	
Mrs A Fraser Moniack Balmaha, by Drymen Stirlingshire Tel: (Balmaha) 036087 357 Fax: 036087 350	HIGHLY COMMENDED ☜ ☜	1 Twin 2 Double	1 En Suite fac 1 Pub. Bath/Show	B&B per person £22.00-£25.00 Single £18.00-£20.00 Double	Open Apr-Oct	
		Unique architect designed modern family home in the heart of this small village, ideal for walkers and fishers.				
Mrs K MacFadyen Dunleen, Milton of Buchanan Balmaha Stirlingshire G63 0JE Tel: (Balmaha) 036087 274	HIGHLY COMMENDED ☜	1 Twin 1 Double	1 Pub. Bath/Show	B&B per person £15.00-£16.00 Double	Open May-Oct	
		Comfortable modern bungalow situated in a quiet spot within easy reach of Loch Lomond. Friendly atmosphere.				
Mrs F MacLuskie Critreoch, Rowardennan Road Balmaha Stirlingshire G63 0AW Tel: (Balmaha) 036087 309		1 Single 1 Twin 1 Double	1 Pub. Bath/Show	B&B per person £15.00-£16.00 Single £15.00-£16.00 Double	Open Apr-Oct	

Mrs Margaret Maxwell Cashel Farm Balmaha, Drymen, Glasgow G63 0AW Tel: (Balmaha) 036087 229	COMMENDED 👑 👑	2 Family	1 En Suite fac 1 Pub. Bath/Show	B&B per person £15.50-£18.50 Double	Open Mar-Sep	

Working farm with Galloway cows and black face sheep. Quiet location overlooking Loch Lomond.

BALQUHIDDER **Perthshire**	Map 1 H3

Auchtubhmor House
BALQUHIDDER, PERTHSHIRE FK19 8NZ
Telephone: (08774) 632

Superbly positioned on its own elevated grounds where herds of wild deer are frequent visitors. An ideal base for touring, walking, fishing, golf, etc. All bedrooms en-suite. Partake of good food and wines after which retreat to a log fire where exchange of the day's pleasantries brings your day to a successful conclusion.

| Auchtubhmor House
Balquhidder, Lochearnhead
Perthshire
FK19 8NZ
Tel: (Strathyre) 08774 632 | COMMENDED
👑 👑 👑 | 1 Twin
2 Double
1 Family | 4 En Suite fac | B&B per person
£20.00-£22.00 Single
£17.00-£20.00 Double | Open Apr-Oct | |

Built for an ancestor of Rob Roy approx 250 years ago. A delightful house with magnificent views of the Trossachs, and surrounding countryside.

| Monachyle Mhor Hotel/
Farmhouse
Balquhidder
by Lochearnhead
Perthshire
FK19 8PQ
Tel: (Strathyre) 08774 622
Fax: 08774 305 | COMMENDED
👑 👑 👑 | 1 Twin
4 Double | 5 En Suite fac | B&B per person
£23.00-£25.00 Double | Open Jan-Dec
Dinner 1930-2200
B&B + Eve. Meal
£37.00-£45.00 | |

18C farmhouse in own 2000 acres. Magnificent situation overlooking Lochs Voil and Doine. Stalking and fishing available. Taste of Scotland.

| Mrs Marshall
Craigruie Farm House
Balquhidder,by Lochearnhead
Perthshire
FK19 8PQ
Tel: (Balquhidder) 08774 262 | COMMENDED
Listed | 1 Twin
2 Family | 1 En Suite fac
1 Pub. Bath/Show | B&B per person
from £20.00 Single
£17.00-£19.00 Double | Open Jan-Dec
Dinner 1800-2130
B&B + Eve. Meal
£26.00-£32.00 | |

Tastefully renovated farmhouse, overlooking Loch Voil, peacefully situated 2 miles (3kms) from Balquhidder. Personally organised sporting facilities.

| **BANAVIE, by Fort William**
Inverness-shire
Mrs Disher
Reneval, Tomonie
Banavie, by Fort William
Inverness-shire
PH33
Tel: (Fort William)
0397 772206 | Map 3
G1 | 1 Twin
2 Double | 1 Pub. Bath/Show | B&B per person
£11.00-£11.50 Single
£11.00-£11.50 Double | Open Jan-Dec
Dinner 1800-1930
B&B + Eve. Meal
£18.00-£20.00 | |

| **BANCHORY**
Kincardineshire
Village Guest House
83 High Street
Banchory
Kincardineshire
AB31 3TJ
Tel: (Banchory) 0330 823307 | Map 4
F1
HIGHLY
COMMENDED
Listed | 2 Twin
2 Double
Suites avail. | 2 Pub. Bath/Show | B&B per person
£18.00-£20.00 Single
from £20.00 Double | Open Jan-Dec | |

Charming Victorian house in centre of Royal Deeside village. Fountain patio. Warm Scottish welcome.

Name & Address	Map Ref	Grading	Rooms	Facilities	B&B Prices	Opening	Symbols
Mrs G Adams, Amulree, Corsee Road, Banchory, Kincardineshire, AB31 3RS, Tel: (Banchory) 03302 2884			1 Twin, 2 Double	2 Pub. Bath/Show	B&B per person to £16.00 Single to £13.00 Double	Open Jan-Dec	
Kathleen Balsamo, Towerbank, 93 High Street, Banchory, Kincardineshire, Tel: (Banchory) 03302 2657/4798		COMMENDED	2 Twin	2 Pub. Bath/Show	B&B per person £18.00-£22.00 Single £16.00-£18.00 Double	Open Jan-Dec	
			Cottage conveniently situated in the main street with south facing views of the Deeside hills.				
Mrs Ellerton, Craigard, Burnett Road, Banchory, Kincardineshire, Tel: (Banchory) 03302 4704		Award Pending	1 Twin, 1 Double, 1 Family	1 Pub. Bath/Show	B&B per person £18.00-£20.00 Single £16.00-£18.00 Double	Open Jan-Dec, Dinner 1800-1900, B&B + Eve. Meal £24.00-£29.00	
Mrs Hampson, The Old Police House, 3 Bridge Street, Banchory, Kincardineshire, AB31 3SX, Tel: (Banchory) 0330 824000		HIGHLY COMMENDED	1 Twin, 1 Double	2 En Suite fac	B&B per person £20.00 Single £16.00 Double	Open Jan-Dec	
			Banchory's original Police Station and Prison. House of great character and warmth. Centrally located and close to all amenities.				
Mrs I Wallace, Kyan, 2 Mill Court, Bredero Drive, Banchory, Kincardineshire, Tel: (Banchory) 0330 824660			1 Twin, 1 Double	2 Priv. NOT ensuite	B&B per person £16.00-£18.00 Double	Open Feb-Nov	
Mrs Wilson, Aldor, 74 Station Road, Banchory, AB31 3YJ, Tel: (Banchory) 03302 4026/ 0330 824026			1 Single, 1 Twin, 1 Double, 1 Family	2 Pub. Bath/Show	B&B per person £16.00-£18.00 Single £16.00-£17.00 Double	Open Jan-Dec	
BY BANCHORY Kincardineshire, Mrs Jean Flavell, The Mill of Eslie, by Banchory, Kincardineshire, AB31 3LD, Tel: (Banchory) 0330 823875	Map 4 F1	Award Pending	1 Twin, 1 Double	2 Pub. Bath/Show	B&B per person £15.00-£20.00 Single £14.00 Double	Open Jan-Dec	
Mrs P Law, Monthammock Farm, Durris, by Banchory, Kincardineshire, AB31 3DX, Tel: (Drumoak) 0330 811421		COMMENDED	1 Twin, 1 Double	1 Pub. Bath/Show	B&B per person from £18.00 Single from £15.00 Double	Open Jan-Dec, Dinner 1800-1930, B&B + Eve. Meal £25.00-£28.00	
			Tranquility and a warm welcome at this sympathetically converted steading with spectacular views over Deeside.				
BANFF Mrs E Addison, Clayfolds Farm, Alvah, Banff, AB45 3UD, Tel: (Eden) 02616 288	Map 4 F7	COMMENDED Listed	1 Double, 1 Family	1 Pub. Bath/Show	B&B per person £13.00-£15.00 Single £13.00-£15.00 Double	Open Jan-Dec	
			Situated on working farm in Deveron Valley. Home cooking and baking. Country and riverside walks. 3 miles (5kms) from Banff.				

Details of Grading and Classification are on page vi.

Key to symbols is on back flap.

	Map Ref	Grade/Award	Rooms	Facilities	Prices	Opening
Dorothy & Alec Clark, Montcoffer House, Montcoffer, Banff, AB45 3LJ, Tel: (Banff) 0261 812979		APPROVED	1 Single, 1 Double, 1 Family	2 En Suite fac, 1 Priv. NOT ensuite	B&B per person to £16.00 Single to £16.00 Double	Open Jan-Dec, Dinner 1800-2000, B&B + Eve. Meal to £23.50

Listed 17C mansion, overlooking Deveron Valley. Ideal centre for walking, golf, fishing, Castle and Whisky trails.

	Map 4 F7					
BY BANFF Eden House, Eden, by Banff, AB45 3NT, Tel: (Eden) 02616 282			2 Twin, 2 Double	3 En Suite fac, 1 Priv. NOT ensuite	B&B per person £30.00-£32.00 Double	Open Jan-Dec, Dinner 1900-2100, B&B + Eve. Meal £48.00-£50.00

		Award Pending				
Mrs J Elrick, Mains of Blackton, King Edward, Banff, AB45 3NJ Tel: (King Edward) 0888 551205			1 Single, 1 Twin, 1 Double, 1 Family	1 En Suite fac, 1 Pub. Bath/Show	B&B per person from £13.00 Single from £13.00 Double	Open Jan-Oct, Dinner 1800-2200, B&B + Eve. Meal from £21.00

	Map 2 A5					
BANKNOCK, by Bonnybridge Stirlingshire, Mrs Pitcairn, Orchard Grove, Banknock, by Bonnybridge, Stirlingshire, FK4 1UA, Tel: (Banknock) 0324 840146			3 Double	3 Priv. NOT ensuite, 2 Pub. Bath/Show	B&B per person to £15.50 Single to £14.00 Double	Open Jan-Dec

	Map 1 G9	COMMENDED				
BARRHILL Ayrshire, Mrs Hughes, Blair Farm, Barrhill, Ayrshire, KA26 0RD, Tel: (Barrhill) 046582 247			1 Double, 1 Family	1 Pub. Bath/Show	B&B per person from £14.00 Single from £14.00 Double	Open Easter-Oct, Dinner from 1800, B&B + Eve. Meal from £21.00

Traditional farmhouse, convenient for Glen Trool Country Park and Ayrshire coast. Fishing available.

	Map 1 H5					
BEARSDEN Dunbartonshire, Mr S McDougall, 2 Baljaffrey Cottages, Grampian Way, Bearsden, Glasgow, G61, Tel: 041 942 9193/942 4145			1 Twin, 3 Double, 1 Family	2 Pub. Bath/Show	B&B per person from £22.00 Single £18.00- Double	Open Jan-Dec

	Map 2 C8	COMMENDED				
BEATTOCK Dumfriesshire, Mrs F Bell, Cogries Farm, Beattock, Dumfriesshire, DG10 9PP, Tel: (Johnstone Bridge) 05764 320			1 Double, 3 Family	1 Pub. Bath/Show	B&B per person from £13.50 Double	Open Feb-Nov

Dairy and mixed farm (275 acres) quietly situated yet convenient for the A74 and Moffat. Good centre for touring.

BEAULY **Inverness-shire** Arkton Guest House West End Beauly Inverness-shire IV4 7BT Tel: (Beauly) 0463 782388	**Map 4** A8	APPROVED ♛	1 Single 4 Twin 1 Double 2 Family	2 Pub. Bath/Show	B&B per person £16.00-£20.00 Single £16.00-£20.00 Double	Open Jan-Dec Dinner 1900-2000 B&B + Eve. Meal £23.00-£27.00

Personally run hotel, situated at the south end of the village square. Ideal for touring Loch Ness and Glen Affric. 12 miles (19kms) from Inverness.

LYNDALE

STATION ROAD, BEAULY IV4 7EH Tel: 0463 782 252

This comfortable family home is situated in the village of Beauly, an ideal centre for touring the Highlands. Inverness is 12 miles away, as is Loch Ness and its facilities. There is ample parking and a large garden for guests' enjoyment.

Mrs S Bruce Lyndale, Station Road Beauly Inverness-shire IV4 7EH Tel: (Beauly) 0463 782252	COMMENDED ♛ ♛	1 Single 1 Twin 1 Double	1 Priv. NOT ensuite 1 Pub. Bath/Show	B&B per person from £13.00 Single from £13.00 Double	Open May-Sep

Situated in residential area of Beauly, with own large garden and ample car parking. Only a few minutes walk from the centre of the village.

Mrs MacKay Ellangowan, Croyard Road Beauly Inverness-shire IV4 7DJ Tel: (Beauly) 0463 782273	COMMENDED ♛	1 Twin 1 Double 1 Family	3 Limited ensuite 1 Pub. Bath/Show	B&B per person £12.00-£14.00 Double	Open Apr-Oct

Comfortable, centrally heated home near priory. Ideal base for touring.

Mrs P Morrison 7 Viewfield Avenue Beauly Inverness-shire IV4 7BW Tel: (Beauly) 0463 782264	COMMENDED Listed	1 Single 2 Double	2 Pub. Bath/Show	B&B per person £12.50 Single £12.50 Double	Open Jan-Dec

In a quiet residential area on the edge of the village, yet within a few minutes walk of shops. Friendly atmosphere and warm welcome.

Mrs E Munro Moniack View Kirkhill, by Inverness Inverness-shire IV5 7PD Tel: (Drumchardine) 0463 831757	HIGHLY COMMENDED ♛	1 Twin 1 Double	1 Pub. Bath/Show	B&B per person to £20.00 Single £12.00-£14.00 Double	Open Apr-Oct

Ranch style bungalow with magnificent views in a rural setting overlooking Moniack Castle. Quiet location and ideal for touring.

Mrs Munro Wester Moniack Farm Kirkhill, by Inverness Inverness-shire IV5 7PQ Tel: (Drumchardine) 0463 831237	COMMENDED Listed	1 Double 1 Family	1 Pub. Bath/Show	B&B per person £13.00-£14.00 Single £13.00-£14.00 Double	Open Jan-Dec Dinner 1830-2000 B&B + Eve. Meal £19.00-£20.00

Farmhouse with family atmosphere in a peaceful setting, next to Castle and Winery. Conveniently situated for Inverness and touring the Highlands.

Mrs M Ritchie Rheindown Farm Beauly Inverness-shire IV4 7AB Tel: (Beauly) 0463 782461	COMMENDED ♛	1 Double 1 Family	1 Pub. Bath/Show	B&B per person £14.00-£14.50 Double	Open Apr-Oct Dinner from 1815 B&B + Eve. Meal £20.00-£22.00

Farmhouse on working farm in elevated position overlooking Beauly and the Firth beyond. Home cooking.

Details of Grading and Classification are on page vi.

Key to symbols is on back flap.

BEITH **Ayrshire** Mrs Gillan Shotts Farm Barrmill, Beith Ayrshire KA15 1LB Tel: (Beith) 0505 502273	Map 1 G6	COMMENDED Listed	1 Double 1 Family	2 Pub. Bath/Show	B&B per person from £11.00 Double B&B + Eve. Meal from £16.00	Open Jan-Dec Dinner 1830-2230
Family run farmhouse accommodation on a 160 acre dairy farm. Ideal base for Burns country, Arran and cultural Glasgow.						
Mrs E Workman Meikle Auchengree, Glengarnock Beith Ayrshire KA14 3BU Tel: (Dalry) 0294 832205		COMMENDED 👑 👑	1 Twin 2 Double	1 En Suite fac 2 Pub. Bath/Show	B&B per person £15.00-£18.00 Single £14.00-£17.00 Double	Open Jan-Dec
Modern comfortable farmhouse, with friendly atmosphere, on dairy farm. Central for Largs, Ayr and Glasgow. Large games room with indoor bowls.						
Mrs Wylie Wester Highgate Farm Beith Ayrshire Tel: (Beith) 05055 2484			1 Double 2 Family	2 En Suite fac 1 Priv. NOT ensuite 1 Pub. Bath/Show	B&B per person £11.00-£13.00 Single £11.00-£13.00 Double B&B + Eve. Meal £11.00-£13.00	Open Jan-Dec Dinner 1800-1900
BERNERAY **North Uist, Western Isles** D A McKillop Burnside Berneray North Uist, Western Isles Tel: (Berneray) 08767 235	Map 3 A7		1 Twin 1 Double	2 En Suite fac	B&B per person £17.00-£21.00 Single £17.00-£21.00 Double B&B + Eve. Meal £23.00-£28.00	Open Jan-Dec Dinner 1800-2030
Mrs Peggy MacLeod Rhu Alainn Berneray North Uist, Western Isles PA82 5BH Tel: (Berneray) 08767 254			1 Single 1 Twin 1 Double	1 Pub. Bath/Show	B&B per person £14.00-£14.50 Single £14.00-£14.50 Double B&B + Eve. Meal £23.00-£23.50	Open Jan-Dec Dinner 1800-1930
BERNISDALE, by Portree **Isle of Skye, Inverness-shire** Mrs MacRae 20 Woodlands Bernisdale Isle of Skye, Inverness-shire Tel: (Skeabost) 047032 388	Map 3 D9		1 Twin 2 Double	2 En Suite fac 1 Pub. Bath/Show	B&B per person £12.00-£15.00 Double	Open Jan-Dec Dinner 1930-2130 B&B + Eve. Meal £20.00-£25.00
BERRIEDALE **Caithness** Mrs Gough Kings Park Llama Farm Berriedale Caithness KW7 6HA Tel: (Berriedale) 05935 202	Map 4 D5		1 Single 1 Double 1 Family	1 En Suite fac 2 Pub. Bath/Show	B&B per person £13.00 Single £14.00 Double	Open Jan-Dec
BETTYHILL **Sutherland** Mrs I MacKay Bruachmhor, 23 Aird Bettyhill Sutherland KW14 7SS Tel: (Bettyhill) 06412 265	Map 4 B3		1 Twin 1 Double	1 Pub. Bath/Show	B&B per person £13.00-£14.00 Double	Open May-Oct

BY BETTYHILL **Sutherland** Mrs H I McPherson 7 Borgie Skerray Sutherland KW14 7TH Tel: (Bettyhill) 06412 428	Map 4 B3		2 Family	2 En Suite fac	B&B per person £21.00-£23.00 Single £16.00-£18.00 Double	Open Jan-Dec Dinner 1830-1930 B&B + Eve. Meal £26.00-£33.00
BIGGAR **Lanarkshire** Mrs Pennie Brown Woodgill, 12 Edinburgh Road Biggar Lanarkshire ML12 6AX Tel: (Biggar) 0899 20324	Map 2 C6		1 Twin 2 Double	2 Pub. Bath/Show	B&B per person £14.00-£17.00 Double	Open Apr-Oct
Mr A & Mrs A L B Dunnet Elmwood 32 Sherrifflats Road Thankerton, by Biggar Lanarkshire ML12 6PA Tel: (Tinto) 08993 740			1 Twin 1 Family	1 Pub. Bath/Show	B&B per person £12.00-£13.00 Double	Open Jan-Dec
Mrs M Dunnet Lyne Cottage, Causewayend Biggar Lanarkshire ML12 6JS Tel: (Biggar) 0899 20141			1 Twin 1 Family	1 En Suite fac 2 Pub. Bath/Show	B&B per person £13.00-£16.00 Double	Open Jan-Dec
Mrs Margaret E Kirby Walston Mansion Farmhouse Walston, Carnwath Lanarkshire ML11 8NF Tel: (Dunsyre) 089981 338		COMMENDED 👑👑👑	1 Twin 1 Double 1 Family	2 En Suite fac 2 Pub. Bath/Show	B&B per person £11.50-£13.50 Single £11.50-£13.50 Double	Open Jan-Dec Dinner 1800-2000 B&B + Eve. Meal £18.50-£20.50
			19C stone built farmhouse situated in small village at south west end of Pentland Hills. 5 miles (8kms) from Biggar.			
Mrs B Miller Walston House, Walston by Carnwath Lanarkshire ML11 8NF Tel: (Dunsyre) 089981 324			1 Double 1 Family	1 Pub. Bath/Show	B&B per person £12.50-£15.00 Single £12.50 Double	Open Jan-Dec Dinner from 1830 B&B + Eve. Meal £16.00-£20.00
Mrs Robbie Biggarshiels Farm Biggar Lanarkshire ML12 6RE Tel: (Biggar) 0899 20545			2 Double 1 Family	2 Pub. Bath/Show	B&B per person £13.00-£15.00 Single £13.00-£14.00 Double	Open Apr-Oct
Mrs M E Stott Lindsaylands Biggar Lanarkshire Tel: (Biggar) 0899 20033/ 21221 Fax: 0899 21009		HIGHLY COMMENDED 👑👑👑	1 Twin 2 Double	2 En Suite fac 1 Priv. NOT ensuite	B&B per person £26.00-£30.00 Single £21.00-£25.00 Double	Open Jan-Dec Dinner 1930-2030 B&B + Eve. Meal £39.00-£40.00
			Attractive country house, set in 6 acres of garden, amidst lovely countryside, with views to Border Hills. Hard tennis court.			

BY BIGGAR **Lanarkshire** Mrs Goldsbrough The Old Manse, Manse Road Symington Lanarkshire ML12 6LN Tel: (Tinto) 08993 242	Map 2 C6		1 Twin 1 Family	2 Priv. NOT ensuite 1 Pub. Bath/Show	B&B per person £15.00-£16.50 Single £14.50-£16.50 Double	Open Jan-Nov
BIRSAY **Orkney** Mrs Balderstone Heatherlea Birsay Orkney KW17 2LR Tel: (Birsay) 085672 382	Map 5 A1	APPROVED ⚜	1 Twin 1 Double	1 Pub. Bath/Show	B&B per person from £13.00 Single from £13.00 Double	Open Apr-Oct
			Beautiful situation overlooking the Loch of Boardhouse. Free trout angling. **Boat for hire. Close to R.S.P.B. reserves and archaeological areas.**			
Mrs Clouston Primrose Cottage Birsay Orkney KW17 2NB Tel: (Birsay) 085672 384		COMMENDED ⚜	1 Single 2 Double	1 Pub. Bath/Show	B&B per person £12.00-£14.00 Single £12.00-£14.00 Double	Open Apr-Oct Dinner 1800-2000 B&B + Eve. Meal £18.00-£21.00
			In quiet location overlooking Marwick Bay, close to RSPB reserves. **Local produce used whenever possible, fresh fish and shellfish.**			
BLACKFORD **Perthshire** Mrs R Robertson Yarrow House, Moray Street Blackford Perthshire PH4 1PY Tel: (Blackford) 0764 682358	Map 2 B3	COMMENDED ⚜ ⚜	1 Single 1 Twin 1 Family	1 En Suite fac 1 Pub. Bath/Show	B&B per person £13.00-£15.00 Single £13.00-£15.00 Double	Open Jan-Dec Dinner from 1800 B&B + Eve. Meal £18.00-£21.00
			Comfortable home in the centre of village with good walks in the **surrounding countryside. Convenient for the A9.**			
BLACKSHIELS, Pathhead **Midlothian** Mrs M Winthrop Fairshiels Blackshiels, Pathhead Midlothian EH37 5SX Tel: (Humbie) 087533 665	Map 2 D5		2 Single 2 Twin	1 En Suite fac 3 Pub. Bath/Show	B&B per person £12.00-£12.50 Single £12.00-£12.50 Double	Open Jan-Dec
BLACKWATERFOOT **Isle of Arran** Mrs G Arthur Broombrae Kilpatrick Isle of Arran Tel: (Shiskine) 077086 435/0770 860435	Map 1 E7		2 Twin	1 Pub. Bath/Show	B&B per person £15.00 Single £15.00 Double	Open Apr-Sep Dinner 1930-2130 B&B + Eve. Meal £23.75

| BLAIR ATHOLL | Map 4 |
| Perthshire | C1 |

THE FIRS

St Andrews Crescent, Blair Atholl
Perthshire. Telephone: 0796 481256

A warm, friendly family run guest house in this peaceful village close to Pitlochry.

Blair Atholl is a quiet holiday centre in the heart of Highland Perthshire. With famous Blair Castle, shops, folk museum, water mill, mountain biking, pony trekking, golf course, etc., the village caters for all.

Extensive woodland, riverside and hill walks around the village.

All rooms en-suite. Excellent weekly terms.

Kirstie and Geoff Crerar look forward to welcoming you.

The Firs St Andrews Crescent Blair Atholl Perthshire PH18 5TA Tel: (Blair Atholl) 0796 481256	COMMENDED 惢 惢 惢	1 Twin 1 Double 2 Family	4 En Suite fac	B&B per person £17.50-£18.00 Double	Open Easter-Oct Dinner from 1930 B&B + Eve. Meal £27.50-£28.00

Friendly family home with half an acre of garden, in a tranquil setting. Fine touring centre, close to Blair Castle.

| BY BLAIR ATHOLL | Map 4 |
| Perthshire | C1 |

Baile na Bruaich

GLENFENDER
BLAIR ATHOLL
PERTHSHIRE
PH18 5TU

Tel: 0796 481329

Bed and Breakfast in a converted croft deep in "Strathblair" country. A warm and comfortable home with open fires and spectacular views. We have 3 rooms, all with H&C and tea/coffee facilities. Nestling at the foot of Beinn a' Ghlo and ideally situated for walking, birdwatching and touring.

Mrs C Booth Bailenabruaich Glen Fender, Blair Atholl Perthshire PH18 5TU Tel: (Blair Atholl) 0796 481329	1 Single 1 Twin 1 Double	1 Pub. Bath/Show	B&B per person £15.00-£16.00 Single £15.00-£16.00 Double	Open Mar-Oct

| BLAIRGOWRIE | Map 2 |
| Perthshire | C1 |

Duan Villa Perth Road Blairgowrie Perthshire PH10 6EQ Tel: (Blairgowrie) 0250 873053	3 Double 2 Family	1 Pub. Bath/Show	B&B per person £16.50-£17.50 Double	Open Jan-Dec Dinner 1830-1930 B&B + Eve. Meal £25.50-£26.50

| BLAIRGOWRIE continued | Map 2 C1 | | | | |

Glenshieling House

Hatton Road, Blairgowrie, Perthshire PH10 7HZ   0250 874605
Located away from noisy, main Balmoral Road in 2 acres of
peaceful tranquillity. Central heating, private facilities, colour TV's.
Very competitive rates. Excellent dinner available, if desired.
Access/Visa accepted.
**Please DO telephone for FULL COLOUR BROCHURE etc.
B&B from £16.**

| Glenshieling House
Hatton Road, Rattray
Blairgowrie
Perthshire
PH10 7HZ
Tel: (Blairgowrie)
0250 874605 | COMMENDED
♛♛♛ | 1 Single
2 Twin
2 Double
2 Family | 4 En Suite fac
2 Pub. Bath/Show | B&B per person
£19.00-£22.50 Single
£17.00-£25.00 Double | Open Jan-Dec
Dinner 1800-2030
B&B + Eve. Meal
£27.00-£41.00 |
| | | Lovely Victorian house tranquilly set in 2 acres of garden and woodland near Blairgowrie. Chef/Proprietor and wife preside. | | | |

| The Laurels Guest House
Golf Course Road
Rosemount
Blairgowrie
Perthshire
PH10 6LH
Tel: (Blairgowrie)
0250 874920 | HIGHLY
COMMENDED
♛♛♛ | 1 Single
3 Twin
2 Double | 4 En Suite fac
1 Pub. Bath/Show | B&B per person
£16.00-£17.00 Single
£15.00-£17.00 Double | Open Jan-Nov
Dinner 1830-1900
B&B + Eve. Meal
£22.50-£25.00 |
| | | Originally a farmhouse dating from 1873, set back from main road, on outskirts of Blairgowrie with own large garden and ample parking. | | | |

| The Old Bank House
Brown Street
Blairgowrie
Perthshire
PH10 6EX
Tel: (Blairgowrie)
0250 872902 | HIGHLY
COMMENDED
♛♛♛ | 4 Twin
2 Double | 6 En Suite fac | B&B per person
£25.00-£30.00 Single
£22.50-£27.50 Double | Open Jan-Dec
Dinner 1900-2000
B&B + Eve. Meal
£35.00-£40.00 |
| | | Former bank dating from 1837 in quiet location, 5 minutes walk from the town centre. Imaginative home cooking. Golf, fishing and shooting packages. | | | |

DRYFESANDS

**BURNHEAD ROAD, BLAIRGOWRIE
PERTHSHIRE PH10 6SY
Tel: 0250 87 3417**

Haven for Non-Smokers   Open All Year

*Ideally placed for golf, hill-walking, skiing
and touring or just relax and be spoilt by our
superb Cordon Bleu cuisine, personal service
and spacious, luxurious accommodation.*

**All bedrooms are en-suite at £28 pp
Half Board or £18 pp B&B**

Our STB Deluxe ♛♛♛ rating
is your guarantee of satisfaction.

| Mr & Mrs Cowan
Dryfesands, Burnhead Road
Blairgowrie
Perthshire
PH10 6SY
Tel: (Blairgowrie)
0250 873417 | DELUXE
♛♛♛ | 1 Twin
2 Double | 3 En Suite fac | B&B per person
from £23.00 Single
from £18.00 Double | Open Jan-Dec
Dinner from 1900
B&B + Eve. Meal
£28.00-£33.00 |
| | | Modern bungalow, ensuite facilities, in quiet residential area. Non smokers haven; mainly fresh produce; regret no children/pets. Ideal for touring | | | |

Mr & Mrs Grant Norwood House, Park Drive Blairgowrie Perthshire PH10 6PA Tel: (Blairgowrie) 0250 874146	COMMENDED ♛	1 Twin 1 Double 1 Family	1 Pub. Bath/Show	B&B per person £14.00 Single £14.00 Double	Open Jan-Dec Dinner 1800-2000 B&B + Eve. Meal £19.50-£21.00	

Comfortable Victorian family house in residential area. Good home cooking; golfers and skiers welcome. Private parking. Ideal for touring Perthshire.

Mrs Koppel Brightview High Street, Rattray Blairgowrie Perthshire PH10 7DL Tel: (Blairgowrie) 0250 875018	APPROVED Listed	1 Twin 1 Double 1 Family	1 Pub. Bath/Show	B&B per person £12.00-£14.00 Single £12.00-£14.00 Double	Open Jan-Dec Dinner 1800-2000 B&B + Eve. Meal £19.00-£21.00	

On the outskirts of the town, overlooking open countryside, detached house with off-street parking.

Duncraggan House

PERTH ROAD · BLAIRGOWRIE PH10 6EJ
Telephone: (0250) 872082

Duncraggan House of character offers peace and relaxation in comfortable and beautiful surroundings with meals of high standard and off-road parking. Ideally situated for tourists, hillwalkers, golfers and skiers alike or just relax in our acre of garden.

STB ♛♛ Commended
AA Listed QQQ

Mrs C McClement Duncraggan, Perth Road Blairgowrie Perthshire PH10 6EJ Tel: (Blairgowrie) 0250 872082	COMMENDED ♛♛	1 Single 1 Twin 1 Double	1 En Suite fac 2 Pub. Bath/Show	B&B per person from £16.00 Single £15.00-£16.00 Double	Open Jan-mid Sep. 2 Nov-Dec Dinner from 1900 B&B + Eve. Meal £23.00-£25.00	

Stone built house of interesting design with large garden, conveniently situated on the main Perth to Blairgowrie road. Town centre 0.5 miles (1km).

Mrs Murray Eildon Bank, Perth Road Blairgowrie Perthshire PH10 6ED Tel: (Blairgowrie) 0250 873648		1 Twin 1 Double	1 Pub. Bath/Show	B&B per person £13.50-£14.00 Single £13.00-£13.50 Double	Open Jan-Dec	

Mrs Marion Paterson Dunmore, Newton Street Blairgowrie Perthshire PH10 9HT Tel: (Blairgowrie) 0250 874451		2 Single 1 Twin 1 Family	2 Pub. Bath/Show	B&B per person £13.50-£14.50 Single £13.50-£14.50 Double	Open Jan-Dec Dinner 1800-1930 B&B + Eve. Meal £20.50-£21.50	

BY BLAIRGOWRIE

Perthshire — Map 2 C1

Mrs Caroline Keen
The Coach House, Kinloch
Blairgowrie
Perthshire
PH10 6SG
Tel: (Essendy) 0250 884308

1 Single · 2 Pub. Bath/Show
1 Twin
1 Family

B&B per person
£12.50-£16.00 Single
£12.50-£16.00 Double

Open Jan-Dec

Mrs H Wightman
Bankhead, Clunie
Blairgowrie
Perthshire
PH10 6SG
Tel: (Essendy) 0250 884281

COMMENDED ♛

1 Twin · 1 Pub. Bath/Show
1 Family

B&B per person
£12.50-£13.00 Double

Open Jan-Dec
Dinner 1830-1900
B&B + Eve. Meal
£18.50-£19.00

Farmhouse on working family farm between Loch Marlee and Clunie.
Ideal for touring, local fishing, golfing and skiing. All home cooking.

BOAT OF GARTEN

Inverness-shire — Map 4 C1

Avingormack Guest House
Boat of Garten
Inverness-shire
PH24 3BT
Tel: (Boat of Garten)
047983 614

HIGHLY COMMENDED ♛♛♛

1 Twin · 2 En Suite fac
2 Double · 2 Pub. Bath/Show
1 Family

B&B per person
from £15.00 Double

Open Jan-Dec
Dinner 1900-2000
B&B + Eve. Meal
from £25.00

Former croft recently redecorated and refurbished, enjoying panoramic views
of Cairngorms. Trad and Veg cuisine. Mountain bike hire. No smoking.

Granlea Guest House
Boat of Garten
Inverness-shire
PH24 3BN
Tel: (Boat of Garten)
047983 601

COMMENDED ♛♛♛

1 Twin · 2 En Suite fac
2 Double · 1 Pub. Bath/Show
1 Family

B&B per person
£15.00-£17.00 Single
£15.00-£17.00 Double

Open Jan-Dec
Dinner 1830-2000
B&B + Eve. Meal
£23.00

Stone built Edwardian house, in village centre, close to Osprey reserve.
Aviemore 6 miles (10 kms). Ski slopes 12 miles (19 kms).

Heathbank –
The Victorian House
Boat of Garten
Inverness-shire
PH24 3BD
Tel: (Boat of Garten)
047983 234

HIGHLY COMMENDED ♛♛♛

2 Twin · 6 En Suite fac
3 Double · 1 Priv. NOT ensuite
2 Family · 1 Pub. Bath/Show

B&B per person
£18.00-£22.00 Single
£18.00-£30.00 Double

Open Dec-Oct
Dinner from 1900
B&B + Eve. Meal
£32.00-£44.00

Victorian stone built house; chef/proprietor committed to fresh produce.
Rooms decorated imaginatively; full of old lace, flowers, pictures, books.

Ryvoan Guest House
Kinchurdy Road
Boat of Garten
Inverness-shire
PH24 3BP
Tel: (Boat of Garten)
047983 654

COMMENDED ♛

1 Twin · 1 En Suite fac
2 Double · 2 Pub. Bath/Show

B&B per person
from £15.00 Double

Open Jan-Dec
Dinner at 1900
B&B + Eve. Meal
from £25.00

Victorian house set in mature woodland with period accommodation and
modern facilities. Near RSPB reserve, golf club and Cairngorms.

Mrs N Clark
Dochlaggie
Boat of Garten
Inverness-shire
PH24 3BU
Tel: (Boat of Garten)
047983 242

1 Twin · 1 Pub. Bath/Show
1 Family

B&B per person
£14.00-£16.00 Double

Open Jan-Dec

Mrs M Cunningham
Steornabhagh, Deshar Road
Boat of Garten
Inverness-shire
PH24 3BN
Tel: (Boat of Garten)
047983 371

COMMENDED ♛♛

1 Twin · 1 En Suite fac
1 Double · 2 Pub. Bath/Show
1 Family

B&B per person
£15.00-£18.00 Single
£15.00-£18.00 Double

Open Jan-Dec
Dinner 1830-1900
B&B + Eve. Meal
£15.00-£18.00

Modern bungalow in quiet setting. Log fires and friendly atmosphere.
Accent on comfort, personal service. Easy access to fishing and bird-watching.

BOAT OF GARTEN continued	Map 4 C1

"LOCHEIL"
BOAT OF GARTEN, INVERNESS-SHIRE PH24 3BX
Telephone: 047 983 603

John and Barbara Davison offer all-year Bed and Breakfast accommodation in their comfortable home 1 mile from the "Osprey Village" on the A95 road midway between Aviemore and Grantown-on-Spey. Dinners and packed lunches on prior notice. Residents CTV lounge. 1-acre garden, ample parking.

Brochure on request.

Mrs B A Davison Locheil Boat of Garten Inverness-shire PH24 3BX Tel: (Boat of Garten) 047983 603	COMMENDED ≈	2 Single 1 Twin 1 Double	1 Pub. Bath/Show	B&B per person £12.50-£14.00 Single £12.50-£14.00 Double	Open Jan-Dec Dinner from 1900 B&B + Eve. Meal £20.50-£22.00
		Stone built house with new guest sitting room. Comfortable bed and breakfast accommodation. Evening meals by arrangement. Offering canoe hire.			
Mrs M M Grant Mullingarroch Croft Boat of Garten Inverness-shire PH24 3BY Tel: (Boat of Garten) 047983 645		2 Double	1 Pub. Bath/Show	B&B per person from £12.00 Single from £12.00 Double	Open Dec-Oct
Mrs S Lyons Glen Sanda, Street of Kincardine Boat of Garten Inverness-shire PH24 3BY Tel: (Boat of Garten) 047983 494	COMMENDED ≈ ≈	1 Twin 1 Double	2 En Suite fac	B&B per person from £14.50 Single from £14.50 Double	Open Jan-Dec
		Modern bungalow with views of Cairngorms on B970. 7 miles (11kms) Aviemore 1 mile (2kms) Boat of Garten. All rooms ensuite.			
Mrs L Sim Croftside, Street of Kincardine Boat of Garten Inverness-shire PH24 3BY Tel: (Boat of Garten) 047983 431	HIGHLY COMMENDED ≈ ≈	2 Twin 1 Double	3 En Suite fac	B&B per person from £15.00 Double	Open Jan-Oct
		Warm welcome at modern house on B970 with splendid views of Cairngorms and close to site of Osprey nest. 7 miles (11kms) north of Aviemore.			

BONAR BRIDGE Sutherland	Map 4 A6

Mrs S THOMSON
Kyle House · Dornoch Road, Bonar Bridge,
Sutherland IV24 3EB Tel: (086 32) 360

This old Scottish house in delightful setting overlooking the Kyle of Sutherland and Ross-shire hills, only 40 miles from Inverness, offers first-class accommodation and comfortable rooms with H&C etc. Convenient for Tourists, Fishermen, Climbers, Golfers (Royal Dornoch 14m) and passengers to Orkney Ferries (1¾ hours away).

Mrs S Thomson Kyle House, Dornoch Road Bonar Bridge Sutherland IV24 3EB Tel: (Ardgay) 08632 360		2 Twin 2 Double	1 En Suite fac 1 Pub. Bath/Show	B&B per person from £15.00 Double	Open Feb-Nov Dinner at 1900 B&B + Eve. Meal from £24.00

BO'NESS
West Lothian
Mr A B Brownlie
Aldersyde
15 Marchlands Terrace
Bo'ness
West Lothian
EH51 9ES
Tel: (Bo'ness) 0506 824084

Map 2
B4

2 Single | 1 Pub. Bath/Show | B&B per person £14.00 Single £12.50 Double | Open Jan-Dec

---

Mrs Caldwell
2 Bonhard Cottages
Bo'ness
West Lothian
EH51 9RR
Tel: (Bo'ness) 0506 823938

1 Twin
1 Double | 1 Pub. Bath/Show | B&B per person £15.00-£16.00 Single £13.50-£14.50 Double | Open Jan-Dec

---

Mrs Nancy Findlay
Gamrie, 63 Dean Road
Bo'ness
West Lothian
EH51 9BA
Tel: (Bo'ness) 0506 824563

COMMENDED
Listed

1 Single
1 Twin
1 Double | 1 Pub. Bath/Show | B&B per person from £15.00 Single from £13.00 Double | Open Apr-Oct

Centrally situated comfortable accommodation on major express bus route to Edinburgh. Private parking.

Mrs J A Harwood
The Knowe, Erngath Road
Bo'ness
West Lothian
EH51 9EN
Tel: (Bo'ness) 0506 825254

COMMENDED
Listed

1 Single
1 Twin
1 Family | 2 Pub. Bath/Show | B&B per person £17.00-£22.00 Single £16.00-£20.00 Double | Open Jan-Dec Dinner 1800-2000 B&B + Eve. Meal £23.00-£30.00

Detached Victorian house retaining many original features, standing in own grounds in elevated position with fine views over River Forth.

Mrs Bunty Kidd
Whigmeleerie, 151 Dean Road
Bo'ness
West Lothian
EH51 0HE
Tel: (Bo'ness)
0506 822707/823333

1 Single
1 Twin
1 Family | 2 Pub. Bath/Show | B&B per person from £17.00 Single from £14.50 Double | Open Jan-Dec

---

BONNYBRIDGE
Stirlingshire
Mrs Jean Forrester
Bandominie Farm
Walton Road
Bonnybridge
Stirlingshire
FK4 2HP
Tel: (Banknock) 0324 840284

Map 2
A4

COMMENDED
Listed

1 Single
1 Twin
1 Double | 1 Pub. Bath/Show | B&B per person £14.00-£15.00 Single £14.00-£15.00 Double | Open Jan-Dec

Working farm 2 miles (3kms) from A80 at Castle Cary (B816). Easy travel to Glasgow, Edinburgh and the North. Lovely views.

BORVE, by Portree
Isle of Skye, Inverness-shire
Mrs MacLean
Grandview, 27 Borve
Borve, by Portree
Isle of Skye, Inverness-shire
IV51
Tel: (Skeabost Bridge)
047032 234

Map 3
D9

COMMENDED
👑 👑

1 Single
1 Twin
1 Double | 1 En Suite fac 1 Pub. Bath/Show | B&B per person £13.50-£15.00 Single £13.50-£15.00 Double | Open May-Sep

Modern croft house on working croft. 3 miles (5kms) from Portree. Fine view of the Skye countryside. Traditional Scottish home fare.

BRAEMAR
Aberdeenshire
Cranford Guest House
15 Glenshee Road
Braemar
Aberdeenshire
AB35 5YQ
Tel: (Braemar) 03397 41675

Map 4
D1

COMMENDED
👑 👑 👑

2 Twin
3 Double
1 Family | 5 En Suite fac 1 Priv. NOT ensuite 1 Pub. Bath/Show | B&B per person £15.00-£16.00 Double | Open Jan-Dec Dinner 1830-1900 B&B + Eve. Meal £25.00-£26.00

Personally run guest house situated near village centre, only 8 miles (13kms) from Glenshee ski run.

VAT is shown at 17.5%: changes in this rate may affect prices. Prices shown are for guidance only. Please send SAE with each enquiry.

Schiehallion Guest House Glenshee Road Braemar Aberdeenshire AB35 5YQ Tel: (Braemar) 03397 41679	COMMENDED 👑 👑 👑	1 Single 4 Twin 4 Double 2 Family	7 En Suite fac 1 Pub. Bath/Show	B&B per person £15.50 Single £14.50-£16.50 Double	Open Jan-Dec Dinner from 1900 B&B + Eve. Meal £25.00-£27.00

Comfortable, tastefully decorated, Victorian house at gateway to Royal Deeside offering personal sevice, home cooking, log fires.

Mrs Bernard An Cromlon, Invercauld Farm Braemar Aberdeenshire AB35 5YQ Tel: (Braemar) 03397 41337		1 Twin 2 Double	2 Pub. Bath/Show	B&B per person to £16.00 Single £13.00 Double	Open Jan-Dec Dinner 1830-1930 B&B + Eve. Meal £18.00

AULD BANK HOUSE
9 INVERCAULD ROAD, BRAEMAR,
ABERDEENSHIRE   Tel/Fax: (03397) 41336

Family-run Victorian villa. Lovely views, centrally heated bedrooms with private facilities, colour TV's, electric blankets, coffee bars and lounge. Next to shops, pubs, golf course and bowling green. Ideal for hillwalking, skiing and visiting Deeside beauty spots and castles.

Mrs D Lamont Auld Bank House Invercauld Road Braemar Aberdeenshire AB35 5YP Tel./Fax: (Braemar) 03397 41336		2 Twin 1 Double 2 Family	5 En Suite fac	B&B per person to £15.50 Double	Open Jan-Dec Dinner 1900-2000 B&B + Eve. Meal to £25.50

BRAES, by Portree **Isle of Skye, Inverness-shire** Nevelee Corry 1/7 Camastianavaig Braes, by Portree Isle of Skye, Inverness-shire IV51 9LQ Tel: (Sligachan) 0478 650325	Map 3 D9	1 Double 1 Family	1 En Suite fac 1 Pub. Bath/Show	B&B per person from £14.00 Single £13.00-£15.00 Double	Open Mar-Oct

Mrs J Goddard Treetops Camustianavaig, Braes Isle of Skye, Inverness-shire IV51 9LQ Tel: (Sligachan) 047852 218/0478 650218	COMMENDED Listed	1 Twin 1 Double	1 Pub. Bath/Show	B&B per person £15.00 Single £13.00-£15.00 Double	Open May-Sep

Modern bungalow in rural area with fine views over bay. Good centre for walking. Tea/coffee served in evenings. 5 miles (8kms) from Portree.

BREAKISH **Isle of Skye, Inverness-shire** Mrs M A B Macgregor Langdale House Waterloo, Breakish Isle of Skye, Inverness-shire IV42 8QE Tel: (Broadford) 0471 822376	Map 3 E1 APPROVED 👑 👑 👑	2 Twin 1 Double	2 En Suite fac 1 Pub. Bath/Show	B&B per person £14.50-£16.00 Double	Open Jan-Dec Dinner 1900-2000 B&B + Eve. Meal £28.50-£30.00

Superb views of sea and mountains from all rooms. Nature watch. Vegetarian and Coeliac food by arrangement.

Details of Grading and Classification are on page vi. | Key to symbols is on back flap. |

BREASCLEIT Lewis, Western Isles Corran View Guest House 22a Breascleit Breascleit Lewis, Western Isles PA86 9EF Tel: (Callanish) 0851 621300	Map 3 C4	HIGHLY COMMENDED 👑 👑 👑	1 Twin 3 Double 1 Family	3 En Suite fac 1 Pub. Bath/Show	B&B per person £20.00 Single £20.00 Double	Open Jan-Dec Dinner 1800-1900 B&B + Eve. Meal £35.00	
			Comfortable modern house overlooking sea loch, within easy reach of ferry and airport. Ideal for touring, walking, sailing and beaches.				

BRECHIN Angus Mrs N Cruickshank Briarton, Little Brechin Brechin Angus DD9 6RQ Tel: (Brechin) 0356 624682	Map 4 F1	COMMENDED Listed	1 Twin 1 Double	1 Pub. Bath/Show	B&B per person £12.00 Double	Open Apr-Oct	
			Quietly situated off main road. Affording superb views of hills. Excellent base for touring.				

Wood of Auldbar Farmhouse

WOOD OF AULDBAR, ABERLEMNO, BRECHIN DD9 6SZ
Telephone: 0307 830 218

Award-winning farmhouse. A warm welcome awaits you at our family farm. Excellent food and accommodation. Tea facilities in all bedrooms. Smoke alarms throughout. Food Hygiene Certificate held. Ideal for touring Glens of Angus, Royal Deeside, Balmoral. Glamis within easy reach. Nature walks, bird-watching, fishing, golf; leisure centres nearby. Aberlemno Standing Stones can be viewed. Aberdeen, Dundee, St Andrews and Edinburgh all within easy reach. **B&B from £13, EM from £8.**

Mrs J Stewart Wood of Auldbar Brechin Angus DD9 6SZ Tel: (Aberlemno) 030783 218/0307 830218		COMMENDED Listed	1 Single 1 Twin 1 Family	2 Pub. Bath/Show	B&B per person from £14.00 Single from £15.00 Double	Open Jan-Dec Dinner 1800-2000 B&B + Eve. Meal from £22.50	
			Farmhouse with large south facing garden on working mixed arable and stock farm in pleasant countryside. 5 miles (8kms) from Brechin.				

A Warm Welcome Awaits . . .

BLIBBERHILL · BRECHIN DD9 6TH
Tel: 0307 830225   **AA Selected QQQQ**

BLIBBERHILL is a spacious, well-appointed farmhouse situated in peaceful, rural surroundings between Angus Glens and Coast, not far from Glamis Castle, Barrie's birthplace and also House of Dun. Ideal for touring, fishing, hill-walking and central to many golf courses. A warm welcome is extended to all guests with all home-cooking, baking and home-made preserves served. Shortbread and porridge our specialities. Dinner optional.

Mrs Margaret Stewart Blibberhill Farmhouse Brechin Angus DD9 6TH Tel: (Aberlemno) 0307 830225		HIGHLY COMMENDED 👑 👑 👑	2 Twin 1 Double	3 En Suite fac 1 Pub. Bath/Show	B&B per person £16.00-£17.50 Single £16.00-£17.00 Double	Open Jan-Dec Dinner from 1800 B&B + Eve. Meal from £24.00	
			18C stone built farmhouse in peaceful situation on mixed working farm. Homemade preserves and home baking and cooking.				

| BRECHIN continued | Map 4 F1 |

FARMHOUSE BED & BREAKFAST
TILLYGLOOM FARM, BRECHIN, ANGUS DD9 7PE
Telephone: 035662 2953
Enjoy the atmosphere of our working farm. Golf courses, country walks, nearby fishing, shooting, riding can be arranged. TV lounge, home cooking. Prices from £12 per night B&B per person; DB&B from £18.50.
Contact Mrs Lorna Watson.

| Mrs L Watson Tillygloom Farm Brechin Angus DD9 7PE Tel: (Brechin) 0356 622953 | | COMMENDED Listed | 1 Twin 1 Family | 1 Pub. Bath/Show | B&B per person £12.00 Single £11.50 Double | Open Apr-Oct Dinner 1800-2000 B&B + Eve. Meal £17.50-£18.50 |

Friendly farmhouse welcome awaits guests at our home near Brechin. In quiet, pleasant surroundings. Easy access to a host of local activities.

| BY BRECHIN Angus Mrs R Beatty Brathinch Farm by Brechin Angus DD9 7QX Tel: (Edzell) 0356 648292 Fax: 0356 648003 | Map 4 F1 | | 2 Double | 1 En Suite fac 1 Priv. NOT ensuite 2 Pub. Bath/Show | B&B per person £14.00 Single £12.00 Double | Open May-Sep |

| Mrs P H Massuch The Station House Farnell, by Brechin Angus DD9 6UH Tel: (Farnell) 067482 208 | | COMMENDED | 3 Twin | 1 En Suite fac 2 Pub. Bath/Show | B&B per person £13.00-£16.00 Double | Open Jan-Dec Dinner 1700-2000 |

Pleasant rural setting in large grounds. Minutes from numerous activities. Spacious accommodation. Large car park. Dog kennels.

| BRIDGE OF ALLAN Stirlingshire Miss M P Grew 94 Henderson Street Bridge of Allan Stirlingshire FK9 4HA Tel: (Bridge of Allan) 0786 832334 | Map 2 A4 | | 1 Twin 1 Family | 1 Priv. NOT ensuite 1 Pub. Bath/Show | B&B per person £13.00-£16.00 Double | Open Apr-Nov |

| BRIDGE OF CALLY Perthshire Mrs Sara Jane Gilbey Mains of Soilzarie Bridge of Cally, Blairgowrie Perthshire PH10 7LS Tel: (Strathardle) 0250 881222 | Map 2 C1 | DELUXE | 1 Twin 1 Double | 2 Priv. NOT ensuite | B&B per person from £20.00 Single from £20.00 Double | Open Jan-Dec |

Beautifully refurbished country house amidst spectacular scenery. Imaginative cooking; own produce. 5 miles (8 kms) north of Bridge of Cally.

BRIDGE OF EARN
Perthshire

Map 2
C3

CRAIGHALL FARMHOUSE

Forgandenny, Bridge of Earn
Perth PH2 9DF Tel: 0738 812415

An ideal touring base — you can visit 90% of population of Scotland in 90 minutes. Situated on B935 ½ mile west from Forgandenny in the historic Valley of the Kings. At the foot of the hills we offer natural good humour and hospitality in our modern and tastefully furnished farmhouse. Through the windows cattle, sheep and pigs graze in fields of our working farm. Golfers are well catered for with an abundance of courses within an hour's drive. Fishing by arrangement in private pond. Hillwalkers' numerous routes through fields — healthy, hearty breakfast sets you up for the day with large and varied choice of home-grown produce. One of the few farmhouses to offer ground floor en-suite rooms.

Mrs M J D Fotheringham Craighall Farm House Forgandenny Bridge of Earn Perthshire PH2 9DF Tel: (Bridge of Earn) 0738 812415 Fax: 0738 812415			2 Twin 1 Family	2 En Suite fac 1 Priv. NOT ensuite 1 Pub. Bath/Show	B&B per person from £15.00 Single from £14.50 Double	Open Jan-Dec Dinner 1800-2100 B&B + Eve. Meal from £20.50

BROADFORD **Isle of Skye, Inverness-shire** Mrs J Donaldson Fairwinds, Elgol Road Broadford Isle of Skye, Inverness-shire IV49 9AB Tel: (Broadford) 0471 822270	Map 3 E1	COMMENDED 👑 👑	1 Twin 2 Double	1 En Suite fac 1 Pub. Bath/Show	B&B per person £14.50-£16.50 Double	Open Apr-Oct
			Peacefully situated bungalow in extensive garden overlooking Broadford River and the mountains. Bicycles for hire.			

Isle of Skye TEL: (0471) 822327
ASHGROVE, BLACK PARK, BROADFORD IV49 9AE

Comfortable accommodation in three-bedroomed bungalow. Two bedrooms with whb, one bedroom with whb, shower and toilet en-suite. Colour TV lounge, tea-making facilities. Cot available. Eight miles from Kyle Ferry. Turn off main road at Lime Park/Black Park junction.

From £13 to £18 per person.

Mrs M Fletcher Ashgrove, 11 Black Park Broadford Isle of Skye, Inverness-shire IV49 9AE Tel: (Broadford) 0471 822327		COMMENDED 👑	1 Twin 1 Double 1 Family	1 En Suite fac 1 Pub. Bath/Show	B&B per person £13.00-£18.00 Double	Open Jan-Dec
			Modern bungalow with fine views of sea and mountains.			

Mrs MacKinnon Failte, 6 Heaste Broadford Isle of Skye, Inverness-shire IV49 8QF Tel: (Broadford) 0471 822268			1 Single 1 Twin 1 Double	1 En Suite fac 1 Pub. Bath/Show	B&B per person £15.00 Single £15.00 Double	Open Apr-Oct Dinner from 1900 B&B + Eve. Meal £20.00-£22.00

Mrs D MacPhie Ptarmigan Broadford Isle of Skye, Inverness-shire IV49 9AQ Tel: (Broadford) 0471 822744 Fax: 0471 822745		**HIGHLY COMMENDED** 👑 👑	1 Twin 2 Double	3 En Suite fac 1 Pub. Bath/Show	B&B per person £20.00-£25.00 Double	Open Jan-Dec	
			Modern family home on seashore of Broadford Bay. Panoramic views across islands to mainland.				
Mrs MacRae Hillcrest, Black Park Broadford Isle of Skye, Inverness-shire IV49 9AE Tel: (Broadford) 0471 822375			1 Twin 1 Double 1 Family	2 Pub. Bath/Show	B&B per person from £14.00 Single from £14.00 Double	Open Jan-Dec	
Mrs Jackie Nelder Ailean Cottage Harrapool, Broadford Isle of Skye, Inverness-shire IV49 9AQ Tel: (Broadford) 0471 822278			1 Single 1 Double 1 Family	1 En Suite fac 2 Pub. Bath/Show	B&B per person £14.00-£18.00 Single £14.00-£18.00 Double	Open Mar-Nov Dinner 1800-2000 B&B + Eve. Meal £23.00-£27.00	
Mrs Robertson Tigh a Croisean, 4 Black Park Broadford Isle of Skye, Inverness-shire IV49 9AE Tel: (Broadford) 0471 822338			1 Twin 2 Double	2 En Suite fac 1 Pub. Bath/Show	B&B per person £13.00-£16.00 Double	Open Apr-Sep	
Mrs M Robertson Earsary, 7-8 Harrapool Broadford Isle of Skye, Inverness-shire IV49 9AQ Tel: (Broadford) 0471 822697		**COMMENDED** 👑 👑	1 Twin 1 Double 1 Family	3 En Suite fac	B&B per person £16.00-£20.00 Single £16.00-£20.00 Double	Open Jan-Dec	
			Modern house with high standard of accomodation on working croft. Panoramic views over Broadford Bay.				
Mrs Scott Tigh-na-Mara Lower Harrapool by Broadford Isle of Skye, Inverness-shire IV49 9AB Tel: (Broadford) 0471 822475			1 Family	2 Pub. Bath/Show	B&B per person £13.00-£14.00 Double	Open Apr-Oct	
Jane Wilcken Corry Lodge, Liveras Broadford Isle of Skye, Inverness-shire IV49 9AA Tel: (Broadford) 0471 822235 Fax: 0471 822318		**HIGHLY COMMENDED** 👑	2 Twin 2 Double	2 En Suite fac 2 Priv. NOT ensuite 2 Pub. Bath/Show	B&B per person £20.00-£25.00 Double	Open Jan-Dec Dinner at 2000 B&B + Eve. Meal £35.00-£45.00	
			Late 18c shooting lodge, totally restored to its former splendour on 80acre estate stretching to the shoreline.				
BY BROADFORD **Isle of Skye, Inverness-shire** Mrs Flora A MacLeod Hazelwood Cottage, Heaste by Broadford Isle of Skye, Inverness-shire IV42 8QF Tel: (Broadford) 0471 822294	Map 3 E1		1 Twin 2 Double	1 Pub. Bath/Show	B&B per person from £13.00 Double	Open May-Oct	
BRODICK **Isle of Arran** Allandale Guest House Brodick Isle of Arran KA27 8BJ Tel: (Brodick) 0770 2278/302278	Map 1 F7	**COMMENDED** 👑 👑 👑	1 Single 2 Twin 1 Double 2 Family	5 En Suite fac 1 Priv. NOT ensuite 1 Pub. Bath/Show	B&B per person £16.00-£20.00 Single £16.00-£20.00 Double	Open Jan-Oct Dinner 1900-1930 B&B + Eve. Meal £25.00-£30.00	
			Comfortable guest house in south-facing postion on the edge of Brodick, only a few minutes walk from the ferry. Some annexe accommodation.				

| BRODICK continued | Map 1
F7 | | |

Glencloy Farmhouse

BRODICK, ISLE OF ARRAN KA27 8DA (0770) 302351

Our farmhouse is a beautiful, century-old sandstone house, situated in a peaceful glen just outside Brodick. We offer cosy rooms, log fires, and excellent food prepared by chef proprietor. We bake our own bread and our vegetables come from our kitchen garden. We are close to golf, castle and mountains.

Glencloy Farm House Brodick Isle of Arran KA27 8BZ Tel: (Brodick) 0770 2351/302351	COMMENDED 👑 👑	1 Single 2 Twin 2 Double	2 En Suite fac 1 Pub. Bath/Show	B&B per person £19.00-£25.00 Single £19.00-£25.00 Double	Open Mar-Nov Dinner 1900-1930 B&B + Eve. Meal £29.00-£35.00
		Farmhouse, set in peaceful glen with views of hills and sea. Within easy reach of Brodick ferry. Chef/proprietor: fresh, homegrown produce.			
Rosa Burn Lodge Brodick Isle of Arran KA27 8DP Tel: (Brodick) 0770 2383/302383		2 Twin 1 Double	3 En Suite fac	B&B per person £27.50-£30.00 Single £17.50-£20.00 Double	Open Jan-Dec
Tighnamara Brodick Isle of Arran KA27 8AN Tel: (Brodick) 0770 2538/302538		2 Twin 3 Double 2 Family	2 En Suite fac 3 Pub. Bath/Show	B&B per person from £15.00 Single from £15.00 Double	Open Apr-Oct
Tuathair House Brodick Isle of Arran KA27 8AJ Tel: (Brodick) 0770 2214/302214	COMMENDED 👑 👑 👑	1 Twin 2 Double 1 Family	4 En Suite fac	B&B per person £17.00-£22.00 Single £17.00-£22.00 Double	Open Jan-Dec Dinner from 1800 B&B + Eve. Meal £27.00-£32.00
		Family run guest house on sea front, open views across Brodick Bay to Goat Fell. Non-smoking establishment.			
Mrs Sutherland Skirza, West Mayish Brodick Isle of Arran KA27 8AF Tel: (Brodick) 0770 2364/302364		1 Twin 1 Double	1 Pub. Bath/Show	B&B per person from £13.00 Double	Open Feb-Nov
BRORA **Sutherland** Mrs J Ballantyne Clynelish Farm Brora Sutherland KW9 6LR Tel: (Brora) 0408 621265	Map 4 C6 COMMENDED 👑 👑	1 Twin 1 Double 1 Family	2 En Suite fac 1 Pub. Bath/Show	B&B per person £14.00-£16.00 Single £14.00-£18.00 Double	Open Nov-Mar Dinner 1830-1900
		Family home, on working farm, in rural setting about a mile from Brora and beaches.			

Mrs Clarkson Tigh Fada, Golf Road Brora Sutherland KW9 6QS Tel: (Brora) 0408 621332 Fax: 0408 621332		COMMENDED 👑👑	1 Twin 1 Double	1 En Suite fac 1 Priv. NOT ensuite 1 Pub. Bath/Show	B&B per person £15.00-£20.00 Double	Open Jan-Dec

Fine sea views and peat fires, home baking and a real Highland welcome. Ideal half way house between Inverness and John O'Groats.

Mrs M Cooper Lynwood, Golf Road Brora Sutherland KW9 6QS Tel: (Brora) 0408 621226		COMMENDED 👑👑👑	2 Twin 1 Double 1 Family	3 En Suite fac 1 Pub. Bath/Show	B&B per person £15.00-£20.00 Double	Open Mar-Dec Dinner 1900-2000 B&B + Eve. Meal £24.00-£29.00

Family home in substantial Edwardian house in its own grounds overlooking Brora harbour. Home cooking. Annexe garden room available on ground floor.

Mrs Fraser Craiglyn, Victoria Road Brora Sutherland Tel: (Brora) 0408 621124		COMMENDED 👑	1 Single 1 Twin 1 Family	2 Pub. Bath/Show	B&B per person £12.00-£14.00 Single £12.00-£14.00 Double	Open Jan-Dec

Comfortable accommodation in friendly bed and breakfast. Ideal touring base.

BROUGHTY FERRY **Angus** Mrs M Laing Auchenean 177 Hamilton Street Broughty Ferry Dundee DD5 2RE Tel: (Dundee) 0382 74782	Map 2 D2	COMMENDED Listed	1 Single 2 Twin	1 Pub. Bath/Show	B&B per person £14.00 Single £14.00 Double	Open Apr-Oct Dinner 1800-2000 B&B + Eve. Meal £21.00

Detached house. Situated in quiet cul-de-sac. Five minutes walk from sea front. Off street parking.

BRUICHLADDICH **Isle of Islay, Argyll** Mrs A MacDonald Anchorage Bruichladdich Isle of Islay, Argyll PA49 7UN Tel: (Port Charlotte) 049685 540	Map 1 B6	Award Pending	1 Twin 2 Double	1 Pub. Bath/Show	B&B per person £13.00-£14.50 Single £13.00-£14.50 Double	Open Jan-Dec B&B + Eve. Meal £22.00-£23.00

BUCHLYVIE **Stirlingshire** Mrs V Golding Upper Gartinstarry Buchlyvie Stirlingshire FK8 3PD Tel: (Buchlyvie) 036085 309	Map 1 H4	COMMENDED 👑👑👑	1 Family	1 En Suite fac	B&B per person £17.50-£20.00 Single	Open Jan-Dec Dinner 1800-2000 B&B + Eve. Meal £25.00-£28.50

Bungalow peacefully situated in 8.5 acres, 2.5 miles (4kms) from the village. Central for touring Loch Lomond and the Trossachs. Home cooking.

BUCKHAVEN **Fife** Mr & Mrs J Murrie 30 College Street Buckhaven Fife KY8 1JX Tel: (Buckhaven) 0592 713534	Map 2 D3		1 Single 1 Double	1 Pub. Bath/Show	B&B per person £11.00-£14.00 Single £12.00-£15.00 Double	Open Jan-Dec Dinner 1800-2000 B&B + Eve. Meal £15.00

BUCKIE **Banffshire** Mrs Marion McKay Rhiconich, 11 Highfield Road Buckie Banffshire AB56 1BE Tel: (Buckie) 0542 31465	Map 4 E7		1 Twin 2 Double	1 Pub. Bath/Show	B&B per person £13.00 Single £13.00 Double	Open Jan-Dec
Mrs Norma Pirie Rosemount 62 East Church Street Buckie Banffshire AB56 1ER Tel: (Buckie) 0542 33434		COMMENDED 👑 👑	1 Twin 1 Double 2 Family	2 En Suite fac 1 Limited ensuite 2 Pub. Bath/Show	B&B per person £13.50-£17.00 Double	Open Jan-Dec
			Modernised Victorian detached house, centrally situated overlooking harbour. Ideal for fishing and golf.			
BUNESSAN **Isle of Mull, Argyll** Mr & Mrs I MacDougall Seawood View, Fountainhead Bunessan Isle of Mull, Argyll PA67 6DP Tel: (Fionnphort) 06817 326	Map 1 C3		1 Twin 1 Double	1 Pub. Bath/Show	B&B per person from £11.00 Single from £10.50 Double	Open May-Sep
Alison Riley Ardchiavaig Cottage Uisken, Bunessan Isle of Mull, Argyll PA67 6DT Tel: (Fionnphort) 06817 286			1 Single 1 Double 1 Family	1 Pub. Bath/Show	B&B per person £12.00-£14.00 Single £12.00-£14.00 Double	Open May-Oct Dinner 1900-2100 B&B + Eve. Meal £19.00-£21.00
BURGHEAD **Moray** Mrs Anne Smith Norland, 26 Granary Street Burghead, Elgin Moray IV30 2UJ Tel: (Burghead) 0343 835212	Map 4 D7		1 Twin 2 Double	1 Pub. Bath/Show	B&B per person from £13.00 Double	Open Jan-Dec
BURNMOUTH, Eyemouth **Berwickshire** Mr & Mrs R Goff Greystonelees Farm House Burnmouth Berwickshire TD14 5SZ Tel: (Ayton) 08907 81709	Map 2 G5	COMMENDED 👑 👑	1 Single 1 Twin 1 Double	2 En Suite fac 1 Pub. Bath/Show	B&B per person £15.00-£25.00 Single £16.00-£18.00 Double	Open Jan-Dec Dinner 1800-2000 B&B + Eve. Meal £24.00-£26.00
			Georgian farmhouse in quiet countryside 200 yards from A1. Good walking country. St Abbs Head 5 miles (8kms); Eyemouth 2 miles (3kms); Home baking.			
BURRELTON, Blairgowrie **Perthshire** Mrs Shonaidh Beattie Shocarjen, The Green Burrelton, Blairgowrie Perthshire PH13 9NU Tel: (Burrelton) 08287 223	Map 2 C2	Award Pending	2 Family	2 En Suite fac	B&B per person £18.00-£20.00 Single £14.00-£16.00 Double	Open Jan-Dec
Mr E M Weaving Burrelton Park Inn High Street Burrelton, Blairgowrie Perthshire PH13 9NX Tel: (Burrelton) 08287 206		COMMENDED 👑 👑 👑	2 Single 3 Twin 1 Family	6 En Suite fac	B&B per person £25.00-£30.00 Single £22.50 Double	Open Jan-Dec Dinner 1800-2200 B&B + Eve. Meal £30.00
			Family run restaurant with rooms. Comfortable ensuite accommodation. Comprehensive all day menu. Taste of Scotland.			

CALLANDER	Map 2					
Perthshire	A3					
Abbotsford Lodge		COMMENDED	1 Single	9 En Suite fac	B&B per person	
Stirling Road		♛ ♛ ♛	4 Twin	4 Pub. Bath/Show	from £24.50 Single	
Callander			5 Double		from £19.50 Double	
Perthshire			8 Family			
FK17 8DA						
Tel: (Callander) 0877 330066			Family run Victorian house in its own grounds with private pa... to town centre. Home cooking and baking.			

ARDEN HOUSE

**BRACKLINN ROAD
CALLANDER
PERTHSHIRE FK17 8EQ**
Jim and Dorothy
McGregor
Tel: 0877 30235/330235
AA 4Q Select/
RAC Highly Acclaimed

Peacefully situated in ... ...dens with marvellous views o... ...ountryside. **Arden House** offers del... ...ome cooking, six comfortable rooms, all en suite, tea/coffee making facilities and central heating. Two lounges, one with colour TV, and a warm, friendly and relaxed atmosphere. Reduced off-season terms. Generous reductions for children and weekly holidays. Ample car parking space. Small putting green.

The TV home of BBC's "Dr Finlay's Casebook"

Arden House Guest House	COMMENDED	1 Single	6 En Suite fac	B&B per person	Open Mar-Nov
Bracklinn Road	♛ ♛ ♛	2 Twin		£16.00-£18.00 Single	Dinner from 1900
Callander		2 Double		£16.00-£18.00 Double	B&B + Eve. Meal
Perthshire		1 Family			£26.00-£28.00
FK17 8EQ					
Tel: (Callander)		Family run, peacefully situated in its own grounds. Superb panoramic			
0877 30235/330235		views to Ben Ledi and the Trossachs. A non-smoking house.			

ARRAN LODGE
LENY ROAD, CALLANDER FK17 8AJ
Telephone: 0877 330976 or 30976

An enchanting period bungalow set on the banks of the River Leny by Callander's western boundary. Relax in the serenity of the tranquil riverside garden. Delight in the luxury of our 4-poster bedrooms and enjoy the mouth-watering cuisine in our elegant Victorian dining-room. Be warmed by a welcome you will never forget.

**RAC: Highly Acclaimed.
AA: Premiere selected QQQQQ
B&B £23.50-£34.50. Dinner £13.50-£17.00.**

An informal, friendly yet elegant atmosphere in which to enjoy an ideal holiday in our home.
Your hosts Pasqua Margarita Moore and Robert Moore.

Arran Lodge	DELUXE	1 Twin	3 En Suite fac	B&B per person	Open Feb-Dec
Leny Road	♛ ♛ ♛	2 Double	1 Priv. NOT ensuite	£35.20-£48.80 Single	Dinner at 1930
Callander		1 Family		£23.50-£30.50 Double	B&B + Eve. Meal
Perthshire					£35.50-£45.00
FK17 8AJ					
Tel: (Callander)		Delightful bungalow on A84 with tranquil riverside garden.			
0877 30976/330976		Friendly welcome, quality cuisine and private parking.			

Campfield Cottage	COMMENDED	1 Twin	1 Pub. Bath/Show	B&B per person	Open Jan-Dec
138 Main Street	Listed	2 Double		£15.00-£17.00 Double	Dinner 1830-1900
Callander					B&B + Eve. Meal
Perthshire					£24.00-£26.00
FK17 8BG					
Tel: (Callander) 0877 330599		Dating from 1759, family cottage off main street with private parking.			
		Evening meals available, children welcome; pets by special arrangement.			

	COMMENDED ☰ ☰	4 Double	4 En Suite fac	B&B per person £18.00-£19.00 Double	Open Apr-Nov	

...der) 0877 30871

Stone built villa in main street, 5 minutes walk from shops and Rob Roy Centre. Own car park with easy access to ground floor bedroom.

INVERTROSSACHS COUNTRY HOUSE

Invertrossachs, By Callander, Perthshire FK17 8HG
Telephone: (0877) 31126/331126
Fax: (0877) 31229/331229

At this splendid lochside Edwardian Mansion we are pleased to offer a superior accommodation and breakfast service complemented with a discreet level of personal attention.

Our Loch Room with private bath, shower and wc is a large double or twin with commanding views over Loch Venachar. Our Victoria Suite in its own private wing sleeps up to 4 in a choice of bedrooms (double, small double and single) with private bath, shower and wc. Both Loch and Victoria have colour TV, d/dial phone, trouser press, hairdryers, video, CD and tea-making facilities. Prices include 5-course Scottish Breakfast served in our conservatory. Dinner reservations may be made at nearby recommended restaurants.

Leisurely walking, cycling, fishing on site. Golf/Watersports close by. Ideal touring base for freedom, flexibility and a complete escape. — Advance booking recommended.

On enquiry, please quote EBB.

Invertrossachs Country House Invertrossachs, by Callander Perthshire FK17 8HG Tel: (Callander) 0877 31126/0877 331126 Fax: 0877 31229/ 0877 331229	HIGHLY COMMENDED ☰ ☰ ☰	1 Twin 2 Double Suite avail.	3 En Suite fac 1 Pub. Bath/Show	B&B per person £35.00-£60.00 Single £29.50-£45.00 Double	Open Jan-Dec	

Edwardian mansion in its own 28 acres of mature woodlands overlooking Loch Venachar. Quiet rural setting 4 miles (6kms) up a private drive.

The Knowe Ancaster Road Callander Perthshire FK17 8EL Tel: (Callander) 0877 30076	COMMENDED ☰ ☰ ☰	1 Twin 3 Double 1 Family	5 En Suite fac	B&B per person £18.00-£25.00 Single £17.00-£18.00 Double	Open Jan-Dec Dinner from 1830 B&B + Eve. Meal £27.00-£28.00	

Family run with a friendly welcome and good cooking. Quietly situated off the main road with magnificent views. Ideal for a peaceful holiday.

Riverview House

LENY ROAD, CALLANDER FK17 8AL
Tel: 0877 30635/330635

Detached Victorian house set in its own grounds near parklands, yet close to shops and other venues. Private facilities in all rooms including colour TV and tea-making. Good home cooking with choice on menu. Ample parking in own grounds.

Riverview House Leny Road Callander Perthshire FK17 8AL Tel: (Callander) 0877 30635/330635	COMMENDED ☰ ☰ ☰	1 Single 1 Twin 3 Double	4 En Suite fac 1 Limited ensuite 1 Pub. Bath/Show	B&B per person £17.50 Single £17.50 Double	Open Apr-Oct Dinner 1900-1915 B&B + Eve. Meal £28.50	

19C house situated back from the main route north out of Callander. All meals with choice of menu, using fresh produce in season.

VAT is shown at 17.5%: changes in this rate may affect prices. Prices shown are for guidance only. Please send SAE with each enquiry.

Mrs O Aitken Achray House 4 Achray Avenue Callander Perthshire FK17 8JZ Tel: (Callander) 0877 30104	COMMENDED 👑	1 Single 1 Twin 1 Double	2 Pub. Bath/Show	B&B per person £13.00-£15.00 Single £13.00-£15.00 Double	Open Easter-Oct Dinner 1800-1930 B&B + Eve. Meal £20.00-£22.00	(symbols)
		Modern family villa in quiet residential area near the edge of town. Private parking. Non-smoking establishment.				
Mr and Mrs G Angiolini Camp View, Stirling Road Callander Perthshire Tel: (Callander) 0877 30349		2 Twin 1 Double	3 Limited ensuite 1 Pub. Bath/Show	B&B per person £17.00-£18.00	Open Jan-Nov	(symbols)
Mrs Collier Inver-Enys, Ancaster Road Callander Perthshire FK17 8EL Tel: (Callander) 0877 30908		1 Twin 1 Double 1 Family	2 Pub. Bath/Show	B&B per person £14.00-£16.00 Single £13.00-£14.00 Double	Open Jan-Dec	(symbols)

ROSLIN COTTAGE GUEST HOUSE
Lagrannoch, Callander, Perthshire FK17 8LE
Telephone: 0877 30638/330638
On the outskirts of Callander, with fine views, our early eighteenth century cottage has been restored, retaining its original stone walls, beams and fireplace in the lounge.
We offer a varied Scottish breakfast, using eggs and honey from our large garden.
Lynne and Alistair Ferguson welcome you to their home.

Mrs Ferguson Roslin Cottage, Lagrannoch Callander Perthshire FK17 8LE Tel: (Callander) 0877 30638/330638		2 Single 1 Twin 1 Double	1 Pub. Bath/Show	B&B per person £15.00-£16.50 Single £12.50-£14.00 Double	Open Jan-Dec Dinner from 1830 B&B + Eve. Meal £23.00-£25.00	(symbols)
Mrs A Lochans The Lochans, 5 Lubnaig Drive Callander Perthshire FK17 8JT Tel: (Callander) 0877 30627	COMMENDED 👑	1 Twin 1 Family	2 En Suite fac	B&B per person £16.00-£17.50 Single £16.00-£17.50 Double	Open Apr-Oct Dinner 1830-1930	(symbols)
		Detached bungalow in quiet residential area on south side of town, 1/2 mile (1km) from town centre. Both bedrooms with en suite facilities.				
Mrs McAlpine Craigburn House North Church Street Callander Perthshire FK17 Tel: (Callander) 0877 30332		1 Single 1 Twin 2 Double 1 Family	2 Pub. Bath/Show	B&B per person £13.00-£14.00 Single £13.00-£14.00 Double	Open Apr-Oct	(symbols)
Mrs E MacKenzie Lamorna, Ancaster Road Callander Perthshire FK17 8EL Tel: (Callander) 0877 30868	COMMENDED 👑	1 Twin 1 Double	1 Pub. Bath/Show	B&B per person £14.00-£15.00 Double	Open Apr-Oct	(symbols)
		Family run, detached bungalow in a quiet area. Comfortable rooms, warm friendly atmosphere. Private parking.				
The Misk 9 Katrine Crescent Callander Perthshire FK17 8JR Tel: (Callander) 0877 30396		1 Twin	1 En Suite fac	B&B per person £17.00 Double	Open Apr-Oct	(symbols)

CALLANDER continued	Map 2 A3

LENY HOUSE

LENY ESTATE · CALLANDER
PERTHSHIRE FK17 8HA   (0877) 31078/331078

Historic LENY HOUSE, a 15th-century listed country family home set in Leny Park and surrounded by acres of farmland. It featured in much of the history of Callander, particularly during the Jacobite Rebellion. It now offers tranquil, comfortable Bed & Breakfast accommodation in beautiful surroundings. The private Leny Glen, in which visitors may walk, and where deer safely graze, contains much wildlife, indeed the resident roe deer family are often seen in the grounds. The paddocks contain a small goat herd, sheep and horses. Magnificent views to the Trossachs and Ben Ledi. Featured on television travel programme.

A & F Roebuck Leny House, Leny Estate Callander Perthshire FK17 8HA Tel: (Callander) 0877 31078/331078			1 Twin 1 Double 1 Family	2 En Suite fac 2 Pub. Bath/Show	B&B per person £20.00-£22.00 Double	Open Apr-Sep	

E Stirrup Sundial House, Leny Estate Callander Perthshire FK17 8HA Tel: (Callander) 0877 331592/330152			2 Twin 1 Double	3 En Suite fac	B&B per person £30.00-£33.00 Single £20.00-£22.00 Double	Open Apr-Oct	

BY CALLANDER Perthshire	Map 2 A3

STABLES COTTAGE

INVERTROSSACHS ESTATE
CALLANDER FK17 8HG
Telephone: 0877 31278/331278

STABLES COTTAGE is on the Invertrossachs Estate to the west of Callander, the main town of "The Trossachs". A cycle path close by leads to the Queen Elizabeth Forest Park and to the final resting place of Rob Roy McGregor.

We offer a comfortable base to pursue your hobby, be it walking, cycling or just relaxing.

Meals are available and snacks can be made for guests arriving late.

For the energetic we have mountain bikes available. Packed lunches supplied by arrangement.

Tranquil location 5 miles (8kms) from Callander; wonderful scenery. All rooms on one level. Ideal for walking, cycling or just relaxing.

Mr & Mrs J Nixon Stables Cottage Invertrossachs Estate by Callander Perthshire FK17 8HG Tel: (Callander) 0877 31278/331278		COMMENDED	3 Double	1 En Suite fac 1 Pub. Bath/Show	B&B per person £17.00-£20.00 Single £13.00-£18.00 Double	Open Jan-Dec Dinner 1900-2030 B&B + Eve. Meal £21.00-£26.00	

CALLANISH **Lewis, Western Isles** Eshcol Guest House 21 Breascleit Callanish Lewis, Western Isles PA86 9ED Tel: (Callanish) 085172 357	Map 3 C5	HIGHLY COMMENDED 👑👑👑	2 Twin 1 Double	2 En Suite fac 1 Priv. NOT ensuite	B&B per person from £20.00 Single from £20.00 Double	Open Mar-Oct Dinner 1700-1900 B&B + Eve. Meal £29.00-£34.00	

Modern detached house with fine views south over Loch Roag.
Near to Callanish Standing Stones and Carloway Broch. En suite facilites.

Mrs A MacLeod The Cairns, 32 Callanish Callanish Lewis, Western Isles PA86 9DY Tel: (Callanish) 085172 248			2 Twin 1 Double	1 Pub. Bath/Show	B&B per person £12.50-£14.00 Single £12.50-£14.00 Double	Open Jan-Dec Dinner from 1900 B&B + Eve. Meal £18.00-£20.00	

Catherine Morrison 27 Callanish Callanish Lewis, Western Isles PA86 9DY Tel: (Callanish) 085172 392		COMMENDED 👑👑	1 Twin 1 Double	1 Priv. NOT ensuite 2 Pub. Bath/Show	B&B per person £13.00-£15.00 Double	Open Mar-Sep	

Comfortable accommodation on working croft close to the standing stones and
overlooking the sea loch.

CALVINE **Perthshire** Mrs Culliven Craigmhor Calvine, Pitlochry Perthshire PH18 5UA Tel: (Blair Atholl) 0796 483250	Map 4 B1		3 Double	1 Pub. Bath/Show	B&B per person £12.50-£13.50 Double	Open May-Oct Dinner from 1800	

CAMPBELTOWN **Argyll** Westbank Guest House Dell Road Campbeltown Argyll PA28 6JG Tel: (Campbeltown) 0586 553660	Map 1 E7	APPROVED 👑👑	1 Single 1 Twin 5 Double	2 En Suite fac 2 Pub. Bath/Show	B&B per person from £16.00 Single from £16.00 Double	Open Jan-Dec	

Mid Victorian, detached, stone built house in quiet residential area
close to town centre.

CANNICH **Inverness-shire** Mr & Mrs E R Venn Kerrow House Cannich, Strathglass Inverness-shire IV4 7NA Tel: (Cannich) 0456 415243 Fax: 0456 415243	Map 3 H9	COMMENDED Listed	1 Double 1 Family	2 Priv. NOT ensuite	B&B per person £15.00-£30.00 Single £15.00-£20.00 Double	Open Jan-Dec	

Large country house 200 years old with many period features. Set in wooded
grounds on banks of River Glass. Bedrooms with own bathrooms.

CANONBIE, by Langholm **Dumfriesshire** Mr & Mrs Carruthers Watchknowe, Watchhill Road Canonbie Dumfriesshire DG14 0TA Tel: (Canonbie) 03873 71805	Map 2 D9		1 Double 1 Family	2 Priv. NOT ensuite	B&B per person £14.00-£16.00 Single £14.00-£16.00 Double	Open Apr-Sep Dinner 1800-1930 B&B + Eve. Meal to £22.00	

Details of Grading and Classification are on page vi.

Key to symbols is on back flap.

Mr & Mrs N Imrie Harelawhill Canonbie Dumfriesshire DG14 0RX Tel: (Canonbie) 03873 71569	COMMENDED Listed	1 Double 1 Family	2 Pub. Bath/Show	B&B per person from £13.50 Double	Open May-Oct Dinner 1800-1930 B&B + Eve. Meal from £20.00	
		Georgian farmhouse on working farm about 3 miles (5kms) from main A7 Carlisle to Edinburgh road. Magnificent views of Pennines and Lake District.				
Mrs Ruth Williams Caulside Head Canonbie Dumfriesshire DG14 0RT Tel: (Canonbie) 03873 71452	COMMENDED	1 Twin 2 Double	1 En Suite fac 1 Pub. Bath/Show	B&B per person £13.00-£15.00 Single £13.00-£15.00 Double	Open Jan-Dec	
		Traditional croft cottage with feature stone fireplace, situated beside the B6357, 12 miles (19kms) from Gretna Green, amidst Border countryside.				
CAOL, by Fort William **Inverness-shire** Map 3 G1 Mrs S Forbes 5 Glenkingie Street Caol, by Fort William Inverness-shire PH33 7DW Tel: (Fort William) 0397 703343		1 Single 1 Twin 1 Family	1 Pub. Bath/Show	B&B per person from £12.00 Single from £15.00 Double	Open Jan-Dec Dinner from 1800 B&B + Eve. Meal from £18.00	
CARDROSS **Dunbartonshire** Map 1 G5						

KIRKTON HOUSE CARDROSS G82 5EZ
COUNTRY HOUSE GUEST ACCOMMODATION
Glasgow Airport 14 miles, Dumbarton & Helensburgh each 4 miles

OLD WORLD CHARMS WITH MODERN AMENITIES

18/19th century converted farmhouse with superb Clyde views. Tranquil rural setting. Informal guest lounge and dining rooms with original stone walls and fireplaces. Drinks licence. Convivial, home cooked dinners by oil lamplight. Real open fire in the guest lounge.

Kirkton House Darleith Road Cardross Dunbartonshire G82 5EZ Tel: (Cardross) 0389 841951 Fax: 0389 841868	HIGHLY COMMENDED	2 Twin 4 Family	6 En Suite fac	B&B per person £31.00-£36.00 Single £22.00-£27.50 Double	Open Jan-Dec Dinner 1930-2030 B&B + Eve. Meal £37.50-£51.50	
		Built around central courtyard in a quiet, elevated rural position commanding magnificent views of the River Clyde.				
Mrs A C G Russell Lea Farm Cardross Dunbartonshire G82 5EW Tel: (Cardross) 0389 63035	Award Pending	1 Twin 1 Family	1 Pub. Bath/Show	B&B per person £16.00-£18.00 Single £14.00-£16.00 Double	Open Jan-Dec	

| CARGILL, by Perth
Perthshire | Map 2
C2 | | | | | |

Cargil House
Cargil, By Perth PH2 6DT
Telephone: (0250) 883 334

Far from the madding crowd . . . Cargil House is an elegant period mansion, set in mature grounds on the banks of the River Tay — the ideal spot for a peaceful holiday, with good company and personal service. The rooms are beautifully appointed, very comfortably furnished, with twin/double beds. All have wash-hand basins and tea/coffee making equipment. En-suite bath and shower facilities are available. Breakfast and optional Evening Meal are taken in a quiet dining room overlooking the river.

Cargil is perfectly situated for a golfing, fishing, hill-walking, sightseeing or ski-ing holiday — or if you simply want to relax.

| Miss C Dorrell
Cargil House
Cargill,by Perth
Perthshire
PH2 6DT
Tel: (Meikleour) 0250 883334 | | | 1 Single
1 Twin
1 Family | 1 En Suite fac
1 Pub. Bath/Show | B&B per person
£16.00-£16.50 Single
£16.00-£17.50 Double | Open Jan-Nov
Dinner 1930-2100
B&B + Eve. Meal
£25.00-£31.00 |

| CARNOUSTIE
Angus
Mrs A Malcolm
Lochty Bank, 20 High Street
Carnoustie
Angus
DD7 6AQ
Tel: (Carnoustie) 0241 54849 | Map 2
E2 | | 2 Twin
1 Double
2 Family | 2 Pub. Bath/Show | B&B per person
£13.50-£14.00 Single
£13.50-£14.00 Double | Open Apr-Oct |

| Mrs S M Penman
Elm Bank, 3 Camus Street
Carnoustie
Angus
DD7 7PL
Tel: (Carnoustie) 0241 52204 | | | 1 Double
1 Family | 1 Pub. Bath/Show | B&B per person
£12.00-£13.00 Single
£12.00-£13.00 Double | Open Apr-Oct |

| Mrs E Watson
Balhousie Farm
Carnoustie
Angus
DD7 6LG
Tel: (Carnoustie) 0241 53533 | | COMMENDED
Listed | 1 Twin
2 Double | 2 Pub. Bath/Show | B&B per person
from £14.00 Single
from £14.00 Double | Open Jan-Dec |

Traditional Victorian family farmhouse on working farm, with sea views. Ideal for golfing and touring.

| CARRADALE
Argyll
Mrs McCormick
The Mains Farm
Carradale
Argyll
PA28 6QG
Tel: (Carradale) 05833 216 | Map 1
E7 | COMMENDED
Listed | 1 Single
1 Double
1 Family | 1 Pub. Bath/Show | B&B per person
from £13.00 Single
from £13.00 Double | Open Apr-Oct
Dinner from 1800
B&B + Eve. Meal
from £18.00 |

Traditional farmhouse on working farm, on the outskirts of the village and a short walk from the beach. Panoramic views across to the Isle of Arran.

Details of Grading and Classification are on page vi.

Key to symbols is on back flap.

CARRBRIDGE **Inverness-shire** Ard-na-Coille Guest House Station Road Carrbridge Inverness-shire PH23 3AN Tel: (Carrbridge) 047984 239	Map 4 C1 Award Pending	1 Twin 1 Double 1 Family	3 En Suite fac	B&B per person £15.00-£16.00 Double	Open Jan-Dec Dinner 1830-1900 B&B + Eve. Meal £23.00-£24.00
Craigellachie House Main Street Carrbridge Inverness-shire PH23 3AS Tel: (Carrbridge) 047984 641	COMMENDED	1 Single 2 Twin 3 Double 2 Family	2 Pub. Bath/Show	B&B per person £13.00-£14.00 Single £13.00-£14.00 Double	Open Jan-Dec Dinner 1900-2000 B&B + Eve. Meal £22.00-£23.00
		Warm comfortable hospitality assured. Proprietor a keen cook. Ample parking. Centre of village. Ideal base for holiday activities.			
Crannich Guest House & Lodges Carrbridge Inverness-shire PH23 3AA Tel: (Carrbridge) 047984 620		1 Single 1 Twin 2 Double 1 Family	3 Pub. Bath/Show	B&B per person £13.00-£14.00 Single £13.00-£14.00 Double	Open Jan-Dec Dinner 1800-1930 B&B + Eve. Meal £20.00-£21.00
The Mariner Guest House Station Road Carrbridge Inverness-shire PH23 3AN Tel: (Carrbridge) 047984 331	COMMENDED	2 Twin 2 Double 1 Family	5 En Suite fac 1 Pub. Bath/Show	B&B per person £19.00-£25.00 Single £17.00-£19.00 Double	Open Dec-Oct Dinner at 1900 B&B + Eve. Meal £25.00-£27.00
		A modern, purpose built house in residential area 800m from main street. All ensuite facilities. Ideally situated for touring and skiing.			
Mrs P Bailey The Lodge, Easter Duthil Carrbridge Inverness-shire PH23 3ND Tel: (Carrbridge) 047984 503	COMMENDED	2 Twin 1 Double	3 En Suite fac	B&B per person £15.00-£17.00 Single £15.00-£17.00 Double	Open Jan-Dec Dinner 1845-1900 B&B + Eve. Meal £21.00-£23.00
		Modern family run guest house in open countryside. Close to R.S.P.B. reserve and all Spey Valley amenities. Home cooking.			
Mrs A S Malcolm Solas, Carr Road Carrbridge Inverness-shire PH23 3AA Tel: (Carrbridge) 047984 557		2 Single 2 Double	2 Pub. Bath/Show	B&B per person from £12.00 Single from £12.00 Double	Open Jan-Dec
Mrs F Ritchie Pine View, Carr Road Carrbridge Inverness-shire PH23 3AB Tel: (Carrbridge) 047984 217	APPROVED Listed	1 Twin 1 Double 1 Family	1 Pub. Bath/Show	B&B per person from £13.00 Single from £13.00 Double	Open Jan-Dec
		Victorian house in quiet residential area of Carrbridge. Convenient for touring. Aviemore 7 miles (11 kms).			
Mrs L J Taulbut Braes of Duthil Carrbridge Inverness-shire PH23 3NP Tel: (Carrbridge) 047984 395	HIGHLY COMMENDED	2 Double 1 Family	3 En Suite fac	B&B per person £15.00-£16.00 Single £15.00-£16.00 Double	Open Dec-Oct Dinner 1830-1900 B&B + Eve. Meal £21.00-£22.00
		Modern country house set in 5 acres, views to Cairngorms, ideal for hill-walking, bird watching.			

CARRONBRIDGE, Denny **Stirlingshire** Jean & Andrew Morton Lochend Farm, Carronbridge Denny Stirlingshire FK6 5JJ Tel: (Denny) 0324 822778	Map 2 B4	HIGHLY COMMENDED 👑	1 Twin 1 Double	1 Pub. Bath/Show	B&B per person from £15.50 Double	Open Easter-Oct

Stone built house on sheep and cattle farm with fine views over Loch Coulter and surrounding countryside. 6 miles (10kms) from Stirling.

CASTLEBAY **Barra, Western Isles** Mrs MacKechnie Ravenscroft, Nask Castlebay Barra, Western Isles PA80 Tel: (Castlebay) 08714 574	Map 3 A1		1 Twin 1 Double	1 Pub. Bath/Show	B&B per person £13.50 Double	Open Apr-Sep Dinner 1800-1900 B&B + Eve. Meal £21.00

CASTLE DOUGLAS **Kirkcudbrightshire** Rose Cottage Guest House Gelston, by Castle Douglas Kirkcudbrightshire DG7 1SH Tel: (Castle Douglas) 0556 502513	Map 2 A1	COMMENDED 👑 👑	3 Twin 2 Double	3 En Suite fac 1 Priv. NOT ensuite 1 Pub. Bath/Show	B&B per person £15.00-£17.50 Double	Open Jan-Dec Dinner at 1830 B&B + Eve. Meal £23.00-£25.50

Friendly welcome in personally run guest house situated in quiet village. Ideal for walkers and birdwatchers. Some accommodation in annexe.

Mrs Margaret Gordon Craig of Balmaghie Farm Laurieston, Castle Douglas Kirkcudbrightshire DG7 2NA Tel: (Laurieston) 06445 287		COMMENDED 👑 👑	1 Twin 2 Double	1 En Suite fac 1 Pub. Bath/Show	B&B per person £14.00-£18.00 Single £12.00-£16.00 Double	Open Mar-Nov Dinner 1800-2000 B&B + Eve. Meal £19.00-£23.00

Warm and friendly working farm set in rolling countryside 2 miles (3kms) north of Laurieston.

Mrs E Henry Knockallan Farm Crossmichael, Castle Douglas Kirkcudbrightshire Tel: (Crossmichael) 055667 242			1 Double 2 Family	2 Priv. NOT ensuite 1 Pub. Bath/Show	B&B per person from £13.00 Single from £13.00 Double	Open Jan-Dec Dinner 1700-1930 B&B + Eve. Meal from £20.00

Mrs J C Herbertson Airieland House Gelston, Castle Douglas Kirkcudbrightshire DG7 1SS Tel: (Bridge of Dee) 0556 680375		DELUXE 👑 👑 👑	1 Twin 1 Double	1 En Suite fac 1 Priv. NOT ensuite	B&B per person £26.00-£30.00 Double	Open Apr-Sep Dinner 1900-1930 B&B + Eve. Meal £41.00-£45.00

Victorian country home peacefully set in 3 acres of woodland garden. Wide views over open country. Non - smokers only please.

Mrs McBride Airds Farm Crossmichael, by Castle Douglas Kirkcudbrightshire DG7 3BG Tel: (Crossmichael) 055667 418		COMMENDED 👑 👑	1 Twin 2 Double 1 Family	2 Pub. Bath/Show	B&B per person from £19.00 Single from £14.00 Double	Open Mar-Nov Dinner from 1830 B&B + Eve. Meal from £21.00

On mixed livestock farm in quiet rural location, with excellent views to Loch Ken. 4 miles (6kms) from Castle Douglas.

Mrs A Muir Milton Park Farm Castle Douglas Kirkcudbrightshire DG7 3JJ Tel: (Haugh-of-Urr) 055666 212		COMMENDED 👑	1 Twin 2 Double	2 Pub. Bath/Show	B&B per person from £15.00 Single from £15.00 Double	Open Apr-Oct

Well appointed farmhouse overlooking a large lawn and down the Urr valley. Free trout and salmon fishing on River Urr.

Details of Grading and Classification are on page vi.

Mrs Anne Rae Dungarry, 41 Abercromby Road Castle Douglas Kirkcudbrightshire Tel: (Castle Douglas) 0556 502642			1 Single 1 Twin	1 Pub. Bath/Show	B&B per person £13.00–£14.00 Single £13.00–£14.00 Double	Open Apr-Oct	
Mrs C Smith Ingleston Farm Castle Douglas Kirkcudbrightshire DG7 1SW Tel: (Castle Douglas) 0556 502936		COMMENDED ♛ ♛	1 Twin 1 Double	2 En Suite fac	B&B per person £17.00 Double	Open Apr-Oct Dinner from 1830 B&B + Eve. Meal £24.00	
			Charming old farmhouse, rich in history; spacious bedrooms with own bathrooms. Outstanding rural views; lovely walking country.				
CAWDOR Nairn Mrs Jennifer MacLeod Dallaschyle Cawdor Nairn IV12 5XS Tel: (Croy) 0667 493422	Map 4 B8	COMMENDED Listed	1 Double 1 Family	1 Pub. Bath/Show	B&B per person from £18.00 Single from £14.00 Double	Open Apr-Oct Dinner 1800-2000 B&B + Eve. Meal from £24.00	
			Spacious modern house in peaceful woodland setting with large garden. Close to Cawdor Castle and Culloden Moor.				
CLACHAN, by Tarbert Argyll Mrs Moller The Old Smithy Clachan, by Tarbert Argyll PA29 6XL Tel: (Clachan) 08804 635	Map 1 E6		2 Family	1 Pub. Bath/Show	B&B per person £12.50–£13.00 Single £12.00–£12.50 Double	Open Apr-Dec Dinner 1800-1930 B&B + Eve. Meal £18.00–£18.50	
CLADDACH KIRKIBOST North Uist, Western Isles Mr W J & Mrs Anne Quarm Sealladh Traigh Claddach Kirkibost North Uist, Western Isles PA82 5EP Tel: (Locheport) 08764 248	Map 3 A8		2 Single 1 Twin 1 Double	2 Pub. Bath/Show	B&B per person from £15.00 Double	Open Jan-Dec Dinner 1800-2100 B&B + Eve. Meal from £24.00	
CLYDEBANK, Glasgow Dunbartonshire Mrs J McCay 13 Southview Dalmuir, Clydebank Dunbartonshire G81 3LA Tel: 041 952 7007	Map 1 H5	COMMENDED Listed	1 Single 1 Twin 1 Double	2 Pub. Bath/Show	B&B per person to £12.50 Single to £12.50 Double	Open Apr-Sep	
			Family home in residential area 9 miles (14kms) from city centre. Close to railway station and bus routes. Convenient for Loch Lomond.				
COATBRIDGE Lanarkshire Mrs Barr Auchenlea, 153 Langmuir Road Bargeddie, by Coatbridge Lanarkshire Tel: 041 771 6870	Map 2 A5		1 Twin 1 Family	1 Priv. NOT ensuite	B&B per person from £15.00 Double	Open Jan-Dec	

COCKBURNSPATH **Berwickshire** Edna D Johnston Pathhead House Cockburnspath Berwickshire TD13 5XB Tel: (Cockburnspath) 03683 208	Map 2 F5	COMMENDED	2 Twin 2 Double	3 Pub. Bath/Show	B&B per person from £16.00 Single from £16.00 Double	Open Apr-Sep	
			Former Victorian farmhouse with many original features set back from the A1, ideal for tourers.				
COLDSTREAM **Berwickshire** Mrs C M Stepanenko Tigh na Bradan, The Lees Stables, Kelso Road Coldstream Berwickshire Tel: (Coldstream) 0890 882445	Map 2 F6	Award Pending	1 Twin 1 Double	1 Pub. Bath/Show	B&B per person £18.00-£20.00 Single £15.00-£18.00 Double	Open Jan-Nov	
BY COLDSTREAM **Berwickshire** Mrs Eleanor Jarvis Tweedview Birgham, by Coldstream Berwickshire TD12 4NF Tel: (Coldstream) 089083 312/0890 88312	Map 2 F6	APPROVED Listed	1 Twin 1 Double	1 Pub. Bath/Show	B&B per person from £12.00 Single from £12.00 Double	Open Jan-Dec	
			In small village between Kelso and Coldstream an interesting terraced cottage – now a family home – ideal for animal lovers.				
COLL, Isle of **Argyll** Mrs Pat Graham Garden House, Castle Gardens Isle of Coll Argyll PA78 6TB Tel: (Coll) 08793 374	Map 1 B1		2 Double	1 Pub. Bath/Show	B&B per person £11.00-£16.00 Single £11.00-£16.00 Double	Open Jan-Dec Dinner from 1900 B&B + Eve. Meal £18.00-£25.00	
Mrs Sturgeon Arinagour Coll, Isle of Argyll PA78 6SY Tel: (Coll) 08793 354			1 Single 2 Twin 3 Double 2 Family	2 En Suite fac 3 Pub. Bath/Show	B&B per person £16.50 Single £16.50 Double	Open Feb-Nov B&B + Eve. Meal £26.50	
Mrs I G Underwood Achamore Isle of Coll Argyll PA78 6TE Tel: (Coll) 08793 430		HIGHLY COMMENDED	1 Twin 1 Family	2 Priv. NOT ensuite 1 Pub. Bath/Show	B&B per person from £16.50 Double	Open Jan-Dec Dinner 1830-2000 B&B + Eve. Meal from £30.00	
			Comfortably refurbished to a high standard, an old stone farmhouse, well placed for exploring this quiet and beautiful isle.				

COLMONELL, by Girvan **Ayrshire** Mrs Shankland Burnfoot Farm Colmonell Ayrshire KA26 0SQ Tel: (Colmonell) 046588 220/265	**Map 1** G9	COMMENDED	1 Double 1 Family	1 Pub. Bath/Show	B&B per person £14.00-£15.00 Double	Open Apr-Oct B&B + Eve. Meal £22.00-£23.00

Farmhouse on 150 acre mixed farm. Ideally situated for touring Ayrshire coast and Burns Country. Excellent home cooking and baking.

COLONSAY, Isle of **Argyll** Mr & Mrs Lawson Seaview Colonsay, Isle of Argyll PA61 7YN Tel: (Colonsay) 09512 315	**Map 1** C4		2 Twin 1 Family	1 Pub. Bath/Show	B&B per person £20.00 Single £20.00 Double	Open Apr-Oct Dinner at 1900 B&B + Eve. Meal £33.00

COMRIE **Perthshire** Mr & Mrs Paterson St Margaret's, Braco Road Comrie Perthshire PH6 2HP Tel: (Comrie) 0764 670413	**Map 2** A2		2 Twin 1 Double	1 En Suite fac 1 Pub. Bath/Show	B&B per person £13.00-£17.00 Single £13.00-£17.00 Double	Open Apr-Oct
Mrs Thomson Schiehallion, Dalginross Comrie Perthshire PH6 2ED Tel: (Comrie) 0764 670127			1 Twin	1 Pub. Bath/Show	B&B per person £13.00-£15.00 Double	Open Jan-Dec Dinner 1800-1900 B&B + Eve. Meal £19.00-£21.00
Mrs Carol Thorburn Fintallich, Glenlednock Comrie, Crieff Perthshire PH6 2LY Tel: (Comrie) 0764 670536			1 Twin 1 Family	1 Pub. Bath/Show	B&B per person £12.00 Single £12.00 Double	Open Mar-Oct

BY COMRIE **Perthshire** Mrs Cuthbert Knowehead Cottage Comrie Perthshire PH6 2LS Tel: (Comrie) 0764 670751	**Map 2** A2		2 Twin 2 Double	4 Limited ensuite 2 Pub. Bath/Show	B&B per person £14.00 Single from £14.00 Double	Open Jan-Dec

CONNEL **Argyll** Mr R Craig Ach-na-Craig, Grosvenor Crescent Connel Argyll Tel: (Connel) 063171 588	**Map 1** E2	COMMENDED	2 Twin 1 Double	3 En Suite fac 1 Pub. Bath/Show	B&B per person from £16.50 Double	Open Jan-Dec Dinner 1830-2000 B&B + Eve. Meal from £23.00

Newly-built family house in quiet village, 5 miles (8kms) from Oban. Secure off-street parking. All rooms on ground floor and en-suite.

CONON BRIDGE **Ross-shire** Mrs C Morrison Dun Eistein, Alcaig Conon Bridge, by Dingwall Ross-shire IV7 8HS Tel: (Dingwall) 0349 62210	**Map 4** A8	COMMENDED	1 Double 1 Family	1 En Suite fac 1 Priv. NOT ensuite	B&B per person £13.50-£15.00 Double	Open Apr-Oct

Highland cottage on country road with views of Ben Wyvis from garden. 11miles (18kms) north of Inverness. Non-smoking.

CORPACH, by Fort William **Inverness-shire** Mrs Joan Cameron, Centre Manager Outward Bound, Loch Eil Corpach,by Fort William Inverness-shire PH33 7NN Tel: (Fort William) 0397 772866	Map 3 G1		4 Twin 12 Pub. Bath/Show 19 Family	B&B per person £9.00-£13.00 Double	Open Jan-Dec, exc Xmas Dinner 1730-1830 B&B + Eve. Meal £18.00-£24.00	
R Cumming Travee Corpach,by Fort William Inverness-shire PH33 7LR Tel: (Corpach) 0397 772380		**COMMENDED** ♛	1 Twin 2 Pub. Bath/Show 2 Double **Friendly welcoming, family home, 4 miles (6kms) from Fort William,** **with super views over Loch Linnhe and Ben Nevis.**	B&B per person to £18.00 Single to £14.00 Double	Open Jan-Dec	
Mrs McCallum The Neuk Corpach,by Fort William Inverness-shire PH33 7LR Tel: (Corpach) 0397 772244			3 Twin 2 Pub. Bath/Show	B&B per person £16.50-£19.00 Single £11.50-£14.00 Double	Open Jan-Dec Dinner 1730-1900 B&B + Eve. Meal £18.50-£26.00	
Mrs MacPhee Tangasdale Corpach,by Fort William Inverness-shire PH33 7LT Tel: (Corpach) 0397 772591			2 Family 1 Pub. Bath/Show	B&B per person from £13.50 Double	Open Jan-Dec	
Mrs Wynne Heston Corpach,by Fort William Inverness-shire PH33 7LT Tel: (Fort William) 0397 772425			1 Twin 1 Pub. Bath/Show 1 Double	B&B per person £13.00 Single £12.00-£13.00 Double	Open Mar-Oct	
CORRIECRAVIE **Isle of Arran** Mrs Adamson Rosebank, Corriecravie Kilmory Isle of Arran KA27 8PD Tel: (Sliddery) 077087 228/0770 870228	Map 1 E7	**COMMENDED** ♛ ♛	1 Single 1 En Suite fac 1 Twin 1 Pub. Bath/Show 1 Family **Traditional farmhouse with warm welcome, home baking and open fires.** **Views over sea to Mull of Kintyre and Ireland.**	B&B per person £15.00-£18.00 Single £15.00-£18.00 Double	Open Jan-Nov	
CORTACHY, by Kirriemuir **Angus** Mrs J F Grant Cullew Farm, Cortachy Kirriemuir Angus DD8 4QP Tel: (Cortachy) 05754 242	Map 2 D1		1 Twin 1 Pub. Bath/Show 1 Family	B&B per person £12.00-£12.50 Single £12.00-£12.50 Double	Open Apr-Sep	
COWDENBEATH **Fife** Mrs Ellen Bruce The Old Manse, 80 Broad Street Cowdenbeath Fife KY4 8JD Tel: (Cowdenbeath) 0383 511908	Map 2 C4		1 Single 2 Pub. Bath/Show 1 Twin 1 Family	B&B per person £13.00-£14.50 Single £13.00-£14.50 Double	Open Jan-Dec	

Details of Grading and Classification are on page vi.

Key to symbols is on back flap.

COYLTON, by Ayr **Ayrshire** Mrs P Hepher Strathcoyle, Hillhead Coylton, Ayr KA6 6JR Tel: (Joppa) 0292 570366	Map 1 H7		1 Twin 1 Family	2 Pub. Bath/Show	B&B per person £16.00 Single £14.00-£15.00 Double	Open Mar-Oct
CRAIGHOUSE **Isle of Jura, Argyll** Mrs Knight Fish Farm House Craighouse Jura Tel: (Jura) 049682 304	Map 1 D5		1 Twin 1 Double	2 Pub. Bath/Show	B&B per person from £15.00 Single from £15.00 Double	Open Jan-Dec Dinner 1800-2000 B&B + Eve. Meal from £23.00
CRAIGNURE **Isle of Mull, Argyll** Redburn Redburn, Lochdon Craignure Isle of Mull, Argyll PA64 6AP Tel: (Craignure) 06802 370	Map 1 D2	COMMENDED 👑 👑	1 Twin 2 Double	3 En Suite fac	B&B per person £16.50-£18.00	Open Jan-Dec Dinner at 1800 B&B + Eve. Meal £26.00-£28.00

Converted croft house in quiet location on lochside. 3 miles (4.8 Km) Craignure Ferry. Area for natural history enthusiasts. Home cooking.

CRAIL **Fife** Hazelton Guest House 29 Marketgate Crail Fife KY10 3TH Tel: (Crail) 0333 50250	Map 2 E3	COMMENDED Listed	1 Single 2 Twin 2 Double 2 Family	2 Pub. Bath/Show	B&B per person £15.00-£17.00 Single £15.00-£17.00 Double	Open Jan-Dec Dinner 1900-1930 B&B + Eve. Meal £28.00-£30.00

In the heart of small fishing town, a friendly guest house personally run by the owners. Fresh local produce used whenever possible.

Selcraig Guest House 47 Nethergate Crail Fife KY10 3TX Tel: (Crail) 0333 50697		COMMENDED 👑	2 Twin 1 Double 2 Family	2 Pub. Bath/Show	B&B per person £15.00-£17.00 Double	Open Jan-Dec Dinner 1800-1900 B&B + Eve. Meal £27.00-£29.00

200 year old listed house in quiet street close to sea shore. Convenient for touring the East Neuk of Fife.

CRAWFORD **Lanarkshire** Field End Guest House The Loaning Crawford Lanarkshire ML12 6TN Tel: (Crawford) 08642 276	Map 2 B7	APPROVED 👑 👑	1 Single 1 Twin 1 Double 1 Family	2 En Suite fac 1 Limited ensuite 2 Pub. Bath/Show	B&B per person £14.00-£18.00 Single £18.00-£20.00 Double	Dinner 1830-1930 B&B + Eve. Meal £20.00-£24.00

Stone villa overlooking fields, located up the hill opposite the church. Ideal half-way house and touring centre. No smoking or pets.

CREETOWN, **by Newton Stewart** **Wigtownshire** Marclaysean Guest House 51 St John's Street Creetown Wigtownshire DG8 7JB Tel: (Creetown) 067182 319	Map 1 H1	COMMENDED Listed	1 Twin 1 Double	1 En Suite fac	B&B per person £14.00-£16.00	Open Apr-Oct Dinner from 1900 B&B + Eve. Meal £21.50-£23.50

Guest house with an en suite bedroom, conveniently situated in centre of village near to Gem Rock museum.

Mrs Oxley Barholm Mains Farm Creetown Wigtownshire DG8 7EN Tel: (Creetown) 067182 346			1 Twin 1 Double	1 Pub. Bath/Show	B&B per person £15.00 Single £13.00-£13.50 Double	Open Apr-Oct	
CRIANLARICH **Perthshire** Craigbank Guest House Crianlarich Perthshire FK20 8QS Tel: (Crianlarich) 08383 279	**Map 1** G2		2 Twin 1 Double 2 Family	1 En Suite fac 1 Pub. Bath/Show	B&B per person from £15.00 Double	Open Jan-Dec Dinner from 1900	
Glenardran Guest House Crianlarich Perthshire FK20 8QS Tel: (Crianlarich) 08383 236		**COMMENDED** **Listed**	1 Single 2 Twin 3 Double	1 En Suite fac 1 Pub. Bath/Show	B&B per person from £19.00 Single from £17.00 Double	Open Jan-Dec Dinner 1915-2000	
			Friendly welcome at recently refurbished house on A84, collection from station available. Excellent base for touring, walking or climbing.				
Mr J C W Christie Inverardran Crianlarich Perthshire Tel: (Crianlarich) 08383 240		**Award** **Pending**	1 Twin 1 Double	1 Pub. Bath/Show	B&B per person £10.00-£15.00 Single £10.00-£15.00 Double	Open Mar-Dec	
CRIEFF **Perthshire** MacKenzie Lodge Broich Terrace Crieff Perthshire PH7 3BD Tel: (Crieff) 0764 653721	**Map 2** B2	**COMMENDED**	2 Twin 2 Double 1 Family	2 En Suite fac 2 Pub. Bath/Show	B&B per person £18.00-£24.00 Single £14.00-£20.00 Double	Open Jan-Dec	
			Elegant Victorian home retaining many original features. **Winner of "Warmest Welcome in Perthshire 1991". Private parking.**				
Mrs Mary Kelly 49 Carrington Terrace Crieff Perthshire PH7 4DZ Tel: (Crieff) 0764 653531			1 Double 1 Family	1 Pub. Bath/Show	B&B per person to £12.50 Single to £12.50 Double	Open Easter-Oct Dinner 1800-1930 B&B + Eve. Meal to £18.50	
Mrs MacLellan Bell House, 1 Broich Terrace Crieff Perthshire PH7 3BD Tel: (Crieff) 0764 654689			1 Twin 2 Double	2 Pub. Bath/Show	B&B per person £13.00 Double	Open Jan-Dec	

CRIEFF continued — Map 2 B2

Mrs Macnaughton
Dalknock, 2 Coldwells Road
Crieff
Perthshire
PH7 4BB
Tel: (Crieff) 0764 655717

2 Double / 1 Family — 1 Pub. Bath/Show — B&B per person £15.00 Single £15.00 Double — Open Jan-Dec

---

W & Mrs N Newbigging
Mill House, South Bridgend
Crieff
Perthshire
PH7 4DH
Tel: (Crieff) 0764 654700

COMMENDED — Listed

1 Single / 1 Twin / 1 Double — 2 Pub. Bath/Show — B&B per person £14.00-£16.00 Single £14.00-£16.00 Double — Open Apr-Oct

Comfortable, friendly home, set back from the road and with the river to the rear. Ideal touring centre.

Mrs Heather Robbins
Craigentor House, Gilmerton
Crieff
Perthshire
Tel: (Crieff) 0764 652858
Fax: 0764 2946

1 Twin / 1 Double — 1 En Suite fac / 1 Priv. NOT ensuite — B&B per person £17.50-£18.50 Double — Open Jan-Dec

---

Mrs Scott
Concraig Farm, Muthill Road
Crieff
Perthshire
PH7 4HH
Tel: (Crieff) 0764 653237

APPROVED — Listed

1 Twin / 1 Double / 1 Family — 1 Pub. Bath/Show — B&B per person £13.50-£14.50 Double — Open Apr-Oct

Comfortable farmhouse with spacious rooms. Peacefully situated just outside Crieff.

Mrs Katie Sloan
Somerton House,
Crieff Holiday Village
Turret Bank, Crieff
Perthshire
PH7 4JN
Tel: (Crieff) 0764 653513

COMMENDED

1 Twin / 1 Family — 2 En Suite fac — B&B per person from £12.50 Double — Open Jan-Dec Dinner 1800-1900

Friendly bed and breakfast within 15 minutes walk of town. Ideal touring base.

BY CRIEFF — Perthshire — Map 2 B2

Mrs Nan Waugh
Fendoch Cottage
Sma' Glen
Perthshire
PH7 3LW
Tel: (Crieff) 0764 653446

1 Twin / 1 Double / 1 Family — 3 En Suite fac — B&B per person £16.00-£18.00 Double — Open Jan-Dec

---

CRIMOND, by Fraserburgh — Aberdeenshire — Map 4 H8

Mrs Gladys Clarke
Strathlea, Spreaderhill
Crimond, by Fraserburgh
Aberdeenshire
AB43 4XR
Tel: (Fraserburgh)
0346 32379/(public)
32458 (private)

APPROVED

3 Single / 1 Twin / 1 Family — 3 En Suite fac / 1 Pub. Bath/Show — B&B per person £13.00-£15.00 Single £13.00-£15.00 Double — Open Jan-Dec Dinner 1800-2000 B&B + Eve. Meal £18.00-£20.00

Modern bungalow just outside village famous for the tune of 24th Psalm. Bird sanctuary closeby. 8 miles (13 kms) from Peterhead and Fraserburgh.

CROWLISTA **Lewis, Western Isles** Helen Skippen 3 Crowlista Uig Lewis, Western Isles Tel: (Timsgarry) 0851 75280	Map 3 B5		1 Twin	1 Pub. Bath/Show	B&B per person £14.00-£16.00 Double	Open Jan-Dec Dinner 1800-2400 B&B + Eve. Meal £21.00-£23.00	
CULLEN **Banffshire** Mrs Angela Kirby Mayfield, Seafield Place Cullen, Buckie Banffshire AB56 2TE Tel: (Cullen) 0542 40819	Map 4 E7	COMMENDED 👑 👑	1 Twin 2 Double	1 En Suite fac 2 Pub. Bath/Show	B&B per person from £14.00 Single from £12.00 Double	Open Jan-Dec Dinner from 1800 B&B + Eve. Meal from £18.00	
			Detached Victorian house in residential area, close to town centre, beach and bowling green. Off street parking.				
Mrs Margaret Kirk Homelea, 7 South Castle Street Cullen, Buckie Banffshire AB56 2RT Tel: (Cullen) 0542 41052			2 Single 1 Twin 1 Double	2 Pub. Bath/Show	B&B per person from £13.00 Single from £13.00 Double	Open Apr-Oct Dinner 1800-1900	
Mrs A Mair Torrach, 147 Seatown Cullen, Buckie Banffshire AB56 2SL Tel: (Cullen) 0542 40724		Award Pending	1 Double 1 Family	1 Pub. Bath/Show	B&B per person from £12.00 Double	Open Apr-Oct	

NORWOOD HOUSE - CULLEN

NORWOOD GUEST HOUSE
11 SEAFIELD PLACE, CULLEN
Telephone: 0542 840314

NORWOOD HOUSE is a late Georgian listed family home quietly situated off the main A98 coast road in the picturesque Banffshire coastal resort of Cullen, and is within easy reach of shops, the sea, and Cullen's unique cliff and links golf course.

Tom and Marian Sleightholm warmly welcome discerning guests to their family home. All bedrooms have hot and cold water, coffee/tea-making facilities, electric blankets and duvets (or conventional bedding if required). Bath and shower facilities with constant hot water on tap. A separate lounge and colour TV room for convenience of guests.

Mrs Marian Sleightholm Norwood House, 11 Seafield Place Cullen, Buckie Banffshire AB56 2TE Tel: (Cullen) 0542 840314		APPROVED 👑	1 Single 2 Twin 2 Double 1 Family	2 Pub. Bath/Show	B&B per person £12.50 Single	Open Apr-Oct Dinner from 1830 B&B + Eve. Meal £20.00	
			Personally run with friendly atmosphere, in quiet residential area, yet with easy access to centre of town and all amenities. Private parking.				

CULLEN continued Mrs Hazel Taylor Stroma, 4 Seafield Place Cullen, Buckie Banffshire AB56 2TF Tel: (Cullen) 0542 40295	Map 4 B5 Award Pending	1 Twin 2 Double	2 Pub. Bath/Show	B&B per person from £13.00 Double	Open Jun-Sep Dinner 1830-1930 B&B + Eve. Meal from £20.00	

CULLODEN MOOR **Inverness-shire** Mrs E M C Alexander Culdoich Farm Culloden Moor, by Inverness Inverness-shire IV1 2EP Tel: (Inverness) 0463 790268	Map 4 B9 COMMENDED	1 Double 1 Family	1 Pub. Bath/Show	B&B per person £14.00-£15.00 Double	Open May-Oct Dinner from 1900 B&B + Eve. Meal £22.00-£23.00	

18C farmhouse on mixed arable and livestock farm, on hillside near Culloden Battlefield and Clava Stones. Home baking and cooking.

Mrs M Campbell Bayview, Westhill Culloden Moor Inverness-shire IV1 2BP Tel: (Inverness) 0463 790386 Fax: 0463 790386	COMMENDED	1 Twin 2 Double	1 Priv. NOT ensuite 1 Pub. Bath/Show	B&B per person £15.00 Single £15.00 Double	Open Apr-Oct Dinner at 1830 B&B + Eve. Meal £22.00-£25.00

Quiet, comfortable house in pleasant country surroundings with magnificent views over the Moray Firth. Evening meals by arrangement; home cooking.

Mrs R MacKay Leanach Farm Culloden Moor, by Inverness Inverness-shire IV1 2EJ Tel: (Inverness) 0463 791027	COMMENDED Listed	2 Twin 1 Double	1 Pub. Bath/Show	B&B per person £20.00-£21.00 Single £15.00-£16.50 Double	Open Jan-Dec

Large family farmhouse on 400 acre sheep and cattle farm, 5 miles (9kms) from Inverness, near Culloden Battlefield.

Mrs M MacLean Woodside of Culloden Westhill, Inverness Inverness-shire IV1 2BP Tel: (Inverness) 0463 790242		1 Twin 2 Double	2 En Suite fac 1 Pub. Bath/Show	B&B per person from £15.00 Double	Open May-Oct

CULROSS **Fife** Mr & Mrs J W Braes Woodhead Farm Culross Fife KY12 8ET Tel: (Newmills) 0383 880270 Fax: 0383 880465	Map 2 B4 COMMENDED Listed	3 Twin	1 Pub. Bath/Show	B&B per person £18.00-£20.00 Single £16.00-£18.00 Double	Open Jan-Dec Dinner 1800-2000 B&B + Eve. Meal £26.00-£30.00	

19C farmhouse of individual character, close to Royal Burgh of Culross. 30 minutes drive to Edinburgh and Glasgow. Family games room, home cooking.

CUMBERNAULD **Dunbartonshire** Mrs M Abercrombie 68 Lammermoor Drive, Greenfaulds Cumbernauld Dunbartonshire G67 4BE Tel: (Cumbernauld) 0236 721307	Map 2 A5 COMMENDED Listed	3 Twin	1 Pub. Bath/Show	B&B per person £16.00 Single £16.00 Double	Open Jan-Dec	

Modern family home, centrally situated situated with easy access to main roads to Glasgow, Stirling and Edinburgh.

CUNNINGHAMHEAD, by Kilmarnock Ayrshire Mrs McKay The Stables Fairlie Crevoch Farm Cunninghamhead by Kilmaurs, Kilmarnock Ayrshire KA2 3PD Tel: (Torranyard) 0294 85333	Map 1 H6		1 Family	1 Priv. NOT ensuite	B&B per person £13.00-£15.00 Single £13.00-£15.00 Double	Open Jan-Dec Dinner 1700-2200 B&B + Eve. Meal £19.00-£21.00
CUPAR Fife Mrs Roma Adam Mill Cottage, Cults Mill Cupar Fife KY15 5RD Tel: (Cupar) 0334 54980	Map 2 D3	COMMENDED ♨ ♨	1 Twin 1 Double	1 En Suite fac 1 Pub. Bath/Show	B&B per person £17.50-£20.00 Double	Open Jan-Dec

Tastefully converted cottage, in tranquil setting overlooking River Eden.
Ideal base for touring and bird watching.

Mrs Yvonne Brady The Grove Dura Den, Cupar Fife KY15 5TJ Tel: (Cupar) 0334 53862			1 Twin 1 Double	2 Pub. Bath/Show	B&B per person £15.00 Double	Open Jan-Dec

'EASTERHILLS'
CASTLEBANK ROAD, CUPAR, FIFE KY15 4BN
Contact: Mrs Lynda Gibson — Telephone: 0334 54275
A Victorian home of charm and character, set in extensive grounds, offering good food and comfortable accommodation with friendly service. Ideal base for touring, golfing, etc. Ladybank, St Andrews, Carnoustie, Gleneagles, all within easy reach.

Lynda M Gibson Easterhills, Castlebank Road Cupar Fife KY15 4BN Tel: (Cupar) 0334 54275		COMMENDED ♨ ♨	1 Twin 1 Double 1 Family	2 Pub. Bath/Show	B&B per person £17.50-£20.00 Double	Open Jan-Dec

Victorian house of charm and character, set in large gardens. Comfortable ,
good food and hospitality. Ideal base for golfing, touring etc.

| BY CUPAR | Map 2 |
| Fife | D3 |

YES — there's golf in Fife, and there's so much more!

Todhall House

Dairsie by Cupar
Fife KY15 4RQ
Tel: 0334 56344

Whether pursuing sporting activities, relaxing, or exploring this lovely corner of the Kingdom of Fife — Todhall House makes an ideal base being close to St. Andrews and Dundee.

En-suite rooms with usual facilities — Guest Lounge, Car Parking, Non-Smoking.

★ *Warmth* ★ *Good Food* ★
★ *Comfort* ★ *Fresh Country Air* ★

Mrs Gillian Donald Todhall House by Cupar Fife KY15 4RQ Tel: (Cupar) 0334 56344	1 Twin 2 Double	2 En Suite fac	B&B per person £17.50-£25.00 Double	Open Easter-Oct Dinner 1900-1930 B&B + Eve. Meal £27.50-£35.00

| DALBEATTIE | Map 2 |
| Kirkcudbrightshire | B1 |

BRIARDALE HOUSE
17 HAUGH ROAD, DALBEATTIE
KIRKCUDBRIGHTSHIRE DG5 4AR
Tel: 0556 611468   Mobile: 0850 267251

John and Verna Woodworth invite you to relax in their elegant Deluxe — 3 Crown Victorian house, furnished with antiques yet providing modern facilities and comfort at a very reasonable price. John is a professional chef producing excellent food with choice on the menu, which changes daily. Bedrooms are large with en-suite bath *and* shower.

An ideal base to explore our beautiful and peaceful Galloway. Car parking; large walled garden. Complimentary bikes available.

Mini breaks — January to March.

Briardale House Haugh Road Dalbeattie Kirkcudbrightshire DG5 4AR Tel: (Dalbeattie) 0556 611468/ 0850 267251 (mobile)	DELUXE	1 Twin 2 Double	3 En Suite fac	B&B per person £19.00 Double	Open Jan-Oct Dinner 1800-1900 B&B + Eve. Meal £30.00
		Detached Victorian villa retaining many original features in residential area on the outskirts of town. Excellent food; no licence, no corkage.			

Mrs M Maddison Broomlands House Haugh Road Dalbeattie Kirkcudbrightshire DG5 4AR Tel: (Dalbeattie) 0556 611463 Fax: 0556 611462	DELUXE	1 Twin 2 Double	3 En Suite fac	B&B per person from £22.00 Double	Open Jan-Dec Dinner 1900-2100 B&B + Eve. Meal from £32.00
		A magnificent granite house, sympathetically refurbished, set in over 3 acres of landscaped grounds – very spacious!			

DALCROSS, by Inverness **Inverness-shire** Mrs Pottie Easter Dalziel Farm Dalcross Inverness-shire IV1 2JL Tel: (Ardersier) 0667 462213	**Map 4** B8	HIGHLY COMMENDED	1 Twin 2 Double	2 Pub. Bath/Show	B&B per person from £15.00 Double	Open Mar-Nov Dinner from 1900 B&B + Eve. Meal from £24.00	

Victorian farmhouse, on stock/arable farm. Friendly atmosphere. Log fire in lounge and home baking. Inverness 7 mls (11kms). Culloden 5 mls (8km).

Mrs E B Simpson Woodend House Dalcross Inverness-shire IV1 2JJ Tel: (Croy) 0667 493234		HIGHLY COMMENDED Listed	2 Twin 1 Double	2 Pub. Bath/Show	B&B per person £13.00-£14.50 Double	Open Apr-Oct Dinner from 1900	

Former Victorian farmhouse in secluded setting, 7 miles (11kms) east of Inverness. Elegantly furnished with accent on comfort. Close to airport.

DALGETY BAY **Fife** Mrs Helen S Eadie 3 Hopeward Mews Dalgety Bay Fife KY11 5TB Tel: (Dalgety Bay) 0383 824136 Fax: 0383 824433	**Map 2** C4		1 Twin 1 Family	2 Pub. Bath/Show	B&B per person £14.00-£16.00 Single £13.00-£15.00 Double	Open Mar-Oct Dinner 1800-2300 B&B + Eve. Meal £20.00-£22.00	

Mrs Punler Seal Bay House, 42 The Wynd Dalgety Bay Fife KY11 5SJ Tel: (Dalgety Bay) 0383 822790		COMMENDED Listed	2 Twin 1 Double	2 Pub. Bath/Show	B&B per person from £18.00 Single from £18.00 Double	Open Jan-Dec Dinner from 1800 B&B + Eve. Meal from £24.00	

A large, modern house situated on the sea-front at Dalgety Bay and enjoying its own heated indoor swimming pool, solarium, jacuzzi and sauna.

DALKEITH **Midlothian** Mrs M Blair 'Woodcot' 22 Bonnyrigg Road Eskbank, Dalkeith Midlothian EH22 3EZ Tel: 031 663 2628	**Map 2** D5		2 Family	1 Pub. Bath/Show	B&B per person £15.00 Single £15.00 Double	Open Jan-Dec	

Mr W Conboy Newbattle Abbey College Dalkeith Midlothian EH22 3LL Tel: 031 663 1921			10 Twin	3 Pub. Bath/Show	B&B per person £18.40 Single £18.40 Double	Open Jan-Dec Dinner 1800-1830 B&B + Eve. Meal £25.50	

Mrs Margaret Jarvis Belmont, 47 Eskbank Road Dalkeith Midlothian Tel: 031 663 8676		COMMENDED Listed	1 Twin 2 Double	1 En Suite fac 1 Pub. Bath/Show	B&B per person £15.00-£17.00 Single £15.00-£17.00 Double	Open Jan-Dec	

Large Victorian house, with original features. Set in extensive landscaped gardens. Off street parking.

BY DALKEITH **Midlothian** Mrs Dorothy Stevenson 1 Hadfast Road Cousland, by Dalkeith Midlothian EH22 2NU Tel: 031 663 1294	**Map 2** D5	COMMENDED Listed	2 Twin 1 Family	1 Pub. Bath/Show	B&B per person £15.00-£17.00 Single £14.00 Double	Open Mar-Oct	

Modern house with paddock and horses in quiet village, 2 miles (3kms) from Dalkeith, approx 9 miles (14kms) from Edinburgh with views of Pentlands.

DALMALLY **Argyll** Craig Villa Guest House Dalmally Argyll PA33 1AX Tel: (Dalmally) 08382 255/06313 63255	**Map 1** F2	COMMENDED ᕯ ᕯ ᕯ	2 Twin 2 Double 2 Family	5 En Suite fac 1 Priv. NOT ensuite	B&B per person £18.00-£22.00 Double	Open Apr-Oct Dinner from 1900 B&B + Eve. Meal £29.00-£34.00

Personally run guest house in own grounds amidst breathtaking scenery. Good touring base. Home cooking.

PORTINNISHERRICH FARM
SOUTH EAST LOCHAWE SIDE, by DALMALLY
ARGYLL PA33 1BW   Telephone: 08664 202
Peaceful picturesque working farm situated on Lochawe side. En-suite bedrooms, loch views, tea/coffee facilities. Guest lounge and dining room where dinner is available using local produce. Ideally positioned for relaxing, forest walks, ornithology. Own jetty provides boating, fishing and sailing close to historic island castle. **NON-SMOKING ESTABLISHMENT**

R N & P B McKenzie Portinnisherrich Dalmally Argyll PA33 1BW Tel: (Loch Avich) 08664 202	2 Family	2 En Suite fac	B&B per person £17.00-£20.00 Double	Open Apr-Sep Dinner 1900-1930 B&B + Eve. Meal £27.50-£30.50

DALMELLINGTON **Ayrshire** Mrs Taveren Benbain, Cumnock Road Dalmellington Ayrshire KA6 7PS Tel: (Dalmellington) 0292 550556	**Map 1** H8	COMMENDED Listed	1 Single 1 Twin 1 Double	2 Pub. Bath/Show	B&B per person £13.00-£16.00 Single £13.00-£16.00 Double	Open Jan-Dec Dinner 1800-2100 B&B + Eve. Meal £22.00-£26.00

17th century house and converted byre with superb views of Galloway hills. Excellent baking, cooking and personal touches.

DAVIOT **Inverness-shire** Pauline Fowler Greystanes Daviot West Inverness-shire IV1 2EP Tel: (Farr) 08083 381	**Map 4** B9	HIGHLY COMMENDED Listed	2 Single 1 Twin 1 Double	1 En Suite fac 1 Pub. Bath/Show	B&B per person £16.00-£19.00 Single £16.00-£23.00 Double	Open Jan-Dec Dinner 1830-2000 B&B + Eve. Meal from £25.00

Spacious modern bungalow in 5.5 acres (1.5 acres woodland). Panoramic views of Strathnairn. Excellent country walks. One ensuite room.

Alex & Margaret Hutcheson Daviot Mains Farm Daviot Inverness-shire IV1 2ER Tel: (Daviot) 0463 772215/ 0850 559478 (mobile) Fax: 0463 772215	HIGHLY COMMENDED ᕯ ᕯ	1 Twin 1 Double 1 Family	1 En Suite fac 1 Priv. NOT ensuite 1 Pub. Bath/Show	B&B per person from £15.00 Single from £15.00 Double	Open Jan-Dec Dinner from 1830 B&B + Eve. Meal from £24.50

19C Highland farmhouse close to Culloden Moor. Good home cooking and a warm, friendly atmosphere.

Mrs M MacLeod Chalna Daviot Inverness-shire IV1 2XQ Tel: (Daviot) 0463 772239	COMMENDED ᕯ ᕯ	1 Twin 1 Double 1 Family	1 En Suite fac 1 Pub. Bath/Show	B&B per person £15.00-£17.50 Double	Open Apr-Dec

Modern, detached, stone built villa, in extensive grounds in rural setting. 7 miles (11kms) South of Inverness. Fishing available.

DENHOLM **Roxburghshire** Mr Douglas Newlands The Fox and Hounds Inn, Main Street Denholm Roxburghshire TD9 8NU Tel: (Denholm) 045087 247 Fax: 045087 500	Map 2 E7	Award Pending	1 Single 1 Double 1 Family	2 Pub. Bath/Show	B&B per person from £17.00 Single £15.00–£17.00 Double	Open Jan-Dec Dinner 1800-2200 B&B + Eve. Meal from £25.00	
DENNY **Stirlingshire** Mrs Jennifer Steel The Topps Farm, Fintry Road Denny Stirlingshire FK6 5JF Tel: (Denny) 0324 822471	Map 2 A4	COMMENDED ♕ ♕ ♕	3 Twin 4 Double 1 Family	8 En Suite fac	B&B per person from £25.00 Single from £17.00 Double	Open Jan-Dec Dinner to 1900 B&B + Eve. Meal from £30.00	
			Modern chalet-style farmhouse on working sheep farm in superb position. Taste of Scotland and Good Room Guides.				
DERVAIG **Isle of Mull, Argyll** Druimard Country House Druimard Dervaig, by Tobermory Isle of Mull, Argyll PA75 6QW Tel: (Dervaig) 06884 345/291	Map 1 C1	HIGHLY COMMENDED ♕ ♕ ♕	2 Twin 3 Double 1 Family Suite avail.	4 En Suite fac 1 Pub. Bath/Show	B&B per person £49.00–£54.50 Single £33.00–£42.50 Double	Open Jan-Dec Dinner 1800-2100 B&B + Eve. Meal £50.50–£62.00	
			Small Victorian country house hotel, with elegant restaurant, interesting cuisine using fresh ingredients. Adjacent to Mull Little Theatre.				
Mrs J Fairbairns Torrbreac, Sea Life Surveys Dervaig, Isle of Mull Argyll PA75 6QL Tel: (Dervaig) 06884 223 Fax: 06884 383		Award Pending	5 Twin	2 Pub. Bath/Show	B&B per person £19.00–£24.00 Single £12.50–£16.50 Double	Open Jan-Dec Dinner 1900-2100 B&B + Eve. Meal £25.00–£30.00	
John and Mary Porter Tigh an Allt Dervaig Isle of Mull, Argyll PA75 6QR Tel: (Dervaig) 06884 247		COMMENDED ♕	1 Twin 1 Double	1 Pub. Bath/Show	B&B per person £13.50–£15.00 Double	Open Jan-Dec Dinner to 1900 B&B + Eve. Meal £22.00–£24.00	
			Modern family house in quiet secluded setting. Close to Mull Little Theatre. Ideally situated for wildlife and bird observation.				
Mrs Smith Achnacraig Dervaig Isle of Mull, Argyll PA75 6QW Tel: (Dervaig) 06884 309		COMMENDED Listed	1 Single 1 Twin 1 Family	1 Pub. Bath/Show	B&B per person £13.00–£14.00 Single £13.00–£14.00 Double	Open Apr-Oct Dinner from 1930 B&B + Eve. Meal £21.00–£22.00	
			Winding river, circling buzzards, stone farmhouse, steep stair, stupendous views. Home grown produce, real cooking.				
DIABAIG **Ross-shire** Mrs B J Peacock Upper Diabaig Torridon, Achnasheen Ross-shire IV22 2HE Tel: (Diabaig) 044581 227	Map 3 F8	COMMENDED Listed	2 Twin 1 Double	1 Pub. Bath/Show	B&B per person from £13.50 Double	Open Apr-Sep Dinner from 1900 B&B + Eve. Meal from £22.50	
			Dramatic drive by Torridon Hills to modern house on working croft. Traditional Scottish hospitality. Warm and comfortable. Good home cooking.				

DIABAIG continued	Map 3 F8						
Miss I A Ross 3 Diabaig Torridon, Achnasheen Ross-shire IV22 2HE Tel: (Diabaig) 044581 240			1 Double 1 Family	1 Pub. Bath/Show	B&B per person £13.00-£13.50 Single £13.00-£13.50 Double	Open Jan-Dec Dinner 1900-2130 B&B + Eve. Meal £21.00-£21.50	
Mrs I Ross Ben Bhraggie, Diabaig Torridon, Achnasheen Ross-shire IV22 2HE Tel: (Diabaig) 044581 268			1 Twin 1 Double	1 Pub. Bath/Show	B&B per person £12.00-£12.50 Single £12.00-£12.50 Double	Open Apr-Nov Dinner 1900-2100 B&B + Eve. Meal £19.00-£19.50	

DINGWALL	Map 4
Ross-shire	A8

THE CROFT

**25 CASTLE STREET
DINGWALL IV15 9HU**

Tel: 0349 63319

FRIENDLY HOME-FROM-HOME ATMOSPHERE. SITUATED IN QUIET AREA OF DINGWALL. WITHIN EASY WALK OF TOWN CENTRE, BUS AND RAIL LINKS.

SPECIAL RATES FOR CHILDREN UNDER 12.

PRICES FROM £14.00 B&B.

Mrs Davis The Croft, Castle Street Dingwall Ross-shire IV15 9HU Tel: (Dingwall) 0349 63319			2 Twin 1 Family	2 Pub. Bath/Show	B&B per person £14.00-£20.00 Single £14.00 Double	Open Jan-Dec	
Mrs J MacLean Duart, 1 Logan Drive Dingwall Ross-shire IV15 9LN Tel: (Dingwall) 0349 62387			2 Twin	1 Pub. Bath/Show	B&B per person from £13.00 Double	Open Feb-Nov	

Kirklee B & B   TEL: 0349 63439

'KIRKLEE', 1 ACHANY ROAD, DINGWALL IV15 9JB

Charming Victorian, family-run house with private garden in a wide exclusive cul-de-sac with free parking near centre of quiet market town — close to bus and rail stations.

Ideal base for exploring the Highlands — day trips are quite feasible to Skye, Orkney, Loch Ness, Dornoch Firth, Moray Firth, Wester Ross and Black Isle.

Mrs M Swan Kirklee, 1 Achany Road Dingwall Ross-shire IV15 9JB Tel: (Dingwall) 0349 63439	COMMENDED Listed	2 Single 1 Twin 1 Double	2 Pub. Bath/Show	B&B per person £14.00 Single	Open Jan-Dec	
		Spacious Victorian family run house in own garden, in quiet cul-de-sac, close to town centre near to rail and bus station.				

DORES **Inverness-shire** Mrs J Morrison Beinn Dhearg, Torr Gardens Dores Inverness-shire IV1 2TS Tel: (Dores) 046375 336	Map 4 A9	COMMENDED 👑 👑	1 Twin 1 Double 1 Family	3 En Suite fac 1 Pub. Bath/Show	B&B per person £14.50-£16.50 Double	Open Apr-Sep

Modern spacious bungalow in quiet setting 8 miles (13kms) south of Inverness. Wonderful views across Loch Ness. All rooms with private facilities.

DORNIE, by Kyle of Lochalsh **Ross-shire** Mrs Clayton Tigh Tasgaidh Dornie, by Kyle of Lochalsh Ross-shire IV40 8EH Tel: (Dornie) 059985 242	Map 3 F1	COMMENDED 👑 👑	1 Twin 2 Double	3 En Suite fac 1 Pub. Bath/Show	B&B per person £14.00-£16.00 Double	Open Feb-Nov

Detached house standing in its own grounds overlooking Loch Long. In a quiet residential area but near main Inverness-Skye road. Non-smoking.

Mrs Alexina Finlayson 2 Sallachy Dornie Ross-shire IV40 8DZ Tel: (Kililan) 059988 238		COMMENDED 👑	1 Twin 1 Double	1 Pub. Bath/Show	B&B per person £13.00-£14.00 Single £13.00-£14.00 Double	Open Apr-Oct Dinner 1900-2000 B&B + Eve. Meal £20.00-£21.00

Modern bungalow on working croft. An elevated position with views across Loch Long.

Mrs Gray Mira House, 15 Francis Street Dornie, by Kyle of Lochalsh Ross-shire IV40 8DT Tel: (Dornie) 059985 221			1 Single 1 Twin 1 Double	2 Pub. Bath/Show	B&B per person £13.00-£13.50 Single £13.00-£13.50 Double	Open 6 Jan-22 Dec

DORNOCH **Sutherland** S M Board Fourpenny Cottage Skelbo, by Dornoch Sutherland IV25 3QF Tel: (Dornoch) 0862 810727	Map 4 B6	HIGHLY COMMENDED 👑 👑 👑	2 Twin 1 Double 1 Family	4 En Suite fac	B&B per person £22.50 Double	Open Jan-Dec Dinner 1800-2000 B&B + Eve. Meal from £32.50

Large detached house in quiet rural position 2 miles (3kms) from Dornoch. Overlooks Loch Fleet. Friendly atmosphere; home baking. Some annexe accom.

'HIGHFIELD'

Evelix Road, Dornoch, Sutherland IV25 3HR   Tel: 0862 810909

Comfortable non-smoking B&B standing in grounds of almost one acre with southerly views over the Dornoch Firth yet only four hundred yards from the centre of this beautiful small town. Bedrooms have private facilities, colour televisions etc. Car park and residents' lounge. **B&B from £18 per person.**

Mrs J Dooley Highfield, Evelix Road Dornoch Sutherland IV25 3HR Tel: (Dornoch) 0862 810909		HIGHLY COMMENDED 👑 👑	1 Twin 2 Double	3 En Suite fac	B&B per person £16.00-£19.00 Double	Open Jan-Dec

A modern house at edge of the picturesque golfing town – a warm welcome assured in this very comfortable family home.

DORNOCH Mrs E A Dunlop Cluaine, Evelix Dornoch Sutherland IV25 3RD Tel: (Dornoch) 0862 810276	Map 4 B6		1 Single 1 Twin 1 Double	1 En Suite fac 1 Pub. Bath/Show	B&B per person £13.00-£15.00 Single £13.00-£15.00 Double	Open May-Sep	
Mrs Audrey Hellier Achandean, The Meadows, off Castle Close Dornoch Sutherland IV25 3SF Tel: (Dornoch) 0862 810413			1 Twin 2 Double	2 En Suite fac 1 Pub. Bath/Show	B&B per person £16.00-£20.00 Double	Open Mar-Dec	
Fiona MacLean 11 Gilchrist Square Dornoch Sutherland Tel: (Dornoch) 0862 811024	Award Pending		3 Twin	1 En Suite fac 1 Pub. Bath/Show	B&B per person £13.00-£16.00 Single £13.00-£16.00 Double	Open Apr-Dec	
Mrs S Young Parfour, Rowan Crescent Dornoch Sutherland IV25 3SF Tel: (Dornoch) 0862 810955	HIGHLY COMMENDED 👑👑		1 Twin 2 Double	3 Limited ensuite	B&B per person £19.50-£26.00 Single £17.50-£19.50 Double	Open Jan-Dec Dinner 1900-2000 B&B + Eve. Meal £27.50-£29.50	
		Homely, modern bungalow. Convenient for town centre, golf course and beach. Private parking.					
DOUGLAS **Lanarkshire** Mrs J Shanks West Glespin Farm Glespin, nr Douglas Lanarkshire ML11 0SQ Tel: (Douglas) 0555 851349	Map 2 B7		1 Twin 1 Double 1 Family	1 Pub. Bath/Show	B&B per person £15.00-£17.50 Single £12.50-£15.00 Double	Open Jun-Sep	
DOUNBY **Orkney** Mr & Mrs D Paice Dounby House Dounby Orkney KW17 2HT Tel: (Harray) 085677 535	Map 5 B1	COMMENDED 👑👑	1 Twin 2 Double	1 En Suite fac 1 Pub. Bath/Show	B&B per person to £13.00 Single to £13.00 Double	Open Feb-Nov B&B + Eve. Meal to £18.00	
		Family run Victorian house in quiet village 17 miles (27kms) from Kirkwall, 9 miles (14kms) from Stromness. Specialises in birdwatching holidays.					
DOUNE **Perthshire** Mrs F J R Graham Mackeanston House Doune Perthshire Tel: (Doune) 0786 850213	Map 2 A3	COMMENDED Listed	1 Twin 1 Double	1 En Suite fac 1 Priv. NOT ensuite	B&B per person £16.00-£18.00 Single £16.00-£20.00 Double	Open Jan-Dec Dinner from 2000 B&B + Eve. Meal £28.00-£32.00	
		Peaceful, comfortable old farmhouse with large garden. Enjoy open fires, home cooking with free range eggs and home-made bread. Ensuite bathrooms.					
DRUMBEG **Sutherland** Drumbeg House Drumbeg Sutherland IV27 4NW Tel: (Drumbeg) 05713 209	Map 3 G4	COMMENDED 👑👑👑	1 Twin 2 Double	3 En Suite fac	B&B per person £20.00 Double	Open Jan-Dec Dinner 1800-1900 B&B + Eve. Meal £30.00-£32.50	
		In house-party style, Ron and Margaret provides a warm welcome, convivial company. Fresh vegetables, self indulgent, wonderfully peaceful situation.					

VAT is shown at 17.5%: changes in this rate may affect prices. Prices shown are for guidance only. Please send SAE with each enquiry.

	Map 4 A9					
DRUMNADROCHIT **Inverness-shire** Glen Rowan Guest House West Lewiston Drumnadrochit Inverness-shire IV3 6UW Tel: (Drumnadrochit) 04562 235/0456 450235	COMMENDED	2 Twin 1 Double	3 En Suite fac	B&B per person £22.00-£32.00 Single £14.50-£19.50 Double	Open Jan-Dec Dinner 1830-1900 B&B + Eve. Meal £25.00-£30.00	
		Modern house with garden running down to river in a quiet village by Loch Ness between Drumnadrochit and Urquhart Castle.				
Mrs Tina Beet Heatherlea, The Beeches, Balmacaan Road Drumnadrochit Inverness-shire IV3 6UR Tel: (Drumnadrochit) 04562 561	COMMENDED Listed	1 Twin 2 Double	1 En Suite fac 1 Pub. Bath/Show	B&B per person £11.00-£18.00 Double	Open Jan-Dec	
		Modern family home in popular Highland village close to Loch Ness. Good views to Loch and hills. Inverness 14 miles (22 kms).				
Mrs A Forrester Linne Dhuinn, Lewiston Drumnadrochit Inverness-shire IV3 6UW Tel: (Drumnadrochit) 0456 450244	COMMENDED	1 Twin 1 Double 1 Family	2 En Suite fac 1 Priv. NOT ensuite	B&B per person from £13.00 Single from £13.00 Double	Open Jan-Dec	
		Modern bungalow in a quiet residential area of this Highland village. Warm hospitality assured.				
Mrs H MacDonald Maeshowe, Walled Garden, Balmacaan Drumnadrochit Inverness-shire IV3 6UP Tel: (Drumnadrochit) 04562 382/0456 450382	HIGHLY COMMENDED Listed	1 Single 1 Twin 1 Double	2 Pub. Bath/Show	B&B per person £13.00 Single £13.00 Double	Open Mar-Oct	
		Modern house in old walled garden, with panoramic views of hills; 2 miles(3kms) from Loch Ness and 14 miles (22kms) from Inverness.				
Capt & Mrs A D MacDonald-Haig Borlum Farm Drumnadrochit Inverness-shire IV3 6XN Tel: (Drumnadrochit) 0456 450358 Fax: 0456 450358	COMMENDED	1 Twin 1 Double 3 Family	2 En Suite fac 2 Pub. Bath/Show	B&B per person £17.50-£20.50 Double	Open Jan-Dec	
		Comfortable country house with many period features, welcomes non smokers. On working farm with fine views of Loch Ness. Riding available.				
Mr R J MacGregor Riverbank, West Lewiston Drumnadrochit Inverness-shire IV3 6UL Tel: (Drumnadrochit) 04562 274/0456 450274	COMMENDED	1 Twin 2 Double	1 En Suite fac 2 Pub. Bath/Show	B&B per person £12.00-£15.00 Double	Open Jan-Dec	
		Modern house with ground floor accommodation peacefully situated. Ample parking. Riverside and woodland walks.				
John & Rosemary MacKenzie Carrachan House, Milton Drumnadrochit Inverness-shire IV3 6UA Tel: (Drumnadrochit) 04562 254/0456 450254	COMMENDED	2 Double 1 Family	2 Pub. Bath/Show	B&B per person £12.00-£13.00 Single £12.00-£13.00 Double	Open Jan-Dec	
		Traditional stone cottage in peaceful village at entrance to Glen Urquhart and under 3 miles (5kms) from Loch Ness. Fishing and golf nearby.				
Mrs MacLennan Benview, Lewiston Drumnadrochit Inverness-shire IV3 6UW Tel: (Drumnadrochit) 04562 379/0456 450379	APPROVED Listed	1 Twin 1 Double	1 Pub. Bath/Show	B&B per person £12.00-£12.50 Double	Open Jan-Dec	
		19C cottage in quiet village. 1/2 mile (800m) walk from Loch Ness. Near to bus stop by Lewiston Arms Hotel. 14 miles (22kms) from Inverness.				

Details of Grading and Classification are on page vi.

Key to symbols is on back flap.

DRUMNADROCHIT continued
Map 4 A9

Mrs E Paterson
Allanmore Farm
Drumnadrochit
Inverness-shire
IV3 6XE
Tel: (Drumnadrochit)
04562 247/0456 450247

COMMENDED
Listed

1 Twin
2 Double

1 Pub. Bath/Show

B&B per person
£12.50-£13.00 Double

Open Apr-Oct

16th Century farmhouse on stock and arable farm in peaceful setting.

Sandra & Bill Silke
Westwood, Lower Balmacaan
Drumnadrochit
Inverness-shire
IV3 6UL
Tel: (Drumnadrochit)
0456 450826

COMMENDED
Listed

2 Twin
1 Double

1 En Suite fac
1 Pub. Bath/Show

B&B per person
£12.00-£16.00 Double
Dinner 1800-2030
B&B + Eve. Meal
£18.00-£22.00

Open Jan-Dec

Modern centrally heated bungalow. Quiet location in
popular Highland village near Loch Ness.

Mrs M Van Loon
Kilmore Farm House
Drumnadrochit
Inverness-shire
IV3 6UW
Tel: (Drumnadrochit)
0456 450524

COMMENDED
👑 👑 👑

1 Twin
2 Double

3 En Suite fac

B&B per person
from £14.00 Double
Dinner 1800-1930
B&B + Eve. Meal
from £21.00

Open Jan-Dec

Modern farmhouse peacefully situated with splendid views of surrounding hills.
Site of Special Scientific Interest. Highland Cattle.

Mrs J Witty
The Haining, Lower Balmacaan
Drumnadrochit
Inverness-shire
IV3 6UR
Tel: (Drumnadrochit)
0456 450837

COMMENDED
Listed

1 Twin
2 Double

1 En Suite fac
1 Pub. Bath/Show

B&B per person
from £13.00 Double

Open Apr-Oct

Peacefully situated at edge of village with fine views. Near Loch Ness and Exhibition.
Ideal for touring the Highlands.

DRYMEN
Stirlingshire
Map 1 H4

Mrs Betty Robb
Ceardach, Gartness Road
Drymen
Stirlingshire
G63 0BH
Tel: (Drymen) 0360 60596

1 Twin
1 Double

1 Pub. Bath/Show

B&B per person
to £15.00 Single
to £12.50 Double

Open Jan-Dec

DUFFTOWN
Banffshire
Map 4 E9

Ms Lynn Cogan
Nashville, 8a Balvenie Street
Dufftown, Keith
Banffshire
AB55 4AB
Tel: (Dufftown) 0340 20553

Award
Pending

1 Twin
1 Double
1 Family

1 Pub. Bath/Show

B&B per person
£10.00-£12.00 Double

Open Jan-Dec

Mrs E MacMillan
Davaar, Church Street
Dufftown, Keith
Banffshire
AB55 4AR
Tel: (Dufftown) 0340 20464

COMMENDED
Listed

1 Twin
2 Double

2 En Suite fac
1 Pub. Bath/Show

B&B per person
£13.00-£15.50 Double
Dinner 1800-2000
B&B + Eve. Meal
from £19.00

Open Jan-Dec

Comfortable and personally run accommodation. Close to Whisky and
Castle Trails. Traditional Scottish home baking.

Mrs D Moir
The Old Schoolhouse,
Kirkton of Mortlach
Dufftown, Keith
Banffshire
AB55 4BR
Tel: (Dufftown) 0340 20076

COMMENDED
Listed

1 Twin
1 Family

1 Pub. Bath/Show

B&B per person
£12.50-£15.00 Single
£12.50-£15.00 Double
Dinner 1800-2000
B&B + Eve. Meal
£20.00-£25.00

Open Jan-Dec

Small cottage southfacing in quiet area of Dufftown, beside historic
Mortlach Kirk. Caters for guests with disabilities.

Mrs Mary M Robertson 11 Conval Street Dufftown, Keith Banffshire AB55 4AE Tel: (Dufftown) 0340 20818		**COMMENDED** ⛄	1 Twin 1 Double	1 Pub. Bath/Show	B&B per person £11.00-£12.00 Double	Open Jan-Dec Dinner 1800-2000 B&B + Eve. Meal £17.00-£18.00	

Warm welcome at quiet modern bungalow, off main street 18 miles (29 kms) south of Elgin. On Whisky Trail.

Mrs Jean D Smart Errolbank, 134 Fife Street Dufftown, Keith Banffshire AB55 4DP Tel: (Dufftown) 0340 20229			1 Single 1 Double 3 Family	1 Pub. Bath/Show	B&B per person £11.50-£13.00 Single £11.50-£13.00 Double	Open Jan-Dec Dinner 1700-2100 B&B + Eve. Meal £18.00-£20.00	

DUMBARTON Mr & Mrs R Muirhead Kilmalid House, 17 Glenpath, off Barnhill Rd Dumbarton Dunbartonshire G82 2QL Tel: (Dumbarton) 0389 32030	Map 1 H5		1 Twin 1 Family	1 Pub. Bath/Show	B&B per person £15.00-£18.00 Single from £15.00 Double	Open Jan-Dec	

DUMFRIES Dalston House Laurieknowe Dumfries DG2 Tel: (Dumfries) 0387 54422 Fax: 0387 54422	Map 2 B9	**COMMENDED** ⛄ ⛄ ⛄	3 Single 3 Twin 7 Double 4 Family	16 En Suite fac 1 Priv. NOT ensuite 1 Pub. Bath/Show	B&B per person £40.00-£50.00 Single £25.00-£30.00 Double	Open mid Jan-Nov Dinner 1800-2200 B&B + Eve. Meal £35.00-£65.00	

Family run establishment close to town centre and all amenities. Varied menu with accent on fresh produce. Special breaks off-season.

Laurelbank Guest House 7 Laurieknowe Dumfries DG2 7AH Tel: (Dumfries) 0387 69388		**COMMENDED** ⛄ ⛄	2 Twin 1 Double 1 Family	3 Limited ensuite 1 Pub. Bath/Show	B&B per person £16.00-£18.00 Double	Open Feb-Nov	

Elevated sandstone villa, a short walk to River Nith, town centre and Bus Station. New Ice Bowl 3 minutes away. Private car park at rear.

Mrs Burdekin Shambellie View, Wellgreen, Glencaple Rd Dumfries DG1 4TD Tel: (Dumfries) 0387 69331		**COMMENDED** Listed	1 Twin 1 Double	2 Pub. Bath/Show	B&B per person from £13.50 Single from £13.50 Double	Open Jan-Dec Dinner 1900-2100 B&B + Eve. Meal from £21.50	

Comfortable home with rural outlook, peacefully situated 1.5 miles (2.5kms) from town centre.

SCOTTISH TOURIST BOARD
QUALITY COMMENDATIONS ARE:

Deluxe — *An EXCELLENT quality standard*
Highly Commended — *A VERY GOOD quality standard*
Commended — *A GOOD quality standard*
Approved — *An ADEQUATE quality standard*

DUMFRIES continued	Map 2 B9					
Mrs M A Conaghan Glencairn Villa, 45 Rae Street Dumfries DG1 1JD Tel: (Dumfries) 0387 62467		COMMENDED Listed	2 Single 2 Family	1 En Suite fac 1 Pub. Bath/Show	B&B per person £13.00-£14.50 Single £13.00-£17.50 Double	Open Jan-Dec Dinner 1700-1800 B&B + Eve. Meal £20.00-£24.50

Comfortable 19C home within walking distance of town centre.
Close to railway station and library. Home cooking.

| Mrs Conners & Mrs Parker
Mouswald Place, Mouswald
Dumfries
DG1 4JS
Tel: (Mouswald) 038783 226 | | | 1 Twin
2 Double | 2 Pub. Bath/Show | B&B per person
£16.00 Single
£13.00 Double | Open Jan-Dec
Dinner 1830-2130
B&B + Eve. Meal
£17.00-£20.00 |

| Mrs E Gray
Charter House,
2 Troqueer Road
Dumfries
Tel: (Dumfries) 0387 52185 | | Award
Pending | 3 Twin | 2 En Suite fac
1 Pub. Bath/Show | B&B per person
£12.00-£16.00 Double | Open Feb-Dec |

| Mrs P Martin
Wheatley, 1 Merkland Road,
Bankend
Dumfries
Dumfriesshire
Tel: (Glencaple) 038777 392 | | | 2 Single
1 Double | 1 Pub. Bath/Show | B&B per person
£13.00-£14.00 Single
£12.00-£13.00 Double | Open Feb-Nov
Dinner 1800-1900
B&B + Eve. Meal
£17.00-£18.00 |

| Mrs A Prentice
North Laurieknowe,
3 North Laurieknowe Pl
Dumfries
DG2 7AL
Tel: (Dumfries) 0387 54136 | | COMMENDED | 1 Single
1 Twin
1 Family | 2 Pub. Bath/Show | B&B per person
£14.00 Single
£14.00 Double | Open Feb-Nov |

Built 1868, substantial detached sandstone villa in large secluded garden.
Short walk to town centre.

| Anne Sharp
The Haven, 1 Kenmure Terrace
Dumfries
DG2 7QX
Tel: (Dumfries) 0387 51281 | | COMMENDED | 1 Single
2 Twin | 1 En Suite fac
1 Limited ensuite
1 Priv. NOT ensuite
1 Pub. Bath/Show | B&B per person
£15.00-£18.00 Single
£15.00-£18.00 Double | Open Jan-Dec |

Comfortable Victorian house on riverside, close to town. Residential area.
Separate kitchen where guests can prepare snacks.

| Mrs Smyth
Henderland Farm,
Crocketford Road
Dumfries
DG2 8QD
Tel: (Lochfoot) 038773 270 | | | 1 Single
1 Twin
1 Double | 2 Limited ensuite
2 Pub. Bath/Show | B&B per person
from £11.00 Single
£15.00-£20.00 Double | Open Jan-Dec |

BY DUMFRIES	Map 2 B9					
Mrs Carson Hemplands Farm Torthorwald, by Dumfries Dumfriesshire DG1 3PP Tel: (Collin) 038775 225		COMMENDED Listed	1 Twin 1 Double	1 Pub. Bath/Show	B&B per person £13.00-£13.50 Double	Open Jun-Sep

On working farm, with panoramic views over Solway Firth and Lakeland hills.
Yachting on nearby loch. Good base for touring Dumfries and Galloway.

| Mr Ireson
Smithy House
Torthorwald, by Dumfries
Dumfriesshire
DG1 3PT
Tel: (Collin) 038775 518 | | | 1 Twin
1 Double | 1 En Suite fac
2 Pub. Bath/Show | B&B per person
£12.50-£15.00 Double | Open Jan-Dec
Dinner 1800-2000
B&B + Eve. Meal
£17.00-£19.50 |

Mrs C M Schooling Locharthur House Beeswing, by Dumfries Dumfriesshire DG2 8JG Tel: (Dumfries) 0387 76235		COMMENDED ⚜	1 Twin 1 Family	1 Pub. Bath/Show	B&B per person £15.00-£18.00 Single £15.00-£16.00 Double	Open Jan-Dec Dinner 1800-2000 B&B + Eve. Meal £22.00-£23.00	
			Late Georgian house set in 3 acres of grounds with access off A711. Excellent views of countryside. Home baking and cooking.				
DUNBAR **East Lothian** Cruachan Guest House East Links Road Dunbar East Lothian EH42 1LT Tel: (Dunbar) 0368 63006/863006	Map 2 E4	Award Pending	1 Single 1 Twin 2 Family	1 Limited ensuite 2 Pub. Bath/Show	B&B per person to £15.00 Single to £15.00 Double	Open Jan-Dec Dinner 1800-1830 B&B + Eve. Meal £20.00-£22.00	
Overcliffe Guest House 11 Bayswell Park Dunbar East Lothian EH42 1AE Tel: (Dunbar) 0368 64004		COMMENDED ⚜ ⚜	3 Double 3 Family	3 En Suite fac 3 Pub. Bath/Show	B&B per person £18.00-£21.00 Single £15.00-£18.50 Double	Open Jan-Dec Dinner 1830-1930 B&B + Eve. Meal £24.00-£27.50	
			Personally run, situated in pleasant residential area. Convenient for town centre and local amenities. Close to sea and cliff tops.				
St Helen's Guest House Queens Road Dunbar East Lothian EH42 1LN Tel: (Dunbar) 0368 863716		COMMENDED ⚜ ⚜	1 Single 4 Twin 1 Double 1 Family	2 En Suite fac 2 Pub. Bath/Show	B&B per person £15.00 Single £14.00-£16.00 Double	Open Jan-Oct	
			Victorian red sandstone house situated in quiet area of Dunbar. Few minutes walk from beach and golf course. Friendly welcome.				
Springfield Guest House Belhaven Road Dunbar East Lothian EH42 1NH Tel: (Dunbar) 0368 62502		COMMENDED ⚜	1 Single 1 Twin 1 Double 2 Family	2 Pub. Bath/Show	B&B per person £17.00 Single £16.00 Double	Open Jan-Nov Dinner at 1800 B&B + Eve. Meal £26.00	
			An elegant 19th century villa with attractive garden and under the personal supervision of the owner.				
Mrs Brown 89 Lammermuir Crescent Dunbar East Lothian EH42 1DP Tel: (Dunbar) 0368 862136			1 Twin	1 Priv. NOT ensuite	B&B per person £16.00-£18.00 Double	Open Apr-Oct	
Mrs Gill Last St Ronan's, East Links Dunbar East Lothian EH42 1LT Tel: (Dunbar) 0368 63634			2 Twin 1 Family	1 Pub. Bath/Show	B&B per person £13.00-£15.00 Double	Open Apr-Oct	
Miss I Taylor Easterbroomhouse Farm Dunbar East Lothian EH42 1RD Tel: (Dunbar) 0368 62738			1 Twin 2 Double	1 Priv. NOT ensuite 1 Pub. Bath/Show	B&B per person £14.00-£18.00 Single £14.00-£18.00 Double	Open Apr-Oct	

Details of Grading and Classification are on page vi.

Key to symbols is on back flap.

DUNBEATH	Map 4						
Caithness	D4						
Mrs M MacDonald			1 Twin	1 Pub. Bath/Show	B&B per person	Open May-Sep	
Tormore Farm			1 Double		£12.00 Single	Dinner from 1800	
Dunbeath			1 Family		£12.00 Double	B&B + Eve. Meal	
Caithness						£17.00-£19.00	
KW6 6EH							
Tel: (Dunbeath) 05933 240							

DUNBLANE	Map 2
Perthshire	A3

MOSSGIEL

DOUNE ROAD · DUNBLANE
PERTHSHIRE · FK15 9ND
Tel: 0786 824325

Conveniently situated near the A9. Mossgiel is an established Bed and Breakfast House situated in a beautiful country setting on the A820. It provides an ideal touring base for Loch Lomond. The Trossachs and Central Scotland.

The House is tastefully furnished and all bedrooms are on the ground floor and equipped with central heating, H&C, wash-basins, radios and tea/coffee-making facilities, 1 double and 1 twin-bedded room provide en-suite facilities. There is a Guest Lounge with colour TV, large garden and off-the-road parking.

Mossgiel offers its guests a comfortable, friendly and relaxing stay.

Mrs Bennett	COMMENDED	1 Twin	2 En Suite fac	B&B per person	Open Apr-Oct	
Mossgiel, Doune Road	❧ ❧	1 Double		£14.00-£16.00 Double		
Dunblane						
Perthshire						
FK15 9ND		**Bungalow in beautiful rural setting, 1 mile (2 km) from Dunblane on A820.**				
Tel: (Dunblane) 0786 824325		**Two ensuite bedrooms.**				

Westwood

DOUNE ROAD
DUNBLANE
PERTHSHIRE
FK15 9ND

Telephone:
0786 822579

❧ ❧

The ideal place to stay whilst holidaying in Central Scotland. Westwood enjoys a quiet country location with lovely views yet is conveniently situated near the A9. It offers safe parking within one acre of pleasant gardens. All comfortable bedrooms enjoy private facilities. Residents' lounge with colour TV.
NO SMOKING

Mrs Elizabeth J Duncan	HIGHLY	1 Twin	1 En Suite fac	B&B per person	Open Mar-Oct	
Westwood, Doune Road	COMMENDED	2 Double	2 Priv. NOT ensuite	£15.50-£17.50 Double		
Dunblane	❧ ❧					
Perthshire						
FK15 9ND		**Modern, in rural and peaceful setting with attractive garden.**				
Tel: (Dunblane) 0786 822579		**Offering relaxed and friendly atmosphere. Ground floor room available.**				

Mrs E A Richardson		1 Twin	2 En Suite fac	B&B per person	Open Jan-Dec	
Rhu House, Lower Auchinlay		1 Double		£15.00-£16.50 Single		
Dunblane				£15.00-£16.50 Double		
Perthshire						
FK15 9NA						
Tel: (Dunblane) 0786 822752						

Name & Address	Map Ref	Grading	Rooms	Facilities	Prices	Opening
DUNDEE **Angus** Aberlaw Guest House 230 Broughty Ferry Road Dundee Angus DD4 7JP Tel: (Dundee) 0382 456929	Map 2 D2	COMMENDED	2 Single 1 Twin 1 Double 1 Family	1 En Suite fac 2 Pub. Bath/Show	B&B per person £15.00-£16.00 Single £14.00-£17.00 Double	Open Jan-Dec
			Family run house with private parking. Close to city centre, overlooking River Tay.			
Anderson's Guest House 285 Perth Road Dundee Angus DD2 1JS Tel: (Dundee) 0382 68585			1 Single 2 Twin 2 Double 2 Family	4 En Suite fac 2 Pub. Bath/Show	B&B per person £16.00-£18.00 Single from £16.00 Double	Open Jan-Dec Dinner 1730-1830 B&B + Eve. Meal from £22.00
Hillside Guest House Hillside, 43 Constitution Street Dundee Angus DD3 6JH Tel: (Dundee) 0382 23443		HIGHLY COMMENDED	2 Twin 1 Family	1 En Suite fac 2 Pub. Bath/Show	B&B per person £19.00-£25.00 Single £17.00-£23.00 Double	Open Jan-Dec
			Victorian family home in quiet residential area close to city centre and all amenities. Off street parking.			
Stonelee Guest House 69 Monifieth Road, Broughty Ferry Dundee Angus DD5 2RW Tel: (Dundee) 0382 737812 Fax: 0382 737812			2 Twin 1 Double 2 Family Suite avail.	5 En Suite fac 1 Priv. NOT ensuite 1 Pub. Bath/Show	B&B per person £17.50-£24.50 Double	Open Jan-Dec
Mrs Julie Cromar Brook House, 86 Brook Street Broughty Ferry, Dundee Angus DD5 1DQ Tel: (Dundee) 0382 79166			2 Twin 2 Double	4 En Suite fac	B&B per person £20.00-£25.00 Single £17.50-£20.00 Double	Open Jan-Dec
Mrs E M & Mr A E Lerpiniere 43 Denoon Terrace Dundee Angus DD2 2EB Tel: (Dundee) 0382 68512			1 Double 1 Family	2 Pub. Bath/Show	B&B per person £14.00 Double	Open Jan-Dec
J Leslie Elmlodge, 49 Seafield Road Dundee Angus DD1 4NW Tel: (Dundee) 0382 28402			1 Single 1 Twin 1 Family	1 Pub. Bath/Show	B&B per person £12.50-£15.00 Single from £12.50 Double	Open Jan-Dec
Mrs E Park 1 Fyne Road, Broughty Ferry Dundee Angus DD5 3JF Tel: (Dundee) 0382 78980			1 Single 1 Twin	1 Pub. Bath/Show	B&B per person £13.00-£15.00 Single £13.00-£15.00 Double	Open Jan-Dec
Mr Reid 149 Arbroath Road Dundee Angus DD4 6LP Tel: (Dundee) 0382 453393		COMMENDED Listed	2 Family	2 Pub. Bath/Show	B&B per person from £15.00 Single from £13.00 Double	Open Jan-Dec
			Detached stone built house in residential area in east end of city. Guests car parking; on main bus route into city centre.			

DUNDEE continued — Map 2 D2

Name/Address	Rating	Rooms	Facilities	B&B	Meals/Open
Mrs Florence Taylor, Ardmoy, 359 Arbroath Road, Dundee, Angus, DD4 7SQ, Tel: (Dundee) 0382 453249	COMMENDED Listed	1 Twin, 1 Double, 1 Family	1 Pub. Bath/Show	B&B per person £20.00 Single £15.00 Double	Open Jan-Dec, Dinner 1700-1900, B&B + Eve. Meal £25.50

Spacious stone built house in own garden on direct route to centre. Private Parking.

| Mrs H Thomson, 251 Perth Road, Dundee, Angus, DD2 1EL, Tel: (Dundee) 0382 66175 | | 1 Single, 1 Twin | 1 Pub. Bath/Show | B&B per person £13.50-£14.50 Single £13.50-£14.50 Double | Open Jan-Dec, Dinner 1700-1900, B&B + Eve. Meal £18.50-£19.50 |

| Mr & Mrs B Wallace, The Bend, 17a Claypotts Rd, Broughty Ferry, Dundee, Angus, DD5 1BS, Tel: (Dundee) 0382 730085 | COMMENDED | 1 Twin | 1 En Suite fac | B&B per person £15.00-£17.00 Double | Open Jan-Dec |

Private suite with secluded garden in quiet area with off-street parking. Convenient for Dundee, East Coast, and golf courses. Regret no smoking.

DUNDONNELL — Ross-shire — Map 3 G7

| Mrs A Ross, 4 Camusnagaul, Dundonnell, Ross-shire, IV23 2QT, Tel: (Dundonnell) 085483 237 | | 1 Twin, 1 Double, 1 Family | 1 Pub. Bath/Show | B&B per person £12.50-£13.00 Single £12.50-£13.00 Double | Open Jan-Dec |

DUNFERMLINE — Fife — Map 2 C4

| Broomfield Guest House, 1 Broomfield Drive, Dunfermline, Fife, KY12 0PJ, Tel: (Dunfermline) 0383 732498 | | 1 Single, 1 Twin, 2 Double, 2 Family | 6 En Suite fac, 1 Pub. Bath/Show | B&B per person from £18.00 Single from £16.00 Double | Open Jan-Dec |

| Garvock Guest House, 82 Halbeath Road, Dunfermline, Fife, KY12 7RS, Tel: (Dunfermline) 0383 734689 | APPROVED Listed | 1 Single, 2 Twin, 2 Double, 1 Family | 3 En Suite fac, 1 Pub. Bath/Show | B&B per person from £14.00 Single £14.00-£16.00 Double | Open Jan-Dec |

19C modernised and converted house situated 1 mile (2kms) from the town centre. Convenient for M90 and on main bus routes.

| Pitreavie Guest House, 3 Aberdour Road, Dunfermline, Fife, KY11 4PB, Tel: (Dunfermline) 0383 724244 | | 2 Single, 2 Twin, 1 Double, 1 Family | 2 Pub. Bath/Show | B&B per person £15.00-£17.00 Single £16.00-£17.00 Double | Open Jan-Dec |

| Mrs Dunsire, The Haven, 82 Pilmuir Street, Dunfermline, Fife, KY12 0LN, Tel: (Dunfermline) 0383 729039 | COMMENDED Listed | 1 Single, 1 Twin, 1 Double | 1 Pub. Bath/Show | B&B per person from £14.00 Single from £13.00 Double | Open Jan-Dec |

Family run Victorian guest house in a central location, with many period features. Warm and friendly welcome.

Mrs E M Fotheringham Bowleys Farm, Roscobie Dunfermline Fife KY12 0SG Tel: (Dunfermline) 0383 721056	COMMENDED 👑	2 Family	1 Pub. Bath/Show	B&B per person £16.00 Single £14.00 Double	Open Apr-Oct

Quite peaceful and relaxing 19C working stock farm set in 130 acres.
Warm welcome and homebaking. Dunfermline 5 miles (8kms).

Mrs Jane Gellan Farm House, Main Street, Kingseat Dunfermline Fife KY12 0TJ Tel: (Dunfermline) 0383.720237		1 Single 1 Twin 1 Double	2 Priv. NOT ensuite 2 Pub. Bath/Show	B&B per person £12.00-£14.00 Single £12.00-£14.00 Double	Open May-Oct

Mrs Hooper Hillview House, 9 Aberdour Road Dunfermline Fife KY11 4PB Tel: (Dunfermline) 0383 726278	COMMENDED 👑 👑	1 Twin 2 Double	1 Limited ensuite 2 Pub. Bath/Show	B&B per person £15.00-£16.00 Single £14.00-£15.00 Double	Open Jan-Dec

Friendly family home on the outskirts of the town. Comfortable and well
appointed rooms, some overlooking attractive rear garden.

Mrs Moffat Cameron Hse, 4 Scobie Place, Halbeath Road Dunfermline Fife KY12 7RX Tel: (Dunfermline) 0383 725894		1 Single 2 Twin	1 Pub. Bath/Show	B&B per person £12.50-£14.00 Single £12.50-£14.00 Double	Open Jan-Dec

Mrs Ward 102 Dewar Street Dunfermline Fife KY12 8AA Tel: (Dunfermline) 0383 725724		1 Twin	1 Pub. Bath/Show	B&B per person to £12.00 Single to £11.50 Double	Open Jan-Dec

DUNKELD **Perthshire** Waterbury Guest House Birnam, by Dunkeld Perthshire PH8 0BG Tel: (Dunkeld) 0350 727324	Map 2 B1 COMMENDED 👑	1 Single 1 Twin 1 Double 2 Family	2 Pub. Bath/Show	B&B per person £14.50-£16.00 Single £14.50-£15.50 Double	Open Jan-Dec

Traditional Scottish hospitality in this listed building in rural village
on Grampian fringe. Ideal for walkers and bird watchers.

Mr & Mrs P Buxton Bheinne Mhor, Perth Road Birnam, by Dunkeld Perthshire PH8 0DH Tel: (Dunkeld) 0350 727779		2 Twin 1 Double	3 En Suite fac 1 Pub. Bath/Show	B&B per person from £19.00 Single from £19.00 Double	Open Jan-Dec Dinner 1830-1900 B&B + Eve. Meal from £31.00

Mrs Hannah S Crozier Balmore, Perth Road Birnam, by Dunkeld Perthshire PH8 0BH Tel: (Dunkeld) 0350 728885	HIGHLY COMMENDED 👑	1 Twin 1 Double	1 Pub. Bath/Show	B&B per person from £16.00 Double	Open Mar-Sep

Friendly welcome at family run house, with well furnished accommodation
in small village, just off A9. 12 miles (19kms) from Perth.

Mrs Flatley Heatherbank, Guthrie Villas, St Marys Rd Birnam, by Dunkeld Perthshire PH8 0BJ Tel: (Dunkeld) 0350 727413		1 Twin 2 Double	1 Pub. Bath/Show	B&B per person £12.00-£13.00 Double	Open Easter-Oct Dinner 1930-2030 B&B + Eve. Meal £21.00-£22.00

DUNKELD continued Joanne & Gordon Gerrie Byways, Perth Road Birnam, by Dunkeld Perthshire PH8 0DH Tel: (Dunkeld) 0350 727542	**Map 2** B1		1 Twin 2 Double	2 En Suite fac 1 Priv. NOT ensuite	B&B per person £16.00-£17.50 Double	Open Apr-mid Nov
The Tap Inn Birnam, by Dunkeld Perthshire PH8 0BQ Tel: (Dunkeld) 0350 727699			6 Twin	6 En Suite fac	B&B per person £25.00-£30.00 Single £15.00-£20.00 Double	Open Jan-Dec Dinner 1800-2000 B&B + Eve. Meal £20.00-£30.00
BY DUNKELD **Perthshire** Mrs Audrey Andrew Letter House, Loch of the Lowes by Dunkeld Perthshire PH8 0HH Tel: (Butterstone) 0350 724229	**Map 2** B1		1 Twin 2 Double	3 En Suite fac	B&B per person from £15.00 Double	Open Jan-Dec
Mrs Jo Andrew Letter Farm, Loch of the Lowes Dunkeld Perthshire PH8 0HH Tel: (Butterstone) 0350 724254		COMMENDED 👑 👑	1 Twin 1 Double 1 Family	3 En Suite fac	B&B per person from £15.00 Double	Open Jan-Dec
			Tastefully renovated farmhouse on working farm 1.5 miles from Scottish Wildfowl Trust Reserve. 3 miles (5kms) from Dunkeld.			
Mrs Jessie Mathieson The Coppers, Inchmagrannachan Dunkeld Perthshire PH8 0JS Tel: (Dunkeld) 0350 727372		COMMENDED Listed	1 Twin 1 Double	1 En Suite fac 1 Pub. Bath/Show	B&B per person £13.00-£17.00 Double	Open Apr-Oct Dinner from 1830 B&B + Eve. Meal £20.00-£24.00
			Typical Highland welcome and home cooking in this bungalow with one en suite bedroom. Access to fishing and golf.			
Mrs McLean Upper Woodinch Dalguise, by Dunkeld Perthshire PH8 0JU Tel: (Dunkeld) 0350 727442			1 Double 1 Family	2 En Suite fac	B&B per person from £20.00 Single £14.00-£16.00 Double	Open Jan-Dec Dinner 1700-2000 B&B + Eve. Meal £24.00-£26.00
Mrs Paterson The Orchard Dalguise, by Dunkeld Perthshire PH8 0JX Tel: (Dunkeld) 0350 727446		COMMENDED 👑 👑 👑	1 Twin 1 Double	2 En Suite fac	B&B per person £15.00-£17.50 Double	Open Jan-Dec Dinner 1800-2100 B&B + Eve. Meal £23.50-£26.00
			Set in over two acres, a detached bungalow in the heart of Beatrix Potter country. Scottish produce used wherever possible.			
DUNLOP **Ayrshire** Struther Farm Guest House 17 Newmill Road Dunlop Ayrshire KA3 4BA Tel: (Stewarton) 0560 484946	**Map 1** H6	APPROVED 👑	1 Twin 1 Double 2 Family	2 Pub. Bath/Show	B&B per person £15.00-£18.00 Single £15.00-£18.00 Double	Open Jan-Dec Dinner 1700-1930 B&B + Eve. Meal £28.00-£32.00
			Old Scottish farmhouse with large garden. Fresh seafood and meat in season. Only 17 miles (27kms) from Glasgow. Good base for touring.			

Name/Address	Map	Grading	Rooms	Bath	B&B Rate	Opening
Mrs W Burns Borland Hills Dunlop Ayrshire KA1 4BU Tel: (Stewarton) 0560 482978			2 Double	2 Pub. Bath/Show	B&B per person £12.50-£15.00 Double	Open Mar-Dec
DUNOON **Argyll** Mrs W Addison Dhailling Lodge, 155 Alexandra Parade Dunoon Argyll PA23 8AW Tel: (Dunoon) 0369 4004	Map 1 G5		1 Twin 1 Double 1 Family	1 Pub. Bath/Show	B&B per person from £14.00 Single from £13.00 Double	Open Jan-Dec
Mrs A Dowds Lismore, Clyde Street, Kirn Dunoon Argyll PA23 8DY Tel: (Dunoon) 0369 5994		COMMENDED	1 Twin 2 Double	1 En Suite fac 1 Pub. Bath/Show	B&B per person £13.00-£15.50 Single £13.00-£15.00 Double	Open Jan-Dec Dinner 1700-1730 B&B + Eve. Meal £19.00-£22.50

Friendly family home in quiet residential area, yet only a short distance from town centre and amenities. On main bus route.

Name/Address	Map	Grading	Rooms	Bath	B&B Rate	Opening
DUNS **Berwickshire** Simon & Tracey Ashby Broomhouse Mains Duns Berwickshire TD11 3PP Tel: (Duns) 0361 83665	Map 2 F5	HIGHLY COMMENDED	1 Twin 1 Double 1 Family	3 En Suite fac	B&B per person £17.00-£23.00 Double	Open Jan-Dec Dinner 1800-1900 B&B + Eve. Meal £28.00-£34.00

Relax in this recently renovated and refurbished farmhouse, set in peaceful surroundings, on 200 acre farm. Home cooking. Salmon and trout fishing.

St Albans
COMMENDED

CLOUDS, DUNS, BERWICKSHIRE TD11 3BB
Telephone: 0361 83285

Clouds is a lane parallel to and behind Newtown Street where police station is situated. Pleasant Georgian house with secluded south-facing garden. Magnificent view over small town to Cheviot Hills. Excellent breakfast in gracious surroundings. Private bathroom available. 3 minutes from town centre.
From £14 per person.

Name/Address	Map	Grading	Rooms	Bath	B&B Rate	Opening
Mrs Hannay St Albans, Clouds Duns Berwickshire TD11 3BB Tel: (Duns) 0361 83285		COMMENDED	1 Twin 1 Double	1 Priv. NOT ensuite 1 Pub. Bath/Show	B&B per person £13.50-£17.50 Double	Open Jan-Dec

Pleasant Georgian house with secluded south facing garden.
Magnificent view over small town to Cheviot Hills. Close to town centre.

Name/Address	Map	Grading	Rooms	Bath	B&B Rate	Opening
BY DUNS **Berwickshire** Mrs E Graham The Smithy, Cranshaws Duns Berwickshire TD11 3SG Tel: (Longformacus) 03617 277	Map 2 F5	COMMENDED Listed	1 Twin 1 Double	1 En Suite fac 1 Limited ensuite 2 Priv. NOT ensuite 2 Pub. Bath/Show	B&B per person £15.00 Single £15.00 Double	Open Mar-Dec Dinner 1800-2200 B&B + Eve. Meal £20.00

Modernised blacksmiths cottage on working croft with tea room.
1 mile (2kms) from Cranshaw village. 11 miles (18kms) from Duns on B6355.

DUNSYRE Lanarkshire Mrs Margaret Armstrong Dunsyre Mains Farm Dunsyre, Carnwath Lanarkshire ML11 8NQ Tel: (Dunsyre) 089981 251	Map 2 C6	COMMENDED ♛	1 Twin 1 Double 1 Family	2 Pub. Bath/Show	B&B per person £15.00 Single £14.00-£15.00 Double	Open Jan-Dec Dinner from 1900 B&B + Eve. Meal £22.00-£23.00

On working farm in quiet rural location near main routes to Edinburgh and Glasgow. Lovely scenery; ideal for walkers and families.

DUNURE, by Ayr Ayrshire Mrs M Wilcox Fisherton Farm Dunure Ayrshire KA7 4LF Tel: (Dunure) 029250 223	Map 1 G8	COMMENDED ♛	2 Twin	1 Pub. Bath/Show	B&B per person from £14.00 Single from £13.00 Double	Open Mar-Nov

Traditional stone-built farmhouse on working mixed farm, with extensive sea views to Arran. 5 miles (8kms) from Ayr.

DUNVEGAN Isle of Skye, Inverness-shire Mrs A E Gracie Silverdale, 14 Skinidin Dunvegan Isle of Skye, Inverness-shire IV55 8ZS Tel: (Dunvegan) 047022 251	Map 3 C9	COMMENDED ♛ ♛	1 Twin 1 Double 1 Family	1 En Suite fac 2 Pub. Bath/Show	B&B per person from £14.00 Double	Open Jan-Dec

Modern house with superb views over Loch Dunvegan. Decor and furnishings to a high standard. Acclaimed restaurant nearby.

Mrs MacDonald Herebost Dunvegan Isle of Skye, Inverness-shire IV55 8GZ Tel: (Dunvegan) 047022 255		COMMENDED ♛	1 Twin 2 Double	1 Pub. Bath/Show	B&B per person to £13.00 Double	Open Apr-Oct

Modern bungalow on working sheep farm situated just off the Dunvegan Road with views to the south. Supper in the lounge in the evening.

DURNESS Sutherland Lesley Smith Choraidh Croft, 94 Laid Loch Eribollside, by Altnaharra Lairg, Sutherland IV27 4UN Tel: (Durness) 0971 511235	Map 3 H3		1 Twin 1 Family	1 En Suite fac 1 Pub. Bath/Show	B&B per person from £12.00 Single £12.00-£13.00 Double	Open Easter-Oct Dinner 1700-2100 B&B + Eve. Meal to £20.00

DUROR OF APPIN Argyll Mrs F C Worthington Lagnaha Farm Duror of Appin Argyll PA38 4BS Tel: (Duror) 063174 207 Fax: 063174 207	Map 1 F1		1 Single 1 Double 1 Family	1 Pub. Bath/Show	B&B per person £12.50-£15.00 Single £12.50-£15.00 Double	Open Easter-October

EAGLESFIELD, by Lockerbie Dumfriesshire Helen Covello Lochaber Cottage, Eaglesfield Lockerbie Dumfriesshire DG11 3PF Tel: (Kirtlebridge) 0461 500546	Map 2 D9	COMMENDED ♛	1 Double 1 Family	1 Pub. Bath/Show	B&B per person £12.50 Single £12.50 Double	Open Jan-Dec

Detached bungalow in extensive grounds in small village, just off the A74. Ideal as a touring base.

Mrs B Crouch Kirtle House Kirtlebridge, by Lockerbie Dumfriesshire DG11 3LZ Tel: (Kirtlebridge) 0461 500221						
Mrs Fletcher Glengower Eaglesfield, by Lockerbie Dumfriesshire DG11 3LU Tel: (Kirtlebridge) 0461 500253			1 Single 1 Twin 2 Double			
Mrs Sherlock Cushathill Cottage Eaglesfield Dumfriesshire DG11 3JT Tel: (Kirtlebridge) 0461 500643 Fax: 0461 500643			1 Double 1 Family	1 Pub. Bath/Show	B&B p £14.00-£1 £14.00-£16.00	

EAGLESHAM
Renfrewshire — Map 1 H6

Mrs Anne Margetts Annecy, 60 Montgomery Street Eaglesham Renfrewshire G76 0AU Tel: (Eaglesham) 03553 2413	HIGHLY COMMENDED Listed	1 Single 1 Twin 1 Family	2 Pub. Bath/Show	B&B per person from £18.00 Single from £17.00 Double	Open Jan-Dec, exc Oct

In conservation village, within easy reach of Glasgow, and an ideal base for touring Ayrshire and the Clyde Valley.

EAST CALDER
West Lothian — Map 2 C5

Near EDINBURGH
OVERSHIEL FARMHOUSE, EAST CALDER
Tel: 0506 880 469
A LOVELY STONE-BUILT FARMHOUSE (6 MILES WEST OF EDINBURGH, 5 MILES FROM EDINBURGH AIRPORT). THE SPACIOUS BEDROOMS LOOK ONTO A LARGE, ATTRACTIVE GARDEN AND ACRES OF FARMLAND. THERE IS A RESIDENTS' LOUNGE WITH A REAL COAL FIRE.
GOLF, FISHING AND HORSE-RIDING AVAILABLE NEARBY.

Mrs Jan Dick Overshiel Farm East Calder West Lothian EH53 0HT Tel: (Mid Calder) 0506 880469	2 Twin 1 Double	2 En Suite fac 2 Pub. Bath/Show	B&B per person £20.00-£22.00 Single £16.00-£18.00 Double	Open Jan-Dec

EAST KILBRIDE
Lanarkshire — Map 2 A6

Mrs Hughes Ambleside Crookedshields Road Nerston, by East Kilbride Lanarkshire G74 4PE Tel: (East Kilbride) 03552 34589	3 Twin	1 Pub. Bath/Show	B&B per person from £17.00 Double	Open Jan-Dec

EAGLESFIELD, by Lockerbie—EAST KILBRIDE

...stone-built,
...t and
...ve to coastal
...arm welcome

...ly Commended

860 410

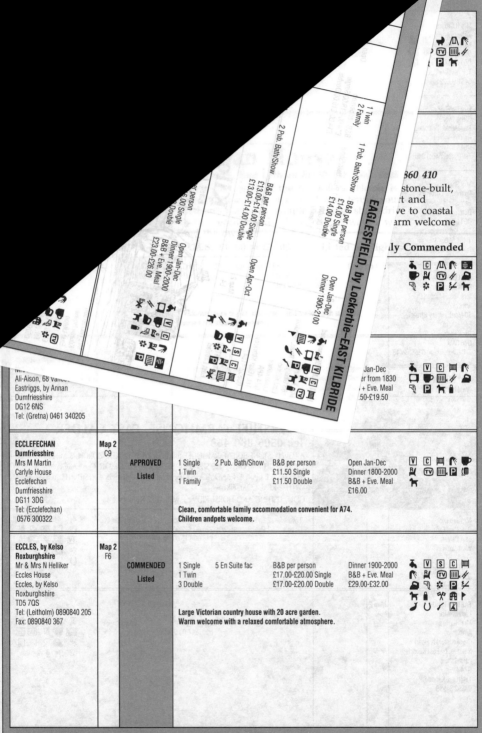

| | | | 2 Pub. Bath/Show | B&B per person
£13.00-£14.00 Single
£13.00-£14.00 Double | Open Apr-Oct |
| | | | | B&B per person
...00 Single
...Double | Open Jan-Dec
Dinner 1900-2000
B&B + Eve. Meal
£23.00-£26.00 |

Ali-Aison, 68 Van...
Eastriggs, by Annan
Dumfriesshire
DG12 6NS
Tel: (Gretna) 0461 340205

...Jan-Dec
...er from 1830
... + Eve. Meal
...50-£19.50

| **ECCLEFECHAN**
Dumfriesshire
Mrs M Martin
Carlyle House
Ecclefechan
Dumfriesshire
DG11 3DG
Tel: (Ecclefechan)
0576 300322 | Map 2
C9 | APPROVED
Listed | 1 Single
1 Twin
1 Family | 2 Pub. Bath/Show | B&B per person
£11.50 Single
£11.50 Double | Open Jan-Dec
Dinner 1800-2000
B&B + Eve. Meal
£16.00 |

Clean, comfortable family accommodation convenient for A74.
Children andpets welcome.

| **ECCLES, by Kelso**
Roxburghshire
Mr & Mrs N Helliker
Eccles House
Eccles, by Kelso
Roxburghshire
TD5 7QS
Tel: (Leitholm) 0890840 205
Fax: 0890840 367 | Map 2
F6 | COMMENDED
Listed | 1 Single
1 Twin
3 Double | 5 En Suite fac | B&B per person
£17.00-£20.00 Single
£17.00-£20.00 Double | Dinner 1900-2000
B&B + Eve. Meal
£29.00-£32.00 |

Large Victorian country house with 20 acre garden.
Warm welcome with a relaxed comfortable atmosphere.

EDAY Orkney Mrs Cockram Skaill Eday Orkney KW17 2AA Tel: (Eday) 08572 271 Fax: 08572 271	Map 5 C1	COMMENDED Listed	1 Twin 1 Double	2 Pub. Bath/Show	B&B per person £16.00-£17.50 Double	Open Jan-Mar, Jun-Dec Dinner 1900-2100 B&B + Eve. Meal £23.00-£24.50	V ⚓ ♨ TV ⊞ ⚡ 🍴 ♿ ❄ P ✕ 🛏 🚲
			Historic farmhouse comfortably furnished in Victorian style, ideal for birdwatching and walking in an unspoilt envirnoment.				

EDINBURGH Aaron Guest House 16 Hartington Gardens Edinburgh EH10 4LD Tel: 031 229 6459 Fax: 031 228 5807	Map 2 D5	COMMENDED Listed	2 Single 4 Twin 2 Double 2 Family	5 En Suite fac 1 Limited ensuite 2 Pub. Bath/Show	B&B per person £18.00-£19.00 Single £18.00-£25.00 Double	Open Jan-Dec	🏧 V S C ⊞ ⚓ ⊡ ⊞ ♨ ♨ TV ⊞ ⚡ ♿ ♨ ⚡ ✕ 🐕 ♿ ♨ ⚐ T
			Family run, in quiet residential area, yet close to the West end of city. Private parking. Many rooms have ensuite facilities.				
Abbeylodge Guest House 137 Drum Street Edinburgh EH17 8RJ Tel: 031 664 9548		COMMENDED 👑 👑 👑	1 Single 2 Twin 1 Double 1 Family	5 En Suite fac	B&B per person £16.00-£25.00 Single £16.00-£25.00 Double	Open Jan-Dec Dinner 1800-2100 B&B + Eve. Meal £26.00-£35.00	🏧 ♨ V S C ⊞ 🍴 ⚓ △ ⊡ ⚡ ⚡ ♨ TV ⊞ ⚡ 🍴 ✕ ♨ ❄ P ⚐ ✂ 🐕 🍴 SP ♨ 🔒 ♿
			New guest house in Edinburgh all on ground level. Close to city centre, A 1 and City Bypass. All rooms ensuite, Sky TV, telephone. Private Parking.				
Acorn Guest House 70 Pilrig Street Edinburgh EH6 5AS Tel: 031 554 2187		APPROVED 👑	1 Twin 1 Double 3 Family	2 Pub. Bath/Show	B&B per person £13.50-£15.50 Double	Open Jan-Dec	🏧 V S C ⚓ ⊡ 🍴 ♨ TV ⊞ ⚐
			Terraced house on bus route to and from city centre.				

ADAM GUEST HOUSE
2 HARTINGTON GARDENS, EDINBURGH EH10 4LD
Telephone: 031-229 8664   Fax: 031-228 5807

ADAM HOUSE is a family-run, non-smoking guest house situated in a quiet cul-de-sac only 15 minutes walk from the city centre. We are close to bus routes, shops, theatres and restaurants. Our bedrooms are bright and comfortable with colour television and hot drinks facilities.
We look forward to welcoming you.

Adam Guest House 2 Hartington Gardens Edinburgh EH10 4LD Tel: 031 229 8664 Fax: 031 228 5807		COMMENDED Listed	1 Single 1 Twin 1 Double 2 Family	1 En Suite fac 1 Priv. NOT ensuite 2 Pub. Bath/Show	B&B per person £16.00-£20.00 Single £16.00-£25.00 Double	Open Jan-Dec	🏧 S C ⊞ ⚓ ⊡ 🍴 ⊞ ⚓ ♨ ⚐ ✕ 🐕 ♨ 🔒 ♨ T
			Family run Victorian terraced house in quiet cul de sac. Easy access to city centre by bus or 15 minute walk. Unrestricted parking. Non smoking.				
A-Haven in Edinburgh 180 Ferry Road Edinburgh EH6 4NS Tel: 031 554 6559 Fax: 031 554 5252		COMMENDED 👑 👑 👑	2 Single 2 Twin 2 Double 4 Family Suite avail.	7 En Suite fac 2 Pub. Bath/Show	B&B per person £20.00-£35.00 Single £16.00-£30.00 Double	Open Jan-Dec Dinner 1830-1930 B&B + Eve. Meal £30.00-£47.00	🏧 V S C ⊞ 🍴 △ ⚓ ♨ ⊡ ⚡ ♨ ♨ P ⚐ 🍴 SP ✕ 🔒 ❄ T 🎻
			Family run city centre guest house with private parking and main bus routes. Scottish welcome and hospitality.				

EDINBURGH continued	Map 2 D5		

AIRLIE GUEST HOUSE
29 MINTO STREET, EDINBURGH EH9 1SB
Tel: 031-667 3562 Fax: 031-662 1399

Peter and Fiona Flynn look forward to welcoming you to their home. Situated 1.5 miles from Princes Street, The Airlie is in an area well serviced by buses. All bedrooms are comfortably furnished, have colour televisions, tea/coffee making facilities and are centrally heated. Private facilities and car parking available.

Airlie Guest House 29 Minto Street Edinburgh EH9 1SB Tel: 031 667 3562 Fax: 031 662 1399	COMMENDED 👑 👑	2 Single 3 Twin 5 Double 2 Family	7 En Suite fac 1 Priv. NOT ensuite 2 Pub. Bath/Show	B&B per person £18.00-£25.00 Single £16.00-£25.00 Double	Open Jan-Dec
		Formerly two terraced houses, some rooms featuring plaster cornicing. **On bus route with easy access to city centre.**			
Akbar Guest House 25 East Hermitage Place Edinburgh EH6 8AD Tel: 031 554 4709		1 Single 3 Twin 1 Double	3 Pub. Bath/Show	B&B per person £14.00-£20.00 Single £14.00-£20.00 Double	Open Jan-Oct Dinner 1800-2000 B&B + Eve. Meal £18.00-£24.00
Amaragua Guest House 10 Kilmaurs Terrace Edinburgh EH16 5DR Tel: 031 667 6775	APPROVED 👑 👑	2 Single 2 Twin 1 Double 1 Family	3 En Suite fac 2 Pub. Bath/Show	B&B per person £16.00-£18.00 Single £17.00-£20.00 Double	Open Jan-Dec
		Victorian terraced house in residential area, close to Prestonfield Golf Course, **Holyrood Park and Commonwealth Pool. Nearby bus routes to centre.**			
Angusbeag Guest House 5 Windsor Street Edinburgh EH7 5LA Tel: 031 556 1905		1 Double 3 Family	1 En Suite fac 2 Limited ensuite 1 Pub. Bath/Show	B&B per person £16.50-£20.00 Single £15.00-£19.50 Double	Open Jan-Dec
Annie Laurie Guest House 3 East Hermitage Place Leith Links Edinburgh EH6 8AA Tel: 031 554 3065		1 Single 1 Twin 1 Double	1 Priv. NOT ensuite 2 Pub. Bath/Show	B&B per person £12.00-£16.00 Single £14.00-£16.00 Double	Open Jan-Dec Dinner 1730-1930 B&B + Eve. Meal £17.00-£21.00
Ardblair Guest House 1 Duddingston Crescent Milton Road Edinburgh EH15 3AS Tel: 031 669 2384	COMMENDED 👑	1 Double 2 Family	2 Pub. Bath/Show	B&B per person £15.00-£18.00 Single £14.00-£17.00 Double	Open Jan-Dec Dinner 1800-2000 B&B + Eve. Meal £21.00-£23.00
		Conveniently placed on main bus route to city centre. Private parking area.			
Ardenlee Guest House 9 Eyre Place Edinburgh EH3 5ES Tel: 031 556 2838	APPROVED Listed	1 Single 2 Twin 2 Double 3 Family	2 En Suite fac 2 Pub. Bath/Show	B&B per person £17.00-£21.00 Single £16.00-£20.00 Double	Open Jan-Dec
		Terraced house on bus routes to city centre which is about 0.75 miles **(1.5kms) away.**			

| Ardmor Guest House
74 Pilrig Street
Edinburgh
EH6 5AS
Tel: 031 554 4944 | COMMENDED
♕ | 2 Twin
1 Double
1 Family | 2 Limited ensuite
2 Pub. Bath/Show | B&B per person
£15.00-£17.00 Single
£15.00-£17.00 Double | Open Jan-Dec | 🛠 Ⓥ Ⓢ Ⓒ 🐾
ℝ 🍽 🐾 📺 🏛 |

Stone built house in residential area overlooking Pilrig Park 0.5 miles (1km) from city centre, with convenient bus routes.

Edinburgh
Ashdene House
23 FOUNTAINHALL ROAD
EDINBURGH EH9 2LN
Tel: 031-667 6026

SHORT BREAK or LONGER STAY, make ASHDENE HOUSE your base. Situated in high amenity, quiet conservation area, typical Victorian town house with many original features preserved. ASHDENE HOUSE has been modernised to a high standard and all centrally heated bedrooms are equipped with:

Private facilities, colour TV, direct-dial telephone, hairdryer, beverage making, warmth, comfort and privacy.

TARIFF (per person): Min £18.00, Max £22.00 including breakfast, individually cooked with fresh ingredients.

SPECIAL BREAKS: November to Easter. Unrestricted parking. Public transport (3-minute walk). City centre 10-minute ride.

AA QQQ RAC "Acclaimed" STB Highly Commended

| Ashdene House
23 Fountainhall Road
Edinburgh
EH9 2LN
Tel: 031 667 6026 | HIGHLY
COMMENDED
♕ ♕ | 1 Twin
2 Double
2 Family | 4 En Suite fac
1 Priv. NOT ensuite
1 Pub. Bath/Show | B&B per person
£18.00-£22.00 Double | Open Jan-Dec | 🛠 Ⓥ Ⓢ Ⓒ 🐾
ℝ ☎ 🖥 🍽 🐾
🏛 🛏 🐾 🅿 ✂
SP 🐾 Ⓣ |

Edwardian town house retaining many features, in quiet residential Conservation area. Convenient for bus route to city centre (10 minutes).

| Ashgrove House
12 Osborne Terrace
Edinburgh
EH12 5HG
Tel: 031 337 5014
Fax: 031 313 5043 | Award
Pending | 3 Single
2 Twin
2 Double
2 Family | 6 En Suite fac
2 Pub. Bath/Show | B&B per person
£20.00-£25.00 Single
£20.00-£28.00 Double | Open Jan-Dec
Dinner 1800-2000 | 🛠 Ⓥ Ⓢ Ⓒ 🏛
🐾 🖥 🖨 🍽 🐾
🐾 📺 🏛 🛏 🐾
🅿 📱 🐾 🈺 |

| Ashlyn Guest House
42 Inverleith Row
Edinburgh
EH3 5PY
Tel: 031 552 2954 | COMMENDED
♕ ♕ ♕ | 2 Single
2 Twin
3 Double
1 Family | 5 En Suite fac
1 Priv. NOT ensuite
3 Pub. Bath/Show | B&B per person
£20.00-£25.00 Single
£18.00-£25.00 Double
B&B + Eve. Meal
£36.00-£43.00 | Open Jan-Dec
Dinner 1730-1900 | 🛠 Ⓥ Ⓢ Ⓒ ℝ
🐾 🖥 🛏 🐾 📺
🏛 🛏 🐾 🐾 📱
🈺 🐾 🐾 🏠 |

Georgian listed building in residential area of city. On main bus route to centre with street parking.

AVERON GUEST HOUSE
44 Gilmore Place, Central Edinburgh EH3 9NQ

★ Excellent accommodation with traditional Scottish Breakfast.
★ All credit cards accepted.
★ Only 10 minutes walk to Princes Street and Castle.

Tel: 031-229 9932   CAR PARK

| Averon Guest House
44 Gilmore Place
Edinburgh
EH3 9NQ
Tel: 031 229 9932 | Award
Pending | 1 Single
4 Twin
2 Double
3 Family | 3 Pub. Bath/Show | B&B per person
£16.00-£22.00 Single
£12.00-£22.00 Double | Open Jan-Dec | Ⓥ Ⓢ Ⓒ ℝ 🖥
🍽 🛏 🏛 🐾 🐾
🅿 📱 🐾 SP 🐾
🐾 🈺 Ⓣ 🏠 |

Details of Grading and Classification are on page vi. · Key to symbols is on back flap. ·

	Map 2 D5						
EDINBURGH continued							
Balmoral Guest House 32 Pilrig Street Edinburgh EH6 5AL Tel: 031 554 1857	COMMENDED ♔	1 Single 3 Twin 1 Double 2 Family	2 Pub. Bath/Show	B&B per person £15.00-£17.00 Single £14.50-£17.00 Double	Open Jan-Dec	
Situated in residential area of city, convenient for all amenities. On main bus route and with easy access to city centre.						
Balquhidder Guest House 94 Pilrig Street Edinburgh EH6 5AY Tel: 031 554 3377	COMMENDED ♔ ♔	1 Single 2 Twin 2 Double 1 Family	5 En Suite fac 1 Limited ensuite 1 Pub. Bath/Show	B&B per person £15.00-£25.00 Single £15.00-£25.00 Double	Open Jan-Dec	
Detached house in its own grounds overlooking public park and on bus routes to the city centre.						
Barrosa Guest House 21 Pilrig Street Edinburgh EH6 5AN Tel: 031 554 3700		1 Twin 2 Double 3 Family	4 En Suite fac 3 Pub. Bath/Show	B&B per person £16.00-£26.00 Double	Open Jan-Dec	
Beechcroft Guest House 46 Murrayfield Avenue Edinburgh EH12 6AY Tel: 031 337 1081		1 Single 3 Twin 3 Double 3 Family	5 En Suite fac 2 Pub. Bath/Show	B&B per person £18.00-£25.00 Single £12.00-£20.00 Double	Open Jan-Dec	

Belford Guest House
13 BLACKET AVENUE · EDINBURGH EH9 1RR
Telephone: 031-667 2422

Small and friendly family run guest house in a quiet tree-lined avenue 1 mile from the city centre. Buses run from either end of the avenue to all attractions in the city.

Private parking.

Belford House 13 Blacket Avenue Edinburgh EH9 1RR Tel: 031 667 2422		3 Twin 4 Family	2 Pub. Bath/Show	B&B per person £20.00-£22.00 Single £17.00-£20.00 Double	Open Jan-Dec	
Bellrock Guest House 105 Ferry Road Edinburgh EH6 4ET Tel: 031 554 2604		1 Single 1 Twin 2 Double 3 Family	1 Limited ensuite 2 Pub. Bath/Show	B&B per person £15.00-£20.00 Single £15.00-£20.00 Double	Open Jan-Dec	

TELEPHONE DIALLING CODES

Many telephone dialling codes have changed this year. If you experience difficulty in connecting a call, please call Directory Enquiries — **192** — where someone will issue the correct number. Please note: a charge will be placed for this service when using a private telephone

BONNINGTON GUEST HOUSE

202 FERRY ROAD, EDINBURGH EH6 4NW
Telephone: 031-554 7610

A comfortable early Victorian house (built 1840), personally run,
where a friendly and warm welcome awaits guests.
Situated in residential area of town on main bus routes.
Private car parking.

For further details contact Eileen and David Watt, Proprietors.

Bonnington Guest House 202 Ferry Road Edinburgh EH6 4NW Tel: 031 554 7610	COMMENDED 👑 👑	1 Twin 2 Double 3 Family	2 En Suite fac 2 Pub. Bath/Show	B&B per person £19.00-£26.00 Double	Open Jan-Dec
		Early Victorian Listed building with private parking on the north side of the city; convenient bus routes to centre.			
Brig O'Doon Guest House 262 Ferry Road Edinburgh EH5 3AN Tel: 031 552 3953	COMMENDED Listed	3 Twin 1 Double 2 Family	3 Pub. Bath/Show	B&B per person £15.00-£18.00 Double	Open Jan-Dec
		Stone built terraced house on North side of city centre, overlooking playing fields with fine views to castle. Bus route to city centre.			
Bruntsfield Guest House 55 Leamington Terrace Edinburgh EH10 4JS Tel: 031 228 6458 Fax: 031 228 6458	COMMENDED Listed	2 Single 2 Twin 2 Double 1 Family	1 En Suite fac 2 Pub. Bath/Show	B&B per person £15.00-£20.00 Single £15.00-£24.00 Double	Open Jan-Dec
		Situated in residential area close to main bus route to city centre. No residents lounge but TV in all bedrooms.			

BUCHANAN GUEST HOUSE

97 Joppa Road, Edinburgh EH15 2HB
Telephone: 031-657 4117

A warm welcome is extended to all visitors
by Margaret and Stewart Buchanan at their
personally run Victorian guest house with
panoramic view overlooking Firth of Forth.
The bedrooms are well equipped with every
comfort in mind and full Scottish breakfast is
provided. Conveniently located. Frequent bus
service to city centre and en-route to main
golf courses. Businessmen welcome. Free
unrestricted parking.

Buchanan Guest House 97 Joppa Road Edinburgh EH15 2HB Tel: 031 657 4117	COMMENDED 👑 👑	2 Twin 1 Double 1 Family	1 En Suite fac 1 Pub. Bath/Show	B&B per person £13.50-£20.00 Double	Open Jan-Dec
		Comfortable personally run guest house, on major bus route to city centre. Unrestricted parking.			

Details of Grading and Classification are on page vi. | **Key to symbols is on back flap.** |

EDINBURGH continued Map 2 D5

Cameron Toll Guest House

299 Dalkeith Road
Edinburgh EH16 5JX   Tel: 031-667 2950

A friendly, family-run guest house with single, double, twin and family rooms, all with private/en-suite shower and toilet. Colour TV and tea/coffee facilities in each bedroom. Full Scottish Breakfast provided. Evening meals, picnics and special diets by arrangement. Spacious guests' lounge. Private parking, frequent bus services, 10 mins. from city centre. Close to Commonwealth Pool and University. Ideal for exploring city and surrounding countryside. We will be pleased to help arrange activities, local tours and bagpiping from our resident piper.

Cameron Toll Guest House 299 Dalkeith Road Edinburgh EH16 5JX Tel: 031 667 2950	COMMENDED ♕ ♕ ♕	2 Single 2 Twin 2 Double 2 Family	7 En Suite fac 1 Priv. NOT ensuite	B&B per person £20.00-£30.00 Single £16.00-£28.00 Double	Open Jan-Dec Dinner 1800-1900 B&B + Eve. Meal £23.00-£37.00

Family run guest house with some private parking. Conveniently located on A7 with frequent bus service to city centre. Close to Commonwealth Pool.

Camus House 4 Seaview Terrace, Joppa Edinburgh EH15 2HD Tel: 031 657 2003	COMMENDED Listed	1 Twin 2 Double	1 Priv. NOT ensuite 2 Pub. Bath/Show	B&B per person £14.00-£20.00 Single £14.00-£20.00 Double	Open Jan-Dec

Late Victorian terraced house with fine sea views. Relaxed and comfortable atmosphere; easy access to the city.

Castle Park Guest House 75 Gilmore Place Edinburgh EH3 9NU Tel: 031 229 1215	Award Pending	1 Single 2 Twin 3 Double 1 Family	2 En Suite fac 2 Limited ensuite 2 Pub. Bath/Show	B&B per person £13.50-£16.00 Single £12.50-£16.00 Double	Open Jan-Dec Dinner 1800-1900

Chalumna Guest House 5 Granville Terrace Edinburgh EH10 4PQ Tel: 031 229 2086	APPROVED ♕	1 Single 2 Twin 2 Double 1 Family	1 Limited ensuite 2 Pub. Bath/Show	B&B per person £18.00-£20.00 Single £15.00-£20.00 Double	Open Jan-Dec

Family run guest house in quiet residential area, close to Kings Theatre and within easy reach of Princes Street.

Classic Guest House 50 Mayfield Road Edinburgh EH9 2NH Tel: 031 667 5847	HIGHLY COMMENDED ♕	1 Single 1 Twin 1 Double 1 Family	3 En Suite fac 1 Priv. NOT ensuite 1 Pub. Bath/Show	B&B per person £15.00-£25.00 Single £15.00-£25.00 Double	Open Jan-Dec Dinner 1800-1900 B&B + Eve. Meal £25.00-£35.00

Friendly welcome at this family home, recently refurbished to a high standard. Short bus ride from city centre. Non smoking.

Claymore Guest House 68 Pilrig Street Edinburgh EH6 5AS Tel: 031 554 2500	COMMENDED ♕ ♕	2 Twin 2 Double 2 Family	3 En Suite fac 1 Priv. NOT ensuite 1 Pub. Bath/Show	B&B per person £15.00-£22.50 Double	Open Jan-Dec

Red sandstone Victorian terraced villa, a former manse, situated close to the city centre and on the main bus routes.

| Crioch Guest House
23 East Hermitage Place
Edinburgh
EH68AO
Tel: 031 554 5494 | | 2 Single
3 Twin
1 Family | 2 Pub. Bath/Show | B&B per person
£13.00-£20.00 Single
£13.00-£20.00 Double | Open Jan-Dec | |

Crion Guest House

33 MINTO STREET, EDINBURGH EH9 2BT
Tel: 031-667 2708   Fax: 031-662 1946

A warm and friendly welcome awaits you at the family-run guest house. Fully refurbished with your comfort in mind, offering outstanding Bed & Breakfast value. 3 en-suite rooms.

Conveniently situated within 1½ miles of the City Centre on an excellent bus route. The ideal base to explore Edinburgh's many tourist attractions and visitors centres, i.e. the Castle, Museums and Art Galleries etc. There are also several top-class golf courses in the surrounding area. Near University and Commonwealth Pool.

For enquiries send s.a.e. or telephone.

| Crion Guest House
33 Minto Street
Edinburgh
EH9 2BT
Tel: 031 667 2708
Fax: 031 662 1946 | COMMENDED
👑 👑 | 1 Single
2 Twin
2 Double
1 Family | 3 En Suite fac
3 Pub. Bath/Show | B&B per person
£17.00-£20.00 Single
£14.00-£25.00 Double | Open Jan-Dec | |
| **Refurbished, friendly family run guest house, close to city centre.** | | | | | | |

| Cruachan Guest House
53 Gilmore Place
Edinburgh
EH3 9NT
Tel: 031 229 6219
Fax: 031 229 6219 | APPROVED
Listed | 1 Single
1 Twin
1 Double
2 Family | 1 Pub. Bath/Show | B&B per person
£16.00-£21.00 Single
£14.00-£19.00 Double | Open Jan-Dec | |
| **Comfortable family run accommodation close to city centre and major bus routes.** | | | | | | |

| Daisy Park Guest House
41 Abercorn Terrace, Joppa
Edinburgh
EH15 2DG
Tel: 031 669 2503 | COMMENDED
👑 👑 | 1 Single
2 Twin
1 Double
2 Family | 3 Pub. Bath/Show | B&B per person
£16.00-£21.00 Single
£15.00-£21.00 Double | Open Jan-Dec | |
| **Family run small guest house with spacious rooms on bus route for city centre. 100 yards from beach. Vegetarians welcome.** | | | | | | |

| Dalwin Lodge Guest House
& Restaurant
75 Mayfield Road
Edinburgh
EH9 3AA
Tel: 031 667 2294 | COMMENDED
👑 | 2 Single
1 Twin
1 Double
1 Family | 2 Pub. Bath/Show | B&B per person
£14.00-£17.00 Single
£14.00-£17.00 Double | Open Jan-Dec
Dinner 1800-2000 | |
| **Stone terraced house, c100 years old, within walking distance of Observatory and Arthur's Seat, with an inhouse licensed restaurant.** | | | | | | |

| Dargil Guest House
16 Mayfield Gardens
Edinburgh
EH9 2BZ
Tel: 031 667 6177 | | 2 Twin
1 Double
1 Family | 2 En Suite fac
2 Pub. Bath/Show | B&B per person
£16.00-£22.00 Single
£10.00-£22.00 Double | Open Jan-Dec | |

EDINBURGH continued	Map 2 D5						
Dene Guest House 7 Eyre Place Edinburgh EH3 5ES Tel: 031 556 2700	APPROVED Listed	2 Single 3 Twin 2 Family	2 En Suite fac 2 Pub. Bath/Show	B&B per person £18.00-£22.00 Single £17.00-£23.00 Double	Open Jan-Dec		

Family run, centrally located guest house, close to Botanic Gardens.

DICKIE GUEST HOUSE "No 22"
22 EAST CLAREMONT ST., EDINBURGH EH7 4JP
Tel: 031-556 4032   Fax: 031-556 9739
City centre Victorian terraced guest house on cobbled street only 15 minutes walk from Princes Street. Four very comfortable and well-equipped bedrooms (2 en-suite). Excellent breakfast choice including Scottish, vegetarian and fish dishes.
Eileen and John Dickie look forward to welcoming you to our family home.

Dickie Guest House No. 22, East Claremont Street Edinburgh EH7 4JP Tel: 031 556 4032 Fax: 031 556 9739	COMMENDED 👑 👑	1 Single 1 Twin 1 Double 1 Family	2 En Suite fac 1 Pub. Bath/Show	B&B per person £19.00-£22.00 Single £18.00-£25.00 Double	Open Jan-Dec	

Small, friendly and family run; a Victorian town house in a cobbled street only 15 minutes walk from Princes Street. Scottish breakfasts a speciality

Dukes of Windsor Street 17 Windsor Street Edinburgh EH7 5LA Tel: 031 556 6046 Fax: 031 556 6046		1 Single 1 Twin 5 Double 1 Family	· 10 En Suite fac	B&B per person £25.00-£45.00 Single £20.00-£35.00 Double	Open Jan-Dec	

Dunedin Guest House
8 PRIESTFIELD ROAD, EDINBURGH EH16 5HH
Telephone: 031-668 1949
Friendly, family-run guest house on south side of Edinburgh (A7) 10 minutes bus journey to city centre. All rooms with private facilities; one suitable for wheelchair access, roll-in shower.
Full breakfast.
Convenient for University, Holyrood and Commonwealth Pool.

Dunedin Guest House 8 Priestfield Road Edinburgh EH16 5HH Tel: 031 668 1949	Award Pending	1 Single 2 Twin 2 Double 1 Family	5 En Suite fac 1 Priv. NOT ensuite 1 Pub. Bath/Show	B&B per person £16.00-£18.00 Single £15.00-£20.00 Double	Open Jan-Dec		

Edinburgh Thistle Guest House 10 East Hermitage Place Leith Links Edinburgh EH6 8AA Tel: 031 554 8457/5864		1 Twin 1 Double 3 Family	1 En Suite fac 2 Pub. Bath/Show	B&B per person £15.00-£18.00 Single £13.00-£16.00 Double	Open Jan-Dec Dinner 1800-1930 B&B + Eve. Meal £17.00-£20.00		

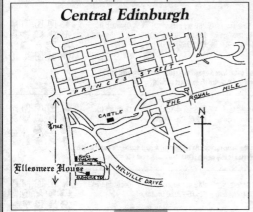

Central Edinburgh

ELLESMERE HOUSE

**11 Glengyle Terrace,
Edinburgh EH3 9LN
Tel: 031-229 4823   Fax: 031-229 5285**

Central location overlooking The Meadows area within easy walking distance to most places of interest. Theatre and various good restaurants situated very nearby. All rooms are decorated and furnished to a very high standard and are equipped with every comfort in mind. Most rooms are en-suite and there is a four-poster bed available. Breakfast menu including full Scottish Breakfast.

Personally run by Celia and Tommy Leishman who extend a very warm welcome to all of their guests.

Ellesmere Guest House	HIGHLY COMMENDED ❧ ❧	1 Single 4 En Suite fac	B&B per person	Open Jan-Dec	
11 Glengyle Terrace		2 Twin 2 Pub. Bath/Show	£17.00-£20.00 Single		
Edinburgh		1 Double	£17.00-£28.00 Double		
EH3 9LN		2 Family			
Tel: 031 229 4823					
Fax: 031 229 5285		**Terraced house overlooking the Meadows. Side street location but near Kings Theatre and bus routes to city centre.**			

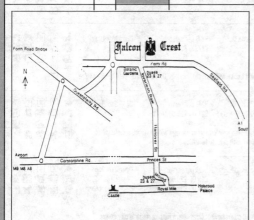

Falcon Crest

**70 South Trinity Road, Edinburgh EH5 3NX
Telephone: 031-552 5294**

A family run guest house in a quiet residential area on the north side of the city. Situated between the Botanic Gardens and Granton Marina. Well served by buses — only 10 minutes from Princes Street. Good road links. All bedrooms have washhand basins, shaver points, TVs and tea/coffee making facilities. Full central heating, 3-course evening meals.

PRICES FROM £12 B&B.

For further details contact Stuart and Kathryn Clark, Proprietors.

Falcon Crest Guest House	APPROVED ❧	1 Single 2 Pub. Bath/Show	B&B per person	Open Jan-Dec	
70 South Trinity Road		1 Twin	£12.00-£20.00 Single	Dinner 1730-1900	
Edinburgh		1 Double	£11.00-£18.00 Double	B&B + Eve. Meal	
EH5 3NX		2 Family		£16.00-£26.00	
Tel: 031 552 5294					
		Victorian terraced family home in attractive residential area, near main bus route to city centre.			

Fountainhall Guest House	APPROVED ❧	1 Single 3 Pub. Bath/Show	B&B per person	Open Jan-Dec	
40 Fountainhall Road		2 Twin	£16.00-£19.00 Single		
Edinburgh		1 Double	£16.00-£19.00 Double		
EH9 2LW		3 Family			
Tel: 031 667 2544					
		Victorian house in quiet residential area, 2 miles (3 kms) from City Centre, with public transport nearby.			

EDINBURGH continued	Map 2 D5						
Galloway Guest House 22 Dean Park Crescent Edinburgh EH4 1PH Tel: 031 332 3672	COMMENDED ✧✧✧		1 Single 3 Twin 3 Double 3 Family	6 En Suite fac 2 Pub. Bath/Show	B&B per person £22.00-£40.00 Single £17.00-£25.00 Double	Open Jan-Dec	
			Friendly, family run guest house beautifully restored and situated in a residential area of the city centre. Free street parking.				
Gifford Guest House 103 Dalkeith Road Edinburgh EH16 5AJ Tel: 031 667 4688	COMMENDED ✧✧		3 Twin 1 Double 2 Family	3 En Suite fac 2 Limited ensuite 2 Pub. Bath/Show	B&B per person £13.00-£26.00 Double	Open Jan-Dec	
			Situated on one of the main routes into Edinburgh. A well appointed guest house with nearby bus service to city centre. Commonwealth pool 100 metres.				
Gil Dun Guest House 9 Spence Street Edinburgh EH16 5AG Tel: 031 667 1368	APPROVED ✧		1 Twin 1 Double 4 Family	2 En Suite fac 3 Pub. Bath/Show	B&B per person £15.00-£20.00 Double	Open Jan-Dec	
			Family guest house situated in cul de sac with private parking. Close to Commonwealth Pool and bus route to city centre.				
Gilmore Guest House 51 Gilmore Place Edinburgh EH3 9NT Tel: 031 229 5008			1 Single 1 Twin 1 Double 3 Family	1 Limited ensuite 2 Pub. Bath/Show	B&B per person £12.00-£20.00 Single £12.00-£18.00 Double	Open Jan-Dec	
Glenalmond Guest House 25 Mayfield Gardens Edinburgh EH9 2BX Tel: 031 668 2392	COMMENDED ✧✧		1 Twin 2 Double 2 Family	5 En Suite fac	B&B per person £17.00-£25.00 Double	Open Mar-Oct	
			Personally run guest house with private parking. On main bus route to city centre.				
Glenerne Guest House 4 Hampton Terrace Edinburgh EH12 5JD Tel: 031 337 1210	COMMENDED ✧✧		1 Twin 2 Double	2 En Suite fac 1 Priv. NOT ensuite	B&B per person £21.00-£25.00 Double	Open Jan-Dec	
			Comfortable family home with off street parking within walking distance of city centre. All rooms with private facilities.				
Glenesk Guest House 39 Liberton Brae Edinburgh EH16 6AG Tel: 031 664 1529 Fax: 031 664 1529	APPROVED Listed		2 Twin 1 Double 1 Family	1 Pub. Bath/Show	B&B per person £15.00-£20.00 Single £13.00-£18.00 Double	Open Jan-Dec Dinner 1800-2000 B&B + Eve. Meal £18.50-£20.50	
			Personally run, small guest house. Convenient for bus route to city centre. Limited car parking available.				

Use the Scottish Tourist Board's Quality Commendations to select the holiday accommodation which is right for you!

VAT is shown at 17.5%: changes in this rate may affect prices. Prices shown are for guidance only. Please send SAE with each enquiry.

GLENORCHY GUEST HOUSE
22 GLENORCHY TERRACE, EDINBURGH EH9 2DH
Telephone: 031-667 5708

Family hotel, 10 minutes from the city centre (just off the main A7 road from the South) catering for B&B and evening meals. Tea-making facilities, colour TV in all rooms, central heating, lounge. Quiet location. Unrestricted parking. Children welcome. 2 Crowns APPROVED

| Glenorchy 22 Glenorchy Terrace Edinburgh EH9 2DH Tel: 031 667 5708 | APPROVED | 1 Single 2 Twin 4 Double 2 Family | 3 En Suite fac 6 Limited ensuite 1 Pub. Bath/Show | B&B per person £18.00-£20.00 Single £20.00-£22.00 Double | Open Jan-Dec Dinner from 1800 B&B + Eve. Meal £28.50-£30.50 | |

Privately owned Victorian house situated in quiet residential area, convenient for bus routes to city centre. Unrestricted parking.

| Hamilton House Guest House 12 Moston Terrace Edinburgh EH9 2DE Tel: 031 667 2540 | COMMENDED | 2 Single 1 Twin 1 Double 2 Family | 1 En Suite fac 1 Limited ensuite 2 Pub. Bath/Show | B&B per person £16.00-£18.00 Single £16.00-£19.00 Double | Open Jan-Dec Dinner 1800-1830 B&B + Eve. Meal £25.00-£28.00 | |

Elegant Victorian villa retaining many original features, in quiet residential area convenient for city centre. One room with private facilities.

HAVRIST
Tel: 031-657 3160
Fax: 031-657 3160
33 STRAITON PLACE, EDINBURGH EH15 2BH

Ideally situated on Portobello beach with excellent outlook to the Firth of Forth. Swimming pool, restaurants and all the fun of the fair nearby, or for the less agile, a stroll along the promenade.
Only 20 minutes by bus (no's 15, 26, 85, 66 or 129) from city centre. Close to A1, off street parking.
B&B £12−£20 per person per night *Contact* **Mr and Mrs Sadol**

| The Havrist Guest House 33 Straiton Pl, The Promenade, Portobello Edinburgh EH15 2BH Tel: 031 657 3160 Fax: 031 657 3160 | Award Pending | 2 Single 1 Twin 2 Double 2 Family | 2 Pub. Bath/Show | B&B per person £12.00-£18.00 Single £10.00-£16.00 Double | Open Jan-Dec | |

| Heatherlea Guest House Mayfield Gardens Edinburgh EH9 2AX Tel: 031 667 3958 | | 1 Single 3 Twin 3 Double 3 Family | 4 En Suite fac 2 Pub. Bath/Show | B&B per person £18.00-£25.00 Single £15.00-£20.00 Double | Open Jan-Dec | |

| Hermitage Guest House 16 East Hermitage Place Leith Links Edinburgh EH6 8AB Tel: 031 555 4868 | Award Pending | 2 Twin 2 Double 1 Family | 2 Pub. Bath/Show | B&B per person £14.00-£20.00 Double | Open Jan-Dec | |

| Highfield Guest House 83 Mayfield Road Edinburgh EH9 3AE Tel: 031 667 8717 | COMMENDED | 1 Single 1 Twin 2 Double 1 Family | 2 Pub. Bath/Show | B&B per person £13.00-£18.00 Single £13.00-£18.00 Double | Open Jan-Dec | |

Stone built Victorian house offering friendly and comfortable accommodation for non-smokers. 10 minutes from city centre on bus routes 40 and 42.

EDINBURGH continued	Map 2 D5		

HIGHLAND PARK GUEST HOUSE

16 Kilmaurs Terrace, Edinburgh EH16 5DR   Tel: 031-667 9204

Comfortable guest house situated in quiet street off Dalkeith Road (A7). Unrestricted street parking. Frequent bus service to city centre. Near Holyrood Park, University and Royal College of Surgeons. Local amenities include restaurant, swimming pool and launderette.

All rooms TV, tea/coffee, central heating, H&C.

Highland Park Guest House 16 Kilmaurs Terrace Edinburgh EH16 5DR Tel: 031 667 9204	COMMENDED ♛	1 Single 2 Twin 2 Family	2 Pub. Bath/Show	B&B per person £14.00-£18.00 Single £13.00-£17.00 Double	Open Jan-Dec

Victorian stone built house retaining many original features in quiet residential area 1.5 miles (3kms) from city centre. On main bus routes.

Hillview 22 Hillview Queensferry Road, Blackhall Edinburgh EH4 2AF Tel: 031 343 2969	HIGHLY COMMENDED ♛ ♛	1 Double 1 Family	1 En Suite fac 1 Priv. NOT ensuite	B&B per person £16.00-£22.00 Double	Open Jan-Dec

Elegant Edwardian terraced family home with easy access to the city centre.

EDINBURGH
Hopetoun Guest House

15 Mayfield Road, Edinburgh EH9 2NG   031-667 7691

Stone-built Victorian terraced house on bus route to City Centre. A pleasant 25-minute walk through quiet suburban streets takes you to the Royal Mile and Castle. Parking. TV, Central Heating, Tea/Coffee-making facilities.

COMPLETELY NON-SMOKING

Prices from £14-£18 including breakfast

Hopetoun Guest House 15 Mayfield Road Edinburgh EH9 2NG Tel: 031 667 7691	COMMENDED ♛	1 Double 2 Family	2 Pub. Bath/Show	B&B per person £14.00-£18.00 Double	Open Jan-Dec

Completely non-smoking, small, friendly guest house on the south side of the city, 1.5 miles (2.5kms) from Princes Street.

Joppa Turrets Guest House 1 Lower Joppa Edinburgh EH15 2ER Tel: 031 669 5806	COMMENDED ♛ ♛	1 Single 1 Twin 3 Double	1 En Suite fac 1 Priv. NOT ensuite 2 Pub. Bath/Show	B&B per person £13.00-£15.00 Single £13.00-£19.00 Double	Open Jan-Dec

Quiet and friendly, with fine sea views and close to sandy beach. Easy access to city centre. Unrestricted street parking.

Kariba Guest House 10 Granville Terrace Edinburgh EH10 4PQ Tel: 031 229 3773	COMMENDED ♛ ♛	2 Twin 4 Double 2 Family	2 En Suite fac 5 Limited ensuite 2 Pub. Bath/Show	B&B per person £16.00-£20.00 Single £16.00-£20.00 Double	Open Jan-Dec

A Victorian house on major bus route to city centre about 10 minutes away. Easy access to country areas.

KENVIE GUEST HOUSE

16 Kilmaurs Road, Edinburgh EH16 5DA   031-668 1964

Quiet and comfortable house situated in a residential area with easy access to City Centre on an excellent bus route. All rooms have tea and coffee-making facilities and TV's. Central heating throughout.

A warm and friendly welcome is guaranteed.

Kenvie Guest House 16 Kilmaurs Road Edinburgh EH16 5DA Tel: 031 668 1964	COMMENDED 👑 👑	2 Twin 1 Double 2 Family	2 En Suite fac 2 Pub. Bath/Show	B&B per person £16.00-£20.00 Single £16.00-£20.00 Double	Open Jan-Dec
		Personally run, situated in quiet residential area close to city centre, and on main bus routes.			
Kew Guest House 1 Kew Terrace, Murrayfield Edinburgh EH12 5JE Tel: 031 313 4407	Award Pending	1 Single 1 Twin 1 Double 2 Family	2 En Suite fac 2 Pub. Bath/Show	B&B per person £19.00-£23.00 Single £19.00-£26.00 Double	Open Jan-Dec
Khwaja Guest House 17 Hopetoun Crescent Edinburgh Tel: 031 556 4262		4 Single 1 Twin 5 Double 2 Family	4 Pub. Bath/Show	B&B per person £14.00-£20.00 Single £14.00-£20.00 Double	Open Jan-Dec
Kilmaurs Guest House 9 Kilmaurs Road Edinburgh EH16 5DA Tel: 031 667 8315	COMMENDED 👑 👑	2 Twin 1 Double 2 Family	3 En Suite fac 2 Pub. Bath/Show	B&B per person £18.00-£24.00 Single £16.00-£24.00 Double	Open Jan-Dec
		Family run guest house in quiet residential area close to Commonwealth Pool and only ten minutes by bus from city centre.			
Kingsley Guest House 30 Craigmillar Park Edinburgh EH16 5PS Tel: 031 667 8439	COMMENDED 👑 👑	2 Twin 1 Double 3 Family	4 En Suite fac 1 Priv. NOT ensuite 2 Pub. Bath/Show	B&B per person £15.00-£20.00 Double	Open Jan-Dec
		Friendly, comfortable and family run with own off street parking. Easy access to city centre.			
Kirklea Guest House 11 Harrison Road Edinburgh EH11 1EG Tel: 031 337 1129/346 7866 Fax: 031 337 1129	COMMENDED 👑	2 Single 2 Twin 1 Double 1 Family	1 En Suite fac 2 Pub. Bath/Show	B&B per person £17.00-£21.00 Single £15.00-£21.00 Double	Open Jan-Dec
		A family run guest house in Victorian terrace convenient for bus routes to city centre and all attractions.			
Kirtle Guest House 8 Minto Street Edinburgh EH9 1RG Tel: 031 667 2813 (office)/ 5353 (guests)	COMMENDED 👑 👑	3 Double 4 Family	4 En Suite fac 3 Limited ensuite 2 Pub. Bath/Show	B&B per person £17.00-£22.00 Double	Open Jan-Dec
		On main bus routes for city centre, 1 mile (2kms). Some private car parking available. Close to Commonwealth Pool.			
Kisimul Guest House 16 Claremont Park Edinburgh EH6 7PJ Tel: 031 554 4203	COMMENDED Listed	1 Single 2 Twin 3 Double	3 Pub. Bath/Show	B&B per person £13.00-£16.00 Single £13.00-£16.00 Double	Open Jan-Dec
		Stone built house overlooking Leith Links. Convenient bus routes to city centre.			

EDINBURGH continued	Map 2 D5					
The Lairg 11 Coates Gardens Edinburgh EH12 5LG Tel: 031 337 1050 Fax: 031 346 2167	APPROVED	2 Single 3 Twin 2 Double 3 Family	7 En Suite fac 1 Limited ensuite 2 Pub. Bath/Show	B&B per person £17.00-£25.00 Single £17.00-£25.00 Double	Open Jan-Dec Dinner from 1715	
		Personally run guest house with large lounge area. **Easy access to city centre and all tourist attractions.**				
Lauderville Guest House 52 Mayfield Road Edinburgh EH9 2NH Tel: 031 667 7788/4005	COMMENDED	1 Single 1 Twin 2 Double 1 Family	3 En Suite fac 1 Priv. NOT ensuite 1 Pub. Bath/Show	B&B per person £17.00-£25.00 Single £17.00-£25.00 Double	Open Jan-Dec Dinner 1830-1930 B&B + Eve. Meal £25.00-£33.00	
		Family run Victorian terraced guest house, on main bus route into **city centre. En-suite facilities available.**				
Lorne Villa Guest House 9 East Mayfield Edinburgh EH9 1SD Tel: 031 667 7159	COMMENDED Listed	1 Single 2 Double 3 Family	2 En Suite fac 1 Priv. NOT ensuite 2 Pub. Dath/Show	B&B per person £12.00-£18.00 Single £15.00-£25.00 Double	Open Jan-Dec	
		Personally run guest house conveniently situated for **city centre bus route with off street parking.**				
Maple Leaf Guest House 23 Pilrig Street Edinburgh EH6 5AN Tel: 031 554 7692		2 Single 2 Twin 2 Double 3 Family	3 En Suite fac 1 Limited ensuite 1 Priv. NOT ensuite 2 Pub. Bath/Show	B&B per person £16.00-£19.00 Single £13.00-£18.00 Double	Open Jan-Dec	
Marrakech Guest House 30 London Street Edinburgh EH3 6NA Tel: 031 556 4444/7293 Fax: 031 557 3615	COMMENDED	2 Single 3 Twin 4 Double 2 Family	9 En Suite fac 2 Pub. Bath/Show	B&B per person £20.00-£30.00 Single £17.00-£25.00 Double	Open Jan-Dec Dinner 1800-2200	
		Family run in New Town. Close to the city centre with its own restaurant **serving North African cuisine and featuring many home made specialities.**				
The Mayfield Guest House 15 Mayfield Gardens Edinburgh EH9 2AX Tel: 031 667 8049 Fax: 031 667 5001	COMMENDED	2 Single 2 Twin 4 Double 3 Family	11 En Suite fac 1 Pub. Bath/Show	B&B per person £23.00-£32.00 Single £23.00-£32.00 Double	Open Jan-Dec Dinner 1830-2030	
		On main route into the city, convenient for all attractions. **Private parking and regular bus service. All rooms double glazed.**				

The Meadows Guest House

Terraced house in quiet location overlooking park. Spacious rooms with colour T.V.'s. Hospitality trays. Most rooms en-suite.
Scottish Tourist Boards 2 crowns and commended.
Guestaccom Good Room Award. Access and Visa accepted.
Metered car parking by day.

Jon and Gloria Stuart, 17 Glengyle Terrace,
Edinburgh EH3 9LN. Tel: 031-229 9559   Fax: 031-229 2226.

| The Meadows Guest House
17 Glengyle Terrace
Bruntsfield
Edinburgh
EH3 9LN
Tel: 031 229 9559
Fax: 031 229 2226 | COMMENDED | 1 Single
2 Twin
1 Double
3 Family | 5 En Suite fac
1 Pub. Bath/Show | B&B per person
£20.00-£38.00 Single
£20.00-£24.00 Double | Open Jan-Dec | |
| | | **Quietly situated terraced house overlooking Bruntsfield Links.**
Convenient for theatre and shops. Family run. | | | | |

Menzies Guest House 33 Leamington Terrace Edinburgh EH10 4JS Tel: 031 229 4629	APPROVED ♛ ♛	2 Double 5 Family	2 En Suite fac 1 Limited ensuite 2 Pub. Bath/Show	B&B per person £12.50-£22.50 Double	Open Jan-Dec	

Situated in residential area near Bruntsfield Links and
close to main bus route to city centre. Private parking.

Meriden Guest House 1 Hermitage Terrace Edinburgh EH10 4RP Tel: 031 447 5152/5155		2 Twin 2 Double 1 Family	2 Pub. Bath/Show	B&B per person £14.00-£19.00 Double	Open Jan-Dec	

Milton House 24 Duddingston Crescent Edinburgh EH15 3AT Tel: 031 669 4072	COMMENDED ♛	1 Twin 3 Double	3 Pub. Bath/Show	B&B per person £16.00-£20.00 Single £15.00-£18.00 Double	Open Jan-Dec	

Friendly family atmosphere with off street parking and easy access
to the city centre. Adjacent to 9 hole golf course.

Muffin Guest House 164 Ferry Road Edinburgh EH6 4NS Tel: 031 554 4162	COMMENDED Listed	1 Single 1 Twin 2 Double 1 Family	1 En Suite fac 1 Pub. Bath/Show	B&B per person £16.00-£19.00 Single £13.00-£22.00 Double	Open Jan-Dec Dinner 1830-1930 B&B + Eve. Meal £19.00-£28.00	

Personally run, situated on main bus route with easy access to
town centre and all amenities.

Newington Guest House 18 Newington Road Edinburgh EH9 1QS Tel: 031 667 3356	COMMENDED ♛ ♛	1 Single 2 Twin 3 Double 2 Family	5 En Suite fac 1 Limited ensuite 1 Pub. Bath/Show	B&B per person £26.00-£30.00 Single £18.50-£28.50 Double	Open Jan-Dec	

Interestingly furnished Victorian house on main road into city from South.
Easy access to centre, most rooms double glazed.

Park View Villa Guest House 254 Ferry Road Edinburgh EH5 3AN Tel: 031 552 3456	COMMENDED ♛ ♛	2 Twin 2 Double 3 Family	4 En Suite fac 2 Pub. Bath/Show	B&B per person £20.00-£26.00 Single £15.00-£20.00 Double	Open Jan-Dec	

Victorian villa retaining original woodwork and enjoying
panoramic views of the city skyline.

Parklands Guest House 20 Mayfield Gardens Edinburgh EH9 2BZ Tel: 031 667 7184	COMMENDED ♛ ♛	2 Twin 3 Double 1 Family	5 En Suite fac 1 Priv. NOT ensuite	B&B per person £19.00-£25.00 Double	Open Jan-Dec	

Look forward to a warm welcome at this late Victorian house with fine
woodwork and ceilings, situated on the south side of the city.

Quendale Guest House 32 Craigmillar Park Edinburgh EH16 5PS Tel: 031 667 3171		1 Single 2 Twin 2 Double 1 Family	2 Pub. Bath/Show	B&B per person from £13.50 Double	Open Jan-Dec	

Robertson Guest House 5 Hartington Gardens Edinburgh EH10 4LD Tel: 031 229 2652/3862	COMMENDED ♛	1 Single 1 Twin 1 Double 4 Family	1 En Suite fac 2 Pub. Bath/Show	B&B per person £15.00-£20.00 Single £15.00-£20.00 Double	Open Jan-Dec Dinner 1900-2100 B&B + Eve. Meal £25.00-£30.00	

Friendly, family run guest house situated in quiet residential area of city.
Easy access to centre and close to main bus routes.

Details of Grading and Classification are on page vi. | Key to symbols is on back flap. | 109

EDINBURGH continued	Map 2 D5						
Roselea House 11 Mayfield Road Edinburgh EH9 2NG Tel: 031 667 6115 Fax: 031 667 3556	HIGHLY COMMENDED ♛ ♛	2 Twin 1 Double 4 Family	4 En Suite fac 1 Priv. NOT ensuite 1 Pub. Bath/Show	B&B per person £20.00-£28.00 Single £18.00-£28.00 Double	Open Jan-Dec Dinner from 1800	
		Family run guest house on bus route to city centre. A short walk from the Commonwealth Pool and Pollock Halls of Residence.				
Rosevale House 15 Kilmaurs Road Edinburgh EH16 5DA Tel: 031 667 4781	Award Pending	1 Twin 2 Double 4 Family	5 En Suite fac 2 Priv. NOT ensuite 2 Pub. Bath/Show	B&B per person £17.00-£20.00 Single £17.00-£20.00 Double	Open Jan-Dec	
Rowan Guest House 13 Glenorchy Terrace Edinburgh EH9 2DQ Tel: 031 667 2463	COMMENDED ♛	2 Single 2 Twin 3 Double 2 Family	2 En Suite fac 2 Pub. Bath/Show	B&B per person £17.00-£21.00 Single £16.00-£20.00 Double	Open Jan-Dec	
		Victorian town house in quiet residential area with easy access to city centre and all amenities.				
Roxzannah 36 Minto Street Edinburgh EH9 2BS Tel: 031 667 8933	Award Pending	1 Twin 1 Double 2 Family	1 Limited ensuite 1 Pub. Bath/Show	B&B per person £13.00-£18.00 Double	Open Jan-Dec	

ST CONAN'S GUEST HOUSE

30 MINTO STREET, EDINBURGH EH9 1SB
Telephone: 031-667 8393

St Conan's is situated on the main A772 into Edinburgh. It is easily accessible to the city centre, in an area well served by buses. Accommodation: twin, double, family rooms most with en-suite, all rooms H&C, CH, TV, tea/coffee facilities. Set of keys. Large private car park.

| St Conans Guest House 30 Minto Street Edinburgh EH9 1SB Tel: 031 667 8393 | | 2 Twin 3 Double 2 Family | 5 En Suite fac 2 Pub. Bath/Show | B&B per person £16.00-£25.00 Single £16.00-£22.00 Double | Open Jan-Dec | |

HERE'S THE DIFFERENCE

STB's scheme has two distinct elements, grading and classification.

GRADING:

measures the quality and condition of the facilities and services offered, eg, the warmth of welcome, quality of food and its presentation, condition of decor and furnishings, appearance of buildings, tidiness of grounds and gardens, condition of lighting and heating and so on.
Grading awards are: **Approved, Commended, Highly Commended, Deluxe.**

CLASSIFICATION:

measures the range of physical facilities and services offered, eg, rooms with private bath, heating, reception, lounges, telephones and so on.
Classification awards are: **Listed or from one to five crowns.**

St Margaret's Guest House

18 CRAIGMILLAR PARK, EDINBURGH EH16 5PS
Telephone: 031-667 2202   *Commended*

A personal welcome awaits you at St Margaret's, a Victorian period house, situated on the south side of Edinburgh on the A701/A772. Excellent bus service to Princes Street, ten minutes away. The University, Castle and Holyrood Palace are within easy reach. Individually decorated bedrooms, several en-suite, all with tea/coffee facilities and colour TV. Children are very welcome. A large, beautifully decorated lounge and an airy spacious dining room with French doors leading to a pretty garden. Own key and access at any time. Private car park. Credit cards accepted.   AA QQQ

St Margaret's Guest House	COMMENDED	2 Twin	1 En Suite fac	B&B per person	Open Mar-Dec
18 Craigmillar Park	♛♛	2 Double	1 Limited ensuite	£20.00-£25.00 Single	
Edinburgh		3 Family	1 Priv. NOT ensuite	£15.00-£20.00 Double	
EH16 5PS			2 Pub. Bath/Show		
Tel: 031 667 2202					

Well appointed Victorian house with comfortable lounge and thoughtfully decorated bedrooms. Private car park.

"The Salisbury"

45 SALISBURY ROAD
EDINBURGH EH16 5AA
Tel/Fax: 031-667 1264

Enjoy real Scottish hospitality in the comfort of this Georgian House, quietly situated yet only two minutes walk from main bus routes to City Centre. Comfortable, centrally-heated bedrooms, all with private facilities, colour TV, tea/coffee making etc. Convenient for bus/railway stations. Private car park. We will be delighted to assist with arranging local tours and activities.

AA/RAC ACCLAIMED.

Contact: **Mr and Mrs William Wright.**

Salisbury Guest House	COMMENDED	2 Single	9 En Suite fac	B&B per person	Open Jan-Dec
45 Salisbury Road	♛♛	3 Twin	3 Priv. NOT ensuite	£20.00-£25.00 Single	
Edinburgh		4 Double		£18.00-£24.00 Double	
EH16 5AA		3 Family			
Tel: 031 667 1264					

Georgian Listed building in quiet conservation area, near Holyrood Park and Royal Commonwealth Pool. (1 mile (2kms) from city centre).

San Marco Guest House	COMMENDED	2 Twin	3 En Suite fac	B&B per person	Open Jan-Dec
24 Mayfield Gardens	♛♛	2 Double	2 Pub. Bath/Show	£13.00-£26.00 Double	
Edinburgh		4 Family			
EH9 2BZ					
Tel: 031 667 8982					
Fax: 031 662 1945					

Friendly guest house with some large spacious rooms, on main A772 route south of the city centre. Some off street parking.

EDINBURGH continued	Map 2 D5					

Shalimar Guest House
20 Newington Road
Edinburgh
EH9 1QS
Tel: 031 667 2827/0789

1 Single	4 En Suite fac
2 Twin	1 Limited ensuite
2 Double	2 Pub. Bath/Show
4 Family	

B&B per person
£20.00-£24.00 Single
£16.00-£18.00 Double

Open Jan-Dec

Sharon Guest House

1 KILMAURS TERRACE
EDINBURGH EH16 5BZ   031-667 2002

Quiet, semi-detached Victorian house in residential area just off A7 (pre-1992 A68) and only 5 minutes by public transport to city centre. Close to Commonwealth Swimming Pool and Royal College of Surgeons.

OFF-STREET PARKING with access all day.

House completely refurbished recently to a high standard. H&C, central heating, shaver point, tea/coffee facilities and colour TV in all rooms.

LARGE traditional Scottish breakfast. Menu available and special diets catered for.

See symbols below for additional facilities.

Sharon Guest House
1 Kilmaurs Terrace
Edinburgh
EH16 5BZ
Tel: 031 667 2002
Fax: 0506 858160

COMMENDED
Listed

2 Single	2 Pub. Bath/Show
1 Twin	
3 Double	
3 Family	

B&B per person
£16.00-£22.00 Single
£12.00-£20.00 Double

Open Jan-Dec

Victorian house in residential area but near bus routes for city centre.

Sheridan Guest House
1 Bonnington Terrace
Edinburgh
EH6 4BP
Tel: 031 554 4107

COMMENDED
👑 👑

6 Twin	2 En Suite fac
1 Family	1 Priv. NOT ensuite
	2 Pub. Bath/Show

B&B per person
£16.50-£24.50 Double

Open Jan-Dec

Situated in residential area on bus route to city centre and its amenities. No parking restrictions.

Six Mary's Place Guest House
6 Mary's Place
Edinburgh
EH4 1JH
Tel: 031 332 8965

COMMENDED
👑 👑

3 Single	2 En Suite fac
2 Twin	2 Pub. Bath/Show
3 Double	

B&B per person
£22.00-£24.00 Single
£23.00-£25.00 Double

Open 10 Jan-Dec
Dinner 1800-2130
B&B + Eve. Meal
£30.00-£32.00

Restored Georgian townhouse in central location offering vegetarian cuisine and a restful homely atmosphere.

Sonas Guest House
3 East Mayfield
Edinburgh
EH9 1SD
Tel: 031 667 2781

COMMENDED
👑 👑

1 Single	8 En Suite fac
2 Twin	
4 Double	
1 Family	

B&B per person
£18.00-£30.00 Single
£18.00-£27.00 Double

Open Jan-Dec

Terraced house situated on south side of city. With private parking. Convenient bus routes to centre and all amenities.

Southdown Guest House
20 Craigmillar Park
Edinburgh
EH16 5PS
Tel: 031 667 2410

COMMENDED
👑 👑

2 Twin	2 En Suite fac
2 Double	4 Limited ensuite
2 Family	2 Pub. Bath/Show

B&B per person
£18.00-£30.00 Single
£16.00-£22.00 Double

Open Feb-Nov

Victorian terraced house in residential area on main A7 (A701) road, with many bus routes to city centre. Friendly and family run. Private car park.

Strathmohr Guest House 23 Mayfield Gardens Edinburgh EH9 2BX Tel: 031 667 8475	COMMENDED 🏵 🏵	2 Twin 1 Double 4 Family	7 En Suite fac 2 Pub. Bath/Show	B&B per person £13.00-£25.00 Double	Open Jan-Dec
		Built in 1867 this Victorian refurbished property retains many original features. Family run. Easy access to city centre.			

Straven Guest House 3 Brunstane Road North Edinburgh EH15 2DL Tel: 031 669 5580	COMMENDED 🏵 🏵	2 Twin 2 Double 3 Family	7 En Suite fac	B&B per person £18.00-£27.00 Single £18.00-£25.00 Double	Open Jan-Dec
		Semi detached Victorian villa in a quiet residential area just off the beach in Joppa. 5 miles (8kms) from Edinburgh city centre.			

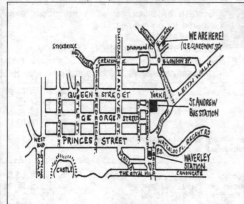

Stuart House

Gloria Stuart invites you to experience hospitality and a truly warm welcome in her traditional Old Town House in city centre.

Beautifully renovated and decorated, the 7 comfortable bedrooms, each with private bath/shower room, are thoughtfully equipped with TV, telephone, hospitality tray and hairdryer.

Delicious breakfast in elegant dining room. No Smoking throughout.

Write to me, Gloria Stuart, at 12 East Claremont Street Edinburgh EH7 4JP. Fax 031-557 0563. 031-557 9030 is my telephone number.

Stuart House 12 East Claremont Street Edinburgh EH7 4JP Tel: 031 557 9030 Fax: 031 557 0563	HIGHLY COMMENDED 🏵 🏵	1 Single 2 Twin 3 Double 1 Family	6 En Suite fac 1 Priv. NOT ensuite	B&B per person £30.00-£50.00 Single £30.00-£35.00 Double	Open Jan-Dec Dinner 1700-2130 B&B + Eve. Meal £36.00-£56.00
		Comfortable, Georgian style house (c1860) situated in the historic New Town. Close to the city centre and Princes Street.			

Sylvern Guest House 22 West Mayfield Edinburgh EH9 1TQ Tel: 031 667 1241	APPROVED Listed	2 Twin 1 Double 3 Family	4 En Suite fac 2 Pub. Bath/Show	B&B per person £17.00-£20.00 Double	Open Jan-Dec
		Detached Victorian House in residential area. Private parking and convenient for main bus routes. Four rooms en suite.			

Tania Guest House 19 Minto Street Edinburgh EH9 1RQ Tel: 031 667 4144	Award Pending	1 Single 1 Twin 1 Double 3 Family	1 En Suite fac 1 Pub. Bath/Show	B&B per person £15.00-£24.00 Single £12.50-£20.00 Double	Open Jan-Dec

EDINBURGH continued	Map 2
	D5

The Thirty-Nine Steps Guest House

62 South Trinity Road, Edinburgh EH5 3NX
Tel: 031-552 1349

Victorian house quietly situated within easy reach of city centre and close to Royal Botanical Gardens. Easy access to main A9 road north. A period house dating back to the late 1800's, named after John Buchan's famous novel. All rooms tastefully decorated with colour TV's, tea/coffee facilities and full central heating. Traditional Scottish breakfast served, with special diets catered for on request.

EASY PARKING
BED & BREAKFAST FROM £14.50

A warm and friendly welcome is assured from resident proprietors Shirley and Derek Mowat.

The Thirty-Nine Steps Guest House 62 South Trinity Road Edinburgh EH5 3NX Tel: 031 552 1349	COMMENDED ☺	1 Single 2 Twin 1 Double 3 Family	3 Pub. Bath/Show	B&B per person £16.50-£20.00 Single £14.50-£18.00 Double	Open Jan-Dec	
		Victorian terraced house in quiet residential area. Convenient bus route for city centre. Unrestricted parking.				
Tiree Guest House 26 Craigmillar Park Edinburgh EH16 5PS Tel: 031 667 7477		1 Single 2 Twin 1 Double 1 Family	3 En Suite fac 1 Limited ensuite 2 Pub. Bath/Show	B&B per person £14.00-£18.00 Single £16.00-£24.00 Double	Open Jan-Dec	
Torivane Guest House 1 Morton Street Edinburgh EH15 2EW Tel: 031 669 1648	COMMENDED Listed	1 Single 1 Double 1 Family	1 Pub. Bath/Show	B&B per person £13.00-£16.00 Single £13.00-£16.00 Double	Open Feb-Nov	
		Stone built house on main bus route to city centre. A one minute walk to beach and seafront promenade.				
The Town House 65 Gilmore Place Edinburgh EH3 9NU Tel: 031 229 1985	COMMENDED ☺ ☺	1 Single 2 Twin 1 Double 1 Family	3 En Suite fac 1 Pub. Bath/Show	B&B per person £18.00-£23.00 Single £18.00-£26.00 Double	Open Jan-Dec	
		A Victorian terraced family house built in 1876. Situated in a residential area within easy walking distance of the town centre.				

Turret Guest House

8 KILMAURS TERRACE, EDINBURGH EH16 5DR
Telephone: 031-667 6704

Friendly family house situated in residential area, 10 minutes by car from city centre. Attractive rooms, some en-suite, all with central heating, television and tea trays. Our extensive breakfast menu also caters for vegetarians. *Contact: Jackie Cameron.*

Turret Guest House 8 Kilmaurs Terrace Edinburgh EH16 5DR Tel: 031 667 6704	HIGHLY COMMENDED 👑 👑	1 Single 2 Twin 2 Double 1 Family	3 En Suite fac 1 Limited ensuite 2 Pub. Bath/Show	B&B per person £16.00-£20.00 Single £13.00-£25.00 Double	Open Jan-Dec	
		Recently refurbished Victorian house in quiet residential area. Convenient for buses to city centre. Commonwealth Pool nearby.				
Villa Nina Guest House 39 Leamington Terrace Edinburgh EH10 4JS Tel: 031 229 2644	APPROVED Listed	1 Twin 2 Double 1 Family	3 Limited ensuite 2 Pub. Bath/Show	B&B per person £13.00-£16.50 Double	Open Jan-Dec	
		Terraced house, close to bus routes to city centre, near King's Theatre and Bruntsfield Links.				
Rachel G Argo 61 Lothian Road Edinburgh EH1 2DJ Tel: 031 229 4054		1 Single 1 Twin 1 Double	1 Pub. Bath/Show	B&B per person £13.00-£17.00 Single £13.00-£17.00 Double	Open May-Sep	
Mrs Armstrong 481 Queensferry Road Edinburgh EH4 7ND Tel: 031 336 5595		1 Twin 1 Double	2 En Suite fac	B&B per person £16.00-£20.00 Double	Open May-Sep	

PRIVATE HOUSE

64 GLASGOW ROAD, CORSTORPHINE, EDINBURGH EH12 8LN
Telephone: 031-334 2610

A warm Scottish welcome awaits you here at this pleasant detached bungalow, situated only 3 miles from City Centre, excellent bus service. There are three comfortable bedrooms, all with modern amenities; these are kept to a very high standard. Tea/coffee making, en-suite facilities. Parking.

Prices from £16 to £19

Mrs H Baird 64 Glasgow Road Edinburgh EH12 8LN Tel: 031 334 2610	HIGHLY COMMENDED 👑 👑	1 Single 1 Twin 1 Double	1 En Suite fac 2 Pub. Bath/Show	B&B per person £17.00-£18.00 Single £17.00-£19.00 Double	Open May-Sep	
		Detached dormer bungalow on the outskirts of the city, offering comfortable and friendly accommodation. Good bus service to town centre.				
Mrs E Banigan 5 Viewforth Terrace Edinburgh EH10 4LH Tel: 031 229 6698	Award Pending	1 Single 1 Twin	1 Pub. Bath/Show	B&B per person £15.00-£16.00 Single £14.00-£15.00 Double	Open Jun-Sep	
Mrs P Birnie Casa Buzzo, 8 Kilmaurs Road Edinburgh EH16 5DA Tel: 031 667 8998	COMMENDED 👑	2 Twin 2 Family	2 Pub. Bath/Show	B&B per person £12.00-£14.00 Double	Open May-Sep	
		A terraced property, conveniently situated for bus routes to the town centre and visitor attractions. Unrestricted parking.				

EDINBURGH continued	Map 2 D5						
Mrs B Blows Fairholme, 13 Moston Terrace Edinburgh EH9 2DE Tel: 031 667 8645	COMMENDED Listed	1 Single 1 Twin 1 Double	2 Pub. Bath/Show	B&B per person £10.00-£15.00 Single £10.00-£14.00 Double	Open May-Sep Dinner 1800-1900 B&B + Eve. Meal from £14.50		
		Comfortable elegant period home, friendly ambience, convenient for city centre.					
Thomas Borland Arrandale House 28 Mayfield Gardens Edinburgh EH9 2BZ Tel: 031 667 6029		1 Twin 1 Double 1 Family	2 En Suite fac 2 Pub. Bath/Show	B&B per person £15.00-£20.00 Double	Open Apr-Oct		
Mrs F Bowman 15 Davidson Road Edinburgh EH4 2PE Tel: 031 332 4445	Award Pending	1 Twin	1 Priv. NOT ensuite	B&B per person £13.50-£16.00 Double	Open May-Sep		
Mrs Maria Boyle Villa Maria 6a Mayfield Gardens Edinburgh EH9 2BU Tel: 031 667 7730	COMMENDED Listed	1 Double 1 Family	1 Pub. Bath/Show	B&B per person £14.00-£15.00 Double	Open May-Sep		
		Victorian house on main road, but with quiet rooms. On bus route to city centre 1 mile (2kms) to Princes Street and all attractions. Parking.					

Birchtree Cottage

1 BARNTON GROVE, EDINBURGH
EH4 6EQ   Telephone: 031-339 3611

Scottish Tourist Board "Highly Commended" — "Listed" "Disabled"

A warm welcome awaits you at Birchtree Cottage — one of Edinburgh's finest B&B's. Situated in north-west Edinburgh, just 3 miles from city centre and 3 miles from Edinburgh Airport. Quiet, residential area close to the sea, with many interesting walks. Opposite one of Scotland's finest golf courses — "The Royal Burgess".

All rooms have central heating, remote-control colour TV, radio/alarm, trouser press, tea and coffee-making facilities, etc. Telephone. Full Scottish Breakfast. The nearby Barnton Hotel with three restaurants offers a wide range of cuisine.

Mrs Bryan Birchtree Cottage 1 Barnton Grove Edinburgh EH4 6EQ Tel: 031 339 3611	HIGHLY COMMENDED Listed	1 Double 1 Family	1 Pub. Bath/Show	B&B per person £18.00-£20.00 Single £18.00-£20.00 Double	Open May-Sep Dinner 1800-2000 B&B + Eve. Meal £24.00-£26.00	
		Detached single storey cottage, 4 miles (7kms) from city centre, just off Forth Bridge route. Large gardens; friendly atmosphere. Close to airport.				

BURNS B&B

Fax: 031-229 9225
Tel: 031-229 1669

67 GILMORE PLACE, EDINBURGH EH3 9NU

Comfortable, homely B&B with free parking, very close to city centre, tourist attractions and 5 mins. Princes Street (buses 10 & 27). Restaurants, theatres etc., nearby. Non-smoking establishment.

Access to the house at all times with your own keys.

Write or telephone Mrs Burns.

Mrs M Burns 67 Gilmore Place Edinburgh EH3 9NU Tel: 031 229 1669 Fax: 031 229 9225	COMMENDED ♛	1 Twin 2 Double	2 Pub. Bath/Show	B&B per person £14.00-£16.00 Double	Open May-Sep	
		Victorian terraced house within easy reach of city centre, stations and tourist attractions. Choice of local restaurants within walking distance.				
Mrs Cairns 28 Cammo Road Edinburgh EH4 8AP Tel: 031 339 3613		2 Double	1 Pub. Bath/Show	B&B per person £16.00 Double	Open May-Sep	

CARRONVALE

38 CORSTORPHINE BANK DRIVE, EDINBURGH EH12 8RN
Telephone: 031-334 3291   Fax: 031-334 3883

Spacious, centrally heated bungalow in quiet residential area 3 miles from city centre and 4 miles from airport. Ground floor bedrooms with wash-basins and tea/coffee making facilities. TV lounge, own keys and full Scottish Breakfast.

Contact: Mrs Eleanor Caven.

Mrs E Caven Carronvale 38 Corstorphine Bank Dr Edinburgh EH12 8RN Tel: 031 334 3291 Fax: 031 334 3883	COMMENDED ♛	2 Twin	1 Pub. Bath/Show	B&B per person £15.00-£17.00 Double	Open May-Sep	
		In quiet residential area, a delightful detached home with colourful gardens. 3 miles (5kms) west of the city centre.				
Mrs M Coleman The Hollies 54 Craigmillar Park Edinburgh EH16 5PS Tel: 031 668 3408	HIGHLY COMMENDED ♛ ♛	1 Twin 2 Double	3 En Suite fac	B&B per person £22.50-£25.00 Double	Open May-Sep	
		Fine town house, many period features. High standard of decor and furnishings. All rooms ground floor. Excellent bus service. Parking available.				

HERE'S THE DIFFERENCE

STB's scheme has two distinct elements, grading and classification.

GRADING: measures the quality and condition of the facilities and services offered, eg, the warmth of welcome, quality of food and its presentation, condition of decor and furnishings, appearance of buildings, tidiness of grounds and gardens, condition of lighting and heating and so on.
Grading awards are: **Approved, Commended, Highly Commended, Deluxe.**

CLASSIFICATION: measures the range of physical facilities and services offered, eg, rooms with private bath, heating, reception, lounges, telephones and so on.
Classification awards are: **Listed or from one to five crowns.**

EDINBURGH continued	Map 2 D5						

Crannoch But & Ben

**467 QUENSFERRY RD
EDINBURGH
EH4 7ND**

Tel: 031-336 5688

STB Grade of Highly Commended and Classification of 🏵️🏵️has been awarded to this outstanding family home. This bungalow has private facilities for all rooms and residents' lounge. Near Airport on A90 and three miles from city centre with excellent bus service and car parking.
All guests receive a warm welcome.

Mrs M Conway Crannoch But & Ben 467 Queensferry Road Edinburgh EH4 7ND Tel: 031 336 5688	HIGHLY COMMENDED 🏵️ 🏵️	1 Twin 1 Family	2 En Suite fac 1 Pub. Bath/Show	B&B per person £19.00-£20.00 Double	Open May-Sep	

Detached bungalow with warm and friendly atmosphere on Forth Road Bridge route, 3 miles (5kms)from city centre. En suite bathrooms, parking.

Mrs Lynn Cooper 24 Gilmore Place Edinburgh EH3 9NQ Tel: 031 228 2136	APPROVED Listed	1 Single 1 Twin 1 Double 1 Family	2 Pub. Bath/Show	B&B per person £15.00-£20.00 Single £12.50-£18.00 Double	Open May-Sep	

Friendly, non smoking Victorian house. Central Edinburgh. Children welcome. Vegetarian breakfast to order.

Mrs M Coutts Meadowplace House, 1 Meadowplace Road Edinburgh EH12 7TZ Tel: 031 334 8459	APPROVED Listed	1 Double 1 Family	2 Pub. Bath/Show	B&B per person £12.00-£14.00 Single £12.00-£14.00 Double	Open May-Sep	

Comfortable, personally run B+B close to major bus route to city centre and airport, own parking.

Mrs Agnes Craig Forthview, 45 Moira Terrace Edinburgh EH7 6TD Tel: 031 657 2912		1 Single 3 Twin	2 En Suite fac 3 Pub. Bath/Show	B&B per person £20.00-£22.00 Single £16.50-£18.50 Double	Open May-Sep	

Mrs V Darlington Borodale, 7 Argyle Place Edinburgh EH9 1JU Tel: 031 667 5578		1 Double 2 Family	2 Limited ensuite 1 Pub. Bath/Show	B&B per person £16.00-£20.00 Single £16.00-£20.00 Double	Open May-Sep	

Mr & Mrs Divine 116 Greenbank Crescent Edinburgh EH10 5SZ Tel: 031 447 9454	APPROVED Listed	1 Single 1 Twin	2 Pub. Bath/Show	B&B per person £12.00-£15.00 Single £12.00-£15.00 Double	Open May-Sep	

Family home in quiet residential area with easy access to city centre. Parking. On main bus routes.

INVERMARK   ♕ COMMENDED

60 Polwarth Terrace, Edinburgh. Tel. 031-337 1066

Invermark is situated in quiet suburbs on main bus route
into city, 5 minutes by car. Private parking.
Accommodation: single, twin, family with wash-hand basins
and tea/coffee-making facilities. TV lounge/dining room,
toilet, bathroom/shower.
Friendly atmosphere, children and pets welcome.

| Mrs H Donaldson
Invermark
60 Polwarth Terrace
Edinburgh
EH11 1NJ
Tel: 031 337 1066 | COMMENDED
♕ | 1 Single
1 Twin
1 Family | 1 Pub. Bath/Show | B&B per person
£15.00-£16.00 Single
£15.00-£16.00 Double | Open May-Sep | 🛆 V C 📺 📖
📞 🖵 📔 🕭 🔥
📺 📖 🚿 🅿
🐾 🐕 |

Victorian house situated in quiet residential area a few minutes from
city centre. Next to main bus route.

| Mrs Egan
157 Craiglea Drive
Edinburgh
EH10 5PT
Tel: 031 447 1580 | | 2 Double | 1 Pub. Bath/Show | B&B per person
£13.00 Double | Open May-Sep | V S 📞 🖵 🕭
📺 📖 🅿 🎿 |

The Hedges

19 HILLSIDE CRESCENT, Off LONDON ROAD
EDINBURGH EH7 5EB   Tel: 031-558 1481

On-street parking. Cosy wee guest house. All facilities. Great breakfast.
Nothing's a problem. Two golden retrievers live here plus a large
marmalade tom cat, so you are guaranteed a welcome. We supply irons,
hair dryers, umbrellas and all the help you need to enjoy Scotland,
especially Edinburgh.   ***SEE YOU SOON!***

| Mr L Essien
The Hedges
19 Hillside Crescent
Edinburgh
EH7 5EB
Tel: 031 558 1481 | | 2 Family | 2 En Suite fac
2 Pub. Bath/Show | B&B per person
£13.00-£15.00 Single
£13.00-£15.00 Double | Open May-Sep | 🛆 C 📞 🖵 📔
🕭 📖 🚿 🅿
🌸 🅿 📰 🐕 ⓘ
🏠 |

| Mrs J Ferguson
20 Restalrig Gardens
Edinburgh
EH7 6HZ
Tel: 031 661 3762 | | 1 Double
1 Family | 1 Pub. Bath/Show | B&B per person
£11.00-£12.00 Double | Open May-Sep | V S C 🐾 📞
🖳 🖵 📔 📖 🚿
🅿 🔍 🅿 🐾 🐕 |

| Mrs D R Frackelton
17 Hope Park Terrace
Edinburgh
EH8 9LZ
Tel: 031 667 7963 | APPROVED
Listed | 1 Single
1 Double | 1 Pub. Bath/Show | B&B per person
£16.00-£17.00 Single
£16.00-£17.00 Double | Open May-Sep | 🛆 V S 📞 🕭
📖 🚿 🅿 🔍 ⓘ |

Ground floor flat on regular bus route to city centre. Restaurants nearby.

| Mrs M R B Garvie
99 Joppa Road
Edinburgh
EH15 5BP
Tel: 031 669 8695 | | 1 Single
2 Twin | 1 Priv. NOT ensuite
1 Pub. Bath/Show | B&B per person
£17.50 Single
£17.50 Double | Open May-Sep
Dinner 1800-2000 | 🕭 V S 📞 🖳
🖵 🔌 📺 📖 🚿
🅿 🔍 🌸 🅿 📰
🍴 🚫 ⓘ 🔞 ▶
🌂 |

| Mrs Alexia Graham
18 Moston Terrace
Edinburgh
EH9 2DE
Tel: 031 667 3466 | HIGHLY
COMMENDED
Listed | 2 Double | 1 Pub. Bath/Show | B&B per person
£13.00-£18.00 Double | Open May-Sep | V S 📞 🖳 📖
🚿 🅿 🔍 🐾 |

Traditionally furnished, elegant Victorian house in quiet, residential area.
Convenient for main bus routes to city centre. Unrestricted parking.

EDINBURGH continued	Map 2 D5					
Mrs Greig 68 Blackford Avenue Edinburgh EH9 3HR Tel: 031 668 1135		2 Twin	1 Pub. Bath/Show	B&B per person £13.00 Double	Open May-Sep	C 📞 🖥 💷 🎬 🛄 🍴 ✕ ⚲
Mrs S Greig Antonville, 3 Millerfield Place Edinburgh EH9 1LW Tel: 031 667 2344	Award Pending	3 Twin	3 En Suite fac 3 Pub. Bath/Show	B&B per person £15.00-£22.00 Single £15.00-£22.00 Double	Open Jun-15 Sep	🛁 C 🎬 📞 💷 📺 TV 🍴 🛄 🅿 🐕 ✕ ⚲

Mrs Helen Hall

"WOODLANDS", 55 BARNTON AVENUE
EDINBURGH EH4 6JJ   Tel: 031-336 1685

Small Mansion House set in two acres of garden and woodlands overlooking Royal Burgess Golf Course. Only 3 miles from West End of Princes Street (nearest main road A90). All bedrooms equipped with tea/coffee making facilities, hairdryers, electric blankets, radios and colour televisions.   ☙ **Commended**

Mrs Hall Woodlands 55 Barnton Avenue Davidson's Mains Edinburgh EH4 6JJ Tel: 031 336 1685	COMMENDED ♛	2 Twin 1 Double	1 En Suite fac 1 Pub. Bath/Show	B&B per person from £20.00 Single £16.00-£18.00 Double	Open May-Sep	🛁 V S 📞 🖥 🖥 💷 🅿 TV 💷 🍴 🛄 🐾 P 🕯 ✕ 🐕
				Stone built house standing in own large garden, overlooking golf course. Situated in quiet area 3 miles (5kms) from city centre.		
Mrs A Hamilton 6 Cambridge Gardens Edinburgh EH6 5DJ Tel: 031 554 3113		1 Double 1 Family	1 Pub. Bath/Show	B&B per person £11.00-£12.50 Single £11.00-£12.50 Double	Open May-Sep	🛁 C 🛏 🖥 💷 🛄 TV 🐕 ✕
Marny Hill 15 Glengyle Terrace Edinburgh EH3 9LN Tel: 031 228 1973		1 Double 2 Twin	3 En Suite fac	B&B per person £25.00-£28.00 Double	Open May-Sep	🛁 V S 📞 🖥 🖥 💷 💷 🍴 🛄 🐾 🕯 ✕ ⚲
Mrs M Holmes South Lodge 2A Dovecot Road Edinburgh EH12 7LG Tel: 031 334 4651	COMMENDED Listed	2 Twin 1 Double	1 En Suite fac 1 Pub. Bath/Show	B&B per person £13.00-£16.00 Double	Open May-Sep	V S C 💷 🛏 📞 🖥 💷 💷 TV 💷 🛄 🐾 ⚲ 🏠
				Victorian home in an historical setting in the west side of Edinburgh near major bus routes. Unrestricted parking.		
Mrs M Hughes 6 Dean Park Crescent Edinburgh EH4 1PN Tel: 031 332 5017		1 Single 1 Twin 2 Double 1 Family	1 En Suite fac 2 Pub. Bath/Show	B&B per person £14.00-£22.00 Single £14.00-£22.00 Double	Open May-Sep	C 💷 🛏 📞 🖥 💷 🍴 💷 🛄 🔥 🐾 🕯 ✕ 🐕

VAT is shown at 17.5%: changes in this rate may affect prices. Prices shown are for guidance only. Please send SAE with each enquiry.

Name / Address	Grading	Rooms	Facilities	B&B Rates	Opening	Symbols
Mrs Valerie Livingstone 50 Paisley Crescent Edinburgh EH8 7JQ Tel: 031 661 6337	COMMENDED Listed	1 Twin 1 Double	1 Pub. Bath/Show	B&B per person £15.00-£18.00 Double	Open May-Sep	
		Modern terraced villa in quiet area adjacent to Arthur's Seat, with fine views over Firth of Forth. Near main bus route to city centre. No smoking.				
Mrs Lyons 14 Zetland Place, Trinity Edinburgh EH5 3LY Tel: 031 552 1608		1 Single 1 Twin 1 Family	2 Pub. Bath/Show	B&B per person £15.00-£16.00 Single £15.00-£16.00 Double	Open May-Sep	
Elizabeth McIntyre 15 McDonald Road Edinburgh EH7 4LX Tel: 031 556 4967	COMMENDED	1 Twin 1 Double 1 Family	3 En Suite fac	B&B per person £25.00 Single £20.00-£25.00 Double	Open May-Sep Dinner 1800-2000 B&B + Eve. Meal £32.00-£35.00	
		Personally run with friendly atmosphere. Situated in residential area with easy access to city centre and station.				
Dorothy M G McKay 41 Corstorphine Bank Drive Edinburgh EH12 8RH Tel: 031 334 4100	COMMENDED Listed	1 Twin 1 Double	1 Priv. NOT ensuite 2 Pub. Bath/Show	B&B per person £13.00-£15.00 Double	Open May-Sep	
		Detached house in quiet residential area. About 3 miles (5kms) from city centre and 4 miles (6kms) from airport. 500 yards from bus stop.				
Mrs E M MacKinnon 5 Bangholm Terrace Edinburgh EH3 5QN Tel: 031 552 3320		1 Twin 1 Double	1 Pub. Bath/Show	B&B per person £14.50-£16.00 Double	Open May-Sep	
Mrs H McKue 1 Moat Street Edinburgh EH14 1PE Tel: 031 443 8020		1 Twin 1 Double 1 Family	2 Pub. Bath/Show	B&B per person from £14.00 Single £12.00-£14.00 Double	Open May-Sep	

Mrs U McLean
7 CRAWFURD ROAD, NEWINGTON
EDINBURGH EH16 5PQ   Tel: 031-667 2283
Centrally located lovely old house with central heating. Rooms have tea/coffee making facilities and television. Situated on excellent bus route, 5 minutes drive from Princes Street, near Arthur's Seat and Commonwealth Pool. *Children welcome.* **Bed and Breakfast from £13.**

Name / Address	Grading	Rooms	Facilities	B&B Rates	Opening	Symbols
Mrs U McLean 7 Crawfurd Road, Newington Edinburgh EH16 5PQ Tel: 031 667 2283		1 Twin 1 Double 1 Family	1 Pub. Bath/Show	B&B per person £14.00-£16.00 Double	Open May-Sep	
Mrs S J McLennan Airdenair, 29 Kilmaurs Road Edinburgh EH16 5DB Tel: 031 668 2336	APPROVED	2 Twin 1 Double	1 Pub. Bath/Show	B&B per person £14.00-£17.00 Single £14.00-£16.00 Double	Open May-Sep	
		Double upper flatted villa. Quiet residential area on south side of city. Near Royal Commonwealth Pool, Holyrood Park. Good bus routes to centre.				

EDINBURGH continued	Map 2 D5					
Mrs J MacLeod 5 Cambridge Gardens Edinburgh EH6 5DH Tel: 031 554 5264		1 Single 1 Twin	1 Pub. Bath/Show	B&B per person £12.00 Single £12.00 Double	Open May-Sep	
Ms A McTavish 9B Scotland Street Edinburgh EH3 6PP Tel: 031 556 5080		1 Single 1 Twin 1 Double	2 Pub. Bath/Show	B&B per person £20.00-£22.00 Single from £20.00 Double	Open May-Sep	
Mrs Eileen McTighe 4 Coinyie House Close Royal Mile Edinburgh EH1 1NL Tel: 031 556 3399		1 Twin 1 Family	1 Pub. Bath/Show	B&B per person £13.00-£17.00 Single £13.00-£17.00 Double	Open May-Sep	
Mrs E Manson Doocote House 15 Moat Street Edinburgh EH14 1PE Tel: 031 443 5455	COMMENDED Listed	1 Twin 1 Family	2 Pub. Bath/Show	B&B per person £15.00-£20.00 Single £12.00-£15.00 Double	Open May-Sep	
Terrace house with attractive garden. On busy bus route to city centre.						
Mrs N Mitchell 19 Meadowplace Road Edinburgh EH12 7UJ Tel: 031 334 8483	COMMENDED Listed	1 Twin 1 Family	1 Pub. Bath/Show	B&B per person £13.50-£17.00 Double	Open May-Sep	
On the West side of the city detached dormer bungalow offering ground floor accommodation and off street parking.						
Mrs Marilyn Nicholl Greenbank House 122 Mayfield Road Edinburgh EH9 3AH Tel: 031 667 2526		1 Single 1 Double 1 Family	2 Pub. Bath/Show	B&B per person £13.50-£17.50 Single £13.00-£17.00 Double	Open May-Sep	
Mrs Helen Olson 20 Esplanade Terrace Edinburgh EH15 2ES Tel: 031 669 1010	Award Pending	2 Double	2 Pub. Bath/Show	B&B per person £14.00-£15.00 Double	Open May-Sep	
Mr & Mrs G Pretsell 40 Drum Brae North Edinburgh EH4 8AZ Tel: 031 339 6811	COMMENDED Listed	1 Twin 1 Double	1 Pub. Bath/Show	B&B per person £14.00-£16.00 Double	Open May-Sep	
Personally run Bed and Breakfast, close to airport and main bus route to city centre. Off road parking.						
Mrs M Rooney 11 Mcdonald Road Edinburgh EH7 4LZ Tel: 031 556 3434	Award Pending	2 Double 2 Family	2 En Suite fac 2 Pub. Bath/Show	B&B per person £16.00-£26.00 Double	Open May-Sep Dinner 1800-1900 B&B + Eve. Meal £22.00-£34.00	
Mrs C M Ross 19 Thirlestane Road Edinburgh EH9 1AL Tel: 031 447 3466		2 Twin	1 Pub. Bath/Show	B&B per person £15.00 Single £15.00 Double	Open May-Sep	

'33 Colinton Road'

33 COLINTON ROAD, EDINBURGH EH10 5DR
Telephone: 031-447 8080

'33 Colinton Road' is a Victorian terraced, 2 crown commended friendly family home. Conveniently situated for all amenities and within walking distance of the city centre. On major bus routes. All rooms non-smoking with private facilities. Diets catered for. Children welcome. Open March-October, other times by arrangement.

| Mrs J Sandeman
33 Colinton Road
Edinburgh
EH10 5DR
Tel: 031 447 8080 | COMMENDED
👑 👑 | 1 Single
1 Twin
1 Double | 2 En Suite fac
1 Priv. NOT ensuite | B&B per person
£20.00-£28.00 Single
£19.00-£25.00 Double | Open May-Sep | |
| End house of a terrace. On main bus route to city centre and near local shops and restaurants. Unrestricted parking. | | | | | | |

Sandilands House

25 QUEENSFERRY ROAD, EDINBURGH EH4 3HB
Telephone: 031-332 2057

Superbly situated only 5 minutes from city centre for exploration of Scotland's capital. Furnished to a high standard with colour TV's, tea-making facilities, hair dryers, vanity units, some en-suite facilities. Includes full Scottish breakfast. Special diets and evening meals on request. Children under 7 years free, under 12 years ½ price. Special weekend rate reductions. Car parking available.

Contact: Mrs Maureen Sandilands.

Mrs Sandilands 25 Queensferry Road Edinburgh EH4 3HB Tel: 031 332 2057	Award Pending	1 Twin 2 Double	1 Limited ensuite 2 Pub. Bath/Show	B&B per person £20.00 Single £15.00-£18.00 Double	Open May-Sep	
Mrs Aurora Sibbet Sibbet House 26 Northumberland Street Edinburgh EH3 6LS Tel: 031 556 1078 Fax: 031 557 9445	DELUXE 👑 👑 👑	1 Twin 1 Double 1 Family	3 En Suite fac	B&B per person £22.50-£30.00 Double Dinner 1800-1930 B&B + Eve. Meal £41.00-£48.50	Open May-Sep	
Georgian town house of considerable character built in 1809 and furnished with antiques. Bagpipes played on request. 5 minutes walk from Princes St.						
Mrs E C Simpson 17 Crawfurd Road Edinburgh EH16 5PW Tel: 031 667 1191	COMMENDED Listed	1 Twin 1 Family	2 Pub. Bath/Show	B&B per person £12.50-£16.50 Double	Open May-Sep	
Friendly welcome in late Victorian family home in quiet residential area, with easy access to city centre. Unrestricted parking.						

Scotland for Golf . . .

Find out more about golf in Scotland. There's more to it than just the championship courses so get in touch with us now for information on the hidden gems of Scotland.

Write to: **Information Unit, Scottish Tourist Board, 23 Ravelston Terrace, Edinburgh EH4 3EU or call: 031-332 2433**

Details of Grading and Classification are on page vi.　　　　　**Key to symbols is on back flap.**

EDINBURGH continued	Map 2 D5

LANSDOWNE
🏵🏵 *Commended*

1 WESTER COATES ROAD, EDINBURGH EH12 5LU
Telephone: 031-337 5002   Proprietor: **Mrs R. Sinclair**
Pleasantly situated villa in a quiet residential area near West End of Princes Street. Very convenient for buses, stations, airport. Private parking. All rooms have wash-hand basins, electric blankets, radio and central heating — one room on ground floor. Spacious and comfortable guests' lounge.
You are assured of a warm welcome.

Mrs R Sinclair Lansdowne 1 Wester Coates Road Edinburgh EH12 5LU Tel: 031 337 5002	COMMENDED 🏵🏵	1 Single 1 Double 1 Family	2 Pub. Bath/Show	B&B per person £14.00-£17.00 Single £14.00-£16.00 Double	Open May-Sep	

Pleasantly situated detached villa in quiet residential area near west end of city. Close to main bus routes, convenient for station and airport.

Mrs J Skidmore 2 Braid Hills Edinburgh EH10 6EZ Tel: 031 447 8848		1 Single 2 Double 1 Family	1 Pub. Bath/Show	B&B per person £15.00-£16.00 Single £14.00-£15.00 Double	Open May-Sep Dinner 1800-2000 B&B + Eve. Meal to £24.00	

28 Northumberland Street

**28 NORTHUMBERLAND STREET
EDINBURGH EH3 6LS
Tel: 031-557 8036   Fax: 558 3453**

28 Northumberland Street is an elegant Georgian house of architectural interest situated in the heart of Edinburgh, 5 minutes walk from Princes Street. It is furnished with antiques and offers a friendly relaxing and comfortable location within a family house. A plentiful breakfast is served within the original dining room of the house with its unusual curved wall. For other meals there is a wide variety of restaurants nearby. The guest rooms are beautifully appointed, centrally heated and have telephone, colour television, radio, hairdryer and tea and coffee making facilities. All have private bath or shower rooms.
B&B from £30 per night.
For brochure and details contact Eirlys Smith.

Mrs Eirlys Smith 28 Northumberland Street Edinburgh EH3 6LS Tel: 031 557 8036 Fax: 031 558 3453	DELUXE 🏵🏵	1 Single 2 Twin	2 En Suite fac 1 Priv. NOT ensuite	B&B per person £28.00-£30.00 Single £25.00-£30.00 Double	Open May-Sep	

Georgian town house and family home in the heart of Edinburgh's New Town. Tastefully decorated and furnished. Telephone and fax facilities.

Mrs Elizabeth Stewart 14 Angle Park Terrace Edinburgh EH11 2JX Tel: 031 337 4157		1 Single 1 Twin 1 Family	1 Pub. Bath/Show	B&B per person £14.00-£15.00 Single £13.00-£15.00 Double	Open Jun-Sep Dinner 1800-2000	

Mrs R C Torrance 15 Viewforth Terrace Edinburgh EH10 4LJ Tel: 031 229 1776		3 Twin	1 Pub. Bath/Show	B&B per person £13.00-£15.00 Double	Open May-Sep	

J Toynbee 21 Dean Park Crescent Edinburgh EH4 1PH Tel: 031 332 3096		COMMENDED 👑 👑	1 Single 1 Double 1 Family	1 Limited ensuite 1 Priv. NOT ensuite 1 Pub. Bath/Show	B&B per person £16.50-£18.50 Single £16.00-£18.00 Double	Open May-Sep	

Terraced Georgian house close to city centre. Within walking distance of shops, restaurants and cultural attractions.

Ms Jennie Tyla
The Green Door
10 Greenhill Terrace
Edinburgh
EH10 4BS
Tel: 031 447 0804 — 1 Double, 1 Family — 1 Limited ensuite, 1 Pub. Bath/Show — B&B per person £14.00-£20.00 Double — Open May-Sep

---

Mr John B Wheelaghan
Sunnyside, 13 Pilrig Street
Edinburgh
Tel: 031 553 2084 — 2 Single, 1 Double, 1 Family — 2 En Suite fac, 1 Limited ensuite, 1 Priv. NOT ensuite, 2 Pub. Bath/Show — B&B per person £18.50-£21.00 Single, £18.00-£21.00 Double — Open Jun-Aug

---

Mrs J Williamson
Hopebank
33 Hope Lane, Portobello
Edinburgh
EH15 2PZ
Tel: 031 657 1149 — COMMENDED 👑 👑 — 1 Twin, 2 Double — 3 Limited ensuite, 1 Pub. Bath/Show — B&B per person to £16.00 Double — Open Jul-Aug

19C terraced villa in quiet residential area with ample parking.
Traditional Scottish hospitality. Good bus service for city centre. Close to beach.

EDZELL
Angus — Map 4 F1

Mrs J Myles
The Gorse, Dunlappie Road
Edzell
Angus
DD9 7UB
Tel: (Edzell) 0356 648207 — COMMENDED 👑 — 2 Twin — 2 Pub. Bath/Show — B&B per person from £11.50 Double — Open Jan-Dec

Quietly situated opposite golf course with open views of hills to rear.
Home baking and a warm welcome. A non-smoking house.

ELGIN
Moray — Map 4 D8

The Lodge Guest House
20 Duff Avenue
Elgin
Moray
IV30 1QS
Tel: (Elgin) 0343 549981 — COMMENDED 👑 👑 — 4 Single, 2 Twin, 1 Double, 1 Family — 8 En Suite fac — B&B per person from £15.00 Single, from £15.00 Double — Open Jan-Dec, Dinner 1830-2000, B&B + Eve. Meal from £25.00

Recently refurbished listred villa in extensive grounds with private parking.
Quietly situated but handy for all amenities.

Mr & Mrs Ken Asher
Rosemount, 5 Mayne Road
Elgin
Moray
IV30 1NY
Tel: (Elgin) 0343 542907
Fax: 0343 542907 — COMMENDED 👑 👑 👑 — 1 Twin, 1 Family — 2 En Suite fac — B&B per person £19.00-£28.00 Single, to £19.00 Double — Open Jan-Dec, Dinner 1830-1900, B&B + Eve. Meal to £29.00

Large house in quiet area on edge of town centre. Private parking.
Emphas is on fresh food and home cooking.

Mrs Frances McMillan
14 South College Street
Elgin
Moray
IV30 1EP
Tel: (Elgin) 0343 541515 — COMMENDED Listed — 1 Twin, 1 Double — 2 En Suite fac — B&B per person £16.00-£18.00 Single, £14.00-£16.00 Double — Open Jan-Dec

Personally run pre-war detached villa, with off street parking. A few minutes
walk from the town centre and Cathedral. No smoking.

Mrs Audrey J Milne
57 Main Street, New Elgin
Elgin
Moray
IV30 3BH
Tel: (Elgin) 0343 545806 — 2 Single, 1 Twin, 1 Double — 2 Pub. Bath/Show — B&B per person £12.00-£15.00 Single, £11.00-£14.00 Double — Open Jan-Dec

---

BY ELGIN Moray	Map 4 D8

ARDGYE HOUSE
ELGIN · MORAY IV30 3UP   TEL/FAX: 0343 85618

ARDGYE HOUSE is a spacious mansion house set in 150 acres, situated close to main Aberdeen to Inverness Road. Superb accommodation in quiet surroundings. Central position ideal for beaches, golf, riding, fishing, castles and distilleries. You are assured of a warm welcome.

For full details contact Carol and Alistair McInnes.

Ardgye House Elgin Moray IV30 3UP Tel: (Alves) 034385 618	**HIGHLY COMMENDED** 👑 👑	1 Single 3 En Suite fac 2 Twin 3 Limited ensuite 3 Double 3 Priv. NOT ensuite 3 Family 2 Pub. Bath/Show **Gracious Edwardian mansion in own extensive grounds easily accessible from A96. 3 miles (5kms) from Elgin. Private facilities available.**	B&B per person £14.00-£16.00 Single £14.00-£16.00 Double Open Jan-Dec
Mrs J Goodwin Foresters House, Newton Elgin Moray IV30 3XW Tel: (Elgin) 0343 552862		1 Twin 1 Pub. Bath/Show 1 Double 2 Limited ensuite	B&B per person £14.00-£16.00 Single £14.00-£16.00 Double Open Jan-Dec
ELIE **Fife** The Elms 14 Park Place Elie Fife KY9 1DH Tel: (Elie) 0333 330404	Map 2 E3 **COMMENDED** 👑 👑 👑	1 Single 4 En Suite fac 3 Twin 2 Pub. Bath/Show 1 Double 2 Family **Privately owned detached Victorian house with large secluded garden, in picturesque coastal village with sandy beach, local golf courses, walks.**	B&B per person £23.50-£45.00 Single £18.00-£24.00 Double Open Apr-Sep Dinner from 1900 B&B + Eve. Meal £28.00-£34.00
Mr & Mrs Cowan Millford House, 19 High Street Elie Fife KY9 1BY Tel: (Elie) 0333 330567		1 Twin 1 Priv. NOT ensuite 1 Double 2 Pub. Bath/Show 1 Family	B&B per person £13.00-£18.00 Single £13.00-£18.00 Double Open Jan-Dec
Mrs P Knottenbelt 33 Park Place Elie Fife KY9 1DH Tel: (Elie) 0333 330391	**APPROVED** Listed	2 Single 1 Pub. Bath/Show 1 Twin **Georgian house, ideal location near seaside. Warm, friendly welcome awaits.**	B&B per person from £16.00 Single from £14.00 Double Open Jan-Dec Dinner from 1800
Mrs E Lamond Craigard, 43 High Street Elie Fife KY9 1BZ Tel: (Elie) 0333 330412		1 Single 1 Pub. Bath/Show 1 Twin 1 Family	B&B per person from £13.00 Single from £13.00 Double Open Apr-Oct
ELLON **Aberdeenshire** Mrs A Deans 77 Ness Circle Ellon Aberdeenshire AB41 9BU Tel: (Ellon) 0358 24145	Map 4 H9 Award Pending	1 Twin 1 Pub. Bath/Show 1 Double	B&B per person £14.00-£16.00 Single £12.00-£14.00 Double B&B + Eve. Meal £17.00-£21.00 Open Jan-Dec Dinner 1800-2100

126   **VAT is shown at 17.5%: changes in this rate may affect prices. Prices shown are for guidance only. Please send SAE with each enquiry.**

Mrs Morrison Claymore, 8 St Mary's Drive Ellon Aberdeenshire AB41 9LW Tel: (Ellon) 0358 20386		**COMMENDED** Listed	1 Single 1 Double	2 Priv. NOT ensuite 1 Pub. Bath/Show	B&B per person £12.50-£14.00 Single £12.50-£15.00 Double	Open Jan-Dec

Modern bungalow in quiet residential area. Easy access to Castle Trail and city of Aberdeen.

Mrs Betty Stevenson Cadha Beag, 14 Turnishaw Hill Ellon Aberdeenshire AB41 8BB Tel: (Ellon) 0358 22383		**COMMENDED** Listed	1 Single 1 Twin	1 Pub. Bath/Show	B&B per person £12.50-£15.00 Single £13.00-£15.00 Double	Open Jan-Dec

Modern bungalow on outskirts of town opposite local golf course.

Mrs Thomson 58 Station Road Ellon Aberdeenshire AB41 9AL Tel: (Ellon) 0358 720263		**COMMENDED**	2 Twin	1 Pub. Bath/Show	B&B per person £15.00-£16.00 Single £12.50-£14.00 Double	Open Jan-Dec

Delightful Victorian house in quiet residential area, close to all local amenities. Warm welcome.

ENOCHDHU, by Pitlochry **Perthshire** Mrs J Catterall Tulloch Enochdhu, by Blairgowrie Perthshire PH10 7PW Tel: (Strathardle) 0250 881404	Map 4 D1		1 Twin 2 Family	1 Pub. Bath/Show	B&B per person £13.00-£14.00 Single £13.00-£14.00 Double	Open Jan-Dec Dinner 1900-2000 B&B + Eve. Meal £19.00-£20.00

ETTRICKBRIDGE, by Selkirk **Selkirkshire** Cross Keys Inn Ettrickbridge, by Selkirk Selkirkshire TD7 5JN Tel: (Selkirk) 0750 52224	Map 2 E7		1 Twin 1 Double	2 En Suite fac	B&B per person from £19.50 Single from £17.50 Double	Open Jan-Dec Dinner 1800-2100

EYEMOUTH **Berwickshire** Mrs Lowther The Hermitage, Paxton Terrace Eyemouth Berwickshire TD14 5EL Tel: (Eyemouth) 08907 50324	Map 2 G5	**COMMENDED**	1 Twin 2 Double	1 Limited ensuite 2 Pub. Bath/Show	B&B per person from £15.00 Single from £15.00 Double	Open Apr-Sep

Warm welcome in this former manse set high above town with splendid seaviews. Convenient for all local amenities.

Mrs McGovern Ebba House, Upper Houndlaw Eyemouth Berwickshire TD14 5BU Tel: (Eyemouth) 08907 50350		**COMMENDED** Listed	2 Single 1 Twin 1 Double	2 Pub. Bath/Show	B&B per person £14.00-£15.00 Single £14.00-£15.00 Double	Open Jan-Dec Dinner 1730-1830 B&B + Eve. Meal £20.00-£23.00

Centrally located terraced house in quiet street. Short walk to beach, harbour and shops. Friendly welcome, home cooking.

Mrs J MacKay Hillcrest, Coldingham Road Eyemouth Berwickshire TD14 5AN Tel: (Eyemouth) 08907 50463		**COMMENDED** Listed	1 Twin 1 Double	1 Pub. Bath/Show	B&B per person from £14.00 Single from £14.00 Double	Open Jan-Dec

Pleasantly situated with own garden in residential area of coastal town. Ideal for touring.

Details of Grading and Classification are on page vi.

Key to symbols is on back flap.

BY EYEMOUTH **Berwickshire** Mr D J Davison The Old Coaching Inn Houndwood Grantshouse Berwickshire TD14 5TB Tel: (Grantshouse) 03615 232	Map 2 G5		1 Single 2 Twin 1 Double 2 Family	6 En Suite fac	B&B per person £15.00-£20.00 Single £15.00-£20.00 Double	Open Jan-Dec Dinner 1830-2030 B&B + Eve. Meal £22.50-£30.00	
Mrs W B Donnelly The White House Lower Burnmouth Eyemouth Berwickshire TD14 5SP Tel: (Eyemouth) 08907 81622		COMMENDED Listed	1 Twin 1 Family	1 Pub. Bath/Show	B&B per person £12.00-£12.50 Single £12.00-£12.50 Double	Open Mar-Oct	
			Friendly welcome awaits in family home on sea front, in picturesque fishing village. Ideal touring base.				
FAIRLIE **Ayrshire** Mrs Gardner Mon Abri, 12 Main Road Fairlie Ayrshire KA29 0DP Tel: (Fairlie) 0475 568241	Map 1 G6	COMMENDED Listed	1 Single 1 Twin 1 Family	1 Pub. Bath/Show	B&B per person £14.00-£16.00 Single £14.00-£16.00 Double	Open Jan-Dec Dinner from 1800 B&B + Eve. Meal £21.00-£23.00	
			Detached bungalow on main tourist route, overlooking the Firth of Clyde. 45 minutes by road from Glasgow. Personally run, evening meals available.				
FALA **Midlothian** Mrs Lothian Fala Hall Farm Fala, Pathhead Midlothian EH37 5SZ Tel: (Humbie) 087533 249	Map 2 D5	COMMENDED Listed	1 Double 1 Family	2 Pub. Bath/Show	B&B per person £13.00-£15.00 Double	Open Jan-Dec	
			Picturesque 17C farmhouse on working farm peacefully set in rolling countryside, yet only 17 miles (27kms) from Edinburgh.				
FALKIRK **Stirlingshire** Mrs C Carruthers-Gannon Chez Nous, Sunnyside Road Brightons, Falkirk Stirlingshire FK2 0RZ Tel: (Polmont) 0324 715953	Map 2 B4		2 Twin 1 Double	1 En Suite fac 1 Pub. Bath/Show	B&B per person from £20.00 Single from £20.00 Double	Open Feb-Nov	
Mrs Helen Jones Ellerslie, Standrigg Road Wallacestone Falkirk Stirlingshire FK2 0EB Tel: (Polmont) 0324 713120		COMMENDED	2 Twin 1 Family	2 En Suite fac 1 Limited ensuite	B&B per person £20.00-£23.00 Single from £20.00 Double	Open Jan-Dec	
			Detached villa in rural surroundings with views over Forth Valley. Close to railway station and motorways. Quiet location.				
Mrs E Rennie Bower's Well 3 Gartcows Road Falkirk Stirlingshire FK1 2AU Tel: (Falkirk) 0324 32352		APPROVED Listed	1 Twin 1 Double	1 Pub. Bath/Show	B&B per person from £15.00 Double	Open Jan-Dec	
			Centrally situated family run B&B. Close to main Edinburgh Glasgow rail link. Private parking, easy reach of town centre.				
Mrs S Taylor Wester Carmuirs Farm Larbert, by Falkirk Stirlingshire FK5 3NW Tel: (Bonnybridge) 0324 812459		COMMENDED	2 Twin 1 Double	2 Pub. Bath/Show	B&B per person from £16.00 Single from £15.00 Double	Open Jan-Dec, exc Xmas	
			Family house on working arable and beef farm. Falkirk leisure centre, 0.5miles (1 km). Bonnybridge 1.5 miles (3kms). Good base for touring.				

FALKLAND
Fife
Map 2 C3

Mrs A Heather
Ladieburn Cottage, High Street
Falkland, Cupar
Fife
KY7 7BZ
Tel: (Falkland)
0337 57016/857016

COMMENDED
👑 👑

1 Twin 2 En Suite fac
1 Family

B&B per person
£18.00-£20.00 Single
£13.00-£15.00 Double

Open Jan-Dec
Dinner 1800-2000
B&B + Eve. Meal
£18.00-£20.00

19C house in centre of village opposite the historic Palace.
Both bedrooms have en suite facilities.

Mrs Sarah G McGregor
Templelands Farm
Falkland
Fife
KY7 7DE
Tel: (Falkland)
0337 57383/857383

COMMENDED
👑

1 Double 2 Pub. Bath/Show
1 Family

B&B per person
£15.00 Double

Open Apr-Oct
Dinner from 1900
B&B + Eve. Meal
£22.00

Farmhouse on side of Lomond Hills with superb views over Howe of Fife.
Taste of Scotland recommended. 20 miles (32 kms) from St Andrews.

FARR
Inverness-shire
Map 4 B9

Mrs J Carter
Inverarnie Cottage
Farr
Inverness-shire
IV1 2XA
Tel: (Farr) 08083 308

APPROVED
Listed

1 Twin 1 Limited ensuite
2 Double 2 Pub. Bath/Show

B&B per person
£15.50-£16.00 Single
£13.50-£15.50 Double

Open Mar-Dec
Dinner 1900-2000
B&B + Eve. Meal
£20.00-£26.00

Traditional farmhouse, beautiful rural setting. Sauna. Sight seeing trips
in light aircraft available. Fishing, birdwatching, riding, walking nearby

---

FEARNAN, by Kenmore
Perthshire
Map 2 A1

LETTERELLAN

LETTERELLAN · FEARNAN · By ABERFELDY PH15 2NY
Telephone: 0887 830 221

Situated in the heart of Scotland with spectacular views over
Loch Tay and Ben Lawers, this rose-fronted (non-smoking) house,
standing in wooded and rhododendroned grounds,
offers tranquillity and a high degree of comfort to visitors.
Tourist attractions and a wide range of sporting activities exist
within easy reach.

Mr G A MacKay
Letterellan
Fearnan, by Aberfeldy
Perthshire
PH15 2NY
Tel: (Kenmore) 0887 830221

COMMENDED
👑 👑

2 Twin 3 Priv. NOT ensuite
1 Double

B&B per person
£17.00-£20.00 Double

Open Mar-Oct

Rose covered house tastefully restored, all bedrooms with
private bathrooms. Superb views over Loch Tay.

FENWICK, by Kilmarnock
Ayrshire
Map 1 H6

Tessie Macnab
Mansefield, 10 Kirkton Road
Fenwick, by Kilmarnock
Ayrshire
KA3 6DH
Tel: (Fenwick) 0560 600834

APPROVED
Listed

2 Twin 1 Pub. Bath/Show
1 Double

B&B per person
£14.00-£17.00 Single
£13.00-£16.00 Double

Open Jan-Dec
Dinner 1700-2200
B&B + Eve. Meal
£20.00-£23.00

Listed manse in conservation village of Fenwick, 9 miles (14kms) from
Glasgow, 3miles (5kms) from Kilmarnock, 15 miles (24kms) from Prestwick.

FETTERCAIRN
Kincardineshire
Map 4 F1

Mrs Monckton
Tillytoghills Farmhouse
Fettercairn
Kincardineshire
AB30 1YJ
Tel: (Fettercairn)
0561 340230

2 Family 2 Pub. Bath/Show

B&B per person
£13.00-£16.00 Single
£13.00-£16.00 Double

Open Mar-Nov

FINDHORN Moray	Map 4 C8

'No 72' FINDHORN
72 FINDHORN, FORRES, MORAY IV36 0YF
Telephone: 0309 690495
Comfortable, homely, tastefully decorated fisherman's cottage in charming small village, on sea with safe bay. Various watersports summer. Near pubs, shops. Warm welcome, friendly atmosphere, log fires.
Double/Twin £25, Single £15.

Heloise Shewan 72 Findhorn Findhorn, Forres Moray IV36 0YF Tel: (Findhorn) 0309 690495	1 Twin 1 Double	1 Pub. Bath/Show	B&B per person £15.00-£16.00 Single £12.50-£14.00 Double	Open Jan-Dec	
Mrs Margaret J Tointon Harbour House Findhorn, by Forres Moray IV36 0YE Tel: (Findhorn) 0309 690328	2 Twin 1 Double	1 Pub. Bath/Show	B&B per person £14.00-£16.00 Single £14.00-£16.00 Double	Open Mar-Oct	

FIONNPHORT Isle of Mull, Argyll Mrs H J Heald Bruach Mhor Fionnphort Isle of Mull, Argyll PA66 6BL Tel: (Fionnphort) 06817 276	Map 1 B3		1 Twin 2 Double	2 Pub. Bath/Show	B&B per person £13.00-£14.00 Double	Open Jan-Dec Dinner 1900-2000 B&B + Eve. Meal £21.00-£22.00	

Mrs Noddings Seaview Fionnphort Isle of Mull, Argyll PA66 6BL Tel: (Fionnphort) 06817 235	COMMENDED Listed	2 Twin 2 Double	1 En Suite fac 2 Pub. Bath/Show	B&B per person £15.00-£17.00 Single £12.00-£19.00 Double	Open Jan-Dec Dinner 1830-1930 B&B + Eve. Meal £21.00-£28.00	

Granite built house with views over the Sound of Iona and only 150 yards from the ferry point to Iona. Friendly atmosphere and home cooking.

Ms A Rimell Dungrianach Fionnphort Isle of Mull, Argyll PA66 6BL Tel: (Fionnphort) 06817 417	COMMENDED 👑👑	2 Twin	2 En Suite fac	B&B per person £18.00-£20.00 Single £14.50 Double	Open Jan-Dec	

Warm friendly cottage close to Iona ferry terminal. Superb views of Iona.

FLODABAY Harris, Western Isles	Map 3 B7

FERNHAVEN
1 FLODABAY, ISLE OF HARRIS, WESTERN ISLES
Telephone: 0859 83 340

Modern house on croft offering accommodation of one double and one twin rooms with w.h.b. Tea/coffee facilities, hairdryers. Residents' lounge with colour TV. Separate dining room. Situated 10 miles from ferry port of Tarbert in quiet lochside setting. Excellent opportunities for hill-walking and bird-watching.

Contact Mrs Catherine MacAulay.

Mrs MacAulay Fernhaven Flodabay Harris, Western Isles PA85 3HA Tel: (Manish) 085983 340	COMMENDED	1 Twin 1 Pub. Bath/Show 1 Double	B&B per person from £17.50 Double	Open Jan-Dec Dinner to 1900 B&B + Eve. Meal £28.00-£30.00

Modern house faced with local stone, on working croft, set amidst rugged mountain scenery of Harris. Home cooking and baking.

FOCHABERS Moray Mrs Phyllis I Cruikshank South View, 42 South Street Fochabers Moray IV32 7ED Tel: (Fochabers) 0343 820478	Map 4 E8	1 Double 2 Priv. NOT ensuite 1 Family 1 Pub. Bath/Show	B&B per person £12.00 Single £12.00 Double	Open Mar-Oct Dinner 1700-1900 B&B + Eve. Meal £18.00

BY FOCHABERS Moray Mrs Mary K Shand Castlehill Cottage, Blackdam Fochabers Moray IV32 7LJ Tel: (Fochabers) 0343 820761	Map 4 E8	COMMENDED Listed	1 Twin 1 Pub. Bath/Show 1 Family	B&B per person from £13.00 Single from £11.00 Double	Open Jan-Dec

Family cottage set back from A96, with own flower garden and ample parking 6 miles (10kms) east of Elgin.

FORDYCE, by Portsoy Banffshire Mrs Leith Academy House, School Road Fordyce Banffshire AB45 2SJ Tel: (Portsoy) 0261 42743	Map 4 F8	DELUXE Listed	1 Twin 2 Pub. Bath/Show 2 Double	B&B per person from £15.00 Single from £13.50 Double	Open Jan-Dec Dinner 1900-2030 B&B + Eve. Meal from £21.00

Scottish hospitality in stylish country home set in beautiful conservation village. Quality cooking with local produce. Well located for touring.

WELCOME

Whenever you are in Scotland, you can be sure of a warm welcome at your nearest Tourist Information Centre.

For guide books, maps, souvenirs, our Centres provide a service second to none—many now offer bureau-de-change facilities. And, of course, Tourist Information Centres offer free, expert advice on what to see and do, route-planning and accommodation for everyone—visitors and residents alike!

FORFAR **Angus** Mrs G Armishaw Inshewan Estate Forfar Angus DD8 3TU Tel: (Forfar) 0307 86313/486313	**Map 2** D1		2 Twin	2 Priv. NOT ensuite 1 Pub. Bath/Show	B&B per person £15.00 Single £15.00 Double	Open Jan-Dec Dinner 1800-2030 B&B + Eve. Meal to £27.50	
Mrs Craig Haven Cottage 20 Craig O' Loch Road Forfar Angus DD8 1BY Tel: (Forfar) 0307 467768			1 Twin 1 Family	2 En Suite fac	B&B per person from £16.00 Single from £13.00 Double	Open Jan-Dec	

Farmhouse Bed & Breakfast
WEST MAINS OF TURIN, FORFAR DD8 2TE
Tel: (0307) 830229 (Aberlemno)

Our stock-rearing farm enjoys a panoramic view over Rescobie Loch on Montrose/Forfar road (B9113). It is an ideal base for exploring places of interest. Golf and fishing nearby.

A friendly welcome and homely atmosphere await guests. Home cooking and baking served. Snooker and croquet for evening entertainment.

Mrs C Jolly West Mains of Turin Rescobie, Forfar Angus DD8 2TE Tel: (Aberlemno) 030783 229/0307 830229	**COMMENDED** 👑 👑	1 Single 1 Double 1 Family	1 En Suite fac 1 Priv. NOT ensuite 1 Pub. Bath/Show	B&B per person £13.00-£16.00 Single £13.00-£16.00 Double	Open Mar-Oct Dinner 1800-1830 B&B + Eve. Meal £20.00-£23.00	

Farmhouse on working stock farm 4 miles (6kms) east of Forfar.
In elevated position with fine views southwards over Rescobie Loch.

WEMYSS FARM
Montrose Road, Forfar   Tel: Forfar (0307) 462887

Situated on the B9113, our 190-acre farm has a wide variety of animals. Glamis Castle nearby. Many other castles etc. within easy reach. Ideal touring base for Glens, Dundee, Perth, St Andrews, Aberdeen, Edinburgh, Balmoral, Deeside and East Coast resorts. Hillwalking, shooting, golf and fishing nearby. Children welcome.

A warm welcome awaits!

Mrs D Lindsay Wemyss Farm Montrose Road Forfar Angus DD8 2TB Tel: (Forfar) 0307 62887/462887	**COMMENDED** Listed	1 Double 1 Family	2 Pub. Bath/Show	B&B per person from £15.50 Single from £12.50 Double	Open Jan-Dec Dinner 1800-1930 B&B + Eve. Meal from £20.00

Family farmhouse on working farm. Centrally situated for touring Angus and
east coast. Home cooking and baking. Children welcome.

BY FORFAR Angus	Map 2 D1

Finavon Farmhouse

Finavon, By Forfar, Angus DD8 3PX 0307 850269

Modern villa with matching amenities set in three acres of grounds with easy access to the Forfar/Aberdeen road (A94). Centrally situated for a wide range of sporting and leisure pursuits. *Guests are assured of a warm welcome and an excellent standard of cuisine using the best of local produce.*

Mrs L Rome Finavon Farmhouse Finavon, by Forfar Angus DD8 3PX Tel: (Finavon) 030785 269/0307 850269	**HIGHLY COMMENDED** 🏅🏅🏅	2 Twin	1 En Suite fac 1 Priv. NOT ensuite	B&B per person £16.00-£18.00 Single £13.50-£14.50 Double	Open Jan-Dec Dinner 1800-1930 B&B + Eve. Meal £21.00-£25.50

Warm welcome assured in this modern house in extensive secluded grounds at foot of Finavon Hill. Offers excellent facilities. Good base for touring.

FORRES Moray	Map 4 C8				
Mr Brian Atkiss Clifton House, Caroline Street Forres IV36 0AQ Tel: (Forres) 0309 673440	**COMMENDED** Listed	2 Twin 2 Double 1 Family	1 En Suite fac 2 Pub. Bath/Show	B&B per person £13.00-£15.50 Double	Open Jan-Dec

Large house in central Forres. Family run and convenient for all local amenities.

Mrs Catherine M Bain Springfield, Croft Road Forres Moray IV36 0JS Tel: (Forres) 0309 676965 Fax: 0309 673376	**Award Pending**	1 Twin 1 Family	2 Priv. NOT ensuite 1 Pub. Bath/Show	B&B per person from £15.00 Single from £13.50 Double	Open Jan-Dec

---

Mrs Barbara MacDonald Morven, Caroline Street Forres Moray IV36 0AN Tel: (Forres) 0309 673788		1 Single 2 Twin	1 Pub. Bath/Show	B&B per person £13.00-£15.00 Single £13.00-£15.00 Double	Open Jan-Dec

---

Mr & Mrs David Ross Heather Lodge, Tytler Street Forres Moray IV36 0EL Tel: (Forres) 0309 672377		3 Single 1 Twin 2 Double 1 Family	5 En Suite fac 2 Limited ensuite	B&B per person £15.00-£16.00 Single £15.00-£16.00 Double	Open Jan-Dec

---

Mrs Lindsay N Ross Tormhor, 11 High Street Forres Moray IV36 0BU Tel: (Forres) 0309 673837	**COMMENDED** 🏅🏅	1 Twin 2 Double	1 En Suite fac 2 Pub. Bath/Show	B&B per person £15.00-£20.00 Double	Open Apr-Oct

Traditional house overlooking 'Britain in Bloom' award winning garden. Large comfortable rooms. Private parking.

Details of Grading and Classification are on page vi. Key to symbols is on back flap.

FORRES continued	Map 4 C8		

SCANIA
ST LEONARD'S ROAD, FORRES, MORAY IV36 0RE
Telephone: 0309 672583

A lovely country house standing in three acres of wooded grounds offering delicious home cooking, comfort and tranquillity along with a warm welcome. Within easy reach of the Malt Whisky Trail and miles of sandy beaches, it stands only ½ mile from Forres Golf Club.

Mrs Norma J Shewan Scania, St Leonards Road Forres Moray IV36 0RE Tel: (Forres) 0309 672583	HIGHLY COMMENDED Listed	2 Twin 1 Double	1 Pub. Bath/Show	B&B per person £15.00-£17.50 Single £13.00-£16.00 Double	Open Apr-Oct

Architect's elegantly designed home set in 3 acres of woods and gardens. Vegetarian breakfast and golf packages available.

BY FORRES Moray Mrs Flora Barclay Moss-Side Farm, Rafford Forres Moray IV36 0SL Tel: (Forres) 0309 672954	Map 4 C8	1 Twin 1 Family	1 Pub. Bath/Show	B&B per person to £12.00 Single to £12.00 Double	Open May-Sep Dinner from 1900 B&B + Eve. Meal to £20.00

Mrs Maureen Bogg Invercairn House, Brodie Forres Moray IV36 0TD Tel: (Brodie) 03094 261	APPROVED	2 Single 2 Twin 1 Family	1 Pub. Bath/Show	B&B per person from £13.00 Single from £12.00 Double	Open Jan-Dec Dinner from 1800 B&B + Eve. Meal £18.00-£19.00

Old Brodie Station House, now family run bed and breakfast on A96 tourist route. Brodie Castle 0.5 miles (1km), Inverness 24 miles (38kms).

Mrs Eileen Bush The Old Custom House Glenburgie Forres Moray IV36 0QU Tel: (Alves) 034385 343	HIGHLY COMMENDED	1 Single 1 Twin	1 Priv. NOT ensuite 1 Pub. Bath/Show	B&B per person £15.00-£17.00 Single £14.00-£16.00 Double	Open Jan-Dec

This well appointed former distillery "Custom House" dispenses in large measure, warmth and family hospitality - the true spirit of the Highlands.

Mrs Elizabeth J Masson Gateside Farm Alves, Forres Moray IV36 0RB Tel: (Alves) 034385 246	HIGHLY COMMENDED	1 Twin 1 Double 1 Family	1 Priv. NOT ensuite 3 Pub. Bath/Show	B&B per person £15.00-£18.00 Double	Open Jan-Dec

Stone built farmhouse approximately 250 years old, situated beside main A96, on mixed arable farm, 4 miles (6km) east of Forres. Home baking.

Mrs Alma Rhind Woodside, Kinloss Forres Moray IV36 0UA Tel: (Forres) 0309 690258 Fax: 0309 690258	COMMENDED	1 Twin 2 Double	2 Pub. Bath/Show	B&B per person from £14.00 Single from £14.00 Double	Open Apr-Oct

Detached farmhouse on mixed farm near village. Real farmhouse welcome with home baking. Farm shop. Sandy beaches 2 miles (3kms).

FORT AUGUSTUS Inverness-shire Mrs J MacKenzie The Old Pier Fort Augustus Inverness-shire PH32 4BX Tel: (Fort Augustus) 0320 6418/366418	Map 3 H1 COMMENDED	1 Twin 1 Double 1 Family	3 En Suite fac	B&B per person £15.00-£25.00 Double	Open Apr-Oct Dinner 1800-2000 B&B + Eve. Meal £25.00-£35.00

50 acre farm by Loch Ness with panoramic views. Friendly atmosphere highland cattle; riding, boating and fishing available.

VAT is shown at 17.5%: changes in this rate may affect prices. Prices shown are for guidance only. Please send SAE with each enquiry.

J G Nairn Appin, Inverness Road Fort Augustus Inverness-shire PH32 4DH Tel: (Fort Augustus) 0320 6541/366541		COMMENDED 👑 👑	1 Twin 1 Double 1 Family	1 En Suite fac 1 Pub. Bath/Show	B&B per person £13.00-£16.00 Double	Open Apr-Oct	

**Detached modern bungalow on the edge of a small village.
Ideal base for touring the Highlands.**

Mrs L H Service Sonas Fort Augustus Inverness-shire PH32 4BA Tel: (Fort Augustus) 0320 6291/366291		HIGHLY COMMENDED 👑 👑	1 Twin 1 Double 1 Family	2 En Suite fac 1 Priv. NOT ensuite	B&B per person £15.00-£20.00 Double	Open Jan-Dec	

**Modern house in elevated position on the northern edge of the village,
with excellent views of surrounding hills.**

FORTEVIOT **Perthshire** Mrs Margaret Drummond Broomhill, Dunning Perth Perthshire PH2 9BU Tel: (Dunning) 0764 684263	Map 2 B3		1 Single 2 Twin	2 Pub. Bath/Show	B&B per person £16.00-£20.00 Single £16.00-£20.00 Double	Open Jan-Dec Dinner from 1900	

FORTINGALL **Perthshire**	Map 2 A1

GARTH HOUSE
by Aberfeldy, Perthshire PH15 2NF
Telephone 0887 830515

Garth House, a Scottish Baronial Manor House, lies on a sheltered bank of the River Lyon in Highland Perthshire.
The B&B suite comprises a lounge-breakfast room with television and double bed, a twin-bedded room, and a panelled shower room.
For details contact: PAULA and STEVEN LODGE.

Mr & Mrs S Lodge Garth House Fortingall Perthshire PH15 2NF Tel: (Kenmore) 0887 830515			1 Twin 1 Double	2 En Suite fac 1 Pub. Bath/Show	B&B per person £16.00-£18.00 Double	Open Jan-Dec	

Mrs Tulloch Fendoch Fortingall Perthshire PH15 2LL Tel: (Kenmore) 0887 830322		Award Pending	1 Twin 1 Double 1 Family	2 En Suite fac 1 Priv. NOT ensuite 1 Pub. Bath/Show	B&B per person £13.00-£15.00 Single £13.00-£15.00 Double	Open Jan-Dec Dinner 1800-2200 B&B + Eve. Meal £23.00-£25.00	

FORTROSE **Ross-shire** Mrs E Cooper West Craig-an-Ron Academy Street Fortrose Ross-shire IV10 8TW Tel: (Fortrose) 0381 21184/621184 Fax: 0381 21184	Map 4 B8		1 Twin 2 Double	3 En Suite fac	B&B per person £13.50-£15.00 Single £13.50-£15.00 Double	Open Jan-Dec Dinner 1800-2000 B&B + Eve. Meal £19.50-£21.00	

FORTROSE Mrs J MacRury 5 Ness Way Fortrose Ross-shire IV10 8SS Tel: (Fortrose) 0381 20988/620988	Map 4 B8		1 Single 1 Twin 1 Double	1 Pub. Bath/Show	B&B per person from £12.00 Single from £12.00 Double	Open Jan-Dec

FORT WILLIAM Map 3
Inverness-shire G1

ASHBURN HOUSE

Achintore Road, Fort William
Highland PH33 6RQ   Tel:/Fax: 0397 706000

Enjoy the comfortable luxury of a unique no
smoking private hotel specialising in B&B. Set in
private grounds yet only 5 mins. from town centre.
Full central heating all rooms, private facilities,
tea-making, hospitality tray, TV. Ample parking.
This is an excellent base for touring the
Highlands (Oban, Mallaig, Inverness all nearby) or
leave your car and day trip to Mallaig by steam
train (summer only) or take coach tours, boat
trips or mountain gondola.

AA QQQQ R.A.C. Highly acclaimed.

Contact: A. W. Henderson for brochure.

B&B £20 to £30 – weekly from £130.

Ashburn House Achintore Road Fort William Inverness-shire PH33 6RQ Tel: (Fort William) 0397 706000 Fax: 0397 706000	**HIGHLY COMMENDED** 👑 👑	1 Single 1 Twin 3 Double 1 Family	6 En Suite fac 2 Pub. Bath/Show	B&B per person £20.00-£30.00 Single £15.00-£30.00 Double	Open Feb-Nov
		Family run totally refurbished Victorian villa in its own grounds, with magnificent views across the Loch. Short distance from town centre.			
Ben View Guest House Belford Road Fort William Inverness-shire PH33 6ER Tel: (Fort William) 0397 702966		1 Single 2 Twin 5 Double 1 Family	8 En Suite fac 6 Pub. Bath/Show	B&B per person £15.00-£18.00 Single £15.00-£21.00 Double	Open Feb-Nov Dinner 1845-1930 B&B + Eve. Meal £23.00-£28.00
Ceilearadh Achintore Road Fort William Inverness-shire PH33 Tel: (Fort William) 0397 703542		2 Twin 3 Double 1 Family	6 En Suite fac	B&B per person £13.00-£18.00 Double	Open Jan-Dec
Craig Nevis Guest House Belford Road Fort William Inverness-shire PH33 6BU Tel: (Fort William) 0397 702023		1 Twin 3 Double 2 Family	2 Pub. Bath/Show	B&B per person from £14.00 Single from £13.00 Double	Open Jan-Dec

Crolinnhe Guest House

GRANGE ROAD, FORT WILLIAM
PH33 6JF Telephone: 0397 70 2709

Set in it's own grounds of 1 acre, stands this elegant Victorian house. In an elevated position, proudly overlooking Loch Linnhe. Relax in the large spacious rooms, tastefully decorated to a very high standard. Enjoy the peace and tranquility of "Crolinnhe", only a 10-minute walk to the town centre. Start the day with a varied menu for breakfast in our charming dining room looking over the Loch to the hills beyond.

We look forward to being of any assistance to making your holiday that bit more memorable. **Ample private parking.**

Crolinnhe Grange Road Fort William Inverness-shire PH33 6JF Tel: (Fort William) 0397 702709	DELUXE	1 Twin 3 Double 1 Family	1 En Suite fac 2 Pub. Bath/Show	B&B per person from £19.00 Double	Open Mar-Nov

Family run detached Victorian villa c1880, refurbished to a high standard. Friendly and welcoming atmosphere. Large colourful garden. Superb views.

DARAICH GUEST HOUSE

CAMERON ROAD, FORT WILLIAM
INVERNESS-SHIRE PH33 6LQ   Tel: 0397 702644

Small Guest House overlooking Loch Linnhe. 5 mins. walk to town. 3 Family, 1 Single, all with wash-basins. Electric blankets, heaters, tea-making facilities. 2 toilets, 1 shower. Colour TV's in all rooms. Private parking.

B&B from £14   OPEN ALL YEAR

Daraich Guest House Cameron Road Fort William Inverness-shire PH33 6LQ Tel: (Fort William) 0397 702644		1 Single 2 Family	2 Pub. Bath/Show	B&B per person £14.00-£15.00 Single £14.00-£15.00 Double	Open Jan-Dec

Distillery House Glenlochy Distillery North Road Fort William Inverness-shire PH33 6LR Tel: (Fort William) 0397 702980/700103 Fax: 0397 706277	HIGHLY COMMENDED	1 Single 4 Twin 3 Double 1 Family	6 En Suite fac 1 Priv. NOT ensuite 1 Pub. Bath/Show	B&B per person £25.00-£35.00 Single £20.00-£32.00 Double	Open Jan-Dec

Distillery house at old Glenlochy Distillery in Fort William. Beside A82, the road to the Isles and Ben Nevis.

FORT WILLIAM continued	Map 3 G1

Glenlochy Guest House

NEVIS BRIDGE, FORT WILLIAM, INVERNESS-SHIRE
PH33 6PF   Telephone: 0397 702909

This comfortable, family-run guest house is situated in its own spacious grounds, overlooking the River Nevis close to Ben Nevis, ¾ mile from town centre. It is an ideal base for touring. Access to rooms at all times. Colour TV and tea/coffee facilities in all rooms. Private parking.

For brochure and details contact Mrs MacBeth.

Glenlochy Guest House Nevis Bridge Fort William Inverness-shire PH33 6PF Tel: (Fort William) 0397 702909	COMMENDED ♛♛♛	4 Twin 5 Double 1 Family	8 En Suite fac 1 Pub. Bath/Show	B&B per person £17.00-£22.00 Single £14.00-£22.00 Double	Open Jan-Dec
		Detached house with garden situated at Nevis Bridge, midway between Ben Nevis and the town centre. 0.5 miles (1km) to railway station.			
Glen Shiel Guest House Achintore Road Fort William Inverness-shire PH33 6RW Tel: (Fort William) 0397 702271	COMMENDED ♛♛	1 Twin 3 Double 1 Family	2 En Suite fac 1 Priv. NOT ensuite 2 Pub. Bath/Show	B&B per person from £13.50 Double	Open Apr-Oct
		Modern house on the outskirts of the town with excellent views over Loch Linnhe. Good touring base.			
Guisachan Guest House Alma Road Fort William Inverness-shire PH33 6HA Tel: (Fort William) 0397 703797/704447	COMMENDED ♛♛♛	2 Single 5 Twin 6 Double 3 Family	15 En Suite fac 1 Pub. Bath/Show	B&B per person £16.00-£24.00 Single £17.00-£24.00 Double	Open Jan-Dec Dinner from 1830 B&B + Eve. Meal £25.00-£32.00
		Family run establishment within easy walking distance of town centre, rail and bus stations. Home cooking. Some annexe accommodation.			
Hillview Guest House Achintore Road Fort William Inverness-shire PH33 6RW Tel: (Fort William) 0397 704349	COMMENDED ♛♛	1 Single 1 Twin 4 Double 2 Family	3 En Suite fac 2 Pub. Bath/Show	B&B per person £15.00-£16.00 Single £13.00-£16.50 Double	Open Jan-Dec
		Family run guest house over looking Loch Linnhe and about 1.5 miles (2.5kms) from Fort William.			
Lochiel Villa Guest House Achintore Road Fort William Inverness-shire PH33 6RQ Tel: (Fort William) 0397 702379/703616	COMMENDED ♛♛	1 Twin 6 Double 1 Family	3 En Suite fac 3 Pub. Bath/Show	B&B per person £15.00-£24.00 Double	Open Feb-Nov
		Granite semi-villa with open views over Loch Linnhe. 500 yards (450 mts) from town centre.			

LOCHVIEW GUEST HOUSE

Heathercroft Road, Fort William PH33 6RE
Telephone: 0397 703149

Lochview is situated on the hillside above the town in a quiet location with panoramic views over Loch Linnhe and the Ardgour Hills. All bedrooms are tastefully decorated and have private facilities, colour TV and tea/coffee facilities. There is a large garden and private parking.

Lochview Guest House Heathercroft, off Argyll Terrace Fort William Inverness-shire PH33 6RE Tel: (Fort William) 0397 703149	COMMENDED ♛♛	1 Single 2 Twin 5 Double	8 En Suite fac	B&B per person £20.00-£25.00 Single £16.00-£21.00 Double	Open Apr-Oct
		Situated on a hillside above the town giving panoramic views over Loch Linnhe and the Ardgour Hills.			

Orchy Villa Guest House Alma Road Fort William Inverness-shire PH33 6HA Tel: (Fort William) 0397 702445		4 Family	3 Pub. Bath/Show	B&B per person £12.50-£15.50 Single £12.50-£15.50 Double	Open Jan-Dec	
Rhu Mhor Guest House Alma Road Fort William Inverness-shire PH33 6BP Tel: (Fort William) 0397 702213	COMMENDED Listed	3 Twin 2 Double 2 Family	2 Pub. Bath/Show	B&B per person £14.30-£15.50 Single £14.30-£15.50 Double	Open Apr-Sep Dinner from 1900 B&B + Eve. Meal £22.80-£24.50	
		Large family house with extensive wild garden in quiet area above town. Short distance from town centre and all amenities.				
Saray Guest House Achintore Road Fort William Inverness-shire Tel: (Fort William) 0397 704422	Award Pending	6 Double	6 En Suite fac	B&B per person £12.00-£30.00 Double	Open Jan-Oct	
Giorgio Boggi Fernbank, 5 Caberfeidh Fassifern Road Fort William Inverness-shire PH33 6BB Tel: (Fort William) 0397 702790		1 Twin 2 Double	1 En Suite fac 1 Pub. Bath/Show	B&B per person £13.00-£19.00 Double	Open Jan-Dec	
Mrs S E Buxton Taransay, Seafield Gardens Fort William Inverness-shire PH33 6RJ Tel: (Fort William) 0397 703303	COMMENDED	1 Single 1 Double 1 Family	1 Priv. NOT ensuite 1 Pub. Bath/Show	B&B per person from £15.00 Single from £13.00 Double	Open New Year-Nov	
		Modern family home in quiet area close to town centre. Excellent views across the Loch. Families especially welcome. No smoking.				
Mrs B Cameron Rodane, Badabrie Banavie, Fort William Inverness-shire PH33 7LX Tel: (Corpach) 0397 772603	COMMENDED	1 Single 2 Family	1 Priv. NOT ensuite 2 Pub. Bath/Show	B&B per person from £14.00 Single from £14.00 Double	Open Jan-Dec Dinner from 1800 B&B + Eve. Meal from £20.00	
		Modern house in quiet residential area 3 miles (5kms) from Fort William. Fine views to Ben Nevis and Loch Linnhe.				
Mrs N Cameron 17 Sutherland Avenue Fort William Inverness-shire PH33 6JS Tel: (Fort William) 0397 704678	COMMENDED Listed	1 Single 1 Twin 1 Family	1 Pub. Bath/Show	B&B per person from £13.00 Single from £13.00 Double	Open Easter-Oct	
		Family home affording splendid views over Loch Linnhe. 1 mile (2kms) from town centre. Non smoking.				
Mrs C Campbell & Mrs I MacLeod 2 Caberfeidh, Fassifern Road Fort William Inverness-shire PH33 6BE Tel: (Fort William) 0397 702533		2 Twin 1 Double	3 Pub. Bath/Show	B&B per person £11.00-£14.00 Double	Open Jan-Dec	

FORT WILLIAM continued	Map 3 G1	COMMENDED ♛	1 Twin 2 Double	1 Pub. Bath/Show	B&B per person £13.00-£13.50 Double	Open Jan-Dec	
Mrs Fiona Campbell Leasona Torlundy, Fort William Inverness-shire PH33 6SW Tel: (Fort William) 0397 704661							

Modern family home in super glen setting, views to Ben Nevis. Ideal base for hillwalking, bird watching, pony trekking and Aonach Mor.

THE GRANGE

Grange Road, Fort William, Inverness-shire PH33 6JF
Tel: 0397 70 5516

The Grange is not a hotel, but we hope more than just B&B. A late Victorian house which has been renovated and refurbished to a very high standard. All rooms have private facilities, two overlooking Loch Linnhe. Set in its own grounds, The Grange is both private and peaceful yet only 10 minutes' walk from Fort William's centre, 2½ hours' drive from Glasgow, 1½ hours from Inverness.
The Grange is a good base for touring the west coast, but why not judge for yourself?

A colour brochure is available on request. Honeymoon breaks also available.

Mrs J Campbell The Grange, Grange Road Fort William Inverness-shire PH33 6JF Tel: (Fort William) 0397 705516	DELUXE ♛ ♛	3 Double	2 En Suite fac 1 Priv. NOT ensuite	B&B per person from £22.00 Double	Open May-Oct

Late Victorian house sympathetically renovated within easy walking distance of Fort William (10 minutes). Views over Loch Linnhe.

Mrs F A Cook Melantee, Achintore Road Fort William Inverness-shire PH33 6RW Tel: (Fort William) 0397 705329	APPROVED ♛	1 Single 1 Twin 1 Double 1 Family	2 Pub. Bath/Show	B&B per person from £14.00 Single £13.00-£15.00 Double	Open Jan-Dec

1.5 miles (3kms) from town centre, overlooking the shores of Loch Linnhe and the Ardgour hills and on the main A82 road.

Mr & Mrs D P Dingwall Tigh na Mara, Achintore Road Fort William Inverness-shire Tel: (Fort William) 0397 702503		1 Twin 2 Double	1 Pub. Bath/Show	B&B per person from £11.00 Double	Open Easter-Sep

Mr & Mrs Fraser Voringfoss, 5 Stirling Place Fort William Inverness-shire PH33 6UW Tel: (Fort William) 0397 704062	COMMENDED ♛	1 Single 1 Twin 1 Double	2 En Suite fac 2 Pub. Bath/Show	B&B per person £13.00-£20.00 Single £13.00-£20.00 Double	Open Jan-Dec

Modern family home in quiet residential area 1 mile (2kms) from town centre. On main bus route.

Mrs E Hamill Westhaven, Achintore Road Fort William Inverness-shire Tel: (Fort William) 0397 705500	HIGHLY COMMENDED ♛ ♛	1 Twin 2 Double	2 En Suite fac 1 Priv. NOT ensuite	B&B per person from £14.50 Double	Open Jan-Dec

Modern detached house over looking Loch Linnhe with all facilities and ample parking. Town centre 1.5 miles (2.4 Km).

Mrs Ann Hearmon Balcarres, Seafield Gardens Fort William Inverness-shire PH33 6RJ Tel: (Fort William) 0397 702377	COMMENDED 👑 👑	1 Twin 1 Double 1 Family	3 En Suite fac	B&B per person £20.00 Single £13.00-£17.00 Double	Open Jan-Oct
		Modern newly-built family home in quiet area. Excellent views across the loch. Close to the town centre.			
Mrs Hutton Alt-An, Achintore Road Fort William Inverness-shire PH33 6RN Tel: (Fort William) 0397 704546		3 Double	1 En Suite fac 2 Limited ensuite 1 Pub. Bath/Show	B&B per person £14.00-£17.00 Single £14.00-£17.00 Double	Open Jan-Dec Dinner 1800-1830 B&B + Eve. Meal £17.00-£22.00
Patricia Jordan Beinn Ard, Argyll Road Fort William Inverness-shire Tel: (Fort William) 0397 704760		1 Single 1 Twin 1 Double	2 En Suite fac 1 Priv. NOT ensuite 2 Pub. Bath/Show	B&B per person £12.00-£16.00 Single £12.00-£16.00 Double	Open Jan-Feb, May-Oct
Mrs A R Lee Leesholme, Cameron Road Fort William Inverness-shire PH33 6LH Tel: (Fort William) 0397 704204	COMMENDED Listed	1 Twin 2 Double	1 Pub. Bath/Show	B&B per person £14.00-£15.00 Single £12.50-£14.00 Double	Open May-Oct
		Modern family home in quiet residential area above the town. Short walk from town centre. Off-street parking. Non-smoking.			
B Lytham Glenmoidart, Fassifern Road Fort William Inverness-shire PH33 6LJ Tel: (Fort William) 0397 705790		1 Twin 2 Double	1 En Suite fac 1 Pub. Bath/Show	B&B per person £15.00-£21.00 Double	Open Jan-Dec
Wilma & Jim McCourt 6 Caberfeidh, Fassifern Road Fort William Inverness-shire PH33 6BE Tel: (Fort William) 0397 703756		1 Single 1 Double 2 Family	1 En Suite fac 1 Pub. Bath/Show	B&B per person £11.00-£14.00 Single £11.00-£19.00 Double	Open Jan-Dec Dinner 1730-1900 B&B + Eve. Meal £19.50-£26.50
Mrs Angela MacIntyre Heatherlie, Argyll Road Fort William Inverness-shire Tel: (Fort William) 0397 700392		1 Twin 1 Double	1 Pub. Bath/Show	B&B per person £12.00-£15.00 Single £12.00-£15.00 Double	Open Jan-Dec
Mrs C MacLeod 5 Grange Terrace Fort William Inverness-shire PH33 6JQ Tel: (Fort William) 0397 702403		1 Twin 1 Double	1 Pub. Bath/Show	B&B per person to £13.50 Double	Open May-Sep

FORT WILLIAM continued	Map 3 G1						
Heather & Charles Moore Abrach House 4 Caithness Place Fort William Inverness-shire PH33 6JP Tel: (Fort William) 0397 702535	COMMENDED 👑	1 Single 1 Double 1 Family	2 Pub. Bath/Show	B&B per person from £12.50 Double	Open Feb-Oct	
		Modern house in elevated position with excellent views over Fort William and surrounding hills and loch.				
R Moreland Dalbreac, Mallaig Road Corpach, by Fort William Inverness-shire PH33 7JR Tel: (Corpach) 0397 772309	COMMENDED 👑 👑	1 Twin 2 Double	2 En Suite fac 1 Priv. NOT ensuite	B&B per person from £16.00 Single from £16.00 Double	Open Jan-Dec	
		Bungalow on the road to-the-isles. Homely atmosphere. Evening meal on request. Home cooking and baking.				
Mrs Nicol Viewfield House, Alma Road Fort William Inverness-shire PH33 6HD Tel: (Fort William) 0397 704763		2 Twin 1 Double	1 Pub. Bath/Show	B&B per person £12.50-£14.00 Double	Open Jan-Sep	
G Ross Dalkeith, Belford Road Fort William Inverness-shire PH33 6BU Tel: (Fort William) 0397 704140		1 Twin 2 Double	3 En Suite fac 2 Pub. Bath/Show	B&B per person £15.00-£22.00 Double	Open Apr-Oct	
Mrs Sweeney Kintail, Seafield Gardens Fort William Inverness-shire PH33 6RJ Tel: (Fort William) 0397 702942		1 Twin 2 Double	3 En Suite fac	B&B per person £12.50-£16.00 Double	Open Mar-Oct	
Mrs Turner Corrie View Lochyside, by Fort William Inverness-shire PH33 7NX Tel: (Fort William) 0397 703608	COMMENDED 👑 👑	1 Twin 2 Double	1 En Suite fac 2 Pub. Bath/Show	B&B per person £13.00-£16.00 Double	Open Jan-Dec	
		Detached family home in quiet residential area 2 miles (3kms) from Fort William. Convenient for touring West Coast.				
Mrs E Walters Melrose, 5 Argyll Road Fort William Inverness-shire PH33 Tel: (Fort William) 0397 702519	APPROVED 👑 👑	2 Single 2 Double	1 En Suite fac 2 Pub. Bath/Show	B&B per person £12.00-£16.00 Single £12.00-£16.00 Double	Open Jan-Dec	
		Modern house with open views over Loch Linnhe, yet close to town centre. Vegetarians welcome.				
Mrs Wardle 16 Perth Place Fort William Inverness-shire PH33 6UL Tel: (Fort William) 0397 704392		1 Double	1 En Suite fac 1 Pub. Bath/Show	B&B per person £10.00-£12.00 Single £10.00-£12.00 Double	Open Jan-Dec Dinner 1800-2100 B&B + Eve. Meal £17.00-£18.00	

Mrs Wiseman 17 Mossfield Drive, Lochyside Fort William Inverness-shire PH33 7PE Tel: (Fort William) 0397 703502		COMMENDED Listed	1 Single 1 Twin 1 Double	1 En Suite fac 1 Pub. Bath/Show	B&B per person from £13.50 Single from £13.50 Double	Open Jan-Dec
			Modern bungalow set in quiet residential area 2.5 miles (4kms) outside Fort William. Restaurants and hotels nearby.			
Mrs R Wynne St Andrews East Fassfern Road Fort William Inverness-shire PH33 6BD Tel: (Fort William) 0397 702337			1 Twin 2 Double	2 Pub. Bath/Show	B&B per person £13.00-£15.00 Double	Open May-Oct
BY FORT WILLIAM **Inverness-shire** Mansefield Guest House Corpach, by Fort William Inverness-shire PH33 7LT Tel: (Corpach) 0397 772262	Map 3 G1	COMMENDED 👑 👑	1 Twin 2 Double 2 Family	1 En Suite fac 2 Pub. Bath/Show	B&B per person £15.00-£20.00 Single £15.00-£18.00 Double	Open Jan-Dec Dinner from 1900 B&B + Eve. Meal £25.00-£30.00
			Victorian house with its own garden. 3 miles (5kms) from Fort William, on the road to Mallaig. Home cooking and preserves, fresh produce.			
Mrs Cameron Strone Farm, by Muirshearlich Banavie, Fort William Inverness-shire PH33 7PB Tel: (Spean Bridge) 039781 773		COMMENDED 👑 👑 👑	1 Twin 2 Double	2 En Suite fac 1 Priv. NOT ensuite 1 Pub. Bath/Show	B&B per person £15.00-£18.00 Double	Open Jan-Sep Dinner from 1900
			Farmhouse situated on working farm overlooking the Caledonian Canal with magnificent view towards Ben Nevis. 7 miles (12kms) North of Fort William.			
Mrs Campbell Lochindaal, Tomonie Banavie, by Fort William Inverness-shire PH33 7LX Tel: (Corpach) 0397 772478			1 Twin 2 Double	1 Pub. Bath/Show	B&B per person £12.50-£14.00 Double	Open Mar-Oct
Mrs Davie Carinbrook Banavie, by Fort William Inverness-shire PH33 7LX Tel: (Corpach) 0397 772318			1 Single 2 Twin 2 Double	2 En Suite fac 2 Pub. Bath/Show	B&B per person from £14.00 Single from £13.00 Double	Open Apr-Oct Dinner 1830-1930 B&B + Eve. Meal from £20.00
Mrs B Grieve Nevis View, 14 Farrow Drive Corpach, by Fort William Inverness-shire PH33 7JW Tel: (Corpach) 0397 772447 Fax: 0397 772800		APPROVED Listed	1 Single 1 Family	1 Pub. Bath/Show	B&B per person from £15.50 Single from £13.00 Double	Open Jan-Dec Dinner 1800-1900 B&B + Eve. Meal from £20.50
			Family home in quiet residential estate. Views of Ben Nevis and Loch Eil. Home cooking.			
Mrs McInnes Taormina Banavie, by Fort William Inverness-shire PH33 7LY Tel: (Corpach) 0397 772217		COMMENDED 👑	1 Single 1 Twin 1 Double	2 Pub. Bath/Show	B&B per person £12.50-£13.00 Single £12.50-£13.00 Double	Open Apr-Oct
			Modern bungalow quietly situated off "Road to the Isles". Restaurant and railway nearby. Caledonian Canal 50 metres, Fort William 1.5 miles (3kms).			

BY FORT WILLIAM continued	Map 3 G1						
Mrs Margaret MacIntyre Algarve, Badabrie Banavie, by Fort William Inverness-shire PH33 7LX Tel: (Corpach) 0397 772461	HIGHLY COMMENDED ♛ ♛	1 Twin 2 Double	1 Priv. NOT ensuite 2 Pub. Bath/Show	B&B per person from £14.50 Double	Open Jan-Dec	
		Detached modern villa in an elevated position overlooking Fort William, Loch Linnhe and the Ben Nevis range.				
Mrs I MacLean Grianan, 4 Lochiel Crescent Banavie, Fort William Inverness-shire PH33 7LZ Tel: (Corpach) 0397 772659	COMMENDED ♛	3 Double	1 Pub. Bath/Show	B&B per person £12.00-£13.00 Double	Open Apr-Oct Dinner from 1830 B&B + Eve. Meal £19.00-£20.00	
		Modern detached bungalow in a quiet residential area near to Neptune's Staircase on the Caledonian Canal. Fine views towards Ben Nevis.				
Mrs McLeod Clintwood, 23 Hillview Drive Corpach, by Fort William Inverness-shire PH33 7LS Tel: (Corpach) 0397 772680	HIGHLY COMMENDED ♛ ♛	1 Twin 2 Double	2 En Suite fac 1 Priv. NOT ensuite	B&B per person £18.00 Double	Open Apr-Oct	
		A warm Highland welcome in this attractively appointed modern villa in village of Corpach. Fort William 4 miles (6kms).				
Mrs Nisbet Dailanna House Kinlocheil, Fort William Inverness-shire PH33 7NP Tel: (Corpach) 0397 722253	COMMENDED ♛ ♛	1 Twin 2 Double	3 En Suite fac 1 Pub. Bath/Show	B&B per person from £14.00 Double	Open Apr-Nov Dinner 1900-2000 B&B + Eve. Meal from £22.50	
		Detached bungalow with large garden in elevated, peaceful position with fine views southwards over Loch Eil to the hills of Ardgour.				
Mrs Wilkinson Fordon, Badabrie Banavie, by Fort William Inverness-shire PH33 7LX Tel: (Corpach) 0397 772737		1 Twin 1 Double 1 Family	1 En Suite fac 2 Pub. Bath/Show	B&B per person £12.00-£16.00 Single £12.00-£17.00 Double	Open Jan-Dec	
Mrs Williamson Aonach View, Hillview Croft Banavie, by Fort William Inverness-shire PH33 7PB Tel: (Corpach) 0397 772794	COMMENDED ♛	1 Twin 2 Double	2 Pub. Bath/Show	B&B per person from £14.00 Single from £13.00 Double	Open Jan-Dec	
		Modern family home in secluded rural location with superb views of Ben Nevis and Aonach Mor. 4 miles (6kms) from Fort William.				
FOYERS **Inverness-shire** Foyers Bay House Foyers Inverness-shire IV1 2YB Tel: (Gorthleck) 0456 486624 Fax: 0456 486337	Map 4 A1	COMMENDED ♛ ♛ ♛	2 Twin 1 Double	3 En Suite fac	B&B per person £20.00-£27.00 Single £18.00-£23.00 Double	Open Jan-Dec Dinner 1800-2000 B&B + Eve. Meal £24.00-£32.00
			Friendly welcome at modernised Victorian house overlooking Loch Ness and set in 4 acres of ground. 500 yards from Falls of Foyers.				

FRASERBURGH Aberdeenshire Mrs M Greig Clifton House 131 Charlotte Street Fraserburgh Aberdeenshire AB43 5LS Tel: (Fraserburgh) 0346 28365	Map 4 H7	COMMENDED 👑 👑	2 Single 1 Double 1 Family	1 En Suite fac 1 Limited ensuite 2 Pub. Bath/Show	B&B per person from £14.00 Single from £14.00 Double	Open Jan-Dec
			Family run guest house in the centre of Fraserburgh, near shopping facilities and on the bus route for Aberdeen. Home cooking.			
FREUCHIE Fife Mrs J Duncan Little Freuchie Freuchie, by Falkland Fife KY7 7AU Tel: (Falkland) 0337 57372/857372	Map 2 D3	COMMENDED Listed	2 Twin	1 Pub. Bath/Show	B&B per person £17.00-£20.00 Single £15.00-£16.00 Double	Open Apr-Oct
			Spacious, comfortable farmhouse in own gardens. Panoramic views. Centrally situated for walking, golf and historic Falkland.			
FYVIE Aberdeenshire Mrs M Wyness Meikle Camaloun Fyvie Aberdeenshire AB53 8JY Tel: (Fyvie) 0651 891319	Map 4 G9	COMMENDED 👑 👑	1 Twin 1 Double	1 En Suite fac 1 Priv. NOT ensuite	B&B per person from £17.00 Single £15.00-£17.00 Double	Open Mar-Nov
			Large comfortable farmhouse, with inviting garden and superb views over rolling farmland. Ideal for Whisky and Castle Trails. Close to Fyvie Castle.			
GAIRLOCH Ross-shire Charleston Guest House Gairloch Ross-shire IV21 2AH Tel: (Gairloch) 0445 2497	Map 3 F7	COMMENDED 👑	2 Single 2 Twin 2 Double 3 Family	2 Pub. Bath/Show	B&B per person from £16.00 Single from £16.00 Double	Open Apr-Oct Dinner from 1900 B&B + Eve. Meal from £21.00
			Large 18C house, situated on sea-loch overlooking Gairloch harbour. Personally run, all home cooking. Children and pets welcome.			
Horisdale House Strath Gairloch Ross-shire IV21 2DA Tel: (Gairloch) 0445 2151		COMMENDED 👑	2 Single 2 Twin 1 Double 1 Family	1 Priv. NOT ensuite 4 Pub. Bath/Show	B&B per person £15.00-£17.00 Single £15.00-£16.00 Double	Open May-Sep Dinner from 1900 B&B + Eve. Meal £25.00-£27.00
			Modern detached house with attractive garden and excellent views. Home cooking with emphasis on fresh produce. Regret no pets allowed.			
Kerrysdale House Gairloch Ross-shire IV21 2AL Tel: (Gairloch) 0445 2292		COMMENDED 👑 👑	1 Twin 2 Double	2 En Suite fac 1 Priv. NOT ensuite	B&B per person £18.00-£20.00 Double	Open Feb-Nov Dinner from 1900 B&B + Eve. Meal £26.50-£28.50
			18C farmhouse recently refurbished and tastefully decorated. Modern comforts in a peaceful setting. 1 mile (2kms) south of Gairloch.			
Little Lodge North Erradale Gairloch Ross-shire IV21 2DS Tel: (North Erradale) 044585 237		HIGHLY COMMENDED 👑 👑 👑	1 Twin 2 Double	3 En Suite fac	B&B per person	Open Feb-Dec Dinner 1900-2000 B&B + Eve. Meal £30.50-£35.50
			Peaceful crofthouse off the beaten track 7 miles (11kms) from Gairloch. Wood burning stove. Emphasis on good food using local produce.			

GAIRLOCH continued — Map 3 F7

The Mountain Restaurant & Lodge
Strath Square
Gairloch
Ross-shire
IV21 2BX
Tel: (Gairloch) 0445 2316

COMMENDED ≈≈

1 Twin	1 En Suite fac	B&B per person	Open Mar-Nov
2 Double	2 Priv. NOT ensuite	£19.95-£39.90 Single	Dinner 1830-2230
		£19.95-£24.95 Double	B&B + Eve. Meal
			from £29.90

In Gairloch's main square, with views across the bay. Day time coffee shop dinners by candlelight in an informal atmosphere.

Whindley Guest House
Auchtercairn
Gairloch
Ross-shire
IV21 2BN
Tel: (Gairloch) 0445 2340

COMMENDED ≈≈≈

1 Twin	4 En Suite fac	B&B per person	Open Jan-Dec
1 Double		£14.00-£20.00 Double	Dinner 1850-2000
2 Family			B&B + Eve. Meal
			£22.75-£28.75

Modern bungalow with large garden in elevated position, with fine views overlooking Gairloch Bay. Some annexe accommodation with steep access.

Lynn Bennett-MacKenzie
Croit Mo Sheanair, 29 Strath
Gairloch
Ross-shire
IV21 2DA
Tel: (Gairloch) 0445 2389

1 Twin	1 Pub. Bath/Show	B&B per person	Open Jan-Dec
1 Double		£14.00-£16.00 Double	Dinner 1800-1930
			B&B + Eve. Meal
			£22.00-£24.00

Mrs M Cuthbertson
Burnbridge House, Shore Street
Gairloch
Ross-shire
IV21 2BZ
Tel: (Gairloch) 0445 2167

1 Twin	1 Pub. Bath/Show	B&B per person	Open Jan-Dec
1 Double		from £15.00 Single	
1 Family		from £13.00 Double	

Miss I MacKenzie
Duisary, 24 Strath
Gairloch
Ross-shire
IV21 2DA
Tel: (Gairloch) 0445 2252

COMMENDED ≈≈

1 Twin	1 Priv. NOT ensuite	B&B per person	Open May-Oct
1 Double	1 Pub. Bath/Show	from £14.00 Single	
1 Family		from £14.00 Double	

Traditional stone built croft house on edge of village, with fine views across Gairloch to the hills of Torridon.

Mrs Mullaney
Wayside, Strath
Gairloch
Ross-shire
IV21 2BZ
Tel: (Gairloch) 0445 2008

| 1 Twin | 1 Pub. Bath/Show | B&B per person | Open Jan-Dec |
| 2 Double | | from £12.00 Double | |

Mr and Mrs J Smith
26 Strath
Gairloch
Ross-shire
IV21 2DA
Tel: (Gairloch) 0445 2064

1 Twin	1 Pub. Bath/Show	B&B per person	Open Apr-Oct
2 Double		£12.00-£13.00 Double	Dinner 1930-2000
			B&B + Eve. Meal
			£19.00-£20.00

GALASHIELS — Selkirkshire — Map 2 E6

Mrs Adam
Morven, 12 Sime Place
Galashiels
Selkirkshire
TD1 1ST
Tel: (Galashiels) 0896 56255

APPROVED
Listed

1 Single	2 Pub. Bath/Show	B&B per person	Open Jan-Dec
1 Twin		£13.50 Single	Dinner 1800-2000
1 Double		£13.50 Double	B&B + Eve. Meal
3 Family			£18.00

Friendly guest house in quiet area of the town with large spacious rooms. Convenient for town centre and bus routes.

Mrs Sheila Bergius Over Langshaw Farm Langshaw, by Galashiels Selkirkshire TD1 2PE Tel: (Blainslie) 089686 244	COMMENDED ♕	1 Double 1 Family	1 En Suite fac 1 Priv. NOT ensuite	B&B per person £16.00-£18.00 Double	Open Jan-Dec B&B + Eve. Meal £26.00-£28.00
		Traditional farmhouse on mixed working farm on 500 acres, 4 miles (6kms) from Galashiels with spectacular views of surrounding countryside.			
Mr Brown Island House, 65 Island Street Galashiels Selkirkshire TD1 1PA Tel: (Galashiels) 0896 2649		2 Twin 1 Double	1 En Suite fac 1 Pub. Bath/Show	B&B per person £13.00-£15.00 Single £13.00-£15.00 Double	Open Jan-Dec
Mrs S Field Ettrickvale 33 Abbotsford Road Galashiels Selkirkshire TD1 3HW Tel: (Galashiels) 0896 55224	COMMENDED Listed	2 Twin 1 Double	1 Pub. Bath/Show	B&B per person from £13.00 Double	Open Jan-Dec B&B + Eve. Meal from £16.00
		Semi-detached bungalow on A7 on outskirts of town but only a short walk from local amenities. Ideally situated for touring.			
Mrs J McLaren Dungallan 30 Abbotsford Road Galashiels Selkirkshire TD1 3HR Tel: (Galashiels) 0896 4257	COMMENDED ♕	2 Twin 1 Double	2 Limited ensuite 1 Pub. Bath/Show	B&B per person from £14.00 Double	Open Jan-Dec
		Comfortable detached house on A7. Open outlook to park, within easy walking distance of town centre. Parking.			
Mr D Peacock Monorene, 23 Stirling Street Galashiels Selkirkshire TD1 1BY Tel: (Galashiels) 0896 3073	COMMENDED ♕	2 Single 3 Twin 1 Double 1 Family	2 Pub. Bath/Show	B&B per person £14.00 Single £14.00 Double	Open Jan-Dec Dinner 1800-1900 B&B + Eve. Meal £19.50
		Stone built house situated near to the town centre, especially convenient for bus station. Recently completely refurbished.			
Mrs A M Platt Wakefield Bank 9 Abbotsford Road Galashiels Selkirkshire TD1 3DP Tel: (Galashiels) 0896 2641	COMMENDED ♕ ♕	1 Twin 2 Double	1 Priv. NOT ensuite 2 Pub. Bath/Show	B&B per person from £14.50 Double	Open Apr-Oct Dinner from 1800 B&B + Eve. Meal from £23.50
		Former mill owner's house, c1840, retaining some original features with large garden and easy access to town centre. No smoking.			
Mr & Mrs D A Ross Springfield 5 Abbotsview Court Galashiels Selkirkshire TD1 3HY Tel: (Galashiels) 0896 59423	COMMENDED ♕ ♕	2 Twin	2 En Suite fac	B&B per person £20.00 Single £16.50-£18.00 Double	Open Mar-Oct
		Modern detached house in quiet location on outskirts of town. Melrose 3 miles (5kms); Edinburgh 35 miles (56kms).			
GALLANACH, Oban Argyll David Doak The Anchorage, By-The-Sea Gallanach Road, Oban Argyll PA34 4QH Tel: (Oban) 0631 62088	Map 1 E2	3 Twin 1 Double 1 Family	3 Pub. Bath/Show	B&B per person from £12.00 Double	Open Apr-Sep

Details of Grading and Classification are on page vi.

Key to symbols is on back flap.

GALSTON Ayrshire Mrs J Bone Auchencloigh Farm Galston Ayrshire KA4 8NP Tel: (Galston) 0563 820567	Map 1 H7	COMMENDED Listed	1 Twin 1 Double	1 Pub. Bath/Show	B&B per person £14.00-£16.00 Double	Open Apr-Oct Dinner from 1830 B&B + Eve. Meal £22.00-£24.00	▢▢▢▥⇥ ⟲⇗▤▦▥ ▥✦▨⇗✿ ▣⇘⌂⋈
			Spacious 18C farmhouse amidst large gardens on 240 acre farm. Non-smokers only please.				

GAMRIE Banffshire	Map 4 G7						

BANKHEAD CROFT (Gardenstown)
GAMRIE · BANFF · AB45 3HN Tel: 0261 851584
Delightful modern country cottage in peaceful surroundings.
One double, one twin, one family bedrooms (all with H&C)
and tea facilities. Bed and Breakfast, Evening Meals. Full or Half
Board. All home cooking. Banff 6 miles; Pennan 4 miles. Large
caravan also available.
Come for a holiday in "Local Hero" country.

Lucy R Smith Bankhead Croft Gamrie Tel: (Gardenstown) 0261 851584		COMMENDED ♛	1 Twin 1 Double 1 Family	2 Pub. Bath/Show	B&B per person from £12.50 Double	Open Jan-Dec Dinner 1800-2000 B&B + Eve. Meal from £17.00	⚒⇗▢▢▢ ⟲⇘⋔▥▤ ▧⇘▥▥▦ ✦⇗✿▣▥⇥ ▶⤵
			Modern country cottage in peaceful surroundings. 2 miles (3 kms) from coast. 6 miles (10 kms) East of Banff. Home cooking.				

GARDENSTOWN, by Banff Banffshire Mrs P Duncan Palace Farm Gamrie,by Banff Banffshire AB45 3HS Tel: (Gardenstown) 0261 851261	Map 4 G7	COMMENDED Listed	1 Double 1 Family	2 Pub. Bath/Show	B&B per person £13.00-£14.00 Single £13.00-£14.00 Double	Open Mar-Nov Dinner 1830-2100 B&B + Eve. Meal £21.00-£22.00	⇘▢▢▢▥ ⇥⚠⋔▨▧ ▥▥▦▥⇗ ⇗✿▣⇥⌂ ⋈▶⤵∪
			Warm welcome in family farmhouse only 2 miles (3kms) from the sea. Excellent home cooking.				

GARELOCHHEAD Dunbartonshire Mr & Mrs N A Constantine Windwhistle, Whistlefield Road Garelochhead Dunbartonshire G84 0EP Tel: (Garelochhead) 0436 810316 Fax: 0436 811401	Map 1 G4		1 Single 1 Double 2 Family	1 Priv. NOT ensuite 1 Pub. Bath/Show	B&B per person £15.00-£20.00 Single £15.00-£18.00 Double	Open Jan-Dec Dinner 1930-2030 B&B + Eve. Meal £21.00-£28.00	⚒⇗▢▢▢ ▥⇥⚠⋔▨ ▧⇘▥▥▦ ✦▣⇗✿▣ ⟨▥⇘▶⤵ ⤴∪⇘⊥

HERE'S THE DIFFERENCE
STB's scheme has two distinct elements, grading and classification.

GRADING: measures the quality and condition of the facilities and services offered, eg, the warmth of
welcome, quality of food and its presentation, condition of decor and furnishings, appearance of buildings,
tidiness of grounds and gardens, condition of lighting and heating and so on.
Grading awards are: **Approved, Commended, Highly Commended, Deluxe.**

CLASSIFICATION: measures the range of physical facilities and services offered, eg, rooms with private
bath, heating, reception, lounges, telephones and so on.
Classification awards are: **Listed or from one to five crowns.**

GARVE Ross-shire	Map 3 H8

MRS HAZEL HAYTON
Birch Cottage, Station Road, Garve 0997 414237

Comfortable, friendly accommodation. Ideal base for touring and walking. All rooms en-suite, TV, tea-making. Guest lounge, garden, patio, parking. Open all year.

Mrs Hayton
Birch Cottage, Station Road
Garve
Ross-shire
Tel: (Garve) 0997 414237

HIGHLY COMMENDED

1 Twin 3 En Suite fac B&B per person Open Jan-Dec
2 Double 1 Pub. Bath/Show £13.00 Double

Traditional Highland cottage enroute to Gairloch/Ullapool. Refurbished to a high standard. Garve railway station 50 metres. 2 annexe bedrooms.

J & P Hollingdale
The Old Manse
Garve
Ross-shire
IV23 2PX
Tel: (Garve) 0997 414201

COMMENDED
Listed

1 Twin 1 En Suite fac B&B per person Open Jan-Nov
2 Double 1 Pub. Bath/Show £12.00-£14.00 Double Dinner from 1900
B&B + Eve. Meal
£19.00-£21.00

A warm, friendly atmosphere assured in this former manse. Set above Ullapool road, an ideal centre for touring, bird watchers, and walkers.

Mrs B MacPhail
Corriemoillie Lodge
by Garve
Ross-shire
IV23 2PY
Tel: (Garve) 0997 414253

COMMENDED

1 Single 2 Pub. Bath/Show B&B per person Open May-Sep
1 Twin £13.00-£15.00 Single
1 Double £13.00-£15.00 Double

Scottish hospitality in former shooting lodge. Ideal touring base. Set in 17 acres of woodland.

Mrs R A Miller
Tigh-na-Drochit
Garve
Ross-shire
IV23 2PU
Tel: (Garve) 0997 414256

1 Twin 1 Pub. Bath/Show B&B per person Open Jan-Dec
1 Family £13.00 Single
from £13.00 Double

Mrs J Wilcox
Keeper's House, Strathgarve
Garve
Ross-shire
IV23 2PU
Tel: (Garve) 0997 414301

COMMENDED
Listed

2 Double 1 Pub. Bath/Show B&B per person Open Jan-Nov
from £12.00 Single
from £12.00 Double

Quiet, secluded home with lovely walks. Ideal base for touring. 34 miles (48 kms) from Ullapool, 30 miles (48 kms) from Inverness.

GATEHOUSE-OF-FLEET Kirkcudbrightshire	Map 2 A1

Mrs W Johnstone
High Auchenlarie Farmhouse
Gatehouse-of-Fleet
Kirkcudbrightshire
DG7 2HB
Tel: (Mossyard) 055724 231

COMMENDED

2 Twin 1 Pub. Bath/Show B&B per person Open Mar-Oct
1 Double from £15.00 Single Dinner from 1800
from £15.00 Double B&B + Eve. Meal
from £22.00

Working beef farm on elevated site with views over Wigtown Bay. Homebaking, open fire in lounge; evening meals available.

Mrs Sheard
Crab Cottage, Sandgreen
Gatehouse of Fleet
Kirkcudbrightshire
Tel: (Gatehouse of Fleet)
0557 814461

HIGHLY COMMENDED

1 Twin 1 En Suite fac B&B per person Open Jan-Dec
1 Family 1 Priv. NOT ensuite £16.00-£20.00 Double

Situated on the shore, overlooking the sea and the hills. Easy access to village and major routes.

Details of Grading and Classification are on page vi. | Key to symbols is on back flap. |

BY GATEHOUSE-OF-FLEET
Kirkcudbrightshire — Map 2 A1

Girthon Kirk Guest House
Sandgreen Road
by Gatehouse-of-Fleet
Kirkcudbrightshire
DG7 2DW
Tel: (Gatehouse) 0557 814352

COMMENDED ♛♛

1 Twin / 2 Double — 3 En Suite fac — B&B per person £19.00-£21.00 Double — Open Mar-Oct — Dinner from 1830 — B&B + Eve. Meal £28.00-£30.00

Lovely country house in idyllic rural setting. Fine home cooking. All rooms with private facilities. 0.5 miles off A75 on Sandgreen road.

GIFFORD
East Lothian — Map 2 E5

Mrs E Whiteford
Long Newton Farm
Gifford
East Lothian
EH41 4JW
Tel: (Gifford) 062081 210

COMMENDED ♛♛

1 Twin / 1 Double / 1 Family — 1 En Suite fac — B&B per person £15.00-£17.00 Single — Open Feb-Nov

Farmhouse (c1650) at foot of Lammermuir Hills with fine views to Forth and Fife. 20 miles (32kms) from Edinburgh. Warm welcome and fine home cooking.

Margaret B Whiteford
Rowan Park, Longnewton Farm
Gifford
East Lothian
EH41 4JW
Tel: (Gifford) 062081 327

HIGHLY COMMENDED Listed

1 Twin / 1 Double — 1 Priv. NOT ensuite — B&B per person £15.00-£17.00 Single £17.00-£19.00 Double — Open Mar-Nov

Modern house furnished to a high standard. Quiet comfortable and relaxing. Close to Lammermuir hills.

GILLOCK
Caithness — Map 4 C3

Mrs Joan Coghill
Royston, Stemster
Gillock, Halkirk
Caithness
KW12 6UX
Tel: (Gillock) 095586 266/0831 224525

DELUXE ♛♛

1 Twin / 1 Double — 1 Priv. NOT ensuite / 2 Pub. Bath/Show — B&B per person £15.00-£17.00 Double — Open Apr-Oct

Semi-detached and former Victorian school set in farmlands, 2 miles (3kms) north of Gillock village on B874. Outdoor activities available locally.

GIRVAN
Ayrshire — Map 1 G9

Thistleneuk Guest House
19 Louisa Drive
Girvan
Ayrshire
KA26 9AH
Tel: (Girvan) 0465 2137

COMMENDED ♛♛♛

1 Single / 2 Twin / 2 Double / 2 Family — 6 En Suite fac / 1 Pub. Bath/Show — B&B per person £17.00-£20.00 Single £15.00-£18.00 Double — Open Jan-Dec — Dinner from 1800 — B&B + Eve. Meal £22.00-£25.00

19C terraced house on seafront overlooking Ailsa Craig. Within easy walking distance of town centre.

Mrs L Hogarth
St Oswalds
5 Golf Course Road
Girvan
Ayrshire
KA26 9HW
Tel: (Girvan) 0465 3786

COMMENDED ♛♛

1 Twin — 1 En Suite fac — B&B per person from £16.50 Double — Open Jan-Dec

Semi detached Victorian seaside villa. Close to beach and harbour and short walk to municipal golf course.

WELCOME

Whenever you are in Scotland, you can be sure of a warm welcome at your nearest Tourist Information Centre.

For guide books, maps, souvenirs, our Centres provide a service second to none—many now offer bureau-de-change facilities. And, of course, Tourist Information Centres offer free, expert advice on what to see and do, route-planning and accommodation for everyone—visitors and residents alike!

Hawkhill Farm

Proprietors; Morton & Isobel Kyle

HAWKHILL FARM
OLD DAILLY, GIRVAN, AYRSHIRE KA26 9RD
Telephone: 0465 87 232

Superb farmhouse hospitality in spacious 17th-century Coaching Inn, where the emphasis is on comfort and good food. Two/three delightful bedrooms with private facilities. Central heating, log fires, Lounge. Peaceful setting perfect for exploring S.W. Scotland: Culzean Castle, Galloway Forest Park, golf, fishing, pony trekking etc.
Phone Mrs Kyle for brochure.

Mrs Isobel Kyle Hawkhill Farm Old Dailly,by Girvan Ayrshire KA26 9RD Tel: (Old Dailly) 046587 232		**HIGHLY COMMENDED**	1 Twin 2 Double	1 En Suite fac 1 Pub. Bath/Show	B&B per person £15.00-£18.00 Double	Open Mar-Oct Dinner at 1900 B&B + Eve. Meal £23.00-£28.00	
			Large traditional farmhouse on mixed farm, 3 miles (5 kms) from Girvan. Friendly, informal atmosphere, home-baking and cooking using fresh produce.				
J & G Mulholland Appin Cottage 27/29 Ailsa Street West Girvan Ayrshire KA26 9AD Tel: (Girvan) 0465 3214			1 Twin 1 Double	2 En Suite fac 1 Pub. Bath/Show	B&B per person £16.00-£18.00 Double	Open May-Sep	
BY GIRVAN Ayrshire Mrs V Dunlop Glengennet Farm Barr,by Girvan Ayrshire KA26 9TY Tel: (Barr) 0465 86220	**Map 1 G9**	**COMMENDED**	1 Twin 1 Double	1 Priv. NOT ensuite 1 Pub. Bath/Show	B&B per person from £16.00 Double	Open May-Oct	
			Former shooting lodge set on hillside overlooking Stinchar Valley, 1.5 miles (3kms) from Barr, a conservation village.				
Mrs S Fergusson The Yett, 4 Manse Road Colmonell Ayrshire KA26 0SA Tel: (Colmonell) 046588 223		**COMMENDED** Listed	1 Twin 2 Double	2 Pub. Bath/Show	B&B per person from £12.50 Single from £12.50 Double	Open Easter-Oct	
			In quiet country location with excellent views over Stinchar Valley. Ideal for touring, fishing and birdwatching.				
Mrs M Whiteford Maxwelston Farm Dailly, by Girvan Ayrshire KA26 9RH Tel: (Dailly) 046581 210		**COMMENDED**	1 Double 1 Family	1 Pub. Bath/Show	B&B per person from £15.00 Single from £13.50 Double	Open Mar-Oct Dinner 1830-1930 B&B + Eve. Meal from £21.00	
			18C Listed farmhouse on working sheep and beef farm, 5 miles (8kms) inland from Girvan.				
GLAMIS Angus Mrs E Wilkie 17 Main Street Glamis Angus DD8 1RU Tel: (Glamis) 030784 419/0307 840419	**Map 2 D1**		2 Twin 1 Double	2 Pub. Bath/Show	B&B per person £15.00-£20.00 Single £13.50-£16.50 Double	Open Jan-Nov	

Details of Grading and Classification are on page vi.

Key to symbols is on back flap.

GLASGOW	Map 1 H5					
Alamo Guest House 46 Gray Street Glasgow G3 7SE Tel: 041 339 2395	APPROVED ♔	2 Single 1 Twin 2 Double 2 Family	3 Pub. Bath/Show	B&B per person from £15.00 Single from £13.00 Double	Open Jan-Dec	

Friendly family run, in quiet location overlooking park. Easy access to centre and within walking distance of SECC, galleries and Transport Museum.

Belle Vue Guest House 163 Hamilton Road Mount Vernon Glasgow G32 9QT Tel: 041 778 1077	Listed	3 Single 4 Twin 3 Double 2 Family	1 En Suite fac 1 Pub. Bath/Show	B&B per person £18.00-£20.00 Single £15.00-£16.00 Double	Open Jan-Dec	

Browns Guest House 2 Onslow Drive Glasgow G31 5LX Tel: 041 554 6797		7 Single 4 Twin 1 Double 2 Family	4 Pub. Bath/Show	B&B per person £14.00-£15.00 Single £13.00-£14.00 Double	Open Jan-Dec	

Chez Nous Guest House 33 Hillhead Street Glasgow G12 Tel: 041 334 2977	COMMENDED ♔ ♔	13 Single 4 Twin 8 Double 7 Family	14 En Suite fac 4 Limited ensuite 6 Pub. Bath/Show	B&B per person £18.50-£27.50 Single £18.50-£27.50 Double	Open Jan-Dec	

Situated in West End of city, close to University and Art Gallery. Within easy reach of M8 and all amenities. Private parking.

Craigielea House 35 Westercraigs Glasgow G31 2HY Tel: 041 554 3446	APPROVED Listed	2 Twin 1 Double 1 Family	1 Limited ensuite 1 Pub. Bath/Show	B&B per person £18.00 Single £14.00-£14.50 Double	Open Jan-Dec	

Victorian semi-villa in East End of city, yet close to centre and all amenities.

Hillview Guest House 18 Hillhead Street Glasgow G12 Tel: 041 334 5585 Fax: 041 353 3155	COMMENDED Listed	4 Single 2 Twin 2 Double 2 Family	3 Pub. Bath/Show	B&B per person £21.00-£25.00 Single £18.00-£20.00 Double	Open Jan-Dec	

Privately owned hotel situated close to Glasgow University and the Kelvin Hall Sports Arena. Convenient for city centre.

Kelvin View Guest House 411 North Woodside Road Glasgow G20 6NN Tel: 041 339 8257		1 Single 4 Twin 1 Double 3 Family	3 En Suite fac 2 Pub. Bath/Show	B&B per person £16.00 Single £15.00 Double	Open Jan-Dec	

McLays Guest House 268 Renfrew Street Glasgow G3 6TT Tel: 041 332 4796 Fax: 041 353 0422	COMMENDED ♔ ♔	16 Single 17 Twin 15 Double 14 Family	39 En Suite fac 9 Pub. Bath/Show	B&B per person £17.50-£19.50 Single £17.50-£19.50 Double	Open Jan-Dec	

Family run guest house in city centre site near Charing Cross. close to University and Kelvingrove Park.

Oakley Guest House 10 Oakley Terrace Glasgow G31 2HX Tel: 041 554 5409	Award Pending	3 Single 3 Twin 2 Double 2 Family	3 Pub. Bath/Show	B&B per person £17.50-£18.00 Single £14.00-£15.00 Double	Open Jan-Dec	

Regent Guest House 44 Regent Park Square Glasgow G41 2AG Tel: 041 422 1199 Fax: 041 423 7531	APPROVED 👑 👑	3 Single 2 Double 2 Family	2 En Suite fac 2 Pub. Bath/Show	B&B per person £20.00-£26.00 Single £20.00 Double	Open Jan-Dec	
		1860 terrace house in quiet, residential area. Ideal for city centre and under 2 miles (3kms) from the Burrell Collection. Warm welcome.				
Scott's Guest House 417 North Woodside Road Glasgow G20 6NN Tel: 041 339 3750		1 Single 4 Twin 1 Double 2 Family	4 Pub. Bath/Show	B&B per person £17.00 Single £15.00 Double	Open Jan-Dec	
Symington Guest House 26 Circus Drive Glasgow G31 2JH Tel: 041 556 1431		1 Twin 1 Double 1 Family	2 Pub. Bath/Show	B&B per person £12.00-£14.00 Single £12.00-£14.00 Double	Open Jan-Dec Dinner 1700-1900	
The Town House 4 Hughenden Terrace Glasgow G12 9XR Tel: 041 357 0862 Fax: 041 339 9605	HIGHLY COMMENDED 👑 👑 👑	3 Twin 5 Double 2 Family	10 En Suite fac	B&B per person £44.00-£48.00 Single £29.00-£29.50 Double	Open Jan-Dec Dinner 1830-2000	
		Elegantly refurbished Victorian town house in quiet conservation area in Glasgow's West End.				
The Victorian House 212 Renfrew Street Glasgow G3 Tel: 041 332 0129 Fax: 041 353 3155	COMMENDED 👑 👑	12 Single 12 Twin 12 Double 9 Family	37 En Suite fac 4 Pub. Bath/Show	B&B per person £21.00-£28.00 Single £18.00-£23.00 Double	Open Jan-Dec	
		Terraced house in quiet location close to city centre.				
Mrs I Adey 4 Holyrood Crescent Glasgow G20 6HJ Tel: 041 334 8390/ 0465 82367	Award Pending	1 Twin 1 Double 1 Family	3 Limited ensuite 2 Pub. Bath/Show	B&B per person £20.00-£22.00 Single £14.00-£15.00 Double	Open Apr-Sep	
Mrs A Bennett 107 Dowanhill Street Glasgow G12 9EQ Tel: 041 337 1307	COMMENDED Listed	2 Twin	1 En Suite fac 1 Pub. Bath/Show	B&B per person £17.50-£20.00 Single £15.00-£17.50 Double	Open Jan-Dec	
		Early Edwardian terraced townhouse in the West End. Convenient for buses and underground to city centre.				
Mrs Jane Black 19 Myrtle Park Crosshill, Glasgow G42 8UQ Tel: 041 423 8014		1 Twin 1 Double	1 Pub. Bath/Show	B&B per person £15.00-£16.00 Single £15.00-£16.00 Double	Open Jan-Dec Dinner 1700-1900 B&B + Eve. Meal £18.00-£20.00	

GLASGOW

GLASGOW continued	Map 1 H5	Award Pending					
John G Bristow 56 Dumbreck Road Glasgow G41 5NP Tel: 041 427 0129		Award Pending	1 Twin 1 Double	2 Priv. NOT ensuite 2 Pub. Bath/Show	B&B per person to £17.00 Single to £17.00 Double	Open Jan-Dec	
Margaret Bruce 24 Greenock Avenue Glasgow G44 5TS Tel: 041 637 0608		COMMENDED ♛♛	1 Single 2 Twin	2 En Suite fac 1 Priv. NOT ensuite 2 Pub. Bath/Show	B&B per person from £15.00 Single from £15.00 Double	Open Jan-Dec	
			Modern, architect designed villa, peacefully situated in residential area, 5 minutes from train station. Private parking.				
Mrs A Couston 13 Carment Drive Glasgow G41 3PP Tel: 041 632 0193			1 Twin 1 Family	2 Pub. Bath/Show	B&B per person £16.00-£18.00 Single £15.00-£17.00 Double	Open Apr-Sep	
Mrs C Divers Kirkland House 42 St Vincent Crescent Glasgow G3 8NG Tel: 041 248 3458		Award Pending	2 Single 1 Twin 1 Double 1 Family	3 En Suite fac 2 Limited ensuite	B&B per person £30.00-£35.00 Single £23.00-£27.50 Double	Open Mar-Oct	
Mrs R Easton 148 Queen's Drive Glasgow G42 8QN Tel: 041 423 3143		COMMENDED ♛	1 Twin 1 Family	1 Pub. Bath/Show	B&B per person to £18.00 Single to £16.00 Double	Open Apr-Sep	
			1st floor flat in B Listed Victorian tenement overlooking Queens Park. Convenient for Burrell Collection; city centre. Unrestricted street parking.				
Mr & Mrs S J Freebairn-Smith 14 Prospect Avenue Cambuslang, Glasgow G72 8BW Tel: 041 641 5055			3 Twin	2 Pub. Bath/Show	B&B per person £12.00-£14.00 Single £12.00-£14.00 Double	Open Jan-Dec Dinner 1700-2000 B&B + Eve. Meal £19.00-£21.00	
Mrs Joan Garner 21 Lamington Road Glasgow G52 2SE Tel: 041 882 1032			1 Twin 1 Double	1 Pub. Bath/Show	B&B per person £20.00 Single £20.00 Double	Open Apr-Sep	
Mrs D Hallam 13 Victoria Park Gardens South Glasgow G11 7BX Tel: 041 339 1559		COMMENDED ♛♛♛	1 Twin 1 Double	1 En Suite fac 2 Pub. Bath/Show	B&B per person £18.00-£22.00 Single £18.00-£22.00 Double	Open Apr-Sep Dinner 1800-2030 B&B + Eve. Meal £27.00-£29.00	
			Large Victorian town house in quiet residential area. Convenient for Clydeside Expressway to city centre.				

Mrs C Mill 41 Tweedsmuir Road Glasgow G52 2RX Tel: 041 883 2508		Award Pending	1 Twin 1 Double	1 Pub. Bath/Show	B&B per person £18.00 Single £18.00 Double	Open Jan-Dec Dinner 1800-2200 B&B + Eve. Meal £20.00-£25.00	
Mrs Margaret Ogilvie Lochgilvie 117 Randolph Road Glasgow G11 7DS Tel: 041 357 1593/ 0831 379732		Award Pending	1 Single 2 Twin	2 Limited ensuite 2 Pub. Bath/Show	B&B per person £20.00-£25.00 Single £18.00-£21.00 Double	Open Jan-Dec	
Mrs A Paterson 16 Bogton Avenue Glasgow G44 3JJ Tel: 041 637 4402		COMMENDED	1 Single 1 Twin	1 Priv. NOT ensuite 2 Pub. Bath/Show	B&B per person £16.00-£16.50 Single £15.00-£16.50 Double	Open Jan-Dec Dinner 1800-1900 B&B + Eve. Meal £22.00-£24.00	
Family home in quiet residential area, 200 yds from railway station with direct access to city centre. On main bus route.							
Mrs M Ross 3 Beech Avenue Glasgow G41 5DE Tel: 041 427 0194			2 Twin	2 En Suite fac	B&B per person £20.00-£25.00 Single £18.00-£20.00 Double	Open Jan-Dec	
Mrs J Sinclair 23 Dumbreck Road Glasgow G41 5LJ Tel: 041 427 1006			1 Twin 1 Double	2 Pub. Bath/Show	B&B per person £16.00-£18.00 Double	Open Apr-Sep Dinner 1800-2100 B&B + Eve. Meal £23.00-£25.00	
Mrs P Wells 21 West Avenue Stepps Glasgow G33 6ES Tel: 041 779 1951 Fax: 041 779 1951			1 Double 1 Family	2 En Suite fac	B&B per person £16.50-£18.00 Double	Open Jan-Dec	
GLENCOE **Argyll** Dorrington Lodge 6 Tigh Phurist Glencoe Argyll PA39 4HN Tel: (Ballachulish) 08552 653	Map 1 F1	COMMENDED	1 Twin 3 Double 1 Family	3 Pub. Bath/Show	B&B per person £16.50-£17.50 Single £13.50-£14.00 Double	Open Feb-Oct Xmas/New Year Dinner 1845-1930 B&B + Eve. Meal £21.50-£22.50	
Comfortable, modern house just off main road, with excellent views over Loch Leven. Home cooked meals using quality local produce.							
Dunire Guest House Glencoe Argyll PA39 4HS Tel: (Ballachulish) 08552 305			2 Twin 3 Double	4 En Suite fac 2 Pub. Bath/Show	B&B per person from £12.00 Double	Open Jan-Dec	

GLENCOE continued	Map 1 F1

GLENCOE   TEL: 08552 244
Strathlachlan, The Glencoe Guest House

A family run guest house in a quiet, peaceful, riverside setting. Spectacular mountain views. Comfortable en-suite rooms. Tea and coffee-making facilities. Central heating. Pleasant residents' lounge. Drying room.
An ideal location for touring and sightseeing the beautiful West Coast or local walking, climbing and skiing.

The Glencoe Guest House Strathlachlan Glencoe Argyll PA39 Tel: (Ballachulish) 08552 244 Fax: 08552 679	COMMENDED ☙☙	2 Twin 3 Double 1 Family	4 En Suite fac 1 Pub. Bath/Show	B&B per person £12.00-£18.00 Double	Open Jan-Dec
		Quiet peaceful riverside setting on edge of village. Magnificent views. Ideal base for touring and for mountain sports. Family run.			
Scorry Breac Guest House Glencoe Argyll PA39 4HT Tel: (Ballachulish) 08552 354	COMMENDED ☙☙	2 Twin 2 Double 1 Family	2 En Suite fac 2 Pub. Bath/Show	B&B per person £14.00-£18.00 Single £13.00-£18.00 Double	Open Jan-Dec Dinner 1800-1830 B&B + Eve. Meal £24.00-£28.00
		Modern single storey house with large garden overlooking Loch Leven. In a quiet secluded situation on the edge of the village with local forest walk.			
GLENDALE Isle of Skye, Inverness-shire Mrs Kernachan 4 Lephin Glendale Isle of Skye, Inverness-shire IV55 8WJ Tel: (Glendale) 047081 376	Map 3 C9 COMMENDED Listed	1 Single 1 Twin 1 Double	1 Pub. Bath/Show	B&B per person £11.50-£13.50 Single £11.50-£13.50 Double	Open Jan-Dec Dinner 1830-2000 B&B + Eve. Meal £18.50-£20.50
		Situated with views across Glendale Valley this is a quiet and beautiful part of north west Skye. Evening meal available.			
GLENESK, by Edzell Angus Mrs I Rawlinson The House of Mark Invermark, Tarfside Glenesk, by Edzell Angus DD9 7YZ Tel: (Tarfside) 0356 670315	Map 4 F1	2 Twin 1 Double	2 Pub. Bath/Show	B&B per person from £18.00 Single from £18.00 Double	Open Jan-Dec Dinner 1700-2100 B&B + Eve. Meal from £28.00
BY GLENFARG Kinross-shire Mrs Susan Lawrie Cuthill Towers by Milnathort Kinross-shire KY13 7SH Tel: (Glenfarg) 0577 830221	Map 2 C3	2 Twin 1 Double	2 Priv. NOT ensuite 1 Pub. Bath/Show	B&B per person £13.00-£16.00 Double	Open Jan-Dec
GLENHINNISDALE Isle of Skye, Inverness-shire M V Butler Mile End House Glenhinnisdale, by Uig Isle of Skye, Inverness-shire Tel: (Uig) 047042 331	Map 3 D8 COMMENDED Listed	1 Twin 1 Double 1 Family	1 Pub. Bath/Show	B&B per person £12.00-£13.00 Single £12.00-£13.00 Double	Open Jan-Dec
		19C former schoolhouse in secluded glen, 6 miles (10 kms) from Uig Ferry. Salmon fishing. Evening meal by prior arrangement. Home cooking.			

Mrs I Nicolson Glenhinnisdale, Snizort Isle of Skye, Inverness-shire IV51 Tel: (Uig) 047042 406		**COMMENDED** ♛	1 Twin 1 Double 1 Family	2 Pub. Bath/Show	B&B per person £12.50-£13.50 Single £12.50-£13.50 Double	Open Apr-Oct Dinner 1830-1930 B&B + Eve. Meal £21.50-£22.50
			Farmhouse in quiet elevated position overlooking Glenhinnisdale. 6 miles (9.6 Km) from Uig Ferry. 100 acre croft. Home cooking.			
GLENISLA, by Kirriemuir **Angus** Mrs M Clark Purgavie Farm Glenisla, by Kirriemuir Angus DD8 5HZ Tel: (Lintrathen) 05756 213/ 0860 392794 (mobile)	**Map 2** C1	**HIGHLY** **COMMENDED** ♛ ♛ ♛	1 Twin 2 Family	2 En Suite fac 1 Priv. NOT ensuite	B&B per person from £16.00 Single from £13.00 Double	Open Jan-Dec Dinner from 1800 B&B + Eve. Meal from £20.00
			19C house on working farm, with views over Strathmore Valley. Glamis Castle, 7 miles (11kms), Kirriemuir 6 miles (11kms). Scottish cooking.			
GLENISLA, by Kirriemuir **Perthshire** S J Evans Glenmarkie Farmhouse Glenisla Perthshire PH11 8QB Tel: (Glenisla) 057582 341	**Map 2** C1	**COMMENDED** ♛ ♛	1 Twin 2 Double	1 En Suite fac 1 Pub. Bath/Show	B&B per person from £15.00 Single from £15.00 Double	Open Jan-Dec Dinner 1800-2200 B&B + Eve. Meal from £25.00
			Family run farmhouse deep in picturesque Glenisla. Home cooking. Ideal for all outdoor pursuits. Own stables. Hacking/trekking in small groups.			
GLEN LETHNOT, by Brechin **Angus** Mrs L Gibb The Post House Glen Lethnot, by Brechin Angus DD9 7UQ Tel: (Menmuir) 0356 660277	**Map 4** F1		1 Twin 1 Double	1 Pub. Bath/Show	B&B per person from £10.00 Single from £10.00 Double	Open Nov-Jul Dinner 1900-2100 B&B + Eve. Meal from £14.00
GLENLIVET **Banffshire** Mrs Jo R Durno Deepdale, Auchbreck Glenlivet, Ballindalloch Banffshire AB37 9EJ Tel: (Glenlivet) 0807 590364	**Map 4** D9	**COMMENDED** ♛	1 Twin 1 Double	1 Pub. Bath/Show	B&B per person £13.00-£16.00 Single £13.00-£16.00 Double	Open Jan-Dec Dinner 1800-2000 B&B + Eve. Meal £19.50-£24.50
			A Highland welcome assured at this comfortable home of farming family. Overlooking the Glenlivet Distillery. Fresh local produce a priority.			
GLENLUCE **Wigtownshire** Rowantree Guest House 38 Main Street Glenluce Wigtownshire DG8 0PS Tel: (Glenluce) 05813 244	**Map 1** G1	**COMMENDED** ♛	1 Twin 1 Double 2 Family	2 Limited ensuite 1 Pub. Bath/Show	B&B per person £12.00-£15.00 Double	Open Jan-Dec Dinner 1830-2000 B&B + Eve. Meal £18.00-£21.00
			Family run house situated in centre of small village, 10 miles (16kms) from Stranraer and the Irish ferry. Car parking; large garden; home cooking.			
Mrs C Marshall Grayhill Farm Glenluce Wigtownshire DG8 0NS Tel: (Glenluce) 05813 400		**COMMENDED** Listed	1 Twin 1 Double	1 Pub. Bath/Show	B&B per person £12.00-£13.00 Single £12.00-£13.00 Double	Open Apr-Oct
			Friendly, family welcome on a traditional farm on outskirts of village (with shooting rights). Centrally situated for touring and leisure pursuits.			

Details of Grading and Classification are on page vi. | Key to symbols is on back flap. |

GLENLUCE continued Mrs M Stewart Bankfield Farm Glenluce Wigtownshire DG8 0JF Tel: (Glenluce) 05813 281	**Map 1** G1	**COMMENDED** ♛	1 Twin 1 Double 1 Family	1 Pub. Bath/Show	B&B per person £13.00–£14.00 Single £13.00–£14.00 Double	Open Apr-Oct

Farmhouse on 370 acre working farm conveniently situated between the village and the main A75 tourist route.

Mr & Mrs Walker Belgrano, 81 Main Street Glenluce Wigtownshire DG8 0PP Tel: (Glenluce) 05813 554			1 Single 1 Double 1 Family	1 En Suite fac 2 Limited ensuite 1 Pub. Bath/Show	B&B per person £13.00–£16.00 Single £13.00–£16.00 Double	Open Feb-Dec Dinner 1700-1830 B&B + Eve. Meal £18.00–£21.00

GLENLYON **Perthshire** Mrs K A Conway Dalchiorlich Glenlyon, Aberfeldy Perthshire PH15 2PX Tel: (Bridge of Balgie) 0887 866226	**Map 2** A1	**APPROVED** Listed	1 Double 1 Family	1 Pub. Bath/Show	B&B per person from £11.00 Single from £11.00 Double	Open Mar-Nov Dinner 1800-2000 B&B + Eve. Meal from £19.00

Remote farmhouse on sheep farm in highland Perthshire. Excellent peaceful setting. Ideal hill walking, fishing, birdwatching.

Mrs Hardy Invervar Lodge Glen Lyon, Aberfeldy Perthshire PH15 2PL Tel: (Glen Lyon) 0887 877206			1 Single 1 Double 1 Family	1 Priv. NOT ensuite 2 Pub. Bath/Show	B&B per person from £13.00 Single	Open Jan-Dec Dinner 1700-2000 B&B + Eve. Meal from £21.00

GLENROTHES **Fife** Jean F Baxter New Inn House, On A92 Markinch Fife KY7 6LR Tel: (Glenrothes) 0592 752623	**Map 2** C3		1 Single 1 Twin 1 Double	1 Pub. Bath/Show	B&B per person £14.00–£15.00 Single	Open Jan-Dec

Mrs Anne Duncan Dunneill, 3 Prestonhall Road Glenrothes Fife KY7 5RL Tel: (Glenrothes) 0592 756827		**HIGHLY** **COMMENDED** Listed	1 Twin 1 Double	1 En Suite fac 1 Pub. Bath/Show	B&B per person £16.00–£18.00 Double	Open Jan-Dec Dinner 1800-2000 B&B + Eve. Meal £23.00–£25.00

Modern bungalow in quiet cul-de-sac on small estate with easy access for all local amenities.

O & H Robertson 13 Laxford Road Glenrothes Fife KY6 2EB Tel: (Glenrothes) 0592 754513		**APPROVED** Listed	1 Single 1 Twin 1 Double	1 Pub. Bath/Show	B&B per person from £12.00 Single from £12.00 Double	Open Jan-Dec Dinner from 1730 B&B + Eve. Meal from £17.00

End terraced house in residential area, west of town centre. On local bus route and close to sports centre.

Carol Tjeransen Wester Markinch Balbirnie Estate Glenrothes Fife KY7 6JN Tel: (Glenrothes) 0592 756719/610062			2 Single 2 Double	1 En Suite fac 1 Pub. Bath/Show	B&B per person to £15.00 Single to £17.50 Double	Open Jan-Dec	
GLENSHEE **Perthshire** Mrs Hardy Blair View Glenshee Perthshire PH10 7LP Tel: (Blacklunans) 0250 882260	Map 4 D1		2 Twin 1 Double	1 En Suite fac 2 Priv. NOT ensuite 1 Pub. Bath/Show	B&B per person £12.50-£15.00 Double	Open Jan-Dec Dinner 1800-2200 B&B + Eve. Meal £20.50-£23.00	
GLENSHIEL **Ross-shire** Mrs Munro Glomach House Glenshiel, by Kyle of Lochalsh Ross-shire Tel: (Glenshiel) 059981 222	Map 3 F1		1 Twin 2 Double	3 Priv. NOT ensuite 2 Pub. Bath/Show	B&B per person £15.00-£17.50 Single £12.50-£17.50 Double	Open Jan-Dec	
GLENURQUHART **Inverness-shire** Mrs Miles Meiklie House Glenurquhart Inverness-shire IV3 6TJ Tel: (Glenurquhart) 0456 476265	Map 4 A9	COMMENDED 👑	3 Twin	2 Pub. Bath/Show	B&B per person £15.00-£16.00 Double	Open Apr-Oct	
			Modern detached house in elevated position set back from the A831 with excellent views over Loch Meiklie and the Western Highlands.				
GOLSPIE **Sutherland** Mrs N Grant Deo Greine Farm, Backies Golspie Sutherland KW10 6SE Tel: (Golspie) 0408 633106	Map 4 B6	COMMENDED 👑👑👑	2 Twin 1 Double 1 Family	3 En Suite fac 1 Priv. NOT ensuite	B&B per person from £14.00 Double	Open Apr-Oct Dinner from 1800 B&B + Eve. Meal from £24.00	
			Crofting farmhouse, situated in hills behind Golspie, in an elevated position overlooking surrounding countryside.				

WELCOME

Whenever you are in Scotland, you can be sure of a warm welcome at your nearest Tourist Information Centre.

For guide books, maps, souvenirs, our Centres provide a service second to none—many now offer bureau-de-change facilities. And, of course, Tourist Information Centres offer free, expert advice on what to see and do, route-planning and accommodation for everyone—visitors and residents alike!

GRANTOWN-ON-SPEY Moray	Map 4 C9

Ardconnel House

Woodlands Terrace, Grantown-on-Spey, Moray PH26 3JU   Tel/Fax: 0479 2104

Ardconnel House is situated at the southern fringe of Grantown-on-Spey opposite Lochan and Pine Forest within a short walk to the famous River Spey. All our bedrooms have en-suite private facilities and are extremely comfortable and equipped with colour televisions, welcome trays and hairdryers. Good Scottish home cooking using fresh local produce is served in our elegant dining room. You can relax with a malt or book in our spacious sitting room where log and peat fires blaze on chillier evenings. 'Taste of Scotland' member.

For further information regarding activities or special interests, please call Jim or Barbara Casey — 0479 2104.

Ardconnel Woodlands Terrace Grantown-on-Spey Moray PH26 3JU Tel: (Grantown-on-Spey) 0479 2104	HIGHLY COMMENDED ♛♛♛	1 Twin 4 Double 2 Family	6 En Suite fac 1 Priv. NOT ensuite	B&B per person from £25.00 Single from £20.00 Double	Open Jan-Dec Dinner from 1900 B&B + Eve. Meal from £30.00	
		Large detached Victorian house with croquet lawn pleasantly situated with open aspects to hills, forests and lochan. Comfortable lounge.				
Brooklynn Grant Road Grantown-on-Spey Moray PH26 3LA Tel: (Grantown-on-Spey) 0479 3113	COMMENDED ♛♛	1 Single 1 Twin 3 Double 1 Family	2 En Suite fac 1 Pub. Bath/Show	B&B per person from £16.00 Single from £16.00 Double	Open Jan-Dec Dinner 1830-1930	
		Attractive villa and garden in quiet area within easy walking distance of town, woods and river. Many personal touches; evening meal by arrangement.				
Crann Tara Guest House High Street Grantown-on-Spey Moray PH26 3EN Tel: (Grantown-on-Spey) 0479 2197	COMMENDED ♛	1 Single 1 Twin 3 Family	2 Pub. Bath/Show	B&B per person £14.00-£16.00 Single £14.00-£16.00 Double	Open Jan-Dec Dinner from 1830 B&B + Eve. Meal £21.00-£24.00	
		19C town house, recently modernised and personally run. Near River Spey, with rod storage and drying room. Cycles for hire. Off-street car parking.				

HERE'S THE DIFFERENCE

STB's scheme has two distinct elements, grading and classification.

GRADING: measures the quality and condition of the facilities and services offered, eg, the warmth of welcome, quality of food and its presentation, condition of decor and furnishings, appearance of buildings, tidiness of grounds and gardens, condition of lighting and heating and so on.
Grading awards are: **Approved, Commended, Highly Commended, Deluxe.**

CLASSIFICATION: measures the range of physical facilities and services offered, eg, rooms with private bath, heating, reception, lounges, telephones and so on.
Classification awards are: **Listed or from one to five crowns.**

Culdearn House

WOODLANDS TERRACE
GRANTOWN-ON-SPEY PH26 3JU
TEL: 0479 872106   FAX: 0479 873641

Private Country House offering house party atmosphere and a warm welcome from the Scottish proprietors. Isobel and Alasdair Little provide freshly prepared food, malt whiskies and a moderately priced wine list. All guest rooms have en-suite private facilities with colour TV, radio and welcome tray. Log and peat fires in season.

Ideal location for birdwatching, walking, salmon and trout fishing. Several golf courses nearby. Horse-riding arranged. Historic sites and many good walks. 3-day and 7-day breaks available.

AA/RAC Highly Acclaimed   Taste of Scotland Members

Please contact Isobel and Alasdair Little
for reservations.

Culdearn House Woodlands Terrace Grantown-on-Spey Moray PH26 3JU Tel: (Grantown-on-Spey) 0479 872106 Fax: 0479 873641	HIGHLY COMMENDED 🏆 🏆 🏆	1 Single 3 Twin 5 Double	9 En Suite fac	B&B per person	Open Mar-Oct Dinner 1845-1930 B&B + Eve. Meal £38.00-£50.00

Elegant Victorian house, retaining many original features. Warm and friendly atmosphere. All rooms en suite facilities. Taste of Scotland member.

KINROSS HOUSE

Woodside Avenue, Grantown-on-Spey
Telephone: 0479 872042

KINROSS HOUSE sits on a quiet avenue an easy stroll from pinewoods and river, and from the centre of this delightful country town.

David and Katherine Elder provide highland hospitality and comfort at its very best in their smoke-free house.

- Bedrooms are bright, warm and spacious. All have welcome tray and colour TV.

- Five bedrooms have en-suite facilities. One of these is suitable for ambulant disabled guests.

- Children from 7 years.

- Delicious traditional Dinner freshly prepared with quality ingredients and served by David wearing his McIntosh kilt.

- 'Taste of Scotland' Member.

Kinross Guest House Woodside Avenue Grantown-on-Spey Moray PH26 3JR Tel: (Grantown-on-Spey) 0479 872042	COMMENDED 🏆 🏆 🏆	1 Single 2 Twin 2 Double 2 Family	4 En Suite fac 2 Pub. Bath/Show	B&B per person £17.00-£21.00 Single £16.00-£23.00 Double	Open Mar-Nov Dinner from 1900 B&B + Eve. Meal £26.50-£34.00

Victorian villa with original features in peaceful residential area. Friendly, informal atmosphere with Scottish hosts. No smoking house.

Parkburn Guest House High Street Grantown-on-Spey Moray PH26 3EN Tel: (Grantown-on-Spey) 0479 3116	COMMENDED 🏆 🏆	1 Twin 3 Double	2 En Suite fac 1 Pub. Bath/Show	B&B per person from £15.00 Single from £15.00 Double	Open Jan-Dec Dinner at 1900 B&B + Eve. Meal from £24.00

Semi detached Victorian villa standing back from main road with ample parking available. Fishing and fishing tuition can be arranged.

	Map 4 C9						
GRANTOWN-ON-SPEY **continued** Rossmor Guest House Woodlands Terrace Grantown-on-Spey Moray PH26 3JU Tel: (Grantown-on-Spey) 0479 872201		COMMENDED ♛ ♛ ♛	1 Twin 4 Double 1 Family	5 En Suite fac 1 Priv. NOT ensuite 1 Pub. Bath/Show	B&B per person £18.00-£20.00 Double	Open Jan-Dec Dinner at 1830 B&B + Eve. Meal £28.00-£30.00	
			Spacious Victorian detached house with original features and large garden. Magnificent views of countryside. Home cooking; a warm welcome. Parking.				
Mrs R Donaldson The Hawthorns Old Spey Bridge Grantown-on-Spey Moray PH26 3NQ Tel: (Grantown-on-Spey) 0479 2016		COMMENDED ♛ ♛ ♛	2 Twin 1 Double	2 En Suite fac 1 Priv. NOT ensuite	B&B per person from £27.00 Single from £17.00 Double	Open Jan-Dec Dinner 1830-2000 B&B + Eve. Meal from £25.00	
			19C country house situated 1 mile (2kms) from town, overlooking the River Spey to the hills beyond.				
Mrs Helen Hunter Bank House, 1 The Square Grantown-on-Spey Moray PH26 3HG Tel: (Grantown-on-Spey) 0479 3256			2 Single 1 Twin 1 Double	1 Pub. Bath/Show	B&B per person £13.00-£15.00 Single £13.00-£15.00 Double	Open Jan-Dec	

THE ANVIL ♛ ♛ TEL: (0479) 3371
16 CASTLE ROAD, GRANTOWN-ON-SPEY PH26 3HL

We offer good food, comfortable beds, log fires and a warm welcome. All rooms have central heating and H&C. Ideal base for golf, fishing, ski-ing, birdwatching or just relaxing in splendid scenery before returning to our delicious home cooking.

DB&B from £21 per person per night.
'Taste of Scotland' Member

Contact:
Mrs O. R. Powell
Proprietor

Mrs O R Powell The Anvil, 16 Castle Road Grantown-on-Spey Moray PH26 3HL Tel: (Grantown-on-Spey) 0479 3371		COMMENDED ♛ ♛	1 Twin 1 Double 1 Family	2 Priv. NOT ensuite 2 Pub. Bath/Show	B&B per person £16.00-£18.00 Single £14.50-£15.50 Double	Open Dec-Oct Dinner 1830-1900 B&B + Eve. Meal £22.00-£24.00	
			Built of local stone, formerly the Blacksmith's house, now offering a warm and friendly atmosphere with home cooking.				
GRANTSHOUSE, by Duns **Berwickshire** Mrs M Burton Harelawside Grantshouse Berwickshire TD11 3RP Tel: (Grantshouse) 03615 209	Map 2 F5	COMMENDED ♛ ♛	1 Twin 2 Double	1 En Suite fac 1 Pub. Bath/Show	B&B per person £18.00-£25.00 Single £16.00-£20.00 Double	Open Jan-Dec Dinner 1830-1930 B&B + Eve. Meal £27.00-£31.00	
			18C farmhouse on family run mixed farm with views of woods and hill. Just off A1. 1 hours drive to Edinburgh. 15 minutes Berwick.				
GREENLAW, Duns **Berwickshire** Mrs Carruthers Bridgend House 36 West High Street Greenlaw, Duns Berwickshire TD10 6XA Tel: (Greenlaw) 03616 270 Fax: 03616 270	Map 2 F6	COMMENDED ♛ ♛	2 Twin 1 Double 2 Family	4 En Suite fac	B&B per person £16.00-£18.00 Double	Open Jan-Dec Dinner 1900-2000 B&B + Eve. Meal £22.00-£26.00	
			Friendly guest house, in the heart of this small village, ideal as a touring base to explore the Borders.				
Mrs S Slater Woodheads Greenlaw Berwickshire TD6 9EJ Tel: (Greenlaw) 03616 446		COMMENDED Listed	1 Twin 1 Double	2 Pub. Bath/Show	B&B per person from £14.50 Double	Open Apr-Oct Dinner 1800-2000 B&B + Eve. Meal from £22.00	
			Traditional farmhouse overlooking surrounding countryside. Fishing, golfing and riding can be arranged locally.				

GREENOCK **Renfrewshire** A Campbell Quarrybank, 10 Fox Street Greenock Renfrewshire PA16 Tel: (Greenock) 0475 25272/888857	Map 1 G5	COMMENDED Listed	1 Double 1 Family	1 En Suite fac 1 Pub. Bath/Show	B&B per person £17.00-£20.00 Single £17.00-£28.00 Double	Open Jan-Dec Dinner 1800-1900 B&B + Eve. Meal £23.00-£26.00	
			Georgian family home close to Esplanade. Easy access to Clyde coast, Cowal Peninsula, Argyll and Glasgow.				
GRETNA **Dumfriesshire** Mr Gary Beattie Guards Mill Farm Gretna Dumfriesshire CA6 5JA Tel: (Gretna) 0461 338358/338707	Map 2 D1		2 Double	2 Limited ensuite 1 Pub. Bath/Show	B&B per person £15.00 Single £13.00 Double	Open Mar-Oct	
Miss M Blackwell New House Farm, Annan Road Gretna Dumfriesshire CA6 5HD Tel: (Gretna) 0461 337711			2 Twin 1 Family	1 Pub. Bath/Show	B&B per person £12.00-£13.00 Double	Open Jan-Dec Dinner 1800-2100 B&B + Eve. Meal £17.00-£18.00	
Mrs Donabie The Beeches, Loanwath Road Gretna Dumfriesshire CA6 5EP Tel: (Gretna) 0461 337448		COMMENDED ♛ ♛	1 Twin 1 Family	2 En Suite fac	B&B per person £15.50-£16.50 Double	Open Jan-Nov	
			Former farmhouse overlooking the Solway and Lakeland hills. A non-smoking house with homely and peaceful atmosphere, ensuite facilities.				
Mrs J L Graham Barrasgate, Millhill Gretna Dumfriesshire CA6 Tel: (Gretna) 0461 337854			1 Double 1 Family	1 En Suite fac 1 Pub. Bath/Show	B&B per person £13.00-£15.00 Double	Open Jan-Dec	
Mrs V Greenhow 164-166 Central Avenue Gretna Dumfriesshire CA6 5AF Tel: (Gretna) 0461 337307/337533		Award Pending	3 Double	1 Pub. Bath/Show	B&B per person £14.00 Single £13.00 Double	Open Mar-Sep	
Mrs S Peacock Rosebank House Glasgow Road Gretna Dumfriesshire CA6 5DT Tel: (Gretna) 0461 338379			2 Twin	1 Pub. Bath/Show	B&B per person £12.00-£13.00 Double	Open Jan-Dec	
GRETNA GREEN **Dumfriesshire** Mrs O Crosbie Alexander House Gretna Green Dumfriesshire CA5 5DU Tel: (Gretna) 0461 337597	Map 2 D1		1 Twin 3 Double	2 En Suite fac 1 Pub. Bath/Show	B&B per person £14.00-£17.00 Double	Open Jan-Dec	

GRANTOWN-ON-SPEY continued Mrs B Moffat Kirkcroft, Glasgow Road Gretna Green Dumfriesshire CA6 Tel: (Gretna) 0461 337403	Map 4 C9	Award Pending	1 Twin 2 Double 1 Family	1 Pub. Bath/Show	B&B per person £20.00 Single £14.00-£15.00 Double	Open Jan-Dec	
GRIMSAY **North Uist, Western Isles** Mrs C MacLeod Glendale, 7 Kallin Grimsay North Uist, Western Isles PA82 5HY Tel: (Benbecula) 0870 2029/0870 602029	Map 3 A8	COMMENDED	2 Twin 1 Family	1 En Suite fac 2 Pub. Bath/Show	B&B per person from £15.00 Double	Open Jan-Dec Dinner 1900-2000 B&B + Eve. Meal from £23.00	
			Modern house with comfortable bedrooms in a quiet position overlooking the harbour.				
GULLANE **East Lothian** Mrs Susan Law Mayfield, East Links Road Gullane East Lothian EH31 2AF Tel: (Gullane) 0620 843288	Map 2 F4		3 Twin	2 Pub. Bath/Show	B&B per person from £15.00 Single from £15.00 Double	Open Jan-Dec Dinner 1930-2100 B&B + Eve. Meal from £30.00	
Mrs Lynch Cruachan, The Beeches off Muirfield Park Gullane East Lothian EH31 2DX Tel: (Gullane) 842033			1 Twin 1 Family	2 Pub. Bath/Show	B&B per person from £14.00 Single from £14.00 Double	Open Jan-Dec	
Mrs McRae Glebewood, Marine Terrace Gullane East Lothian EH31 2AZ Tel: (Gullane) 0620 842593		COMMENDED Listed	1 Twin	1 Priv. NOT ensuite	B&B per person £15.00 Double	Open Apr-Oct	
			Semi detached house overlooking beach and Firth of Forth. Golf courses within walking distance. 20 miles (32 kms) east of Edinburgh.				
Mrs A H Miller Home Cottage, Goose Green Gullane East Lothian Tel: (Gullane) 0620 843236			1 Twin	1 En Suite fac	B&B per person £20.00-£22.00 Double	Open Apr-Oct	
Mr & Mrs Nisbet Faussett Hill House Main Street Gullane East Lothian EH31 2DR Tel: (Gullane) 0620 842396		COMMENDED	1 Twin 2 Double	2 En Suite fac 1 Priv. NOT ensuite 1 Pub. Bath/Show	B&B per person from £18.00 Double	Open Mar-Dec	
			Detached Edwardian house with pleasant garden and views towards Lammermuir Hills. Sandy beaches and several golf courses nearby.				
HADDINGTON **East Lothian** Mrs Clark Upper Bolton Haddington East Lothian EH41 4HW Tel: (Gifford) 062081 346	Map 2 E5	APPROVED Listed	1 Twin 1 Double 1 Family	1 Priv. NOT ensuite 2 Pub. Bath/Show	B&B per person £13.00-£16.00 Single £13.00-£16.00 Double	Open Jan-Dec Dinner from 1800 B&B + Eve. Meal £22.00-£24.00	
			Homely farmhouse accommodation in peaceful rural situation yet only half an hour's drive from Edinburgh. Local produce when available.				

Mrs Horsburgh Hillview, 10 Abbots View Haddington East Lothian EH41 3QG Tel: (Haddington) 062082 2987	COMMENDED Listed	1 Single 1 Twin	1 Pub. Bath/Show	B&B per person to £12.00 Single to £12.00 Double	Open Jan-Dec
Warm and comfortable modern house only half an hours drive from Edinburgh.					

BARNEY MAINS FARMHOUSE
BARNEY MAINS, HADDINGTON, EAST LOTHIAN

Beautiful Georgian farmhouse with spectacular views of lovely countryside within 20 minutes drive to Edinburgh. Close to many golf courses, fine beaches, historic houses and castles, and heather-covered hills. Relax in the peace and comfort of our home.
Prices from £14 pp per night.
For further details contact Katie Kerr, Proprietor on:
Tel: 062 088 310   Fax: 062 088 639. (Changing in 1994 to:
Tel: 0620 880 310   Fax: 0620 880 639.)

Mrs Kerr Barney Mains Farm House Haddington East Lothian EH41 3SA Tel: (Athelstaneford) 062088 310 Fax: 062088 639	COMMENDED Listed	2 Twin 1 Double	1 En Suite fac 1 Priv. NOT ensuite 2 Pub. Bath/Show	B&B per person from £15.00 Single from £15.00 Double	Open Mar-Nov
Peaceful and comfortable farmhouse with superb views of surrounding countryside. Half an hour's drive from Edinburgh.					

Mrs A Kinghorn 12 Traprain Terrace Haddington East Lothian EH41 3QD Tel: (Haddington) 062082 4635	COMMENDED Listed	2 Double	1 Pub. Bath/Show	B&B per person £12.00-£13.00 Double	Open Jan-Dec
Personally run B and B in quiet location, close to A1, Edinburgh 17 miles (27kms). Ideal for touring East Lothian.					

The Plough Tavern 13 Court Street Haddington East Lothian EH41 3DS Tel: (Haddington) 062082 3326		2 Twin 2 Family	4 En Suite fac	B&B per person £15.00-£25.00 Single £17.50-£25.00 Double	Open Jan-Dec

Mrs N D Steven Under Bolton Haddington Tel: (Gifford) 062081 318	HIGHLY COMMENDED	3 Twin	2 En Suite fac 1 Priv. NOT ensuite 2 Pub. Bath/Show	B&B per person £14.00-£16.00 Double	Open Mar-Oct Dinner 1930-2100 B&B + Eve. Meal £26.00-£30.00
Elegantly furnished farmhouse, peacefully situated 3 miles (5 kms) from Haddington. Within easy reach of East Coast golfing resorts.					

Mrs Williams Eaglescairnie Mains Haddington East Lothian EH41 4HN Tel: (Gifford) 062081 491/ 0620 810491 Fax: 062081 491	COMMENDED	2 Single 1 Twin 1 Double	1 En Suite fac 1 Priv. NOT ensuite 2 Pub. Bath/Show	B&B per person £15.50-£17.50 Single £15.50-£18.50 Double	Open Jan-Dec
In quiet rural situation, on working mixed farm, large family house with magnificent views of Fife and Lammermuirs, 4 miles (6kms) from Haddington.					

HALKIRK **Caithness** Mrs M Banks Glenlivet, Fairview Halkirk Caithness KW12 6XF Tel: (Halkirk) 084783 302	Map 4 C3 COMMENDED	2 Single 1 Twin 1 Double	2 Pub. Bath/Show	B&B per person from £12.00 Single from £12.00 Double	Open Jan-Dec
Modern house on outskirts of the village, close to river and 6 miles (10kms) South of Thurso.					

Details of Grading and Classification are on page vi.   Key to symbols is on back flap.

HALKIRK continued

	Map 4 C3						

Sandy & Jessie Waters
The Bungalow
Banachmore Farm
Harpsdale, Halkirk
Caithness
KW12 6UN
Tel: (Westerdale) 084784 216

COMMENDED ♛ ♛ ♛

1 Twin
1 Double
1 Family

1 En Suite fac
1 Priv. NOT ensuite
1 Pub. Bath/Show

B&B per person
£14.00-£16.00 Double

Open Jan-Dec
Dinner 1830-2000
B&B + Eve. Meal
£23.50-£25.50

Modern detached house on a working farm in a quiet rural setting,
¾ mile(1.5kms) from salmon fishing on River Thurso.

HAMILTON
Lanarkshire
Map 2 A6

Mr G A Reid
96 High Blantyre Road
Burnbank, Hamilton
Lanarkshire
Tel: (Hamilton) 0698 822245

APPROVED
Listed

1 Twin
1 Family

1 Pub. Bath/Show

B&B per person
£16.00-£17.00 Single
£13.00-£14.00 Double

Open Jan-Dec

Family run, situated 1 mile (1.5 kms) from town centre, 10 minutes from
local train service. Ideal base for all local amenities.

HARTHILL, by Shotts
Lanarkshire
Map 2 B5

Mrs Ireland
Blair Mains Farm
Harthill, by Shotts
Lanarkshire
ML7 5TJ
Tel: (Harthill) 0501 51278

4 Single
2 Twin
1 Double
1 Family

3 Pub. Bath/Show

B&B per person
£14.50-£16.00 Single
£14.50-£16.00 Double

Open Jan-Dec
Dinner 1800-2000
B&B + Eve. Meal
£19.50-£21.00

HAUGH OF URR
Kirkcudbrightshire
Map 2 B10

Woodburn House

HAUGH OF URR, CASTLE DOUGLAS
DUMFRIES & GALLOWAY DG7 3YB
Telephone: 055 666 217

A warm welcome awaits you at Woodburn — a comfortable 18th-century former Coaching Inn centrally situated for the beautiful Solway Coast and Galloway Hills. Ideal for touring, fishing, golf, walking, birdwatching, or just relaxing and enjoying the peace and quiet. Excellent home cooking using mainly home-grown produce. Home-made bread and preserves. Friendly atmosphere, personal attention assured. Ample private parking. 10% reduction on weekly bookings. Leaflet available on request.

Mrs M E Wormald
Woodburn House
Haugh of Urr, Castle Douglas
Kirkcudbrightshire
DG7 3YB
Tel: (Haugh-of-Urr) 055666 217

HIGHLY COMMENDED ♛ ♛

1 Twin
2 Double

1 En Suite fac
1 Priv. NOT ensuite
2 Pub. Bath/Show

B&B per person
£15.00-£18.00 Double

Open Jan-Dec
Dinner 1800-2000
B&B + Eve. Meal
£23.00-£26.00

Personally run 200 year old former coaching inn in centre of village.
Ideal for touring Solway coast and Galloway hills.

HAWICK
Roxburghshire
Map 2 E8

Mrs H Allan
Hillview, 4 Weensland Road
Hawick
Roxburghshire
TD9 9NP
Tel: (Hawick) 0450 74100

COMMENDED
Listed

1 Twin
1 Double

1 Pub. Bath/Show

B&B per person
to £15.00 Single
to £12.50 Double

Open Jan-Dec

Comfortable, terraced house on main tourist route near town centre.
Public car park opposite. Near leisure centre.

Mrs A Bell Kirkton Farmhouse Hawick Roxburghshire TD9 8QJ Tel: (Hawick) 0450 72421		COMMENDED Listed	1 Twin 2 Double	1 Pub. Bath/Show	B&B per person £17.00-£18.00 Single £14.00-£16.00 Double	Open Mar-Nov Dinner 1800-2100 B&B + Eve. Meal £23.00-£25.00	
			Spacious Border farmhouse with friendly family welcome. Private loch fishing. Golf packages.				
Mrs M Jackson Colterscleugh, Teviothead Hawick Roxburghshire TD9 0LF Tel: (Teviotdale) 045085 247			1 Single 1 Twin 1 Family	1 Limited ensuite 1 Pub. Bath/Show	B&B per person £14.00 Single £13.00 Double	Open Jan-Dec Dinner from 1900 B&B + Eve. Meal £19.00-£20.00	
Mrs M V Park Dunira House, Buccleuch Road Hawick Roxburghshire TD9 0EL Tel: (Hawick) 0450 78493		COMMENDED	1 Twin 2 Double	3 En Suite fac	B&B per person £22.00-£24.00 Single £18.00-£19.00 Double	Open Jan-Dec	
			Victorian mill owners house, retaining many original features, with large garden overlooking river. All rooms with en suite facilities.				
Mrs E Smith Ellistrin, 6 Fenwick Park Hawick Roxburghshire TD9 9PA Tel: (Hawick) 0450 74216		COMMENDED Listed	1 Twin 2 Double	2 En Suite fac 1 Pub. Bath/Show	B&B per person £12.50-£16.00 Single £12.50-£16.00 Double	Open Mar-Oct Dinner 1830-1930 B&B + Eve. Meal £20.50-£24.00	
			Comfortable Victorian villa within spacious grounds in an elevated position overlooking Hawick. 2 rooms ensuite.				
Mrs Telfer Craig-Ian, 6 Weensland Road Hawick Roxburghshire TD9 9NP Tel: (Hawick) 0450 73506		COMMENDED	1 Twin 2 Double	2 Pub. Bath/Show	B&B per person from £13.00 Double	Open Apr-Oct	
			Large Victorian terraced house, set above main A698 tourist route and close to centre of historic Borders town. Public car park opposite.				
Mrs Margaret Young Flex Farm Hawick Roxburghshire TD9 0PB Tel: (Hawick) 0450 75064		COMMENDED Listed	1 Twin 1 Family	1 Pub. Bath/Show	B&B per person £12.00-£14.00 Single £12.00-£14.00 Double	Open May-Oct	
			19c Borders farmhouse set in quiet countryside, 2 miles (3km) from Hawick. Fishing, shooting & golf nearby.				
BY HAWICK **Roxburghshire** Mrs M Irving Whitchesters Farm Hawick Roxburghshire TD9 0NR Tel: (Hawick) 0450 72604	Map 2 E8	COMMENDED Listed	1 Twin 1 Family	1 Pub. Bath/Show	B&B per person £14.00-£15.00 Single £13.00-£14.00 Double	Open May-Oct Dinner 1800-1900 B&B + Eve. Meal £20.00-£22.00	
			Traditional farmhouse on working farm of 840 acres, 4 miles (6.4 Km) south of Hawick.				
Mrs S Shell Wiltonburn Farm Hawick Roxburghshire TD9 7LL Tel: (Hawick) 0450 72414/78000 Fax: 0450 78545		COMMENDED Listed	1 Single 1 Double 1 Family	1 Limited ensuite 1 Pub. Bath/Show	B&B per person £14.00-£15.00 Single £14.00-£15.00 Double	Open Jan-Dec	
			A friendly welcome at this comfortable farmhouse, in a sheltered valley, under 2 miles (3kms) from Hawick.				

HELENSBURGH **Dunbartonshire** Mrs E Blackwell Longleat, 39 East Argyle Street Helensburgh Dunbartonshire G84 7EN Tel: (Helensburgh) 0436 72465	**Map 1** **G4**	COMMENDED ♛	1 Twin 2 Double	1 Pub. Bath/Show	B&B per person from £16.00 Single from £16.00 Double	Open Jan-Dec

Magnificently situated family house in quiet residential area overlooking Firth of Clyde. Non smoking.

Mrs Janet Cowie Garemount Lodge Shandon, Helensburgh Dunbartonshire Tel: (Helensburgh) 0436 820780			1 Twin 1 Double	1 Pub. Bath/Show	B&B per person to £17.50 Single to £15.00 Double	Open Jan-Dec

Mrs Elinor Grummitt Carnmoss, Station Road Shandon Helensburgh Dunbartonshire G84 8NX Tel: (Rhu) 0436 820817		COMMENDED ♛	1 Twin 1 Double 1 Family	1 Pub. Bath/Show	B&B per person £18.00-£20.00 Single £15.00-£17.00 Double	Open Jan-Dec

Comfortable family house in secluded garden. Locally situated for touring Loch Lomond and the Trossachs. Private parking.

Mrs Margaret Irvine Fasgadh, 1 Shiskine Place Helensburgh Dunbartonshire G84 9DZ Tel: (Helensburgh) 0436 75987		Award Pending	1 Single 1 Double	1 Pub. Bath/Show	B&B per person £14.00-£16.00 Single from £16.00 Double	Open Apr-Oct

Mrs Paton Kyra, 100 West Clyde Street Helensburgh Dunbartonshire G84 8BE Tel: (Helensburgh) 0436 75576			1 Single 1 Twin 1 Family	2 Pub. Bath/Show	B&B per person £15.00-£16.00 Single £13.00-£14.00 Double	Open Jan-Dec

Mrs M K Paul Middledrift, 85 James Street Helensburgh Dunbartonshire G84 9LE Tel: (Helensburgh) 0436 74867		COMMENDED ♛	1 Single 1 Twin 1 Family	1 Pub. Bath/Show	B&B per person from £16.00 Single from £14.00 Double	Open Jan-Dec

1860 sandstone family home of character with large established garden. Children and pets welcome.

Mrs M Richards Ravenswood, 32 Suffolk Street Helensburgh Dunbartonshire G84 9PA Tel: (Helensburgh) 0436 72112		COMMENDED ♛ ♛	2 Single 1 Twin 1 Double	2 En Suite fac 2 Priv. NOT ensuite 1 Pub. Bath/Show	B&B per person £17.50-£25.00 Single £17.50-£20.00 Double	Open Jan-Dec Dinner 1900-2030 B&B + Eve. Meal £25.00-£35.00

Victorian family home. Quiet location with mature gardens, close to Hillhouse, town centre and Loch Lomond.

Mrs Dorothy Ross Eastbank, 10 Hanover Street Helensburgh Dunbartonshire G84 7AW Tel: (Helensburgh) 0436 73665			1 Twin 1 Family	1 Pub. Bath/Show	B&B per person £14.00-£17.00 Double	Open Jan-Dec

Mrs D M Smith & Mrs L A Canty Hapland East Abercromby Street Helensburgh Dunbartonshire G84 7SD Tel: (Helensburgh) 0436 74042/79243	COMMENDED 👑 👑	1 Twin 1 Double	2 En Suite fac	B&B per person £19.00-£20.00 Single £16.50-£17.50 Double	Open Jan-Dec
		Large Victorian family home in extensive grounds 10 minutes from Loch Lomond, from the Upper Station and golf course. Warm friendly atmosphere.			

Thorndean House

64 COLQUHOUN ST.
HELENSBURGH
G84 9JP
Tel: 0436 74922
(From spring 1994:
Tel:0436 674922.)

Warm Scottish welcome, good food, spacious comfort, modern amenities and private facilities. Large gardens with off-street parking. No smoking.

Excellent touring centre for Loch Lomond, Trossachs, Clyde Coast. Glasgow airport only 40 mins.

Mrs Urquhart Thorndean 64 Colquhoun Street Helensburgh Dunbartonshire G84 9JP Tel: (Helensburgh) 0436 74922	COMMENDED 👑 👑	1 Twin 1 Double 1 Family	2 En Suite fac 1 Pub. Bath/Show	B&B per person £14.50-£21.00 Single £14.50-£21.00 Double	Open Jan-Dec
		Spacious family home in quiet residential area within easy walking distance of a fine selection of shops and quality restaurants.			

HELMSDALE **Sutherland** Mrs S Blance Broomhill House Helmsdale Sutherland KW8 6JS Tel: (Helmsdale) 04312 259	Map 4 C5 COMMENDED 👑 👑 👑	1 Twin 1 Double	2 En Suite fac 1 Pub. Bath/Show	B&B per person £16.00-£19.00 Double	Open Apr-Oct Dinner 1700-1900 B&B + Eve. Meal £23.00-£27.00
		Victorian, stone built house with turret. Magnificent panoramic view over Helmsdale to the sea.			

Mrs H Clegg Alderwood 157 West Helmsdale Helmsdale Sutherland KW8 6HH Tel: (Helmsdale) 04312 538	COMMENDED 👑	1 Twin 1 Double	1 Pub. Bath/Show	B&B per person £15.00-£17.00 Single £15.00-£17.00 Double	Open Jan-Dec
		Family home in detached house on the edge of Helmsdale in a quiet crofting area. Convenient touring centre. Cycle hire available.			

Mrs B Grainger Fir Brae, 189 Marrel Helmsdale Sutherland KW8 6HU Tel: (Helmsdale) 04312 223		1 Single 1 Twin 1 Family	1 Pub. Bath/Show	B&B per person £12.00 Single £12.00 Double	Open Mar-Nov Dinner 1800-1900 B&B + Eve. Meal £18.00

Mrs L Holmes Toshlair, Strathnaver Street Helmsdale Sutherland KW8 6JH Tel: (Helmsdale) 04312 485		1 Twin 1 Double 1 Family	2 Pub. Bath/Show	B&B per person £12.50-£15.00 Single £12.50-£15.00 Double	Open Mar-Oct

	Map	Grading	Rooms	Facilities	Rates	Open	

HELMSDALE continued — Map 4 C5

Mrs M C Polson
Torbuie, Navidale
Helmsdale
Sutherland
KW8 6JS
Tel: (Helmsdale) 04312 424

COMMENDED

2 Double — 1 En Suite fac / 1 Priv. NOT ensuite — B&B per person £13.00-£16.00 Single / £13.00-£16.00 Double — Open Apr-Oct

Well appointed house with superb views overlooking sea. Good base for touring.

HORGABOST — Map 3 B6
Harris, Western Isles
Mrs Lena MacLennan
1 Horgabost
Horgabost
Harris, Western Isles
PA85 3HR
Tel: (Scarista) 085985 285

1 Twin / 2 Double — 1 Pub. Bath/Show — B&B per person to £20.00 Single / to £20.00 Double — Open Apr-Oct, Dinner 1800-2000, B&B + Eve. Meal to £34.00

HOUSTON — Map 1 H5
Renfrewshire
The Houston Inn
North Street
Houston
Renfrewshire
PA6 7HF
Tel: (Bridge of Weir) 0505 614315

2 Double / 2 Family — 1 Pub. Bath/Show — B&B per person £26.00-£28.00 Single / £21.00-£22.00 Double — Open Jan-Dec

---

HOWNAM, by Kelso — Map 2 F7
Roxburghshire
Mrs J Harris
Greenhill
Hownam
Roxburghshire
TD5 8AW
Tel: (Morebattle) 0573 440505

2 Single / 1 Twin / 1 Double — 2 Priv. NOT ensuite / 2 Pub. Bath/Show — B&B per person £16.00-£18.00 Single / £16.00-£18.00 Double — Open Jan-Dec, Dinner from 1900, B&B + Eve. Meal £25.00-£28.00

HOY — Map 5 A1
Orkney
Mrs Leslye Budge
Burnhouse
Longhope, Hoy
Orkney
Tel: (Longhope) 085670 263

COMMENDED

2 Twin — 1 Pub. Bath/Show — B&B per person £13.00-£14.00 Single / £13.00-£14.00 Double — Open Jan-Dec, Dinner 1700-1830, B&B + Eve. Meal £19.50-£20.50

A welcoming warm active family atmosphere on this island working farm.

Select your holiday accommodation with confidence,

 DELUXE
 HIGHLY COMMENDED
 COMMENDED
 APPROVED

use The Scottish Tourist Board's Grading and Classification Scheme

	Map 4						
HUNTLY **Aberdeenshire** Mrs I Bell Glenburn, 19 Castle Street Huntly Aberdeenshire AB54 5BP Tel: (Huntly) 0466 792798	F9	**COMMENDED** ♛	1 Twin 1 Double 1 Family	2 Pub. Bath/Show	B&B per person £12.50-£14.00 Double	Open Jan-Dec	

Granite built Listed Victorian house with south facing garden. Situated on Castle and Whisky Trails. Fishing and golf available locally.

"BRAESIDE"

Provost Street, Huntly, Aberdeenshire AB54 5BB
Tel: 0466 793825

Modern detached chalet bungalow situated in quiet residential conservation area, close to town centre and railway station. Local amenities within walking distance. Many country pursuits and sporting activities available locally. Ideal centre for touring. On Castle Trail and within easy reach of Whisky Trail and Moray Coast.

Mr D Calcraft Braeside, Provost Street Huntly Aberdeenshire AB54 5BB Tel: (Huntly) 0466 793825	**COMMENDED** Listed	1 Single 1 Twin 1 Double	1 En Suite fac 1 Pub. Bath/Show	B&B per person to £14.00 Single £14.00-£17.00 Double	Open Apr-Sep	

Modern detached house with private parking close to town centre in quiet location.

Mrs Manson Greenmount, 43 Gordon Street Huntly Aberdeenshire AB54 5EQ Tel: (Huntly) 0466 792482	**COMMENDED** ♛ ♛ ♛	2 Single 4 Twin 2 Family	4 En Suite fac 1 Priv. NOT ensuite 1 Pub. Bath/Show	B&B per person £14.00-£17.00 Single £14.00-£20.00 Double	Open Jan-Dec Dinner from 1800 B&B + Eve. Meal £23.00-£26.00	

c1854 town house with annexe. Friendly personal attention; laundry room; private parking. In town centre but quiet. On Castle and Whisky Trails.

Mrs A J Morrison Haddoch Farm Huntly Aberdeenshire AB54 4SL Tel: (Rothiemay) 0466 81217	**COMMENDED** Listed	2 Double	2 Pub. Bath/Show	B&B per person £12.00-£15.00 Double	Open May-Sep Dinner 1800-2000 B&B + Eve. Meal £16.00-£18.00	

Mixed stock/arable farm near River Deveron, 3 miles (5kms) and 15 miles (24kms) from coast. Fine views of countryside. Home cooking.

Mrs R M Thomson Southview, Victoria Road Huntly Aberdeenshire AB54 5AH Tel: (Huntly) 0466 792456	**COMMENDED** Listed	2 Twin 1 Double 1 Family	2 Pub. Bath/Show	B&B per person £13.00-£15.00 Single £13.00-£15.00 Double	Open Jan-Dec Dinner 1700-1800 B&B + Eve. Meal £17.00-£19.00	

Detached Victorian house in quiet residential area close to town centre. Overlooking the bowling green.

	Map 4						
BY HUNTLY **Aberdeenshire** Mrs Margaret I Grant Faich Hill Gartly, Huntly Aberdeenshire AB54 4RR Tel: (Gartly) 046688 240	F9	**COMMENDED** ♛ ♛ ♛	1 Twin 1 Double	1 En Suite fac 1 Priv. NOT ensuite	B&B per person from £16.00 Double	Open Jan-Dec Dinner at 1830 B&B + Eve. Meal from £24.00	

Traditional granite built farmhouse on 500 acre mixed arable working farm 3 miles (5kms) south of Huntly. 1989 Farmhouse of the Year Award Winner.

Mrs Paula Ross Yonder Bognie Forgue, by Huntly Aberdeenshire AB54 6BR Tel: (Forgue) 046682 375	**COMMENDED** Listed	2 Double	1 Pub. Bath/Show	B&B per person to £12.00 Single to £12.00 Double	Open Jan-Dec Dinner from 1700 B&B + Eve. Meal to £17.00	

Traditional family farmhouse on mixed 152 acre farm. 7 miles (11 kms) from Huntly, 12 miles (19 kms) from Banff; on A97. French and Italian spoken.

	Map 2 C2						
INCHTURE **Perthshire** Mrs M Howard Old School House, Main Street Inchture Perthshire PH14 9RH Tel: (Inchture) 0828 86275			1 Double 1 Family	1 Pub. Bath/Show	B&B per person to £15.00 Single to £15.00 Double	Open Jan-Dec	

	Map 2 D6	COMMENDED ✿ ✿					
INNERLEITHEN **Peeblesshire** Caddon View Guest House 14 Pirn Road Innerleithen Peeblesshire EH44 6HH Tel: (Innerleithen) 0896 830208			1 Single 2 Twin 1 Double 1 Family	2 En Suite fac 1 Priv. NOT ensuite 1 Pub. Bath/Show	B&B per person £15.00-£16.00 Single £14.00-£17.00 Double	Open Jan-Dec Dinner 1830-1900 B&B + Eve. Meal £23.00-£26.00	

A warm welcome and home cooking at this substantial Victorian house, with many period features. Ideal for touring the Borders.

	Map 4 B1	HIGHLY COMMENDED ✿					
INSH, Kingussie **Inverness-shire** Ian & Pamela Grant Greenfield Croft Insh Inverness-shire PH21 1NT Tel: (Kingussie) 0540 661010			1 Twin 2 Double	3 En Suite fac	B&B per person from £16.00 Double	Open Jan-Dec Dinner from 1900 B&B + Eve. Meal from £25.00	

Newly built house on a working croft in quiet Highland village with superb views. Home cooking; log fire; all rooms with en suite facilities.

	Map 1 F3	COMMENDED Listed					
INVERARAY **Argyll** Mrs Crawford Brenchoille Farm Inveraray Argyll PA32 8XN Tel: (Furnace) 04995 662			1 Twin 1 Family	1 Pub. Bath/Show	B&B per person from £15.00 Double	Open Apr-Oct Dinner from 1830 B&B + Eve. Meal from £21.00	

Peacefully located on working farm 7 miles (11kms) south of Inveraray close to the Auchindrain Farming Museum. Views over the Cowal Hills.

Mrs MacLaren Old Rectory Inveraray Argyll PA32 Tel: (Inveraray) 0499 302280			1 Single 4 Double 4 Family	3 Pub. Bath/Show	B&B per person £12.00-£20.00 Single £12.00-£16.00 Double	Open Jan-Dec	

VAT is shown at 17.5%: changes in this rate may affect prices. Prices shown are for guidance only. Please send SAE with each enquiry.

CREAG DHUBH
INVERARAY, ARGYLL PA32 8XT
Telephone: 0499 2430

Situated in own grounds and gardens with views of Loch Fyne and the Cowal Hills. Scenic and historic area ideal for touring.

Mrs MacLugash
Creag Dhubh
Inveraray
Argyll
PA32 8XT
Tel: (Inveraray) 0499 2430

COMMENDED

1 Twin   1 En Suite fac   B&B per person   Open Mar-Nov
2 Double   3 Priv. NOT ensuite   £13.50-£18.00 Double
1 Family   2 Pub. Bath/Show

Large stone built house with extensive garden and excellent views over Loch Fyne.

Mrs McPherson
10 Argyll Court
Inveraray
Argyll
PA32 8UT
Tel: (Inveraray) 0499 2273

1 Double   1 Pub. Bath/Show   B&B per person   Open Apr-Oct
£13.00-£14.00 Single
£13.00-£14.00 Double

Mrs Semple
Killean House
Inveraray
Argyll
PA32 8XT
Tel: (Inveraray) 0499 2474

2 Double   2 Pub. Bath/Show   B&B per person   Open Apr-Oct
2 Family   £13.50-£15.00 Double

INVERBEG, by Luss
Dunbartonshire   Map 1   G4
Mrs Robertson
Doune of Glen Douglas Farm
Inverbeg, Luss
Dunbartonshire
G83 8PD
Tel: (Arrochar) 03012 312

Award Pending

2 Double   1 En Suite fac   B&B per person   Open Apr-Oct
1 Family   1 Pub. Bath/Show   £14.00-£18.00 Single
£14.00-£22.00 Double

BY INVERBERVIE
Angus   Map 4   G1
Mrs M A Sunderland
Pipers Cottage
Haughs of Benholm
Gourdon, by Inverbervie
Angus
DD10 0LZ
Tel: (Inverbervie) 0561 361117

1 Twin   1 En Suite fac   B&B per person   Open Jan-Dec
1 Family   1 Limited ensuite   £15.00-£17.00 Double   Dinner 1700-1900
B&B + Eve. Meal
£23.00-£26.00

INVERGARRY
Inverness-shire   Map 3   H1
Forest Lodge Guest House
South Laggan
Invergarry, by Spean Bridge
Inverness-shire
PH34 4EA
Tel: (Invergarry) 08093 219

COMMENDED

2 Twin   5 En Suite fac   B&B per person   Open Jan-Dec
3 Double   2 Priv. NOT ensuite   £15.00-£17.00 Double   Dinner from 1930
2 Family   B&B + Eve. Meal
£23.00-£25.00

Family run guest house in the heart of the Great Glen where Caledonian Canal joins Lochs Lochy and Oich. Ideal centre for outdoor activities.

Details of Grading and Classification are on page vi.   **Key to symbols is on back flap.**   173

INVERGARRY continued	Map 3 H1					
Lundie View Guest House Invergarry Inverness-shire PH35 4HN Tel: (Invergarry) 08093 291	HIGHLY COMMENDED	1 Single 1 Twin 2 Double 2 Family	4 En Suite fac 2 Pub. Bath/Show	B&B per person £15.00–£20.00 Single £15.00–£20.00 Double	Open Jan-Dec Dinner 1830-1930 B&B + Eve. Meal £23.50-£28.50	

Family run, with all accommodation on ground level and some private facilities. Set in open countryside. Craft shop adjacent.

| Mr & Mrs Buswell
Nursery Cottages
Invergarry
Inverness-shire
PH35 4HL
Tel: (Invergarry) 08093 297 | APPROVED | 1 Double
1 Family | 1 Priv. NOT ensuite
2 Pub. Bath/Show | B&B per person
£12.50–£14.50 Single
£12.00–£14.50 Double | Open Jan-Dec
Dinner 1800-1900
B&B + Eve. Meal
£20.00-£22.50 | |

Mid 19th century homely cottage. 7 miles (11kms) south of Fort Augustus. Centrally located for touring the Highlands.

| Mrs H Fraser
Ardfriseal, Mandally Road
Invergarry
Inverness-shire
PH35 4HR
Tel: (Invergarry) 08093 281 | COMMENDED | 1 Twin
2 Double | 1 Pub. Bath/Show | B&B per person
from £15.50 Single
from £12.50 Double | Open May-Oct
Dinner 1900-1930
B&B + Eve. Meal
from £20.50 | |

Modern family home in secluded area with magnificent views of surrounding hills. 1 mile (2kms) from Invergarry.

| Mrs F I Jamieson
Lilac Cottage, South Laggan
Spean Bridge
Inverness-shire
PH34 4EA
Tel: (Invergarry) 08093 410 | | 1 Twin
1 Double | 1 Pub. Bath/Show | B&B per person
from £12.00 Single
from £12.00 Double | Open Jan-Dec
Dinner 1900-2000
B&B + Eve. Meal
from £20.00 | |

| Mr & Mrs MacKenzie Rogers
Tigh-na-car-Ruadh
Invergarry
Inverness-shire
PH35 4HG
Tel: (Invergarry) 08093 359 | | 1 Single
1 Twin | 1 Pub. Bath/Show | B&B per person
£12.50–£13.00 Single
£12.50–£13.00 Double | Open Jan-Dec
Dinner from 1930
B&B + Eve. Meal
£19.00-£20.00 | |

North Laggan Farmhouse
By SPEAN BRIDGE, INVERNESS PH34 4EB
Telephone: Invergarry 080 93 335

Overlooking the Caledonian Canal and Loch Oich, set ½ mile off A82, 2 miles south of Invergarry, amidst sheep farming country. A completely modernised croft house which retains much of its original character. Two comfortable bed/sitting rooms. Home-made bread, good food and individual attention guaranteed.

| Mrs Waugh
North Laggan Farmhouse
by Spean Bridge
Inverness-shire
PH34 4EB
Tel: (Invergarry) 08093 335 | COMMENDED
Listed | 1 Twin
1 Family | 1 Pub. Bath/Show | B&B per person
from £14.50 Double | Open May-Sep
Dinner from 1900
B&B + Eve. Meal
from £23.50 | |

In peaceful open countryside overlooking the Caledonian Canal and Loch Oich. Warm welcome, home made bread and good home cooking.

INVERGLOY Inverness-shire	Map 3 H1

Riverside · Invergloy

RIVERSIDE, INVERGLOY, SPEAN BRIDGE, INVERNESS-SHIRE PH34 4DY   Tel: 0397 712 684

Our bungalow is set in spectacular rhododendron gardens and woodland, 14 miles N.E. of Fort William, adjacent to the A82 trunk route but completely hidden from it. We take a maximum of five guests in 1 double (private bathroom, not en-suite) and 1 twin/family (en-suite shower room). The sitting room has a log fire and fine views over Loch Lochy. Ample car parking. Private beach; free fishing. Three restaurants within 3 miles.

Mrs D Bennet Riverside Invergloy, by Spean Bridge Inverness-shire PH34 4DY Tel: (Spean Bridge) 0397 712684	**HIGHLY COMMENDED** 👑 👑	1 Double 1 Family	1 En Suite fac 1 Priv. NOT ensuite	B&B per person £24.00 Single £18.00 Double	Open Jan-Dec

Cosy bungalow in secluded lochside setting. Extensive grounds with over 200 varieties of rhododendron. Ideal base for Great Glen and West Coast.

INVERGORDON **Ross-shire** Mrs Gillies Sweeny Cottage Newmore, Rhicullen by Invergordon Ross-shire Tel: (Invergordon) 0349 853400	Map 4 B7		2 Twin	1 Pub. Bath/Show	B&B per person £12.00-£14.00 Double	Open Jan-Dec

INVERINATE, Glenshiel **Ross-shire** Mrs Jane Croy Mo Dhachaidh Inverinate Tel: (Glenshiel) 059981 351	Map 3 F1		1 Single 1 Twin 1 Family	1 Pub. Bath/Show	B&B per person £13.00-£15.00 Single £13.00-£15.00 Double	Open Jan-Dec

Mrs J MacIntosh Foresters Bungalow, Inverinate Glenshiel, by Kyle of Lochalsh Ross-shire IV40 8HE Tel: (Glenshiel) 059981 329			1 Twin 1 Double	1 Pub. Bath/Show	B&B per person from £13.00 Double	Open Apr-Sep

INVERKEITHING **Fife** Mrs Gibbon The Roods 16 Bannerman Avenue Inverkeithing Fife KY11 1NG Tel: (Inverkeithing) 0383 415049/413816	Map 2 C4	**COMMENDED** Listed	2 Twin	1 Pub. Bath/Show	B&B per person £13.00-£14.00 Single £13.00-£14.00 Double	Open Jan-Dec

Modern house with quiet garden close to Forth Bridges, near town centre and railway station. Conveniently situated for touring Forth Valley and Fife

INVERKIP **Renfrewshire** Mrs Russell Ellenbank Inverkip Renfrewshire PA16 0AX Tel: (Wemyss Bay) 0475 521209	**Map 1** G5	COMMENDED 👑 👑	2 Twin	1 En Suite fac 2 Pub. Bath/Show	B&B per person £24.00-£28.00 Single £17.00-£19.00 Double	Open Apr-Sep
			Late Georgian 'B' Listed house retaining many original features situated above village overlooking Firth of Clyde and Inverkip marina.			
Mrs Wallace The Foresters, Station Road Inverkip Renfrewshire PA16 Tel: (Wemyss Bay) 0475 521433 Fax: 0475 522000			1 Twin 2 Family	1 Pub. Bath/Show	B&B per person £15.00-£20.00 Single £11.00-£16.00 Double	Open Jan-Dec
INVERMORISTON **Inverness-shire** Mr & Mrs M Douglas Burnside, Dalcataig Glenmoriston Inverness-shire IV3 6YG Tel: (Glenmoriston) 0320 51262/351262	**Map 4** A1	COMMENDED 👑 👑	1 Single 1 Twin 1 Double	2 En Suite fac 1 Priv. NOT ensuite	B&B per person £15.00-£17.00 Single £15.00-£17.00 Double	Open Apr-Oct Dinner at 1900 B&B + Eve. Meal £24.00-£26.00
			Warm Highland hospitality at this modern bungalow 1 mile (2kms) from Invermoriston and near Loch Ness. Peace and tranquillity with birdsong.			
Mrs I Greig Georgeston Invermoriston Inverness-shire IV3 Tel: (Glenmoriston) 0320 51264/351264		COMMENDED 👑	1 Twin 2 Double	1 Pub. Bath/Show	B&B per person £13.00-£16.00 Single £13.00-£16.00 Double	Open Jan-Dec
			Detached bungalow on outskirts of village and just off main road. Ample parking and nice views.			
INVERNESS Aberfeldy Lodge Guest House 11 Southside Road Inverness IV2 3BG Tel: (Inverness) 0463 231120	**Map 4** B8	COMMENDED 👑 👑 👑	3 Twin 3 Double 3 Family	9 En Suite fac	B&B per person £19.00-£25.00 Double	Open Jan-Dec Dinner 1800-1830 B&B + Eve. Meal £31.00-£37.00
			Substantial detached house with large garden in quiet residential area. Close to town centre and convenient for bus and railway stations.			
Ach Aluinn Guest House 27 Fairfield Road Inverness IV3 5QD Tel: (Inverness) 0463 230127		COMMENDED 👑 👑	2 Twin 2 Family	4 En Suite fac	B&B per person £16.00-£20.00 Double	Open Jan-Dec
			Newly refurbished, detached, Victorian house with private parking in quiet residential road. 10 minutes walk from town centre. All rooms ensuite.			
Ardnacoille Guest House 1a Annfield Road Inverness IV2 3HP Tel: (Inverness) 0463 233451		COMMENDED 👑 👑	1 Twin 1 Double 1 Family	1 Priv. NOT ensuite 2 Pub. Bath/Show	B&B per person £15.00-£17.00 Double	Open Mar-Oct
			1865 red sandstone house in residential area. Spacious bedrooms. 10 minute walk from town centre. Ample parking.			
Atherstone Guest House Lynholme, 42 Fairfield Road Inverness IV3 5QD Tel: (Inverness) 0463 240240		COMMENDED 👑 👑	1 Single 1 Double 1 Family	3 En Suite fac	B&B per person £14.00-£17.00 Single £14.00-£17.00 Double	Open Jan-Dec
			Attractively decorated and comfortably furnished with a homely atmosphere. Evening supper on request. All rooms en-suite.			

Atholdene House 20 Southside Road Inverness IV2 3BG Tel: (Inverness) 0463 233565	COMMENDED 👑 👑 👑	1 Single 4 Twin 2 Double 2 Family	6 En Suite fac 2 Pub. Bath/Show	B&B per person £25.00-£35.00 Single £19.00-£22.00 Double	Open Jan-Dec Dinner 1800-1900 B&B + Eve. Meal £29.00-£32.00

Late Victorian stone villa, modernised throughout with ample parking.
Short walk from bus and railway stations.

Clisham House 43 Fairfield Road Inverness IV3 5QP Tel: (Inverness) 0463 239965	COMMENDED 👑 👑	2 Double 2 Family	4 En Suite fac	B&B per person from £18.00 Double	Open Jan-Dec

Large detached town house with interior woodwork of character.
Ample parking. Within walking distance of town centre.

Craigside Lodge 4 Gordon Terrace Inverness IV2 3HD Tel: (Inverness) 0463 231576 Fax: 0463 713409	COMMENDED 👑 👑	3 Twin 3 Double	4 En Suite fac 1 Pub. Bath/Show	B&B per person £18.00-£20.00 Single £16.00-£18.00 Double	Open Mar-Jan

Detached Victorian house set in quiet elevated position.
Outstanding views of Castle, river and town.

Felstead House 18 Ness Bank Inverness IV2 4SF Tel: (Inverness) 0463 231634	COMMENDED 👑	2 Single 2 Twin 2 Double 1 Family	4 Pub. Bath/Show	B&B per person from £16.00 Single from £16.00 Double	Open May-Sep

Family run Georgian house overlooking River Ness; 5 minutes walk
to town centre and 4 minutes walk to Eden Court Theatre.

Oakfield Guest House 1 Darnaway Road, Kingsmills Inverness IV2 3LF Tel: (Inverness) 0463 237926	COMMENDED 👑 👑	1 Twin 3 Double 1 Family	2 En Suite fac 2 Pub. Bath/Show	B&B per person £16.00-£21.00 Single £14.00-£19.00 Double	Open Jan-Dec Dinner 1800-1900 B&B + Eve. Meal £24.00-£29.00

Detached house with private parking in peaceful residential area
within easy walking distance of town centre. Home cooking.

The Old Rectory Guest House 9 Southside Road Inverness IV2 3BG Tel: (Inverness) 0463 220969	HIGHLY COMMENDED 👑 👑	1 Twin 2 Double 1 Family	3 En Suite fac 1 Priv. NOT ensuite	B&B per person £16.00-£19.00 Double	Open Jan-Dec

Privately owned former Victorian manse with large garden situated
in residential area close to town centre. Good car parking. Non-smoking.

Your key to quality accommodation in Scotland:

The Scottish Tourist Board's
Grading and Classification Scheme

INVERNESS

INVERNESS	Map 4 B8						
The Old Royal Guest House 10 Union Street Inverness IV1 1PL Tel: (Inverness) 0463 230551 Fax: 0463 230551	COMMENDED 👑 👑	2 Single 2 Twin 4 Double 2 Family	5 En Suite fac 3 Pub. Bath/Show	B&B per person £20.00-£24.00 Single £17.50-£24.00 Double	Open Feb-Nov		
		Four storey terraced guest house in the heart of the town centre and a few hundred yards from the railway station.					
Mrs C D Aird Pitfarrane, 57 Crown Street Inverness IV2 3AY Tel: (Inverness) 0463 239338	COMMENDED 👑	1 Single 2 Twin 2 Double	4 Limited ensuite 1 Pub. Bath/Show	B&B per person £11.00-£14.00 Single £16.00 Double	Open Jan-Dec		
		End terraced house in quiet residential area within 10 minutes walk from town centre. Some private parking.					
Mrs Boynton 12 Annfield Road Inverness IV2 3HX Tel: (Inverness) 0463 233188	COMMENDED 👑	1 Double 1 Family	2 Pub. Bath/Show	B&B per person £13.00 Double	Open Jan-Dec		
		Family run house in quiet residential area within easy walking distance of town centre. Home baking and preserves.					
Mrs L Cameron Tay Villa, 40 Harrowden Road Inverness IV3 5QN Tel: (Inverness) 0463 232984	COMMENDED 👑 👑	1 Twin 1 Double	2 En Suite fac 1 Pub. Bath/Show	B&B per person £13.00-£14.00 Double	Open Jan-Dec		
		Stone built house, recently refurbished, in quiet residential area, yet within easy access to town centre. All bedrooms with private facilities.					
Mr & Mrs J Campbell 12A Diriebught Road Inverness IV2 3QW Tel: (Inverness) 0463 224717	COMMENDED 👑 👑	1 Twin 1 Double 1 Family	2 En Suite fac 1 Priv. NOT ensuite	B&B per person £13.50-£16.50 Double	Open Jan-Dec		
		Newly built modern spacious family house in quiet residential area. Close to town centre and all amenities. Private parking.					
Mrs Carson Cambeth Lodge 49 Fairfield Road Inverness IV3 5QP Tel: (Inverness) 0463 231764	APPROVED 👑 👑	2 Twin 1 Family	1 En Suite fac 1 Pub. Bath/Show	B&B per person £12.50-£16.00 Double	Open Jan-Dec Dinner from 1800 B&B + Eve. Meal £22.50-£23.50		
		Victorian, stone building with private parking in quiet residential area. 10 minutes walk to town centre.					
Mrs Elizabeth Chisholm Carbisdale, 43 Charles Street Inverness IV2 3AH Tel: (Inverness) 0463 225689	HIGHLY COMMENDED 👑	1 Twin 2 Double	2 Pub. Bath/Show	B&B per person from £13.00 Single from £12.00 Double	Open Jan-Dec		
		Terraced family home furnished to high standard. Warm welcome. Close to town centre, and easy walk from rail station.					

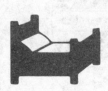

Book your accommodation anywhere in Scotland the easy way—through your nearest Tourist Information Centre.

A booking fee of £2.50 is charged, and you will be asked for a small deposit.

Local bookings are usually free, or a small fee will be charged.

VAT is shown at 17.5%: changes in this rate may affect prices. Prices shown are for guidance only. Please send SAE with each enquiry.

Mrs I Donald Kerrisdale, 4 Muirfield Road Inverness IV2 4AY Tel: (Inverness) 0463 235489	COMMENDED 👑 👑	1 Twin 1 Double 1 Family	1 En Suite fac 1 Pub. Bath/Show	B&B per person £15.00-£17.00 Double	Open Jan-Dec Dinner from 1800 B&B + Eve. Meal £23.00-£25.00	
		Spacious Victorian house with large garden, situated in quiet residential area within walking distance of the town centre. Home cooking.				
Mrs K Dunnett 30 Culduthel Road Inverness IV2 4AP Tel: (Inverness) 0463 710017 Fax: 0463 233130	COMMENDED 👑 👑	1 Single 1 Double	1 En Suite fac 1 Pub. Bath/Show	B&B per person £15.00-£17.50 Single £15.00-£20.00 Double	Open Jan-Dec Dinner 1830-1900 B&B + Eve. Meal £22.50-£27.50	
		Bungalow in quiet residential area just 1 mile (2kms) from centre of town.				
Mrs Margaret Edwards St Kilda, 28 Rangemore Road Inverness IV3 5EA Tel: (Inverness) 0463 235200	COMMENDED 👑	1 Single 1 Double 1 Family	2 Pub. Bath/Show	B&B per person £12.00-£15.00 Single £12.00 Double	Open Jan-Dec	
		Victorian house in quiet residential area and close to city centre and all amenities.				

Clach Mhuilinn

**7 HARRIS ROAD
INVERNESS
IV2 3LS
Tel: 0463 237059**

Let us welcome you to our no-smoking detached house in a quiet, residential area 20 minutes stroll from Inverness centre. Stay a while and unwind, enjoying delicious breakfasts overlooking the lovely garden. Explore the beautiful Highlands, returning nightly to your comfortable room. Bar meals available nearby. **Contact: Mrs Jacqi Elmslie.**

Mrs J R Elmslie Clach Mhuilinn, 7 Harris Road Inverness IV2 3LS Tel: (Inverness) 0463 237059	HIGHLY COMMENDED 👑 👑	1 Single 1 Twin 1 Double	1 En Suite fac 1 Pub. Bath/Show	B&B per person from £16.00 Single from £15.00 Double	Open Mar-Nov	
		Modern, non-smoking family home in residential area with attractive garden and off street parking.				
Mrs L Fraser Edenview, 26 Ness Bank Inverness IV2 4SF Tel: (Inverness) 0463 234397	COMMENDED 👑	1 Double 1 Family	2 Pub. Bath/Show	B&B per person £16.00-£17.00 Double	Open Jan-Dec	
		A large and spacious house on the riverside close to the town centre. Friendly and homely atmosphere.				
Mrs D Gander Canmore, 3 Heathcote Gdns, Muirfield Rd Inverness IV2 4AZ Tel: (Inverness) 0463 230228	HIGHLY COMMENDED 👑	1 Single 1 Twin 1 Double	1 Pub. Bath/Show	B&B per person from £16.00 Single from £15.00 Double	Open Jun-Sep	
		Detached family house situated in secluded cul-de-sac with private parking. Within walking distance of town centre.				
Mrs Geddes Sandale, 37 Midmills Road Inverness IV2 3NZ Tel: (Inverness) 0463 235382	COMMENDED 👑	1 Twin 2 Double	1 Pub. Bath/Show	B&B per person from £14.00 Double	Open Jan-Dec	
		Detached late Victorian house with large garden to rear, in quiet residential area close to town centre. Convenient for bus and railway.				
Mrs M Gillan St Giles Ldg,5 Ladies Wlk, Island Bank Rd Inverness IV2 4TB Tel: (Inverness) 0463 225406	COMMENDED 👑 👑	1 Twin 2 Double	1 En Suite fac 1 Pub. Bath/Show	B&B per person £13.00-£20.00 Double	Open Jan-Dec	
		19C Listed property overlooking the River Ness, 10 minutes walk from the town centre. Attractive river walks.				

Details of Grading and Classification are on page vi.

Key to symbols is on back flap.

INVERNESS continued	Map 4 B8					
Mrs Agnes Gordon Sunnyholm, 12 Mayfield Road Inverness IV2 4AE Tel: (Inverness) 0463 231336	COMMENDED 👑 👑	3 Twin 1 Double	4 En Suite fac	B&B per person £15.00-£25.00 Single £15.00-£17.50 Double	Open Jan-Dec	
		Bungalow situated in quiet residential area close to town centre and Castle. All bedrooms en suite. Private car park.				
Neil & Margaret Hart Melrose Villa 35 Kenneth Street Inverness IV3 5DH Tel: (Inverness) 0463 233745	COMMENDED Listed	1 Single 2 Double 3 Family	3 En Suite fac 1 Pub. Bath/Show	B&B per person £15.00-£20.00 Single £13.00-£18.00 Double	Open Jan-Dec	
		Family run guest house within a few minutes walk of the town centre. Warm and friendly atmosphere.				
Mrs Joan Hendry Tamarue, 70A Ballifeary Road Inverness IV3 5PF Tel: (Inverness) 0463 239724	COMMENDED 👑	1 Twin 2 Double	1 Pub. Bath/Show	B&B per person £12.50-£14.50 Double	Open Apr-Oct	
		Situated in quiet residential area, close to town centre, River Ness, off course and Eden Court Theatre. Off street parking.				
Mrs Maureen Hutcheson Mardon, 37 Kenneth Street Inverness IV3 5DH Tel: (Inverness) 0463 231005	Award Pending	1 Single 2 Twin 3 Double 1 Family	3 En Suite fac 1 Pub. Bath/Show	B&B per person £14.00-£15.00 Single £13.00-£16.00 Double	Open Jan-Dec Dinner 1800-1830 B&B + Eve. Meal £18.00-£20.00	
Mrs Johnstone 55 Crown Street Inverness IV2 3AX Tel: (Inverness) 0463 230448	COMMENDED Listed	1 Twin	1 Priv. NOT ensuite	B&B per person to £16.00 Single £15.00-£16.00 Double	Open Jan-Dec	
		Cosy semi-detached cottage in quiet street. Convenient for all town centre facilities. Private bathroom with bath and shower.				
Mrs F Kennedy 7 Broadstone Park Inverness IV2 3JZ Tel: (Inverness) 0463 236807	COMMENDED Listed	3 Twin	1 Pub. Bath/Show	B&B per person £12.00-£14.00 Double	Open Jan-Dec	
		Detached family house in a quiet residential area near town centre and railway station.				
Mrs Helen Kennedy Kendon, 9 Old Mill Lane Inverness IV2 3XP Tel: (Inverness) 0463 238215	COMMENDED 👑 👑	1 Twin 1 Double	2 En Suite fac	B&B per person from £15.00 Double	Open Mar-Nov	
		Modern bungalow. A family home in quiet residential area. 1 mile (2kms) from town centre, easy access from A9. All bedrooms ensuite.				

SCOTTISH TOURIST BOARD
QUALITY COMMENDATIONS ARE:

Deluxe — *An EXCELLENT quality standard*
Highly Commended — *A VERY GOOD quality standard*
Commended — *A GOOD quality standard*
Approved — *An ADEQUATE quality standard*

Millwood
36 OLD MILL ROAD
INVERNESS IV2 3HR
Tel: 0463 237254

Set in a beautiful secluded garden, the charm of "Millwood" we are sure will make you feel genuinely welcome to stay awhile and relax, enjoying our hospitality. A five-minute stroll takes you to hotels serving first-class evening meals. Inverness airport 15 minutes by car, golf course 5 minutes' walk. Pony trekking and fishing can be arranged. All the splendour of the Highlands is just a short drive away from the house.

♛ Highly Commended

Mrs Gillian Lee Millwood, 36 Old Mill Road Inverness IV2 3HR Tel: (Inverness) 0463 237254	HIGHLY COMMENDED ♛	1 Single 1 Twin 1 Double	2 Pub. Bath/Show	B&B per person £18.00-£19.00 Single £16.00-£17.00 Double	Open Jan-Dec
		A warm friendly welcome in comfortable family home. Large secluded garden, in pleasant residential area close to town centre.			
Mrs B MacBean 9 Victoria Terrace Inverness IV2 3QA Tel: (Inverness) 0463 236198	COMMENDED ♛	1 Double 1 Family	1 Pub. Bath/Show	B&B per person £12.00-£14.00 Single £12.00-£14.00 Double	Open Jan-Dec
		Family run Victorian terrace house in quiet residential area. South facing with views of farmland. 5 minutes from the town centre.			
Mrs D McClorey Bunillidh, 47 Montague Row Inverness IV2 3RS Tel: (Inverness) 0463 225079		1 Single 1 Double 1 Family	1 Pub. Bath/Show	B&B per person £12.00-£15.00 Single £12.00-£20.00 Double	Open Jan-Dec Dinner 1800-2100 B&B + Eve. Meal from £20.00
Isabella McColl Heathfield, 2 Kenneth Street Inverness IV2 5NR Tel: (Inverness) 0463 230547	COMMENDED ♛ ♛	1 Single 1 Double 1 Family	1 En Suite fac 1 Pub. Bath/Show	B&B per person £15.00-£17.00 Single £12.00-£17.00 Double	Open Jan-Dec
		Semi-detached stone house. Close to town centre, Eden Court Theatre and all amenities.			
Mrs MacCuish 1 Caulfield Park Inverness IV1 2GB Tel: (Inverness) 0463 792882	HIGHLY COMMENDED ♛ ♛	1 Twin 1 Double	1 En Suite fac 1 Pub. Bath/Show	B&B per person £13.00-£15.00 Double	Open May-Sep
		Modern detached house with large garden on eastern outskirts of Inverness. 3 miles (5kms) from Culloden Battlefield.			
Mrs MacCuish 50 Argyle Street Inverness IV2 3BB Tel: (Inverness) 0463 235150	APPROVED Listed	1 Double 1 Family	1 Pub. Bath/Show	B&B per person £12.00 Double	Open Apr-Oct
		Terraced house within 10 minutes walk of the town centre.			
Mrs B Macdonald Hebrides 120A Glenurquhart Road Inverness IV3 5TD Tel: (Inverness) 0463 220062	COMMENDED Listed	1 Double 1 Family	1 En Suite fac 1 Priv. NOT ensuite	B&B per person £14.00-£17.00 Double	Open Jan-Dec
		Family home situated beside the Caledonian Canal and opposite Bught Park with its leisure facilities. Town centre 2 miles (3kms).			

INVERNESS continued	Map 4 B8						
Mrs L M MacDonald Baemore, 48 Fairfield Road Inverness IV3 5QD Tel: (Inverness) 0463 234095			1 Twin 1 Family	1 Pub. Bath/Show	B&B per person £11.00-£12.00 Double	Open May-Sep	
Mrs Zandra MacDonald 5 Muirfield Gardens Inverness IV2 4HF Tel: (Inverness) 0463 238114		COMMENDED ♛	1 Twin 2 Double	2 Pub. Bath/Show	B&B per person £12.00-£14.00 Double	Open Jan-Dec	
			Family home in quiet residential area, 15 minutes stroll from the town centre. All accommodation on the ground floor.				
Ms H MacGregor 9 Sunnybank Avenue Inverness IV2 4HD Tel: (Inverness) 0463 715383		COMMENDED Listed	2 Twin	1 Pub. Bath/Show	B&B per person £13.00-£16.00 Double	Open Jan-Dec	
			Modern semi-detached house on the outskirts of the city. Homely atmosphere and a friendly welcome.				
Mrs C McInnes 39 Fairfield Road Inverness IV3 5QD Tel: (Inverness) 0463 236158			1 Twin 1 Double 1 Family	2 En Suite fac 1 Priv. NOT ensuite 1 Pub. Bath/Show	B&B per person £18.00 Double	Open Jan-Dec Dinner 1800-2000	
E A Mackay 12 Glenburn Drive Inverness IV2 4ND Tel: (Inverness) 0463 223809		COMMENDED Listed	1 Twin 1 Double	1 Pub. Bath/Show	B&B per person from £11.00 Single from £11.00 Double	Open Jan-Dec	
			Friendly welcome awaits you in quiet residential area. Ideal base for touring. On main bus route to centre and leisure facilities. (15 mins walk).				
Mrs A MacKenzie 5 Crown Circus Inverness IV2 3NH Tel: (Inverness) 0463 224222		COMMENDED ♛	1 Single 1 Double 1 Family	2 Pub. Bath/Show	B&B per person from £13.00 Double	Open Jan-Dec	
			Traditional stone built Victorian villa in residential area of Inverness with easy access to town centre and all amenities.				
A MacKenzie Ardconnel House 21 Ardconnel Street Inverness IV23 3EU Tel: (Inverness) 0463 240455		COMMENDED Listed	1 Single 1 Twin 1 Double 3 Family	2 Pub. Bath/Show	B&B per person from £15.00 Single from £15.00 Double	Open Jan-Dec Dinner 1730-1830 B&B + Eve. Meal from £23.00	
			Listed, Victorian, terraced house in residential area. Convenient for town centre and railway station.				
Mrs MacKintosh Ardentorrie House 2 Gordon Terrace Inverness IV2 3HD Tel: (Inverness) 0463 230090		COMMENDED ♛ ♛	1 Double 2 Family	3 En Suite fac 2 Pub. Bath/Show	B&B per person £16.00-£18.00 Double	Open Feb-Nov	
			Modern house within easy walking distance of town centre and River Ness.				
Mrs M MacLennan The Bungalow 21 Planefield Road Inverness IV3 5DL Tel: (Inverness) 0463 230337		COMMENDED ♛ ♛	1 Twin 1 Double	2 En Suite fac	B&B per person £14.00-£15.50 Double	Open Jan-Nov	
			Modern detached bungalow in quiet residential area. Own parking. Short walk from town centre and all amenities.				

Mrs Mactaggart 1 Ross Avenue Inverness IV3 5QJ Tel: (Inverness) 0463 236356	COMMENDED Listed	2 Twin 1 Double	2 En Suite fac 1 Pub. Bath/Show	B&B per person from £15.00 Single £14.00-£18.00 Double	Open Jan-Dec	
		Terraced house in quiet residential area, close to town centre, bus and railway stations.				
Mrs U Moffat Lorne House, 40 Crown Drive Inverness IV2 3QG Tel: (Inverness) 0463 236271	HIGHLY COMMENDED 👑 👑	1 Double 1 Family	1 En Suite fac 1 Pub. Bath/Show	B&B per person £16.00-£19.00 Double	Open Jan-Dec	
		Victorian detached house in quiet residential area, close to town centre and railway station. Guest car parking. Private facilities.				
Mrs G Moffat Fernhill, 74 Kingsmills Road Inverness IV2 3LL Tel: (Inverness) 0463 221713	Award Pending	2 Twin 1 Double	3 En Suite fac	B&B per person £18.00-£20.00 Single £18.00-£20.00 Double	Open Jan-Dec	
Caroline A Moyes Annellan Villa, 39 Union Road Inverness IV2 3JY Tel: (Inverness) 0463 241414	Award Pending	1 Twin 1 Double	2 En Suite fac	B&B per person from £17.50 Single £17.50 Double	Open Jan-Dec	

'Bonnieview'

Towerbrae (North), Westhill,
Inverness IV1 2BW   Tel: 0463 792468

At 'Bonnieview' experience a special warmth and hospitality rare in its sincerity — look out from the dining room with marvellous views stretching over the Beauly and Moray Firths, whilst enjoying highly acclaimed home cooking and baking. Excellent as a touring base for day trips around the Highlands.

Comprehensive private facilities in all rooms. You can relax with tea and conversation in the lounge beside a soothing coal fire on those chilly days.

A fine welcome awaits you all.

B&B £16. Evening meal £9.
OPEN ALL YEAR.

Details from *Marjory O'Connor*

Ms Marjory O'Connor Bonnieview Tower Brae North, Westhill Inverness IV1 2BW Tel: (Inverness) 0463 792468	COMMENDED 👑 👑	1 Single 1 Double 1 Family	1 En Suite fac 2 Limited ensuite 1 Pub. Bath/Show	B&B per person £16.00 Single £16.00 Double	Open Jan-Dec Dinner from 1800 B&B + Eve. Meal £25.00	
		Friendly welcome at this modern house quietly located overlooking the Moray Firth.2 miles (3kms) from Culloden Moor, 4 miles (6kms) from Inverness.				
Mrs Reid 101 Kenneth Street Inverness IV3 5QQ Tel: (Inverness) 0463 237224	Award Pending	2 Single 1 Twin 1 Double 2 Family	3 Pub. Bath/Show	B&B per person £13.00-£14.00 Single £12.00-£13.00 Double	Open Jan-Dec	
Mrs M Shields Ardgowan, 45 Fairfield Road Inverness IV3 5QP Tel: (Inverness) 0463 236489	COMMENDED 👑 👑	1 Twin 1 Family	1 En Suite fac 1 Pub. Bath/Show	B&B per person from £14.00 Single from £13.00 Double	Open Jan-Dec	
		A large semi-detached house with spacious rooms within a few minutes walk of the town centre.				

INVERNESS continued	Map 4 B8				
Miss Storrar, Abb Cottage 11 Douglas Row Inverness IV1 1RE Tel: (Inverness) 0463 233486		3 Twin	1 Pub. Bath/Show	B&B per person £14.00-£16.00 Double	Open Mar-Dec Dinner from 1800 B&B + Eve. Meal £22.00-£24.00
Mrs F Thomson Loanfern, 4 Glenurquhart Road Inverness IV3 5NU Tel: (Inverness) 0463 221660	APPROVED Listed	1 Twin 2 Double	2 En Suite fac 1 Pub. Bath/Show	B&B per person £12.00-£20.00 Single £12.00-£16.00 Double	Open Jan-Dec
		Family-run Victorian semi-detached villa, 5 minutes from town centre and all amenities. Situated on Loch Ness Road.			
Mrs Wallace 1 Broadstone Park Inverness IV2 3JZ Tel: (Inverness) 0463 231822	COMMENDED	2 Single 3 Twin 1 Double	2 Pub. Bath/Show	B&B per person £13.00-£14.00 Single £13.00-£14.00 Double	Open Jan-Dec
		Detached villa in quiet residential area but near the centre of town. Scots Pine is a feature of the house.			
Mrs J Wilson Cairnsmore, 41 Charles Street Inverness IV2 3AH Tel: (Inverness) 0463 233485	HIGHLY COMMENDED Listed	1 Twin 2 Double	1 Pub. Bath/Show	B&B per person from £13.50 Double	Open Jan-Dec
		Terraced house in quiet residential area, renovated to a high standard, close to shops, town centre, rail and bus centre.			
BY INVERNESS	Map 4 B8				
Inchberry House Lentran Inverness IV3 6RJ Tel: (Drumchardine) 0463 831342	HIGHLY COMMENDED ♔ ♔ ♔	2 Twin 3 Double 1 Family	3 En Suite fac 1 Priv. NOT ensuite 1 Pub. Bath/Show	B&B per person £20.00-£36.00 Single £18.50-£20.00 Double	Open Jan-Dec Dinner from 1830 B&B + Eve. Meal £29.00-£37.00
		Tastefully decorated 19C country house situated off main road, with views of Beauly Firth. Home cooking. 5 miles (8kms) from Inverness.			
Sky House Upper Cullernie Balloch, by Inverness Inverness-shire IV1 2HU Tel: (Inverness) 0463 792582	COMMENDED ♔ ♔	3 Twin	2 En Suite fac 1 Priv. NOT ensuite	B&B per person £18.00-£24.00 Double	Open Jan-Dec Dinner from 1930 B&B + Eve. Meal £28.00-£34.00
		A friendly and relaxed welcome at this modern house with superb views over Moray Firth to Black Isle. 4 miles (6kms) from Inverness.			
Pamela Beveridge Edgewood, Nairnside Inverness IV12 2BX Tel: (Inverness) 0463 791884	APPROVED Listed	1 Twin 1 Double 1 Family	1 Priv. NOT ensuite 1 Pub. Bath/Show	B&B per person from £15.00 Double	Open Jan-Dec Dinner 1700-2200 B&B + Eve. Meal from £27.50
		Attractively sited; 5 acre woodland, garden and livestock including rare breeds. Conservatory dining. Excellent cuisine. Video and CD library.			
Mrs T M Honnor Westhill House, Westhill by Inverness IV1 2BP Tel: (Inverness) 0463 793225 Fax: 0463 792503	COMMENDED ♔	2 Twin	2 En Suite fac	B&B per person to £16.00 Double	Open Mar-Oct
		Modern family home, own grounds, open countryside. 1 mile (2kms) Culloden Battlefield. 4 miles (6kms) Inverness. Two rooms one annexe. Warm welcome.			
Mrs M Mansfield 3a Resaurie Smithton, by Inverness Inverness-shire IV1 2NH Tel: (Inverness) 0463 791714	COMMENDED ♔ ♔	1 Twin 2 Double	1 En Suite fac 1 Pub. Bath/Show	B&B per person £13.00-£18.00 Double	Open Jan-Dec Dinner 1800-2000 B&B + Eve. Meal £22.50-£27.50
		Modern house set in quiet residential area 4 miles (6kms) from Inverness with panoramic views across the Moray Firth. Warm and friendly stay assured			

Mrs Munro Taransay Lower Muckovie Farm Inverness IV1 2BB Tel: (Inverness) 0463 231880		COMMENDED 👑 👑	1 Twin 1 Double	1 En Suite fac 1 Pub. Bath/Show	B&B per person from £14.50 Double	Open Apr-Oct	
			Modern bungalow in quiet situation on farm with panoramic views over the Moray Firth. 2 miles (3kms) from Inverness. 4 miles (6kms) from Culloden.				
Mrs E S Saggers Laggan View Ness Castle Fishings Dores Road, by Inverness Inverness-shire IV1 2DH Tel: (Inverness) 0463 235996 Fax: 0463 711552		COMMENDED 👑 👑	2 Twin 1 Double	2 En Suite fac 1 Priv. NOT ensuite	B&B per person from £16.00 Double	Open Jan-Dec Dinner 1900-2100 B&B + Eve. Meal from £22.00	
			Quiet secluded house in countryside with magnificient views. Close to Inverness; ideal for walkers and fishermen.				
Mrs J Thom 47 Culloden Road Balloch, by Inverness Inverness-shire IV1 2HQ Tel: (Inverness) 0463 790643		APPROVED 👑	1 Twin 2 Doubles	1 Pub. Bath/Show	B&B per person £13.00-£15.50 Single £13.00-£15.50 Double	Open Jun-Oct	
			Modern, comfortable accommodation with large garden in quiet suburb overlooking Moray Firth. Warm and friendly atmosphere.				
INVERSHIN, by Lairg **Sutherland** Mrs Alford Birkenshaw Invershin Sutherland IV27 4ET Tel: (Invershin) 054982 226	**Map 4** **A6**		2 Twin	2 En Suite fac	B&B per person £13.00-£13.50 Single £13.00-£13.50 Double	Open May-Sep	
Mrs W Brinklow Gneiss House, Balchraggan Invershin, by Lairg Sutherland IV27 4ET Tel: (Invershin) 054982 282		COMMENDED 👑 👑	1 Twin 1 Double	2 En Suite fac	B&B per person £15.00-£20.00 Single £15.00-£17.00 Double	Open Jan-Dec	
			Modern bungalow set back from road with fine river views. Warm, friendly atmosphere. Proprietor has reputation as local poet.				
Mrs M MacLean Invershin Farm Invershin, by Lairg Sutherland IV27 4ET Tel: (Invershin) 054982 206			2 Twin 1 Double	2 Pub. Bath/Show	B&B per person from £13.00 Double	Open Apr-Oct Dinner 1800-1900 B&B + Eve. Meal from £18.00	
INVERURIE **Aberdeenshire** West High Street Guest House 7 West High Street Inverurie Aberdeenshire Tel: (Inverurie) 0467 21434	**Map 4** **G9**	Award Pending	2 Single 2 Double	2 Pub. Bath/Show	B&B per person to £16.00 Single to £16.00 Double	Open Jan-Dec	
Mrs Black Breaslann, Old Chapel Road Inverurie Aberdeenshire AB51 Tel: (Inverurie) 0467 621608		COMMENDED 👑 👑	3 Twin	3 En Suite fac 1 Pub. Bath/Show	B&B per person £20.00-£22.00 Single £15.00-£18.00 Double	Open Jan-Dec	
			Modern comfortable bungalow with attractive gardens and off street parking. 10 minutes walk from town centre.				
Mrs Milne Earlsmohr, 85 High Street Inverurie Aberdeenshire Tel: (Inverurie) 0467 20606		COMMENDED Listed	1 Single 1 Double 1 Family	1 Pub. Bath/Show	B&B per person from £15.00 Single from £15.00 Double	Open Jan-Dec	
			Detached Edwardian granite built house with own garden situated ¹/₂ mile from town centre. Non smoking.				

Details of Grading and Classification are on page vi.　　　　Key to symbols is on back flap.　　185

BY INVERURIE **Aberdeenshire** Mrs Wilma Crosland Homefarm of Logie Pitcaple, by Inverurie Aberdeenshire AB51 9EE Tel: (Pitcaple) 0467 681481	**Map 4** G9	**HIGHLY COMMENDED** **Listed**	2 Twin 1 Double	1 Pub. Bath/Show	B&B per person £16.50-£18.00 Single £15.00-£16.00 Double	Open Jan-Nov	**Delightful country home on working farm in pleasant countryside yet convenient for the A96. Excellent home cooking.**
Mrs Thorp Meikle Pitinnan Farm Oldmeldrum Aberdeenshire AB51 0EH Tel: (Inverurie) 0467 671276		**HIGHLY COMMENDED**	2 Family	1 En Suite fac 1 Pub. Bath/Show	B&B per person from £15.00 Double	Open Apr-Oct Dinner 1800-2000 B&B + Eve. Meal £20.00-£24.00	**Recently refurbished farmhouse on working farm, 4½ miles (7kms) from Old Meldrum. Families welcome to join in farm activities.**
IONA, Isle of **Argyll** Miss A M Wagstaff Finlay, Ross Limited Iona, Isle of Argyll PA76 Tel: (Iona) 06817 357/365	**Map 1** B3	**COMMENDED** **Listed**	1 Single 8 Twin 2 Double 2 Family	3 En Suite fac 1 Priv. NOT ensuite 2 Pub. Bath/Show	B&B per person from £18.00 Single	Open Jan-Dec	**Purpose built rooms all on one level and convenient for the ferry. Continental breakfast only provided in bedrooms.**
IRVINE **Ayrshire** Mrs Angus The Laurels, 29 West Road Irvine Ayrshire KA12 8RE Tel: (Irvine) 0294 78405	**Map 1** G7		1 Single 1 Twin 1 Double	1 Pub. Bath/Show	B&B per person £12.50-£14.00 Single £12.00-£13.50 Double	Open Mar-Dec	
Mr J Daunt The Conifers 40 Kilwinning Road Irvine Ayrshire KA12 8RY Tel: (Irvine) 0294 278070		**APPROVED**	1 Twin 1 Double 1 Family	2 Pub. Bath/Show	B&B per person £15.00 Single £12.50-£15.00 Double	Open Jan-Dec	**Bungalow with large well maintained garden, convenient for town centre. Ample off-street parking in safe location.**
Mr & Mrs J Ferguson Laurelbank Guest House 3 Kilwinning Road Irvine Ayrshire KA12 8RR Tel: (Irvine) 0294 277153		**Award Pending**	2 Single 1 Twin 1 Double 1 Family	2 Pub. Bath/Show	B&B per person £15.00-£18.00 Single £13.00-£15.00 Double	Open Jan-Dec Dinner 1700-1900	
Mrs Martin Arran View 11 Kilwinning Road Irvine Ayrshire KA12 8RR Tel: (Irvine) 0294 78474			3 Twin	2 Limited ensuite 1 Pub. Bath/Show	B&B per person £16.00-£17.00 Single £13.00-£15.00 Double	Open Jan-Dec	
ISLEORNSAY **Isle of Skye, Inverness-shire** Mrs MacDonald 6 Duisdale Beag Isleornsay, Sleat Isle of Skye, Inverness-shire Tel: (Isleornsay) 04713 230	**Map 3** E1	**COMMENDED**	1 Twin 2 Double	1 En Suite fac 2 Pub. Bath/Show	B&B per person £13.00-£16.00 Double	Open Mar-Sep	**Modern bungalow in elevated position in small country village overlooking the sea. Home baking in lounge in evening.**

 VAT is shown at 17.5%: changes in this rate may affect prices. Prices shown are for guidance only. Please send SAE with each enquiry.

| JEDBURGH | Map 2 |
| Roxburghshire | E7 |

FROYLEHURST

THE FRIARS, JEDBURGH TD8 6BN
Tel: (0835) 862477

Detached late-Victorian house offering large comfortable guest rooms and residents' lounge. Situated in a large garden in a quiet residential area of the town, with ample private off-street parking yet only 2 minutes from town centre. All bedrooms have wash basins, shaver points, tea/coffee-making facilities and colour TV. Full Scottish breakfast. Edinburgh is only one hour away. Golf, pony-trekking, fishing and sports centre all local. This is a family home, and guests are made welcome by the owner.

Further details and tariff available from Mrs H. Irvine.

AA Listed

Mrs H Irvin Froylehurst Guest House The Friars Jedburgh Roxburghshire TD8 6BN Tel: (Jedburgh) 0835 62477/862477 Fax: 0835 62477/862477	HIGHLY COMMENDED ♨	1 Twin 2 Double 1 Family	2 Pub. Bath/Show	B&B per person £14.00-£15.00 Double	Open Mar-Oct	

Detached Victorian house with large garden and private parking.
Spacious rooms. Overlooking town, 2 minutes walk from the centre.

KENMORE BANK

OXNAM ROAD, JEDBURGH TD8 6JJ
Tel: (0835) 862369

A charming, family-run hotel with restricted licence. Situated above the Jed Water, just off the A68, it enjoys panoramic views of the Abbey and ancient town of Jedburgh, yet just 5 minutes walk from town.
Excellent cuisine, choice of menu, wines and snacks.

All bedrooms en suite with colour TV.
PRICES from £17.50 B&B.
Proprietors: Charles and Joanne Muller.

♨♨♨ **COMMENDED**   **AA** **QQQ**

Kenmore Bank Guest House Oxnam Road Jedburgh Roxburghshire TD8 6JJ Tel: (Jedburgh) 0835 62369/862369	COMMENDED ♨♨♨	2 Twin 2 Double 2 Family	6 En Suite fac	B&B per person £27.00-£33.00 Single £17.50-£21.00 Double	Open Jan-Dec Dinner 1830-1930 B&B + Eve. Meal £31.50-£35.50	

Situated just off A68 overlooking the Abbey.
Excellent base for touring the Borders.

Willow Guest House Willow Court, The Friars Jedburgh Roxburghshire TD8 6BN Tel: (Jedburgh) 0835 63702/863702	HIGHLY COMMENDED ♨♨♨	1 Twin 2 Double 1 Family	3 En Suite fac 1 Priv. NOT ensuite	B&B per person £18.00-£25.00 Single £15.00-£18.00 Double	Open Jan-Dec Dinner 1800-1900 B&B + Eve. Meal £24.00-£27.00	

Set in 2 acres above the town; excellent views. Family run with home cooking,
home grown produce in season. Ground floor accommodation available.

Details of Grading and Classification are on page vi.   Key to symbols is on back flap.   187

JEDBURGH continued Mrs I Balderston Nisbet Mill Farm Jedburgh Roxburghshire TD8 6TT Tel: (Crailing) 08355 228	**Map 2** E7	COMMENDED 👑 👑	2 Double	1 En Suite fac 1 Priv. NOT ensuite	B&B per person £15.50 Double	Open Apr-Sep Dinner 1700-2000 B&B + Eve. Meal £22.00	
Spacious farmhouse overlooking River Teviot on working farm. Central situation for touring. Woodland walks. Home baking and cooking.							
Mrs Clark Strowan, Oxnam Road Jedburgh Roxburghshire TD8 6QJ Tel: (Jedburgh) 0835 62248/862248		COMMENDED Listed	2 Single 1 Twin 1 Double	1 Limited ensuite 1 Pub. Bath/Show	B&B per person £14.50-£15.00 Single £14.50-£16.50 Double	Open Apr-Oct	
Old manse house of character on the edge of the town, set in its own grounds of nearly 2 acres. One room with own shower.							
Mrs M Crone 15 Hartrigge Crescent Jedburgh Roxburghshire TD8 6HT Tel: (Jedburgh) 0835 62738/862738		COMMENDED Listed	1 Twin 1 Double	1 Pub. Bath/Show	B&B per person £12.50-£13.00 Double	Open Jan-Dec	
Friendly family house in quiet residential area within walking distance of the town.							
Mrs Margaret Harrison Normanie, The Friars Jedburgh Roxburghshire TD8 6BN Tel: (Jedburgh) 0835 63382		COMMENDED Listed	2 Family	1 Pub. Bath/Show	B&B per person £21.00-£23.00 Single £14.00-£16.00 Double	Open Mar-Nov	
A large detached Victorian house with many original features. Warm friendly family atmosphere. Close to local amenities and attractions.							
Mrs M Hume Meadhon House, 48 Castlegate Jedburgh Roxburghshire TD8 6BB Tel: (Jedburgh) 0835 62504/862504			1 Double 3 Family	4 En Suite fac	B&B per person from £25.00 Single from £18.50 Double	Open Jan-Dec	
Mrs Pat McNab The Broch, Lanton Road Jedburgh Roxburghshire TD8 6SY Tel: (Jedburgh) 0835 63542			1 Twin 2 Double	3 En Suite fac	B&B per person from £20.00 Single from £17.00 Double	Open Jan-Dec	
Mrs Till Mayfield, Sharplaw Road Jedburgh Roxburghshire TD8 6SG Tel: (Jedburgh) 0835 63696		COMMENDED 👑	1 Double 1 Family	2 Pub. Bath/Show	B&B per person £14.00-£14.50 Double	Open Apr-Oct	
Handsome detached 19C stone built house in own grounds in elevated position, overlooking town. Free range eggs; home made preserves.							
BY JEDBURGH Roxburghshire Spinney Guest House The Spinney, Langlee Jedburgh Roxburghshire TD8 6PB Tel: (Jedburgh) 0835 63525/ 863525 Fax: 0835 63525/863525	**Map 2** E7	DELUXE 👑 👑	1 Twin 2 Double	2 En Suite fac 1 Priv. NOT ensuite	B&B per person from £18.00 Double	Open mid Mar-Oct	
A warm welcome at this attractive house recently modernised and with large pleasant garden lying just off main A68. All rooms have private facilities							

CRAILING OLD SCHOOL
BY JEDBURGH, ROXBURGHSHIRE TD8 6TL
Telephone: 08355-382

Tastefully converted former school, peacefully situated in own grounds with private parking. Midway between Kelso and Jedburgh, with panoramic views of surrounding countryside. Comfortable and spacious lounge with log-fire and tea/coffee making facilities. Ideal base for touring, sightseeing, walking, fishing and golfing. Families welcome.

Mrs D Skea Crailing Old School Jedburgh Roxburghshire TD8 6TW Tel: (Crailing) 08355 382	COMMENDED Listed	1 Twin 1 Family	2 Pub. Bath/Show	B&B per person £11.00-£13.00 Double	Open Apr-Oct
		Originally a village school now converted into a family home which welcomes non-smokers, peacefully situated just off Jedburgh/Kelso road.			
Mrs Whittaker Hundalee House Jedburgh Roxburghshire TD8 6PA Tel: (Jedburgh) 0835 63011/863011	DELUXE	1 Twin 2 Double 1 Family	3 En Suite fac 1 Pub. Bath/Show	B&B per person £20.00-£25.00 Single £15.00-£20.00 Double	Open Mar-Oct
		Extensively refurbished country home 1 mile (2kms) south of Jedburgh with excellent views of Cheviot Hills. One bedroom with a four poster bed.			
JOHN O'GROATS Caithness Caber-feidh Guest House John O'Groats Caithness KW1 4YR Tel: (John O'Groats) 095581 219	Map 4 E2	4 Single 3 Twin 2 Double 3 Family	3 En Suite fac 3 Pub. Bath/Show	B&B per person £13.50-£14.50 Single £12.50-£13.50 Double	Open Jan-Dec Dinner 1830-2000 B&B + Eve. Meal £17.50-£18.50
Mrs Barton Bencorragh House Upper Gills, Canisbay Caithness KW1 4YB Tel: (John O'Groats) 095581 449	Award Pending	2 Twin 1 Double	3 En Suite fac	B&B per person £15.00-£17.00 Double	Open Jan-Dec Dinner 1800-2030
Mrs M S Green Haven Gore John O'Groats Caithness KW1 4YL Tel: (John O'Groats) 095581 314		1 Twin 1 Double 1 Family	1 Pub. Bath/Show	B&B per person £12.00-£13.00 Double	Open Jan-Dec
BY JOHN O'GROATS Caithness Mrs C G Manson Post Office Canisbay Caithness KW1 4YH Tel: (John O'Groats) 095581 213	Map 4 E2 COMMENDED	1 Twin 2 Double	1 En Suite fac 2 Limited ensuite 1 Pub. Bath/Show	B&B per person £18.00-£20.00 Single £15.00-£17.00 Double	Open Easter-Oct
		100 year old Post Office house. Panoramic views of Pentland Firth, close to John O'Groats and Orkney Ferries. Personally run.			
JOHNSTONE Renfrewshire Mrs C Capper Auchans Farm Johnstone Renfrewshire PA6 7EE Tel: (Johnstone) 0505 20131	Map 1 H5	2 Double 1 Family	3 Priv. NOT ensuite 2 Pub. Bath/Show	B&B per person £15.00-£18.00 Single £15.00-£18.00 Double	Open Jan-Dec

KEITH **Banffshire** Mrs Barbara Allan Barlane, 66 Fife Street Keith Banffshire AB55 3EG Tel: (Keith) 05422 2651	**Map 4** E8		2 Twin 1 Double	1 Pub. Bath/Show	B&B per person £13.00–£15.00 Single £11.50–£12.00 Double	Open Jan-Dec Dinner 1800-1930
Mr and Mrs Bernard Watts Craighurst, Seafield Avenue Keith Banffshire AB55 3BS Tel: (Keith) 05422 6063		**COMMENDED** 👑 👑	2 Twin 1 Double	3 En Suite fac	B&B per person £16.50 Single £16.50 Double	Open Jan-Dec
			A fine detached Victorian House in spacious grounds on Whisky Trail. Sensitively restored retaining many period features. Friendly atmosphere.			
BY KEITH **Banffshire** Mrs Eileen Fleming Chapelhill Croft, Grange Keith Banffshire AB55 3LQ Tel: (Grange) 0542870 302	**Map 4** E8	**COMMENDED** Listed	1 Twin 1 Double	1 En Suite fac 1 Pub. Bath/Show	B&B per person £12.50–£15.50 Double	Open Jan-Dec Dinner 1730-2000 B&B + Eve. Meal £20.00–£23.00
			Warm, friendly welcome on working croft. Guests welcome to participate in running of the croft. Home cooking.			
Mrs Jean Jackson The Haughs Keith Banffshire AB55 3QN Tel: (Keith) 0542 882238		**COMMENDED** 👑 👑 👑	2 Twin 2 Double	3 En Suite fac 1 Priv. NOT ensuite 3 Pub. Bath/Show	B&B per person £13.50–£17.00 Double	Open May-Oct Dinner 1800-1930 B&B + Eve. Meal £22.00–£25.00
			Traditional farmhouse on 165 acre farm near town just off main road. On Whisky Trail; many local sports; golf available at numerous courses.			
KELSO **Roxburghshire** Mrs E Bentham Wooden Kelso Roxburghshire Tel: (Kelso) 0573 224204	**Map 2** F6	**HIGHLY** **COMMENDED** 👑 👑	1 Twin 2 Double	3 En Suite fac	B&B per person £20.00–£22.50 Single £20.00–£22.50 Double	Open May-Sep
			A beautiful Georgian castellated house standing in 400 acres of grounds and farmland bordered by the River Tweed. 0.5 miles (1km) from Kelso.			
Mrs E Blackie 159 Roxburgh Street Kelso Roxburghshire TD5 7DU Tel: (Kelso) 0573 224821		**APPROVED** Listed	1 Twin 1 Family	2 Pub. Bath/Show	B&B per person £13.00 Single £13.00 Double	Open Jan-Dec
			Warm welcome in this town house. Close to all amenities and ideal for touring the Borders.			
Ms Olive Gordon Ivy Neuk, 62 Horsemarket Kelso Roxburghshire TD5 7AE Tel: (Kelso) 0573 224428		**COMMENDED** Listed	1 Single 1 Double 1 Family	1 En Suite fac 1 Limited ensuite 1 Pub. Bath/Show	B&B per person £13.50 Single from £13.50 Double	Open Jan-Dec
			Attractive listed house, 2 minutes from town centre. A warm welcome and full Scottish breakfast.			
Mrs McCririck Whitmuirhaugh, Sprouston Kelso Roxburghshire TD5 8HP Tel: (Kelso) 0573 224615		**COMMENDED** Listed	1 Twin 1 Double	2 En Suite fac	B&B per person to £15.00 Single to £15.00 Double	Open Apr-Oct Dinner 1800-2030 B&B + Eve. Meal to £30.00
			18C farmhouse, 3 miles (5kms) from Kelso (B6350) on 600 acre farm with views of River Tweed. Trout fishing available.			

Mrs Jan McDonald Craignethan House Jedburgh Road Kelso Roxburghshire TD5 8BZ Tel: (Kelso) 0573 224818		COMMENDED Listed	1 Twin 2 Double	2 Pub. Bath/Show	B&B per person to £16.00 Single to £16.00 Double	Open Jan-Dec
			Delightful detached house overlooking the town centre with panoramic views of Floors Castle and surrounding countryside. Ground floor bedroom.			
Mrs J M Middlemas Charlesfield, Edenside Road Kelso Roxburghshire TD5 7BS Tel: (Kelso) 0573 224583		HIGHLY COMMENDED Listed	1 Twin 1 Double	1 Pub. Bath/Show	B&B per person from £16.00 Double	Open Jan-Dec
			Stone built Victorian house with large garden. Situated within a few minutes walk of the historic town centre.			
Mrs D M Playfair Morebattle Tofts Kelso Roxburghshire TD5 8AD Tel: (Morebattle) 0573 440364 Fax: 0573 420227		COMMENDED ♛ ♛	1 Twin 2 Double	1 En Suite fac 1 Pub. Bath/Show	B&B per person £14.00 Single £14.00-£16.00 Double	Open Apr-Oct Dinner 1900-2000 B&B + Eve. Meal £23.00-£25.00
			Elegant C18th farmhouse set in idyllic location beside the kale water. Ideal base for touring, walking, fishing, golf.			
Mr and Mrs A C Robertson Duncan House Chalkheugh Terrace Kelso Roxburghshire TD5 7DX Tel: (Kelso) 0573 225682			1 Twin 1 Double 1 Family	2 En Suite fac 2 Pub. Bath/Show	B&B per person from £13.00 Single £13.00-£13.50 Double	Open Jan-Dec Dinner 1800-2000
Mrs B Smith Whitehill Farm Nenthorn, by Kelso Roxburghshire TD5 7RZ Tel: (Stichill) 0573 470203		HIGHLY COMMENDED ♛ ♛	2 Single 2 Twin	1 En Suite fac 1 Pub. Bath/Show	B&B per person £15.00-£16.00 Single £15.00-£16.00 Double	Open Jan-Dec Dinner 1900-2000 B&B + Eve. Meal £26.00-£27.00
			18C farmhouse with large garden and superb views on mixed farm. Ideally placed for touring the Borders region and just off the Kelso/Edinburgh road.			
Mr & Mrs Archie Stewart Cliftonhill Farm Kelso Roxburghshire TD5 7QE Tel: (Kelso) 0573 225028 Fax: 0573 226416		COMMENDED ♛	1 Twin 1 Double 1 Family	1 En Suite fac 1 Priv. NOT ensuite 1 Pub. Bath/Show	B&B per person £20.00-£30.00 Double	Open Jan-Dec Dinner 1800-2000 B&B + Eve. Meal £30.00-£40.00
			On working farm, large detached farmhouse with extensive garden, 2 miles (3 kms) from Kelso.			
Mr D Watson Clashdale, 26 Inchmead Drive Kelso Roxburghshire TD5 7LW Tel: (Kelso) 0573 223405		COMMENDED Listed	1 Single 1 Double	1 Pub. Bath/Show	B&B per person £12.00 Single £12.00 Double	Open Jan-Dec
			Quietly situated in cul-de-sac, only 10 mintues from town centre and 2 minutes from swimming pool. Parking available.			
BY KELSO **Roxburghshire** Mrs Ruth McGrath Barn Owl Lodge Smailholm, Kelso Roxburghshire TD5 7PH Tel: (Morebattle) 0573 460373 Fax: 0573 460373	Map 2 F6	Award Pending	2 Twin 1 Double	3 En Suite fac	B&B per person £15.00-£20.00 Double	Open Jan-Dec

Details of Grading and Classification are on page vi.

Key to symbols is on back flap.

KENMORE **Perthshire** MrsDott 13 Taymouth Drive Kenmore, by Aberfeldy Perthshire PH15 2NV Tel: (Kenmore) 0887 830271	Map 2 A1		1 Twin 2 Double	1 En Suite fac 1 Pub. Bath/Show	B&B per person £12.50-£15.00 Double	Open Mar-Nov Dinner 1830-2030 B&B + Eve. Meal £23.00-£25.00	
BY KENMORE **Perthshire** Mrs S I McConnel Caochan House Lawers, by Aberfeldy Perthshire PH15 2PA Tel: (Killin) 0567 820738	Map 2 A1		1 Single 1 Twin	1 En Suite fac 1 Pub. Bath/Show	B&B per person £11.00 Single £15.00 Double	Open Jan-Dec	
KILAULEY, Iochdar **South Uist, Western Isles** Mrs Myra MacDonald Monach View Kilauley, Lochdar South Uist, Western Isles PA81 5RE Tel: (Carnan) 08704 347	Map 3 A9		3 Twin	2 Pub. Bath/Show	B&B per person £12.00-£14.00 Single £12.00-£14.00 Double	Open Jan-Dec Dinner from 1830 B&B + Eve. Meal £18.00-£20.00	
KILBARCHAN **Renfrewshire** Mrs Douglas Gladstone Farmhouse Kilbarchan, by Johnstone Renfrewshire PA10 2PB Tel: (Kilbarchan) 05057 2579	Map 1 H5	COMMENDED Listed	1 Twin 1 Family	1 Pub. Bath/Show	B&B per person £15.00 Single £14.00 Double	Open Jan-Dec Dinner 1800-1900	
			300 year old farmhouse on working farm. 7 miles (11kms) from Airport. **Convenient for touring Ayrshire and Loch Lomond.**				
KILCHOAN, by Ardnamurchan **Argyll** Mr and Mrs R Thompson Far View Cottage Pier Road, Mingary Kilchoan, Acharacle Argyll PH36 4LH Tel: (Kilchoan) 09723 357	Map 1 C1	Award Pending	1 Twin 2 Double	2 En Suite fac 1 Priv. NOT ensuite	B&B per person £18.00-£22.00 Single £16.00-£24.00 Double	Open Apr-Oct Dinner at 1930 B&B + Eve. Meal £24.00-£32.00	
KILDRUMMY **Aberdeenshire** Dukeston of Brux Kildrummy Aberdeenshire AB33 8RX Tel: (Kildrummy) 09755 71344	Map 4 E1	Award Pending	1 Twin 1 Double	2 En Suite fac	B&B per person £20.00 Double	Open Feb-Oct Dinner at 1930 B&B + Eve. Meal £32.00	

KILLIECRANKIE **Perthshire** Mrs E Goodfellow Tighdornie, Aldclune Killiecrankie Perthshire PH16 5LR Tel: (Pitlochry) 0796 473276	Map 4 C1		1 Single 2 Double 1 Family	2 En Suite fac 1 Priv. NOT ensuite 1 Pub. Bath/Show	B&B per person from £15.00 Single £16.00-£17.00 Double	Open Jan-Dec
Mrs R MacPherson McDougall Dalnasgadh House Killiecrankie Perthshire PH16 5LN Tel: (Pitlochry) 0796 473237			1 Single 2 Twin 2 Double	2 Pub. Bath/Show	B&B per person £17.50-£18.50 Single £16.50-£17.50 Double	Open Apr-Oct
KILLIN **Perthshire** Breadalbane House Main Street Killin Perthshire FK21 8UT Tel: (Killin) 0567 820386 Fax: 0567 820386	Map 1 H2	COMMENDED 👑👑👑	1 Twin 2 Double 2 Family	5 En Suite fac	B&B per person £17.00-£19.00 Double Traditional stone built house in centre of small village. Ideal base for touring central Scotland.	Open Jan-Dec Dinner 1900-1945 B&B + Eve. Meal £27.00-£29.00
Fairview House Main Street Killin Perthshire FK21 8UT Tel: (Killin) 0567 820667		COMMENDED 👑👑	1 Single 2 Twin 4 Double	3 En Suite fac 2 Pub. Bath/Show	B&B per person £14.00-£16.00 Single £14.00-£16.00 Double Small family run guest house specialising in home cooking. Excellent touring centre, good walking and climbing area.	Open Jan-Dec Dinner from 1930 B&B + Eve. Meal £22.00-£24.00
KILMARNOCK **Ayrshire** Dean Park Guest House 27 Wellington Street Kilmarnock Ayrshire KA3 1DW Tel: (Kilmarnock) 0563 72794/32061	Map 1 H7	Award Pending	1 Single 2 Twin 2 Double 1 Family	2 En Suite fac 2 Pub. Bath/Show	B&B per person £14.00-£18.00 Single £14.00-£18.00 Double	Open Jan-Dec
Eriskay Guest House 2 Dean Terrace Kilmarnock Ayrshire KA3 1RJ Tel: (Kilmarnock) 0563 32061/72794		COMMENDED 👑👑	2 Single 1 Twin 2 Double 1 Family	2 En Suite fac 2 Pub. Bath/Show	B&B per person £14.00-£18.00 Single £14.00-£18.00 Double Detached villa conveniently situated on main bus route and close to Dean Park and Castle. Enclosed secure car park.	Open Jan-Dec
Mrs A Grant 177 Dundonald Road Kilmarnock Ayrshire KA2 0AB Tel: (Kilmarnock) 0563 22733		COMMENDED 👑👑	2 Twin 1 Double	1 En Suite fac 1 Pub. Bath/Show	B&B per person from £15.00 Single from £12.50 Double Modern detached home with attractive enclosed patio and garden on town outskirts. Golf and good touring base. Under 30 miles (48kms) from Glasgow.	Open May-Oct
Mrs Mary Howie Hillhouse Farm Grassyards Road Kilmarnock Ayrshire KA3 6HG Tel: (Kilmarnock) 0563 23370		COMMENDED 👑👑	1 Twin 2 Family	1 En Suite fac 2 Pub. Bath/Show	B&B per person £13.00-£16.00 Single £12.50-£16.00 Double Working dairy farm (500 acres) with fine views of Ayrshire countryside situated about 2 miles (4 kms) East of Kilmarnock.	Open Jan-Dec

Details of Grading and Classification are on page vi.　Key to symbols is on back flap.　193

KILMARNOCK continued	Map 1 H7	COMMENDED ☺☺	1 Twin 1 Double 1 Family	1 En Suite fac 2 Pub. Bath/Show	B&B per person £14.00-£17.00 Single £13.00-£17.00 Double	Open Jan-Dec Dinner 1800-1900 B&B + Eve. Meal £21.00-£26.00

Mrs M Love, Muirhouse Farm, Gatehead, by Kilmarnock, Ayrshire, KA2 0BT, Tel: (Kilmarnock) 0563 23975

Large family farmhouse on 170 acre dairy farm 2 miles (3kms) from Kilmarnock. Quiet rural position.

"Tamarind"
24 ARRAN AVENUE, KILMARNOCK KA3 1TP
Telephone: 0563 71788 Fax: 0563 71787
The accommodation at "Tamarind" was created with the International visitor in mind. Rooms are equipped with remote control TV's and all are en-suite. A heated swimming pool (in season) is also available for your enjoyment.
Discerning travellers will feel at home here.

Mrs C Turner, Tamarind, 24 Arran Avenue, Kilmarnock, Ayrshire, KA3 1TP, Tel: (Kilmarnock) 0563 71788, Fax: 0563 71787	COMMENDED ☺☺☺	1 Single 2 Twin 1 Double 1 Family	5 En Suite fac	B&B per person £22.50-£25.00 Single £17.50-£20.00 Double	Open Jan-Dec Dinner at 1900 B&B + Eve. Meal £30.00-£35.00

Ranch style bungalow with small heated swimming pool in residential area. Convenient base for touring.

BY KILMARNOCK, Ayrshire, Mrs L Howie, Muirhouse Farm, Symington, by Kilmarnock, Ayrshire, KA1 5PA, Tel: (Kilmarnock) 0563 830218	Map 1 H7	COMMENDED ☺	1 Twin 1 Double	1 Pub. Bath/Show	B&B per person £14.00-£17.00 Single £14.00-£17.00 Double	Open Jan-Dec

Traditional farmhouse peacefully situated and convenient for A77. Provides a good base for touring Ayrshire coast, golfing, fishing, walking etc.

KILMARTIN, by Lochgilphead, Argyll, Jessie M Gordon, Ri-Cruin, Kilmartin, by Lochgilphead, Argyll, PA30 8QF, Tel: (Kilmartin) 05465 231	Map 1 E4		1 Twin 1 Double 1 Family	2 Pub. Bath/Show	B&B per person from £15.00 Single from £15.00 Double	Open Apr-Oct

Mrs C C McAuslan, Cornaig, Kilmartin, by Lochgilphead, Argyll, PA30 8RQ, Tel: (Kilmartin) 05465 224	COMMENDED ☺☺	1 Single 2 Twin 1 Double 1 Family	1 En Suite fac 2 Pub. Bath/Show	B&B per person from £15.00 Single £13.00-£15.00 Double	Open Jan-Dec Dinner 1800-2000 B&B + Eve. Meal from £20.00

19C former manse situated on the outskirts of small historic village in an area of archaeological interest. Attractive rural views.

DUNCHRAGAIG HOUSE

0546 605209

by Kilmartin, Lochgilphead Argyll PA31 8RG

Attractive 19th-century house of lovely character, upgraded and finished to a high standard, giving every comfort to our guests. Situated in the heart of Mid-Argyll amidst a conservation area surrounded by historical cairns and henges. It is an ideal centre for touring the West from Campbeltown, Fort William, Oban and also the numerous islands off this coast. A friendly, personal welcome awaits. We offer a varied Scottish breakfast and evening meal. *We pride ourselves on value for money and excellent service.*

Bed and Breakfast from £13.50, Dinner £8.00.

Mrs J MacGillivray Dunchragaig Kilmartin, by Lochgilphead Argyll PA31 8RG Tel: (Lochgilphead) 0546 605209	**COMMENDED** 👑👑	1 Single 1 Twin 2 Double	1 En Suite fac 1 Pub. Bath/Show	B&B per person £13.50-£14.50 Single £13.00-£16.00 Double	Open Mar-Oct Dinner 1900-2000 B&B + Eve. Meal £20.50-£24.00
		Family run home with personal service. All home cooking.			

KILMAURS, by Kilmarnock **Ayrshire** Mrs W Steel Laigh Langmuir Farm Kilmaurs, by Kilmarnock Ayrshire KA3 2NU Tel: (Kilmarnock) 0563 38270	Map 1 H6	**COMMENDED** 👑👑	1 Single 1 Twin 1 Family	1 En Suite fac 2 Pub. Bath/Show	B&B per person £14.00-£15.00 Single £13.00-£16.00 Double
		Open Jan-Dec			
		100 acre farm on outskirts of a small village. Convenient for Ayrshire coast. **Log fire and home baking. Runner-up Scottish Farmhouse of Year 1989.**			

KILMICHAEL GLEN **Argyll** Mr Bracey Kirnan Country House Kilmichael Glen, by Lochgilphead Argyll PA31 8QL Tel: (Dunadd) 0546 605217	Map 1 E4	**COMMENDED** 👑👑	2 Twin 1 Family	1 En Suite fac 2 Pub. Bath/Show	B&B per person £16.00-£19.00 Single £16.00-£17.50 Double
		Open Jan-Dec			
		Victorian, former shooting lodge in 12 acres of landscaped grounds. **Enjoys elevated, peaceful situation in scenic glen south of Loch Awe.**			

KILMORE, Sleat **Isle of Skye, Inverness-shire** Mrs Julia MacDonald 3 Kilmore Sleat Isle of Skye, Inverness-shire IV44 8RG Tel: (Ardvasar) 04714 272	Map 3 E1	**APPROVED** Listed	2 Single 1 Twin 1 Double	1 Limited ensuite 1 Pub. Bath/Show	B&B per person £12.00-£14.00 Single £12.00-£14.00 Double
		Open Apr-Oct			
		Modern bungalow in elevated position. On working croft with panoramic views **towards Knoydart Hills. 2.5 miles (4 kms) from Armadale Ferry.**			

KILMORE, by Oban **Argyll** Braeside Guest House Kilmore, by Oban Argyll PA34 4QR Tel: (Kilmore) 063177 243	Map 1 E2		3 Twin 2 Double 1 Family	5 En Suite fac 1 Limited ensuite 1 Pub. Bath/Show	B&B per person
		Open Mar-Oct Dinner 1830-1900 B&B + Eve. Meal £19.50-£22.50			

KILMORY
Isle of Arran
Mrs N C McLean
Torlin Villa
Kilmory
Isle of Arran
KA27 8PH
Tel: (Sliddery) 0770 870340

Map 1 F7

COMMENDED

1 Twin	1 En Suite fac	B&B per person	Open Jan-Dec
2 Double	2 Pub. Bath/Show	£15.00-£18.00 Double	

Family run guest house with views over local countryside and sea.

KILMUIR, Uig
Isle of Skye, Inverness-shire

Map 3 D7

Kilmuir House
KILMUIR
Nr UIG
ISLE OF SKYE
Tel: 047 042 262

Lovely old manse in large walled garden overlooking Loch Snizort and Outer Hebrides. Furnished with antiques and centrally heated throughout, we offer excellent home cooking using local produce and our own free range eggs. Kilmuir is steeped in history and Gaelic culture and tradition is still much in evidence here.

Mrs S Phelps
Kilmuir House
Kilmuir, by Uig
Isle of Skye, Inverness-shire
IV51 9YN
Tel: (Uig) 047042 262

COMMENDED
Listed

1 Twin	2 Pub. Bath/Show	B&B per person	Open Jan-Dec
1 Double		from £13.50 Double	Dinner 1900-2000
1 Family			B&B + Eve. Meal from £21.50

Former manse in superb situation overlooking Loch to Outer Isles.
Warm hospitality and high standard of home cooking using fresh local produce.

KILSYTH
Stirlingshire
Mrs Margaret Clark
Fairfield, Glasgow Road
Kilsyth
Stirlingshire
G65 9JZ
Tel: (Kilsyth) 0236 825745

Map 2 A5

1 Single	1 Pub. Bath/Show	B&B per person	Open Jan-Dec
1 Twin		£15.50-£17.00 Single	B&B + Eve. Meal
1 Double		£15.50-£17.00 Double	£25.50-£30.00

Mrs Dunlop
Mashobra, Coach Road
Kilsyth
Stirlingshire
G65
Tel: (Kilsyth) 0236 822122

2 Twin	2 En Suite fac	B&B per person	Open Jan-Dec
1 Family	1 Pub. Bath/Show	£12.00-£13.00 Single	Dinner 1800-2000
		£12.00-£13.00 Double	

KILTARLITY
Inverness-shire
Mrs C Hayward
Tigh Bea
Kiltarlity, by Beauly
Inverness-shire
IV4 7JH
Tel: (Kiltarlity) 046374 425

Map 4 A9

Award Pending

1 Twin	2 Priv. NOT ensuite	B&B per person	Open Jan-Dec
1 Double		£13.00-£16.00 Double	

KILWINNING
Ayrshire
Mrs Filby
Claremont House, 27 Howgate
Kilwinning
Ayrshire
KA13 6EW
Tel: (Kilwinning) 0294 53905

Map 1 G6

1 Single	1 Pub. Bath/Show	B&B per person	Open Jan-Dec
1 Family		£12.00-£15.00 Single	
		£12.00-£15.00 Double	

Mrs C Harris Woodburn Cottage Woodwynd Kilwinning Ayrshire Tel: (Kilwinning) 0294 51657 Fax: 0294 58297			1 Single 1 Twin 1 Double	1 Pub. Bath/Show	B&B per person £14.00-£15.00 Single £14.00-£15.00 Double	Open Jan-Dec
KINCARDINE-ON-FORTH **Fife** Mrs C Hughes Inch House Kincardine-on-Forth Fife FK10 4AH Tel: (Kincardine) 0259 730466	Map 2 B4	COMMENDED ♛	1 Twin 1 Family	1 Pub. Bath/Show	B&B per person from £18.00 Single from £15.50 Double	Open Apr-Oct Dinner from 1900 B&B + Eve. Meal £24.00-£26.50
			Fine 18C house in walled gardens overlooking the River Forth. **Easy access to Edinburgh and Glasgow.**			
KINCRAIG **Inverness-shire** Grampian View Kincraig Inverness-shire PH21 1NA Tel: (Kincraig) 0540 651383	Map 4 B1	COMMENDED ♛ ♛	1 Single 2 Twin 2 Double	4 En Suite fac 1 Priv. NOT ensuite	B&B per person £16.00-£18.00 Single £16.00-£18.00 Double	Open Feb-Oct
			Family run Victorian house, over 100 years old, with original fire places **and woodwork; close to old railway station.**			
Insh House Guest House Kincraig Inverness-shire PH21 1NU Tel: (Kincraig) 0540 651377		COMMENDED ♛	2 Single 1 Twin 1 Double 1 Family	2 En Suite fac 1 Pub. Bath/Show	B&B per person from £15.00 Single from £15.00 Double	Open Jan-Dec Dinner from 1900 B&B + Eve. Meal from £22.00
			Fine example of a Telford House in 2 acres of secluded grounds. Close to **Loch Insh, 10 minutes to Aviemore. Skiing, watersports, riding, gliding.**			
March House Guest House Feshiebridge Kincraig Inverness-shire PH21 1NG Tel: (Kincraig) 0540 651388 Fax: 0540 657388		COMMENDED ♛ ♛	3 Twin 2 Double 1 Family	5 En Suite fac 1 Priv. NOT ensuite	B&B per person from £18.00 Single from £18.00 Double	Open Dec-Oct Dinner from 1900 B&B + Eve. Meal from £28.00
			Situated in beautiful Glenfeshie. Excellent views of surrounding hills. **Personally run relaxed atmosphere. Emphasis on fresh food.**			
Insh Hall Lodge Kincraig Kingussie Inverness-shire PH21 1NU Tel: (Kincraig) 0540 651272 Fax: 0540 651208			7 Twin 8 Family	13 En Suite fac 6 Pub. Bath/Show	B&B per person £10.50-£14.00 Single £10.50-£14.00 Double	Open Jan-Dec Dinner 1800-2200 B&B + Eve. Meal £19.50-£20.00
J Knapp-Holland Kincraig House Kincraig Inverness-shire PH21 1ND Tel: (Kincraig) 0540 651685			1 Double 1 Family	1 Pub. Bath/Show	B&B per person from £16.00 Single from £16.00 Double	Open Jan-Dec Dinner 1900-2100 B&B + Eve. Meal from £24.00

KINGCRAIG continued	Map 2 E3

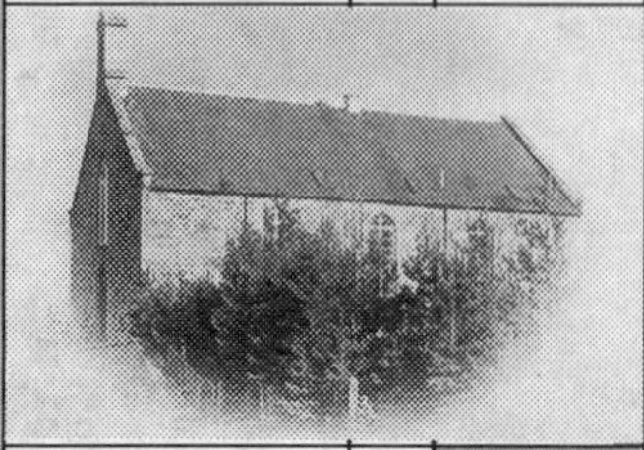

Kirkbeag

0540 651 298

KINCRAIG, KINGUSSIE, INVERNESS-SHIRE PH21 1ND

Enjoy a Highland Welcome and home cooking in our comfortable family home, located on the B9152, 1 mile north of Kincraig Village. Ideal for watersports, walking, touring, bird-watching, skiing, or learning to woodturn, carve or silversmith. Children welcome. Regret no pets. **B&B from £14.00 per person per night. Dinners by arrangement.** *Full details from Sheila Paisley.*

Mr & Mrs J Paisley
Kirkbeag, Milehead
Kincraig
Inverness-shire
PH21 1ND
Tel: (Kincraig) 0540 651298

COMMENDED
Listed

1 Twin 2 Pub. Bath/Show
1 Double

B&B per person
£14.00-£18.00 Single
£13.50-£15.50 Double

Open Jan-Dec
Dinner 1800-2000
B&B + Eve. Meal
£21.50-£23.50

19c church converted to family home. Spiral staircase and craft workshop. Aviemore 5 miles (8kms). Ski slopes 25 minutes. Craft courses available.

KINGSBARNS
Fife
Mrs Farida Hay
Kingsbarns Bed & Breakfast
3 Main Street
Kingsbarns
Fife
KY16 8SL
Tel: (Boarhills) 033488 234

Map 2 E3

COMMENDED
Listed

1 Single 1 Pub. Bath/Show
1 Twin
1 Double
1 Family

B&B per person
£14.00-£16.00 Single

Open Mar-Oct

Family run, 6 miles (10kms) from St Andrews. Off street parking and only 0.5 mile (1km) from the beach. Wide choice of golf courses.

KINGSBURGH
Isle of Skye, Inverness-shire
Mrs MacLean
Iulan Dubh
12 Kingsburgh
Isle of Skye, Inverness-shire
Tel: (Skeabost Bridge)
047032 293

Map 3 D9

1 Single 1 En Suite fac
1 Twin 1 Pub. Bath/Show
2 Double

B&B per person
£13.00-£16.00 Single
£13.00-£18.00 Double

Open Apr-Oct
Dinner 1800-1900
B&B + Eve. Meal
£22.00-£27.00

KINGUSSIE
Inverness-shire
Avondale Guest House
Newtonmore Road
Kingussie
Inverness-shire
PH21 1HF
Tel: (Kingussie) 0540 661731

Map 4 B1

HIGHLY COMMENDED
👑 👑

1 Single 3 En Suite fac
3 Twin 2 Pub. Bath/Show
2 Double
1 Family

B&B per person
£16.00-£19.00 Single
£16.00-£19.00 Double

Open Jan-Dec
Dinner from 1900
B&B + Eve. Meal
£24.00-£27.00

Stone built house with own large garden near centre of village. Friendly atmosphere, ample parking. Skiing and fishing can be arranged.

Sonnhalde Guest House
East Terrace
Kingussie
Inverness-shire
PH21 1JS
Tel: (Kingussie) 0540 661266
Fax: 0540 661266

COMMENDED
👑

1 Single 3 Pub. Bath/Show
2 Twin
2 Double
3 Family

B&B per person
from £16.00 Single
from £16.00 Double

Open Jan-Oct
Dinner from 1830
B&B + Eve. Meal
from £24.50

Warm welcome at Victorian villa overlooking Cairngorms. Home cooking with mainly fresh produce. Natural history. Photographic tours arranged.

J Gibson
Bhuna Monadh, 85 High Street
Kingussie
Inverness-shire
PH21 1HX
Tel: (Kingussie) 0540 661186

Award Pending

1 Twin 2 En Suite fac
1 Double 1 Pub. Bath/Show

B&B per person
£15.00-£18.00 Double

Open Jan-Dec
Dinner from 1900

Mrs Jarratt St Helens, Ardbroilach Road Kingussie Inverness-shire PH21 1JX Tel: (Kingussie) 0540 661430		**HIGHLY COMMENDED** 👑👑	1 Twin 2 Double	2 En Suite fac 1 Priv. NOT ensuite	B&B per person £18.00-£19.00 Double	Open Jan-Dec Dinner from 1900 B&B + Eve. Meal £28.00-£29.00	
			\multicolumn{5}{l}{Stone built house c1895 in elevated position with excellent views over village and to Cairngorm beyond, but only 2 minutes walk from centre.}				

| Mrs A Johnstone
Greystones, Acres Road
Kingussie
Inverness-shire
PH21 1LA
Tel: (Kingussie) 0540 661052
Fax: 0540 661052 | | | 1 Single
1 Double
1 Family | 1 Priv. NOT ensuite
2 Pub. Bath/Show | B&B per person
£14.00-£15.00 Single
£14.00-£15.00 Double | Open Jan-Dec
Dinner from 1900
B&B + Eve. Meal
£22.00-£23.00 | |

GLENGARRY

👑👑 COMMENDED

EAST TERRACE, KINGUSSIE, INVERNESS-SHIRE PH21 1JS
Telephone: 0540 661386

Beautifully situated in its own grounds, this first-class establishment, with an enviable reputation, is located in a quiet, residential area just 5 minutes walk from the centre of town. Rooms are tastefully furnished, and there is ample parking space.

For brochure and details contact: Mel & Ann Short, Proprietors.

Mr & Mrs M B Short Glengarry, East Terrace Kingussie Inverness-shire PH21 1JS Tel: (Kingussie) 0540 661386		**COMMENDED** 👑👑	2 Single 2 Double	1 Priv. NOT ensuite 1 Pub. Bath/Show	B&B per person from £15.00 Single from £15.00 Double	Open Jan-Dec Dinner at 1900 B&B + Eve. Meal from £23.00	
			\multicolumn{5}{l}{Stone built house c1900 with large garden and summer house, in quiet residential area, only a few minutes walk from centre of Kingussie.}				

KINLOCHBERVIE **Sutherland** Mr & Mrs Neame GarbetRooms Kinlochbervie Sutherland IV27 4RP Tel: (Kinlochbervie) 0971 521275 Fax: 0971 521438	Map 3 G3		1 Twin 2 Double 4 Family	5 En Suite fac 1 Pub. Bath/Show	B&B per person £27.00-£32.00 Single £19.00-£24.00 Double	Open May-Sep Dinner 1800-2100	

KINLOCHLEVEN **Argyll** Mrs Robertson Edencoille, Garbhien Road Kinlochleven Argyll PA40 4SE Tel: (Kinlochleven) 08554 358	Map 1 F1	**COMMENDED** 👑	3 Twin	2 Pub. Bath/Show	B&B per person £12.00-£14.00 Double	Open Jan-Dec Dinner 1800-2100 B&B + Eve. Meal £18.00-£22.00	
			\multicolumn{5}{l}{Family home on scenic road from Glencoe. Central for walking, climbing and skiing in the Lochaber area.}				

BUNRANNOCH HOUSE

Kinloch Rannoch, Perthshire
PH16 5QB. Tel: (0882) 632 407

Lovely Victorian house set in 2 acres of grounds on the outskirts of Kinloch Rannoch. A warm welcome awaits you, together with a complimentary tea tray of home cooking on arrival. Comfortable accommodation includes 3 double, 2 twin and 2 family rooms, most en-suite. All rooms have uninterrupted highland views and tea/coffee-making facilities. Two guest lounges. Fire Certificate.

Fishing, walking, cycling, bird-watching, boating and horse riding provide ample choice. Log fires and good cooking.

B&B FROM £16.00.

Mrs J Skeaping Bunrannoch House Kinloch Rannoch Perthshire PH16 5QB Tel: (Kinloch Rannoch) 0882 632407		APPROVED 👑👑	1 Single 1 Twin 3 Double 2 Family	5 En Suite fac 2 Pub. Bath/Show	B&B per person £16.00-£18.00 Single £17.00-£19.00 Double	Open Jan-Dec, exc Xmas/New Year Dinner 1900-2130 B&B + Eve. Meal £28.00-£30.00	
			With supreme hospitality Jenny welcomes you into her warm, friendly home, a former shooting lodge. Taste of Scotland home cooking with local produce				
Mrs Steffen Cuilmore Cottage Kinloch Rannoch Perthshire PH16 5QB Tel: (Kinloch Rannoch) 0882 632218		DELUXE 👑👑👑	1 Twin 1 Double	2 Priv. NOT ensuite	B&B per person to £20.00 Double	Open Feb-Nov Dinner 1900-2100 B&B + Eve. Meal to £40.00	
			Traditional, cosy 18C croft. Best of local produce, own fruit and vegetables, home baking. Taste of Scotland special award winner.				
KINLOCHSPELVE **Isle of Mull, Argyll** Mrs Railton-Edwards Barrachandroman Kinlochspelve Loch Buie Isle of Mull, Argyll PA62 6AA Tel: (Kinlochspelve) 06804 220	Map 1 D2	HIGHLY COMMENDED 👑👑👑	2 Double	2 Priv. NOT ensuite	B&B per person £12.00-£18.00 Double	Open Jan-Dec Dinner 1800-2200 B&B + Eve. Meal £18.00-£24.00	
			Luxuriously converted barn in secluded lochside location, both rooms with private facilities. Accent on fresh fish and seafood.				
KINROSS The Grouse & Claret Heatheryford Kinross KY13 7NQ Tel: (Kinross) 0577 864212 Fax: 0577 864212	Map 2 C3	APPROVED 👑👑👑	2 Twin 2 Double	4 En Suite fac	B&B per person £23.50-£27.50 Single £18.50-£22.50 Double	Open Mar-Jan Dinner 1900-2100 B&B + Eve. Meal £35.00-£40.00	
			Overlooking the trout farm and situated just off the M90 motorway. Annexe accommodation.				

THE MUIRS INN

49 MUIRS, KINROSS KY13 7AU
Telephone: 0577 862270
👑 👑 👑 **Commended**

A quaint Scottish Country Inn — at its best. Offering traditional en-suite bedroom comfort and value for money with award nominated home-cooked country cuisine served at sensible prices in its popular "Maltings" restaurant plus a connoisseur's choice of Scottish Real Ales and Malt Whiskies in addition to the Inn's own branded beers and cyders.

Situated in the Historical Town of Kinross, this well appointed Inn is great for sporting and touring holidays with all Scotland's cities and 120 golf courses within driving distance plus local trout fishing on Loch Leven or walking and pony trekking in the surrounding hills. It's ideal and The Inn is *Really* — Simply Something Special.

The Muirs Inn Kinross 49 Muirs Kinross KY13 7AU Tel: (Kinross) 0577 862270	COMMENDED 👑 👑 👑	2 Twin 3 Double	5 En Suite fac	B&B per person to £35.00 Single £25.00-£27.50 Double	Open Jan-Dec Dinner 1700-2100 B&B + Eve. Meal to £40.00
Scottish country Inn. Award nominated restaurant. Simply something special.					
The Roxburghe Guest House 126 High Street Kinross KY13 7DA Tel: (Kinross) 0577 862498	APPROVED Listed	1 Twin 1 Double 2 Family	1 Pub. Bath/Show	B&B per person from £14.00 Single from £14.00 Double	Open Jan-Dec Dinner 1800-2000 B&B + Eve. Meal from £25.00
Personally run guest house in centre of town. Convenient for touring Perthshire. Close to Loch Leven and Castle.					
Mrs A Bell Hillview House, Gairneybank Kinross Tel: (Kinross) 0577 863802		2 Twin 1 Family	3 En Suite fac 2 Pub. Bath/Show	B&B per person £13.00-£15.00 Single £14.00-£16.00 Double	Open Mar-Nov Dinner 1700-2000 B&B + Eve. Meal £18.00-£22.00
BY KINROSS Mrs W Attewell Devon Bank Crook of Devon, by Kinross Kinross-shire KY13 7UL Tel: (Fossoway) 0577 840367	Map 2 C3	1 Double 1 Family	1 Pub. Bath/Show	B&B per person £13.00-£14.00 Single from £14.00 Double	Open Apr-Oct
Agnes Shand Schichallion Crook of Devon, by Kinross Kinross-shire KY13 7UL Tel: (Fossoway) 0577 840356	COMMENDED Listed	1 Twin 1 Double 1 Family	2 Pub. Bath/Show	B&B per person £15.00 Single £13.00-£14.00 Double	Open Apr-Oct
On the outskirts of the village, a peaceful situation, family home with comfortable rooms. Non smokers preferred.					
KINTORE **Aberdeenshire** Major Frank Rose Wester Tillybin, Leylodge Kintore Aberdeenshire AB51 0YB Tel: (Dunecht) 03306 689	Map 4 G1	1 Single 1 Double	1 Pub. Bath/Show	B&B per person £15.00-£17.00 Single £14.00-£16.00 Double	Open Jan-Dec, exc Xmas/New Year Dinner 1900-2030 B&B + Eve. Meal £22.00-£24.00

KIPPFORD, by Dalbeattie **Kirkcudbrightshire** Orchardknowes Kippford, by Dalbeattie DG5 4LG Tel: (Kippford) 055662 639 Fax: 055662 325	Map 2 B1		1 Single 1 Twin 3 Family	3 En Suite fac 2 Pub. Bath/Show	B&B per person £13.00-£15.00 Single £17.00-£23.00 Double	Open Apr-Oct	

Mrs J Muir Rosemount, On Sea Front Kippford, by Dalbeattie Kirkcudbrightshire DG5 4LN Tel: (Kippford) 055662 214		COMMENDED 👑 👑	2 Twin 2 Double 1 Family	3 En Suite fac 2 Priv. NOT ensuite 2 Pub. Bath/Show	B&B per person from £24.00 Single £18.00-£20.00 Double	Open Feb-Nov Dinner from 1900 B&B + Eve. Meal from £29.00	
Small friendly guest house overlooking the Rough Firth and hills beyond. Smoking and non-smoking lounges.							

Gillian L Williams Boundary Cottage Barnbarroch, by Dalbeattie Kirkcudbrightshire DG5 4QF Tel: (Kippford) 055662 247		COMMENDED 👑 👑	2 Double 1 Family	1 Priv. NOT ensuite 2 Pub. Bath/Show	B&B per person £15.00 Double	Open Jan-Dec	
Detached granite built cottage with large secluded garden. 2 miles (3 kms) from Dalbeattie on Solway coast road near Kippford.							

KIRKBEAN **Dumfriesshire** Mrs J I Ballard Drumpagan Cottage Kirkbean Dumfriesshire DG2 8DW Tel: (Kirkbean) 038788 203	Map 2 B1	Award Pending	2 Twin	1 Pub. Bath/Show	B&B per person £22.00-£25.00 Single £17.50-£19.50 Double	Open May-Sep Dinner from 1830 B&B + Eve. Meal £27.50-£32.50	

KIRKCALDY **Fife** Mrs Linda Duffy Invertiel House, 21 Pratt Street Kirkcaldy Fife KY1 1RZ Tel: (Kirkcaldy) 0592 264849/640103	Map 2 D4	COMMENDED 👑	1 Single 1 Twin 1 Family	1 Pub. Bath/Show	B&B per person £16.00-£18.00 Single £15.00-£18.00 Double	Open Jan-Dec Dinner 1800-1900 B&B + Eve. Meal £24.00-£26.00	
Detached, Victorian, former manse recently refurbished. Large secluded garden with parking. Antique furnishings feature in public rooms.							

Mrs Elizabeth Duncan Bennochy Bank 26A Carlyle Road Kirkcaldy Fife KY1 1DB Tel: (Kirkcaldy) 0592 200733		COMMENDED 👑 👑	1 Twin 1 Double 1 Family	1 En Suite fac 1 Pub. Bath/Show	B&B per person £16.00-£18.00 Single £15.00-£18.00 Double	Open Jan-Dec	
Comfortable accommodation on upper floors of large Victorian house in residential area, close to town centre and railway station. Private parking.							

Mrs B Linton Nor View, 59 Normand Road Dysart, Kirkcaldy Fife KY1 2XP Tel: (Kirkcaldy) 0592 652804/655320			2 Twin 1 Double	1 Pub. Bath/Show	B&B per person £11.00-£12.50 Single £11.00-£12.50 Double	Open Jan-Dec B&B + Eve. Meal from £NNNNNN.NN	

Mrs Nicol Cherrydene 44 Bennochy Road Kirkcaldy Fife KY2 5RB Tel: (Kirkcaldy) 0592 202147		COMMENDED 👑	1 Single 1 Double 1 Family	1 Pub. Bath/Show	B&B per person £13.00-£16.00 Single £14.00-£NN.NN Double	Open Jan-Dec Dinner 1800-2000 B&B + Eve. Meal £21.00-£23.00	
Victorian, end terraced house in quiet residential area, yet within easy reach of all amenities.							

Bob & Vera Scotland Rowan Cottage 5 Melrose Crescent Kirkcaldy Fife KY2 5BN Tel: (Kirkcaldy) 0592 267305			2 Single 1 Twin 1 Double	1 Pub. Bath/Show	B&B per person £12.00-£15.00 Single £12.00-£13.00 Double	Open Jan-Dec	
Mrs Helaine Scott Scotties B&B, 213 Nicol Street Kirkcaldy Fife KY1 1PF Tel: (Kirkcaldy) 0592 268596			2 Twin 1 Family	3 Limited ensuite 1 Pub. Bath/Show	B&B per person £15.00-£17.00 Double	Open Jan-Dec Dinner 1700-1900 B&B + Eve. Meal £21.00-£23.00	
KIRKCOWAN **Wigtownshire** Mrs S Pope Church End, 6 Main Street Kirkcowan Wigtownshire DG8 0HG Tel: (Kirkcowan) 067183 246	Map 1 G1	Award Pending	1 Twin 1 Double 1 Family	3 En Suite fac	B&B per person £13.00-£16.00 Single £13.00-£16.00 Double	Open Jan-Dec Dinner 1900-2030 B&B + Eve. Meal £19.00-£22.00	
KIRKCUDBRIGHT Gladstone House 48 High Street Kirkcudbright DG6 4JX Tel: (Kirkcudbright) 0557 331734	Map 2 A1	HIGHLY COMMENDED 👑 👑	3 Double	3 En Suite fac	B&B per person £24.00-£27.00 Double	Open Jan-Dec	
			Elegance and comfort in sympathetically restored Georgian town house in a quiet corner of the old town. Secret garden.				
Len Rutter Millburn House Millburn Street Kirkcudbright DG6 4ED Tel: (Kirkcudbright) 0557 330926		COMMENDED 👑 👑	2 Twin 1 Double	2 En Suite fac 1 Priv. NOT ensuite	B&B per person £20.00 Double	Open Jan-Dec	
			A warm, friendly welcome awaits you at this small guest house. Listed building, situated in a quiet area close to the centre of the town.				
Mrs I C Sturrock Blue Gate, Atkinson Close 11a High Street Kirkcudbright Tel: (Kirkcudbright) 0557 330785			1 Single 1 Double	1 Pub. Bath/Show	B&B per person £15.00-£17.50 Single £15.00-£17.50 Double	Open Jan-Dec	
KIRKGUNZEON, by Dumfries **Dumfriesshire** Cowans Farm Guest House Kirkgunzeon, Dumfries Dumfriesshire DG2 8JY Tel: (Kirkgunzeon) 038776 284	Map 2 B1		1 Single 2 Twin 2 Family	5 En Suite fac	B&B per person £15.00-£16.50 Single £13.00-£13.50 Double	Open Jan-Dec Dinner 1800-2000 B&B + Eve. Meal £19.00-£22.50	
KIRKMICHAEL **Perthshire** Mrs Finch Cruachan Kirkmichael, Pitlochry Perthshire PH10 7NZ Tel: (Strathardle) 0250 881226	Map 2 C1		1 Twin 1 Double 1 Family	1 En Suite fac 2 Pub. Bath/Show	B&B per person £14.00 Single £14.00-£15.00 Double	Open Jan-Dec Dinner 1900-2000 B&B + Eve. Meal £21.50-£22.50	

Details of Grading and Classification are on page vi. | Key to symbols is on back flap. | 203

KIRKMICHAEL continued Mr & Mrs Mills Ardlebrig Kirkmichael Perthshire PH10 7NY Tel: (Strathardle) 0250 881350	Map 2 C1	APPROVED ♔	1 Single 1 Twin 1 Family	1 Pub. Bath/Show	B&B per person £12.00 Single £12.00 Double	Open Jan-Dec Dinner 1800-2100 B&B + Eve. Meal £18.00	
			Family run B & B, set among the scenic splendour of Perthshire, offering quality home cooking.				
Mr and Mrs A Van der Veldt Curran House Kirkmichael, Blairgowrie Perthshire PH10 7NA Tel: (Strathardle) 0250 881229		COMMENDED ♔ ♔	1 Twin 2 Double	1 En Suite fac 2 Pub. Bath/Show	B&B per person £13.00-£15.00 Single £13.00-£15.00 Double	Open Jan-Nov	
			19c house with large garden in peaceful rural setting, yet only 0.5 miles (1km) from the centre of the village.				
KIRKMUIRHILL, Lesmahagow **Lanarkshire** I H McInally Dykecroft Farm Kirkmuirhill, Lesmahagow Lanarkshire ML11 0JQ Tel: (Lesmahagow) 0555 892226	Map 2 A6	COMMENDED Listed	1 Twin 2 Double	1 Pub. Bath/Show	B&B per person £15.50-£17.00 Single £14.50-£16.00 Double	Open Jan-Dec	
			Modern farmhouse bungalow in rural situation 20 miles (32kms) South of Glasgow.				
KIRKPATRICK FLEMING **Dumfriesshire** Kathleen M Smith Grahamshill Kirkpatrick Fleming, by Lockerbie Dumfriesshire DG11 3BQ Tel: (Kirkpatrick Fleming) 04618 603	Map 2 D10		2 Twin 2 Family	4 En Suite fac	B&B per person £13.50-£15.00 Single £13.50-£15.00 Double	Open Jan-Dec Dinner 1800-2200	
KIRKWALL **Orkney** Sanderlay Guest House 2 Viewfield Drive Kirkwall Orkney Tel: (Kirkwall) 0856 872343 Fax: 0856 876350	Map 5 B1	COMMENDED ♔ ♔	1 Twin 2 Double 2 Family	3 En Suite fac 1 Pub. Bath/Show	B&B per person £12.00-£18.00 Double	Open Jan-Dec	
			Comfortable modern house in quiet residential area on outskirts of town. Some ensuite and 2 self-contained family units.				
Mrs E Bain 6 Albert Street Kirkwall Orkney KW15 1HP Tel: (Kirkwall) 0856 873379			2 Family	1 Pub. Bath/Show	B&B per person £10.00 Single £10.00 Double	Open Jun-Nov	
Mrs M Bain 6 Frasers Close Kirkwall Orkney KW15 1DT Tel: (Kirkwall) 0856 872862		APPROVED ♔ ♔	1 Twin 2 Double	1 En Suite fac 3 Pub. Bath/Show	B&B per person £12.00-£14.00 Single £12.00-£14.00 Double	Open Jan-Dec	
			House of character, situated in quiet lane in the centre of town. Car park adjacent.				
Mrs M Flett Briar Lea, 10 Dundas Crescent Kirkwall Orkney KW15 1JQ Tel: (Kirkwall) 0856 872747		COMMENDED Listed	2 Single 2 Twin	2 Pub. Bath/Show	B&B per person £13.00-£15.00 Single £13.00-£15.00 Double	Open Jan-Dec	
			19C stone built house retaining many original features with large walled garden. Residential area with easy access to town centre.				

Mrs Golding Kemuel, Bignold Park Road Kirkwall Orkney KW15 1PT Tel: (Kirkwall) 0856 873092		COMMENDED ♛	1 Single 1 Twin 1 Double	1 Pub. Bath/Show	B&B per person £12.50-£18.50 Single £12.50-£18.50 Double	Open Apr-Sep Dinner 1900-2130 B&B + Eve. Meal £18.50-£24.50	
			Detached house on main road 10 minutes walk from town centre close to creamery and distillery.				
Mrs M Hourie Heathfield Farmhouse, St Ola Kirkwall Orkney KW15 1TR Tel: (Kirkwall) 0856 872378		COMMENDED ♛	1 Twin 2 Double	1 Pub. Bath/Show	B&B per person £11.50-£13.00 Single £11.50-£13.00 Double	Open Jan-Dec Dinner from 1730 B&B + Eve. Meal £17.00-£19.50	
			Traditional farmhouse on 500 acre working dairy farm 2 miles (3kms) from Kirkwall.				
Mr & Mrs E Linklater Craigwood, Cromwell Road Kirkwall Orkney KW15 1LN Tel: (Kirkwall) 0856 872006		COMMENDED Listed	1 Twin 1 Double	2 Pub. Bath/Show	B&B per person £10.00-£12.00 Single £10.00-£12.00 Double	Open Jan-Dec	
			Warm hospitality. Set in easy walking distance of town centre.				
W A & E P Smith Argyll, Weyland Terrace Kirkwall Orkney KW15 1LS Tel: (Kirkwall) 0856 874858		COMMENDED Listed	1 Double 1 Family	1 Pub. Bath/Show	B&B per person £11.00-£12.00 Single £11.00-£12.00 Double	Open Apr-Mar	
			Comfortable bungalow, overlooking Kirkwall Harbour. 5 minutes walk from the cathedral and town centre.				
Mrs Tonge Orkrest, Annfield Crescent Kirkwall Orkney KW15 1NS Tel: (Kirkwall) 0856 872172		COMMENDED ♛	2 Twin 1 Double	1 Pub. Bath/Show	B&B per person from £14.00 Double	Open Apr-Oct	
			Modern house within walking distance of town centre. Ground floor rooms. Lovely views over the harbour to the North Islands.				
KIRRIEMUIR **Angus** Mrs B Ewart Middlefield House Knowehead Kirriemuir Angus DD8 5AA Tel: (Kirriemuir) 0575 72924	Map 2 D1		1 Single 1 Twin 1 Double	1 Pub. Bath/Show	B&B per person £11.00-£12.50 Single £11.00-£12.50 Double	Open Jan-Dec	
Mrs J Lindsay Crepto, Kinnordy Place Kirriemuir Angus DD8 4JW Tel: (Kirriemuir) 0575 72746		COMMENDED Listed	1 Single 1 Twin 1 Double	1 Pub. Bath/Show	B&B per person £11.50-£12.50 Single £11.50-£12.50 Double	Open Jan-Dec	
			Modern house in quiet cul de sac. 10 minutes walk from centre of town. Gateway to Angus glens.				
Mrs M Marchant The Welton of Kingoldrum Kirriemuir Angus DD8 5HY Tel: (Kirriemuir) 0575 74743		COMMENDED ♛ ♛ ♛	1 Twin 2 Double	1 En Suite fac 1 Pub. Bath/Show	B&B per person £14.00-£17.50 Single £14.00-£17.50 Double	Open Jan-Dec Dinner 1830-2130 B&B + Eve. Meal £21.00-£24.50	
			Self-contained flat on working hill farm. Situated in an Angus glen with panoramic views. Access to local hills.				

BY KIRRIEMUIR **Angus** Mrs D Grimmond Lismore Airlie, by Kirriemuir Angus DD8 5NP Tel: (Craigton) 05753 213	**Map 2** D1	**COMMENDED** Listed	1 Twin 1 Double	1 Pub. Bath/Show	B&B per person £12.00 Single £12.00 Double	Open Apr-Oct Dinner 1900-2100 B&B + Eve. Meal £17.00	

Detached bungalow, in the heart of the country, but within easy reach of Perth, Dundee and Angus glens. Warm welcome. Home baking.

Mrs Myra Miller Braes of Coul Lintrathen, by Kirriemuir Angus DD8 5JR Tel: (Lintrathen) 05756 344			1 Twin 1 Double	1 Pub. Bath/Show	B&B per person £12.00-£13.50 Single £12.00-£13.50 Double	Open Jan-Dec Dinner 1800-2100 B&B + Eve. Meal £20.00-£21.50	
KISHORN **Ross-shire** Mrs A Finlayson An Dail Kishorn Ross-shire IV54 8XB Tel: (Kishorn) 05203 455	**Map 3** F9	**Award** **Pending**	2 Twin 1 Double	1 En Suite fac 2 Pub. Bath/Show	B&B per person £18.00-£20.00 Single £14.00-£17.00 Double	Open Jan-Dec Dinner 1800-2000 B&B + Eve. Meal £21.00-£24.00	
Mrs P Van Hinsbergh Craigellachie, Achintraid Kishorn Ross-shire IV54 8XB Tel: (Kishorn) 05203 253			1 Twin 1 Double	1 Pub. Bath/Show	B&B per person £13.00 Double	Open Apr-Sep Dinner 1800-2000 B&B + Eve. Meal £21.00	
KYLE OF LOCHALSH **Ross-shire** Mr & Mrs Cumine The Old Schoolhouse Licensed Restaurant Erbusaig, Kyle of Lochalsh Ross-shire IV40 8BB Tel: (Kyle) 0599 4369	**Map 3** F1	**Award** **Pending**	2 Double	2 En Suite fac	B&B per person £18.00-£24.00 Double	Open Mar-Nov Dinner 1900-2230	
Mrs I Finlayson Sunnybank, Main Street Kyle of Lochalsh Ross-shire IV40 8DA Tel: (Kyle) 0599 4265			2 Twin 1 Double	1 Pub. Bath/Show	B&B per person £13.00-£15.00 Double	Open Jan-Dec	
Mrs Virginia MacRae Cnocgorm Farm Sallachy, Dornie Kyle of Lochalsh Ross-shire IV40 8DZ Tel: (Kyle of Lochalsh) 059988 227		**APPROVED** Listed	1 Twin 1 Double	1 Pub. Bath/Show	B&B per person £13.00 Double	Open Apr-Oct Dinner 1800-1900 B&B + Eve. Meal from £20.00	

Working hill farm high on hill side overlooking Sallachy and the Loch. About 4 miles (6kms) from Dornie and main road to Isle of Skye.

KYLESKU **Sutherland** Newton Lodge Newton Kylesku Sutherland IV27 4HW Tel: (Scourie) 0971 502070	**Map 3** G4	**HIGHLY** **COMMENDED** 👑 👑 👑	2 Single 2 Twin 4 Double	8 En Suite fac	B&B per person £20.00-£25.00 Single £20.00-£25.00 Double	Open Jan-Dec Dinner 1830-1930 B&B + Eve. Meal £32.00-£37.00	

A large, purpose-built guest house surrounded by an inspiring panorama of mountains and lochs.

KERRACHER
KYLESKU, SUTHERLAND IV27 4HW
Telephone: 05713 288
Remotest DB&B in Britain. Walk 1½ miles with spectacular Highland views to Kerracher Croft House. Completely private setting on the beach with deer, seals, otters and seabirds. For guests, canoeing, boat trips to seal colonies, secluded walks. Superb home cooking, cosy, comfortable rooms, log fires.
Telephone for brochure.

| Mrs L N Ley-Wilson
Kerracher
Kylesku, by Lairg
Sutherland
IV27 4HW
Tel: (Drumbeg) 05713 288 | | | 1 Twin
1 Double | 1 Pub. Bath/Show | B&B per person
from £18.00 Single
from £16.00 Double | Open Jan-Dec
Dinner 1900-2030
B&B + Eve. Meal
from £25.00 | |

Non-Smokers' Sanctuary
"Linne Mhuirich", Unapool Croft Road, Kylesku, via Lairg,
Sutherland IV27 4HW   Tel: 0971 502227
Fiona and Diarmid MacAulay welcome non-smokers to their modern crofthouse, "Taste of Scotland" recommended. Their guests return year after year for the peace, comfort and attention, wonderful views and excellent food. Varied and interesting menus: local fish, seafood, pâtés, soups, casseroles, vegetarian dishes, delicious home baking. 1 twin has private bathroom. EARLY BOOKING ESSENTIAL.

| Mrs F MacAulay
Linne Mhuirich
Unapool Croft Road
Kylesku, via Lairg
Sutherland
IV27 4HW
Tel: (Scourie) 0971 502227 | COMMENDED
👑 👑 | 2 Twin
1 Double | 1 Priv. NOT ensuite
1 Pub. Bath/Show | B&B per person
to £22.50 Single
£17.50-£20.50 Double | Open Easter-Oct
Dinner at 1930
B&B + Eve. Meal
£27.50-£20.50 | |

Friendly and attentive Taste of Scotland recommended croft house.
Peacefully situated near Kylesku Bridge. Directions for walks provided.

| LAIDE
Ross-shire | Map 3
F6 | |

'CUL NA MARA'
SAND PASSAGE, LAIDE, ROSS-SHIRE IV22 2ND
Tel: 0445 731 295
A stay at "Cul Na Mara" (*Gaelic — Song of the Sea*) is an enjoyable experience. Superior bed and breakfast accommodation. Guest rooms fully en-suite and fitted with colour television.
Private dining room — dinner a speciality — fully laid out garden overlooking the Minch. Private parking. *Early booking advisable.*

| Mr & Mrs W T Hart
Cul na Mara, Sand Passage
Laide
Ross-shire
IV22 2ND
Tel: (Aultbea) 0445 731295 | Award
Pending | 1 Double
1 Family | 2 En Suite fac | B&B per person
from £15.00 Double | Open Jan-Dec
Dinner from 1900
B&B + Eve. Meal
from £24.00 | |

Details of Grading and Classification are on page vi.   Key to symbols is on back flap.

LAIDE continued	Map 3 F6		

The Old Smiddy
LAIDE, ROSS-SHIRE IV22 2NB
Telephone: 0445 731425

The Macdonald family, offers you a warm, friendly atmosphere in this delightful country cottage. High standard, home cooking, open fire in guest lounge. Famous Inverewe Gardens 8 miles. Boat hire, loch fishing arranged. Ideal situation for hill, coastal walks and exploring Wester Ross.

Mrs K MacDonald The Old Smiddy Laide Ross-shire Tel: (Aultbea) 0445 731425		HIGHLY COMMENDED ♕ ♕ ♕	1 Double 1 Family	1 En Suite fac 1 Priv. NOT ensuite	B&B per person £15.00-£17.50 Single £15.00-£17.50 Double	Open Jan-Dec Dinner 1830-1900 B&B + Eve. Meal £27.50-£30.00	

Our country cottage on coastal crofting village offers you a warm welcome, home cooking and baking. Loch fishing and boat hire available.

LAIRG Sutherland	Map 4 A6						
Mrs M K Fraser Ambleside, Lochside Lairg Sutherland IV27 4EG Tel: (Lairg) 0549 2130		Award Pending	1 Twin 2 Double	3 En Suite fac	B&B per person £13.50-£15.00 Double	Open Apr-Sep	
Mrs R MacKenzie Carnbren Lairg Sutherland IV27 4AY Tel: (Lairg) 0549 2259		Award Pending	1 Twin 2 Double	1 Pub. Bath/Show	B&B per person from £13.50 Double	Open Jan-Dec	
Mrs B M Paterson Strathwin Lairg Sutherland IV27 4AZ Tel: (Lairg) 0549 2487			1 Double 1 Family	1 Pub. Bath/Show	B&B per person £12.00-£12.50 Double	Open Apr-Sep	
Margaret Walker Park House Lairg Sutherland IV27 4JG Tel: (Lairg) 0549 2208			1 Twin 1 Double 1 Family	3 En Suite fac	B&B per person £15.50-£18.00 Double	Open Jan-Dec Dinner from 1900 B&B + Eve. Meal £25.50-£28.00	

LAMLASH Isle of Arran	Map 1 F7						
Mrs H Driver Glenscorrodale Farm Ross Road Lamlash Isle of Arran KA27 8NX Tel: (Sliddery) 077087 241/ 0770 870241		COMMENDED Listed	1 Single 1 Double 1 Family	2 Pub. Bath/Show	B&B per person from £16.00 Single from £16.00 Double	Open Apr-Oct Dinner from 1800 B&B + Eve. Meal from £21.00	

Traditional stonebuilt farmhouse (C1778) on small working farm amidst scenic Glenscorrodale. Friendly welcome with home cooking.

VAT is shown at 17.5%: changes in this rate may affect prices. Prices shown are for guidance only. Please send SAE with each enquiry.

LANARK	**Map 2 B6**						
Mrs Margaret Allen Roselea, 9 Cleghorn Road Lanark ML11 7QT Tel: (Lanark) 0555 662540		COMMENDED Listed	1 Single 1 Double	1 Pub. Bath/Show	B&B per person £15.00-£16.00 Single £15.00-£16.00 Double	Open Jan-Dec	
			Warm welcome in late Victorian House with many original features. Centrally situated to all amenities. Ideal base for touring. Golfing, fishing.				
Mr & Mrs J Dean Northwoodside Drove Road, Caldwellside Lanark ML11 7SA Tel: (Lanark) 0555 662799			1 Twin 1 Double	1 En Suite fac 1 Pub. Bath/Show	B&B per person £14.00-£17.00 Single £14.00-£17.00 Double	Open Jan-Dec Dinner 1700-1900 B&B + Eve. Meal £22.00-£26.00	

Jerviswood Mains Farm

LANARK ML11 7RL   Telephone: 0555 663987

Good hospitality is offered in this early 19th-century traditional farmhouse, 1 mile from Lanark on the A706, heading northwards. We are near a trout and deer farm and provide good food in a relaxed atmosphere. We combine old world charm with modern amenities.

The unique 1758 industrial village of NEW LANARK, now a world heritage site, and many places of historical interest are nearby, equidistant between Glasgow and Edinburgh. This is an excellent touring base.

Mrs M Findlater Jerviswood Mains Farm Lanark ML11 7RL Tel: (Lanark) 0555 663987		COMMENDED ♛	1 Twin 2 Double	2 Pub. Bath/Show	B&B per person £16.00-£22.00 Single £15.00-£18.00 Double	Open Jan-Dec	
			19C stone built farmhouse of considerable character, 1 mile (2 kms) from historic market town.				
Mrs Faye Hamilton Corehouse Home Farm Lanark ML11 9TQ Tel: (Lanark) 0555 661377		COMMENDED ♛	1 Double 1 Family	1 Pub. Bath/Show	B&B per person £15.00-£16.00 Single £13.00-£15.00 Double	Open Jan-Dec	
			Warm family welcome on traditional mixed farm close to Falls of Clyde and nature reserve.				
Mrs J Lamb Hillhouse Farm, Sandilands Lanark ML11 9TX Tel: (Douglas Water) 055588 661			1 Twin 1 Family	1 Pub. Bath/Show	B&B per person £12.50 Single £12.50 Double	Open Jan-Dec Dinner 1830-2030 B&B + Eve. Meal from £19.00	
Mrs E Young The Old Nursery 77 Braxfield Road Lanark ML11 9BX Tel: (Lanark) 0555 665488 Fax: 0555 665519			1 Double 2 Family	2 En Suite fac 1 Priv. NOT ensuite	B&B per person £22.00-£23.00 Single £19.00-£20.00 Double	Open Jan-Dec	
LANGHOLM Dumfriesshire T Fenwick Border House, 28 High Street Langholm Dumfriesshire DG13 0JH Tel: (Langholm) 03873 80376	**Map 2 D9**		1 Single 1 Twin 1 Double	1 Pub. Bath/Show	B&B per person from £17.00 Single from £18.00 Double	Open Jan-Dec Dinner 1900-2100 B&B + Eve. Meal from £23.00	

	Map 2						
LANGHOLM continued	D9						
Mrs S Geddes Esk Brae Langholm Dumfriesshire DG13 Tel: (Langholm) 03873 80377		COMMENDED Listed	1 Twin 1 Double	1 Pub. Bath/Show	B&B per person £15.00 Single £15.00 Double	Open Apr-Oct	
			Bungalow with own garden in quiet residential area of village, overlooking the River Esk.				
Mr W Riding Whiteshiels Langholm Dumfriesshire DG13 0HG Tel: (Langholm) 03873 80494			1 Twin 1 Family	1 Pub. Bath/Show	B&B per person £11.00-£12.00 Single	Open Jan-Dec Dinner from 1800 B&B + Eve. Meal to £15.00	
LARGS **Ayrshire**	Map 1 G6						
Belmont House 2 Broomfield Place Largs Ayrshire KA30 8DR Tel: (Largs) 0475 676264		HIGHLY COMMENDED 👑 👑	1 Twin 2 Double	1 En Suite fac 2 Priv. NOT ensuite	B&B per person £16.50-£23.00 Double	Open Easter-mid Oct	
			Interesting early 19C house on the waterfront of South Largs with views of Arran, Cumbrae and Bute.				
Lea-Mar Guest House 20 Douglas Street Largs Ayrshire KA30 8PS Tel: (Largs) 0475 672447		COMMENDED 👑 👑	2 Twin 2 Double	4 En Suite fac 1 Pub. Bath/Show	B&B per person £19.00-£20.00 Double	Open Feb-Nov	
			Detached bungalow in quiet area, yet close to town. 100 yards from the promenade and beach. Ideal base for touring.				
Tigh-na-Ligh Guest House 104 Brisbane Road Largs Ayrshire KA30 8NN Tel: (Largs) 0475 673975		COMMENDED 👑 👑 👑	2 Twin 2 Double 1 Family	4 En Suite fac 1 Priv. NOT ensuite	B&B per person £19.00-£20.00 Double	Open Jan-Dec Dinner from 1800 B&B + Eve. Meal £27.00-£28.00	
			Red sandstone house in quiet residential area, close to local amenities and convenient for touring Firth of Clyde area and Burns Country.				

WHIN PARK

16 DOUGLAS STREET, LARGS, AYRSHIRE KA30 8PS   0475-673437

Spacious Guest House in an attractive area of Largs close to the seafront and amidst the scenic beauty of the Firth of Clyde, offers comfortable surroundings and good food. All rooms en-suite with modern facilities. An ideal base for touring or relaxing in a friendly atmosphere.

AA QQQ   *Overseas visitors welcome!*

Whin-Park Guest House 16 Douglas Street Largs Ayrshire KA30 8PS Tel: (Largs) 0475 673437		HIGHLY COMMENDED 👑 👑	1 Single 1 Twin 1 Double 1 Family	4 En Suite fac 1 Pub. Bath/Show	B&B per person from £19.00 Single from £19.00 Double	Open Jan-Dec	
			Warm, comfortable and relaxing atmosphere; near seafront and swimming pool.				

Mrs M L Russell Rutland Guest House 22 Charles Street Largs Ayrshire KA30 8HJ Tel: (Largs) 0475 675642			1 Single 1 Twin 1 Family	2 Pub. Bath/Show	B&B per person from £14.00 Single from £13.00 Double	Open Jan-Dec	
Mrs M Watson South Whittlieburn Farm Brisbane Glen Largs Ayrshire KA30 8SN Tel: (Largs) 0475 675881		COMMENDED 👑 👑	1 Twin 1 Double 1 Family	1 En Suite fac 2 Pub. Bath/Show	B&B per person from £15.00 Single from £14.50 Double	Open Jan-Dec	
				**Working 150 acre sheep farm, warm friendly atmosphere, comfortable rooms. Beautiful quiet location only 5 minutes by car from the centre of Largs.**		

Working 150 acre sheep farm, warm friendly atmosphere, comfortable rooms. Beautiful quiet location only 5 minutes by car from the centre of Largs.

LARKHALL **Lanarkshire** Mrs C Caven Carlin Cottage 109 Machan Road Larkhall Lanarkshire ML9 1HU Tel: (Larkhall) 0698 884084	Map 2 A6		1 Single 3 Twin 1 Family	2 En Suite fac 1 Pub. Bath/Show	B&B per person from £15.00 Single £15.00-£19.00 Double	Open Jan-Dec Dinner from 1800 B&B + Eve. Meal from £21.00	
LASSWADE **Midlothian** Mrs M R Dewton 5 Elm Row Lasswade Midlothian EH18 1AG Tel: 031 663 1741	Map 2 D5		1 Twin 1 Double	1 Pub. Bath/Show	B&B per person £14.00-£16.00 Single £14.00-£16.00 Double	Open Jan-Dec Dinner 1700-1800 B&B + Eve. Meal £19.00-£21.00	
Rosemary M Noble Glenlea, Hawthornden Lasswade Midlothian EH18 1EJ Tel: 031 440 2079			2 Double 1 Family	2 Pub. Bath/Show	B&B per person from £14.00 Single from £13.00 Double	Open Jan-Dec	
Mrs Ann O'Brien Droman House Lasswade Midlothian EH18 1HA Tel: 031 663 9239		APPROVED Listed	1 Single 2 Twin 1 Family	2 Pub. Bath/Show	B&B per person from £13.00 Single from £13.00 Double	Open May-Oct	

Former Georgian Manse in secluded setting. Informal and warm welcome assured. Enclosed parking.

LATHERON **Caithness** Mrs Falconer Tacher Latheron Caithness KW5 6DX Tel: (Latheron) 05934 313	Map 4 D4	Award Pending	1 Double 1 Family	1 En Suite fac 2 Pub. Bath/Show	B&B per person £12.00-£14.00 Single £12.00-£14.00 Double	Open May-Sep Dinner 1700-1830 B&B + Eve. Meal £15.00-£17.00	
Mrs C Sinclair Upper Latheron Farm Latheron Caithness KW5 6DT Tel: (Latheron) 05934 224		HIGHLY COMMENDED Listed	1 Twin 1 Double 1 Family	1 Pub. Bath/Show	B&B per person from £14.00 Single from £13.00 Double	Open May-Sep Dinner 1800-2000	

Farmhouse bed and breakfast with riding/pony trekking available. Fine views of this dramatic coastline.

LAUDER **Berwickshire** Mr P Gilardi The Grange, 6 Edinburgh Road Lauder Berwickshire TD2 6TW Tel: (Lauder) 0578 722649	Map 2 E6	COMMENDED ♛	2 Twin 1 Double	1 Pub. Bath/Show	B&B per person £13.50-£15.00 Single £13.50-£15.00 Double	Open Jan-Dec	

Detached house standing in large garden with lovely views of surrounding countryside. Good home cooking and a warm welcome. A non-smoking house.

BY LAURENCEKIRK **Kincardineshire** Mrs M Anderson Ringwood, Fordoun By Laurencekirk Kincardineshire AB30 1JS Tel: (Auchenblae) 0561 320313	Map 4 G1		2 Double 1 Family	3 En Suite fac	B&B per person £20.00-£22.00 Single £16.00-£18.00 Double	Open Apr-Oct	

LAXDALE **Lewis, Western Isles** Mrs M MacKay 16 Guershader Laxdale Lewis, Western Isles PA86 0DP Tel: (Stornoway) 0851 703463	Map 3 D4	COMMENDED Listed	1 Single 1 Double	1 Limited ensuite 1 Priv. NOT ensuite 2 Pub. Bath/Show	B&B per person £14.00-£16.00 Single £14.00-£16.00 Double	Open Apr-Sep	

Extended croft house, fully renovated, about 1.5 miles (4kms) from Stornoway overlooking the town and sea beyond.

LEACKLEE **Harris, Western Isles** Siamara 6 Leacklee Harris, Western Isles PA85 3EH Tel: (Manish) 085983 314	Map 3 C6	HIGHLY COMMENDED ♛ ♛ ♛	2 Twin 1 Double	3 En Suite fac	B&B per person from £26.00 Single from £26.00 Double	Open Jan-Dec Dinner from 1900 B&B + Eve. Meal from £36.00	

Recently modernised house with warm and friendly atmosphere overlooking Loch Stockinsh. All rooms with private facilities.

LERWICK **Shetland** Bona Vista Guest House 26 Church Road Lerwick Shetland ZE1 0AE Tel: (Lerwick) 0595 2269	Map 5 G4		5 Single 1 Twin	1 En Suite fac 2 Limited ensuite 1 Pub. Bath/Show	B&B per person £19.00-£22.00 Single £17.00 Double	Open Jan-Dec	

Breiview Guest House 43 Kanterstead Road Lerwick Shetland Tel: (Lerwick) 0595 5956		COMMENDED ♛ ♛ ♛	3 Twin 1 Double 1 Family	5 En Suite fac	B&B per person to £23.00 Single to £19.00 Double	Open Jan-Dec Dinner 1800-2000 B&B + Eve. Meal £26.00-£30.00	

Modern house on outskirts of town with fine views. Owner formerly chef on cross channel ferry speaks French and German. All rooms en-suite.

Glen Orchy House 20 Knab Road Lerwick Shetland ZE1 0AX Tel: (Lerwick) 0595 2031		COMMENDED ♛	2 Single 3 Twin 1 Double 1 Family	1 En Suite fac 2 Pub. Bath/Show	B&B per person £20.50 Single £19.50-£22.50 Double	Open Jan-Dec Dinner 1830-2030 B&B + Eve. Meal £29.00-£37.00	

A stone built former manse, situated in quiet residential area, yet only a few minutes walk from town centre.

Name / Address	Grading	Rooms	Facilities	Prices	Open	
Knysna Guest House 6 Burgh Road Lerwick Shetland ZE1 0LB Tel: (Lerwick) 0595 4865	COMMENDED Listed	1 Single 1 Twin 1 Family	1 Pub. Bath/Show	B&B per person £14.00–£16.00 Single £12.00–£13.00 Double	Open Jan-Dec	

Personally run guest house in quiet residential area close to town centre and all amenities. Residents' kitchen available.

Name / Address	Grading	Rooms	Facilities	Prices	Open	
Mrs Gifford 12 Burgh Road Whinrig, Lerwick Shetland ZE1 0LB Tel: (Lerwick) 0595 3554		2 Twin 1 Double	1 En Suite fac 1 Limited ensuite 1 Pub. Bath/Show	B&B per person £14.00–£16.00 Single £12.00–£14.00 Double	Open Jan-Dec	

Name / Address	Map	Grading	Rooms	Facilities	Prices	Open
LETHAM GRANGE by Arbroath, Angus Mrs Mary Soutar Templeton Farm Letham Grange, by Arbroath Angus DD11 4RP Tel: (Gowanbank) 024189 220	Map 2 E1		1 Twin 1 Double 1 Family	2 Priv. NOT ensuite 2 Pub. Bath/Show	B&B per person from £13.00 Single from £13.00 Double	Open Apr-Oct

Name / Address	Map	Grading	Rooms	Facilities	Prices	Open
LEURBOST Lewis, Western Isles Mrs Elizabeth Miller 65 Leurbost Lochs Lewis, Western Isles PA86 9NS Tel: (Crossbost) 085186 483	Map 3 C5	COMMENDED Listed	1 Single 1 Family	1 Pub. Bath/Show	B&B per person £15.00–£16.00 Single £15.00–£16.00 Double B&B + Eve. Meal £22.00–£30.00	Open Jan-Dec Dinner 1750-2050

Comfortable modern home in crofting township beside sea loch. All types of diet catered for including vegetarians.

Name / Address	Map	Grading	Rooms	Facilities	Prices	Open
LEVEN Fife Mrs Hamilton Forth Bay, Promenade Leven Fife KY8 4HZ Tel: (Leven) 0333 23009/ 423009	Map 2 D3		1 Twin 2 Double 1 Family	2 En Suite fac 2 Pub. Bath/Show	B&B per person £12.50–£15.00 Single £12.50–£15.00 Double B&B + Eve. Meal £17.50–£20.00	Open Jan-Dec Dinner 1700-1930

Name / Address	Map	Grading	Rooms	Facilities	Prices	Open
LEVERBURGH Harris, Western Isles Mrs C MacKenzie Garryknowe, Ferry Road Leverburgh Harris, Western Isles PA83 3UA Tel: (Leverburgh) 085982 246	Map 3 B7	COMMENDED 🥂🥂	1 Twin 2 Double	1 En Suite fac 2 Pub. Bath/Show	B&B per person £14.00–£18.00 Double B&B + Eve. Meal £21.00–£25.00	Open Apr-Oct Dinner 1800-2000

Renovated house in the township of Leverburgh. Near sea and passenger ferry to Uist. 21 miles (34kms) from Tarbert.

Name / Address	Grading	Rooms	Facilities	Prices	Open
Mrs MacKenzie Caberfeidh House Leverburgh Harris, Western Isles PA83 3TL Tel: (Leverburgh) 085982 276	COMMENDED Listed	1 Twin 1 Double 1 Family	1 Pub. Bath/Show	B&B per person from £14.00 Single from £14.00 Double B&B + Eve. Meal £20.00–£21.00	Open Apr-Oct Dinner 1800-2000

Detached family house with own garden, in centre of village, overlooking the Millpool.

Name / Address	Grading	Rooms	Facilities	Prices	Open
Mrs Massey St Kilda House Leverburgh Harris, Western Isles Tel: (Leverburgh) 085982 419	HIGHLY COMMENDED Listed	2 Twin	2 Pub. Bath/Show	B&B per person £30.00 Single £20.00 Double B&B + Eve. Meal £30.00–£40.00	Open Jan-Dec Dinner 1900-2000

19th century schoolhouse with views across the Carminish Islands and close to the Uist ferry terminal. Home baking a speciality.

LILLIESLEAF, by Melrose **Roxburghshire** J R Barrington Satchells Farm Lilliesleaf, Melrose Roxburghshire TD6 9JV Tel: (Lilliesleaf) 0835 7335	**Map 2** E6	COMMENDED Listed	2 Double 1 Family	3 En Suite fac 1 Priv. NOT ensuite	B&B per person £15.00 Double	Open Jan-Dec Dinner 1800-2000 B&B + Eve. Meal £20.00-£25.00	
			A traditional working family farm in rural position, 7 miles (11kms) from Hawick. Ideal for children.				
LINICLATE **Benbecula, Western Isles** Inchyra Guest House 27 Liniclate Liniclate Benbecula, Western Isles PA88 5PY Tel: (Benbecula) 0870 2176/ 602176	**Map 3** A9	COMMENDED 🏆🏆🏆	1 Single 3 Twin 1 Double 1 Family	5 En Suite fac 1 Pub. Bath/Show	B&B per person £16.00-£26.00 Single £16.00-£20.00 Double	Open Jan-Dec Dinner 1800-2000 B&B + Eve. Meal £22.00-£34.00	
			Family run guest house, on working croft on main Lochmaddy to Lochboisdale road, about 6 miles (10 kms) from Benbecula airport.				
LINICRO **Isle of Skye, Inverness-shire** Mrs C MacDonald Creagan-Ban Linicro, by Portree Isle of Skye, Inverness-shire IV51 9YN Tel: (Uig) 047042 286	**Map 3** D8		1 Single 1 Twin 1 Double	1 Pub. Bath/Show	B&B per person £14.00-£15.00 Single £14.00-£15.00 Double	Open Apr-Oct	
LINLITHGOW **West Lothian** Mrs W Erskine Woodcockdale Farm Lanark Road Linlithgow West Lothian EH49 6QE Tel: (Linlithgow) 0506 842088	**Map 2** B5		1 Single 1 Twin 1 Family	1 En Suite fac 2 Pub. Bath/Show	B&B per person from £17.00 Single from £14.00 Double	Open Jan-Dec	
Mrs M Findlay 43 Clarendon Crescent Linlithgow West Lothian EH49 6AW Tel: (Linlithgow) 0506 842574			1 Twin 2 Double	1 En Suite fac 1 Pub. Bath/Show	B&B per person £12.00-£15.00 Single £12.00-£15.00 Double	Open Jan-Dec	
Mrs A Hay Belsyde House/Farm Lanark Road Linlithgow West Lothian EH49 6QE Tel: (Linlithgow) 0506 842098 Fax: 0506 847611		COMMENDED 🏆🏆	2 Single 1 Double 1 Family	1 En Suite fac 2 Pub. Bath/Show	B&B per person from £16.00 Single from £16.00 Double	Open Jan-Dec, exc Xmas B&B + Eve. Meal from £25.00	
			Late 18C house set on a 100 acre sheep and cattle farm beside Union Canal. Views over Forth Estuary and Ochil Hills.				

| Anne M Watt
130 Baronshill Avenue
Linlithgow
West Lothian
EH49 7JG
Tel: (Linlithgow) 0506 843746 | | | 1 Single
1 Twin
1 Double | 1 Pub. Bath/Show | B&B per person
from £15.00 Double | Open Apr-Sep | |

| **BY LIVINGSTON**
West Lothian | **Map 2**
C5 | | | | | | |

ASHCROFT FARMHOUSE
EAST CALDER EH53 0ET
Tel: 0506 881810   Fax: 0506 884327

New, tastefully furnished house. All rooms on ground floor. All bedrooms have tea-making facilities plus colour TV. Ashcroft is surrounded by farmland yet only 10m city centre, 6m airport, 5m city bypass and M8/M9. Ideal base for touring, golfing or sightseeing. Early morning tea is provided for guests before they are tempted with a full Scottish breakfast with home-made sausage, local produce and even whisky marmalade. Four-poster bedroom. All bedrooms en-suite.

Derek and Elizabeth Scott extend a warm Scottish welcome to all guests.

★ **Fire Certificate** ★ **AA Selected QQQQ** ★
SORRY NO SMOKING

| Derek and Elizabeth Scott
Ashcroft Farmhouse
7 Raw Holdings
East Calder, by Livingston
West Lothian
EH53 0ET
Tel: (Mid Calder) 0506 881810
Fax: 0506 884327 | **HIGHLY COMMENDED**
👑 👑 | 3 Twin
1 Double
2 Family | 6 En Suite fac | B&B per person
from £22.00 Single
from £18.00 Double | Open Jan-Dec | |
| | | **Large, modern family run bungalow in own grounds with private parking.**
All rooms en-suite. Totally non-smoking. | | | | |

| **LOCHBOISDALE**
South Uist, Western Isles
Mrs M MacDonald
Lochside Cottage
27 Lochboisdale
Lochboisdale
South Uist, Western Isles
PA81
Tel: (Lochboisdale) 08784 472 | **Map 3**
A1 | | 1 Twin
1 Double | 1 Pub. Bath/Show | B&B per person
from £12.50 Single
from £12.50 Double | Open Jan-Dec
Dinner 1830-2100
B&B + Eve. Meal
from £18.00 | |

| Mrs A MacLellan
Riverside
Lochboisdale
South Uist, Western Isles
PA81
Tel: (Lochboisdale) 08784 250
Fax: 08784 380 | | | 1 Single
1 Twin
1 Double | 2 Pub. Bath/Show | B&B per person
from £12.50 Single
from £12.50 Double | Open Jan-Dec | |

| Mrs C MacLeod
Innis Ghorm
422 Lochboisdale
Lochboisdale
South Uist, Western Isles
PA81 5TH
Tel: (Lochboisdale) 08784 232 | **COMMENDED**
👑 | 1 Twin
1 Double | 1 Pub. Bath/Show | B&B per person
£14.00 Single
£14.00 Double | Open Jan-Dec | |
| | | **Croft house situated close to bus route and 0.5 miles (1km) from ferry terminal.**
Washbasins in all bedrooms. | | | | |

LOCHBOISDALE **continued** Mrs Christina MacPhee 363 Leth Meadhanach South Boisdale Lochboisdale South Uist, Western Isles PA81 5UB Tel: (Lochboisdale) 08784 586	**Map 3** A1		1 Twin 1 Double	2 Pub. Bath/Show	B&B per person from £13.00 Single from £13.00 Double	Open Jan-Dec Dinner from 1800 B&B + Eve. Meal from £19.00	
Mrs Murray Brae Lea Lochboisdale South Uist, Western Isles PA81 5TH Tel: (Lochboisdale) 08784 497			2 Single 1 Twin 1 Double	4 En Suite fac	B&B per person £15.00-£20.00 Single £15.00-£20.00 Double	Open Jan-Dec Dinner 1800-2100 B&B + Eve. Meal £22.00-£30.00	
Mrs Morag Walker Karingheidha, Daliburgh Lochboisdale South Uist, Western Isles PA81 Tel: (Lochboisdale) 08784 495			2 Double	2 Limited ensuite 2 Pub. Bath/Show	B&B per person £16.00-£17.00 Single £17.00-£18.00 Double	Open Jan-Dec Dinner 1800-1900 B&B + Eve. Meal £22.00-£25.00	
LOCHCARRON **Ross-shire** Mrs Flora Catto The Creagan Lochcarron Ross-shire IV54 8YH Tel: (Lochcarron) 05202 430	**Map 3** F9	COMMENDED ♛	1 Double 1 Family	1 Pub. Bath/Show	B&B per person from £13.00 Single from £13.00 Double	Open Apr-Oct Dinner 1900-1930	
			Modern bungalow, peacefully situated, with magnificent views **over Loch Carron and the hills beyond.**				
Mrs K Coppock Corrack, Main Street Lochcarron Ross-shire Tel: (Lochcarron) 05202 647			1 Single 2 Twin	2 Pub. Bath/Show	B&B per person £12.50-£14.50 Single £12.50-£14.50 Double	Open Jan-Dec Dinner 1800-2000 B&B + Eve. Meal from £20.00	
Susan Duncan Kinloch House Lochcarron Ross-shire Tel: (Lochcarron) 05202 417		COMMENDED ♛ ♛	1 Double 1 Family	2 En Suite fac	B&B per person £17.50-£20.00 Double	Open Apr-Oct	
			Spacious Victorian house by golf course, near sea loch and village. **All rooms ensuite. Breakfasts to suit your taste.**				
Ms M F Innes Aultsigh, Croft Road Lochcarron Ross-shire IV54 8YA Tel: (Lochcarron) 05202 558		COMMENDED Listed	1 Twin 2 Double	2 Pub. Bath/Show	B&B per person £15.00-£16.00 Single £12.50-£14.00 Double	Open Jan-Dec	
			Detached modern bungalow in elevated position, with magnificent panoramic **views of Loch Carron and hills.**				

Mrs E MacKay Strathardle, Croft Road Lochcarron Ross-shire IV54 8YA Tel: (Lochcarron) 05202 301		COMMENDED 👑 👑	1 Twin 2 Double	1 En Suite fac 1 Pub. Bath/Show	B&B per person £14.00-£16.00 Single £14.00-£16.00 Double	Open Apr-Oct
			Modern, comfortable house with garden, on hillside overlooking village, with views over Loch Carron to hills of Ross-shire.			
Mrs A MacKenzie Chuillinn, Croft Road Lochcarron Ross-shire IV54 8YA Tel: (Lochcarron) 05202 460		COMMENDED 👑 👑	1 Twin 1 Family	1 En Suite fac 1 Pub. Bath/Show	B&B per person £14.00-£17.00 Double	Open Apr-Oct
			New bungalow in quiet location overlooking the village, with fine views across Loch Carron.			
Mrs C Michael Castle Cottage, Main Street Lochcarron Ross-shire IV54 8YB Tel: (Lochcarron) 05202 564		COMMENDED 👑 👑	1 Twin 2 Double	1 En Suite fac 1 Pub. Bath/Show	B&B per person £13.00-£16.00 Double	Open Jan-Dec
			Modernised detached house in village centre with fine views across Loch Carron from all rooms.			
Mr Pillinger Glaisbheinn Lochcarron Ross-shire IV54 8YB Tel: (Lochcarron) 05202 367		COMMENDED 👑	2 Twin 1 Double	2 Pub. Bath/Show	B&B per person £13.50-£15.00 Double	Open Apr-Oct
			Comfortable house overlooking the loch. Traditionally furnished. Centrally heated house with open fire in lounge. TV on request.			
LOCHEPORT **North Uist, Western Isles** Sandra MacLean Glen-Eval, 20 Locheport Lochmaddy North Uist, Western Isles PA82 5EU Tel: (Locheport) 08764 317	Map 3 A8		1 Double 1 Family	1 En Suite fac 1 Pub. Bath/Show	B&B per person from £15.00 Single from £15.00 Double	Open Jan-Dec Dinner 1800-1900 B&B + Eve. Meal from £27.00
LOCHGOILHEAD **Argyll** Shore House Inn Lochgoilhead Argyll Tel: (Lochgoilhead) 03013 340/580	Map 1 G4		1 Single 3 Twin 1 Double 2 Family	2 En Suite fac 1 Pub. Bath/Show	B&B per person £15.00-£16.00 Single £13.00-£18.00 Double	Open Jan-Dec Dinner 1730-2100 B&B + Eve. Meal £21.00-£26.00
LOCHINVER **Sutherland**	Map 3 G5					
Ann H Brown Suilven, Badnaban Lochinver, by Lairg Sutherland IV27 4LR Tel: (Lochinver) 05714 358		COMMENDED 👑	1 Twin 1 Double	1 Pub. Bath/Show	B&B per person £14.50-£19.50 Single to £14.50 Double	Open Jan-Dec Dinner 1830-2000 B&B + Eve. Meal to £24.00
			Bungalow with superb views across Loch Inver. The best of home cooking. Boat trips and sea angling.			
Mr & Mrs McBain Ardglass Lochinver, Lairg Sutherland IV27 4LI Tel: (Lochinver) 05714 257		COMMENDED 👑	1 Single 2 Twin 3 Double 2 Family	3 Pub. Bath/Show	B&B per person £14.00-£15.00 Single £14.00-£15.00 Double	Open Jan-Dec
			Set above this popular fishing village with spectacular harbour, sea and mountain views. Homely atmosphere.			

Details of Grading and Classification are on page vi.

Key to symbols is on back flap.

LOCHMABEN **Dumfriesshire** Mr and Mrs G C Pickering Broomhill Farmhouse Lochmaben Dumfriesshire DG11 1LT Tel: (Dumfries) 0387 811600	Map 2 C9		1 Twin 1 Double	1 Pub. Bath/Show	B&B per person £13.50-£15.00 Single £13.50-£15.00 Double	Open Apr-Nov	
LOCHMADDY **North Uist, Western Isles** Mrs A Morrison Old Bank House Lochmaddy North Uist, Western Isles PA82 Tel: (Lochmaddy) 08763 275	Map 3 A8		2 Single 1 Twin 1 Double	1 Pub. Bath/Show	B&B per person £15.00-£16.00 Single £15.00-£16.00 Double	Open Jan-Dec	
LOCH MAREE, **by Achnasheen, Ross-shire** Mrs I Grant Garbaigh House Loch Maree, by Achnasheen Ross-shire IV22 2HW Tel: (Gairloch) 0445 2412	Map 3 F7	COMMENDED 👑	1 Double 2 Family	2 Pub. Bath/Show	B&B per person £12.50-£13.00 Single £12.50-£13.00 Double	Open Jan-Dec Dinner 1830-1900 B&B + Eve. Meal £20.00-£21.00	
Modernised, detached bungalow on working croft with fine views over Loch Maree to hills beyond. Warm welcome with simple plain home cooking.							
LOCHRANZA **Isle of Arran** Kincardine Lodge Guest House Lochranza Isle of Arran KA27 8HL Tel: (Lochranza) 077083 267/0770 830267	Map 1 E6		2 Twin 2 Double 2 Family	3 En Suite fac 1 Pub. Bath/Show	B&B per person £15.00-£17.00 Single £15.00-£17.00 Double	Open Mar-Oct Dinner 1830-1900 B&B + Eve. Meal £23.00-£25.00	
LOCKERBIE **Dumfriesshire** Rosehill Guest House Carlisle Road Lockerbie Dumfriesshire DG11 Tel: (Lockerbie) 0576 202378	Map 2 C9	COMMENDED 👑	1 Single 1 Twin 1 Double 2 Family	1 En Suite fac 3 Pub. Bath/Show	B&B per person £16.00-£17.00 Single £15.00-£16.00 Double	Open Jan-Dec	
Family guest house in residential area, 5 minutes walk from town centre. Ample car parking.							
Mrs Dempster Castlehill Farm, Tundergarth Lockerbie Dumfriesshire DG11 2PX Tel: (Bankshill) 05767 223		COMMENDED Listed	1 Double 1 Family	2 Priv. NOT ensuite 1 Pub. Bath/Show	B&B per person from £12.00 Single from £12.00 Double	Open Apr-Oct Dinner 1800-2000 B&B + Eve. Meal from £18.00	
Traditional stone farmhouse on 230 acre breeding farm. Home cooking and baking. 3.5 miles (5.5 kms) from Lockerbie. Fishing and golf courses nearby.							
Mrs J Hastings Riggheads Farm Johnstone Bridge Dumfriesshire DG11 1ET Tel: (Johnstone Bridge) 05764 337			1 Twin 1 Family	1 Pub. Bath/Show	B&B per person from £13.00 Single from £13.00 Double	Open Apr-Oct Dinner from 1800	
Mrs C Hislop Carik Cottage Waterbeck, Lockerbie Dumfriesshire DG11 3EU Tel: (Waterbeck) 0461 600652		COMMENDED Listed	1 Twin 2 Double	1 En Suite fac 1 Pub. Bath/Show	B&B per person £12.50 Single £11.50-£14.00 Double	Open Mar-Oct	
Tastefully converted cottage in peaceful rural setting yet only 3 miles (5kms) from the A74. Ideal for touring the Border countryside.							

VAT is shown at 17.5%: changes in this rate may affect prices. Prices shown are for guidance only. Please send SAE with each enquiry.

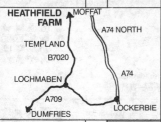

HEATHFIELD FARM
MOFFAT
A74 NORTH
TEMPLAND
B7020
LOCHMABEN
A74
A709
DUMFRIES
LOCKERBIE

HEATHFIELD FARM

TEMPLAND, LOCKERBIE DG11 1HR   TEL: 05764 488

Ideal family accommodation in this tastefully modernised early 18th-century farmhouse enjoying full central heating on our 206-acre dairy farm. Situated 2 miles north of Templand on the B7020 Lochmaben to Moffat Road only a short distance from the A74. It's ideal for an overnight stay. Lovely walks with an abundance of wildlife. Golf, fishing and pony trekking close by.

B&B £14.00

Mrs J M McDougal Heathfield Farm, Templand Lockerbie Dumfriesshire DG11 Tel: (Johnstone Bridge) 05764 488	COMMENDED 👑	1 Twin 1 Family	1 Pub. Bath/Show	B&B per person £13.00-£14.00 Single £13.00-£14.00 Double	Open Mar-Oct

On 206 acre dairy farm with lovely walks and an abundance of wildlife. Golf, fishing and pony trekking nearby.

NETHER BORELAND FARM

BORELAND, LOCKERBIE, DUMFRIESSHIRE DG11 2LL
Telephone: 05766 248

Sample Scottish hospitality. Peaceful, friendly surroundings, hearty breakfasts with our free range eggs and home-made preserves. The spacious comfortable farmhouse has two en-suite bedrooms and one with private bathroom, tea/coffee trays, hair-dryers and clock-radios. En-suites with TV. *Ideal base for touring, golfing, walking or simply relaxing.* **Brochure available.**

Mrs M Rae Nether Boreland Farm Boreland Lockerbie Dumfriesshire DG11 2LL Tel: (Boreland) 05766 248	HIGHLY COMMENDED 👑👑	1 Twin 2 Double	2 En Suite fac 1 Priv. NOT ensuite	B&B per person £18.00-£20.00 Double	Open Mar-Nov

Stone built farmhouse situated beside B723, in centre of small village. Excellent views of surrounding hill country.

Mrs I D Woodburn Bankshill Tundergarth, by Lockerbie Dumfriesshire DG11 2QA Tel: (Bankshill) 05767 694		1 Twin 1 Double	1 Pub. Bath/Show	B&B per person £11.00-£12.00 Single £11.00-£12.00 Double	Open Apr-Oct Dinner from 1800 B&B + Eve. Meal from £16.50

LONGNIDDRY **East Lothian** Mrs M Anderson 5 Stevenson Way Longniddry East Lothian EH32 0PF Tel: (Longniddry) 0875 53395	Map 2 D5	2 Double	1 Pub. Bath/Show	B&B per person to £15.00 Single £12.50-£15.00 Double	Open May-Sep

Mrs Peace Coates Farm Longniddry East Lothian EH32 0PL Tel: (Haddington) 062082 2131	COMMENDED 👑👑	1 Twin 1 Double	1 En Suite fac 1 Priv. NOT ensuite	B&B per person from £17.50 Double	Open Apr-Sep

Set in large garden, on a working arable farm, attractive farmhouse with spacious accommodation. 2 miles (3kms) from the village.

LOSSIEMOUTH **Moray** Mrs M Jean D Cox Mormond, Prospect Terrace Lossiemouth Moray IV31 6JS Tel: (Lossiemouth) 0343 813143	Map 4 D7	HIGHLY COMMENDED	1 Twin 2 Double	2 Pub. Bath/Show	B&B per person £13.00–£14.00 Single £13.00–£14.00	Open Jan-Nov Double	
			Traditional villa in quiet residential area with outstanding view across Moray Firth. Close to all amenities. Friendly, happy atmosphere.				
Mrs Marjorie MacKenzie Moray View, 1 Seatown Road Lossiemouth Moray IV31 6JL Tel: (Lossiemouth) 0343 813915		COMMENDED	1 Twin 2 Double	1 Pub. Bath/Show	B&B per person £16.00–£18.00 Single £12.50–£13.50 Double	Open Jan-Dec	
			350 year old house of character immediately on sea front, overlooking harbour and beach. Convenient for town centre and all amenities.				
Mrs Anne Main Letchworth Lodge Dunbar Street Lossiemouth Moray IV31 6AN Tel: (Lossiemouth) 0343 812132			1 Twin 1 Double 1 Family	1 Pub. Bath/Show	B&B per person £15.00 Single £12.50–£13.50 Double	Open Jan-Dec	
Mrs Frances Reddy Lossiemouth House 33 Clifton Road Lossiemouth Moray IV31 6DP Tel: (Lossiemouth) 0343 813397		COMMENDED Listed	1 Single 1 Double 1 Family	2 Pub. Bath/Show	B&B per person £14.00–£15.00 Single £13.00–£14.00 Double	Open Jan-Dec	
			200 year old former Dower House, situated in its own grounds in the residential area of the town, a mere 2 minute walk from the seafront.				
Mrs Mabel Stewart Skerryhill, 63 Dunbar Street Lossiemouth Moray IV31 6AN Tel: (Lossiemouth) 0343 813035			1 Twin 2 Double	1 Pub. Bath/Show	B&B per person £12.00–£15.00 Single £12.00–£13.00 Double	Open Jan-Dec	
LUIB, by Broadford **Isle of Skye, Inverness-shire** Mrs Dobson Luib House Luib, by Broadford Isle of Skye, Inverness-shire IV49 9AN Tel: (Broadford) 0471 822724	Map 3 E1		1 Twin 1 Double	2 En Suite fac 1 Pub. Bath/Show	B&B per person £10.00–£14.00 Single £10.00–£14.00 Double	Open Jan-Dec Dinner 2000-2100 B&B + Eve. Meal from £15.00	
LUMPHANAN **Kincardineshire** Mrs A E Baker Little Beck, 8 MacBeth Place Lumphanan Kincardineshire AB31 4SG Tel: (Lumphanan) 03398 83480	Map 4 F1	HIGHLY COMMENDED Listed	1 Double 1 Family	1 Pub. Bath/Show	B&B per person to £14.50 Single to £14.50 Double	Open Apr-Oct	
			Friendly welcome at modern bungalow in quiet village on the site of Macbeth's last battle. Close to Castle Trail. 9 miles (14kms) from Banchory.				

LUNAN, by Arbroath **Angus** Mrs A MacKintosh Lunan Lodge Lunan, by Arbroath Angus DD10 9TG Tel: (Inverkeilor) 02413 267 Fax: 02413 435	**Map 2** E1	COMMENDED ♛	2 Twin 1 Double	2 Pub. Bath/Show	B&B per person from £20.00 Single from £15.00 Double	Open Apr-Oct	

Warm welcome at modernised 18C manse in quiet countryside overlooking Lunan Bay. 15 mins walk from sea. 4 miles (5kms) Montrose and Bird Sanctuary.

LUNCARTY, by Perth **Perthshire** Mrs Haddow Ordie House Luncarty, Perth Perthshire PH1 4PR Tel: (Stanley) 0738 828471	**Map 2** C2		1 Twin 2 Double	2 En Suite fac 1 Limited ensuite 1 Pub. Bath/Show	B&B per person £17.00 Single £14.00-£15.00 Double	Open May-Oct B&B + Eve. Meal £20.00-£21.00	

LUSS, by Alexandria **Dunbartonshire** Mrs A Lennox Shantron Farm Cottage Shantron Farm Luss, by Alexandria Dunbartonshire Tel: (Arden) 038985 231 Fax: 038985 239	**Map 1** G4	APPROVED Listed	1 Twin 1 Family	1 Pub. Bath/Show	B&B per person £14.00-£18.00 Double	Open Easter-Sep	

Cottage, in elevated position with superb views over Loch Lomond. Farm is used regularly for film of "Take the High Road".

Mrs J T K Short Ardallie House Luss, by Alexandria Dunbartonshire G83 8NU Tel: (Luss) 043686 272		COMMENDED ♛ ♛	2 Twin 1 Double	2 Pub. Bath/Show	B&B per person £14.00-£18.00 Double	Open Mar-Oct B&B + Eve. Meal £24.00-£28.00	

Charming country house on hillside in woodland garden. Impressive views over Loch Lomond.

Mrs Wragg Glenmollochan Farm Luss Dunbartonshire Tel: (Luss) 0436 86246		COMMENDED ♛ ♛		2 En Suite fac	B&B per person £14.00-£19.00 Double	Open Easter-Oct	

Situated on working sheep farm, 2 miles (3 kms) from Luss. Ensuite bedrooms both with superb views of Loch Lomond.

LYBSTER **Caithness** Mrs Lamont Seaview Mid Clyth, Lybster Caithness KW3 6BA Tel: (Lybster) 05932 513	**Map 4** D4		1 Twin 1 Double	1 Pub. Bath/Show	B&B per person to £12.00 Single to £12.00 Double	Open May-Sep	

MACDUFF **Banffshire** Mrs Kathleen Greig 11 Gellymill Street Macduff Banffshire AB44 1TN Tel: (Macduff) 0261 33314	**Map 4** F7	COMMENDED Listed	2 Double	1 Pub. Bath/Show	B&B per person from £12.00 Single from £11.00 Double	Open Jan-Dec Dinner 1930-2000 B&B + Eve. Meal from £16.00	

Comfortable family home in quiet street near to harbour in small fishing town. Home cooking and baking.

MALLAIG
Inverness-shire
Map 3
E1

Western Isles Guest House East Bay Mallaig Inverness-shire PH41 4QG Tel: (Mallaig) 0687 2320	COMMENDED 👑	1 Single 1 Double 1 Family	3 Pub. Bath/Show	B&B per person £16.00-£18.00 Single £14.00-£16.00 Double	Open Jan-Dec Dinner 1800-1930 B&B + Eve. Meal £24.00-£26.00	

Modern house overlooking the harbour and fishing boats, well situated for ferries to the islands. 4 miles (6kms) from renowned Morar sands.

Mrs J Crocket 1 Loch Nevis Crescent Mallaig Inverness-shire PH41 4QJ Tel: (Mallaig) 0687 2171	1 Twin 1 Double	1 Pub. Bath/Show	B&B per person from £12.00 Double	Open May-Sep	

Mabel Crocket The Moorings Mallaig Inverness-shire PH41 4PQ Tel: (Mallaig) 0687 2225	1 Twin 1 Family	2 Pub. Bath/Show	B&B per person from £10.00 Double	Open Jan-Dec	

May Forbes Glencairn, East Bay Mallaig Inverness-shire PH41 Tel: (Mallaig) 0687 2412	1 Twin 1 Double	2 En Suite fac	B&B per person £16.00-£18.00 Double	Open Apr-Sep	

Mrs C King Seaview Mallaig Inverness-shire PH41 4QS Tel: (Mallaig) 0687 2059	1 Twin 1 Double	2 Pub. Bath/Show	B&B per person £12.00-£14.00 Double	Open Apr-Sep	

John S Summers The Anchorage, Gillies Park Mallaig Inverness-shire PH41 4QU Tel: (Mallaig) 0687 2454	1 Double 1 Family	1 En Suite fac 2 Pub. Bath/Show	B&B per person from £12.50 Double	Open Apr-Sep	

MARKINCH
Fife
Map 2
D3

Mrs C Craig Shythrum Farm Markinch, by Glenrothes Fife KY7 6HB Tel: (Glenrothes) 0592 758372	COMMENDED Listed	1 Twin 1 Family	1 Pub. Bath/Show	B&B per person £14.00-£15.00 Single £14.00-£15.00 Double	Open Jan-Dec Dinner from 1800 B&B + Eve. Meal £22.00-£23.00	

Farm with some buildings dating from Mary Queen of Scots. Balgonie Castle 0.5 miles (1km), Falkland Palace 5 miles (8kms), Glenrothes 2 miles (3kms)

MARYBANK, by Muir of Ord **Ross-shire** Mrs J S Bell Birchgrove, Arcan Marybank, by Muir of Ord Ross-shire IV6 7UL Tel: (Urray) 09973 245	Map 4 A8		1 Double 1 Family	1 Pub. Bath/Show	B&B per person £13.50-£14.50 Single £13.50-£14.50 Double	Open Easter-Oct Dinner from 1900 B&B + Eve. Meal £21.50-£22.50	
Mrs E Gammie Wester Balloan Farm Marybank, by Muir of Ord Ross-shire IV6 7UU Tel: (Urray) 09973 212			1 Twin 2 Double	2 Pub. Bath/Show	B&B per person £13.00-£14.00 Single £13.00-£14.00 Double	Open Apr-Oct	
MARYBURGH **Ross-shire** Mrs P Whyte Corriegarth, 9 Proby Street Maryburgh, Dingwall Ross-shire IV7 8DZ Tel: (Dingwall) 0349 61936	Map 4 A8		1 Twin 1 Family	1 En Suite fac 1 Limited ensuite 1 Pub. Bath/Show	B&B per person £11.50-£15.00 Double	Open May-Sep	
MAUCHLINE **Ayrshire** Mrs M MacMillan Knowehead Mauchline Ayrshire KA5 6EY Tel: (Mauchline) 0290 50566	Map 1 H7		1 Single 1 Twin 1 Double	2 Priv. NOT ensuite 3 Pub. Bath/Show	B&B per person from £12.50 Single from £12.50 Double	Open Jan-Dec	
Mrs Smith Dykefield Farm Mauchline Ayrshire KA5 6EY Tel: (Mauchline) 0290 50328		**APPROVED** Listed	1 Double 1 Family	1 Pub. Bath/Show	B&B per person from £10.00 Double	Open Jan-Dec Dinner 1800-2200 B&B + Eve. Meal from £15.00	
			Working dairy farm, 2 miles (3kms) from Mauchline in the centre of Burns country. **Evening meal and home baking.**				
MAUD, by Peterhead **Aberdeenshire** Mrs Burdon Horsedrawn Holidays Tillypestle Maud, Peterhead Aberdeenshire AB42 8PB Tel: (Maud) 07714 422	Map 4 G8		1 Twin 1 Double	1 Pub. Bath/Show	B&B per person £12.00-£15.00 Double	Open Jan-Dec B&B + Eve. Meal £17.00-£20.00	
MAYBOLE **Ayrshire** Mrs J McKellar Homelea, 62 Culzean Road Maybole Ayrshire KA19 8AH Tel: (Maybole) 0655 82736 Fax: 0655 83557	Map 1 G8		1 Double 1 Family	2 Pub. Bath/Show	B&B per person from £15.00 Single from £13.50 Double	Open Mar-Oct	

MEIGLE **Perthshire** Ray & May Eskdale Stripside, Longleys Meigle Perthshire PH12 8QX Tel: (Meigle) 08284 388	Map 2 D1	COMMENDED 👑 👑 👑	1 Twin 2 Double	3 En Suite fac	B&B per person £15.00-£16.00 Double	Open Jan-Dec Dinner 1830-2000 B&B + Eve. Meal £22.00-£23.00

Renovated farmhouse with a ground floor bedroom, set back from the A94. Open rural views. Registered cattery.

MELROSE **Roxburghshire** Dunfermline House Guest House Buccleuch Street Melrose Roxburghshire TD6 9LB Tel: (Melrose) 089682 2148	Map 2 E6	HIGHLY COMMENDED 👑 👑	1 Single 2 Twin 2 Double	4 En Suite fac 1 Priv. NOT ensuite	B&B per person £19.00-£20.00 Single £19.00-£20.00 Double	Open Jan-Dec

Comfortable family home overlooking Melrose Abbey. Ideal base for touring Scott country and Edinburgh. No smoking.

Mrs M Aitken The Gables, Darnick Melrose Roxburghshire TD6 9AL Tel: (Melrose) 089682 2479	COMMENDED 👑	1 Single 1 Twin 1 Double	1 Pub. Bath/Show	B&B per person £14.00-£15.00 Single £14.00-£15.00 Double	Open Jan-Dec Dinner 1800-1930 B&B + Eve. Meal £22.00-£23.00

Georgian villa in centre of quiet village, 1 mile (2kms) from Melrose. Ideal base for touring the borders. 14 golf courses easily accessible.

Mrs E M Cripps Chiefswood, Chiefswood Road Melrose Roxburghshire TD6 9BA Tel: (Melrose) 089682 2172	COMMENDED 👑 👑	1 Twin 1 Double	1 En Suite fac 1 Priv. NOT ensuite	B&B per person £16.00-£18.00 Double	Open Apr-Sep

Set in 9 acres of grounds, a delightful house once occupied by the daughter of Sir Walter Scott.

Mrs Christine Dalgetty Little Fordel, Abbey Street Melrose Roxburghshire TD6 9PX Tel: (Melrose) 089682 2206	COMMENDED 👑 👑	1 Twin 1 Double	2 En Suite fac	B&B per person £18.00-£19.00 Double	Open Jan-Dec

Former school house, quietly situated near the centre of town, own car parking in rear courtyard.

Mrs G Graham Craigard, Huntly Avenue Melrose Roxburghshire TD6 9SD Tel: (Melrose) 089682 2041	HIGHLY COMMENDED 👑	1 Twin 1 Double	1 Pub. Bath/Show	B&B per person £15.00 Double	Open Jan-Dec

Modern spacious bungalow in quiet part of town, yet only 5 minutes walk from town centre and Abbey.

Mrs M Graham Braidwood, Buccleuch Street Melrose Roxburghshire TD6 9LD Tel: (Melrose) 089682 2488	HIGHLY COMMENDED 👑	1 Single 1 Twin 1 Double	1 En Suite fac 1 Pub. Bath/Show	B&B per person £15.00 Single £15.00-£18.00 Double	Open Jan-Dec Dinner 1800-1930 B&B + Eve. Meal £22.00-£25.00

Friendly welcome in attractive Listed town house only a stone's throw from Melrose Abbey and Priorwood Gardens. Home baking.

Mrs E Haldane Priory View, 15 Priors Walk Melrose Roxburghshire TD6 9RB Tel: (Melrose) 089682 2087	COMMENDED Listed	2 Double	1 Pub. Bath/Show	B&B per person £14.00-£15.00 Double	Open Jan-Dec Dinner from 1800 B&B + Eve. Meal £22.00-£24.00

Situated in quiet residential area with views to Abbey, and a short distance from the centre of Melrose.

Mrs A Paterson Fiorlin, Abbey Street Melrose Roxburghshire TD6 9PX Tel: (Melrose) 0896 822984		COMMENDED 👑 👑	1 Double 1 Family	2 En Suite fac	B&B per person £20.00-£22.00 Single £18.00-£20.00 Double	Open Jan-Dec
			Modern detached house set in quiet residential area with private parking. Convenient for town centre and restaurants, ideal touring base.			
Mrs Schofield Torwood Lodge High Cross Avenue Melrose Roxburghshire TD6 9SU Tel: (Melrose) 089682 2220		COMMENDED 👑 👑	1 Twin 1 Double	2 En Suite fac	B&B per person £18.00-£19.00 Double	Open Jan-Dec
			Large comfortable Victorian family house in attractive location. Easy walking distance to town, River Tweed and Eildon Hills. Private facilities.			
Mrs S Sugden Collingwood, Waverley Road Melrose Roxburghshire TD6 9AA Tel: (Melrose) 089682 2670		COMMENDED 👑 👑	2 Twin 1 Double	2 En Suite fac 1 Priv. NOT ensuite	B&B per person £25.00 Single £18.00-£20.00 Double	Open Mar-Oct
			Detached Victorian house on outskirts of Melrose with enclosed garden and good parking.			
MELVICH **Sutherland** Shieling Guest House Melvich Sutherland KW14 7YJ Tel: (Melvich) 06413 256 Fax: 06413 356	Map 4 B3	HIGHLY COMMENDED 👑 👑 👑	1 Twin 2 Double	2 En Suite fac 1 Priv. NOT ensuite 2 Pub. Bath/Show	B&B per person £20.00-£22.00 Double	Open Apr-Sep Dinner 1800-2030 B&B + Eve. Meal £32.00-£35.00
			Genuine Highland hospitality, home cooked meals, choice of menu. Spectacular views over bay. Picture window in coffee lounge; separate TV lounge.			
METHLICK **Aberdeenshire** Mrs C Staff Sunnybrae Farm, Gight Methlick, Ellon Aberdeenshire AB41 0JA Tel: (Methlick) 0651 806456	Map 4 G9	APPROVED 👑 👑	1 Single 1 Twin 1 Double	2 En Suite fac	B&B per person £15.00-£18.00 Single £15.00-£18.00 Double	Open Jan-Dec B&B + Eve. Meal £NNNNNN.NN
			Traditional croft on working farm, in rural position offering magnificent views. Situated on the Methlick - Fyvie Road (B9005).			
MEY **Caithness** Mrs M MacKay The Hawthorns Mey KW14 8XL Tel: (Barrock) 084785 710	Map 4 D2		1 Twin 2 Double	3 En Suite fac 1 Pub. Bath/Show	B&B per person £13.00-£15.00 Double	Open Jan-Dec Dinner 1800-2000 B&B + Eve. Meal £20.00-£22.00
MILNGAVIE, Glasgow Mrs E J Chapman Arnish, 14 Blane Drive Milngavie, Glasgow G62 8HG Tel: 041 956 1767	Map 1 H5		1 Single 1 Twin	1 Pub. Bath/Show	B&B per person £13.00-£14.00 Single £14.00 Double	Open Jan-Dec Dinner 1800-1900 B&B + Eve. Meal £19.00-£21.00

Establishment	Map	Grade	Accommodation	Facilities	Prices	Opening
MILNGAVIE, Glasgow continued Mrs O Daly 93 Drumlin Drive Milngavie, Glasgow G62 6NF Tel: 041 956 1596	Map 1 H5		1 Twin 1 Double	1 En Suite fac 1 Limited ensuite 2 Pub. Bath/Show	B&B per person £16.00-£18.00 Single £16.00-£18.00 Double	Open Jan-Dec
Graneag House 55 Drumlin Drive Milngavie, Glasgow G62 Tel: 041 956 6681			1 Twin 2 Double	1 En Suite fac 1 Pub. Bath/Show	B&B per person £14.50-£16.50 Single £14.50-£16.50 Double	Open Jan-Dec
Mrs G Groves 58 Keystone Quadrant Milngavie, Glasgow G62 6LP Tel: 041 956 5615			1 Single 1 Twin	1 Pub. Bath/Show	B&B per person £14.00-£15.00 Single £14.00-£16.00 Double	Open Jan-Dec Dinner 1700-1900 B&B + Eve. Meal from £20.00
J M & J G McColl Westview 1 Dougalston Gardens South Milngavie, Glasgow G62 Tel: 041 956 5973			2 Twin 1 Double	3 En Suite fac	B&B per person to £17.00 Single to £15.00 Double	Open Jan-Dec
MINARD, by Inveraray Argyll Mrs J MacVicar Victoria House Minard, by Inveraray Argyll PA32 8YB Tel: (Minard) 0546 86224	Map 1 F4	COMMENDED	1 Single 2 Double	1 Pub. Bath/Show	B&B per person £12.50-£13.50 Single £12.50-£13.50 Double	Open Apr-Oct
			Stone built villa in centre of village with uninterrupted views over Loch Fyne.			
MINTLAW Aberdeenshire Mrs J M Scroggie Ivydene, Mintlaw Station Mintlaw, by Peterhead Aberdeenshire AB42 8EB Tel: (Mintlaw) 0771 23118	Map 4 H8		1 Single 1 Twin 1 Double 1 Family	1 Pub. Bath/Show	B&B per person £12.00 Single £12.00 Double	Open Jan-Dec Dinner 1800-2100 B&B + Eve. Meal £17.00
MOFFAT Dumfriesshire Barnhill Springs Country Guest House Moffat Dumfriesshire DG10 Tel: (Moffat) 0683 20580	Map 2 C8	COMMENDED	2 Twin 2 Double 1 Family	1 Priv. NOT ensuite 2 Pub. Bath/Show	B&B per person £17.50-£19.50 Single £17.50-£19.50 Double	Open Jan-Dec Dinner from 1830 B&B + Eve. Meal £28.00-£30.00
			Early Victorian country house, ideally situated for walking the Southern Upland Way. Access from A74 via South bound slip road at Moffat junction.			
Ivy Cottage Guest House High Street Moffat Dumfriesshire DG10 9HG Tel: (Moffat) 0683 20279			2 Twin 1 Double 1 Family	1 Pub. Bath/Show	B&B per person £14.50-£16.50 Single from £14.50 Double	Open Jan-Dec

| Rockhill Guest House
14 Beech Grove
Moffat
Dumfriesshire
DG10 9RS
Tel: (Moffat) 0683 20283 | COMMENDED
👑 👑 | 2 Single
1 Twin
3 Double
4 Family | 5 En Suite fac
2 Pub. Bath/Show | B&B per person
£15.00-£18.00 Single
£15.00-£18.00 Double | Open Jan-Nov
Dinner from 1830
B&B + Eve. Meal
£21.50-£25.00 | |

Victorian house overlooking bowling green and park, in quiet area close to town centre. Open outlook to hills. Own private car park, ensuite rooms.

| Mrs Eileen Baty
Thai-Ville, 3 Dundanion Place
Moffat
Dumfriesshire
DG10 9GD
Tel: (Moffat) 0683 20922 | DELUXE
👑 👑 | 2 Twin | 2 En Suite fac | B&B per person
£15.00 Double | Open Mar-Nov | |

Modern detached bungalow with individual style, in quiet residential area, close to town centre. Warm and friendly welcome, en suite rooms.

| Mrs K Clarke
Hopetoun House
Academy Road
Moffat
Dumfriesshire
DG10 9HW
Tel: (Moffat) 0683 21251 | | 1 Twin
2 Double | 1 Pub. Bath/Show | B&B per person
£13.50 Single
£13.50 Double | Open Jan-Dec | |

| Mrs Durno
St Nicolas House
Ballplay Road
Moffat
Dumfriesshire
DG10 9JU
Tel: (Moffat) 0683 20274 | | 1 Twin
2 Double | 2 En Suite fac
1 Limited ensuite | B&B per person
£15.00 Single
£14.00-£16.00 Double | Open Mar-Oct
Dinner from 1830
B&B + Eve. Meal
£22.00-£24.00 | |

| Mrs Gourlay
Fernhill, Grange Road
Moffat
Dumfriesshire
DG10 9HT
Tel: (Moffat) 0683 20077 | DELUXE
👑 👑 | 1 Twin
1 Double | 2 Pub. Bath/Show | B&B per person
to £20.00 Single
£14.00-£16.00 Double | Open May-Sep | |

Every comfort and care in this quietly situated house in delightful gardens, a few minutes walk from town centre.

| Gary Hall
The Lodge,
Sidmount Avenue, Well Road
Moffat
Dumfriesshire
DG10 9BS
Tel: (Moffat) 0683 20440 | | 1 Twin
1 Double
1 Family | 1 Limited ensuite
1 Pub. Bath/Show | B&B per person
£13.00-£15.00 Single
£13.00-£15.00 Double | Open Jan-Dec | |

| Mrs Jackson
Woodhead Farm
Moffat
Dumfriesshire
DG10 9LU
Tel: (Moffat) 0683 20225 | HIGHLY
COMMENDED
👑 👑 👑 | 2 Twin
1 Double | 3 En Suite fac | B&B per person
to £35.00 Single
£22.50-£25.00 Double | Open Jan-Dec
Dinner 1900-2000
B&B + Eve. Meal
£35.50-£38.00 | |

Luxuriously furnished farmhouse situated on 220 acre working stock farm and commanding panoramic views of the surrounding countryside. All ensuite.

| Robert H Jackson
Ericstane
Moffat
Dumfriesshire
DG10 9LT
Tel: (Moffat) 0683 20127 | COMMENDED
👑 👑 | 1 Twin
1 Double | 1 En Suite fac
1 Priv. NOT ensuite | B&B per person
from £15.00 Single
from £20.00 Double | Open Jan-Dec | |

Tastefully restored period farmhouse in peaceful valley, 4 miles (6kms) from Moffat. An ideal base for hill walking.

| Mrs Jappy
Craigie Lodge, Ballplay Road
Moffat
Dumfriesshire
DG10 9JU
Tel: (Moffat) 0683 21037 | COMMENDED
👑 👑 | 1 Twin
1 Double
1 Family | 3 En Suite fac | B&B per person
£15.00-£16.50 Double | Open Mar-Nov
Dinner from 1830
B&B + Eve. Meal
£24.00-£26.00 | |

Large Victorian family house set in mature ½ acre garden. All rooms private facilities. Reduced rates 3 days.

Details of Grading and Classification are on page vi.

Key to symbols is on back flap.

MOFFAT

MOFFAT continued	Map 2 C8						
Evelyn Lindsay Alba House, 20 Beechgrove Moffat Dumfriesshire DG10 9RS Tel: (Moffat) 0683 20418	DELUXE 👑 👑	1 Twin 1 Double 1 Family	3 En Suite fac	B&B per person £16.50 Double		Open Apr-Oct	
		On outskirts of town, a delightful old house c1830 with beamed dining room, inglenook, colourful garden. Warm and friendly welcome.					
Mrs S Long Coxhill Farm, Old Carlisle Road Moffat Dumfriesshire DG10 9QN Tel: (Moffat) 0683 20471	HIGHLY COMMENDED 👑 👑	1 Twin 2 Double	3 Pub. Bath/Show	B&B per person £20.00 Single £15.00-£18.00 Double		Open Mar-Oct Dinner at 1900 B&B + Eve. Meal £25.00-£30.00	
		Modern farmhouse in peaceful setting with fine views over open countryside 1 mile (2kms) from Moffat.					

BROOMLANDS FARM
BEATTOCK, MOFFAT, DUMFRIES-SHIRE DG10 9PQ
Telephone: 06833 320

A lovely spacious farmhouse in the scenic Annandale Valley, only 2 miles from the popular town of Moffat. An ideal base for touring, golfing, walking, fishing. High standard bedrooms, all en-suite, colour TV, tea/coffee facilities. Convenient for A/M74. Safe private parking. Personal attention, wonderful breakfasts.

B&B from £16 per person.

Mrs K Miller Broomlands Farm Beattock, Moffat Dumfriesshire DG10 9PQ Tel: (Beattock) 06833 320	HIGHLY COMMENDED 👑 👑	1 Single 1 Twin 1 Double	3 En Suite fac	B&B per person from £18.00 Single from £16.00 Double		Open Apr-Oct	
		Farmhouse on a working 200 acre mixed farm. Convenient to A74 and 2 miles (3kms) from Moffat. Self catering cottage available.					
Mrs Vivienne Murray Queensberry House 12 Beechgrove Moffat Dumfriesshire DG10 9RS Tel: (Moffat) 0683 20538	HIGHLY COMMENDED 👑 👑	3 Double	3 En Suite fac	B&B per person £15.00 Double		Open Feb-Nov	
		Recently refurbished Victorian house in quiet area opposite park and bowling green and within a few minutes walk of the town centre.					
Mrs P Pirie Annavah, 23 Beechgrove Moffat Dumfriesshire DG10 9RS Tel: (Moffat) 0683 20550	HIGHLY COMMENDED 👑	2 Twin 1 Double	1 Pub. Bath/Show	B&B per person £14.00-£14.50 Double		Open Easter-Oct Dinner 1800-1930 B&B + Eve. Meal £22.00-£22.50	
		Attractive and quietly situated opposite the park, 5 minutes walk from the centre. Home cooking using fresh local produce when available.					
Mr & Mrs A Poynton Gilbert House, Beechgrove Moffat Dumfriesshire DG10 9RS Tel: (Moffat) 0683 20050	HIGHLY COMMENDED 👑 👑 👑	1 Single 1 Twin 1 Double 3 Family	4 En Suite fac 2 Limited ensuite 1 Pub. Bath/Show	B&B per person £15.00-£18.00 Single £15.00-£18.00 Double		Open Jan-Dec Dinner from 1830 B&B + Eve. Meal £24.00-£27.00	
		Spacious family run guest house in quiet position, 5 minutes walk from the town centre. Fresh local produce used when available.					
I Toni Villa Toscana, Alton Road Moffat Dumfriesshire DG10 9LB Tel: (Moffat) 0683 20358	COMMENDED 👑 👑	2 Twin 1 Double	3 En Suite fac	B&B per person to £20.00 Single to £16.00 Double		Open Apr-Oct	
		Modern family home with large quiet garden in residential area, close to town centre.					

Mrs G T Walker Springbank, Beechgrove Moffat Dumfriesshire DG10 9RS Tel: (Moffat) 0683 20070		HIGHLY COMMENDED	1 Twin 1 Double	2 Pub. Bath/Show	B&B per person from £13.00 Double	Open Mar-Nov	

Early 19C detached house in quiet residential area. Home baking a speciality. Private parking and colourful garden.

Mrs B C Williams Corehead Farm, Annanwater Moffat Dumfriesshire DG10 9LT Tel: (Moffat) 0683 20973/21087		HIGHLY COMMENDED	1 Twin 1 Double	2 En Suite fac	B&B per person from £25.00 Single £21.00-£23.00 Double	Open Mar-Oct Dinner 1830-1900 B&B + Eve. Meal £33.00-£36.00	

Stone farmhouse dating in part from 16C. Rural location 5 miles (8kms) from Moffat. Excellent views of hills and Devils Beef Tub. Taste of Scotland.

Mrs Wilson Longbedholm Farm Moffat Dumfriesshire DG10 9SN Tel: (Beattock) 06833 414		APPROVED Listed	2 Twin 1 Double	1 Pub. Bath/Show	B&B per person £15.00-£20.00 Double	Open Jan-Dec Dinner 1800-1900 B&B + Eve. Meal £23.00-£28.00	

Traditional farmhouse c1700's in open countryside adjacent to A74. Ideal stopover travelling north or south.

MONIAIVE **Dumfriesshire** Mrs Alison Boon Bainoon, High Street Moniaive Dumfriesshire DG3 4HN Tel: (Moniaive) 08482 266	Map 2 A9	COMMENDED Listed	2 Single 1 Family	1 Pub. Bath/Show	B&B per person £12.00 Single £12.00 Double	Open Jan-Nov	

In the centre of a small village, a warm and friendly welcome is assured at this 250 year old family home. Home-baking. Enclosed garden.

MONREITH, by Port William **Wigtownshire** Mr & Mrs B Hayes Larroch Cottage Monreith Wigtownshire DG8 8NH Tel: (Port William) 09887 520	Map 1 H1		1 Twin 2 Double	1 Pub. Bath/Show	B&B per person £11.50-£13.50 Single £11.50-£13.50 Double	Open Jan-Dec	

MONTGREENAN **by Kilwinning, Ayrshire** Mrs K Melville Tarcoola, Montgreenan Kilwinning Ayrshire KA13 7QZ Tel: (Torranyard) 0294 85379 Fax: 0294 85379	Map 1 G6	COMMENDED Listed	1 Single 1 Double	1 Pub. Bath/Show	B&B per person £12.50-£13.50 Single £12.50-£13.50 Double	Open Jan-Dec	

Modern bungalow in peaceful country setting. Ideal centre for touring Ayrshire and the Clyde Coast. 30 minutes drive from Glasgow.

MONTROSE **Angus** Cranes Meadow Guest House 28 The Mall Montrose Angus DD10 8NW Tel: (Montrose) 0674 72296	Map 2 E1		1 Single 1 Twin 2 Double 2 Family	4 Limited ensuite 3 Pub. Bath/Show	B&B per person from £16.00 Single £14.00-£15.00 Double	Open Jan-Dec	

The Limes Guest House 15 King Street Montrose Angus DD10 8NL Tel: (Montrose) 0674 77236 Fax: 0674 77236		COMMENDED	2 Single 4 Twin 4 Double 2 Family	4 En Suite fac 4 Limited ensuite 2 Priv. NOT ensuite 3 Pub. Bath/Show	B&B per person from £18.00 Single from £16.50 Double	Open Jan-Dec Dinner from 1800	

Family run, centrally situated in quiet, residential part of town. A few minutes walk from the centre, railway station and beach. Private parking..

Details of Grading and Classification are on page vi.

Key to symbols is on back flap.

MONTROSE continued	Map 2 E1						
Murray Lodge 2-8 Murray Street Montrose Angus DD10 8LB Tel: (Montrose) 0674 78880 Fax: 0674 78877	Award Pending	4 Single 3 Twin 5 Double	12 En Suite fac	B&B per person £23.50-£35.25 Single £20.56-£23.50 Double	Open Jan-Dec Dinner 1730-1900 B&B + Eve. Meal £27.00-£42.00	
Oaklands Guest House 10 Rossie Island Road Montrose Angus DD10 9NN Tel: (Montrose) 0674 72018	COMMENDED ≋ ≋	1 Single 3 Twin 2 Double 1 Family	4 En Suite fac 1 Pub. Bath/Show	B&B per person from £15.00 Single £14.00-£17.00 Double	Open Jan-Dec	
		En suite facilities available at this comfortable family house within walking distance of Montrose town centre. Parking. Boat fishing available.				
Mrs M Docherty Byeways, 11 Rossie Terrace Ferryden, by Montrose Angus DD10 9RX Tel: (Montrose) 0674 78510	COMMENDED ≋ ≋	1 Twin 2 Double	1 En Suite fac 2 Pub. Bath/Show	B&B per person £12.00-£16.00 Double	Open Apr-Dec	
		Situated in quiet coastal fishing village. Walks, fishing and agate collection from beach. Comfortable accommodation.				
Mrs H Robertson Stone of Morphie Montrose Angus DD10 0AA Tel: (Hillside) 067483 388	COMMENDED Listed	2 Twin 1 Family	1 Pub. Bath/Show	B&B per person from £14.00 Single	Open Jan-Dec Dinner 1800-2000 B&B + Eve. Meal from £22.00	
		Friendly working farm, with large garden overlooking Montrose. Nearby beaches and Nature Reserve. Children and pets welcome.				
Mrs A Ruxton Muirshade of Gallery Farm Montrose Angus DD10 9JU Tel: (Northwaterbridge) 067484 209	COMMENDED ≋ ≋	1 Twin 2 Double	2 En Suite fac 1 Pub. Bath/Show	B&B per person from £14.50 Double	Open Apr-Oct Dinner from 1800 B&B + Eve. Meal from £21.50	
		Farmhouse on working stock and cereal farm 5 miles (8kms) from Montrose and sandy beaches. Ideal for touring coast and Angus glens. Home baking.				
Mrs M Scott Fairfield, 24 The Mall Montrose Angus DD10 8NW Tel: (Montrose) 0674 76386		2 Twin 1 Double	1 Pub. Bath/Show	B&B per person £14.00-£15.00 Single from £14.00 Double	Open Jan-Dec	
Mrs J Scrimgeour Grey Harlings House Dorward Road Montrose Angus DD10 8SW Tel: (Montrose) 0674 73980		1 Single 2 Twin 2 Double 2 Family	1 En Suite fac 3 Pub. Bath/Show	B&B per person £15.00-£18.00 Single £15.00-£18.75 Double	Open Jan-Dec	
MORAR, by Mallaig **Inverness-shire** Mrs C MacDonald Shilo Morar, by Mallaig Inverness-shire PH40 4PB Tel: (Mallaig) 0687 2167 Fax: 0687 2167	Map 3 E1	1 Twin 1 Double	2 En Suite fac	B&B per person from £15.00 Double	Open Apr-Oct	

MOREBATTLE **Roxburghshire** Mrs Taylor Kaleview, Main Street Morebattle Roxburghshire TD5 6QQ Tel: (Morebattle) 0573 440345	Map 2 F7	COMMENDED Listed	1 Single 2 Twin	1 Priv. NOT ensuite 2 Pub. Bath/Show	B&B per person from £14.00 Single from £14.00 Double	Open Jan-Dec Dinner 1800-2000 B&B + Eve. Meal from £22.00

Friendly and comfortable. South facing secluded patio in attractive garden. Village inn and fishing available. French and Italian spoken.

MOTHERWELL **Lanarkshire** Strathclyde Guest House 90 Hamilton Road Motherwell Lanarkshire ML1 3DG Tel: (Motherwell) 0698 264076/263691	Map 2 A5		2 Single 2 Twin 2 Double 2 Family	1 Pub. Bath/Show	B&B per person £14.50-£17.00 Single £13.00 Double	Open Jan-Dec
Mr William Cumming Fir Trees 92 Main Street, Holytown Motherwell Lanarkshire ML1 4TJ Tel: (Holytown) 0698 832818/ 2832818			1 Double 2 Family	1 En Suite fac 1 Pub. Bath/Show	B&B per person £15.00-£17.50 Single £13.00-£15.50 Double	Open Jan-Dec Dinner 1730-1930 B&B + Eve. Meal £17.00-£21.00
MUASDALE **Argyll** Mrs MacMillan Seafield Muasdale, by Tayinloan Argyll PA29 6XD Tel: (Glenbarr) 05832 240	Map 1 D6	COMMENDED Listed	2 Double 1 Family	1 Pub. Bath/Show	B&B per person from £14.00 Double	Open Mar-Oct

House standing in its own grounds under 1 mile (2kms) from small village on west coast of Kintyre. Lovely seascapes towards Gigha, Islay and Jura.

MUIR OF AIRD **Benbecula, Western Isles** Mrs Emma MacDonald Lennox Cottage 24 Muir of Aird Muir of Aird Isle of Benbecula Western Isles Tel: (Benbecula) 0870 602965	Map 3 A9		1 Twin 1 Double	1 En Suite fac 1 Pub. Bath/Show	B&B per person £12.00-£14.00 Single £12.00-£14.00 Double	Open Jan-Dec Dinner from 1830 B&B + Eve. Meal £17.00-£19.00
MUIR OF ORD **Ross-shire** The Dower House Highfield Muir of Ord Ross-shire IV6 7XN Tel: (Muir of Ord) 0463 870090 Fax: 0463 870090	Map 4 A8		3 Twin 2 Double Suite avail.	5 En Suite fac	B&B per person £35.00-£70.00 Single £35.00-£90.00 Double	Open Jan-Dec Dinner 2000-2130 B&B + Eve. Meal £60.00-£70.00
Mrs E Brown Hawthorn Bank Black Isle Road Muir-of-Ord Ross-shire IV6 7RR Tel: (Muir of Ord) 0463 870188			1 Double 1 Family	1 Pub. Bath/Show	B&B per person from £12.50 Single from £12.50 Double	Open Apr-Oct

Details of Grading and Classification are on page vi.

Key to symbols is on back flap.

MUIR OF ORD continued

Map 4 A8

Mrs A B G Fraser
Gilchrist Farm
Muir of Ord
Ross-shire
IV6 7RS
Tel: (Muir of Ord)
0463 870243

COMMENDED

1 Twin   1 Pub. Bath/Show   B&B per person   Open Apr-Oct
1 Double   from £14.00 Single
                            from £14.00 Double

Traditional farmhouse on mixed arable and livestock farm with attractive garden.
Home cooking, baking and preserves.

Mrs W A Keir
Monadh Liath, Ord Wood
Muir-of-Ord
Ross-shire
IV6 7XS
Tel: (Muir of Ord)
0463 870587

COMMENDED

2 Twin   1 Pub. Bath/Show   B&B per person   Open Jan-Dec
1 Double   from £12.50 Double

In quiet residential area, on the outskirts of the town, large modern house
set in extensive gardens.

Mrs E Urquhart
Vulcan Cottage, Main Street
Muir of Ord
Ross-shire
IV6 7TP
Tel: (Muir of Ord)
0463 870462

2 Twin   2 Pub. Bath/Show   B&B per person   Open Jan-Dec
1 Double   £12.50 Single
                            £12.50 Double

BY MUIR OF ORD
Ross-shire

Map 4 A8

Mrs M MacKenzie
Argyll Cottage, Drynie Park
by Muir of Ord
Ross-shire
Tel: (Muir of Ord)
0463 871022

1 Single   1 Pub. Bath/Show   B&B per person   Open Jan-Dec
1 Twin   £12.50-£13.50 Single
                              £12.50-£13.50 Double

MUSSELBURGH
East Lothian

Map 2 D5

Craigesk Guest House
10 Albert Terrace
Musselburgh
East Lothian
EH21 7LR
Tel: 031 665 3344/3170

APPROVED

1 Single   2 Pub. Bath/Show   B&B per person   Open Jan-Dec
2 Twin   from £14.00 Single
2 Family   from £14.00 Double

Victorian terraced house with private parking, overlooking golf and racecourse.
Convenient bus route to city centre (20 minutes).

Mrs Elizabeth Aitken COMMENDED

18 WOODSIDE GARDENS, MUSSELBURGH, EAST LOTHIAN EH21 7LJ
Telephone: 031-665 3170/3344

Well-appointed bungalow within 6 miles of Edinburgh in quiet suburb with private parking. Excellent bus service to city. 2 minutes from oldest golf course in world and race course. Easy access to beaches and beautiful countryside.

All rooms hot and cold, colour TV and tea/coffee. Private parking.

Mrs J M Aitken 18 Woodside Gardens Musselburgh East Lothian EH21 7LJ Tel: 031 665 3170/3344	COMMENDED	1 Single 1 Twin 1 Family	2 Pub. Bath/Show	B&B per person from £14.00 Single from £14.00 Double **Detached bungalow in quiet residential area, close to Musselburgh Racecourse and golf course. Private parking.**	Open Jan-Dec
Mrs Bouglas Melville House, 103a North High Street Musselburgh East Lothian EH21 6JE Tel: 031 665 5187		1 Twin 1 Double 1 Family	2 Pub. Bath/Show	B&B per person from £16.00 Single from £13.50 Double	Open Apr-Oct
Mrs C Douglas 5 Craighall Terrace Musselburgh East Lothian EH21 7PL Tel: 031 665 4294		1 Double 1 Family	1 Pub. Bath/Show	B&B per person from £14.00 Single from £12.50 Double	Open Jun-Oct
Mrs McGowan 23 Linkfield Road Musselburgh East Lothian EH21 7LQ Tel: 031 665 7436		1 Double 1 Family	1 Pub. Bath/Show	B&B per person £15.00-£20.00 Single £15.00-£18.00 Double	Open Jan-Dec
Mrs Millar 3 Beulah Musselburgh East Lothian EH21 7LH Tel: 031 665 2317		1 Single 1 Double 1 Family	2 Pub. Bath/Show	B&B per person from £14.00 Single £13.00-£15.00 Double	Open Jan-Dec
Mrs Moffat Arden House 26 Linkfield Road Musselburgh East Lothian EH21 7LL Tel: 031 665 0663		1 Single 1 Twin 1 Family	1 Limited ensuite 2 Pub. Bath/Show	B&B per person from £16.00 Single from £13.50 Double	Open Apr-Oct
Mrs E Raistrick St Michaels, Inveresk Musselburgh East Lothian EH21 7BD Tel: 031 665 3055		1 Twin 1 Double	2 Pub. Bath/Show	B&B per person £18.00 Double	Open May-Sep

MUSSELBURGH continued Mr & Mrs L Shearer Rosehill Cottages, Rosehill Steadings Musselburgh East Lothian EH21 8QQ Tel: 031 665 4444	Map 2 D5		1 Twin 1 Double	2 Pub. Bath/Show	B&B per person £12.50-£15.00 Single from £15.00 Double	Open Jan-Dec	
Mr W Wilson 17 Windsor Park Musselburgh East Lothian EH21 7QL Tel: 031 665 2194			1 Single 1 Twin	1 Pub. Bath/Show	B&B per person £14.00-£16.50 Single £14.00-£16.50 Double	Open May-Sep	
MUTHILL **Perthshire** Mrs Stewart Highfield, 104 Willoughby Street Muthill, Crieff Perthshire Tel: (Muthill) 0764 681340	Map 2 B3		1 Twin 1 Double 1 Family	1 Pub. Bath/Show	B&B per person £13.00-£17.00 Single £13.00 Double	Open Jan-Dec Dinner 1800-2130 B&B + Eve. Meal £20.00-£24.00	
NAIRN Roy & Irene Busby Winkfield, Tradespark Road Nairn IV12 5NP Tel: (Nairn) 0667 456168	Map 4 C8	COMMENDED	1 Twin 2 Double	2 En Suite fac 1 Priv. NOT ensuite	B&B per person from £15.00 Double	Open Jan-Nov	
			Welcoming family home, 10 minutes from safe beach. Convenient for golf, marina and the airport. Ideal base for exploring Highlands. Pets welcome.				
Mrs Patricia Robertson Langdale, Merryton Crescent Nairn IV12 5AQ Tel: (Nairn) 0667 452878		HIGHLY COMMENDED Listed	2 Twin 1 Double	1 Pub. Bath/Show	B&B per person £16.00-£18.00 Single £15.00-£17.00 Double	Open Apr-Oct	
			Modern bungalow in residential area 200 yards from golf course, and 5 minutes walk from town centre.				
BY NAIRN Mr & Mrs G Pearson Brightmony Farm House Auldearn Nairn IV12 5PP Tel: (Nairn) 0667 455550	Map 4 C8	COMMENDED Listed	1 Twin 2 Double	1 Pub. Bath/Show	B&B per person £12.50-£14.00 Single £12.50-£14.00 Double	Open Jan-Dec	
			A listed, Georgian farmhouse overlooking Moray Firth, Easter Ross and beyond. Open fire, walled gardens ensures peaceful accommodation.				
NETHY BRIDGE **Inverness-shire** Mrs Anderson Tigh-na-Drochit Nethy Bridge Inverness-shire PH25 3DW Tel: (Nethy Bridge) 0479 821666	Map 4 C1	COMMENDED	1 Twin 2 Double	1 Pub. Bath/Show	B&B per person £12.00-£12.50 Single £12.00-£12.50 Double	Open Jan-Dec Dinner 1800-1900 B&B + Eve. Meal £16.00-£16.50	
			In centre of Highland village, period house with large garden and access to the river. All home cooking. Ideally situated for touring Spey Valley.				

Aultmore House

NETHY BRIDGE, INVERNESS-SHIRE
PH25 3ED   Tel: 0479 821473

Aultmore, lingering in time, is a home from home of the highest quality in the heart of the Scottish Highlands.

It's purpose, to offer a few house guests the pleasures of some of the world's most breathtaking scenery, the timeless search for flora and fauna, the solitude of forest and mountain, the challenge of club and fly or simply beautiful surroundings in which to relax with colleagues of compatible interests.

More, much more, than any guest house or hotel, Aultmore offers the welcome once reserved for the traditional guest of a Scottish country estate, enjoying friendship and true Highland hospitality.

Location / Address	Map	Grade	Rooms	Bathrooms	Prices	Terms	Symbols
Mr A G Edwards, Aultmore House, Nethy Bridge, Inverness-shire, PH25 3ED, Tel: (Nethy Bridge) 0479 821473			1 Twin, 2 Double	2 En Suite fac, 2 Pub. Bath/Show	B&B per person £16.50 Single £16.50-£25.00 Double	Open Apr-Oct, Dinner 1900-1930, B&B + Eve. Meal £24.00-£32.50	
NEW ABERDOUR, by Pennan, Aberdeenshire Mrs J White, Pennywells, 20 High Street, New Aberdour, Fraserburgh, Tel: (New Aberdour) 03466 482	Map 4 G7		1 Twin, 1 Double	1 Pub. Bath/Show	B&B per person from £13.00 Single from £13.00 Double	Open Jan-Dec, B&B + Eve. Meal from £20.00	
NEWBURGH Fife Mrs Barbara Baird, Ninewells Farm, Woodriffe Road, Newburgh, Fife, KY14 6EY, Tel: (Newburgh) 0337 40307/840307	Map 2 C3	Award Pending	2 Twin	2 Pub. Bath/Show	B&B per person from £14.50 Double	Open mid May-Sep	
Mrs A Duff, Hillview, 46 Scotland Terrace, Newburgh, Fife, KY14 6AR, Tel: (Newburgh) 0337 40570/840570		COMMENDED Listed	1 Twin, 1 Double	1 Pub. Bath/Show	B&B per person £13.00-£15.00 Double	Open Apr-Sep, Dinner 1900-2100, B&B + Eve. Meal £18.00-£20.00	

Family home in quiet residential area of Fife village. Ideal centre for touring.
12 miles (19kms) from Perth, 20 miles (32kms) from Dundee.

Location / Address	Map	Grade	Rooms	Bathrooms	Prices	Terms	Symbols
NEW GALLOWAY Kirkcudbrightshire Mr McPhee, The Smithy, Licensed Rest. & Craft Shop, New Galloway, Kirkcudbrightshire, DG7 3RN, Tel: (New Galloway) 06442 269	Map 2 A9		1 Twin, 1 Double	1 Pub. Bath/Show	B&B per person £13.50 Single £13.50 Double	Open Mar-Oct, Dinner 1000-2100	

NEW GALLOWAY continued	Map 2 A9

CAIRN EDWARD (06442) 244
NEW GALLOWAY, KIRKCUDBRIGHTSHIRE DG7 3RZ

Comfortable Victorian country house in several acres of garden and grounds, one mile from village centre and golf course. All rooms centrally heated and en-suite.
"Guestaccom". good room award.
Golf, fishing, walking, sailing available nearby.

Open April to October.

Mrs P M Murray Cairn Edward New Galloway Kirkcudbrightshire DG7 3RZ Tel: (New Galloway) 06442 244		1 Twin 2 Double	3 En Suite fac	B&B per person £16.00-£18.00 Double	Open Apr-Sep

NEWMILLS Fife	Map 2 B4				
Mrs P McFarlane Langlees Farm Newmills, by Culross Fife Tel: (Newmills) 0383 881152		1 Twin 1 Double	1 En Suite fac 2 Pub. Bath/Show	B&B per person from £14.00 Single from £14.00 Double	Open Jan-Dec Dinner 1700-2000 B&B + Eve. Meal from £20.00

BY NEWPORT-ON-TAY Fife	Map 2 D2	HIGHLY COMMENDED			
Forgan House Forgan Newport-on-Tay Fife DD6 8RB Tel: (Newport-on-Tay) 0382 542760			2 Twin 2 Double	3 En Suite fac 1 Priv. NOT ensuite	B&B per person £25.00-£30.00 Double	Open Jan-Dec Dinner 1900-2000 B&B + Eve. Meal £35.00-£40.00

Georgian country house set in 5 acres of grounds and gardens located between Dundee and St Andrews.

NEWTON, by South Queensferry West Lothian	Map 2 C5				
Newton Guest House Newton Village by South Queensferry West Lothian EH52 6QE Tel: 031 331 3298		1 Twin 1 Double 2 Family	2 Pub. Bath/Show	B&B per person to £18.00 Single to £15.00 Double	Open Jan-Dec

NEWTONMORE Inverness-shire	Map 4 B1	Award Pending			
Celia Ferrie Ben-y-Gloe, Laggan Road Newtonmore Inverness-shire PH20 1DR Tel: (Newtonmore) 0540 673633		1 Twin 2 Double	3 En Suite fac	B&B per person from £14.00 Single from £14.00 Double	Open Jan-Dec

		Award Pending			
Mrs M Johnston Ardnabruach, Glen Road Newtonmore Inverness-shire PH20 1DZ Tel: (Newtonmore) 0540 673339		1 Twin 1 Family	1 Pub. Bath/Show	B&B per person £12.00-£14.00 Single £12.00-£14.00 Double	Open Jan-Dec

Mrs A Morrison Laggan Road Newtonmore Inverness-shire PH20 1DG Tel: (Newtonmore) 0540 673839		**COMMENDED** Listed	1 Double 1 Family	1 Pub. Bath/Show	B&B per person £13.00-£15.00 Single £13.00-£15.00 Double	Open Jan-Dec
			Stone built house on edge of quiet Highland village. Comfortable stay assured in this welcoming family home. Garden nursery business in grounds.			
Mrs D E Muir Greenways, Golf Course Road Newtonmore Inverness-shire PH20 1AT Tel: (Newtonmore) 0540 673325		**Award Pending**	1 Single 1 Double 1 Family	1 Pub. Bath/Show	B&B per person £12.50 Single £12.50 Double	Open Jan-Dec
Mrs Mullender Falls of Truim Newtonmore Inverness-shire PH20 1BE Tel: (Newtonmore) 0540 673211			1 Twin 1 Family	1 Pub. Bath/Show	B&B per person £13.00-£15.00 Double	Open Mar-Sep
Mrs K Sharp Spey Valley Lodge, Station Road Newtonmore Inverness-shire PH20 1AR Tel: (Newtonmore) 0540 673398		**COMMENDED** Listed	1 Twin 1 Double 1 Family	2 Pub. Bath/Show	B&B per person from £14.00 Single from £14.00 Double	Open Jan-Dec Dinner 1800-1900
			Detached house standing in its own grounds, at the edge of the village, with views of the Monadhliath Hills. Warm welcome.			
Valerie Tonkin Eagle View, Perth Road Newtonmore Inverness-shire PH20 1AP Tel: (Newtonmore) 0540 673675		**COMMENDED** 👑 👑	2 Twin 2 Double	3 En Suite fac 1 Priv. NOT ensuite	B&B per person £14.00-£19.00 Single £14.00-£15.00 Double	Open Jan-Dec Dinner from 1900 B&B + Eve. Meal £21.00-£22.50
			Traditional stone built house with large garden and ample parking. Warm and friendly atmosphere, situated near centre of village.			
NEWTON STEWART Wigtownshire Flower Bank Guest House Minnigaff Newton Stewart Wigtownshire DG8 6PJ Tel: (Newton Stewart) 0671 2629	**Map 1** H1	**COMMENDED** 👑	1 Single 1 Twin 3 Double 2 Family	2 Pub. Bath/Show	B&B per person £15.00-£17.00 Single £15.00-£16.00 Double	Open Jan-Dec Dinner from 1830 B&B + Eve. Meal £22.50-£24.50
			Detached 18C house set in 1 acre of grounds on banks of River Cree. Quiet peaceful location 0.5 miles (1km) from town centre.			
Mrs P Adams Clugston Farm Newton Stewart Wigtownshire DG8 9BH Tel: (Kirkcowan) 067183 338		**COMMENDED** Listed	1 Twin 2 Double	1 Pub. Bath/Show	B&B per person £13.00-£14.00 Single £12.00-£13.00 Double	Open Apr-Oct Dinner from 1800 B&B + Eve. Meal £19.00-£20.00
			About 5 miles (8kms) off the A75. Near the sea, hill walking and easy access to 3 golf courses. Two ground floor rooms.			
Mrs H Dickson Kilwarlin, Corvisel Road Newton Stewart Wigtownshire DG8 Tel: (Newton Stewart) 0671 3047			1 Single 1 Twin 1 Double	1 Pub. Bath/Show	B&B per person £13.50-£14.00 Single £13.50-£14.00 Double	Open Apr-Oct

Details of Grading and Classification are on page vi.

Key to symbols is on back flap.

NEWTON STEWART continued Mrs J Gustafson Lynwood, Corvisel Road Newton Stewart Wigtownshire DG8 6LN Tel: (Newton Stewart) 0671 2074	Map 1 H1	COMMENDED ♛	1 Twin 1 Double 1 Family	2 Pub. Bath/Show	B&B per person £13.00-£14.00 Double	Open Jan-Dec Dinner from 1830 B&B + Eve. Meal £21.00-£22.00
			Spacious Victorian house in quiet residential area, close to the town centre. Ideal for families and young children.			
Mrs M Hewitson Auchenleck Farm Newton Stewart Wigtownshire DG8 7AA Tel: (Newton Stewart) 0671 2035		COMMENDED ♛♛	1 Twin 2 Double	1 En Suite fac 2 Priv. NOT ensuite	B&B per person £16.00-£17.00 Single £16.00-£17.00 Double	Open Easter-Oct
			Turreted former shooting lodge on farm with cattle and sheep. Set within Glen Trool National Park. Ideally situated for walking and touring.			
NORTH BALLACHULISH **Inverness-shire** Mr Houston Glenlea North Ballachulish Inverness-shire PH33 6SA Tel: (Onich) 08553 324	Map 1 F1		1 Twin 2 Double	1 En Suite fac 1 Priv. NOT ensuite 1 Pub. Bath/Show	B&B per person £12.00-£16.00 Double	Open Jan-Dec
Mrs E MacMillan Brudair, Bail Ur North Ballachulish Argyll PH33 6SB Tel: (Onich) 08553 431			1 Twin 1 Double	1 Pub. Bath/Show	B&B per person from £13.00 Single from £13.00 Double	Open Jan-Dec Dinner 1900-2030 B&B + Eve. Meal from £20.00
NORTH BERWICK **East Lothian** Craigview Guest House 5 Beach Road North Berwick East Lothian EH39 4AB Tel: (North Berwick) 0620 2257	Map 2 E4		1 Twin 2 Double	1 En Suite fac 2 Pub. Bath/Show	B&B per person from £13.50 Double	Open Jan-Dec Dinner at 1900
Mrs May Barbour Windygates Windygates Road North Berwick East Lothian EH39 4QP Tel: (North Berwick) 0620 2936			2 Single 1 Twin 1 Double	2 Pub. Bath/Show	B&B per person £14.00-£16.00 Single £14.00-£16.00 Double	Open Apr-Oct
Mrs I Brown 14 Marine Parade North Berwick East Lothian EH39 4LD Tel: (North Berwick) 0620 2063			1 Single 1 Twin 1 Double	1 Pub. Bath/Show	B&B per person £11.00-£13.50 Single £11.00-£13.50 Double	Open Jan-Dec

Mrs S Clelland Cragside, 16 Marine Parade North Berwick East Lothian EH39 4LD Tel: (North Berwick) 0620 2879		3 Twin	2 Pub. Bath/Show	B&B per person £16.00-£17.50 Double	Open Jan-Dec
Mrs Fife Beehive Cottage, Kingston North Berwick East Lothian EH39 5JE Tel: (North Berwick) 0620 4785		1 Double	1 En Suite fac	B&B per person £15.00-£17.00 Double	Open Jun-Sep
Mrs S Gray Seabank, 12 Marine Parade North Berwick East Lothian EH39 4LD Tel: (North Berwick) 0620 2884		2 Twin 3 Family	1 Pub. Bath/Show	B&B per person £13.00-£17.00 Single	Open Jan-Dec
Mrs Morrison Lanwyn, 19 St Baldred's Road North Berwick East Lothian EH39 4PY Tel: (North Berwick) 0620 4847		1 Double 2 Family	1 Pub. Bath/Show	B&B per person £12.50-£16.50 Single £12.50-£16.50 Double	Open Jan-Dec Dinner 1800-1900 B&B + Eve. Meal £17.50-£21.50
Mrs K Patrick Cosyden, 16 Marly Green North Berwick East Lothian EH39 4QX Tel: (North Berwick) 0620 3069/4052	COMMENDED 👑 👑	1 Double	1 Priv. NOT ensuite	B&B per person £18.00-£20.00 Double	Open Jan-Dec
		Completely private self contained accommodation. South facing in peaceful surroundings. Attractive garden. Private parking. Golf by arrangement.			
Mrs Moira Ralph Craigmore, 13 Westgate North Berwick East Lothian EH39 4AE Tel: (North Berwick) 0620 2782		1 Twin 1 Double	1 Pub. Bath/Show	B&B per person £15.00-£16.00 Single £15.00-£16.00 Double	Open Jan-Dec
Mrs M Ramsay The Studio, Grange Road North Berwick East Lothian EH39 4QT Tel: (North Berwick) 0620 5150		1 Double	1 Priv. NOT ensuite	B&B per person £18.00-£20.00 Double	Open Jan-Dec
Mrs P Swanston Chestnut Lodge 2A Ware Road North Berwick East Lothian EH39 4BN Tel: (North Berwick) 0620 4256	COMMENDED 👑 👑	2 Twin 1 Double	2 En Suite fac 1 Pub. Bath/Show	B&B per person £12.00-£16.00 Double	Open Mar-Nov
		Modern well appointed house in quiet location. Close to transport. Ideal base for golfing and other sporting activities. Private parking.			

NORTH KESSOCK Ross-shire Mrs Grigor Redfield Farm North Kessock Ross-shire IV1 1XD Tel: (Munlochy) 046381 228	Map 4 B8	COMMENDED 🏵 🏵	1 Single 1 Twin 1 Double	1 En Suite fac 2 Pub. Bath/Show	B&B per person from £12.00 Single £15.00-£16.00 Double	Open Jan-Dec Dinner 1900-2000 B&B + Eve. Meal £22.00-£23.00	

On mixed working farm, 4 miles (7kms) north of Inverness, large family farmhouse. Home baking.

OBAN Argyll	Map 1 E2

Ardblair
AA QQQ & RAC Acclaimed

OBAN'S LEADING GUEST HOUSE
DALRIACH ROAD, OBAN, ARGYLL PA34 5JD
Telephone: 0631-62668

We're the third generation of this family-run business. We specialise in home-cooking and good old-fashioned friendly welcome and comfort. Our spacious sun-lounge and our garden have magnificent views over Oban Bay, and yet we're very central — only 3 minutes' walk from the town centre. Our safe car park takes 10 cars.

We're very easy to find: just turn left half way down the hill coming into Oban, up past the tennis courts and swimming pool, and there we are!

We'll gladly send you a brochure, or why not phone IAN & MONIKA SMYTH.

Ardblair Guest House Dalriach Road Oban Argyll PA34 5JB Tel: (Oban) 0631 62668		3 Single 3 Twin 6 Double 3 Family Suite avail.	12 En Suite fac 1 Limited ensuite 2 Pub. Bath/Show	B&B per person £16.00-£20.00 Single £16.00-£20.00 Double	Open May-Sep Dinner from 1830 B&B + Eve. Meal £25.00-£29.00	
Beechgrove Guest House Croft Road Oban Argyll PA34 5JL Tel: (Oban) 0631 66111	COMMENDED 🏵 🏵 🏵	1 Twin 1 Double 1 Family	3 En Suite fac 1 Pub. Bath/Show	B&B per person from £17.00 Double	Open Mar-Oct Dinner from 1800 B&B + Eve. Meal from £27.00	

Family run guest house a short walk from the harbour and shops, with pleasant views of Oban Bay and the Sound of Kerrera.

Scotland for Golf . . .

Find out more about golf in Scotland. There's more to it than just the championship courses so get in touch with us now for information on the hidden gems of Scotland.

Write to: **Information Unit, Scottish Tourist Board, 23 Ravelston Terrace, Edinburgh EH4 3EU or call: 031-332 2433**

Braehead Guest House Albert Road Oban Argyll PA34 5EJ Tel: (Oban) 0631 63341	APPROVED 👑	2 Twin 3 Double 1 Family	1 En Suite fac 2 Pub. Bath/Show	B&B per person £15.00-£17.00 Double	Open Jan-Dec	

Attractive house convenient for town centre. Ground floor ensuite. Private parking area.

Elmbank Guest House Croft Road Oban Argyll PA34 5JN Tel: (Oban) 0631 62545		1 Single 2 Twin 4 Double	2 En Suite fac 2 Limited ensuite 2 Pub. Bath/Show	B&B per person from £15.00 Single from £15.00 Double	Open Feb-Nov	

Glenara Guest House Rockfield Road Oban Argyll PA34 5DQ Tel: (Oban) 0631 63172	COMMENDED 👑 👑	1 Single 5 Double	3 En Suite fac 1 Limited ensuite 1 Priv. NOT ensuite 1 Pub. Bath/Show	B&B per person £16.00-£18.00 Single £16.00-£17.50 Double	Open Jan-Dec	

Family run guest house close to the town centre and all amenities. Private parking.

Glenbervie Guest House Dalriach Road Oban Argyll PA34 5NL Tel: (Oban) 0631 64770		2 Single 2 Twin 2 Double 2 Family	3 Limited ensuite 1 Pub. Bath/Show	B&B per person £15.00-£19.00 Single £15.00-£19.00 Double	Open Jan-Dec Dinner 1830-2000 B&B + Eve. Meal £22.00-£25.00	

Glenroy Guest House Rockfield Road Oban Argyll PA34 5DQ Tel: (Oban) 0631 62585	COMMENDED 👑 👑	1 Single 1 Twin 4 Double 1 Family	3 En Suite fac 3 Pub. Bath/Show	B&B per person to £16.00 Single £15.00-£17.50 Double	Open Jan-Dec	

Family run guest house overlooking Oban Bay. Centrally situated and convenient for all amenities. Private parking.

Maridon Guest House Dunuaran Road Oban Argyll PA34 4NE Tel: (Oban) 0631 62670		1 Single 2 Twin 5 Double 1 Family	2 En Suite fac 1 Pub. Bath/Show	B&B per person £12.00-£18.00 Single £12.00-£18.00 Double	Open Jan-Dec	

Roseneath Guest House
DALRIACH ROAD, OBAN PA34 5EQ
Telephone: 0631 62929

Situated in quiet location ten minutes' walk from ferry, bus and rail terminals. Three minutes' walk from town centre close to swimming pool, bowling green, squash and tennis courts. Splendid views over Oban Bay to Mull. Built in 1888, this fine house has a warm and friendly atmosphere.

Roseneath Guest House Dalriach Road Oban Argyll PA34 5EQ Tel: (Oban) 0631 62929	COMMENDED 👑 👑	2 Single 3 Twin 5 Double	3 En Suite fac 4 Limited ensuite 2 Pub. Bath/Show	B&B per person £13.00-£16.00 Single £13.00-£18.00 Double	Open Jan-Dec	

Victorian house overlooking town and bay, near seafront and shops. Private parking.

Details of Grading and Classification are on page vi. | Key to symbols is on back flap. |

OBAN

OBAN continued	Map 1 E2						
Sand Villa Guest House Breadalbane Street Oban Argyll PA34 Tel: (Oban) 0631 62803			6 Twin 3 Double 6 Family	3 Pub. Bath/Show	B&B per person £12.00-£15.00 Double	Open Jan-Nov Dinner from 1800	
Sgeir Mhaol Guest House Soroba Road Oban Argyll PA34 4JF Tel: (Oban) 0631 62650	COMMENDED 👑 👑		1 Twin 2 Double 3 Family	5 En Suite fac 1 Priv. NOT ensuite 1 Pub. Bath/Show	B&B per person £14.00-£22.00 Single £14.00-£19.00 Double	Open Jan-Dec Dinner from 1830 B&B + Eve. Meal £21.00-£27.00	
			Bungalow style, with ample private car parking and only a short walk from the town centre. All rooms and facilities on the ground floor.				
Mrs Adams Westmount, Dalriach Road Oban Argyll PA34 Tel: (Oban) 0631 62884			5 Family	2 Pub. Bath/Show	B&B per person £16.00-£18.00 Double	Open Apr-Sep	
Mrs Calderwood The Torrans, Drummore Road Oban Argyll Tel: (Oban) 0631 65342	COMMENDED 👑 👑		1 Twin 2 Double	2 En Suite fac 1 Priv. NOT ensuite	B&B per person £14.00-£17.00 Single £14.00-£17.00 Double	Open Jan-Dec	
			Comfortable family house in quiet residential cul-de-sac. 1 mile (2kms) from town centre and all amenities.				
Mundi Cooper 1 Lonan Drive Oban Argyll PA34 4NN Tel: (Oban) 0631 63164	COMMENDED Listed		1 Twin 1 Double	1 Pub. Bath/Show	B&B per person from £14.00 Double	Open Jan-Dec	
			Informal family atmosphere in comfortable modern home.				
W S Currie Whinhurst, Glenshellach Road Oban Argyll PA34 4PP Tel: (Oban) 0631 64094			1 Twin 2 Double	2 Pub. Bath/Show	B&B per person £11.00-£13.00 Double	Open Jan-Dec Dinner 1700-2030 B&B + Eve. Meal £16.00-£18.00	
Mrs J Driver Kinnaird, Villa Road Oban Argyll Tel: (Oban) 0631 62320	COMMENDED 👑 👑		1 Twin 2 Double	2 En Suite fac 1 Priv. NOT ensuite	B&B per person £16.00-£17.50 Double	Open Apr-Sep	
			Family home in residential area 0.5 miles (1km) from town centre. On hillside with extensive views arcoss Oban. Private parking.				
Mrs Griffin Kenmore, Soroba Road Oban Argyll Tel: (Oban) 0631 63592			1 Twin 3 Double 2 Family	3 Pub. Bath/Show	B&B per person from £14.00 Double	Open Jan-Dec	
Mrs Hopkin Ardview, Ardconnel Road Oban Argyll PA34 5DP Tel: (Oban) 0631 65112	COMMENDED Listed		1 Twin 1 Double	1 Pub. Bath/Show	B&B per person £14.00-£16.00 Single £14.00-£16.00 Double	Open Jan-Dec	
			In an elevated position with views to Oban Bay and backing onto famous McCaig's Tower. Only 5 minutes walk from the town.				

| J & D Ledwidge
Drumriggend, Drummore Road
Oban
Argyll
PA34 4JL
Tel: (Oban) 0631 63330 | COMMENDED
♔ ♔ ♔ | 1 Twin
1 Double
1 Family | 3 En Suite fac | B&B per person
£15.00-£17.00 Double | Open Jan-Dec
Dinner 1800-1830
B&B + Eve. Meal
£21.00-£23.00 | |

Detached house in quiet residential area. Situated on the south side of town about 1 mile (2kms) from the centre.

| Mrs MacCalman
Duncarden, Rowan Road
Oban
Argyll
PA34 5TQ
Tel: (Oban) 0631 64947 | COMMENDED
♔ ♔ | 1 Double
1 Family | 1 En Suite fac
1 Priv. NOT ensuite | B&B per person
£15.00-£18.00 Double | Open Apr-Sep | |

Spacious modern villa overlooking Oban with large garden and private parking. Seafront within 5 minutes walk.

| Mrs B MacColl
Glengorm, Dunollie Road
Oban
Argyll
PA34 5PH
Tel: (Oban) 0631 65361 | COMMENDED
♔ | 1 Twin
3 Double | 2 Pub. Bath/Show | B&B per person
£13.00-£15.00 Double | Open Apr-Sep | |

Attractively decorated, Victorian terraced house on level ground near town centre, convenient for entertainments, shops and ferries.

BRACKER

Polvinister Road, Oban, Argyll PA34 5TN
Telephone/Fax: (0631) 64302

Modern bungalow situated in beautiful quiet residential area within walking distance of town (approx. 8-10 mins.) and the golf course. All bedrooms have private facilities and tea/coffee-making. TV lounge, private parking.

| Mrs C MacDonald
Bracker, Polvinister Road
Oban
Argyll
PA34 5TN
Tel: (Oban) 0631 64302 | COMMENDED
♔ ♔ | 1 Twin
2 Double | 3 En Suite fac | B&B per person
£15.00-£17.00 Double | Open Mar-Nov | |

Modern family bungalow in secluded residential area. Short distance from town centre and all amenities. Private parking.

| Mrs K MacDonald
Mingulay, Laurel Crescent
Oban
Argyll
PA34 5ED
Tel: (Oban) 0631 62627
Fax: 0631 66482 | | 1 Twin
1 Double | 2 En Suite fac | B&B per person
£14.00-£18.00 Double | Open Mar-Oct | |

| Mrs MacDougall
Harbour View, Shore Street
Oban
Argyll
PA34 4LQ
Tel: (Oban) 0631 63462
Fax: 0631 66482 | APPROVED
♔ | 2 Twin
3 Family | 2 Pub. Bath/Show | B&B per person
£12.50-£15.50 Double | Open Jan-Dec | |

Centrally situated and convenient for a level stroll to ferry, railway station and shops.

| Mrs MacDougall
Glen Maree, Mossfield Drive
Oban
Argyll
PA34 4EN
Tel: (Oban) 0631 62420 | | 3 Double | 2 Pub. Bath/Show | B&B per person
£12.50-£13.50 Double | Open Apr-Oct | |

OBAN continued	Map 1 E2						
Mrs McGill Argyll Villa, Albert Road Oban Argyll PA34 5JE Tel: (Oban) 0631 66897		1 Twin 2 Double	1 Pub. Bath/Show	B&B per person £15.00-£18.00 Double	Open Jan-Dec		

YULARA

Glen Cruitten, Oban, Argyll PA34 4QA
Telephone: 0631 66986

We are situated one mile from town centre in a peaceful location. We are an ideal base for walking, golf and pony trekking. It is a modern property with a large garden and parking. Two double rooms with bathroom and shower to yourselves.
COME AND HAVE A GREAT HOLIDAY!

Mrs R MacKinnon Yulara, Glencruitten Oban Argyll Tel: (Oban) 0631 66986		2 Double	1 Pub. Bath/Show	B&B per person £12.00-£15.00 Double	Open Apr-Oct		
Mrs E M MacLean Lorne View, Ardconnel Road Oban Argyll PA34 5DW Tel: (Oban) 0631 65500	COMMENDED	1 Twin 2 Double	3 Limited ensuite 2 Pub. Bath/Show	B&B per person £30.00-£32.00 Single £15.00-£16.00 Double	Open Mar-Oct Dinner at 1815 B&B + Eve. Meal £25.00-£26.00		
		Quiet location overlooking Oban Bay. Convenient for local sports amenities and town centre. Evening meals with advance notice except Sundays.					
Mrs P Robertson Don-Muir, Pulpit Hill Oban Argyll PA34 4LY Tel: (Oban) 0631 64536 Fax: 0631 63739	COMMENDED	1 Single 1 Twin 3 Double	2 En Suite fac 1 Priv. NOT ensuite 2 Pub. Bath/Show	B&B per person £14.00-£15.00 Single £16.00-£17.00 Double	Open Feb-Oct Dinner 1830-1930 B&B + Eve. Meal £25.00-£27.00		
		Set in quiet residential area, high up on Pulpit Hill and close to public transport terminals. Parking available.					

"Dungrianach"

(Gaelic — "the sunny house on the hill")

Highly Commended

Although only a few minutes walk from Oban ferry piers and town centre, Dungrianach sits in private woodland, right above the yacht moorings, and enjoys unsurpassed views of sea and islands.
Accommodation 1 twin and 1 double room, each with private facilities.
Contact: Mrs Elaine Robertson, "Dungrianach", Pulpit Hill, Oban, Argyll PA34 4LX. Tel: 0631 62840.

Mrs Robertson Dungrianach, Pulpit Hill Oban Argyll PA34 Tel: (Oban) 0631 62840	HIGHLY COMMENDED	1 Twin 1 Double	2 En Suite fac	B&B per person £16.50-£18.50 Double	Open Apr-Sep		
		Secluded, in 4 acres of wooded garden on top of Pulpit Hill. Magnificent views over Oban Bay and the islands.					

Mrs R Rodaway Pinmacher, Polvinister Road Oban Argyll PA34 5TN Tel: (Oban) 0631 63553	COMMENDED 👑 👑 👑	1 Twin 2 Double	3 En Suite fac	B&B per person £15.00-£17.00 Single £15.00-£17.00 Double	Open Mar-Oct Dinner 1900-2100 B&B + Eve. Meal £23.00-£25.00	
		Comfortable modern bungalow quietly situated only 10 minutes walk from town centre. Private parking.				
Mrs S Scott Verulam, Drummore Road Oban Argyll PA34 4JL Tel: (Oban) 0631 66115	COMMENDED 👑 👑	1 Twin 2 Double	2 En Suite fac 1 Priv. NOT ensuite	B&B per person £12.00-£16.00 Double	Open Mar-Sep	
		Modern family bungalow in quiet residential area, close to town centre. Off-street parking. All rooms ground floor.				
Mrs Stewart Glenview, Soroba Road Oban Argyll PA34 4JF Tel: (Oban) 0631 62267		2 Twin 2 Family	1 Pub. Bath/Show	B&B per person £12.50-£15.00 Single £12.50-£15.00 Double	Open Jan-Dec Dinner 1800-2000 B&B + Eve. Meal £20.00-£22.00	
Mrs Morven Wardhaugh Kathmore, Soroba Road Oban Tel: (Oban) 0631 62104		1 Twin 3 Double 1 Family	4 En Suite fac 1 Pub. Bath/Show	B&B per person £18.00-£25.00 Single £15.00-£21.00 Double	Open Jan-Dec Dinner from 1830 B&B + Eve. Meal £20.00-£28.00	
Mrs Worthington Willowdene, Glencruitten Road Oban Argyll PA34 4EW Tel: (Oban) 0631 64601		2 Double 1 Family	1 Pub. Bath/Show	B&B per person £11.00-£13.00 Single £11.00-£13.00 Double	Open Jan-Dec	
OLD KILPATRICK **Dunbartonshire** Mr & Mrs A Hunter Elmhurst 2 Mount Pleasant Drive Old Kilpatrick Dunbartonshire G60 5HJ Tel: (Duntochter) 0389 74341	Map 1 H5	1 Single 2 Twin	1 Pub. Bath/Show	B&B per person £13.00-£15.00 Single £13.00-£15.00 Double	Open Jan-Dec	

OLD RAYNE	Map 4
Aberdeenshire	F9

✂ MILL CROFT GUEST HOUSE

Lawrence Road, Old Rayne, Aberdeenshire AB52 6RY

Telephone: (046 45) 210

Homely cottage and working croft in the heart of Grampian countryside/Castle Trail under personal management of Dorothy and Peter Thomson. Woodcraft courses for hobby minded. Ideal for walking, hill-climbing, fishing, etc. Fire Certificate.

Mill Croft Guest House Old Rayne, by Inverurie Aberdeenshire AB52 6RY Tel: (Old Rayne) 04645 210	COMMENDED ♛♛	1 Twin 1 Double 1 Family	1 En Suite fac 2 Priv. NOT ensuite	B&B per person £15.00-£17.00 Single £15.00-£17.00 Double	Open Jan-Dec Dinner 1830-1930 B&B + Eve. Meal £21.00-£23.00

Friendly welcome at working croft with excellent views over Grampian countryside, on Castle Trail. Residential wood craft courses.

ONICH	Map 1
Inverness-shire	F1

Camus House Lochside Lodge Onich Inverness-shire PH33 6RY Tel: (Onich) 08553 200	COMMENDED ♛♛	1 Single 2 Twin 3 Double 3 Family	7 En Suite fac 1 Pub. Bath/Show	B&B per person £17.50-£28.00 Single £17.50-£28.00 Double	Open Jan-Nov Dinner to 1915 B&B + Eve. Meal £32.00-£42.50

Large well appointed house, comfortably furnished, superb views of the sealoch and hills. Fort William 10 miles (16kms), Glen Coe 5 miles (8kms).

Glendevin Inchree Onich Inverness-shire PH33 6SE Tel: (Onich) 08553 330	APPROVED ♛♛	1 Twin 2 Double	1 En Suite fac 2 Pub. Bath/Show	B&B per person from £14.50 Single from £13.00 Double	Open Jan-Dec Dinner 1800-2000 B&B + Eve. Meal from £21.50

Situated off main road. Convenient for Glencoe and Fort William. Ideal base for touring and activity holidays.

Mr Collins Tom-na-Creige North Ballachulish Onich Inverness-shire PH33 6RY Tel: (Onich) 08553 405	COMMENDED ♛♛	1 Twin 1 Double	2 En Suite fac	B&B per person £16.00-£18.00 Double	Open Jan-Dec

Modern comfortable en suite accommodation with inspiring views over Loch Linnhe.

Mrs Reen Hall Inveree, Oldtown Onich Inverness-shire PH33 6RZ Tel: (Onich) 08553 383	APPROVED Listed	1 Twin 1 Double	1 Pub. Bath/Show	B&B per person £10.50-£11.00 Single £10.50-£11.00 Double	Open Feb-Nov Dinner 1800-2000 B&B + Eve. Meal £15.50-£16.00

Informal hospitality in a homely atmosphere. Evening meal, facilities for babies. Special off season rates for senior citizens.

Mrs M MacLean Janika, Bunree Onich Inverness-shire PH33 6SE Tel: (Onich) 08553 359		1 Twin 2 Double	1 Pub. Bath/Show	B&B per person £13.00-£14.00 Double	Open Apr-Oct

Mr & Mrs I Rae Lismore House North Ballachulish Onich Inverness-shire PH33 6RZ Tel: (Onich) 08553 344		**COMMENDED** Listed	1 Twin 1 Double 1 Family	2 Pub. Bath/Show	B&B per person from £14.00 Single from £13.00 Double	Open Jan-Dec Dinner 1800-1900 B&B + Eve. Meal from £21.00	

Modern detached villa in beautiful situation with uninterrupted views over Loch Linnhe and Glencoe. 11 miles (17kms) south of Fort William.

OUT SKERRIES Shetland Mrs K Johnson Rocklea, East Isle Out Skerries Shetland ZE2 9AS Tel: (Out Skerries) 08065 228	Map 5 H3	**COMMENDED** 👑	1 Single 1 Twin 1 Double	2 Pub. Bath/Show	B&B per person £13.00-£14.00 Single £13.00-£14.00 Double	Open Jan-Dec Dinner 1800-2100 B&B + Eve. Meal £18.00-£19.00	

Family run, fully modernised house close to the pier.
Bird watching, sealwatching and sea fishing available.

PAISLEY Renfrewshire Ardgowan Guest House 92 Renfrew Road Paisley Renfrewshire PA3 4BJ Tel: 041 889 4763	Map 1 H5		2 Single 2 Twin 2 Double 4 Family	2 Pub. Bath/Show	B&B per person £22.00-£30.00 Single £18.00-£20.00 Double	Open Jan-Dec Dinner 1830-2030	

Dryfesdale Guest House 37 Inchinnan Road Paisley Renfrewshire PA3 2PR Tel: 041 889 7178/887 7751		**APPROVED** Listed	1 Single 3 Twin 2 Family	2 Pub. Bath/Show	B&B per person £18.00-£20.00 Single £15.00-£17.00 Double	Open Jan-Dec Dinner 1800-2000	

Privately owned guest house 0.5 mile (1km) from Glasgow Airport and M8 access.
Close to Paisley and all facilities.

Myfarrclan Guest House 146 Corsebar Road Paisley Renfrewshire PA2 9NA Tel: 041 884 8285		**DELUXE** 👑 👑	1 Double 1 Family	1 En Suite fac 1 Priv. NOT ensuite	B&B per person from £35.00 Single £22.50-£25.00 Double	Open Jan-Dec	

Detached bungalow in residential area, convenient for Glasgow Airport.
Non smoking house.

Mrs A Wadsworth 25 Main Road, Castlehead Paisley Renfrewshire PA2 6AN Tel: 041 889 5766 Fax: 041 332 8224			1 Twin 2 Double	2 En Suite fac	B&B per person £25.00-£30.00 Single £20.00-£25.00 Double	Open Feb-Nov	

BY PAISLEY Renfrewshire Ashburn Guest House Milliken Park Road Kilbarchan, by Paisley Renfrewshire PA10 2DB Tel: (Kilbarchan) 05057 5477/ 0505 705477 Fax: 0505 705477	Map 1 H5	**APPROVED** 👑 👑	1 Single 3 Twin 2 Family	1 En Suite fac 2 Pub. Bath/Show	B&B per person £22.00-£31.00 Single £19.00-£26.50 Double	Open Jan-Dec Dinner 1800-2000 B&B + Eve. Meal £29.00-£41.00	

19C country house in an acre of garden, 5 minutes drive to Glasgow Airport.

PATHHEAD **Midlothian** Mrs L Matthewson Soutra Mains Blackshiels, Pathhead Midlothian EH37 5TF Tel: (Humbie) 087533 224	Map 2 D5		1 Single 2 Double	2 Pub. Bath/Show	B&B per person to £12.00 Single to £12.00 Double	Open May-Sep B&B + Eve. Meal to £12.00	
PATNA **Ayrshire** Sheila Campbell Parson's Lodge, 15 Main Street Patna Ayrshire KA6 7LN Tel: (Patna) 0292 531306	Map 1 H8	COMMENDED Listed	1 Twin 1 Double 1 Family	1 En Suite fac 2 Pub. Bath/Show	B&B per person £15.00-£18.50 Single £15.00-£18.50 Double	Open Jan-Dec Dinner 1830-2100	
Traditional Scottish hospitality at former manse built from local Ballochmyle sandstone.							
PEAT INN **Fife** Mrs J Aird Falfield House Peat Inn Fife KY15 5LJ Tel: (Peat Inn) 033484 224	Map 2 D3		1 Twin 2 Double	2 Pub. Bath/Show	B&B per person £16.00-£18.00 Double	Open Jan-Dec	
Mrs I Grant West Mains Farm Peat Inn Fife KY15 5LF Tel: (Peat Inn) 033484 313		COMMENDED Listed	1 Twin 1 Double	1 Pub. Bath/Show	B&B per person £12.50-£14.00 Double	Open Apr-Oct	
Home baking on mixed farm with open views of countryside. Good base for touring Fife fishing villages. 7 miles (11kms) from St Andrews.							
PEEBLES Mrs D Davidson Hillside, 44 Edinburgh Road Peebles EH45 8EB Tel: (Peebles) 0721 729817	Map 2 C6	COMMENDED Listed	1 Double 1 Family	1 En Suite fac 1 Pub. Bath/Show	B&B per person £13.00-£15.00 Double	Open Jan-Dec	
Detached house with delightful gardens situated on the outskirts of the town – ideal as a touring base.							
Mrs Fawcett Woodlands, Venlaw Farm Road Peebles Tel: (Peebles) 0721 729882		HIGHLY COMMENDED Listed	1 Twin 1 Double	2 Priv. NOT ensuite	B&B per person £12.00-£14.00 Single £12.00-£14.00 Double	Open Jan-Dec	
Modern detached house in peaceful walled garden setting. Ample parking. Totally secluded, yet only 1 mile (2kms) from town centre.							
Mrs Sheila Goldstraw Venlaw Farm Peebles EH45 8QG Tel: (Peebles) 0721 722040		COMMENDED 👑👑	1 Twin 2 Double 1 Family	1 En Suite fac 1 Priv. NOT ensuite 2 Pub. Bath/Show	B&B per person £14.00-£16.00 Double	Open Apr-Oct	
Personally run modern farmhouse by Peebles. Ideal for walking, fishing and golfing. Good base for touring.							
Mrs Haydock Winkston Farmhouse Peebles EH45 8PH Tel: (Peebles) 0721 721264		HIGHLY COMMENDED 👑	1 Twin 2 Double	2 Pub. Bath/Show	B&B per person £14.00-£15.00 Double	Open Apr-Oct	
'B' Listed Georgian farmhouse of historical interest, in own grounds. Friendly family atmosphere. On main bus route, 21 miles (34kms) from Edinburgh							

Evelyn Inglis Robingarth 46 Edinburgh Road Peebles EH45 8EB Tel: (Peebles) 0721 720226		COMMENDED Listed	2 Twin 1 Double	1 En Suite fac 1 Pub. Bath/Show	B&B per person from £13.00 Double	Open Jan-Dec

Detached pink-faced stone bungalow offering comfortable accommodation on the edge of town. Friendly atmosphere and small craft display. Non-smoking.

Mrs A Kampman 12 Dukehaugh Peebles EH45 9DN Tel: (Peebles) 0721 720118		COMMENDED Listed	1 Single 2 Double	1 Pub. Bath/Show	B&B per person £13.00-£14.00 Single £13.00-£14.00 Double	Open Jan-Dec

Comfortable, non-smoking, house in quiet residential area. 2 minutes from the Tweed and 5 minutes from hourly bus service to Edinburgh.

Mrs C Lane Lindores, Old Town Peebles EH45 8JE Tel: (Peebles) 0721 720441		COMMENDED	2 Twin 2 Double 1 Family	1 En Suite fac 2 Pub. Bath/Show	B&B per person £14.50-£15.50 Single £14.00-£16.00 Double	Open Jan-Dec

Stone built late Victorian town house near edge of town, situated on main A72 tourist route. Convenient for touring the Borders and Edinburgh.

Mrs E McTeir Colliedean, 4 Elibank Road Eddleston Peebles EH45 8QL Tel: (Eddleston) 07213 281/ 0721 730281		COMMENDED Listed	1 Twin 1 Double	1 Pub. Bath/Show	B&B per person to £14.00 Double	Open Apr-Oct

Quietly situated in small village on main bus route to Edinburgh and Borders towns. Homely and friendly atmosphere.

Mrs Morrison 9 Witchwood Crescent Peebles EH45 9AJ Tel: (Peebles) 0721 721206		COMMENDED Listed	1 Single 1 Double	1 Pub. Bath/Show	B&B per person from £15.00 Single from £14.00 Double	Open Apr-Oct

Quiet, comfortable, modern house in pleasant surroundings. Homely atmosphere.

Mrs Muir Whitestone House Innerleithen Road Peebles EH45 8BD Tel: (Peebles) 0721 720337			1 Twin 1 Double 1 Family	2 Pub. Bath/Show	B&B per person £14.00-£15.00 Double	Open Jan-Dec

Mrs J K Phillips Drummore, Venlaw High Road Peebles EH45 8RL Tel: (Peebles) 0721 720336 Fax: 0721 723004		COMMENDED	1 Twin 1 Family	1 Pub. Bath/Show	B&B per person £14.50-£15.50 Double	Open Apr-Oct Dinner 1900-1930 B&B + Eve. Meal £26.50-£28.00

Hillside house in quiet cul-de-sac off the A703. Ideally situated for visiting Edinburgh and the Borders. Taste of Scotland.

	Map 2 C6						
PEEBLES Mrs R Smith Chapel Hill Farm Peebles EH45 8PQ Tel: (Peebles) 0721 720188		COMMENDED	1 Twin 2 Double	1 Pub. Bath/Show	B&B per person £14.00 Double	Open May-Sep	

Farmhouse c1695 on working farm offering warm welcome. Peaceful rural setting yet only 1 mile (2kms) from Peebles. 23 miles (38kms) Edinburgh.

	Map 2 C6						
BY PEEBLES Mrs M Dennison Brookside, Eshiels Peebles EH45 8NA Tel: (Peebles) 0721 721178		COMMENDED Listed	1 Twin 1 Double	1 Pub. Bath/Show	B&B per person to £13.00 Double	Open Mar-Dec	

Large modern bungalow in country 1 mile (2kms) from town and close to Glentress Forest. Home baking. A non-smoking house.

	Map 2 C5						
PENICUIK **Midlothian** Mrs Margaret Kidd Eastfield House 1A Eastfield Drive Penicuik Midlothian EH26 8AY Tel: (Penicuik) 0968 674154		COMMENDED	4 Twin 1 Double	1 En Suite fac 2 Pub. Bath/Show	B&B per person from £17.00 Single from £14.00 Double	Open Jan-Dec	

Friendly welcome in modern, purpose built accommodation only 10 miles (16kms) from Edinburgh city centre.

Mrs A Noble Peggyslea Farm Nine Mile Burn Penicuik Midlothian EH26 9LX Tel: (Penicuik) 0968 60930		COMMENDED Listed	1 Twin 2 Double	2 Pub. Bath/Show	B&B per person £14.00 Single £13.00 Double	Open Jan-Dec	

Warm welcome assured in tastefully furnished modern house on working farm. 20 minutes from Edinburgh on main A702.

Woodhouselee Lodge

Easter Howgate, Penicuik, Midlothian EH26 0PF
Telephone: 031-445 2265

Relax in the delightful surroundings of the Pentland Hills Country Park, with all the attractions of historic Edinburgh just 7 miles away. Plenty of good walking; we can arrange golf, riding and fishing nearby.

The house is comfortably modernised but retains a great deal of its original character and charm.

Dan & Jean Thompson Woodhouselee Lodge Easter Howgate, Penicuik Midlothian EH26 0PF Tel: 031 445 2265		Award Pending	1 Double 1 Family	1 Pub. Bath/Show	B&B per person £16.00-£20.00 Single from £14.00 Double	Open Jan-Dec	

	Map 2 C5						
BY PENICUIK **Midlothian** M & R Marwick Walltower Farm Howgate, by Penicuik Midlothian EH26 8PY Tel: (Penicuik) 0968 672277		COMMENDED	2 Twin 1 Double	1 En Suite fac 1 Pub. Bath/Show	B&B per person £13.00-£18.00 Double	Open Jan-Dec	

Traditional country farmhouse, set in mature garden, only 10 miles (16 kms) from Edinburgh and airport. Easy access to Borders.

	Map 2 C2						
PERTH Adam Guest House 6 Pitcullen Crescent Perth PH2 7HT Tel: (Perth) 0738 27179		COMMENDED	1 Single 1 Twin 2 Double 1 Family	2 En Suite fac 1 Priv. NOT ensuite 1 Pub. Bath/Show	B&B per person £15.00-£17.50 Single £15.00-£17.50 Double	Open Jan-Dec Dinner 1830-1930 B&B + Eve. Meal £23.00-£25.50	

Small and friendly guest house beside A94, with private off road parking. Good home cooking.

Albert Villa Guest House 63 Dunkeld Road Perth PH1 5RP Tel: (Perth) 0738 22730	COMMENDED 👑 👑	3 Single 2 Twin 2 Double 2 Family	6 En Suite fac 1 Pub. Bath/Show	B&B per person £15.00-£20.00 Single £15.00-£16.00 Double	Open Jan-Dec

Family guest house with ample car parking, close to sports centre and swimming pool. Ground floor bedrooms each have their own entrance.

Almond Villa Guest House 51 Dunkeld Road Perth PH1 5RP Tel: (Perth) 0738 29356	COMMENDED 👑 👑	1 Single 1 Twin 1 Double 2 Family	1 En Suite fac 2 Pub. Bath/Show	B&B per person £15.00-£18.00 Single £15.00-£18.00 Double	Open Jan-Dec Dinner from 1830 B&B + Eve. Meal £22.00-£27.50

Semi detached Victorian villa, close to town centre, Bells Sports Centre, the North Inch and River Tay.

Arisaig Guest House 4 Pitcullen Crescent Perth PH2 7HT Tel: (Perth) 0738 28240	COMMENDED 👑 👑	1 Single 1 Twin 1 Double 2 Family	4 En Suite fac 1 Priv. NOT ensuite	B&B per person from £16.00 Single from £16.00 Double	Open Jan-Dec

Comfortable family run guest house, with off street parking. Close to city's many facilities; local touring base. Ground floor bedroom.

Beechgrove Guest House Dundee Road Perth PH2 7AD Tel: (Perth) 0738 36147	HIGHLY COMMENDED 👑 👑	1 Single 2 Twin 2 Double 1 Family	6 En Suite fac	B&B per person from £25.00 Single £20.00-£27.50 Double	Open Jan-Dec

Listed building and former manse set in extensive grounds. Peaceful and quiet, yet only a few minutes walk from the city centre. 1 annexe room.

Clunie Guest House 12 Pitcullen Crescent Perth PH2 7HT Tel: (Perth) 0738 23625	COMMENDED 👑 👑 👑	1 Single 3 Twin 2 Double 1 Family	7 En Suite fac	B&B per person from £17.00 Single from £17.00 Double	Open Jan-Dec Dinner from 1800 B&B + Eve. Meal from £25.00

Personally run in residential part of town. Easy access to town centre and on main bus route.

Hazeldene Guest House Pitcullen Crescent Perth PH2 7HT Tel: (Perth) 0738 23550	COMMENDED 👑 👑 👑	1 Single 1 Twin 2 Double 1 Family	5 En Suite fac	B&B per person £18.00-£20.00 Single £14.00-£18.00 Double	Open Jan-Dec

Family run guest house, on main tourist route to north east but near to city centre. Private car parking available.

Iona Guest House 2 Pitcullen Crescent Perth PH2 7HT Tel: (Perth) 0738 27261	COMMENDED 👑 👑	2 Single 1 Twin 1 Double 1 Family	2 En Suite fac 2 Pub. Bath/Show	B&B per person £15.00-£17.00 Single £15.00-£17.00 Double	Open Jan-Dec Dinner 1800-1930 B&B + Eve. Meal £23.00-£25.00

In residential area, 10 minutes from the town centre with private parking. Over 30 golf courses within 30 miles (48kms) radius.

Kinnoull Guest House 5 Pitcullen Crescent Perth PH2 7HT Tel: (Perth) 0738 34165	COMMENDED 👑 👑 👑	1 Twin 2 Double 1 Family	4 En Suite fac	B&B per person £15.00-£24.00 Single £14.00-£18.00 Double	Open Jan-Dec Dinner 1800-1900

Family run guest house on main tourist route north (A94), within easy reach of city centre. Private facilities for all bedrooms.

PERTH continued	Map 2 C2						
Park Lane Guest House 17 Marshall Place Perth PH2 8AG Tel: (Perth) 0738 37218 Fax: 0738 43519	HIGHLY COMMENDED ⚜ ⚜	1 Single 2 Twin 2 Double 1 Family	6 En Suite fac	B&B per person £16.50-£20.00 Single £16.50-£20.00 Double	Open Jan-Dec	
		Georgian house overlooking Perth South Inch but near to city centre. All ensuite rooms, private car park. Walking distance to golf courses.				
Pitcullen Guest House 17 Pitcullen Crescent Perth PH2 7HT Tel: (Perth) 0738 26506/28265	COMMENDED ⚜ ⚜	1 Single 3 Twin 1 Double 1 Family	3 En Suite fac 2 Pub. Bath/Show	B&B per person from £17.00 Single from £17.00 Double	Open Jan-Dec Dinner from 1800	
		Personally run and conveniently situated on A94 tourist route. Only 5 minutes from City Centre. Private parking.				

ROWANBANK GUEST HOUSE
3 PITCULLEN CRESCENT, PERTH PH2 7HT
Telephone: 0738 21421   Fax: 0738 444110

A late Victorian house tastefully decorated to a high standard. An ideal base for touring and visiting the many interesting visitor attractions in the area, or play golf over some of the finest courses in Britain. You are assured of a warm welcome and a comfortable holiday.

Rowanbank Guest House 3 Pitcullen Crescent Perth PH2 7HT Tel: (Perth) 0738 21421	HIGHLY COMMENDED ⚜ ⚜	1 Twin 1 Double 2 Family	2 En Suite fac 1 Limited ensuite 1 Pub. Bath/Show	B&B per person £16.00-£25.00 Single £16.00-£18.00 Double	Open Jan-Dec Dinner from 1830 B&B + Eve. Meal £24.00-£26.00	
		Friendly, family run guest house with off street parking in an ideal touring area. One ensuite room on ground floor.				
Tigh Mhorag Guest House 69 Dunkeld Road Perth PH1 5RP Tel: (Perth) 0738 22902	Award Pending	2 Single 2 Twin 2 Double	3 En Suite fac 1 Pub. Bath/Show	B&B per person £14.00-£15.00 Single £28.00-£30.00 Double	Open Jan-Dec Dinner from 1800 B&B + Eve. Meal £20.00	
Mrs C Booth Bellview, 38 Hay Street Perth Perthshire PH1 5HS Tel: (Perth) 0738 2858£/38375		2 Double 1 Family	1 Pub. Bath/Show	B&B per person to £14.50 Single from £13.50 Double	Open Jan-Dec, exc Xmas/New Year	
Mrs Buchan Lochiel House Pitcullen Crescent Perth PH2 7HT Tel: (Perth) 0738 33183	HIGHLY COMMENDED ⚜ ⚜	1 Twin 2 Double	1 Priv. NOT ensuite 2 Pub. Bath/Show	B&B per person £14.00-£18.00 Single £14.00-£18.00 Double	Open Jan-Dec	
		Delightful, comfortable Victorian terrace house, own parking close to town centre. One room with private bathroom. Exceptional breakfast selection.				
Alastair Calder 7 King's Place Perth PH2 8AA Tel: (Perth) 0738 25708 Fax: 0738 25708	COMMENDED ⚜ ⚜	1 Twin 2 Double 2 Family	1 En Suite fac 1 Pub. Bath/Show	B&B per person £11.00-£15.00 Single £11.00-£15.00 Double	Open Jan-Dec	
		Terraced house overlooking public park near bus and railway station. Only 600 yards from town centre. Off street car parking.				

Mr & Mrs J Cattanach Clark Kimberley 57-59 Dunkeld Road Perth PH1 5RP Tel: (Perth) 0738 37406	COMMENDED 👑👑	2 Single 2 Twin 2 Double 2 Family	6 En Suite fac 1 Pub. Bath/Show	B&B per person £15.00-£17.00 Single £15.00-£17.00 Double	Open Jan-Dec	
		Detached house on main Inverness road out of the city. City centre within walking distance. Private parking.				
Mrs J Davidson Fernlea, 37 Needless Road Perth PH2 0LE Tel: (Perth) 0738 27766		1 Family	1 Pub. Bath/Show	B&B per person £12.00-£13.00 Double	Open Jan-Dec	
Mr& Mrs Dawson Castleview, 166 Glasgow Road Perth PH2 0LY Tel: (Perth) 0738 26415		2 Twin 1 Family	3 En Suite fac	B&B per person £16.00-£18.00 Double	Open Feb-Dec Dinner 1830-1900 B&B + Eve. Meal £24.00-£26.00	
Mrs J Glennie 54 Glasgow Road Perth PH2 0PB Tel: (Perth) 0738 26723		1 Single 1 Twin 1 Double	2 Pub. Bath/Show	B&B per person from £13.00 Double	Open Apr-Oct	
Mrs V Harding Rhodes Villa, 75 Dunkeld Road Perth PH1 5RP Tel: (Perth) 0738 28466	COMMENDED 👑👑	2 Twin 1 Double	2 En Suite fac 2 Pub. Bath/Show	B&B per person £13.50-£15.00 Single £13.50-£15.00 Double	Open Jan-Dec Dinner 1700-1930 B&B + Eve. Meal £18.00-£20.00	
		Personal attention and a friendly welcome. Close to amenities with private parking. En route to the north; ideally situated for touring.				
Mr & Mrs Livingstone Westview, 49 Dunkeld Road Perth PH1 5RP Tel: (Perth) 0738 27787		2 Twin 1 Double	1 En Suite fac 1 Pub. Bath/Show	B&B per person £13.00-£14.00 Single £14.00-£16.00 Double	Open Jan-Dec Dinner 1800-2100	
Mr & Mrs McNicol Abbotsford, 23 James Street Perth PH2 8LX Tel: (Perth) 0738 35219	COMMENDED Listed	1 Single 2 Twin 3 Family	6 Limited ensuite	B&B per person £14.00-£16.00 Single £16.00-£18.00 Double	Open Jan-Dec	
		Victorian villa, in quiet residential area, a few minutes walk from the town centre, station and bus station. All rooms have shower and colour TV.				
Mr J R Muir Brae Lodge, 140 Glasgow Road Perth PH2 0LX Tel: (Perth) 0738 28473	APPROVED 👑	1 Twin 1 Double 1 Family	2 Limited ensuite 1 Pub. Bath/Show	B&B per person £14.00-£16.00 Double	Open Jan-Dec Dinner 1800-2000 B&B + Eve. Meal £18.25-£20.25	
		Semi-detached house now double glazed. Off street parking available. Ideal base for touring the Highlands.				
Mr & Mrs Napier Lindally, 10-12 North William Street Perth PH1 5PT Tel: (Perth) 0738 36728 Fax: 0738 36728		2 Twin 2 Double 1 Family	1 Pub. Bath/Show	B&B per person £13.50-£15.50 Single £13.50-£15.50 Double	Open Jan-Dec Dinner 1800-1900 B&B + Eve. Meal £20.50-£22.50	

PERTH continued	Map 2 C2						
Mr A P Normand Richmond House 50 Glasgow Road Perth PH2 0PB Tel: (Perth) 0738 27548		APPROVED Listed	1 Single 1 Twin 1 Family	1 En Suite fac 2 Pub. Bath/Show	B&B per person from £14.00 Single from £13.00 Double	Open Jan-Dec	

Personally run, close to town and the Leisure Pool and ice rink.

| Orana
21 Marshall Place
Perth
PH2 8AG
Tel: (Perth) 0738 28482 | | | 3 Single
1 Twin
3 Family | 2 En Suite fac
2 Pub. Bath/Show | B&B per person
£16.50-£17.00 Single
£15.50-£17.50 Double | Open Jan-Dec | |

| Mr & Mrs Reid
Ballabeg, 14 Keir Street
Bridgend
Perth
PH2 7HJ
Tel: (Perth) 0738 20434 | | COMMENDED | 1 Single
1 Double
1 Family | 1 Pub. Bath/Show | B&B per person
£14.50-£17.00 Single
£14.50-£17.00 Double | Open Jan-Dec | |

Friendly, family run house in quiet street off A94. Evening snacks available in rooms. 10 minutes from the city centre.

| Mrs P Smith
Beeches, 2 Comely Bank
Perth
PH2 7HU
Tel: (Perth) 0738 24486 | | COMMENDED | 1 Single
1 Twin
1 | 1 En Suite fac
1 Pub. Bath/Show
Double | B&B per person
from £15.00 Single
from £15.00 Double | Open Jan-Dec
Dinner 1800-2000 | |

Semi-detached villa with ample car parking, conveniently situated on A94 tourist route.

BY PERTH	Map 2 C2						
Waterybutts Lodge Grange Errol Perthshire PH2 7SZ Tel: (Errol) 0821 642894 Fax: 0821 642523		HIGHLY COMMENDED	3 Twin 4 Double	7 En Suite fac	B&B per person £30.00-£33.00 Single £25.00-£27.50 Double	Open Jan-Dec Dinner 1900-2200 B&B + Eve. Meal £40.00-£44.00	

Beautiful Georgian Lodge with fine grounds, shrubs and trees and a unique herb garden. Set in the gentle climatic region of the Carse of Gowrie.

Sandabel House

Netherlea, Scone, Perthshire PH3 6QA
Telephone: (0738) 51062

Beautiful and spacious luxury bungalow with large extensive gardens in a quiet residential area just off the main A94. Scone is only 2 miles from Perth town centre. We can assure you of a warm and friendly welcome and personal attention at all times. Our rooms have private facilities, colour TV, tea/coffee, hairdryers, trouser presses. Ample private parking. Activities such as golf, fishing, pony-trekking and hill-walking can be arranged if required. A full Scottish breakfast every morning should start your day off really well and Perthshire is a lovely place to see.

This establishment is Deluxe.

| Mrs S Dewar
Sandabel House, Netherlea
Scone
Perthshire
PH2 6RQ
Tel: (Scone) 0738 51062 | | DELUXE
Listed | 1 Twin
1 Double | 2 En Suite fac
2 Pub. Bath/Show | B&B per person
£15.00-£20.00 Single
£15.00-£18.50 Double | Open Jan-Dec | |

Delightful and spacious luxury bungalow with extensive gardens in quiet residential area, 2 miles (3kms) from Perth.

VAT is shown at 17.5%: changes in this rate may affect prices. Prices shown are for guidance only. Please send SAE with each enquiry.

Mrs Dorothy Dow Tophead Farm, Tullybelton Stanley, by Perth Perthshire PH1 4PT Tel: (Stanley) 0738 828259	COMMENDED	2 Twin 1 Double	1 En Suite fac 1 Priv. NOT ensuite 1 Pub. Bath/Show	B&B per person £14.00–£18.00 Double	Open Jan-Dec
		A very warm Scottish welcome in this traditional farmhouse on 200 acre dairy farm. Perth 4 miles (6kms). Extensive views over rural Perthshire.			
Mrs A Guthrie Newmill Farm Stanley, Perth Perthshire PH1 4QD Tel: (Stanley) 0738 828281		1 Twin 2 Double	2 En Suite fac 2 Pub. Bath/Show	B&B per person £15.00–£18.00 Single £14.00–£18.00 Double	Open Apr-Oct Dinner 1800-1830 B&B + Eve. Meal £24.00-£28.00
Mrs H Lindsay Huntingtower House by Perth Perthshire PH1 3JJ Tel: (Perth) 0738 24681	Award Pending	2 Twin 1 Double	1 Pub. Bath/Show	B&B per person £13.00–£15.00 Single £13.00–£15.00 Double	Open Jan-Dec
Mrs D McFarlane Letham Farm Bankfoot Perthshire PH1 4EF Tel: (Bankfoot) 073887 322	COMMENDED	1 Twin 1 Double 1 Family	2 Pub. Bath/Show	B&B per person £15.00 Single £13.00–£14.00 Double	Open Mar-Oct Dinner from 1830 B&B + Eve. Meal £22.00-£23.00
		300 acre arable and raspberry farm in beautiful countryside, yet only 10 minutes from Perth. Warm welcome and home cooking.			
Mrs M Niven Braeknowe Tibbermore Perthshire PH1 1QJ Tel: (Perth) 0738 840295		1 Twin 1 Double	1 Pub. Bath/Show	B&B per person £12.00–£15.00 Single £12.00–£15.00 Double	Open May-Oct
Mrs C Smith Pitmurthly Farm Redgorton, by Perth Perthshire PH1 3HX Tel: (Perth) 0738 828363	HIGHLY COMMENDED Listed	1 Single 1 Twin 1 Double	1 En Suite fac 1 Pub. Bath/Show	B&B per person £15.00–£18.00 Double	Open Jan-Dec
		Traditional Scottish hospitality at this comfortable farmhouse set in peaceful countryside 5 mins from historic Perth. Ideal for touring. Close			
Mrs Stirrat Fingask Farm Rhynd, by Perth Perthshire PH2 8QF Tel: (Perth) 0738 812220	COMMENDED Listed	1 Single 1 Twin 1 Double	1 Pub. Bath/Show	B&B per person from £14.00 Single from £14.00 Double	Open Feb-Nov Dinner from 1830 B&B + Eve. Meal from £24.00
		Enjoy the lovely garden and home cooking on this traditional farmhouse on mixed working farm, approximately 6 miles (10kms) south east of Perth.			
PETERHEAD **Aberdeenshire** Carrick Guest House 16 Merchant Street Peterhead Aberdeenshire AB42 6DU Tel: (Peterhead) 0779 70610 Fax: 0779 70610	Map 4 H8 COMMENDED	2 Single 3 Twin 2 Family	7 En Suite fac	B&B per person £15.00–£17.50 Single £15.00–£17.50 Double	Open Jan-Dec
		Personally run, terraced house close to town centre, harbour and beach. All bedrooms double glazed.			

| PITLOCHRY | Map 2 |
| Perthshire | B1 |

Craigroyston House

2 LOWER OAKFIELD, PITLOCHRY PH16 5HQ
Telephone: 0796-472053

A Victorian Country House set in own grounds with views of the surrounding hills. Centrally situated, there is direct pedestrian access to the town centre.

★ All rooms have private facilities and are equipped to a high standard.
★ Colour TV, welcome tray, central heating.
★ Residents' lounge.
★ Dining room with separate tables.
★ Safe private parking. **OPEN**
★ Dinner available. **ALL YEAR**
★ Table licence.

AA Listed QQQ

BED & BREAKFAST FROM £16 PER PERSON.

Craigroyston Guest House 2 Lower Oakfield Pitlochry Perthshire PH16 5HQ Tel: (Pitlochry) 0796 472053	COMMENDED 👑 👑 👑	3 Twin 3 Double 2 Family	8 En Suite fac	B&B per person £16.00-£25.00 Double	Open Jan-Dec Dinner 1815-1845 B&B + Eve. Meal £29.00-£39.00	

Family run Victorian villa near town centre with large garden overlooking wooded hills. 10 minutes walk from theatre.

Derrybeg Guest House

18 Lower Oakfield, Pitlochry. Tel: 0796 472070

DERRYBEG is set in a quiet location only a few minutes' walk from the town centre, enjoying magnificent views of the Vale of Atholl. The resident proprietors, Derek and Marion Stephenson, ensure only the finest hospitality, comfort, and good home cooking.

● Open all year for B&B or DB&B. Unlicensed, but guests welcome to supply own table wine.
● Full central heating throughout.
● Colour television and welcome tea/coffee tray in all bedrooms.
● All bedrooms with private facilities.
● Comfortable lounge and dining room.
● Food Hygiene Excellent Award.
● Ample parking in the grounds.
● Leisure activities can easily be arranged, i.e. theatre bookings, golf, fishing, pony-trekking, etc.

👑 👑 👑
COMMENDED

Colour brochure/tariff and details of weekly reductions available on request.

Derrybeg Guest House 18 Lower Oakfield Pitlochry Perthshire PH16 5DS Tel: (Pitlochry) 0796 472070	COMMENDED 👑 👑 👑	2 Single 2 Twin 6 Double 1 Family	11 En Suite fac	B&B per person £16.00-£21.00 Single £16.00-£21.00 Double	Open Jan-Nov Dinner 1815-1845 B&B + Eve. Meal £26.50-£31.50	

Privately owned detached house with large south facing garden in quiet, but central location. Elevated position overlooking Tummel Valley.

DUNDARAVE HOUSE

Situated in one of the most enviable areas of Pitlochry, in its own grounds of approx. ½ acre. Dundarave offers the tourist of the nineteen-nineties every comfort and amenity required.

- *All rooms, colour TV and tea/coffee making facilities.*
- *All double/twin bedded rooms with bathrooms en-suite.*
- *Fully heated.*
- *Residents lounge — open all day.*

For your ovenight stay or longer please contact your hosts: Mae and Bob Collier.

SPECIAL AA QUALITY AWARD
STB ♛♛♛ COMMENDED

STRATHVIEW TERRACE, PITLOCHRY
Tel: (0796) 473109

Dundarave House Strathview Terrace Pitlochry Perthshire PH16 5AT Tel: (Pitlochry) 0796 473109	COMMENDED ♛♛♛	2 Single 2 Twin 2 Double 1 Family	5 En Suite fac 2 Pub. Bath/Show	B&B per person £20.00-£26.00 Single £20.00-£26.00 Double	Open Apr-Oct Dinner 1800-1900 B&B + Eve. Meal £35.00-£41.00	
Charming Victorian house, quiet location and stunning views close to centre of Pitlochry. Ground floor room; personal, attentive service.					

DUNTRUNE

22 East Moulin Road, Pitlochry, Perthshire PH16 5HY
Telephone: 0796 472172

Standing in mature gardens overlooking Pitlochry and surrounding countryside — yet within walking distance of all local amenities. Duntrune offers a personal service, comfortably appointed bedrooms with private facilities, and freshly prepared home cooking. Short break terms available throughout the season. **AA Listed**

Duntrune Guest House 22 East Moulin Road Pitlochry Perthshire PH16 5HY Tel: (Pitlochry) 0796 472172	COMMENDED ♛♛♛	2 Single 2 Twin 2 Double 1 Family	5 En Suite fac 1 Pub. Bath/Show	B&B per person £17.00-£18.00 Single £17.00-£19.00 Double	Open Mar-Oct Dinner from 1800 B&B + Eve. Meal from £26.00	
Stone built house in quiet residential area overlooking town, with warm friendly atmosphere and excellent views of surrounding area.					
Mrs Beattie Cresta, 15 Lettoch Terrace Pitlochry Perthshire PH16 5BA Tel: (Pitlochry) 0796 472204		1 Twin 1 Double	1 Pub. Bath/Show	B&B per person to £14.00 Double	Open Apr-Oct	
Mrs C A Bell Silver Howe, Perth Road Pitlochry Perthshire PH16 5LY Tel: (Pitlochry) 0796 472181	HIGHLY COMMENDED ♛♛	2 Twin 2 Double	2 En Suite fac 1 Limited ensuite 1 Pub. Bath/Show	B&B per person £17.00-£20.00 Double	Open Jan-Dec	
Detached modern bungalow on town outskirts with large south facing garden and open outlook to Tummel Valley. Evening home-bakes.					

Details of Grading and Classification are on page vi.

Key to symbols is on back flap.

PITLOCHRY continued	Map 2 B1					
Mrs Bruce Atholl Villa, 29 Atholl Road Pitlochry Perthshire PH16 5BX Tel: (Pitlochry) 0796 473820		COMMENDED ♛	4 Twin 3 Double 2 Family	9 En Suite fac	B&B per person from £23.00 Single £19.50-£21.00 Double	Open Feb-Nov
			Comfortable and elegant ensuite accommodation, centrally situated for all facilities. Non smoking.			
Mrs L Fraser Lyndon, 4A Higher Oakfield Pitlochry Perthshire PH16 5HT Tel: (Pitlochry) 0796 472663			1 Twin 1 Double	2 Pub. Bath/Show	B&B per person £14.00-£14.50 Double	Open Apr-Oct
Mr R Gordon Rosehill, 47 Atholl Road Pitlochry Perthshire PH16 5BX Tel: (Pitlochry) 0796 472958			4 Double 3 Family	4 En Suite fac 2 Pub. Bath/Show	B&B per person £15.00-£18.00 Double	Open Apr-Oct
Mr & Mrs Henderson Oakbank, 20 Lower Oakfield Pitlochry Perthshire PH16 5BS Tel: (Pitlochry) 0796 473441			2 Double	1 En Suite fac 1 Priv. NOT ensuite	B&B per person to £16.00 Single	Open Apr-Sep
Mr Ian Hendry Four Seasons Higher Oakfield, Pitlochry Perthshire PH16 5HT Tel: (Pitlochry) 0796 472080			1 Single 1 Twin 1 Double	2 Pub. Bath/Show	B&B per person £12.00-£14.00 Single £12.00-£14.00 Double	Open Jan-Dec
Mrs Howman Auchnahyle, Tomcroy Terrace Pitlochry Perthshire PH16 5JA Tel: (Pitlochry) 0796 472318 Fax: 0796 473657			3 Twin	3 En Suite fac	B&B per person £28.00-£40.00 Single £28.00-£30.00 Double	Open Jan-Dec Dinner from 1900 B&B + Eve. Meal £42.00-£58.50
Mrs M MacNicoll Morag Cottage 163 Atholl Road Pitlochry Perthshire PH16 5QL Tel: (Pitlochry) 0796 472973			1 Double 2 Family	1 Pub. Bath/Show	B&B per person £13.00-£14.50 Double	Open Jan-Dec
Mr & Mrs A Norris Kinnaird House Kirkmichael Road Pitlochry Perthshire PH16 5JL Tel: (Pitlochry) 0796 472843		COMMENDED Listed	1 Twin 2 Double	2 En Suite fac 1 Pub. Bath/Show	B&B per person £16.00-£25.00 Double	Open Jan-Dec
			Detached Victorian villa in rural setting 1.5 miles (2.5 kms) from the town. Superb views of the surrounding countryside.			

Mr S Robertson Catherine Bank West 5 Lower Oakfield Pitlochry Perthshire PH16 5DS Tel: (Pitlochry) 0796 473851			1 Single 1 Twin 1 Double	2 En Suite fac 1 Pub. Bath/Show	B&B per person £15.00-£16.00 Single £17.00-£18.00 Double	Open Apr-Oct	
Mrs Robertson Lavalette, Manse Road, Moulin Pitlochry Perthshire PH16 5EP Tel: (Pitlochry) 0796 472364			1 Double 1 Fam/Twin	2 En Suite fac	B&B per person from £13.50 Double	Open Mar-Oct	
Mrs P Robinson Manseholm, Manse Road Moulin Pitlochry Perthshire PH16 5EP Tel: (Pitlochry) 0796 473700 Fax: 0796 473774	Award Pending		2 Double 1 Family	1 En Suite fac 1 Pub. Bath/Show	B&B per person £14.00-£17.50 Double	Open Jan-Dec	
Mrs Kathleen Scott Landscape, Larchwood Road Pitlochry Perthshire PH16 5AS Tel: (Pitlochry) 0796 472765			3 Double	3 En Suite fac	B&B per person £17.50-£20.00 Double	Open May-Oct	
Mrs Vickers Lonaig, Lettoch Terrace Pitlochry Perthshire PH16 5BA Tel: (Pitlochry) 0796 472422			2 Double	1 Pub. Bath/Show	B&B per person from £12.50 Double	Open May-Oct	

Dun-Donnachaidh
9 Knockard Road, Pitlochry, Perthshire PH16 5HJ
Telephone/Fax: 0796 474018

Enjoy a warm welcome in our beautiful Victorian home, which has the finest views in Pitlochry. The charm and elegance of the drawing room and dining room and all the comforts in the en-suite bedrooms are there to make your holiday a pleasure. *Please contact Mrs Lorraine Wallace.*

| Mrs Lorraine Wallace
Dundonnachaidh
Knockard Road
Pitlochry
Perthshire
Tel: (Pitlochry) 0796 474018 | | | 1 Twin
2 Double | 3 En Suite fac | B&B per person
£16.00-£22.00 Double | Open Jan-Dec | |

PITLOCHRY continued	Map 2 B1

Comar House

STRATHVIEW TERRACE · PITLOCHRY
Tel: (0796) 473531 Fax: (0796) 473811

The idyllic situation and character of Comar House offers the tourist traveller something special. Comar enjoys panoramic views and is an ideal base for the many and varied attractions for which Perthshire is noted, not least the world-renowned Pitlochry Festival Theatre and the nearby Hydro-Electric Board Dam with its famous salmon ladder.

A warm welcome awaits from Isabel and Bill Watson.

Mr & Mrs W Watson Comar House Strathview Terrace Pitlochry Perthshire PH16 5AT Tel: (Pitlochry) 0796 473531	COMMENDED 👑👑	1 Single 3 Twin 1 Double 1 Family	3 En Suite fac 1 Pub. Bath/Show	B&B per person £15.00–£17.50 Single £15.00–£20.50 Double	Open Apr-Oct	

Elegant turreted period house standing high above town with panoramic views.

PITTENWEEM Fife Mrs S Hart Victoria Cottage 11 Viewforth Place Pittenweem Fife KY10 2PZ Tel: (Pittenweem) 0333 311998	Map 2 E3 COMMENDED Listed	1 Twin 1 Double	1 Pub. Bath/Show	B&B per person £13.00–£16.00 Single £13.00–£16.00 Double	Open Apr-Oct	

Warm welcome awaits in charming Victorian House. Conveniently situated near harbour. Ideal base for coastal villages, St Andrews. Non smoking.

PLOCKTON Ross-shire Mrs Alice Byrne Minvouch, 2 Railway Cottages Plockton Ross-shire IV52 Tel: (Plockton) 059984 333	Map 3 F9	2 Double 1 Family	1 Pub. Bath/Show	B&B per person £11.50–£12.00 Single £11.50–£12.00 Double	Open Jan-Dec	

Mrs Heaviside Craig Highland Farm Plockton Ross-shire IV52 8UB Tel: (Plockton) 059984 205	APPROVED Listed	1 Twin 1 Double 1 Family	1 Limited ensuite 1 Pub. Bath/Show	B&B per person from £15.00 Single £14.00–£16.00 Double	Open Jan-Dec	

Converted croft house. Farm now a sanctuary for rare and ancient breeds of farm animals. Family loft room.

Mrs J Jones 4 Frithard Road Plockton Ross-shire IV52 8TQ Tel: (Plockton) 059984 321		Award Pending	1 Twin 1 Double 1 Family	2 Pub. Bath/Show	B&B per person £12.50 Double	Open Jan-Dec
Mrs Jane MacDonald The Sheiling Plockton Ross-shire IV52 8TL Tel: (Plockton) 059984 282		COMMENDED 👑 👑	2 Double 1 Family	1 En Suite fac 1 Pub. Bath/Show	B&B per person £13.00-£17.00 Double	Open Apr-Oct
			Family run home with a beautiful view over Loch Carron. Short walk to shops and hotels. Ideal centre for touring and walking.			
Mrs Rowe 25 Harbour Street Plockton Ross-shire IV52 8TN Tel: (Plockton) 059984 356			1 Twin 2 Double	2 En Suite fac 1 Priv. NOT ensuite	B&B per person £16.00-£18.50 Double	Open Jan-Dec
Mrs B Townend Achnahenich Farm Plockton Ross-shire IV52 8TY Tel: (Plockton) 059984 238			2 Twin 1 Family	1 En Suite fac 1 Pub. Bath/Show	B&B per person £13.00-£15.00 Single £13.00-£15.00 Double	Open Apr-Oct Dinner 1800-2000 B&B + Eve. Meal £17.00-£19.00
Mrs J Williams Obanduine, Harbour Street Plockton Ross-shire IV52 8TG Tel: (Plockton) 059984 261			1 Single 1 Double 1 Family	1 Pub. Bath/Show	B&B per person from £13.00 Single from £13.00 Double	Open Jan-Dec
POOLEWE **Ross-shire** Mrs K MacDonald Benlair, Near Cove Poolewe Ross-shire IV22 2LS Tel: (Poolewe) 044586 354	Map 3 F7	COMMENDED 👑	2 Twin	1 En Suite fac 1 Priv. NOT ensuite	B&B per person from £19.00 Double	Open Apr-Oct Dinner from 1800
			Family run cottage in tranquil setting with superb views over the sea, 200 yards from sandy beach, near village of Cove. Occasional evening meals.			
PORT APPIN **Argyll** Linnhe House Port Appin Argyll PA38 4DE Tel: (Appin) 063173 245	Map 1 E1	COMMENDED 👑 👑 👑	3 Twin 1 Double	4 En Suite fac 1 Pub. Bath/Show	B&B per person £22.00-£25.00 Single £22.00-£25.00 Double	Open Jan-Dec Dinner at 1900 B&B + Eve. Meal £30.00-£33.00
			Family run detached 19thC house in own grounds overlooking Loch Linnhe and the Morven Hills. Home cooking and baking.			
PORT ASKAIG **Isle of Islay, Argyll** Mrs M McMillan Meadowbank, Keills Port Askaig Isle of Islay, Argyll Tel: (Port Askaig) 049684 679	Map 1 C5		1 Twin 2 Double	1 Pub. Bath/Show	B&B per person £13.00 Single £13.00 Double	Open Jan-Dec Dinner 1800-1830 B&B + Eve. Meal £18.00

Details of Grading and Classification are on page vi. | Key to symbols is on back flap. |

PORT CHARLOTTE **Isle of Islay, Argyll** Mrs P Halsall Nerabus Port Charlotte Isle of Islay, Argyll PA48 7UE Tel: (Port Charlotte) 049685 431 Fax: 049685 431	Map 1 B6		2 Twin	2 En Suite fac 1 Pub. Bath/Show	B&B per person £12.00-£15.00 Single £12.00-£15.00 Double	Open Jan-Dec Dinner 1830-2030 B&B + Eve. Meal £19.00-£22.00

Carole & David Harris   TEL: 049 685 261

7 SHORE STREET, PORT CHARLOTTE, ISLAY PA48 7TR

A PEACEFUL ISLAND SETTING

10 metres from lochside, rooms with uninterrupted views over hills and loch. A friendly atmosphere with good service.
REAL FOOD using **ALL** fresh produce (including real vegetarian food)
We are a small B&B offering something different.
NO SMOKING ★ Open all year ★ Minibus/Taxi service.
THE TASTE OF SCOTLAND COMMENDED

Carole & David Harris Taigh-na-Creag, 7 Shore Street Port Charlotte Isle of Islay, Argyll PA48 7TR Tel: (Port Charlotte) 049685 261			1 Twin 1 Double	2 Pub. Bath/Show	B&B per person £18.50 Single £16.00 Double	Open Jan-Dec Dinner 1800-1900 B&B + Eve. Meal £26.50
PORT ELLEN **Isle of Islay, Argyll** Pat & John Kent Tighcargaman Port Ellen Isle of Islay, Argyll PA42 7BX Tel: (Port Ellen) 0496 2345	Map 1 C6		2 Twin 1 Double	2 Pub. Bath/Show	B&B per person from £15.00 Double	Open Jan-Dec Dinner from 1900 B&B + Eve. Meal from £23.00

GLENMACHRIE FARMHOUSE

Glenmachrie, Port Ellen, Isle of Islay, Argyll PA42 7AW
Telephone: Mrs Rachel Whyte on 0496 2560

Escape the pressures of modern life!
Sample true Highland hospitality within the peace and beauty of Glenmachrie Farmhouse nestling between Machrie Golf Links and Duich Nature Reserve. Quality food using the best of Islay's larder, private fishing for wild brown trout and wonderful memories is our pledge to guests.

Mrs R Whyte Glenmachrie Farmhouse Port Ellen Isle of Islay, Argyll PA42 7AW Tel: (Port Ellen) 0496 2560		👑 👑 👑	3 Twin 2 Double	5 En Suite fac 1 Pub. Bath/Show	B&B per person £18.00-£22.00 Double	Open Jan-Dec Dinner 1800-2030 B&B + Eve. Meal £26.00-£30.00
BY PORT ELLEN **Isle of Islay, Argyll** Mrs Underwood Carraig Fhada Farm by Port Ellen Isle of Islay, Argyll PA42 7AX Tel: (Port Ellen) 0496 2114	Map 1 C6		1 Single 2 Twin	1 Pub. Bath/Show	B&B per person £12.00-£14.50 Single £12.50-£15.00 Double	Open Jan-Dec Dinner 1830-1900 B&B + Eve. Meal £18.50-£23.00

PORTNAHAVEN **Isle of Islay, Argyll** Mrs MacLean Glenview House Portnahaven Isle of Islay, Argyll PA47 7SL Tel: (Portnahaven) 049686 303	Map 1 B6		1 Twin 1 Double 1 Family	1 Pub. Bath/Show	B&B per person £13.50-£15.50 Double	Open Jan-Dec Dinner 1800-1930 B&B + Eve. Meal £21.00-£23.00

PORT OF MENTEITH **Perthshire** Mrs Norma Erskine Inchie Farm Port of Menteith Perthshire FK8 3JZ Tel: (Port of Menteith) 0877 385233	Map 1 H3	COMMENDED 👑	1 Twin 1 Family	1 Pub. Bath/Show	B&B per person £12.00-£14.00 Double	Open Apr-Oct Dinner from 1800 B&B + Eve. Meal £19.00-£21.00

Family farm on the shores of Lake of Menteith. Traditional, comfortable farmhouse. Home baking and hospitality a priority.

Mrs C Tough Collymoon Pendicle Port of Menteith Perthshire FK8 3JY Tel: (Buchlyvie) 036085 222/268		COMMENDED 👑	1 Single 1 Double 1 Family	1 Pub. Bath/Show	B&B per person £12.00-£14.00 Single £12.00-£14.00 Double	Open Apr-Oct Dinner 1800-1900 B&B + Eve. Meal £19.00-£21.00

Family run modern bungalow in country setting surrounded by panoramic views. Home cooking a speciality. Salmon and trout fishing available.

PORT OF NESS **Lewis, Western Isles** Michael Allen Harbour View Port of Ness Lewis, Western Isles PA86 0XA Tel: (Port of Ness) 085181 735	Map 3 D3	COMMENDED 👑	1 Twin 1 Double	1 Pub. Bath/Show	B&B per person £14.50-£18.00 Single £14.50-£18.00 Double	Open Easter-Nov Dinner to 1900

Originally a boat builder's house C1880, now sympathetically converted. Tea room adjacent with home baking and cooking; vegetarians welcome.

Catriona MacLeod Eisdean, 12 Fivepenny Ness Lewis, Western Isles PA86 0XG Tel: (Port of Ness) 085181 240		COMMENDED Listed	1 Single 1 Twin 1 Family	1 Pub. Bath/Show	B&B per person from £14.00 Single from £14.00 Double	Open Jan-Dec Dinner 1900-2200 B&B + Eve. Meal from £21.00

Working croft with home baking and cooking within 1 mile (2kms) of Butt of Lewis with several sandy beaches in surrounding area. Gaelic spoken.

PORTPATRICK **Wigtownshire** Carlton Guest House South Crescent Portpatrick Wigtownshire DG9 8JR Tel: (Portpatrick) 077681 253	Map 1 F1	COMMENDED 👑 👑 👑	2 Twin 3 Double 2 Family	6 En Suite fac 1 Pub. Bath/Show	B&B per person £18.00-£25.00 Single £16.00-£20.00 Double	Open Jan-Dec Dinner 1800-1900 B&B + Eve. Meal £24.00-£26.00

Comfortable, and overlooking picturesque harbour with superb views over the Irish Sea. Fresh local produce.

Mrs McPherson Pinminnoch Farmhouse Portpatrick Wigtownshire DG9 9AB Tel: (Portpatrick) 077681 362			2 Twin 1 Double	2 Pub. Bath/Show	B&B per person to £13.00 Single to £13.00 Double	Open Easter-Oct Dinner 1800-1900 B&B + Eve. Meal to £20.00

Mrs A Moffat Braefield House Portpatrick Wigtownshire DG9 8TA Tel: (Portpatrick) 077681 255			1 Single 2 Twin 3 Double 1 Family	4 En Suite fac 1 Pub. Bath/Show	B&B per person £17.00-£18.00 Single £17.00-£18.00 Double	Open Jan-Dec

PORTPATRICK **Wigtownshire** Roger and Evelyn O'Meara The Knowe, 1 North Crescent Portpatrick Wigtownshire DG9 8SX Tel: (Portpatrick) 077681 441	Map 1 F1		1 Twin 5 Double 1 Family	5 En Suite fac 1 Limited ensuite 1 Pub. Bath/Show	B&B per person to £17.00 Single £15.00–£17.00 Double	Open Jan-Dec	
PORTREE **Isle of Skye, Inverness-shire** Mrs M J Gilmour Myrtlebank, Achachork Portree Isle of Skye, Inverness-shire IV51 9HT Tel: (Portree) 0478 2597/ 612597	Map 3 D9		1 Single 1 Double 1 Family	1 Pub. Bath/Show	B&B per person from £13.00 Single from £13.00 Double	Open Apr-Sep	
Mrs J MacDonald 10 Achachork, Staffin Road Portree Isle of Skye, Inverness-shire IV51 9HP Tel: (Portree) 0478 2213/ 612213			1 Single 1 Double 1 Family	2 Pub. Bath/Show	B&B per person from £14.00 Single from £14.00 Double	Open Mar-Nov	
Mrs MacFarlane Quiraing, Viewfield Road Portree Isle of Skye, Inverness-shire IV51 9ES Tel: (Portree) 0478 612870			1 Twin 1 Double 2 Family	4 En Suite fac	B&B per person £15.00–£17.00 Single £15.00–£17.00 Double	Open Jan-Dec	
Mrs MacLeod An Airidh, Viewfield Road Portree Isle of Skye, Inverness-shire IV51 9EU Tel: (Portree) 0478 612250			2 Single 1 Double 3 Family	4 En Suite fac 2 Priv. NOT ensuite 1 Pub. Bath/Show	B&B per person £15.00 Single £17.00–£18.00 Double	Open Mar-Sep Dinner from 1800 B&B + Eve. Meal £25.00–£38.00	
Mrs McPhie Balloch, Viewfield Road Portree Isle of Skye, Inverness-shire IV51 9ES Tel: (Portree) 0478 2093/ 612093			2 Twin 1 Double	2 Pub. Bath/Show	B&B per person from £15.00 Single from £15.00 Double	Open Mar-Dec	
Mrs C Murray Conusg, Coolin Hills Gardens Portree Isle of Skye, Inverness-shire IV51 9NR Tel: (Portree) 0478 2426/ 612426			2 Single 1 Twin 1 Double	1 Pub. Bath/Show	B&B per person £14.00–£14.50 Single £14.00–£14.50 Double	Open Mar-Oct	
Mrs E Nicolson Almondbank, Viewfield Road Portree Isle of Skye, Inverness-shire IV51 9EU Tel: (Portree) 0478 2696/ 612696 Fax: 0478 3114			2 Double 2 Family	2 En Suite fac 2 Pub. Bath/Show	B&B per person from £15.00 Single from £15.00 Double	Open Jan-Dec Dinner from 1800 B&B + Eve. Meal from £25.00	

Mrs Nicolson 16 Martin Crescent Portree Isle of Skye, Inverness-shire IV51 9DW Tel: (Portree) 0478 2342			2 Family	1 Pub. Bath/Show	B&B per person from £12.00 Double	Open Jan-Dec	
Mrs P M Thorpe Jacamar, Achachork Road Portree Isle of Skye, Inverness-shire IV51 9HT Tel: (Portree) 0478 2274/ 612274		Award Pending	1 Double 1 Family	1 En Suite fac 1 Pub. Bath/Show	B&B per person £14.00-£15.00 Single £13.00-£18.00 Double	Open Jan-Dec Dinner 1830-1930 B&B + Eve. Meal £20.00-£26.00	

BY PORTREE Map 3 D9
Isle of Skye, Inverness-shire

The Shielings Guest House Torvaig Portree Isle of Skye, Inverness-shire IV51 9HU Tel: (Portree) 0478 3024/ 613024	COMMENDED ≝ ≝	2 Double 2 Family	1 En Suite fac 2 Pub. Bath/Show	B&B per person £14.00-£21.00 Double	Open Jan-Dec Dinner at 1830 B&B + Eve. Meal £23.00-£30.00	

Converted croft cottage with superb views. Situated just 2 miles (3kms)
outside Portree. Home cooking and a warm homely atmosphere.

Mrs J MacLeod Storr Lochs Cottage by Portree Isle of Skye, Inverness-shire Tel: (Portree) 04781 612894	Award Pending	1 Twin	1 Priv. NOT ensuite 1 Pub. Bath/Show	B&B per person from £12.00 Double	Open Apr-Sep	

PORT WILLIAM Map 1 H1
Wigtownshire

Mrs M McMuldroch Jacob's Ladder Mochrum, by Port William Wigtownshire DG8 9BD Tel: (Mochrum) 098886 227	COMMENDED ≝ ≝	1 Twin 2 Double	2 En Suite fac 1 Pub. Bath/Show	B&B per person £15.00-£20.00 Single £13.00-£19.00 Double	Open Jan-Dec Dinner from 1800 B&B + Eve. Meal £19.00-£25.00	

Farmhouse in a peaceful location. Excellent centre for touring, golf,
fishing and birdwatching. Friendly atmosphere and all home cooking.

PRESTWICK Map 1 G7
Ayrshire

Fernbank Guest House 213 Main Street Prestwick Ayrshire KA9 1SU Tel: (Prestwick) 0292 75027	COMMENDED ≝ ≝	2 Single 2 Twin 2 Double 1 Family	4 En Suite fac 1 Priv. NOT ensuite 3 Pub. Bath/Show	B&B per person £14.00-£16.00 Single £17.00-£18.00 Double	Open Jan-Dec	

Modernised Edwardian villa near beach and local sports. 1 mile (2kms) from airport.

Miss R Allan 25 Central Esplanade Prestwick Ayrshire KA9 1RD Tel: (Prestwick) 0292 78097	COMMENDED Listed	1 Single 1 Twin 1 Family	1 Pub. Bath/Show	B&B per person £15.00-£16.00 Single £15.00-£16.00 Double	Open Jan-Dec	

Personally run Victorian seaside villa on the promenade, with extensive sea views.
Close to town centre. Secluded garden.

Mrs R Auld 66 Adamton Road Prestwick Ayrshire KA9 2HD Tel: (Prestwick) 0292 70399		1 Single 1 Twin 1 Family	2 Pub. Bath/Show	B&B per person from £11.50 Single from £11.00 Double	Open Apr-Sep	

PRESTWICK continued Mrs Anne Murphy Westmount, 79 Ayr Road Prestwick Ayrshire KA9 1TF Tel: (Prestwick) 0292 74888	**Map 1** G7		1 Twin 1 Double 1 Family	2 En Suite fac 1 Pub. Bath/Show	B&B per person £16.00-£20.00 Single £14.00-£18.00 Double	Open Jan-Dec
Mrs M Young Balgownie, 115 Ayr Road Prestwick Ayrshire KA9 1TN Tel: (Prestwick) 0292 77055		**APPROVED** **Listed**	2 Twin 1 Double	2 Pub. Bath/Show	B&B per person from £13.00 Single from £13.00 Double	Open Jan-Dec
			Comfortable family accommodation personally run by owner. **Near to beaches and mid-way between Ayr and Prestwick.**			
QUARFF **Shetland** Mrs B A Laurenson The Sparl, Wester Quarff Road Quarff Shetland Tel: (Cunningsburgh) 09503 301 Fax: 09503 301	**Map 5** G5		1 Twin 1 Double	2 Pub. Bath/Show	B&B per person £12.00-£15.00 Double	Open Jan-Dec Dinner 1800-2000 B&B + Eve. Meal £15.00-£20.00
RENDALL **Orkney** Mrs I Sinclair Riff Rendall Orkney KW17 2PB Tel: (Finstown) 085676 541	**Map 5** B1	**COMMENDED** ♛	1 Twin 1 Double	2 Pub. Bath/Show	B&B per person £10.00-£11.00 Double	Open Jan-Dec Dinner 1900-2000 B&B + Eve. Meal £16.00-£17.00
			A fine example of Orcadian hospitality. Mrs Sinclair, in her farmhouse by the shore, **treats you as one of the family. Close to Rousay ferry.**			
RENFREW Renfrew Guest House 4 West Avenue Renfrew PA4 0SZ Tel: 041 886 4350	**Map 1** H5	**APPROVED** **Listed**	1 Twin 1 Family	1 Pub. Bath/Show	B&B per person £18.00-£22.00 Single £14.50-£18.00 Double	Open Jan-Dec Dinner 1800-2000 B&B + Eve. Meal £23.00-£25.00
			Family home in quiet residential street. Conveniently situated for airport, **M8 and rail transport. On bus route to Glasgow.**			
RESTON, by Eyemouth **Berwickshire** Chris & Sheila Olley Stoneshiel Hall Reston, by Eyemouth Berwickshire TD14 5LU Tel: (Eyemouth) 08907 61267	**Map 2** F5	**COMMENDED** ♛	1 Twin 1 Double	1 Pub. Bath/Show	B&B per person to £20.00 Double	Open Jan-Dec Dinner 1800-2100 B&B + Eve. Meal to £35.00
			A warm welcome awaits at this tranquil and historic mansion house, **where home cooking is of particular interest and enjoyment.**			

ROCKCLIFFE, by Dalbeattie **Kirkcudbrightshire** Millbrae Guest House Rockcliffe, by Dalbeattie Kirkcudbrightshire DG5 4QG Tel: (Rockcliffe) 055663 217	Map 2 B1	HIGHLY COMMENDED ♕ ♕	3 Twin 2 Double	4 En Suite fac 1 Pub. Bath/Show	B&B per person £15.00-£17.00 Double	Open Jan-Dec Dinner from 1900 B&B + Eve. Meal £25.00-£27.00

19C guest house close to beach and forest; an ideal base for walkers and nature lovers.

Torbay Guest House Torbay Farmhouse Rockcliffe, by Dalbeattie Kirkcudbrightshire DG5 4QE Tel: (Rockcliffe) 055663 403		HIGHLY COMMENDED ♕ ♕ ♕	1 Twin 2 Double	2 En Suite fac 1 Priv. NOT ensuite	B&B per person £22.00-£24.00 Single £15.00-£18.00 Double	Open Easter-Oct Dinner 1830-1930 B&B + Eve. Meal £22.00-£25.00

Family house in former farmhouse peacefully situated 0.5 miles (1km) from picturesque village of Rockcliffe. French and German spoken. Pets welcome.

ROGART **Sutherland** Mrs J Corbett Benview Morness, Rogart Sutherland IV28 3XG Tel: (Rogart) 0408 641222	Map 4 B6	COMMENDED ♕	1 Single 1 Twin 1 Double	2 Pub. Bath/Show	B&B per person from £12.50 Single from £12.50 Double	Open May-Oct Dinner 1830-2000

Traditional modernised croft house in lovely setting, but only 3 mls (5kms) from Rogart. Splendid views in all directions over countryside.

ROTHESAY **Isle of Bute** Mrs E K Anderson Venetzia, 12a Argyle Place Rothesay Isle of Bute PA20 0BA Tel: (Rothesay) 0700 502203	Map 1 F5		2 Single 1 Double	1 Pub. Bath/Show	B&B per person £12.50-£13.50 Single £12.50-£13.50 Double	Open Apr-Sep Dinner 1700-1800 B&B + Eve. Meal £17.50

Mr & Mrs Clegg Glenarch, 21 Craigmore Road Rothesay Isle of Bute PA20 9LB Tel: (Rothesay) 0700 502033		HIGHLY COMMENDED ♕	1 Single 1 Twin 2 Double	2 Pub. Bath/Show	B&B per person £16.50 Single £16.50 Double	Open Jan-Dec

Large family house in quiet residential area. Town centre 1.5 miles (3kms). On main bus route. On seafront with extensive views across Clyde estuary.

ROY BRIDGE **Inverness-shire** Anne M Buchanan Tardis, Bunroy Roy Bridge Inverness-shire PH31 4AG Tel: (Spean Bridge) 039781 348	Map 3 H1		2 Double	1 En Suite fac 1 Pub. Bath/Show	B&B per person to £15.00 Single to £18.50 Double	Open Jan-Dec Dinner 1800-2030

	Map 3 H1						
ROY BRIDGE continued Mrs Grieve Station House Roy Bridge Inverness-shire PH31 4AG Tel: (Spean Bridge) 0397 712285		COMMENDED 🌢	1 Twin 1 Double	2 Pub. Bath/Show	B&B per person from £13.50 Double	Open Apr-Oct Dinner from 1830 B&B + Eve. Meal from £20.00	

Secluded detached bungalow in ¼ acre of garden situated 200 metres from the main A86. Close to railway station. Tea making facilities in bedrooms.

| Mrs C MacDonald
Tulloch Farm
Roy Bridge
Inverness-shire
Tel: (Tulloch) 039785 217
Fax: 039785 309 | | Award
Pending | 1 Twin
1 Double | 1 En Suite fac
1 Pub. Bath/Show | B&B per person
£13.00-£15.00 Single
£13.00-£15.00 Double | Open Mar-Sep
Dinner 1900-1930
B&B + Eve. Meal
£21.00-£24.00 | |

ST ABBS Berwickshire	Map 2 G5						
Castle Rock Guest House Murrayfield St Abbs Berwickshire TD14 5PP Tel: (Coldingham) 08907 71715 Fax: 08907 71520		COMMENDED 🌢 🌢 🌢	1 Single 1 Twin 1 Double 1 Family	4 En Suite fac 1 Pub. Bath/Show	B&B per person from £21.00 Single from £21.00 Double	Open Easter-Oct Dinner 1900-1930 B&B + Eve. Meal from £34.00	

Good food and comfort plus sea views from all rooms are features of this attractive house. Close to nature reserve and 3 miles (5kms) from A1.

| Wilma Wilson
7 Murrayfield
St Abbs
Berwickshire
TD14 5PP
Tel: (Coldingham)
08907 71468 | | COMMENDED
Listed | 1 Twin
1 Family | 1 Pub. Bath/Show | B&B per person
£12.50 Single
£12.50 Double | Open Jan-Dec | |

Former fisherman's cottage, in quiet village, close to beach, harbour and nature reserve. Home baking.

ST ANDREWS Fife	Map 2 E3						
Aslar Guest House 120 North Street St Andrews Fife KY16 9AF Tel: (St Andrews) 0334 73460 Fax: 0334 73460		HIGHLY COMMENDED 🌢 🌢	1 Single 1 Twin 2 Double 1 Family	5 En Suite fac	B&B per person £20.00-£25.00 Single £20.00-£25.00 Double	Open Jan-Dec	

Victorian, family run terraced house centrally situated for shops, golf courses, restaurants and cultural pursuits. All rooms en suite.

| Cadzow Guest House
58 North Street
St Andrews
Fife
KY16 9AH
Tel: (St Andrews) 0334 76933 | | COMMENDED
🌢 🌢 | 1 Single
2 Twin
4 Double
1 Family | 6 En Suite fac
1 Pub. Bath/Show | B&B per person
£22.00-£27.00 Single
£14.00-£22.00 Double | Open Feb-Nov | |

Privately owned Victorian terraced house. Close to castle, cathedral and sea front and within walking distance of shops. Good parking available.

Edenside House

EDENSIDE
ST ANDREWS
FIFE KY16 9SQ
Tel: (0334) 838108
Fax: (0334) 838493

Waterfront 18thC listed former Scottish farmhouse set back from A91 on bird sanctuary/nature reserve. Only 2½ miles St Andrews (5 mins by car). Exclusively non-smoking, well appointed double/twin rooms, all en-suite, some ground floor. Guaranteed parking space. Colour televisions, beverage trays. Extensive breakfast menu. Golf booking advice. Quality accommodation at realistic prices.

Edenside House Edenside St Andrews Fife KY16 9SQ Tel: (Leuchars) 0334 838108 Fax: 0334 838493	COMMENDED 👑 👑 👑	6 Twin 3 Double	9 En Suite fac	B&B per person £20.00-£25.00 Double	Open Jan-Dec Dinner at 1900 B&B + Eve. Meal £36.00-£41.00	
		Visible from A91 on approach to St Andrews 2.5 miles (4 kms) in superb setting on Eden estuary shore. All rooms ensuite and own parking. Non smoking				
Glenderran Guest House 9 Murray Park St Andrews Fife KY16 9AW Tel: (St Andrews) 0334 77951 Fax: 0334 77908	COMMENDED 👑 👑	2 Single 1 Twin 2 Double	3 En Suite fac 2 Priv. NOT ensuite	B&B per person £18.00-£25.00 Single £18.00-£25.00 Double	Open Jan-Dec	
		Victorian town house retaining some original features. Warm and comfortable. Close to all amenities. Non-smoking.				
Shorecrest Guest House 23 Murray Park St Andrews Fife KY16 9AW Tel: (St Andrews) 0334 75310 Fax: 0334 75310		2 Single 3 Twin 3 Double 4 Family	12 En Suite fac 1 Pub. Bath/Show	B&B per person £17.00-£28.00 Single £17.00-£28.00 Double	Open Jan-Dec Dinner from 1800 B&B + Eve. Meal £28.00-£39.00	
Mrs M Allan 2 King Street St Andrews Fife KY16 8JQ Tel: (St Andrews) 0334 76326	APPROVED Listed	1 Twin 1 Double	1 Pub. Bath/Show	B&B per person £13.00-£15.00	Open Easter-Oct Double	
		Friendly welcome awaits. Quiet. Fairly central. Within walking distance of town centre its many amenities.				

TELEPHONE DIALLING CODES

Many telephone dialling codes have changed this year. If you experience difficulty in connecting a call, please call Directory Enquiries — **192** — where someone will issue the correct number. Please note: a charge will be placed for this service when using a private telephone

Shorecrest Guest House

Personally managed by Pat and Jim Ledder

★ All rooms with en suite shower, toilet, washbasin and colour T.V.

★ Reasonable prices — Seasonal rates.

★ Good food — traditional home-cooking.

★ Tea/Coffee making facilities in the bedrooms.

★ Separate dining-room.

★ Comfortable lounge.

★ Full central heating.

★ Electric blankets.

★ Hot water available at all times.

★ 110/240v shaver points in bedrooms.

★ Pay phone available for local, long distance and international calls.

★ Early breakfast by arrangement.

★ Access is available at all times.

Shorecrest Guest House
21-23 Murray Park, St Andrews
Fife, Scotland KY16 9AW.
Tel: (0334) 75310
Fax: (0334) 75310

VAT is shown at 17.5%: changes in this rate may affect prices. Prices shown are for guidance only. Please send SAE with each enquiry.

ST ANDREWS continued
Fife

Map 2
E3

Stravithie
Country Estate

STRAVITHIE·ST ANDREWS·FIFE·KY16 8LT
Tel/Fax: 0334 88251

Bed and Breakfast on a beautiful old Scottish Country Estate with 30 acres of wooded grounds and gardens.
Rooms within east wing of Castle.
Facilities within the grounds include horse-riding, trout fishing, open air badminton, table tennis, putting, golf-net, nature trail, launderette and telephone.
How to find us — 3 miles from St Andrews on the Anstruther road. Signpost on right (near Dunino).
B&B FROM £25.00. *Reductions for children.*

John Chalmers Stravithie Country Estate St Andrews Fife KY16 8LT Tel: (Boarhills) 033488 251			2 Twin 2 Double	4 En Suite fac	B&B per person to £35.00 Single £22.50-£25.00 Double	Open Apr-Dec	
Mrs Bodil Fjord 151 South Street St Andrews Fife KY16 9UN Tel: (St Andrews) 0334 75913			1 Single 1 Twin 1 Double	2 Pub. Bath/Show	B&B per person £13.00-£16.00 Single £13.00-£15.00 Double	Open Jun-Oct	
Mrs A Hippisley Rockview, 15 The Scores St Andrews Fife KY16 9AR Tel: (St Andrews) 0334 75844			1 Twin 2 Double	2 En Suite fac 1 Pub. Bath/Show	B&B per person £20.00-£35.00 Single £15.00-£25.00 Double	Open May-Oct	
Mrs Lily Mason 4 Cairnsden Gardens St Andrews Fife KY16 8QS Tel: (St Andrews) 0334 72433	Award Pending		1 Twin 1 Double	2 Pub. Bath/Show	B&B per person £16.00 Single £12.00-£16.00 Double	Open Jan-Dec Dinner 1700-2000 B&B + Eve. Meal £20.00-£24.00	
Mrs Methven Ardmore, 1 Drumcarrow Road St Andrews Fife KY16 8SE Tel: (St Andrews) 0334 74574	COMMENDED Listed		2 Twin	1 Pub. Bath/Show	B&B per person £11.00-£13.00 Double	Open Jan-Dec	
			Family house in quiet residential area within walking distance of town centre. Convenient for all amenities.				
Mrs J Pumford Linton, 16 Hepburn Gardens St Andrews Fife KY16 9DD Tel: (St Andrews) 0334 74673	COMMENDED 👑👑		1 Twin 2 Double	1 En Suite fac 1 Pub. Bath/Show	B&B per person £14.00-£17.50 Double	Open Apr-Oct	
			Spacious family house, within a few minutes walk of the town. Private parking, open views to parkland and beyond.				

Details of Grading and Classification are on page vi.

Key to symbols is on back flap.

ST ANDREWS continued Fife Mrs V Rhind Hazlehead, 16 Lindsay Gardens St Andrews Fife KY16 8XB Tel: (St Andrews) 0334 75677	**Map 2** E3	COMMENDED Listed	1 Double 1 Family	1 Pub. Bath/Show	B&B per person £13.00-£15.00 Double	Open Jan-Dec Dinner 1800-2000 B&B + Eve. Meal £20.00-£22.50

Modern detached villa in quiet residential area 1 mile (2kms) from town centre.
Easy parking. Home cooking.

DRUMRACK FARM

By St Andrews KY16 8QQ — 0333-310520

Drumrack is a family run working farm in Fife, where you are
welcome to stay in the comfort of our farmhouse. Only six miles
from St Andrews, we are centrally situated for many East Neuk
attractions — golf, beaches, historical buildings and quaint
fishing villages dotted around the coast.

Mrs H Watson Drumrack Farm by St Andrews Fife KY16 8QQ Tel: (Anstruther) 0333 310520	1 Single 2 Pub. Bath/Show 1 Twin 1 Double	B&B per person £14.00-£14.50 Single £14.00-£14.50 Double	Open Jan-Nov Dinner 2000-2100 B&B + Eve. Meal £21.00-£21.50

BY ST ANDREWS Fife Romar Guest House 45 Main Street Strathkinness Fife KY16 9RZ Tel: (Strathkinness) 0334 85308 Fax: 0334 85308	**Map 2** E3	COMMENDED ♛	2 Single 1 En Suite fac 1 Twin 2 Pub. Bath/Show 1 Double	B&B per person £15.00-£20.00 Single £14.00-£18.00 Double	Open Jan-Dec

Spacious modern house in pleasant rural surroundings,
3 miles (5kms) from St Andrews.

Seggie House

CUPAR ROAD
Nr GUARDBRIDGE
ST ANDREWS
Tel: 0334 839209

*A gracious mansion set in a private 5-acre
garden conveniently situated on the A91 four
miles from St Andrews. Individually heated
spacious rooms have TV and tea/coffee-making
facilities. Elegant drawingroom for guests. Full
Scottish breakfast. Moderate rates. Sorry, no
smoking or pets but a warm welcome from:
Heather Douglas, Proprietor.*

♛♛ **Commended**

Heather Douglas Seggie House, Cupar Road Guardbridge, by St Andrews Fife KY16 0UP Tel: (Leuchars) 0334 839209	COMMENDED ♛ ♛	1 Twin 2 En Suite fac 4 Family 2 Limited ensuite 3 Priv. NOT ensuite	B&B per person £17.00-£20.00 Double	Open May-Sep

Gracious Victorian mansion in 5 acres of wooded ground with walled garden.
4 miles (6kms) from St Andrews and its golf courses. Ample parking.

Mr Peter Erskine Cambo House Kingsbarns, by St Andrews Fife KY16 8QD Tel: (Crail) 0333 50313 Fax: 0333 50987	COMMENDED ♛ ♛ ♛	1 Twin 1 En Suite fac 2 Double 2 Priv. NOT ensuite 2 Pub. Bath/Show	B&B per person £25.00-£45.00 Double	Open Dec-Jan Dinner 1800-2000 B&B + Eve. Meal £40.00-£65.00

Elegant Victorian mansion on wooded coastal estate, close to St Andrews
with handsome four poster bed in principal guest bedroom.

"The Larches"

7 River Terrace, Guardbridge, by St Andrews KY16 0XA
Telephone: 0334 838008   Fax: 0334 838008

Guardbridge is situated on the A919 between St Andrews (3 miles) and Dundee (6 miles). Convenient for golf, riding, beautiful countryside and beaches. All rooms have H&C, TV, tea/coffee facilities. Centrally heated throughout. Residents' lounge always available, video player with selection of films, games etc. Early breakfast on request. Comprehensive menu.   *Every home comfort!*

Mrs Valerie Mayner The Larches, 7 River Terrace Guardbridge, by St Andrews Fife KY16 0XA Tel: (Guardbridge) 033483 8008	COMMENDED ⚜	1 Twin 1 Double 1 Family	2 Pub. Bath/Show	B&B per person £16.00-£20.00 Single from £16.00 Double	Open Jan-Dec

A former memorial hall, now converted into a family home, near centre of Guardbridge and R.A.F. Leuchars. 4 miles (6kms) from St. Andrews.

Easter Craigfoodie

DAIRSIE · CUPAR · FIFE KY15 4SW
Telephone: 0334 870 286

Comfortable Farmhouse with wonderful views over bay only 6 miles from St Andrews. Residents' lounge with TV. Ample parking. Ideal golf or touring base.

Mrs C Scott Easter Craigfoodie Dairsie, by Cupar Fife KY15 4SW Tel: (Cupar) 0334 870286	HIGHLY COMMENDED Listed	1 Twin 1 Double 1 Family	1 Pub. Bath/Show	B&B per person £16.00-£18.00 Single £14.50-£15.50 Double	Open Jan-Dec

Traditional, Victorian farmhouse with panoramic views across Fife to Firth of Tay and Angus coast. 7 miles (11kms) from St Andrews. Ideal golf base.

ST BOSWELLS **Roxburghshire** Mrs Shirley Sloggie Struan, off Jenny Moore's Road St Boswells Roxburghshire TD6 0AN Tel: (St Boswells) 0835 822711 Fax: 0835 823945	**Map 2** **E7** COMMENDED ⚜	1 Twin 1 Family	1 Limited ensuite 1 Pub. Bath/Show	B&B per person £15.00-£20.00 Single £13.50-£16.00 Double	Open Jan-Dec

Stone built family house, in quiet residential area. Off street parking. Near to town centre. Easy access to countryside and attractions.

ST CYRUS **Kincardineshire** Mrs A Coates Burnmouth St Cyrus Kincardineshire DD10 0DL Tel: (St Cyrus) 067485 430	**Map 4** **G1** Award Pending	1 Single 1 Twin 2 Double 1 Family	2 En Suite fac 1 Priv. NOT ensuite 2 Pub. Bath/Show	B&B per person £14.00-£16.50 Single £14.00-£16.00 Double	Open Mar-Oct Dinner 1800-2000 B&B + Eve. Meal £20.00-£22.00

Mrs Alison Williamson Kirkside Bothy St Cyrus Nature Reserve St Cyrus Kincardineshire DD10 0AQ Tel: (Montrose) 0674 83780		3 Twin 1 Family	4 En Suite fac	B&B per person £17.00-£20.00 Single £17.00-£20.00 Double	Open Jan-Dec

---

ST FILLANS
Perthshire
Map 2 A2
Mrs April D'Arcy
Inverearn House
St Fillans
Perthshire
PH6 2NF
Tel: (St Fillans) 0764 685322

Award Pending

2 Twin / 1 Double — 1 Limited ensuite / 2 Pub. Bath/Show

B&B per person
£15.00-£20.00 Single
£15.00-£20.00 Double

Open Jan-Dec

Mrs U Ross
Earngrove Cottage
St Fillans
Perthshire
PH6 2ND
Tel: (St Fillans) 0764 685224

2 Twin — 2 Pub. Bath/Show

B&B per person
£12.50 Double

Open Mar-Oct
Dinner 1830-2030
B&B + Eve. Meal
£19.00

Mrs Spearing
Ardsheean
St Fillans
Perthshire
PH6 2ND
Tel: (St Fillans) 0764 685245

COMMENDED

1 Twin / 1 Double / 1 Family — 2 En Suite fac / 1 Priv. NOT ensuite

B&B per person
£15.00 Double

Open Jan-Dec

Spacious Edwardian House with tennis court in grounds of 3.5 acres,
close to village centre and Loch Earn. Ensuite bathroom with sauna.

ST MARGARET'S HOPE
Orkney
Map 5 B1
Mrs A Brown
Blanster House
St Margaret's Hope
Orkney
KW17 2TG
Tel: (St Margaret's Hope)
085683 549

COMMENDED

1 Twin / 2 Double — 1 Priv. NOT ensuite / 1 Pub. Bath/Show

B&B per person
£10.00-£12.00 Single
£10.00-£12.00 Double

Open Jan-Dec
Dinner 1900-2100
B&B + Eve. Meal
£15.00-£17.00

19C farmhouse standing in own grounds on outskirts of village. Near Scapa Flow
and Churchill Barriers. 7 miles (11kms) to John O' Groats ferry.

ST MONANS
Fife
Map 2 E3
Miss M Aitken
Inverforth, 20 Braehead
St Monans
Fife
KY10 2AN
Tel: (St Monans) 0333 730205

COMMENDED
Listed

2 Twin / 1 Double — 1 Pub. Bath/Show

B&B per person
£14.00-£15.00 Double

Open mid May-
mid Oct

Overlooking the harbour in this attractive small fishing village,
a Victorian house with spacious bedrooms. Home-baking.

Mrs L Rennie
Stenton Farm
St Monans
Fife
KY10 2DF
Tel: (St Monans)
0333 730213

1 Twin / 2 Double — 1 Pub. Bath/Show

B&B per person
£12.00-£15.00 Single
£10.00-£14.00 Double

Open Jan-Dec
Dinner 1800-2100
B&B + Eve. Meal
£16.00-£20.00

SALEN
Isle of Mull, Argyll
Map 1 D2
Mrs I T Adam
Cuilgown
Salen
Isle of Mull, Argyll
PA72 6JB
Tel: (Aros) 0680 300386

2 Twin / 1 Double — 2 Pub. Bath/Show

B&B per person
from £14.00 Single
from £14.00 Double

Open Feb-Nov

SALINE, by Dunfermline
Fife
Map 2 B4
Mrs J Cousar
Lynn Farm
Saline, by Dunfermline
Fife
KY12 9LR
Tel: (New Oakley) 0383 852261

1 Twin / 1 Family — 2 Priv. NOT ensuite / 1 Pub. Bath/Show

B&B per person
£18.00 Single
£13.00-£15.00 Double

Open Mar-Oct

SANDWICK **Orkney** Mrs M Grieve Dencraigon Sandwick, by Stromness Orkney KW16 3JB Tel: (Sandwick) 085684 647	Map 5 A1	COMMENDED Listed	2 Twin 1 Double	1 Pub. Bath/Show	B&B per person £11.00-£12.50 Single £11.00-£12.50 Double	Open Apr-Oct

Bungalow on A967 overlooking Loch Harray, 6 miles (10kms) from Stromness and 3 miles (5kms) from Skara Brae. Washbasins in bedrooms.

Mrs Kirkpatrick Millburn Sandwick, by Stromness Orkney KW16 3JB Tel: (Sandwick) 085684 656		HIGHLY COMMENDED Listed	2 Twin 1 Double	1 Priv. NOT ensuite 2 Pub. Bath/Show	B&B per person £14.00-£16.00 Double	Open Apr-Oct

Modern house right on the shore of Loch Harray with lovely open views. Fishing, bird watching. Stromness 6 miles (10kms); Skara Brae 4 miles (6kms).

SANDWICK **Shetland** Mrs M Inkster Marelda Park Sandwick Shetland ZE2 9HP Tel: (Sandwick) 09505 379 Fax: 09505 582	Map 5 G5		1 Single 1 Twin 1 Family	2 Pub. Bath/Show	B&B per person £12.00-£14.00 Single £11.00-£13.00 Double	Open Jan-Dec Dinner 1900-2000 B&B + Eve. Meal £16.00-£19.00

SCANIPORT **Inverness-shire** Mrs C M Fraser Borlum House Scaniport Inverness-shire IV1 2DL Tel: (Dores) 046375 306	Map 4 A9	COMMENDED	1 Twin 2 Double	2 Pub. Bath/Show	B&B per person £15.00-£18.00 Single from £14.00 Double	Open Jan-Dec

18C farmhouse built on castle ruins in quiet countryside overlooking River Ness and Caledonian Canal. 3 miles (5kms) from both Dores and Inverness.

SCONSER **Isle of Skye, Inverness-shire** Mrs C M MacLeod Old Schoolhouse Sconser Isle of Skye, Inverness-shire IV48 Tel: (Sligachan) 0478 650313	Map 3 D9		1 Twin 1 Double 1 Family	2 Pub. Bath/Show	B&B per person from £12.50 Double	Open Jan-Dec

SCOTLANDWELL, by Kinross **Kinross-shire** Mrs S M Wardell 6 Bankfoot Park Scotlandwell, by Kinross Kinross-shire KY13 7JP Tel: (Scotlandwell) 059284 515	Map 2 E3	COMMENDED	1 Single 1 Twin	1 Priv. NOT ensuite 1 Pub. Bath/Show	B&B per person from £14.00 Single from £14.00 Double	Open Jan-Dec

Family home near Loch Leven. Easy access to Lomond Hills and Fife Coast. Bee keeping, gliding, fishing, bird watching, country parks.

SCOURIE **Sutherland** Mrs Sarah Thomson Braeval, Scourie More Scourie Sutherland IV27 4TG Tel: (Scourie) 0971 502076	Map 3 G4	COMMENDED Listed	2 Twin 1 Double	2 Pub. Bath/Show	B&B per person £12.50-£14.00 Single	Open May-Sep

Modern bungalow set up above this typical west coast Highland village. Fine views of Scourie Bay and Handa Island in the distance.

Details of Grading and Classification are on page vi.

Key to symbols is on back flap.

SEAMILL
Ayrshire
Spottiswood Guest House
3 Sandy Road
Seamill
Ayrshire
KA23 9NN
Tel: (Seamill) 0294 823131

Map 1
G6

DELUXE

1 Twin | 1 En Suite fac | B&B per person | Open Jan-Dec
2 Double | 1 Pub. Bath/Show | from £16.00 Double | Dinner at 1900
| | | B&B + Eve. Meal
| | | from £26.00

Victorian shore-side home. Tea in garden, island views, imaginative menus,
flowers, music, books. Base for golf, Ayrshire coast, being pampered.

SELKIRK

Mrs P Dickson
Sunnybrae House
75 Tower Street
Selkirk
TD7 4LS
Tel: (Selkirk) 0750 21156

Map 2
E7

COMMENDED

1 Twin | 2 En Suite fac | B&B per person | Open Jan-Dec
1 Double | | to £17.00 Single | Dinner 1800-2000
| | to £17.00 Double | B&B + Eve. Meal
| | | to £28.00

Two suites (own sitting room) in friendly family home. Private parking.
Ideal for touring the Borders. Edinburgh only 38 miles (60kms).

Mrs T Donaldson
Alwyn, Russell Place
Selkirk
TD7 4NF
Tel: (Selkirk) 0750 22044

COMMENDED

1 Twin | 1 Pub. Bath/Show | B&B per person | Open Apr-Oct
1 Double | | £13.00-£15.00 Double

Large bungalow situated on outskirts of historic town.
Ideal centre for exploring lovely surrounding countryside.

Mrs D J Hannah
Hillholm, 36 Hillside Terrace
Selkirk
TD7 4ND
Tel: (Selkirk) 0750 21293

COMMENDED

2 Twin | 2 En Suite fac | B&B per person | Open Mar-Dec
1 Double | 1 Priv. NOT ensuite | from £14.00 Double | Dinner from 1800
| 2 Pub. Bath/Show | | B&B + Eve. Meal
| | | from £20.00

Elegant semi-detached Victorian house on outskirts of town. Small interesting
garden with rockery and Alpine plants. Ideal centre for touring.

Mrs Lindores
Dinsburn, 1 Shawpark Road
Selkirk
TD7 4DS
Tel: (Selkirk) 0750 20375

1 Twin | 1 Pub. Bath/Show | B&B per person | Open Jan-Dec
1 Double | | from £14.00 Single | Dinner from 1800
1 Family | | from £12.50 Double | B&B + Eve. Meal
| | | from £18.00

Mrs J F MacKenzie
Ivybank, Hillside Terrace
Selkirk
TD7
Tel: (Selkirk) 0750 21270

COMMENDED

1 Twin | 1 Pub. Bath/Show | B&B per person | Open Feb-Nov
1 Double | | from £13.00 Single | Dinner 1830-1930
| | from £13.00 Double | B&B + Eve. Meal
| | | from £22.00

Set back from A7 with fine views over the hills beyond.
Breakfast served at 8.00 am or earlier Monday - Friday, term time.

Mrs H Murray
Collingwood, The Green
Selkirk
TD7 5AA
Tel: (Selkirk) 0750 20018

COMMENDED

1 Twin | 2 En Suite fac | B&B per person | Open Jan-Dec
2 Double | 1 Pub. Bath/Show | £16.00 Double | Dinner 1700-2100

Friendly and family run. All bedrooms have private facilities.
Easy walking distance from town centre.

Mrs S M Todd
34 Hillside Terrace
Selkirk
TD7 4ND
Tel: (Selkirk) 0750 20792

COMMENDED

2 Twin | 1 Priv. NOT ensuite | B&B per person | Open Mar-Oct
1 Double | 2 Pub. Bath/Show | from £13.50 Double

Family run house in a small, historic border town.
An ideal centre for touring and hillwalking.

BY SELKIRK Mr & Mrs Thurston Greenwells, Yarrow Feus Selkirk TD7 5LB Tel: (Selkirk) 0750 82228 Fax: 0750 82243	Map 2 E7	HIGHLY COMMENDED Listed	1 Twin 1 Double	1 Pub. Bath/Show	B&B per person from £15.00 Single from £15.00 Double	Open Apr-Oct	

Shepherds cottage with large garden, overlooking Yarrow Water 11 miles (18kms) from Selkirk. Private fishing. A haven for non smokers.

SELLAFIRTH, Yell **Shetland** Mrs E Gott Bayanne House Sellafirth, Island of Yell Shetland	Map 5 G2		1 Family	1 Pub. Bath/Show	B&B per person from £11.50 Single from £11.50 Double	Open Jan-Dec Dinner 1800-2000	
SHIELDAIG **Ross-shire** Mrs T Blaxter Drumacosh Shieldaig, by Strathcarron Ross-shire IV54 8XN Tel: (Shieldaig) 05205 218	Map 3 F8		1 Twin 1 Double	1 Pub. Bath/Show	B&B per person £12.00-£15.00 Double	Open Jan-Dec	
Mrs M C Calcott Tigh Fada, 117 Doireanor Shieldaig, Strathcarron Ross-shire IV54 8XH Tel: (Shieldaig) 05205 248		Award Pending	1 Twin 1 Double 1 Family	2 Pub. Bath/Show	B&B per person from £12.00 Double	Open Jan-Dec Dinner from 1900 B&B + Eve. Meal from £18.00	
SOUTHEND, by Campbeltown **Argyll** Mrs M Ronald Ormsary Farm Southend, by Campbeltown Argyll PA28 6RN Tel: (Southend) 058683 665	Map 1 D8	COMMENDED	1 Twin 1 Double 1 Family	2 En Suite fac 1 Pub. Bath/Show	B&B per person from £14.00 Double	Open Apr-Sep Dinner from 1800 B&B + Eve. Meal from £20.00	

Beautifully situated family farm only 2 miles (3kms) from beach and 18 hole golf course. Children especially welcome.

SOUTH SHAWBOST **Lewis, Western Isles** Mr I MacLean Airigh, 1 Teachers House South Shawbost Lewis, Western Isles PA86 9BJ Tel: (Shawbost) 0851 710478	Map 3 C4		1 Twin 2 Double	2 En Suite fac 1 Priv. NOT ensuite 2 Pub. Bath/Show	B&B per person from £17.00 Double	Open Jan-Dec Dinner 1900-2000 B&B + Eve. Meal from £27.00	

WELCOME

Whenever you are in Scotland, you can be sure of a warm welcome at your nearest Tourist Information Centre.

For guide books, maps, souvenirs, our Centres provide a service second to none—many now offer bureau-de-change facilities. And, of course, Tourist Information Centres offer free, expert advice on what to see and do, route-planning and accommodation for everyone—visitors and residents alike!

SPEAN BRIDGE Inverness-shire	Map 3 H1

Barbagianni Guest House
Speanbridge PH34 4EV   Tel: 0397 712437

This is a family run guest house, situated in its own grounds, overlooking Ben Nevis mountain range on outskirts of Spean Bridge. Ideal base for touring. Central heating, tea/coffee facilities (all with private facilities). Comfortable lounge with TV. Home cooking. Parking. Enjoy tea at 10 p.m.

Barbagianni Guest House
Tirindrish
Spean Bridge
Inverness-shire
PH34 4EU
Tel: (Spean Bridge)
0397 712437

HIGHLY COMMENDED
🏅🏅🏅

1 Single 4 En Suite fac
1 Twin   2 Pub. Bath/Show
5 Double

B&B per person
£15.50 Single
£15.50-£17.50 Double

Open Easter-20 Oct
Dinner from 1930
B&B + Eve. Meal
£25.50-£27.50

Detached modern house of interesting design, in its own grounds with excellent views over Ben Nevis and beyond. Friendly atmosphere, home baking.

Coire Glas Guest House
Spean Bridge
Inverness-shire
PH34 4EU
Tel: (Spean Bridge)
0397 712272

COMMENDED
🏅🏅

2 Single 8 En Suite fac
4 Twin   3 Pub. Bath/Show
6 Double
2 Family

B&B per person
£14.00-£16.00 Single
£13.00-£18.00 Double

Open Jan-Oct
Dinner 1900-2000
B&B + Eve. Meal
£23.00-£28.00

Family run guest house set back from A86 tourist route, only 8 miles (13kms) from Aonach Mor gondola station. Views of the Ben Nevis mountain range.

Distant Hills Guest House
Spean Bridge
Inverness-shire
PH34 4EU
Tel: (Spean Bridge)
039781 452

HIGHLY COMMENDED
🏅🏅🏅

4 Twin   7 En Suite fac
3 Double 1 Pub. Bath/Show

B&B per person
from £15.00 Double

Open Jan-Dec
Dinner 1700-2030

Modern bungalow at edge of quiet village. Friendly and personal attention. Excellent views of Aonach Mhor; ideally situated for touring and skiing.

Druimandarroch House
Spean Bridge, by Fort William
Inverness-shire
PH34 4EU
Tel: (Spean Bridge)
039781 335/0397 712335

APPROVED
🏅🏅

2 Twin   2 En Suite fac
3 Double 2 Pub. Bath/Show
2 Family

B&B per person
from £16.00 Single
from £15.00 Double

Open Mar-Nov
Dinner 1900-2000
B&B + Eve. Meal
from £25.00

House at the centre of this small but busy Highlands village. Ideal for touring; Fort William 10 miles (16kms), Aonach Mor Gondola 8 miles (11kms).

Grey Corries Guest House
Spean Bridge
Inverness-shire
PH34
Tel: (Spean Bridge)
0397712 579

COMMENDED
🏅🏅

1 Twin   4 En Suite fac
2 Double 2 Priv. NOT ensuite
3 Family 2 Pub. Bath/Show

B&B per person
£10.50-£16.50 Single
£10.50-£16.50 Double

Open Jan-Dec
Dinner 1700-2100
B&B + Eve. Meal
£19.50-£24.50

Modern house on A82 Fort William to Inverness Road. Family run; home cooking with wild game and fish. Open all the year round.

Inverour Guest House
Spean Bridge
Inverness-shire
PH34
Tel: (Spean Bridge)
039781 218

Award Pending

2 Single 3 En Suite fac
2 Twin   2 Pub. Bath/Show
3 Double

B&B per person
from £14.00 Single
from £13.00 Double

Open Jan-Dec
Dinner 1900-2000
B&B + Eve. Meal
from £25.00

Old Pines

Gairlochy Road, Spean Bridge, Inverness-shire PH34 4EG
Telephone: 0397 712 324   Fax: 0397 712 433

Quiet situation. Breathtaking views of Aonach Mor and Ben Nevis. Ideal base for touring the West Highlands. Happy family home with a relaxing, informal atmosphere, pretty en-suite bedrooms, flowers, books and log fires. Imaginative fresh food carefully prepared and presented.

Contact: Niall or Sukie Scott   "A Very Special Place"

Niall & Sukie Scott, Old Pines Gairlochy Road Spean Bridge Inverness-shire PH34 4EG Tel: (Spean Bridge) 0397 712324 Fax: 0397 712433	HIGHLY COMMENDED 👑👑👑	2 Single 2 Twin 2 Double 2 Family	7 En Suite fac 1 Priv. NOT ensuite 1 Pub. Bath/Show	B&B per person £20.00-£25.00 Single £20.00-£25.00 Double	Open Jan-Dec Dinner from 2000 B&B + Eve. Meal £35.00-£40.00

Scandinavian log cabin set among pine trees with panoramic views of Aonach Mor. Friendly family home. A flair for imaginative fresh food.

INVERGLOY HOUSE 0397 712681

SPEAN BRIDGE · INVERNESS-SHIRE PH34 4DY

100-year-old coach house offering three twin-bedded rooms with wash-basins, 2 bath/shower rooms. Overlooking Loch Lochy in 50 acres of rhododendron woodland. 5 miles north of Spean Bridge on A82 to Inverness, signposted on left along wooded drive. Fishing, rowing boats, tennis court. Youngsters over 8 years. "Non-smoking" house.
S.A.E. for brochure to Mrs M. H. Cairns.
B&B from £15.00. Evening meal on request £9.00.

Mrs M Cairns Invergloy House, Invergloy Spean Bridge Inverness-shire PH34 4DY Tel: (Spean Bridge) 0397 712681	HIGHLY COMMENDED 👑	3 Twin	3 Limited ensuite 2 Pub. Bath/Show	B&B per person £15.00 Single £15.00 Double	Open Jan-Dec Dinner from 1930 B&B + Eve. Meal £23.00

A warm welcome is offered in our peaceful country home.

Mrs D Horner Highbridge Spean Bridge Inverness-shire PH34 4EX Tel: (Fort William) 0397 712493	COMMENDED 👑👑	1 Twin 1 Double	1 En Suite fac 1 Limited ensuite 1 Pub. Bath/Show	B&B per person £12.00-£15.00 Double	Open Apr-Oct

Secluded cedar wood, family home. Excellent views of Ben Nevis and Aonach Mor. Fort William 9 Miles (14kms), Spean Bridge 1.5 miles (2kms).

Mr Andrew Simpson Roseisle Spean Bridge Inverness-shire PH34 4EU Tel: (Spean Bridge) 039781 563		1 Twin 1 Double 1 Family	2 En Suite fac 1 Priv. NOT ensuite 1 Pub. Bath/Show	B&B per person £15.00-£21.00 Single £12.50-£16.50 Double	Open Jan-Nov

Peter & Jean Wilson Tirindrish House Spean Bridge Inverness-shire PH34 4EU Tel: (Spean Bridge) 039781 520		1 Twin 1 Double 1 Family	3 Priv. NOT ensuite	B&B per person £15.00-£18.00 Double	Open Jan-Dec Dinner 1900-2000 B&B + Eve. Meal £24.00-£27.00

SPITTALFIELD, by Murthly **Perthshire** Mrs A W Smith Stralochy Farm Spittalfield, by Murthly Perthshire PH1 4LQ Tel: (Caputh) 073871 447	**Map 2** C2	**COMMENDED** Listed	1 Twin 1 Double 1 Family	2 Pub. Bath/Show	B&B per person £13.00-£17.00 Single £13.00-£14.00 Double	Open May-Sep Dinner from 1830 B&B + Eve. Meal £20.00-£21.00	

Real farmhouse hospitality on working farm overlooking the House of Strathmore, enjoying superb open views.

STAFFIN **Isle of Skye, Inverness-shire** Mrs M McDonald Ben Edra, 1 Maligar Staffin, by Portree Isle of Skye, Inverness-shire IV51 9JF Tel: (Staffin) 047062 291	**Map 3** D8	**COMMENDED** Listed	1 Twin 1 Family	1 Pub. Bath/Show	B&B per person to £14.00 Single £12.00-£14.00 Double	Open May-Sep Dinner 1800-2000 B&B + Eve. Meal £19.00-£21.00	

Traditional working croft house. Warm island welcome, home baking, cooking. Peat fires. Superb views of the Storr. Salmon/trout fishing available.

Mrs K Money Quiraing Lodge Staffin Isle of Skye, Inverness-shire Tel: (Staffin) 047062 330			2 Twin 1 Double 4 Family	3 Pub. Bath/Show	B&B per person from £15.00 Double	Open Jan-Dec Dinner 1900-2100 B&B + Eve. Meal from £22.50	

STANLEY **Perthshire** Mrs Howden Stanley Farm Stanley Perthshire PH1 4QQ Tel: (Stanley) 0738 828334	**Map 2** C2	**COMMENDED** Listed	1 Double 1 Family	2 Pub. Bath/Show	B&B per person £15.00-£18.00 Single £13.00-£16.00 Double	Open Apr-Oct Dinner 1900-2030 B&B + Eve. Meal £21.00-£25.00	

Friendly family farmhouse central for touring Perthshire. Home cooking and baking. Children especially welcome.

Mrs G Lax The Old Manse Stanley Perthshire PH1 4PA Tel: (Stanley) 0738 828796		**COMMENDED** Listed	2 Double	2 Priv. NOT ensuite	B&B per person from £18.00 Single from £15.00 Double	Open Jan-Dec	

Elegant family home on the edge of village. Variety of sporting and leisure activities can be arranged.

STENNESS **Orkney** Mrs Scott Upper Nist House Stenness Orkney KW16 3HE Tel: (Finstown) 085676 378	**Map 5** B1	**COMMENDED** Listed	1 Twin 1 Double 1 Family	1 Pub. Bath/Show	B&B per person from £10.00 Single from £10.00 Double	Open May-Oct	

Working farm midway between Stromness and Kirkwall. Lovely views of hills and lochs; ideal for birdwatchers.

STEWARTON **Ayrshire** Lochridge House Stewarton Ayrshire KA3 5LH Tel: (Stewarton) 0560 484334	**Map 1** H6	**COMMENDED**	1 Twin 1 Family	1 En Suite fac 2 Pub. Bath/Show	B&B per person £15.00-£17.50 Single £15.00-£17.50 Double	Open Jan-Dec	

Large family house, dating back to C1635, set in wooded grounds with own tennis court. Warm welcome and friendly atmosphere.

STIRLING	Map 2 A4					
Bannockburn Lodge 24/32 Main Street Bannockburn, Stirling Stirlingshire FK7 8LY Tel: (Bannockburn) 0786 812121/816501 Fax: 0786 817628	COMMENDED Lodge	3 Twin 2 Double 1 Family	6 En Suite fac	B&B per person £22.00-£24.00 Single £17.00-£19.00 Double	Open Jan-Dec Dinner at 1800 B&B + Eve. Meal £23.00-£28.00	

Purpose built 1990's facilities in a 1760's building! Ideal touring centre 1 mile (2kms) from motorway.

| Castlecroft Ballengeich Road Stirling FK8 1TN Tel: (Stirling) 0786 474933 | HIGHLY COMMENDED | 2 Twin 3 Double 1 Family | 6 En Suite fac 1 Pub. Bath/Show | B&B per person £25.00-£30.00 Single £16.00-£19.00 Double | Open Jan-Dec | |

Nestling on elevated site under Stirling Castle, this comfortable, modern house offers warm welcome. Private facilities, some suitable for disabled.

| Forth Guest House 23 Forth Place, Riverside Stirling FK8 1UD Tel: (Stirling) 0786 471020 Fax: 0786 447220 | HIGHLY COMMENDED | 1 Twin 2 Double | 3 En Suite fac | B&B per person £20.00-£30.00 Single £17.50-£19.00 Double | Open Jan-Dec Dinner 1730-1830 B&B + Eve. Meal £24.50-£26.00 | |

Terraced house close to railway station and town centre. Good location for touring.

| Mia-Roo Guest House 37 Snowdon Place Stirling FK8 2JP Tel: (Stirling) 0786 473979 | | 2 Single 2 Twin 2 Double 2 Family | 1 Pub. Bath/Show | B&B per person £16.50-£18.00 Single £16.50-£18.00 Double | Open Jan-Dec | |

| Woodside Guest House 4 Back Walk Stirling FK8 2QA Tel: (Stirling) 0786 475470 | APPROVED | 1 Single 1 Twin 2 Double 1 Family | 2 En Suite fac 3 Limited ensuite 1 Pub. Bath/Show | B&B per person £16.00-£18.00 Single £16.00-£17.00 Double | Open Jan-Dec | |

Character building on historic wall of Stirling. A warm welcome assured. Centrally located.

| Mrs J Bremner Spittal Villa 26 Causewayhead Road Stirling FK9 5EU Tel: (Stirling) 0786 478864 | | 1 Twin 2 Double | 1 En Suite fac 1 Limited ensuite 1 Priv. NOT ensuite 1 Pub. Bath/Show | B&B per person from £16.50 Single £16.00-£18.50 Double | Open Jan-Dec | |

| Mrs R Henderson Ravenswood 94 Causewayhead Road Stirling Tel: (Stirling) 0786 472950 | | 1 Twin 2 Double | 2 Pub. Bath/Show | B&B per person £18.00-£20.00 Single £13.00-£15.00 Double | Open Mar-Nov | |

| Mrs Ann Hume Myreton, 4 Clarendon Place Stirling FK8 2QW Tel: (Stirling) 0786 461741 | HIGHLY COMMENDED Listed | 1 Twin 2 Double | 1 Pub. Bath/Show | B&B per person £15.00-£17.00 Double | Open Apr-Sep | |

Elegantly refurbished Victorian town house in quiet residential area close to town centre.

| Mrs R Johnson Shalom, 15 1/2 Manse Cresent Stirling FK7 9AJ Tel: (Stirling) 0786 471092 | COMMENDED | 1 Single 1 Twin | 1 Pub. Bath/Show | B&B per person £14.00-£16.00 Single £14.00-£16.00 Double | Open Jan-Dec | |

Bungalow with character in quiet cul-de-sac, 3 minutes walk to frequent bus service, 15 minutes walk to town centre. Off street parking.

Details of Grading and Classification are on page vi.

Key to symbols is on back flap.

STIRLING continued	Map 2 A4						
Mrs M Johnston West Plean House Denny Road Stirling FK7 8HA Tel: (Stirling) 0786 812208		COMMENDED 👑 👑	1 Single 1 Double 1 Family	2 En Suite fac 1 Priv. NOT ensuite	B&B per person £20.00-£25.00 Single £18.00-£22.00 Double	Open Feb-Nov	
			200 year old country house on working farm with extensive grounds and woods. Spacious comfort; warm Scottish farming hospitality.				
Mrs K Logie Marclair 39 Kenninknowles Road Stirling FK7 9JF Tel: (Stirling) 0786 479194			2 Double	1 Pub. Bath/Show	B&B per person £12.00-£13.00 Double	Open Easter-Oct	
Miss F McGuinness St Margarets 8 Causewayhead Road Stirling FK9 5EU Tel: (Stirling) 0786 447332			1 Single 1 Twin 1 Double 1 Family	1 Pub. Bath/Show	B&B per person £16.50-£17.50 Single £21.00-£23.00 Double	Open Jan-Dec Dinner 1800-2100 B&B + Eve. Meal £24.00-£30.00	
Moira E McPhail Wellgreen Guest House 8 Pitt Terrace Stirling FK8 2EZ Tel: (Stirling) 0786 472675			1 Single 1 Twin 2 Family	2 Pub. Bath/Show	B&B per person £14.00-£16.00 Single £14.00-£16.00 Double	Open Jan-Dec	
Mr & Mrs J Nicol Danskine Villa, Main Street Fallin, by Stirling Stirlingshire Tel: (Stirling) 0786 813810/811111 Fax: 0786 811447		Award Pending	1 Twin 1 Double 1 Family	3 Limited ensuite 1 Pub. Bath/Show	B&B per person £14.00 Double	Open Jan-Dec	
Mrs Agnes Thomson Tiroran, 45 Douglas Terrace Stirling FK7 9LW Tel: (Stirling) 0786 464655		HIGHLY COMMENDED Listed	1 Twin 1 Double	1 Pub. Bath/Show	B&B per person £13.50-£14.00 Double	Open Apr-Oct	
			A warm welcome in this modern house, with easy access to the town centre.				
STOER **Sutherland** Mrs F Mackenzie Lochview, 216 Clashmore Stoer, Lochinver Sutherland IV27 4JQ Tel: (Stoer) 05715 226	Map 3 G5		1 Twin 1 Double	1 Pub. Bath/Show	B&B per person from £13.00 Double	Open May-Sep Dinner 1800-2030 B&B + Eve. Meal from £20.00	

'MacPhails'

TEL: 057 15 295

216 CLASHMORE, STOER, LOCHINVER, SUTHERLAND IV27 4JQ

A warm welcome awaits you in our traditional crofthouse modernised to a high standard with many original features and peat/log fires. A lochside situation overlooking the sea to the Hebrides. Sandy beaches and mountains nearby to explore, or simply relax in peaceful surroundings. Enjoy our "Taste of Scotland" recommended meals. House open all day.

Mr & Mrs P MacPhail 216 Clashmore Stoer, Lochinver Sutherland IV27 4JQ Tel: (Stoer) 05715 295			1 Twin 2 Double	1 En Suite fac 1 Pub. Bath/Show	B&B per person £14.00-£22.00 Double	Open May-Oct Dinner from 1900 B&B + Eve. Meal £26.00-£34.00	
STONEHAVEN **Kincardineshire** Mrs V Craib Car-Lyn-Vale Rickarton, by Stonehaven Kincardineshire AB3 2TD Tel: (Stonehaven) 0569 762406	Map 4 G1	HIGHLY COMMENDED 👑 👑	1 Twin 2 Double	3 En Suite fac	B&B per person £18.00-£20.00 Single £16.00-£17.00 Double	Open Jan-Dec	
			Friendly B and B. Non smoking. 10 minutes from Stonehaven in rural setting at gateway to Royal Deeside. Ensuite facilities. Ample, safe parking.				
Mrs Lana Gibson Malcolm's Mount Broomhill Road Stonehaven Kincardineshire AB3 2NH Tel: (Stonehaven) 0569 63937			1 Single 1 Twin 1 Double	2 Priv. NOT ensuite 2 Pub. Bath/Show	B&B per person £15.00-£20.00 Single £15.00-£20.00 Double	Open Jan-Dec	
STORNOWAY **Lewis, Western Isles** Hebridean Guest House Bayhead Stornoway Lewis, Western Isles PA87 2DZ Tel: (Stornoway) 0851 702268	Map 3 D4	Award Pending	5 Single 3 Twin 2 Double 2 Family	7 En Suite fac 2 Pub. Bath/Show	B&B per person £18.00-£24.00 Single	Open Jan-Dec Dinner 1830-2030 B&B + Eve. Meal £26.00-£30.00	
Roddy & Catherine Afrin Park Guest House 30 James Street Stornoway Lewis, Western Isles PA87 2QN Tel: (Stornoway) 0851 702485		COMMENDED 👑	1 Single 2 Twin 2 Double	1 En Suite fac 3 Pub. Bath/Show	B&B per person from £20.00 Single from £19.00 Double	Open Jan-Dec Dinner 1800-2030 B&B + Eve. Meal from £32.00	
			Victorian house, sympathetically refurbished to retain its character. Convenient for ferry and airport. Taste of Scotland.				

STORNOWAY continued	Map 3 D4		

ARNSIDE · 12 Churchill Drive
STORNOWAY, ISLE OF LEWIS PA87 2NP
Tel: 0851 704893
COMFORTABLE ACCOMMODATION WITH MANY PLACES
OF INTEREST TO VISIT. FISHING AND GOLF AVAILABLE.
5-10 MINUTES WALK FROM FERRY AND TOWN CENTRE.
BACKPACKERS WELCOME.
— B&B FROM £13 —

Mrs M Campbell Arnside, 12 Churchill Drive Stornoway Lewis, Western Isles PA87 2NP Tel: (Stornoway) 0851 704893	**COMMENDED** Listed	1 Single 1 Pub. Bath/Show 1 Twin Quietly situated in a residential area but convenient for ferries and all facilities. Backpackers welcome.	B&B per person £12.00-£13.00 Single £12.00-£13.00 Double Open Jan-Dec
Mrs A C MacLeod Ravenswood 12 Matheson Road Stornoway Lewis, Western Isles PA87 2LR Tel: (Stornoway) 0851 702673	**HIGHLY COMMENDED** 👑👑	2 Single 2 En Suite fac 1 Twin 1 Pub. Bath/Show 1 Double Turn of the century villa in a quiet area of Stornoway yet a short stroll to the harbour and town centre.	B&B per person from £16.00 Single from £16.00 Double Open Jan-Dec
Mrs J Skinner Ardlonan, 29 Francis Street Stornoway Lewis, Western Isles PA87 2NF Tel: (Stornoway) 0851 703482		2 Twin 2 Pub. Bath/Show 2 Double 1 Family	B&B per person £16.00-£17.00 Single £17.00 Double Open Jan-Dec
Mrs Smith 40 Goathill Road Stornoway Lewis, Western Isles PA87 2NS Tel: (Stornoway) 0851 703681		1 Twin 2 Pub. Bath/Show 2 Double	B&B per person from £13.00 Single from £13.00 Double Open Jan-Dec
STRAITON **Ayrshire** H R Henry Three Thorns Farm Straiton Ayrshire Tel: (Straiton) 06557 221	Map 1 H8 **COMMENDED** 👑👑	1 Twin 1 En Suite fac 1 Double 2 Limited ensuite 1 Family 2 Priv. NOT ensuite 1 Pub. Bath/Show Farm house on working farm in rural area, 1 mile (2kms) from Conservation Village of Straiton. Trout pond on the farm; fishing and golf available.	B&B per person from £20.00 Single from £18.00 Double Open Jan-Dec

STRANRAER **Wigtownshire** Fernlea Guest House Fernlea, Lewis Street Stranraer Wigtownshire DG9 7AQ Tel: (Stranraer) 0776 3037	Map 1 F1	COMMENDED 👑 👑 👑	1 Twin 2 Double	2 En Suite fac 1 Pub. Bath/Show	B&B per person £13.00-£18.00 Double	Open Jan-Dec Dinner 1800-1900 B&B + Eve. Meal £20.00-£25.00	

Personally run, with friendly atmosphere. Close to town centre, Stranraer and Cairnryan ferries. En suite facilities and ample parking. Non-smoking.

Jan-da-Mar Guest House 1 Ivy Place, London Road Stranraer Wigtownshire DG9 8ER Tel: (Stranraer) 0776 6194		COMMENDED 👑 👑	2 Single 3 Twin 3 Family	2 En Suite fac 2 Pub. Bath/Show	B&B per person £15.00 Single £13.00-£17.50 Double	Open Jan-Dec	

Early 19C townhouse, modernised yet retaining some original features. Conveniently situated for town centre and ferry terminal.

Mrs F Hull Hartforth, 33 London Road Stranraer Wigtownshire DG9 8AF Tel: (Stranraer) 0776 4832			1 Twin 2 Double 1 Family	2 Pub. Bath/Show	B&B per person £14.00-£15.00 Double	Open Jan-Dec	

Mr & Mrs R King Kingsway, Dalrymple Street Stranraer Wigtownshire DG9 7OH Tel: (Stranraer) 0776 2126		COMMENDED 👑 👑	2 Single 1 Twin 1 Double	1 En Suite fac 1 Pub. Bath/Show	B&B per person £13.00-£15.00 Single £13.00-£15.00 Double	Open Jan-Dec Dinner 1700-1800 B&B + Eve. Meal £18.00-£20.00	

Personally run family home, close to town centre and ferries. Ideal base for touring, golf, fishing and leisure pursuits.

Mrs McDonald Auld Ayre, 4 Park Lane Stranraer Wigtownshire DG9 0DS Tel: (Stranraer) 0776 4500		COMMENDED 👑 👑 👑	1 Twin 1 Double 1 Family	2 En Suite fac 1 Priv. NOT ensuite 1 Pub. Bath/Show	B&B per person £15.00-£18.00 Single £13.00-£15.00 Double	Open Jan-Dec Dinner 1700-1830 B&B + Eve. Meal £18.00-£20.00	

Large detached house in quiet residential area close to seafront, ferry and town centre. Own parking.

Mrs P Parker Low Balyett Farm, Cairnryan Road Stranraer Wigtownshire DG9 8QL Tel: (Stranraer) 0776 3395		COMMENDED 👑 👑 👑	1 Twin 1 Double 1 Family	1 En Suite fac 1 Priv. NOT ensuite 1 Pub. Bath/Show	B&B per person £17.00-£20.00 Single £14.00-£17.00 Double	Open Jan-Dec Dinner 1800-1900 B&B + Eve. Meal £20.50-£23.50	

Working farmhouse on edge of town. Convenient for both ferries. Children specially welcome. Home cooking using own farm produce.

Mrs A Rafferty Neptune's Rest 25 Agnew Crescent Stranraer Wigtownshire Tel: (Stranraer) 0776 4729			1 Single 1 Double 1 Family	2 Pub. Bath/Show	B&B per person £13.00-£15.00 Single from £13.00 Double	Open Jan-Dec	

Mr & Mrs Whitworth Kildrochet House Stranraer Wigtownshire DG9 9BB Tel: (Lochans) 077682 216		COMMENDED 👑 👑 👑	2 Twin 1 Double	2 En Suite fac 1 Priv. NOT ensuite	B&B per person £22.00 Single £22.00 Double	Open Jan-Dec Dinner at 1930 B&B + Eve. Meal £32.00-£35.00	

18C Adam Dower House set in peaceful 6 acres of gardens, pasture and woodlands with open views over Rhins of Galloway. Non smoking. Home cooking.

Details of Grading and Classification are on page vi.   Key to symbols is on back flap.   285

STRATHAIRD, by Broadford **Isle of Skye, Inverness-shire** Strathaird House Strathaird Isle of Skye, Inverness-shire IV49 9AX Tel: (Loch Scavaig) 04716 269/ (0444 452990 off season)	**Map 3** D1	**APPROVED** Listed	2 Single 1 Double 4 Family	4 Pub. Bath/Show	B&B per person £15.30-£24.00 Single £13.50-£22.00 Double	Open Apr-Sep B&B + Eve. Meal £23.50-£34.00	

Family run guest house in own extensive grounds with views of sea and Cuillins.
10 miles (16 kms) west of Broadford.

STRATHCARRON Ross-shire	**Map 3** F9	

"THE SHIELING"
ACHINTEE, STRATHCARRON,
ROSS-SHIRE IV54 8YX   Tel: 05202 364

Only minutes from a railway station, surrounded by spectacular scenery, a comfortable base for many leisure activities, particularly hill walking and climbing. Central for day trips to such places as Skye and Inverewe Gardens. Evening meals served if given advance notice.

Mrs J Levy The Shieling, Achintee Strathcarron Ross-shire IV54 8YX Tel: (Lochcarron) 05202 364	**Award** **Pending**	1 Single 2 Twin	1 En Suite fac 1 Pub. Bath/Show	B&B per person £13.50-£14.00 Single £13.50-£17.00 Double	Open Jan-Dec Dinner 1900-2030 B&B + Eve. Meal £22.50-£26.00	

STRATHDON **Aberdeenshire** Mrs Denise Jones The Smiddy House Glenkindie Aberdeenshire AB33 8RX Tel: (Glenkindie) 09756 41216	**Map 4** E1	**COMMENDED** Listed	1 Single 1 Twin 1 Double	1 Pub. Bath/Show	B&B per person £10.00-£12.00 Single £10.00-£12.00 Double	Open Jan-Dec Dinner 1800-1900 B&B + Eve. Meal £16.00-£18.00

Friendly bed and breakfast on Highland route and Castle Trail.
Set in pleasant surroundings.

Mrs E Ogg Farmhouse Bed & Breakfast Buchaam Holiday Properties Buchaam Farm Strathdon Aberdeenshire AB36 8TN Tel: (Strathdon) 09756 51238	**COMMENDED** Listed	1 Twin 1 Double 1 Family	2 Pub. Bath/Show	B&B per person £13.00 Double	Open Apr-Oct Dinner 1800-1930 B&B + Eve. Meal £20.00

Large farmhouse on 600 acre mixed farm with sporting facilities including
badminton, table tennis and putting green. Free river fishing.

STRATHPEFFER **Ross-shire** Gardenside Guest House Strathpeffer Ross-shire IV14 9BJ Tel: (Strathpeffer) 0997 421242	**Map 4** A8	**COMMENDED** ♛ ♛ ♛	3 Twin 4 Double	4 En Suite fac 1 Pub. Bath/Show	B&B per person £14.00-£17.00 Double	Open Mar-Dec Dinner 1830-2000 B&B + Eve. Meal £26.00-£30.00

Friendly welcome at family run guest house in Spa village.
Good walking country and touring base. 18 miles (27kms) from Inverness.

Mrs G P Cameron White Lodge Strathpeffer Ross-shire IV14 9AL Tel: (Strathpeffer) 0997 421730	COMMENDED 👑 👑 👑	1 Twin 2 Double	3 En Suite fac	B&B per person £16.00-£18.00 Double	Open Apr-Oct Dinner 1830-1930 B&B + Eve. Meal £26.50-£28.50	🛇 Ⅴ ⒞ 📟 ☐ 🌙 🍴 🐾 🐕 📺 🛏 ⚜ 🦮 🛁 🐾 ☐ 🎵 ⛵
				'B' Listed 18C lodge overlooking charming square of small Highland spa village.		

INVER LODGE
STRATHPEFFER, ROSS-SHIRE IV14 9DL
Telephone: 0997 421392

A WARM WELCOME AWAITS YOU AT INVER LODGE.
LOG FIRES, HOME BAKING, GOOD FOOD. A FRIENDLY
RELAXED ATMOSPHERE.

BED & BREAKFAST FROM £14.
DINNER AND PACKED LUNCHES AVAILABLE.

Mrs Derbyshire Inver Lodge Strathpeffer Ross-shire Tel: (Strathpeffer) 0997 421392	Award Pending	1 Twin 1 Family	2 Pub. Bath/Show	B&B per person £16.00-£18.00 Single £14.50 Double	Open Mar-Dec Dinner 2000-2030 B&B + Eve. Meal £26.00	🛇 Ⅴ ⒞ 📟 🍴
Mrs J MacDonald Scoraig, 8 Kinnettas Square Strathpeffer Ross-shire IV14 9BD Tel: (Strathpeffer) 0997 421847		1 Twin 1 Double 1 Family	1 En Suite fac 1 Priv. NOT ensuite 2 Pub. Bath/Show	B&B per person £12.00-£14.00 Single £12.00-£14.00 Double	Open May-Sep Dinner 1800-2000 B&B + Eve. Meal from £20.00	🛇 Ⅴ ⒞ 📟 🍴
Mrs M MacKenzie Francisville Strathpeffer Ross-shire IV14 9AX Tel: (Strathpeffer) 0997 421345	COMMENDED 👑	2 Family	1 Pub. Bath/Show	B&B per person from £13.00 Single from £13.00 Double	Open Apr-Oct	🛇 ⒞ 📟 ☐
				Small cottage located on a quiet road above Strathpeffer with views across the valley, but 5 minutes walk from the centre.		
Mrs Kay MacLean Linnmhor, Park Road Strathpeffer Ross-shire IV14 9BY Tel: (Strathpeffer) 0997 421528		5 Twin 3 Double 1 Family	3 En Suite fac 2 Pub. Bath/Show	B&B per person £14.00 Single £12.00 Double	Open Jan-Dec Dinner 1830-2000	🛇 Ⅴ ⒞ 📟 🍴

STRATHPEFFER continued	Map 4 A8

CRAIGVAR

THE SQUARE, STRATHPEFFER IV14 9DL Tel: 0997 421 622

Beautifully situated overlooking the square in this charming Victorian spa village. This distinctive Georgian House offers superb luxury facilities.
* All rooms have colour TV, tea/coffee facilities, direct-dial telephone.
* All bedrooms with attractive en-suite bathrooms.
* Four-poster bedroom/open fires.
* Excellent parking.
* Ideal touring base.

Mrs M Scott
Craigvar, The Square
Strathpeffer
Ross-shire
IV14 9DL
Tel: (Strathpeffer)
0997 421622

HIGHLY COMMENDED

1 Single
1 Twin
1 Double

3 En Suite fac

B&B per person
from £19.00 Single
£13.00-£19.00 Double

Open Apr-Oct

Beautifully situated overlooking the square in charming spa village,
this distinctive Georgian house offers attractive ensuite rooms. 4 poster bed.

STRATHTAY
Perthshire
Bendarroch Guest House
Strathtay
Perthshire
PH9 9PG
Tel: (Strathtay) 0887 840420
Fax: 0887 840438

Map 2
B1

1 Single
4 Twin

5 En Suite fac

B&B per person
from £25.00 Single
from £25.00 Double

Open Jan-Dec
Dinner 1900-2000
B&B + Eve. Meal
from £40.00

Mrs P Orr
Ballinduin Bothy
Strathtay, Aberfeldy
Perthshire
PH9 0LP
Tel: (Strathtay) 0887 840460

COMMENDED

3 Twin

3 En Suite fac
1 Pub. Bath/Show

B&B per person
£16.00-£20.00 Double

Open Jan-Dec

Tastefully converted ground floor accommodation separate from main house.
Superb views over Strathtay.

STRATHY POINT, by Thurso
Sutherland
Mrs A Spry
Curlew Cottage, Aultivullin
Strathy Point, by Thurso
Sutherland
KW14 7RY
Tel: (Strathy) 06414 315

Map 4
B3

1 Twin

1 Priv. NOT ensuite

B&B per person
£14.00-£16.00 Single
£12.00-£14.00 Double

Open Jan-Dec
Dinner 1800-2030
B&B + Eve. Meal
£19.00-£21.00

STRATHYRE
Perthshire
Miss E Haydock &
Mrs M Mylne
Stroneslaney Farmhouse
Strathyre
Perthshire
FK18 8NF
Tel: (Strathyre) 0877 384676

Map 1
H3

COMMENDED

1 Twin
1 Double

1 Pub. Bath/Show

B&B per person
from £17.00 Single
from £14.00 Double

Open Jun-Sep
Dinner from 1845
B&B + Eve. Meal
from £24.00

Restored 18C farmhouse in idyllic location in the midst of the Trossachs.
Peaceful riverside setting. Trout fishing available.

STRICHEN
Aberdeenshire
Mrs Mutch
Findon House, 36 High Street
Strichen
Aberdeenshire
AB43 4SR
Tel: (Strichen) 07715 469

Map 4
H8

COMMENDED

1 Twin
1 Family

2 Pub. Bath/Show

B&B per person
£13.00 Single
£13.00 Double

Open May-Oct

A warm welcome awaits you at this family house in the heart of a small village,
approximately 9 miles (14kms) West of Fraserburgh.

VAT is shown at 17.5%: changes in this rate may affect prices. Prices shown are for guidance only. Please send SAE with each enquiry.

STROMEFERRY **Ross-shire** Mrs P Davey Soluis Mu Thuath Braeintra, Achmore Stromeferry Ross-shire IV53 8UN Tel: (Stromeferry) 059987 219	**Map 3** F9	COMMENDED 👑 👑	2 Twin 1 Double 1 Family	4 En Suite fac	B&B per person £15.00-£18.00 Double	Open Feb-Nov	

Purpose built by owners set amidst quiet countryside. Excellent centre for Skye and Lochalsh.

STROMNESS **Orkney** Mrs Alison M Clouston Thira, Innertown Stromness Orkney KW16 3JP Tel: (Stromness) 0856 851181	**Map 5** A1	COMMENDED 👑 👑 👑	2 Single 2 Double	4 En Suite fac	B&B per person to £22.00 Single to £22.00 Double	Open Jan-Nov Dinner 1900-2000 B&B + Eve. Meal to £30.00	

Custom built guest house in a quiet location with unrivalled views of Hoy Sound. Home cooking with fresh produce.

Mrs C Hourston 15 John Street Stromness Orkney KW16 3AD Tel: (Stromness) 0856 850642		COMMENDED Listed	2 Single 1 Twin 1 Double	1 Pub. Bath/Show	B&B per person to £15.00 Single to £15.00 Double	Open Jan-Dec	

In quiet situation above harbour, convenient for ferry terminal, shops and all local amenities. Exceptional breakfast menu and many 'extras'.

Mrs S Thomas Stenigar, Ness Road Stromness Orkney KW16 3DW Tel: (Stromness) 0856 850438		COMMENDED 👑 👑 👑	2 Twin 1 Double	2 En Suite fac 1 Priv. NOT ensuite	B&B per person £17.50-£25.00 Single £17.50-£20.00 Double	Open Apr-Oct Dinner 1800-2100	

Rambling historic house with bags of character. Comfortable lounge with sea views to Hoy. Golf course and yacht club nearby.

STRUAN **Isle of Skye, Inverness-shire** Mrs Beaton 3 Balmeanach Struan Isle of Skye, Inverness-shire Tel: (Struan) 047072 300	**Map 3** C9		1 Twin 1 Double 1 Family	1 En Suite fac 1 Pub. Bath/Show	B&B per person £11.00-£13.00 Double	Open Apr-Oct	

Mrs Moira Campbell The Anchorage, 9 Ebost West Struan Isle of Skye, Inverness-shire IV55 8FE Tel: (Struan) 047072 206		COMMENDED 👑 👑	1 Twin 2 Double	1 En Suite fac 2 Pub. Bath/Show	B&B per person £13.00-£15.00 Single £13.00-£15.00 Double	Open Jan-Dec Dinner 1800-1930 B&B + Eve. Meal £21.50-£23.50	

Modern bungalow standing in its own grounds with views over Loch Bracadale. Home cooking and family atmosphere.

Mrs Morrison Loch Mor Struan Isle of Skye, Inverness-shire IV56 8FB Tel: (Struan) 047072 283			1 Twin 2 Double	2 Pub. Bath/Show	B&B per person £13.00-£13.50 Double	Open Apr-Sep	

SYMINGTON **Ayrshire** Danepark House 1 Kilmarnock Road Symington Ayrshire KA1 5PT Tel: (Kilmarnock) 0563 830246 Fax: 0563 830246	Map 1 H7	**HIGHLY COMMENDED** 👑 👑 👑	2 Twin 1 Double	3 En Suite fac	B&B per person £35.00-£40.00 Single £22.50-£28.50 Double	Open Jan-Dec Dinner 1900-2000 B&B + Eve. Meal £37.50-£43.50	
			Country residence set in 2.5 acres of grounds. Very convenient for Prestwick Airport, golf courses and Ayr racecourse.				
TAIN **Ross-shire** Golf View Guest House 13 Knockbreck Road Tain Ross-shire Tel: (Tain) 0862 892856	Map 4 B7	**HIGHLY COMMENDED** 👑 👑	3 Twin 1 Double 1 Family	1 En Suite fac 2 Pub. Bath/Show	B&B per person £15.00-£20.00 Single £13.00-£15.00 Double	Open Jan-Dec	
			Secluded Victorian house with panoramic views over Golf Course and across the Dornoch Firth. Centrally situated in Scotland's oldest Royal Burgh.				
Mrs Anderson Rosslyn, 2 Moss Road Tain Ross-shire IV19 1HQ Tel: (Tain) 0862 892697			1 Twin 1 Family	1 Pub. Bath/Show	B&B per person from £13.00 Single £13.00 Double	Open Jan-Dec	
Mrs M MacLean 23 Moss Road Tain Ross-shire IV19 1HH Tel: (Tain) 0862 894087		**COMMENDED** 👑	1 Single 1 Twin 1 Double	2 Pub. Bath/Show	B&B per person £13.00-£13.50 Single £13.00-£13.50 Double	Open Jan-Dec	
			Comfortable family-run home in quiet location. Log burning stove in lounge and a warm welcome assured.				
Mrs Roberts Carringtons, Morangie Road Tain Ross-shire IV19 1PY Tel: (Tain) 0862 892635		**COMMENDED** 👑	1 Double 2 Family	2 Limited ensuite 2 Pub. Bath/Show	B&B per person from £13.00 Single from £13.00 Double	Open Jan-Dec	
			Detached family home on the outskirts of Tain overlooking the sea.				
TARBERT **Harris, Western Isles** Mrs A Morrison Hillcrest West Tarbert Harris, Western 'sles PA85 3BG Tel: (Harris) 0859 2119	Map 3 B6	**COMMENDED** 👑 👑	1 Twin 1 Double 1 Family	1 En Suite fac 2 Pub. Bath/Show	B&B per person £13.00-£14.00 Single £13.00-£14.00 Double	Open Apr-Oct Dinner from 1900 B&B + Eve. Meal £22.00-£24.00	
			Modern croft house in elevated position with fine view over West Loch Tarbert. About 1 mile (2kms) from ferry terminal.				

Book your accommodation anywhere in Scotland the easy way—through your nearest Tourist Information Centre.

A booking fee of £2.50 is charged, and you will be asked for a small deposit.

Local bookings are usually free, or a small fee will be charged.

Flora Morrison Tigh na Mara Tarbert Harris, Western Isles Tel: (Harris) 0859 2270		**COMMENDED** ♛	1 Single 1 Twin 1 Family	1 Pub. Bath/Show	B&B per person £13.00-£15.00 Single £13.00-£15.00 Double	Open Jan-Dec Dinner 1900-2000 B&B + Eve. Meal £20.00-£22.00	
			Detached house with scenic views over East Loch Tarbert. Only about 500 metres from ferry terminal. Ideal centre for touring Harris.				
TARBERT, Loch Fyne **Argyll** Mrs Peden The Hollies Tarbert, Loch Fyne Argyll PA29 6YF Tel: (Tarbert) 0880 820742	Map 1 E5		2 Twin 1 Double	2 Pub. Bath/Show	B&B per person from £15.00 Single from £15.00 Double	Open Jan-Dec	
TARBET, by Arrochar **Dunbartonshire** Mrs E Fairfield Lochview Tarbet, by Arrochar Dunbartonshire G83 7DD Tel: (Arrochar) 03012 200	Map 1 G3	Award Pending	1 Twin 2 Double	1 Pub. Bath/Show	B&B per person £13.00-£15.00 Single £13.00-£15.00 Double	Open Jan-Dec B&B + Eve. Meal £13.00-£16.00	
Mrs C Harvey Tarbet House Tarbet, Loch Lomond Dunbartonshire G83 7DE Tel: (Arrochar) 03012 349		**COMMENDED** ♛ ♛	1 Twin 2 Double	1 En Suite fac 2 Pub. Bath/Show	B&B per person £18.00-£25.00 Single £15.00-£25.00 Double	Open Jan-Oct	
			Modern country house in 7 acres. Panoramic view south across Loch Lomond. Dinner by arrangement. Sailing, walking and other activities.				
Mrs Kelly Bon-Etive Tarbet, by Arrochar Dunbartonshire G83 Tel: (Arrochar) 03012 219		**COMMENDED** Listed	1 Twin 1 Double	1 Pub. Bath/Show	B&B per person £13.00-£13.50 Double	Open Apr-Oct	
			Conveniently situated in quiet cul-de-sac close to the A82, with fine views of Loch Lomond and 'The Ben'.				
Mrs M McDonald Aye Servus, Tighloan Tarbet, by Arrochar Dunbartonshire G83 7DD Tel: (Arrochar) 03012 491			1 Twin 1 Double	1 Pub. Bath/Show	B&B per person £13.00-£15.00 Double	Open Apr-Oct	
TARBOLTON, by Ayr **Ayrshire** Mrs Maurice Harrison Scoutts Farm Tarbolton, by Ayr Ayrshire KA5 5NQ Tel: (Tarbolton) 0292 541218	Map 1 H7	**APPROVED** ♛	1 Twin 1 Double 1 Family	1 Pub. Bath/Show	B&B per person £14.00-£15.00 Single £14.00-£15.00 Double	Open Jan-Dec	
			19th Century farmhouse on a hill in the heart of Burns Country, with dramatic views across Prestwick and Ayr to Arran.				

TARVES **Aberdeenshire** Mrs E Cook Little Meldrum Tarves, by Ellon Aberdeenshire AB41 0NB Tel: (Schivas) 0358 761261	Map 4 G9	**COMMENDED** Listed	1 Twin 1 Double 1 Family	3 Pub. Bath/Show	B&B per person from £15.00 Single from £15.00 Double	Open May-Sep
Family farmhouse, modernised and extended with sauna, solarium and billiard table. Home cooking. Central for National Trust Properties.						
TAYNUILT **Argyll** J Pearson Aros Taynuilt Argyll PA35 1JE Tel: (Taynuilt) 08662 236	Map 1 F2		2 Double	1 Pub. Bath/Show	B&B per person £13.00-£15.00 Single £13.00-£15.00 Double	Open Apr-Dec Dinner 1900-2100 B&B + Eve. Meal £19.00-£21.00
TEANGUE, Sleat **Isle of Skye, Inverness-shire** B & J Shaw Alltan House Ferindonald, Sleat Isle of Skye, Inverness-shire IV44 8RQ Tel: (Ardvasar) 04714 342	Map 3 E1	**COMMENDED** Listed	1 Twin 2 Double	2 Pub. Bath/Show	B&B per person £17.00-£20.00 Single £15.00-£17.00 Double	Open Mar-Nov Dinner from 1900 B&B + Eve. Meal £27.00-£29.00
Modern house in elevated position offering panoramic views over the Sound of Sleat to the mountains of Knoydart, 4 miles (6kms) from Armadale ferry.						
THORNHILL **Dumfriesshire** Mrs G Crawford 47-48 Drumlanrig Street Thornhill Dumfriesshire DG3 5LJ Tel: (Thornhill) 0848 330566	Map 2 B8		1 Twin 2 Family	1 En Suite fac 2 Pub. Bath/Show	B&B per person £12.50-£15.00 Double	Open Jan-Dec Dinner 1800-2000 B&B + Eve. Meal £20.00-£22.00
Mrs Hill Drumcruilton Thornhill Dumfriesshire DG3 5BG Tel: (Durisdeer) 08485 210		**Award** **Pending**	1 Single 2 Double 1 Family	1 En Suite fac 1 Priv. NOT ensuite 2 Pub. Bath/Show	B&B per person from £18.00 Single £17.00-£22.00 Double	Open May-Nov Dinner 1830-1930 B&B + Eve. Meal £29.00-£34.00
Mrs Maxwell Druidhall Farm Thornhill Dumfriesshire DG3 4NE Tel: (Marrburn) 08486 271			1 Twin 2 Double	2 Pub. Bath/Show	B&B per person £8.50-£9.50 Single £8.50-£9.50 Double	Open Mar-Dec Dinner 1800-1900 B&B + Eve. Meal £17.50-£18.50
THORNHILL **Perthshire** Mrs S Duke Norrieston Thornhill, by Stirling Perthshire FK8 3QE Tel: (Thornhill) 0786 850234	Map 2 A4	**COMMENDED** Listed	3 Twin	2 Pub. Bath/Show	B&B per person £15.00 Single £15.00 Double	Open May-Sep
19C former manse in quiet rural setting, convenient for touring.						
THURSO **Caithness** Mrs J Anderson 3 Castle Street Thurso Caithness KW14 7JB Tel: (Thurso) 0847 63820	Map 4 C3		1 Twin 1 Double 2 Family	1 Pub. Bath/Show	B&B per person £12.00-£13.00 Single from £15.00 Double	Open Jan-Dec

Mrs Bews Ashley House 21 Durness Street Thurso Caithness KW14 8BD Tel: (Thurso) 0847 63906			1 Twin 2 Double	2 Pub. Bath/Show	B&B per person £13.00-£15.00 Single £13-£15.00 Double	Open Jan-Dec
Mrs Brown Borlum, 26 Sinclair Street Thurso Caithness KW14 7AG Tel: (Thurso) 0847 65830			1 Single 2 Twin 1 Double 1 Family	2 En Suite fac 1 Pub. Bath/Show	B&B per person from £12.00 Single £12.00-£15.00 Double	Open Jan-Dec Dinner from 1800 B&B + Eve. Meal £16.00-£19.00
Mrs J Falconer 1 Campbell Street Thurso Caithness KW14 7HD Tel: (Thurso) 0847 65759			1 Single 1 Twin 1 Family	2 Pub. Bath/Show	B&B per person £13.50-£15.00 Double	Open Jan-Dec
Mrs M Fisher Carlingwark, 5 Mears Place Thurso Caithness KW14 7EW Tel: (Thurso) 0847 64124			1 Single 1 Twin 1 Double	2 Pub. Bath/Show	B&B per person to £13.50 Single to £12.50 Double	Open Jun-Sep
Mrs McDonald Seaview Farm, Hill of Forss Thurso Caithness KW14 7XQ Tel: (Thurso) 0847 62315	COMMENDED		1 Twin 2 Double	1 Pub. Bath/Show	B&B per person £12.50-£13.00 Single £12.50-£13.00 Double	Open Jan-Dec
		Working farm, warm welcome and homebakes; display of Highland Dancing and trophies.				
Mrs Murray 1 Granville Crescent Thurso Caithness KW14 7NP Tel: (Thurso) 0847 62993	COMMENDED		2 Twin	1 Limited ensuite 1 Pub. Bath/Show	B&B per person £13.00-£14.00 Double	Open Jan-Dec
		Quietly situated, yet within easy reach of station and all facilities. All ground floor rooms, one with private shower.				
Mrs Oag 9 Couper Street Thurso Caithness KW14 8AR Tel: (Thurso) 0847 64529			2 Single 1 Double	1 Pub. Bath/Show	B&B per person £12.00-£13.00 Single £12.00-£13.00 Double	Open Jan-Dec
Mrs M Sinclair Shinval, Glengolly Thurso Caithness KW14 7XN Tel: (Thurso) 0847 64306	COMMENDED		1 Twin 1 Double 1 Family	2 Pub. Bath/Show	B&B per person £12.50-£13.50 Single £12.50-£13.50 Double	Open Jan-Dec
		Family home in quiet rural setting. 2 miles (3kms) from Thurso. Extensive countryside views.				
Mrs J Sutherland 11 Park Avenue Mountpleasant Thurso Caithness KW14 8JP Tel: (Thurso) 0847 64269	COMMENDED Listed		1 Single 1 Twin	1 Pub. Bath/Show	B&B per person from £13.00 Double	Open Jan-Dec Dinner 1800-1930
		Homely, warm and comfortable house in quiet residential district only a short walk from town centre.				

	Map	Beds	Bath	B&B Price	Opening	

THURSO continued
Caithness
Mrs Swanson
47 Princes Street
Thurso
Caithness
KW14 7AB
Tel: (Thurso) 0847 63180

Map 4 C3

1 Twin / 1 Double / 1 Family — 3 Pub. Bath/Show — B&B per person £13.50-£15.00 Single £12.50-£13.50 Double — Open Jan-Dec

---

Mrs D Thomson
Annandale
2 Rendel Govan Road
Thurso
Caithness
KW14 7EP
Tel: (Thurso) 0847 63942

2 Twin / 1 Double — 2 Pub. Bath/Show — B&B per person £13.50-£14.00 Double — Open May-Sep

---

Mrs B Tuck
Seaview, Dixonfield
Thurso
Caithness
KW14 8YN
Tel: (Thurso) 0847 64511

DELUXE

1 Twin / 2 Double — 2 Pub. Bath/Show — B&B per person from £13.00 Double — Open Jan-Dec

Modern bungalow with panoramic views over Thurso harbour and across the sea to Orkney. A warm welcome and most comfortable stay assured.

TIGHNABRUAICH
Argyll
Mrs P C McLachlan
Ferguslie, Seafront
Tighnabruaich
Argyll
PA21 2BE
Tel: (Tighnabruaich)
0700 811414

Map 1 F5

2 Double — 1 Pub. Bath/Show — B&B per person from £13.50 Single from £12.50 Double — Open Apr-Sep Dinner from 1800 B&B + Eve. Meal from £20.00

TILLICOULTRY
Clackmannanshire
Mrs Goddard
Wyvis, 70 Stirling Street
Tillicoultry
Clackmannanshire
FK13 6EA
Tel: (Tillicoultry) 0259 751513

Map 2 B4

COMMENDED
Listed

1 Twin — 1 Pub. Bath/Show — B&B per person from £17.00 Single £15.00-£17.00 Double — Open Jan-Dec Dinner 1900-2030 B&B + Eve. Meal £23.00-£25.00

Cottage in conservation area overlooking the Ochil Hills and ideally situated for hillwalking. Friendly atmosphere, home cooking and baking.

WESTBOURNE

10 Dollar Road, Tillicoultry FK13 6PA. Tel: (0259) 750314

Victorian Mill Owner's Mansion set in wooded grounds beneath Ochil Hills. Warm, friendly atmosphere with unusual collection of arts and curios from around the world. Delicious home cooking using local produce. Vegetarian food a speciality. Log fires. Centrally situated for Edinburgh, Glasgow, Perth, Stirling — motorways 15 minutes. Secure off-street parking.

Mrs J O'Dell
Westbourne, 10 Dollar Road
Tillicoultry
Clackmannanshire
FK13 6PA
Tel: (Tillicoultry) 0259 750314

COMMENDED

2 Twin / 1 Double — 1 En Suite fac / 1 Pub. Bath/Show — B&B per person from £20.00 Single from £17.00 Double — Open Jan-Dec Dinner 1830-2030 B&B + Eve. Meal from £27.00

Victorian mansion, full of character, on the Mill Trail below Ochil Hills. Home baking and cooking. Log fire. Secure off-road parking.

TOBERMORY **Isle of Mull, Argyll** Baliscate Guest House Tobermory Isle of Mull, Argyll PA75 6QA Tel: (Tobermory) 0688 2048	Map 1 C1	COMMENDED 👑 👑	1 Twin 3 Double 1 Family	2 En Suite fac 2 Pub. Bath/Show	B&B per person £16.00-£20.00 Double	Open Jan-Dec
			Set in 1.5 acres of garden and woodland with magnificent views over The Sound of Mull.			
Carnaburg 55 Main Street Tobermory Isle of Mull, Argyll PA75 6NT Tel: (Tobermory) 0688 2479			2 Twin 3 Double 1 Family	2 Pub. Bath/Show	B&B per person £16.00-£17.50 Double	Open Jan-Dec
Failte Guest House Main Street Tobermory Isle of Mull, Argyll PA75 6NU Tel: (Tobermory) 0688 2495 Fax: 0688 2232		Award Pending	3 Twin 3 Double 1 Family	7 En Suite fac 2 Pub. Bath/Show	B&B per person £25.00-£30.00 Single £20.00-£25.00 Double	Open Mar-Oct
Staffa Cottages Guest House Tobermory Isle of Mull, Argyll PA75 6PL Tel: (Tobermory) 0688 2464 Fax: 0688 2464		COMMENDED 👑 👑	2 Twin 3 Double	3 En Suite.fac 2 Priv. NOT ensuite	B&B per person £16.00-£18.00 Double	Open Jan-Dec Dinner from 1900 B&B + Eve. Meal £28.00-£30.00
			In quiet residential area on slopes above Tobermory with large garden. Fine views over bay to Sound of Mull and Morvern Hills.			
D E McAdam Fairways Lodge Tobermory Isle of Mull, Argyll PA75 6PX Tel: (Tobermory) 0688 2238 Fax: 0688 2142		HIGHLY COMMENDED 👑 👑	1 Single 2 Twin 1 Double 1 Family	5 En Suite fac	B&B per person from £28.00 Single from £28.00 Double	Open Jan-Dec
			Situated between 3rd and 4th fairways on golf course. Commanding view across Tobermory Bay and Sound of Mull.			
TOMINTOUL **Banffshire** Mrs Michele Birnie Livet House, 34 Main Street Tomintoul, Ballindalloch Banffshire AB37 9EX Tel: (Tomintoul) 08074 205	Map 4 D1		1 Single 2 Double	2 Pub. Bath/Show	B&B per person from £12.00 Single from £12.00 Double	Open Jan-Dec
BY TOMINTOUL **Banffshire** Mrs M C McIntosh Milton Farm Tomintoul, Ballindalloch Banffshire AB37 9EQ Tel: (Tomintoul) 0807 580288	Map 4 D1	COMMENDED Listed	1 Double 1 Family	1 Pub. Bath/Show	B&B per person £13.00-£15.00 Double	Open Jan-Dec
			Warm welcome at 18C farmhouse with panoramic views over hills. Tomintoul 0.5 miles (1km). Good base for walking, touring. Ground floor accommodation			
Mrs Anne Shearer Croughly Farm Tomintoul, Ballindalloch Banffshire AB37 9EN Tel: (Tomintoul) 0807 580476		COMMENDED 👑 👑	1 Double 1 Family	1 En Suite fac 1 Priv. NOT ensuite	B&B per person £12.50-£14.00 Double	Open Apr-Oct
			18th century listed farmhouse, overlooking the River Conglass with stunning views of the Cairngorms. 2 miles (3kms) from Tomintoul.			

Details of Grading and Classification are on page vi.

Key to symbols is on back flap.

BY TOMINTOUL continued Mrs Elma Turner Findron Farm, Braemar Road Tomintoul Banffshire AB37 9ER Tel: (Tomintoul) 08074 382	Map 4 D1	**Award Pending**	1 Double 1 Family	1 Pub. Bath/Show	B&B per person £12.00-£13.00 Single £12.00-£13.00 Double	Open Jan-Dec Dinner 1800-1930 B&B + Eve. Meal £17.00-£18.00	
TONGUE **Sutherland** Mrs S Mackay Rhian Cottage Tongue Sutherland IV27 Tel: (Tongue) 084755 257	Map 4 A3	**COMMENDED** **Listed**	1 Twin 1 Double 1 Family	1 En Suite fac 1 Pub. Bath/Show	B&B per person £15.00-£16.00 Double	Open Jan-Dec	
			Charming modernised croft cottage, with peacocks, 0.5 miles (1km) outside village. Dramatic views of Ben Loyal. Owner's painting gallery next door.				
Mrs H Sutherland Woodend Tongue Sutherland IV27 4XW Tel: (Tongue) 084755 332		**COMMENDED** **Listed**	1 Single 1 Double 1 Family	1 Pub. Bath/Show	B&B per person £15.00-£17.00 Single £14.00-£16.00 Double	Open Jan-Dec	
			With excellent views over Tongue Bay this cottage is situated just 1 mile (1.5 kms) outside Tongue village.				
TORE, by Muir of Ord **Ross-shire** Mrs E MacKenzie Fiveways Tore, by Muir of Ord Ross-shire Tel: (Munlochy) 046381 408	Map 4 A8		1 Twin 2 Double	2 Pub. Bath/Show	B&B per person £14.00-£15.00 Single £13.00-£14.00 Double	Open Easter-Oct	
TORRIDON **Ross-shire** Ben Damph Lodge Torridon Ross-shire Tel: (Torridon) 0445 791242 Fax: 0445 791296	Map 3 F8		14 Family	14 En Suite fac	Price per room from £25.00	Open Jan-Dec Dinner 1830-2030	
Mrs M MacDonald Grianan, Alligin Torridon, Achnasheen Ross-shire IV22 2HB Tel: (Torridon) 0445 791264		**COMMENDED** **Listed**	1 Twin 1 Double	1 Pub. Bath/Show	B&B per person from £13.00 Double	Open Apr-Sep Dinner from 1900 B&B + Eve. Meal from £21.50	
			Modern bungalow with panoramic views over Loch Torridon to the mountains beyond. Ideal for walking.				
Mrs P J Rose Heather Cliff, Inveralligin Torridon, Achnasheen Ross-shire IV22 2HB Tel: (Torridon) 0445 791256			1 Single 1 Double 1 Family	1 Pub. Bath/Show	B&B per person from £13.50 Single from £13.50 Double	Open Feb-Nov Dinner from 1900 B&B + Eve. Meal from £21.50	

TRANENT **East Lothian** Mrs R Harrison Rosebank House 161 High Street Tranent East Lothian EH33 1LP Tel: (Tranent) 0875 610967	**Map 2** D5	**APPROVED** ♛	1 Twin 3 Double 1 Family	2 Pub. Bath/Show	B&B per person £13.00-£16.00 Single £13.00-£15.00 Double	Open Jan-Dec
			Stone built house near centre of Tranent. 10 miles (16kms) to Edinburgh city centre. Ideal base for golfing and touring East Lothian.			
Mrs H C Harvey North Elphinstone Farm Tranent East Lothian EH33 2ND Tel: (Tranent) 0875 610329		**COMMENDED** Listed	1 Twin 1 Double 1 Family	2 Pub. Bath/Show	B&B per person £15.00-£16.00 Single £14.00-£16.00 Double	Open Jun-Sep
			Large farmhouse set in quiet rural area. 10 miles (16 Km) from city centre and convenient for numerous golf courses. Non smoking house.			
TREASLANE **Isle of Skye, Inverness-shire** Mrs M Cameron Hillcroft, 2 Treaslane by Portree Isle of Skye, Inverness-shire IV51 9NX Tel: (Edinbane) 047082 304	**Map 3** D8	**HIGHLY** **COMMENDED** ♛♛	1 Twin 1 Double	1 En Suite fac 1 Priv. NOT ensuite 1 Pub. Bath/Show	B&B per person £12.50-£16.00 Double	Open Jan-Dec
			Friendly welcome at modernised house on working croft overlooking Loch Snizort. On A850 9 miles (14 kms) north of Portree.			
TROON **Ayrshire** Mrs L Devine 5 St Meddans Street Troon Ayrshire KA10 6JU Tel: (Troon) 0292 311423	**Map 1** G7	**COMMENDED** ♛♛	2 Twin 1 Double	2 En Suite fac 1 Priv. NOT ensuite	B&B per person from £15.00 Double	Open Jan-Dec
			Stone built house, centrally located near to beach and golf courses. All rooms with private facilities.			
Mrs Hamilton Fin' me oot, 30a South Beach Troon Ayrshire KA10 6EF Tel: (Troon) 0292 313270			2 Twin 1 Double	2 Pub. Bath/Show	B&B per person from £14.00 Double	Open Apr-Sep
Mrs A R Jamieson Knockmarloch, 57 St Meddans Street Troon Ayrshire KA10 6NN Tel: (Troon) 0292 312840			2 Twin 1 Double	1 Limited ensuite 2 Pub. Bath/Show	B&B per person from £14.50 Double	Open Jan-Dec
Mrs N Livingstone 31 Victoria Drive Troon Ayrshire KA10 6JF Tel: (Troon) 0292 311552			1 Single 1 Twin 1 Family	2 Pub. Bath/Show	B&B per person £12.50-£16.00 Single £12.50-£16.00 Double	Open Jan-Dec
Mrs Christine McGeachin Marvay, 87 Bentinck Drive Troon Ayrshire KA10 6HZ Tel: (Troon) 0292 311626		**COMMENDED** ♛♛	1 Single 1 Twin 1 Family	2 En Suite fac 1 Priv. NOT ensuite	B&B per person from £16.00 Single from £16.00 Double	Open Jan-Dec
			Red sandstone traditional semi-villa in residential area, off street parking. Convenient for beach and golf course. 10 minutes to railway station.			

TROON **Ayrshire** Mrs Irene Sharpe Cairndale, 7 Kilkerran Drive Barassie, Troon Ayrshire KA10 6TN Tel: (Ayr) 0292 312417	**Map 1** G7	**APPROVED** Listed	1 Twin 1 Double	1 Pub. Bath/Show	B&B per person from £15.00 Single from £14.00 Double	Open Apr-Oct	

Comfortable modern accommodation near to seafront. Children welcome, homebaking, warm and friendly atmosphere.

Mrs M Tweedie The Cherries, 50 Ottoline Drive Troon Ayrshire KA10 7AW Tel: (Troon) 0292 313312		**COMMENDED** 👑 👑	1 Twin 1 Family	1 En Suite fac 1 Pub. Bath/Show	B&B per person from £15.00 Single £15.00-£17.00 Double	Open Jan-Dec	

Warm welcome in family home. Quiet residential area backing onto golf course.

TROSSACHS, by Callander **Perthshire**	**Map 1** H3

Dundarroch Country House

Brig o'Turk, Trossachs
Perthshire FK17 8HT
Tel/Fax: Trossachs (0877) 376200

Enjoy AWARD-WINNING HOSPITALITY in this small Victorian Country House set in the heart of the Trossachs. Three luxurious bedrooms, each en-suite, with colour TV, direct-dial telephone, refrigerator, trouser-press, ironing centre, hairdryer and tea/coffee maker. The Residents' Lounge and Breakfast Room, furnished with tapestries, paintings and fine antiques, have superb views to river and mountains. Chef's speciality meals are served in the Byre Restaurant in the grounds of Dundarroch House, a splendid holiday base from which to explore this area of outstanding scenic beauty.
STB 👑 👑 👑 Highly Commended
AA QQQQ "Selected" Guesthouse

Dundarroch Country House Brig O'Turk Trossachs, by Callander Perthshire FK17 8HT Tel: (Trossachs) 0877 376200 Fax: 0877 376200		**HIGHLY** **COMMENDED** 👑 👑 👑 👑	1 Twin 2 Double	3 En Suite fac	B&B per person £39.75 Single £25.50-£29.50 Double	Open Mar-Oct Dinner 1900-2100	

A friendly welcome in this restored Victorian house, peacefully set in 14 acres, with spectacular mountain views. Own fishing available.

TUMMEL BRIDGE **Perthshire** Mrs Sheena Forsythe Heatherbank Tummel Bridge Perthshire PH16 5NX Tel: (Tummel Bridge) 0882 634324	**Map 2** A1	**Award** **Pending**	1 Twin 1 Double	1 En Suite fac 1 Pub. Bath/Show	B&B per person £14.00-£17.00 Double	Open Apr-Sep	

TURRIFF **Aberdeenshire** Mrs Margaret Beattie Meikle Colp Turriff Aberdeenshire AB53 8DT Tel: (Turriff) 0888 62728	**Map 4** F8	**COMMENDED** 👑	1 Twin 1 Family	1 Pub. Bath/Show	B&B per person £15.00-£18.00 Single £15.00-£18.00 Double	Open Apr-Oct Dinner 1800-1900 B&B + Eve. Meal £22.00-£25.00	

Stone built farmhouse in working arable farm, set amidst rolling countryside, yet only 1 mile (2km) from Turriff.

Mrs Rae Silverwells Farm St Mary's Well Turriff Aberdeenshire AB53 8BS Tel: (Turriff) 0888 62469		COMMENDED 👑👑	1 Twin 1 Double	2 Priv. NOT ensuite	B&B per person £15.00 Single £14.00-£15.00 Double	Open Jan-Dec Dinner 1800-1900 B&B + Eve. Meal £22.00-£23.00	

Working stock farm with extensive views. 3 miles (5kms) south of Turriff.
Good base for touring coast and castles. Home cooking.

Mrs Strong Carlotta Cottage Muiresk, Turriff Aberdeenshire AB53 7HE Tel: (Turriff) 0888 62025		COMMENDED Listed	1 Double 1 Family	1 Pub. Bath/Show	B&B per person £12.50 Single £11.00-£12.50 Double	Open Jan-Dec	

Cottage set in elevated position in hamlet. Attractive bedrooms
feature combed ceilings. Turriff 2 miles (5kms).

BY TURRIFF **Aberdeenshire** Mrs C R M Roebuck Lendrum Farm, Birkenhills by Turriff Aberdeenshire AB53 8HA Tel: (Cuminestown) 08883 285	Map 4 F8	COMMENDED 👑👑	1 Twin 1 Family	1 En Suite fac 1 Pub. Bath/Show	B&B per person £14.00-£16.00 Single £14.00-£16.00 Double	Open Jan-Dec	

Historic working farm in Buchan countryside. Near picturesque coast, castles,
gardens, distilleries. Warm welcome, comfortable, good food, peaceful.

TWYNHOLM **Kirkcudbrightshire** Mrs M McMorran Miefield Farm Twynholm Kirkcudbrightshire DG6 4PS Tel: (Twynholm) 05576 254	Map 2 A1	APPROVED Listed	2 Family	1 Pub. Bath/Show	B&B per person £12.00-£12.50 Single £12.00-£12.50 Double	Open Apr-Oct Dinner from 1730 B&B + Eve. Meal £16.00-£16.50	

Working sheep and beef farm at the head of a quiet glen.
See sheep dogs and shepherds at work.

UDDINGSTON **Lanarkshire** Northcote Guest House 2 Holmbrae Avenue Uddingston, Glasgow Lanarkshire G71 6AL Tel: (Uddingston) 0698 813319	Map 2 A5		1 Single 1 Double 1 Family	1 Pub. Bath/Show	B&B per person £13.00-£13.50 Single £13.00-£13.50 Double	Open Jan-Dec	

UIG **Isle of Skye, Inverness-shire** Mrs Campbell Oronsay, Idrigill Uig Isle of Skye, Inverness-shire IV51 9UX Tel: (Uig) 047042 316	Map 3 D8	COMMENDED 👑👑	1 Single 1 Twin 1 Double	1 En Suite fac 1 Pub. Bath/Show	B&B per person £12.00-£15.00 Single £12.00-£15.00 Double	Open Jan-Dec	

Detached modern house overlooking Uig Bay and near to Uig ferry terminal.
Only 20 minutes in a car from Portree.

Mrs P MacKenzie 5 Glenconnon Uig Isle of Skye, Inverness-shire Tel: (Uig) 047042 311			1 Twin 1 Double	2 Pub. Bath/Show	B&B per person £13.00 Single £13.00 Double	Open Apr-Sep	

Mrs K A MacKinnon Harris Cottage Uig Isle of Skye, Inverness-shire IV51 Tel: (Uig) 047042 268			1 Twin 2 Double	2 Pub. Bath/Show	B&B per person from £14.00 Double	Open Apr-Sep Dinner 1830-2000 B&B + Eve. Meal from £22.00	

Details of Grading and Classification are on page vi. | Key to symbols is on back flap. |

UIG **Isle of Skye, Inverness-shire** Mrs R MacKinnon Braigh-Uige Uig Isle of Skye, Inverness-shire Tel: (Uig) 047042 228	**Map 3** D8	**HIGHLY COMMENDED** 👑 👑	1 Twin	1 Priv. NOT ensuite 1 Pub. Bath/Show	B&B per person from £15.00 Double	Open Apr-Oct	

Small and personally run, situated in magnificent position overlooking Uig Bay to the Waternish Peninsula.

Mrs MacLeod 11 Earlish Uig Isle of Skye, Inverness-shire IV51 9XL Tel: (Uig) 047042 319		**COMMENDED** Listed	1 Twin 1 Double 1 Family	2 Pub. Bath/Show	B&B per person £12.00-£13.00 Single £12.00-£13.00 Double	Open Apr-Nov	

Farmhouse on working sheep farm about 2 miles (3kms) from Uig Ferry terminal. Quiet location.

Mrs Anne Morrison Braeholm Uig Isle of Skye, Inverness-shire IV51 9XX Tel: (Uig) 047042 396		**COMMENDED** 👑	1 Single 1 Twin 1 Family	1 Pub. Bath/Show	B&B per person £13.00-£14.00 Single £13.00-£14.00 Double	Open Jan-Dec Dinner 1830-1900 B&B + Eve. Meal £21.00-£23.00	

Traditional cottage at water's edge. Approximately 100 metres to Uig ferry. Home cooking and baking provided in a friendly warm setting.

Mrs Wilson Garybuie, 4 Balmeanach Glenhinnisdale, Snizort Isle of Skye, Inverness-shire IV51 9UX Tel: (Uig) 047042 310		**APPROVED** Listed	1 Single 1 Double 2 Family	2 Pub. Bath/Show	B&B per person £12.00-£14.00 Single £12.00-£14.00 Double	Open Apr-Oct Dinner to 1900 B&B + Eve. Meal £21.00-£23.00	

Former croft in secluded glen, yet 4 miles (6kms) from Uig and ferry to Outer Isles.

ULBSTER **Caithness** Mrs Helen M MacLeod Norlands Ulbster Caithness KW2 6AA Tel: (Thrumster) 095585 265	**Map 4** D4		2 Twin 1 Double	2 Pub. Bath/Show	B&B per person £12.50-£15.50 Double	Open Jun-Sep	

ULLAPOOL **Ross-shire** Ardvreck Guest House Morefield Brae Ullapool Ross-shire IV26 2TH Tel: (Ullapool) 0854 612028/ 612561 Fax: 0854 612028	**Map 3** G6	**HIGHLY COMMENDED** 👑 👑	2 Single 2 Twin 4 Double 2 Family	10 En Suite fac	B&B per person £20.00-£25.00 Single £20.00-£24.00 Double	Open Jan-Dec Dinner 1830-1930 B&B + Eve. Meal from £32.50	

Quiet secluded guest house with spectacular views over Loch Broom. All rooms ensuite. Ullapool 1.5 miles (2.5 kms).

Dromnan Guest House Garve Road Ullapool Ross-shire IV26 2SX Tel: (Ullapool) 0854 612333		**Award Pending**	2 Twin 3 Double 2 Family	7 En Suite fac	B&B per person £17.00-£20.00 Double	Open Jan-Dec	

The Sheiling Guest House Garve Road Ullapool Ross-shire IV26 2SX Tel: (Ullapool) 0854 612947		3 Twin 4 Double	7 En Suite fac	B&B per person £16.00-£20.00 Double	Open Jan-Dec	
Strathmore Guest House & The Highlander Restaurant Morefield Ullapool Ross-shire IV26 2TH Tel: (Ullapool) 0854 612423	**COMMENDED** 👑 👑	1 Single 1 Twin 4 Double	4 En Suite fac 1 Pub. Bath/Show	B&B per person £14.00-£18.00 Single £14.00-£20.00 Double	Open Apr-Oct Dinner 1800-2100	
		Guest house enjoying panoramic views over Loch Broom and Ullapool. **Local game and seafood is a speciality in the Highlander Restaurant.**				
Mrs Allan The Kist, Moss Road Ullapool Ross-shire IV26 2TF Tel: (Ullapool) 0854 612269		1 Twin 2 Double	1 Pub. Bath/Show	B&B per person £12.50 Double	Open May-Oct	

HARRIS HOUSE

CUSTOM HOUSE STREET, ULLAPOOL IV26 2XF
Telephone: 0854-612801

Modern, comfortable accommodation. TV in bedrooms plus
tea/coffee making facilities. Situated in quiet street in the village.
1 twin room, 1 family room. From £13.50 pp.

Open Easter to October   **Mrs Harold Baldwin, Proprietor**

Mrs V I Baldwin Harris House Custom House Street Ullapool Ross-shire IV26 2XF Tel: (Ullapool) 0854 612801		1 Twin 1 Family	1 Pub. Bath/Show	B&B per person £15.00 Single £13.50 Double	Open Easter-Oct	
Mrs I Boa The Bens, Ardmair Ullapool Ross-shire Tel: (Ullapool) 0854 612220	**Award Pending**	2 Twin 1 Double	1 Priv. NOT ensuite 2 Pub. Bath/Show	B&B per person from £13.00 Double	Open Apr-Oct	
Mrs B Brinkler Old Bank House, Argyle Street Ullapool Ross-shire IV26 2UB Tel: (Ullapool) 0854 612166		1 Single 2 Twin 1 Double	2 Pub. Bath/Show	B&B per person from £15.00 Single from £14.00 Double	Open Jan-Dec	
Mrs A Campbell Clisham, 56 Rhue Ullapool Ross-shire IV26 2TJ Tel: (Ullapool) 0854 612498/ (except Sunday)	**COMMENDED** 👑	2 Family	1 Pub. Bath/Show	B&B per person £13.00 Single £13.00 Double	Open May-Oct	
		Small working croft peacefully situated in elevated position, **giving superb views over Loch Broom. 3 miles (5kms) north of Ullapool.**				

ULLAPOOL

ULLAPOOL continued Map 3 G6						
Mrs Downey Oakworth, Riverside Terrace Ullapool Ross-shire IV26 2TE Tel: (Ullapool) 0854 612290	COMMENDED 👑 👑	1 Twin 2 Double	2 En Suite fac 1 Pub. Bath/Show	B&B per person £13.00-£16.00 Double	Open Jan-Dec	
		Modern bungalow set in quiet residential area of this Highland town. Fine views. Home baking.				
Mrs H MacDonald Broomvale, 26 Market Street Ullapool Ross-shire IV26 2XE Tel: (Ullapool) 0854 612559	Award Pending	1 Twin 2 Double	1 Pub. Bath/Show	B&B per person from £12.50 Double	Open Apr-Oct	
Mrs C Mackenzie 25 Ladysmith Street Ullapool Ross-shire Tel: (Ullapool) 0854 612123		2 Double	1 Pub. Bath/Show	B&B per person from £12.50 Double	Open May-Sep	
Mrs MacRae Fyffe House, Pulteney Street Ullapool Ross-shire IV26 2HD Tel: (Ullapool) 0854 612452		1 Single 1 Twin 1 Double	2 Pub. Bath/Show	B&B per person from £15.50 Single from £13.50 Double	Open Apr-Oct	
Mrs I MacRae 18 Pulteney Street Ullapool Ross-shire IV26 2UP Tel: (Ullapool) 0854 612397		1 Twin 1 Double 1 Family	1 Pub. Bath/Show	B&B per person £12.50-£13.50 Single £13.50-£14.00 Double	Open Jan-Dec	
Mrs K Stewart Rhue Ullapool Ross-shire IV26 2TJ Tel: (Ullapool) 0854 612435		1 Double 1 Family	1 Pub. Bath/Show	B&B per person £12.00 Double	Open Apr-Oct	
Mrs C Sykes The Bungalow, Garve Road Ullapool Ross-shire IV26 2SX Tel: (Ullapool) 0854 612233	COMMENDED 👑	2 Twin 1 Double	2 Pub. Bath/Show	B&B per person £13.00-£13.50 Double	Open Apr-Sep	
		The only 2 storey Bungalow in Ullapool, set back from the main road, with fine views of the harbour and town. ¼ mile to centre. Parking available.				
Mrs Urquhart Ardlair, Morefield Ullapool Ross-shire IV26 2TH Tel: (Ullapool) 0854 612087	COMMENDED 👑 👑	2 Double 2 Family	2 En Suite fac 2 Pub. Bath/Show	B&B per person £13.00-£16.00 Double	Open May-Oct	
		Purpose built modern house in elevated position, giving excellent views over Loch Broom. Under 2 miles (3kms) north of Ullapool.				

VAT is shown at 17.5%: changes in this rate may affect prices. Prices shown are for guidance only. Please send SAE with each enquiry.

BY ULLAPOOL **Ross-shire** Mrs F Campbell Corrieshalloch House, Fasnagrianach, Garve Road Loch Broom, by Ullapool Ross-shire IV23 2RH Tel: (Lochbroom) 085485 204	**Map 3** G6	**Award** **Pending**	1 Twin 2 Double	1 En Suite fac 1 Pub. Bath/Show	B&B per person £11.00-£16.00 Single £11.00-£16.00 Double	Open Jan-Dec Dinner 1830-1930 B&B + Eve. Meal £18.00-£24.00

Clachan Farmhouse
NO SMOKING HOUSEHOLD

Lochbroom, Ullapool, Ross-shire IV23 2RZ
Telephone: 0854 85 209

Excellent accommodation is provided in this modern farmhouse seven miles south of Ullapool. Under one hour from Inverness; two minutes off the A835. Electric blankets on beds. Three-course breakfast. Lounge is available all day. The exotic Inverewe Gardens. Corrieshalloch Gorge, and nature reserves are within easy reach.
No Sunday enquiries.

Mrs I Renwick Clachan Farm House Lochbroom, by Ullapool Ross-shire IV23 2RZ Tel: (Lochbroom) 085485 209	**COMMENDED** ♛	1 Single 1 Twin 1 Double	1 Pub. Bath/Show	B&B per person from £13.00 Single from £13.00 Double	Open Apr-Nov

Peacefully situated on a working farm 7 miles (11kms) south of Ullapool, 2 minutes off A835. Home baking. Log fire in the lounge.

Mrs Wheatley Glenview House Clachan, Lochbroom Ullapool Ross-shire IV23 2RZ Tel: (Lochbroom) 085485 217		2 Single 1 Twin 1 Double	1 Pub. Bath/Show	B&B per person to £14.00 Single to £14.00 Double	Open Mar-Nov

UNST, Island of **Shetland** F E Wilson Barns, New-Gord Westing, Unst Shetland ZE2 9DW Tel: (Uyeasound) 095785 249 Fax: 095785 305	**Map 5** G1	**COMMENDED** **Listed**	2 Twin	2 Pub. Bath/Show	B&B per person £14.00-£15.00 Single £14.00-£15.00 Double	Open Jan-Dec Dinner 1800-2000 B&B + Eve. Meal £20.00-£21.00

Comfortable family house with magnificent coastal views. Ideal for bird watching, local fishing and walking. Special diets catered for.

UPLAWMOOR **Renfrewshire** Mrs J MacLeod East Uplaw Farm Uplawmoor Renfrewshire G78 4DA Tel: (Uplawmoor) 0505 850383	**Map 1** H6	**COMMENDED** **Listed**	1 Twin 1 Double 1 Family	1 En Suite fac 2 Pub. Bath/Show	B&B per person £13.00-£15.00 Single £13.00-£15.00 Double	Open Jan-Dec Dinner 1800-2200 B&B + Eve. Meal £22.00-£25.00

Modern comfortable accommodation, convenient for Burns country on 320 acre beef farm. Good farmhouse cooking, mainly fresh produce. Children welcome.

Details of Grading and Classification are on page vi.　　　　Key to symbols is on back flap.

WALKERBURN **Peeblesshire** Mrs A Barbour Willowbank, 13 High Cottages Walkerburn Peeblesshire EH43 6AZ Tel: (Walkerburn) 089687 252	**Map 2** D6	COMMENDED Listed	2 Twin 1 Double	2 Pub. Bath/Show	B&B per person from £14.00 Single from £14.00 Double	Open Jan-Dec Dinner 1900-1930 B&B + Eve. Meal from £22.00	

Personally run, stone built semi-detached villa, situated on main tourist route through the Borders. Outstanding views of surrounding countryside.

WATERNISH **Isle of Skye, Inverness-shire** Amanda Broughton 25 Lochbay Waternish Inverness-shire Tel: (Waternish) 047083 346	**Map 3** C8		1 Twin 1 Double	1 En Suite fac 1 Priv. NOT ensuite	B&B per person £14.50-£16.00 Double	Open Apr-Oct	

Mrs Greenhalgh Loch Bay Tearoom & Seafood Restaurant Waternish Isle of Skye, Inverness-shire IV55 Tel: (Waternish) 047083 235			1 Twin 2 Family	1 Pub. Bath/Show	B&B per person £15.50 Single £15.50 Double	Open Mar-Nov Dinner 1830-2100	

WEST LINTON **Peeblesshire** Mrs Cottam Rowallan, Mountain Cross West Linton Peeblesshire EH46 7DF Tel: (West Linton) 0968 60329	**Map 2** C6	COMMENDED 👑	1 Double 1 Family	1 Pub. Bath/Show	B&B per person from £14.00 Double	Open May-Oct	

A warm welcome at modern house on A701, about half an hours drive from Edinburgh. Fine views over the valley. Well situated for touring Borders.

Mrs McCallum Lynehurst, Carlops Road West Linton Peeblesshire EH46 7DS Tel: (West Linton) 0968 60795		COMMENDED 👑👑👑	1 Twin 2 Double	2 En Suite fac 1 Priv. NOT ensuite 1 Pub. Bath/Show	B&B per person £24.00-£29.00 Double	Open Jan, Apr-Oct Dinner at 2000 B&B + Eve. Meal £35.00-£40.00	

Detached Tudor style house set in 2.5 acres in conservation village.
On A702, 20 minutes from Edinburgh.

WHITEKIRK **East Lothian** Mrs Tuer Whitekirk Mains Whitekirk East Lothian EH42 1XS Tel: (Whitekirk) 062087 245/ 0620870 245 Fax: 062087 245/0620870 245	**Map 2** E4	HIGHLY COMMENDED 👑👑	1 Twin 1 Double 1 Family	2 En Suite fac 1 Priv. NOT ensuite	B&B per person £16.00-£18.00 Single £16.00-£18.00 Double	Open Easter-Oct	

Large comfortable Georgian farmhouse in small historic village.
4 miles (6kms) from North Berwick. 3 miles (5kms) from the sea.

WHITHORN **Wigtownshire** Mrs E Forsyth Baltier Farm Whithorn Wigtownshire DG8 8HA Tel: (Garlieston) 09886 241	Map 1 H1	COMMENDED Listed	1 Double 1 Family	2 Pub. Bath/Show	B&B per person £14.00-£15.00 Single £14.00-£15.00 Double	Open Mar-Nov Dinner from 1830 B&B + Eve. Meal £22.00-£24.00

Stone built house on dairy farm with large garden and sun room.
High position gives fine views over surrounding countryside.

Mrs M Forsyth Mid Bishopton Farm Whithorn Wigtownshire DG8 8DE Tel: (Whithorn) 0988 500315		COMMENDED Listed	1 Double	1 Pub. Bath/Show	B&B per person £14.00-£15.00 Double	Open Apr-Oct B&B + Eve. Meal £20.00

Working dairy farm about 1 mile (2kms) from village and 3 miles (5kms)
from Isle of Whithorn. Ideal for couple wanting a quiet holiday.

WHITING BAY **Isle of Arran** Mr and Mrs Frank Ferguson Fourwinds Whiting Bay Isle of Arran Tel: (Whiting Bay) 0770 700545	Map 1 F7		2 Double 2 Family	2 Pub. Bath/Show	B&B per person from £12.50 Single from £12.50 Double	Open Apr-Oct

Mrs Green Silverhill North Whiting Bay Isle of Arran KA27 8QR Tel: (Whiting Bay) 07707 414/ 0770 700414			2 Twin 1 Double	1 Pub. Bath/Show	B&B per person £13.50-£15.00 Double	Open Jan-Dec

WICK **Caithness** Mrs Bremner The Clachan, South Road Wick Caithness KW1 5NH Tel: (Wick) 0955 5384	Map 4 E3	COMMENDED	1 Twin 2 Double	3 En Suite fac	B&B per person £17.00-£20.00 Double	Open Jan-Dec

Family run recently refurbished, detached house dating back to 1938
on quiet main street with off street parking.

Mrs E Calder 9 Francis Street Wick Caithness KW1 5PZ Tel: (Wick) 0955 2136			1 Double 2 Family	2 Pub. Bath/Show	B&B per person from £12.50 Double	Open Jan-Dec

WICK continued	Map 4 E3						
Mrs Coghill Dunelm, 7 Sinclair Terrace Wick Caithness KW1 5AD Tel: (Wick) 0955 2120/5791			1 Single 1 Double 1 Family	2 Pub. Bath/Show	B&B per person from £13.00 Single from £12.00 Double		Open Jan-Dec
Mrs Gunn Sibster Mains Wick Caithness KW1 4TB Tel: (Wick) 0955 3270			1 Twin 2 Double	1 Pub. Bath/Show	B&B per person £13.00-£14.00 Double		Open Jan-Dec Dinner 1800-2000
Mrs S Gunn Papigoe Cottage, Papigoe Wick Caithness KW1 4RD Tel: (Wick) 0955 3363		APPROVED Listed	1 Twin 1 Double 1 Family	2 Pub. Bath/Show	B&B per person from £11.00 Double		Open Jan-Dec Dinner 1900-2030 B&B + Eve. Meal from £15.25
			A warm welcome is assured as you are treated as one of the family in this modest bungalow. Mrs Gunn quite knowledgeable on this historic area.				
Mr & Mrs J Johnston Greenvoe, George Street Wick Caithness Tel: (Wick) 0955 3942		HIGHLY COMMENDED Listed	1 Single 1 Twin 1 Double	2 Pub. Bath/Show	B&B per person £12.00 Single £12.00 Double		Open Jan-Dec
			A large modern comfortable house, 0.5 miles (1km) from town centre. A non-smoking establishment.				

BILBSTER HOUSE
5 miles from Wick, phone Watten (095582) 212

An attractive country house situated in about 5 acres of garden and woodland.

Leave Wick on A882 (Wick-Watten-Thurso). After 5 miles see line of trees on right and signboard. Turn right down lane. Gates face you after 450 yards. (Bilbster House is shown on Ordnance Survey Map. Reference 282533.)

| Mr A Stewart
Bilbster House
Wick
Caithness
KW1 5TB
Tel: (Watten) 095582 212 | | COMMENDED
♔ | 1 Twin
2 Double | 2 Pub. Bath/Show | B&B per person
£13.00 Single
£13.00 Double | | Open May-Sep |
| | | | Listed country house dating from late 1700's set in 5 acres of grounds. Traditionally furnished. | | | | |

	Map 1 H1						
WIGTOWN Mr & Mrs W B Cairns Glaisnock House, 20 South Main Street Wigtown DG8 9EH Tel: (Wigtown) 09884 2249		COMMENDED 😁 😁	1 Single 1 Twin 1 Family	1 En Suite fac 1 Limited ensuite 2 Pub. Bath/Show	B&B per person £12.50-£13.50 Single £13.50-£14.50 Double	Open Jan-Dec Dinner 1800-2030 B&B + Eve. Meal £20.00-£22.00	

Family run guest house with restaurant in the heart of the town.

	Map 5 G2						
YELL, Island of **Shetland** Pinewood Guest House South Aywick, East Yell Shetland ZE2 9AX Tel: (Mid Yell) 0957 2077 Fax: 0957 2410		COMMENDED 😁 😁	2 Twin 1 Double	2 En Suite fac 1 Limited ensuite 1 Pub. Bath/Show	B&B per person £25.00-£30.00 Single £20.00-£25.00 Double	Open Jan-Dec Dinner from 1900 B&B + Eve. Meal £25.00-£30.00	

Modernised crofthouse with large garden, enjoying fine views eastwards over the sea to islands of Fetlar, Unst and Skerries.

TELEPHONE DIALLING CODES

Many telephone dialling codes have changed this year. If you experience difficulty in connecting a call, please call Directory Enquiries — **192** — where someone will issue the correct number.

Please note: a charge will be placed for this service when using a private telephone.

Le secret de très

Lorsque vous choisissez vos vacances par correspondance, la qualité et le confort sont trop importants pour être laissés au hasard.

C'est pourquoi, depuis 1985, le STB inspecte systématiquement les hôtels, pensions de famille et "bed & breakfasts", déterminant la qualité à laquelle nos visiteurs s'attendent et aidant les propriétaires et les organisateurs à offrir cette qualité. Les établissements dans tout le pays, du plus simple au plus sophistiqué, sont NOTES en fonction de leur qualité et CLASSES en fonction des aménagements offerts.

Voici comment le système fonctionne.

Repérez des plaques ovales bleues arborées par les établissements adhérant au système de NOTATION et de CLASSEMENT. ·

Le centre de la plaque vous indique si l'établissement est noté APPROVED (qualité raisonnable), COMMENDED (bonne qualité), HIGHLY COMMENDED (très bonne qualité) ou DELUXE (excellente qualité).

Ces NOTES sont attribuées par les inspecteurs du STB une fois qu'ils ont vérifié tous les facteurs importants contribuant à la qualité d'un établissement. Comme vous le feriez, ils recherchent un cadre propre et agréable, bien meublé et bien chauffé. Ils goûtent aux repas, dorment dans les lits et parlent au personnel. Comme vous, ils apprécient une ambiance et un cadre agréable et un sourire accueillant.

bonnes vacances!

Scottish Tourist Board

COMMENDED

Facilities

Le bas de la plaque indique le classement par COURONNES, en fonction de la gamme d'aménagements et de services proposés - le classement va de LISTED à 5 COURONNES. Les critères se cumulent et tous les critères doivent être satisfaits pour chaque niveau jusqu'au nombre de COURONNES affiché.

Le tableau ci-dessous vous donnera une idée de certains des aménagements auxquels vous pouvez vous attendre à chaque niveau. Pour recevoir une liste complète de tous les critères de classement par COURONNES, contactez le STB, 23 Ravelston Terrace, Edinburgh EH4 3EU Tél.: (0)31 332 2433

	1 ♔	2 ♔	3 ♔	4 ♔	5 ♔
Etablissement propre et confortable	•	•	•	•	•
Moyens de chauffage adéquats sans supplément de prix petit déjeuner	•	•	•	•	•
Lavabo dans la chambre ou dans une salle de bains attenante	•	•	•	•	•
Clef de chambre fournie		•	•	•	•
Coin salon commun		•	•	•	•
TV couleur dans les chambres ou dans le salon 20% des chambres ont une salle de bains attenante		•	•	•	•
Possibilité de se faire servir thé/café dans la chambre le matins			•	•	•
Repas chaud le soir jusqu'à 19H			•	•	•
50% des chambres ont une salle de bains attenante			•	•	•
Accès 24 heures sur 24 pour les clients inscrits			•	•	•
Radio, TV couleur et téléphone dans toutes les chambres				•	•
Boissons et en-cas servis dans la chambre entre 7H et 23H				•	•
Salle de bains attenante avec baignoire et douche dans toutes les chambres				•	•
Au moins 1 suite et diverses possibilités de service dans la chambre					•
Restaurant ouvert pour le petit déjeuner, le déjeuner et le dîner					•

En 1993 le STB a introduit un classement pour les bungalows. Ce mode d'hébergement vous propose une salle de bains attenante dans toutes les chambres, des possibilités de restauration sur place ou non loin, mais des services supplémentaires restreints.

Plus de 3300 établissements avec service - 38000 chambres - partout en Ecosse, sont membres du système de notation et de classement.

RESERVATIONS DIRECTES? RESERVATIONS PAR LE BIAIS DU TOURIST INFORMATION CENTRE? N'OUBLIEZ PAS DE VERIFIER LA NOTATION ET LE CLASSEMENT PAR COURONNES DE L'ETABLISSEMENT CHOISI.

Ihr Schlüssel zu einem

Bei der Auswahl Ihrer Urlaubsunterkunft sollten Sie Qualität und Komfort nicht dem Zufall überlassen.

Daher unterzieht der STB seit 1985 alljährlich Hotels, Pensionen und "Bed & Breakfast"-Unterkünfte einer Prüfung. Wir definieren die Standards, die unsere Gäste von uns erwarten, und helfen Eigentümern und Veranstaltern dabei, diese Standards einzuhalten. Von Bedienungspersonal versorgte Unterkünfte in ganz Schottland – von den einfachsten bis zu den anspruchsvollsten – werden mit einer GRADIERUNG als Qualitätsauszeichnung sowie einer KLASSIFIKATION je nach Zahl der vorhandenen Einrichtungen versehen.

Und so funktioniert es:
Achten Sie auf die ovalen blauen Plaketten, die von Mitgliedern des GRADIERUNGS- und KLASSIFIKATIONS-Schemas ausgehängt werden.

Auf dem Mittelteil der Plakette wird die jeweilige Unterkunft folgendermaßen eingestuft: APPROVED (angemessener Standard), COMMENDED (guter Standard), HIGHLY COMMENDED (sehr guter Standard) oder DELUXE (ausgezeichneter Standard).

Diese GRADIERUNGEN werden von Prüfern des STB vergeben, nachdem diese alle wichtigen Faktoren untersucht haben, auf die es bei der Qualität einer Unterkunft ankommt. Wie auch Sie achten die Prüfer auf saubere, attraktive Unterkünfte, gut eingerichtet und beheizt. Sie essen und übernachten in den Unterkünften und unterhalten sich mit dem Personal. Wie auch Sie legen die Prüfer Wert auf Atmosphäre und ein freundliches Lächeln zur Begrüßung.

großartigen Urlaub!

Scottish Tourist Board

COMMENDED

Facilities

Der untere Teil der Plakette zeigt die KRONEN-Klassifikation, welche den Umfang der vorhandenen Einrichtungen angibt. Die niedrigste Klassifikation ist LISTED, der bis zu 5 KRONEN hinzugefügt werden können. Höhere Klassifikationen bauen auf jeweils niedrigeren auf, und die Gesamtzahl der KRONEN gewährleistet die volle Zahl an Einrichtungen für diese Klassifikationsstufe.

Die folgende Tabelle gibt Ihnen eine Vorstellung von einigen der Einrichtungen, die Sie für jede der Stufen erwarten können. Ein vollständiges Verzeichnis aller Kriterien des KRONEN-Klassifikationssystems erhalten Sie von: STB, 23 Ravelston Terrace, Edinburgh EH4 3EU Tel.: (0)31 332 2433.

	1 ♛	2 ♛	3 ♛	4 ♛	5 ♛
Saubere, komfortable Unterkunft	•	•	•	•	•
Angemessene Beheizung ohne Aufpreis	•	•	•	•	•
Waschbecken im Zimmer oder in eigenem Bad	•	•	•	•	•
Eigener Zimmerschlüssel		•	•	•	•
Gemeinschaftsbereich (Lounge)			•	•	•
Farbfernsehen im Zimmer oder in Gäste-Lounge			•	•	•
Tee/Kaffee frühmorgens			•	•	•
Warme Küche bis 19.00 Uhr			•	•	•
50% aller Zimmer mit eigenem Bad			•	•	•
24 Stunden Zugang für eingetragene Gäste			•	•	•
Radio, Farbfernsehen und Telefon in allen Zimmern				•	•
Zimmerservice mit Getränken und Snacks von 19.00-23.00 Uhr				•	•
Alle Zimmer mit eigenem Bad und Dusche				•	•
Mindestens 1 Suite und ausgedehnter Zimmerservice					•
Restaurant für Frühstück, Mittag- und Abendessen					•

1993 hat der STB auch eine Klassifikation für Ferienwohnungen eingeführt. Hier sind alle Unterkünfte mit eigenem Bad, und Abendmahlzeiten sind entweder auf dem Gelände oder in der Nähe verfügbar; zusätzliche Einrichtungen sind jedoch nur beschränkt vorhanden.

Über 3.300 von Bedienungspersonal versorgte Unterkünfte in allen Landesteilen Schottlands, mit insgesamt über 38,000 Zimmern, sind Mitglieder des Gradierungs- und Klassifikationsschemas.

DIREKTBUCHUNG? BUCHUNG ÜBER EIN TOURIST INFORMATION CENTRE? ACHTEN SIE STETS AUF DIE GRADIERUNG UND KRONEN-KLASSIFIKATION DER UNTERKUNFT IHRER WAHL.

INFORMATION FOR PEOPLE
WITH DISABILITIES

Establishments in the accommodation guides displaying one of the four wheelchair access symbols are now inspected under the Scottish Tourist Board's Grading and Classification Scheme. The four symbols indicate:

&. Access for wheelchair users without assistance

Adequate parking or letting down area for visitor in wheelchair.

Clear, safe approach and entrance in wheelchair.

Access to reception and social area in wheelchair.

Public toilets fully suitable for all disabled use.

At least one bedroom on ground floor, or accessible by lift, with appropriate dimensions and facilities with suitable private bathroom for unattended visitor in wheelchair.

&.A Access for wheelchair users with assistance

Parking, letting down and approach and entrance possible for the visitor in wheelchair with attendant help.

Access by permanent or portable ramps, or by lift, to reception and social areas.

Public toilets suitable for wheelchair use with attendant help.

At least one bedroom with appropriate dimensions and bathroom facilities, accessible by wheelchair user, or other disabled person, with attendant help.

&.P Access for ambulant disabled visitors (other than wheelchair users)

Parking, letting down, approach and entrance with safe steps or ramps, not too steep and preferably with hand rails.

Access to reception and social areas all accessible on same level, by lift or safe steps.

Public toilets suitable for walking, disabled visitor.

At least one bedroom suitable for visitor with walking disability with bathroom and toilet facility nearby.

&.R Access for disabled residents only

At least one bedroom suitable for disabled residents, equipped to &. or &.A or &.P standard. Bathroom and toilet facilities also equipped to the appropriate standard.

Please use your discretion and telephone the establishments in advance if you require further information.

312

INDEX OF ACCOMMODATION PROVIDING DISABLED FACILITIES

The following establishments have been inspected under the Scottish Tourist Board's Grading, and Classification Scheme and have attained one of the four possible awards for access facilities for their disabled visitors.

Accommodation for Ambulant Disabled Visitors (other than wheelchair users)
Ballater, Gairnshiel Lodge
Brora, Mrs M Cooper
Dufftown, Mrs D Moir
Eaglesfield, by Lockerbie, Helen Covello
Edinburgh, Abbeylodge Guest House
Edinburgh, Mrs Bryan
Grantown-on-Spey, Kinross Guest House
Jedburgh, Mrs Whittaker

Accommodation for Wheelchair Users with Assistance
Old Rayne, Mill Croft Guest House
Spean Bridge, Niall & Sukie Scott, Old Pines

Accommodation for Wheelchair Users without Assistance
Buchlyvie, Mrs V Golding
Strathtay, Mrs P Orr

Melvich, GAIRLOCH

RUA REIDH LIGHTHOUSE
MELVAIG, GAIRLOCH IV21 2EA   Tel: 0445 85 263

A spectacular and remote location for an overnight or longer stay. Comfortable accommodation is provided in the old lighthouse keeper's house. Home cooked evening meal also available. A great base for walking, bird watching or just sitting looking out to sea and getting away from it all!

Sanquhar, DUMFRIESSHIRE

Mrs N. Turnbull
28 High Street · Sanquhar · Dumfriesshire DG4 6BL
Telephone: 0659 58143

Sanquhar in Upper Nithsdale is central for Dumfries, Ayr and Kilmarnock. Accommodation in large family flat. Friendly household. Pleasant private garden. No objection to dogs if controlled. Lots of different walks. Local museum and oldest Post Office in Britain.
Annual Festival Week in mid-August — Riding of The Marches.

315

BOOKS TO HELP YOU

SCOTLAND: HOTELS AND GUEST HOUSES 1994   £7.90

Almost 2,000 places to stay in Scotland, from luxury hotels to budget-priced guest houses.
Details of prices and facilities, with location maps. Completely revised each year.
Includes Grading and Classification quality assurance throughout.

SCOTLAND: BED AND BREAKFAST 1994   £5.80

Almost 2,000 B&B establishments throughout Scotland offering inexpensive accomodation.
The perfect way to enjoy a budget trip – and meet Scottish folk in their own homes. Details of
prices and facilities, with location maps. Completely revised each year. Includes Grading and
Classification quality assurance.

SCOTLAND: SELF CATERING ACCOMMODATION 1994   £6.50

Over 1,500 cottages, apartments, houses and chalets to let – many in scenic areas. Details of
prices and facilities, with location maps. Completely revised each year. Includes Grading and
Classification quality assurance. Full colour throughout.

SCOTLAND: CAMPING AND CARAVAN PARKS 1994   £4.70

Over 300 parks detailed with prices, available facilities and other useful information.
Parks inspected under the British Holiday Parks Grading Scheme. Also includes caravan
holiday homes for hire. Location maps. Completely revised each year. Entries graded.

ENJOY SCOTLAND PACK   £8.10

A handy plastic wallet containing the Scottish Tourist Board's Touring Map of Scotland
(5 miles to inch) showing historic sites, gardens, museums, beaches and other places of
interest. Enclosed with its **Touring Guide to Scotland**, which gives locations and details of
these places, as well as opening times and admission charges. Details of access for the disabled.

TOURING MAP OF SCOTLAND   £3.50

As above, available separately.

TOURING GUIDE TO SCOTLAND   £4.60

As above, available separately.

POSTERS

A series of colourful posters is available, illustrating a wide range of Scotland's attractions.
All posters printed on high quality paper and the entire range is also available with a plastic
coating for extra hard wear and it has an attractive glossy finish. They represent excellent value
for money as a souvenir of Scotland.

Paper posters cost £2.80 inc p&p
Plastic coated cost £3.90 inc p&p

To order these publications, fill in the coupon.

PASTIME PUBLICATIONS

To complement your visit to Scotland, Pastime have produced a series of guides·
Scotland, Home of Golf including details of over 400 courses and clubs;
Scotland for Fishing with full details of permits, fishing clubs, boat and
tackle hire and much more; **Scotland for the Motorist**; places of
interest, theatres, galleries, historic buildings, gardens and wildlife
reserves. All are available through Tourist Information Centres
and good bookshops, priced £3.50 (£4.10 incl. p&p).

ALL PRICES INCLUDE POSTAGE & PACKAGE

ORDER FORM OVER PAGE

PUBLICATIONS ORDER FORM

Please mark the publications you would like, cut out this section and send it with your cheque, postal order (made payable to the Scottish Tourist Board) or credit card details to:

Scottish Holidays, 80 Berkeley Street, Glasgow G3 7DS

Scotland: Hotels and Guest Houses	£7.90	☐
Scotland: Bed and Breakfast	£5.80	☐
Scotland: Self Catering Accommodation	£6.50	☐
Scotland: Camping and Caravan Parks	£4.70	☐
Enjoy Scotland Pack	£8.10	☐
Touring Map of Scotland	£3.50	☐
Touring Guide to Scotland	£4.60	☐
Pastime Publications	(each) £4.10	☐

	Plastic Coated £3.90	Paper £2.80
POSTERS		
Piper (24" x 34")	☐	☐
Edinburgh Castle (24" x 34")	☐	☐
Land o' Burns (27" x 40")	☐	☐
Isle of Skye (27" x 40")	☐	☐
Highland Cattle (24" x 34")	☐	☐
Curling (24" x 34")	☐	☐
Scottish Post Boxes (24" x 34")	☐	☐
Five Sisters of Kintail (27" x 40")	☐	☐
Loch Eilt (24" x 34")	☐	☐

BLOCK CAPITALS PLEASE:

NAME (Mr/Mrs/Ms) _____

ADDRESS _____

_____

POST CODE _____ TELEPHONE NO. _____

SIGNATURE _____ DATE _____

TOTAL REMITTANCE ENCLOSED £ _____

PLEASE CHARGE MY *VISA/ACCESS ACCOUNT (*delete as appropriate)

| Card No. | | | | | | | | | | | | | | | Expiry Date | | | | |

To order BY PHONE ring 0800 636 660 (free) quoting the items you require and your credit card details.

For FREE BROCHURES phone 0800 636 660 or mark the brochures you would like.

☐ Short Breaks   ☐ Activity Holidays   ☐ Ski-ing   ☐ Wild Brown Trout Fishing

NOTES

NOTES